SECOND EDITION

# A Guide to LATEX 2ε

## Document Preparation for Beginners and Advanced Users

Helmut Kopka

Patrick W. Daly

*Max-Planck-Institut für Aeronomie*

ADDISON-WESLEY PUBLISHING COMPANY

WOKINGHAM, ENGLAND • READING, MASSACHUSETTS • MENLO PARK, CALIFORNIA • NEW YORK
DON MILLS, ONTARIO • AMSTERDAM • BONN • SYDNEY • SINGAPORE
TOKYO • MADRID • SAN JUAN • MILAN • PARIS • MEXICO CITY • SEOUL • TAIPEI

The programs in this book have been included for their instructional value. They have been tested with care but are not guaranteed for any particular purpose. The publisher does not offer any warranties or representations, nor does it accept any liabilities with respect to the programs.

Many of the designations used by manufacturers and sellers to distinguish their products are claimed as trademarks. Addison-Wesley has made every attempt to supply trademark information about manufacturers and their products mentioned in this book. A list of the trademark designations and their owners appears at the bottom of this page.

Cover designed by Designers & Partners of Oxford and
printed by The Riverside Co. (Reading) Ltd.
Typeset by the authors with the LaTeX Documentation System.
Printed in Great Britain by TJ Press, Padstow, Cornwall

First edition published 1993. Reprinted 1994.
Second edition printed 1995.

**British Library Cataloguing in Publication Data**
A catalogue record for this book is available from the British Library.

**Library of Congress Cataloging in Publication Data**
Kopka, Helmut.
    A guide to Latex2[epsilon] : document preparation for beginnners
  and advanced users / Helmut Kopka, Patrick W. Daly. -- 2nd ed.
    p. cm
    Rev. ed. of: A guide to LATEX. 1993
    Includes index.
    ISBN 0-201-42777-X
    1. LaTeX (Computer file)  2. Computerized typesetting.   I. Daly,
  Patrick W.  II. Title.  III. Series: Kopka, Helmut.  Guide to LATEX.
  Z253.4.L38K66  1995
  686.2'2544536--dc20                                        95-3376
                                                             CIP

# Preface

The great success of Helmut Kopka's book *LaTeX, eine Einführung* in Germany has led to many requests for an English translation, especially from non-German speaking visitors to our Institute. The standard manual on LaTeX by Leslie Lamport, *LaTeX, A Documentation Preparation System*, provides a reasonable introduction to this text formatting program, but leaves many open questions about advanced topics and user-defined extensions. Kopka's book includes many tips and practical examples for solving common problems that are not to be found in the Lamport manual.

A straightforward translation of the German book would not be particularly useful, since it contains considerable information on the application to German texts. For this reason, Patrick W. Daly has undertaken to produce an English version of Kopka's work, adding the sections on international and multilingual LaTeX, and including some applications from his own experience.

At the time of the first edition, late 1992, LaTeX was undergoing major revisions. Some test versions of the new extensions were described in that book, but were in fact out of date before it appeared. Now the revised and consolidated new LaTeX has been released, mid-1994, with many improvements and additions.

This second edition of the *Guide* attempts to present both the classical version (designated 2.09) and the new official standard, named LaTeX$2_\varepsilon$. Of course, the emphasis is on the newer version.

The entire book has been revised in the light of LaTeX$2_\varepsilon$, although the basic material in Chapters 2–7 is much the same. The Advanced Features of Chapter 8 now include the New Font Selection Scheme, a list of standard packages, and the slides class (formerly SliTeX, which had an appendix to itself previously). The error messages of Chapter 9 have been extended. Appendix C is totally new, describing the advanced programming features of LaTeX, with useful examples. Finally, Appendix D, on Extensions, has been expanded; it also contains a description of the CTAN network, the electronic source for TeX and its accessories.

As for the first edition, it is hoped that this book will be particularly useful to those readers who wish to go beyond the basic features of the LaTeX system but who do not want to venture into the murky depths of the TeX world on which it is all based. The Command Summary and Summary

Tables and Figures in Appendix F should become standard reference tools for any LaTeX user of any degree of experience.

*Helmut Kopka and Patrick W. Daly*
*March 1995*

# Contents

# Appendices

# List of Tables

# List of Figures

# Introduction

## I Text formatting

The electronic processing of text, one of the most common functions of computers today, consists essentially of four stages:

1. the text is *entered* into the computer for storage and later corrections, extensions, deletions;

2. the input text is *formatted* into lines of equal length and pages of a certain size;

3. the output text is *displayed* on the computer monitor screen;

4. the final output is sent to a *printer*.

Many word processing systems handle all four functions together in one package so that the user is not aware of this division of labor. Furthermore, stages 3 and 4 are actually one and the same: sending the results of the formatting to an output device, which is in one case a monitor, in the other, a printer.

A *text formatting program*, such as TEX, is only concerned with the second stage. Any text *editor* program may be used to enter and modify the input text. If you have an *editor* with which you are familiar and comfortable, then you may use it. A *word processor* program is not always appropriate for this purpose because it normally adds many unseen *control characters*. It may very well be that 'what you see is what you get' with a *word processor*, but what you see is not necessarily what you've got.

The text that is produced with the *editor* as input for the *formatting program* must also contain special commands or instructions, but these are written with normal characters that are not hidden. To some extent, the instruction set for a *formatter* is much like a *markup language*, indicating where paragraphs, sections, chapters, etc. begin without explicitly

formatting them in the text itself. How these instructions are to be interpreted during formatting depends on the layout that is chosen. The same
text may be formatted quite differently if another layout is selected.

A formatter can also be much more. In fact TeX is also a powerful
*programming language* that allows knowledgeable users to write code
for all sorts of additional features. LaTeX itself is just such a set of
complex macros. Furthermore, anyone can program extra *extensions* to
LaTeX, or make use of public ones that have been contributed by other
programmers. The capabilities of TeX and LaTeX are by no means limited
to those of the original package.

The last stage of text processing with a formatter is to send the results
to an output device, either a printer or the computer monitor or a file.
The programs that accomplish this are called *drivers*; they translate the
encoded output of the formatter program into the specific instructions
for the particular printers that the user has at hand. This means that for
each type of printer, one has to have the corresponding driver program.

## 1.2    TeX and its offspring

The most powerful formatting program for producing book quality text
of scientific and technical works is that of Donald E. Knuth (Knuth, 1984,
1986a, 1986b, 1986c, 1986d). The program is called TeX, which is a
rendering in capitals of the Greek letters $\tau\epsilon\chi$. For this reason the last
letter is pronounced not as an *x*, but as the *ch* in Scottish *loch* or German
*ach*, or as the Spanish *j* or Russian *kh*. The name is meant to emphasize
that the printing of mathematical texts is an integral part of the program
and not a cumbersome add-on. In addition to TeX, the same author has
developed a further program called METAFONT for the production of
character fonts. The standard TeX program package contains 75 fonts
in various design sizes, each of which is also available in up to eight
magnification steps. All these fonts were produced with the program
METAFONT. With additional applications, further character fonts have
been created, such as for Cyrillic and even Japanese, with which texts in
these alphabets can be printed in book quality.

### 1.2.1    The TeX program

The basic TeX program understands only a set of very primitive commands that are adequate for the simplest of typesetting operations and
programming functions. However, it does allow more complex, higher-
level commands to be defined in terms of the primitive ones. In this way,
a more user-friendly environment can be constructed out of the low-level
building blocks.

During a processing run, the program first reads in a so-called *format file* which contains the definitions of the higher-level commands in terms of the primitive ones, and which also contains the hyphenation patterns for word division. Only then does it read in the *source file* containing the actual text to process, including formatting commands that are predefined in the format file.

Creating new formats is something that should be left to very knowledgeable programmers. The definitions are written to a source file which is then processed with a special version of the TeX program called initex. It stores the new format file in a compact manner so that it can be read in quickly by the regular TeX program.

Although the normal user will almost never write such a format, he or she may be presented with a new format source file that will need to be installed with initex. For example, this is just what must be done to update to the new LaTeX 2ε format, as described in Section D.4.

## 2.2    Plain TeX

Knuth has provided a basic format named *Plain TeX* to interact with TeX at its simplest level. This is such a fundamental part of word processing with TeX that one tends to forget the distinction between the actual processing program TeX and this particular format. Most people who claim to 'work only with TeX' really mean that they only work with Plain TeX.

Plain TeX is also the basis of every other format, something that only reinforces the impression that TeX and Plain TeX are one and the same.

## 2.3    LaTeX

The emphasis of Plain TeX is still very much at the typesetter's level, rather than that of the author's. Furthermore, the exploitation of all its potential demands considerable experience with programming techniques. Its application thus remains the exclusive domain of typographic and programming professionals.

For this reason, the American computer scientist Leslie Lamport has developed the LaTeX format (Lamport, 1985), which provides a set of higher-level commands for the production of complex documents. With it, even the user with no knowledge of typesetting or programming is in a position to take extensive advantage of the possibilities offered by TeX, and to be able to produce a variety of text outputs in book quality within a few days, if not hours. This is especially true for the production of complex tables and mathematical formulas.

LaTeX is very much more a *markup language* than the original Plain TeX, on which it is based. It contains provisions for automatic running heads, sectioning, tables of contents, cross-referencing, equation numbering, citations, floating tables and figures, without the author having to know just how these are to be formatted. The layout information is stored in additional *class files* which are referred to but not included in the source text. The layouts may be altered if need be, or the standard layouts accepted as they are.

Since its introduction in the mid-1980s, LATEX has been periodically updated and revised, like all software products. For many years now the version number has been fixed at 2.09 and the revisions are only identified by their dates. The last major update occurred on December 1, 1991, with some minor corrections up to March 25, 1992.

## 1.2.4   LATEX 2ε

The enormous popularity of LATEX and its expansion into fields for which it was not originally intended, together with improvements in computer technology, especially dealing with cheap but powerful laser printers, have created a diversity of formats bearing the LATEX label. In an effort to re-establish a genuine, improved standard, the LATEX3 Project was set up in 1989 by Leslie Lamport, Frank Mittelbach, Chris Rowley, and Rainer Schöpf. Their goal is to construct an optimized and efficient set of basic commands complemented by various *packages* to add specific functionality as needed.

As the name of the project implies, its aim is to achieve a version 3 for LATEX. However, since that is the long-term goal, a first step towards it has been the release of LATEX 2ε in mid-1994 together with the publication of the second edition of Lamport's basic manual (Lamport, 1994) and of a new book (Goosens *et al.*, 1994) describing many of the extension packages available and LATEX programming in the new system. LATEX 2ε is now the standard version, pending the appearance of the promised LATEX3 around the millennium.

Even before the release of LATEX 2ε, some parts of it dealing with font installation and selection had been made public as the *New Font Selection Scheme*, or NFSS, which has already been incorporated by many organizations and individuals. There are two versions of it, which unfortunately possess incompatibilities not only with each other, but also with both LATEX 2.09 and LATEX 2ε. The latter re-implements NFSS in a manner that is fully compatible with the 2.09 version.

## 1.2.5   TEX on various computers

TEX and LATEX were originally designed to run on central mainframe computers, but with the development of *work stations* and of ever more powerful *personal computers*, or *PCs*, TEX packages including the LATEX macros have become available for these mighty midgets too. Everything in this book about writing LaTeX text files applies equally well to both central and personal computers.

This poses a new problem for the user. On a mainframe computer, there is an operator responsible for the installation and maintenance of the TeX program and its accessories. However, the user of a work station or PC must take on the role of computer manager as well, meaning that he or she must learn something more about the setting up of both TeX and LaTeX than was previously necessary. Or, as is more often the case, somebody must be found who will do this for them. This person is normally referred to as the local *TeX guru*.

One extremely useful output driver available with work stations and PCs is a screen previewer, which prints the output to the monitor. This is very practical for checking the appearance of the printed page before it is actually committed to paper, something that is most appreciated when working with complicated tables or mathematical formulas. The results of the exercises in this book are best viewed on the monitor.

There are also *shells* on PCs and work stations that permit one to switch from editor to processor to previewer and back at the touch of a button or click of a mouse. With such systems, TeX becomes practically WYSIWYG ('what-you-see-is-what-you-get').

## 3 What's new in LaTeX 2ε?

This section is intended primarily for readers who are familiar with the older LaTeX 2.09. It gives a brief overview of the new features of LaTeX 2ε.

### 3.1 Classes and packages

The most fundamental difference between LaTeX 2.09 and LaTeX 2ε is the very first command which declares the overall layout: this difference actually makes compatibility between the two versions possible.

In LaTeX 2.09, one must state the *main style* that one wants, together with any options that go with it, as for example:

```
\documentstyle[ifthen,12pt,titlepage]{article}
```

Here the main style is *article*, stored in a file named `article.sty`, with 12 pt as the basic font size, and with the title on a separate page. The additional option `ifthen` is not understood by the main style; instead a file named `ifthen.sty` is read in.

This method of treating undefined options is the principal way in which LaTeX extensions, or supplemental coding, are read into a document. The hundreds of such additional files available are therefore referred to as *style options* or *sub-styles*.

Under LATEX 2$_\varepsilon$, a clear distinction is made between such supplements and true internal options to the main layout. The main style is now renamed the *class* and any extension files are called *packages*. The above initial declaration now becomes:

```
\documentclass[12pt,titlepage]{article}
\usepackage{ifthen}
```

The layout information is contained in the file `article.cls`, which is designed to handle the options `12pt` and `titlepage`. The file `ifthen.sty` is read in as before; however, the new feature here is that it too may have its own internal options. Not only that, but those options listed in the `\documentclass` command are considered global and are therefore valid for all further packages (see Section 3.1.2).

The initial declaration `\documentstyle` may still be used in LATEX 2$_\varepsilon$, in which case it switches to a compatibility mode to reproduce the behavior of LATEX 2.09.

A number of new features have been added to assist LATEX programmers, those intrepid individuals who write class and package files. The handling of options has been improved, and, as mentioned above, it is also possible to add options to packages. Some safety devices have been included to ensure that version numbers match. Better tests exist for reading in other files so that alternative action may be taken if they are not found. These programming elements are described in Appendix C.

## 1.3.2    Font management

Under LATEX 2.09, TEX's Computer Modern fonts were firmly hard-wired into the format. This was acceptable in the days when these were the only fonts that one was likely to use, but today when so many other fonts are available, especially with PostScript printers, a more flexible system is required. The New Font Selection Scheme (NFSS) meets this demand and is fully incorporated in LATEX 2$_\varepsilon$. Changing the basic fonts from Computer Modern to something else is only a matter of a few simple redefinitions (see Section 8.5).

NFSS also changes the way in which fonts are addressed within the document. LATEX 2.09 inherited the TEX font commands like `\bf` (bold) and `\it` (italic) which rigidly select a particular font. Only the size of the font remains unchanged by these commands. Under NFSS, fonts are described by certain *attributes* that may be selected independently of one another. Thus it is possible to select first bold and then italic to obtain a bold, italic font, something that was not allowed in LATEX 2.09.

LATEX 2$_\varepsilon$ encourages the use of *font commands* as opposed to *declarations*. For example, to emphasize some text, the command `\emph{word}` is preferred to the declaration `{\em word}`. Such commands are more logical to the beginner, although the experienced LATEX 2.09 user who is thoroughly used to the latter form might object.

The use of text fonts in math mode is achieved by special *math alphabet commands* rather than with the older font declarations. That is, the declarations \rm, \bf, \cal and so on are no longer allowed in math mode, and are replaced by the commands \mathrm, \mathbf, \mathcal which operate on arguments.

## 3.3 Float placement

One annoying problem in LATEX 2.09 is getting floats (figures and tables) to end up where one would optimally prefer to see them. There are very complicated rules for placing floats and the human does not always see through them. LATEX 2ε provides two new mechanisms to intervene in this process, one to discourage and the other to encourage the placement.

The current page may be declared to be free of floats by issuing the command \suppressfloats. Optionally, one may specify an argument t or b to suppress only the floats at the top or bottom of the current page.

On the other hand, a new float location specifier ! suspends all restrictions for that one float on the amount of text and number of floats that may appear on one page. This overcomes a very common grievance which is normally assuaged only by redefining \textfraction or some other float placement parameter, and that with much trial and error. The float location specifier ! is given just like the others: for example,

    \begin{figure}[!]

It is now possible to define horizontal rules to be drawn above or below floats, in order to set them off better from the text. All these features are described in Section 6.6.

## 3.4 Extended syntaxes

Several commands in LATEX 2ε have an extended syntax compared to that in version 2.09. The older, limited syntax still functions as before, of course.

- The commands \newcommand, \renewcommand, \newenvironment, and \renewenvironment may be used to define new commands and environments that contain one optional argument in addition to several mandatory ones (Sections 7.3 and 7.4).

- The box commands \makebox, \framebox, and \savebox can refer to their natural dimensions while specifying their actual size. That is, one can make them to be, say, twice their natural width. See Section 4.7.

- The `\parbox` command and `minipage` environment can now specify a vertical size in additional to the horizontal width. A new internal placement parameter determines whether the text in the box is to be shoved to the top, centered, pushed to the bottom, or even stretched to fill the whole box (Section 4.7.5).

- Previously it was possible to measure the width of some text with the command `\settowidth`; this is now complemented with `\settoheight` and `\settodepth` (Section 7.2).

## 1.3.5   Compatibility with LaTeX 2.09

Every effort has been made to make LaTeX $2_\varepsilon$ as compatible as possible with version 2.09. This means that documents written for the older standard should produce the same results under the new one. It also means that most style options (or sub-styles) should function just as before as a package, without any revisions.

That at least is the theory. In practice, incompatibilities must exist. How likely is it that one will encounter them?

- If only upper-level commands are used, those not containing any @ signs in their names, then the compatibility should be 100%.

- If internal commands have been manipulated, there could be problems, especially if they involve boxes or output routines.

- If internal font control commands have been used, especially those from the `lfonts.tex` file, problems are likely to appear. However, it should be pointed out that even here there are fewer incompatibilities than were present in the first and second releases of NFSS.

From our own experience so far, we have found very few packages that do not work under LaTeX $2_\varepsilon$, even when boxes and output routines are involved. Our worst case was when we explicitly loaded a support file from LaTeX 2.09 that is not supposed to exist under LaTeX $2_\varepsilon$. It was loaded anyway, causing serious error messages to be issued.

## 1.3.6   'Which version do I have?'

If you do not know whether or not LaTeX $2_\varepsilon$ is installed on your system, there are a number of ways to find out. At the start of any LaTeX job, the name and date of the format is printed, both on the monitor screen and in the transcript file, for example

```
LaTeX Version 2.09 <25 March 1992>    for LaTeX 2.09, or
LaTeX2e <1994/06/01>    for LaTeX 2ε.
```

Your dates may differ from these.

Alternatively, try processing a LaTeX file with \documentclass on the first line. If you receive the error message

```
! Undefined command sequence
        \documentclass
```

then you do not have LaTeX2ε.

## 3.7 Upgrades to LaTeX2ε

It is intended to issue upgrades to LaTeX every June and December, consisting not only of improved internal coding, but also of additional features. This means that as time goes on, it will not be sufficient to state that a document has been written for LaTeX2ε, but rather one must specify the necessary version as well as the date when it was released.

In this book, any commands that were not present in the first official release of LaTeX2ε on June 1, 1994 are so indicated, along with their release date, both in the main text and in the command summary of Appendix F.

It is possible to declare in a document file the earliest possible version date needed to be able to process all the features it employs. This is done by placing an identification command near the beginning (Section C.2.1). For the first release, this would be

```
\NeedsTeXFormat{LaTeX2e}[1994/06/01]
```

The date must be numerical, in exactly the format shown above, as year/month/day, including slashes and zeros. If a file with this command is processed by an earlier version of LaTeX, a warning message is printed.

## 4   How to use this book

This *Guide* is meant to be a mixture of textbook and reference manual. It explains all the basic elements of LaTeX, especially those of the new standard LaTeX2ε, restricting itself as much as possible to what is in the standard distribution. Compared to Lamport (1985, 1994), it goes into more detail at times, offers more examples and exercises, and describes many 'tricks' based on the authors' experiences. Unlike *The LaTeX Companion* (Goosens *et al.*, 1994), it does not go into detail about the many additional packages available outside the standard distribution, since these may not always be easily obtainable for all readers. An exception to this is necessarily Appendix D, dealing with some of these extra features.

This book is designed for LaTeX users who have little or no experience with computers. It contains no information about computers or system-dependent activities such as *logging on, calling the editor,* or *using the editor.*

There is considerable repetition in the text, especially within the first half, so that the reader, having learned a brief definition of some expression, is not expected to have fully mastered it when it reappears a few pages later. Nevertheless, the user should become familiar right from the beginning with the basic elements described in Sections 2.1–2.4.

The authors have tried to avoid *computer slang*, even when this has not been entirely successful. It is hoped that such expressions as *file* and *editor* are sufficiently well known today that no further explanation is required.

In the description of command syntax, typewriter type is used to indicate those parts that must be entered exactly as given, while *italic* is reserved for those parts that are variable or for the text itself. For example, the command to produce tables is presented as follows:

`\begin{tabular}{`*col form*`}`     *lines*     `\end{tabular}`

The parts in typewriter type are obligatory, while *col form* stands for the definition of the column format that must be inserted here. The allowed values and their combinations are given in the detailed descriptions of the commands. In the above example, *lines* stands for the line entries in the table and are thus part of the text itself.

!

Sections of text that are printed in a smaller typeface together with the boxed exclamation mark at the left are meant as an extension to the basic description. They may be skipped over on a first reading. This information presents deeper insight into the workings of LaTeX than is necessary for everyday usage, but which is invaluable for creating more refined control over the output.

## 1.4.1   Distinguishing LaTeX 2$_\varepsilon$ from version 2.09

Since LaTeX 2$_\varepsilon$ is now the current standard, all the descriptions of syntax and functions given here will conform to it. However, we believe that many users will still be working with version 2.09 for several years to come, either because they do not have the possibility of upgrading, or because they do not have the inclination to change. This book must also serve these clients.

For this reason, those commands that are new to LaTeX 2$_\varepsilon$, or existing ones that have been extended in some way, are marked with the symbol $\boxed{2\varepsilon}$. Similarly, any sections of text that apply strictly to LaTeX 2.09 are marked with $\boxed{2.09}$.

Since LaTeX 2$_\varepsilon$ is downward compatible with LaTeX 2.09, it should not be necessary to mark any command as belonging only to the older version. Nevertheless, some commands have been retained strictly for compatibility reasons (such as `\bf` and `\rm`) and are discouraged in LaTeX 2$_\varepsilon$, while in LaTeX 2.09 they are indispensable.

# 5   Basics of a LaTeX file

## .1   Text and commands

Every text consists of *characters* which are put together to make *words*. The words make up *sentences*, which in turn produce *paragraphs*. The paragraphs can be part of larger units, such as *sections* or *chapters*.

Words consist of one or more characters and are terminated by *blanks* or *carriage returns*. TeX interprets both blanks and carriage returns as the end of a word. It is irrelevant how many blanks come between the words; multiple blanks have no effect on the spacing between the words.

Paragraphs are separated from one another by one or more *empty lines*. Once again, the spacing between the paragraphs is not affected by the number of empty lines. TeX treats the words of a paragraph as one long string of words, selecting the spacing between them to be as uniform as possible such that the individual lines are left and right justified. Lines are broken up *automatically* independently of the text input.

The line spacing depends on the selected font size. Paragraphs are indicated either by indenting the first line or by increasing the line spacing between them. Both the paragraph and line spacings are slightly variable. TeX (and LaTeX) select these spacings so that the top and bottom edges of a full page appear at the required locations. These locations may be varied within the document. Page breaking takes place automatically just as line breaking does.

In the simplest case, a text file contains only the input text. TeX will process this text using a standard width and height; that is, the breaking up into lines, paragraphs, and pages occurs justified on all pages, as with typeset text.

However, each LaTeX document normally contains not only the *text* to be processed but also *commands* to specify how the processing is to be done. It is therefore necessary to be able to distinguish between text and commands. Commands consist either of certain single characters that cannot be used as text characters, or of words preceded immediately by a special character, the backslash \.

## 5.2   Structure of a LaTeX document

In every LaTeX file there must be a *preamble* and a *body*.

The preamble is a collection of commands that specify the global processing parameters for the following text, such as the paper format, the height and width of the text, the form of the output page with its pagination and automatic page heads and footlines. As a mininum, the preamble must contain the command \documentclass to specify the document's overall processing type. This is normally the first command in the preamble.

If there are no other commands in the preamble, LaTeX selects standard values for the line width, margins, paragraph spacing, page height and width, and much more. In the original version, these specifications are tailored to the American norms. For European applications, built-in options exist to alter the text height and width to the A4 standard. Furthermore, there are language-specific packages to translate certain headings such as 'Chapter' and 'Abstract'.

The preamble ends with \begin{document}. Everything that follows this command is interpreted as *body*. It consists of the actual text mixed with additional commands. In contrast to those in the preamble, these commands have only a local effect, meaning they apply only to a part of the text, such as *indentation*, *equations*, temporary change of *font*, and so on. The body ends with the command \end{document}. This is normally the end of the file as well.

The general syntax of a LaTeX file is as follows:

> $\boxed{2\varepsilon}$  \documentclass [*options*] {*class*}
> *Further global commands and specifications*
> \begin{document}
> *Text mixed with additional commands of local effect*
> \end{document}

The possible *options* and *classes* that may appear in the \documentclass command are presented in Section 3.1.1.

For LaTeX 2.09, or for compatibility with it under LaTeX 2$\varepsilon$, the initial command \documentclass must be replaced by \documentstyle. Thus the general syntax would appear as follows in version 2.09:

> $\boxed{2.09}$  \documentstyle [*options*] {*class*}
> . . . . . . . . . .
> \begin{document}
> . . . . . . . . . .
> \end{document}

At a computing center, information about the available LaTeX classes and packages is described in a so-called *Local Guide*. This should also include how the LaTeX program is to be run, as well as what output devices are installed, such as printer, microfilm, plotters, etc., and how they are to be implemented. The device drivers may also recognize options to produce the output in various discrete magnifications.

## 1.5.3    LaTeX processing modes

$\boxed{!}$  (This section is marked with a boxed exclamation mark and is printed in a smaller type face. For the meaning of this, see the end of Section 1.4 on page 10.)

During processing, LaTeX is always in one of three modes:

1. paragraph mode,
2. math mode,
3. LR, or left-to-right mode.

The *paragraph mode* is the normal processing mode in which LaTeX treats the input text as a sequence of words and sentences to be broken up (automatically) into lines, paragraphs, and pages.

LaTeX switches to *math mode* when it encounters certain commands that tell it that the following text represents a *formula*. In math mode, blanks are ignored. The two texts `is` and `i s` are both interpreted as the product of `i` and `s` and appear as *is*. LaTeX switches back to paragraph mode when it encounters the corresponding command that the formula is completed.

*LR mode* is similar to paragraph mode: LaTeX treats the text input from left to right as a string of words *that cannot be split up by a line break*. LaTeX will be in this mode when, for example, normal text is to appear embedded within a formula, or with a special command `\mbox{`*short text*`}` that forces *short text* to be printed on one line.

Understanding and recognizing the processing modes is important since some commands are allowed only in certain modes or their effects are different depending on the mode.

In the following we will refer to paragraph and LR modes as *text mode* to the extent that their properties are identical. This is to distinguish them from *math mode*, which is normally quite different.

## 1.4  Producing a LaTeX document

The creation of a LaTeX document from text input to printer output is a three-stage process. First a text file is created (or corrected) using the computer editor. This text file consists of the actual text mixed with LaTeX commands.

The full name of the text file consists of a *root* name plus the *extension* `.tex` (for example, `sample.tex`). The operating system of the computer usually puts additional limitations on the choice of file name, such as the maximum number of characters in the name and extension, or the exclusion of special characters. For example, if the root name is limited to 8 characters, `finances.tex` is an allowed name, but `financial.tex` is not.

The text file is then processed by LaTeX. As explained in Section 1.2.1, this means running the TeX program with the LaTeX format. Most installations have a special shorthand command, called `latex`, to accomplish this, followed by the name of the text file, *without* the extension `.tex`.

For example, if the name of the text file is `sample.tex`, one would start the LaTeX processing with the call

```
latex sample
```

During the processing, the terminal monitor displays the page numbers together with possible warnings and error messages. Chapter 9 deals with the interpretation of these error messages and their consequences. After LATEX has finished processing, it creates a new file with the selected root name and the extension `.dvi`. In the above example, this would be `sample.dvi`.

This `.dvi` (*device-independent*) file contains the *formatted* text along with information about the required character fonts, but in a form that is independent of the characteristics of the printer to be used. Such a device-independent file is called a *metafile*.

Finally the information in the `.dvi` metafile has to be converted to a form that can be output on the chosen printer by means of a so-called *printer driver* that is specific for that printer type. The call to the driver contains only the root name of the file, just like the LATEX call, that is, without the ending `.dvi`. After processing with the printer driver, another file is created with the selected root name and an extension specifying the printer type.

For example, if the output is to go to a LaserJet printer, the driver might be called as

```
dvilj sample
```

which either produces a file `sample.lj` or sends the output directly to the printer.

Other drivers exist for letter-quality dot-matrix printers as well as for PostScript. However, it is not the purpose of this book to describe the DVI drivers, since there are a great many available, with different names and extra features, such as printing only certain pages or printing them in reverse order. A computing center will have the important drivers installed for the output devices available. A summary of these calls and further information should be available in a TEX or LATEX *Local Guide* that is accessible to all system users. The best source of information, however, is often other experienced users, the *gurus* mentioned previously.

# 2 Commands and Environments

The text that is to be the input to a LATEX processing run must be prepared with a *text editor* (any one will do) in a file with the extension .tex. The contents of this file are printable characters only—there are no invisible characters or commands hiding behind the screen. However, commands are still necessary to issue instructions to LATEX. These commands are visible in the input text but will not appear in their literal form in the output. It is therefore vital to know how commands are distinguished from text that is to be printed, and, of course, how they function.

## Command names and arguments

The characters # $ & ~ _ ^ % { } represent special commands, whose meanings are explained later. If these characters are to appear as text characters, they must be preceded by a \ (backslash).

About twenty commands consist of two characters, the \ followed immediately by another character that is not a letter. In this manner, for example, \$ means *suspend the meaning of the command $ and instead print this character as text*.

The great majority of commands consist of \ followed immediately by one or more letters, ending with the first character that is not a letter. Many commands have *arguments*, or variable extensions to the corresponding command. Arguments may be *optional*, that is, they may or may not be included, or *mandatory*, at least one of the permitted values must be present. The syntax of such commands is

$$\backslash commandname\,[optional\_argument]\,\{mandatory\_argument\}$$

where the optional arguments are put into square brackets [ ] and the mandatory ones into curly braces { }. A command may have several optional arguments, each one in its set of brackets in the specified sequence. If no optional argument is used, the square brackets may be omitted. Any number of blanks may appear between the command name and the arguments.

Two problems can arise with optional arguments: if none of them are to be used and the next character in the text is [, or if the text of an optional argument contains ], then LaTeX will misinterpret the argument. This may be avoided by hiding the offending bracket within braces as {[} or {]}.

Some commands have several mandatory arguments. Each one must be put into a { } pair and their sequence must be maintained as given in the command description. For example,

> \rule[*lift*]{*width*}{*height*}

produces a black rectangle of size *width* and *height*, raised by an amount *lift* above the current baseline. A rectangle of width 10 mm and height 3 mm sitting on the baseline is made with \rule{10mm}{3mm}. The optional argument *lift* is not given here. The arguments must appear in the order fixed by the syntax and may not be interchanged.

Some commands appear in two forms, one the standard and the other a so-called *-form. The latter is marked by the fact that the command name ends in a *, which comes before the bracket pairs [ ] or { } for optional or mandatory arguments. The difference between the standard and *-form is explained in the description of the individual commands.

Command names end before the first character that is not a letter. If there are optional or mandatory arguments following the command name, then it ends before the [ or { bracket, since these characters are not letters. Many commands, however, possess no arguments and are composed of only a name, such as the command \LaTeX which produces the LaTeX logo. If such a command is followed by a punctuation mark, such as comma or period, it is obvious where the command ends. If it is followed by a normal word, the blank between the command name and the next word is interpreted as the command terminator: The \LaTeX logo results in 'The LaTeXlogo', that is, the blank was seen only as the end of the command and not as spacing between two words. This is a result of the special rules for blanks, described in Section 2.5.1.

In order to insert a space after a command that consists only of a name, either an empty structure {} or a space command (\ and blank) must be placed after the command. The proper way to produce 'The LaTeX logo' is to type either The \LaTeX{} logo or The \LaTeX\ logo. Alternatively, the command itself may be put into curly braces, as The {\TeX} logo, which also produces the correct output with the inserted blank: 'The TeX logo'. Incidentally, the LaTeX 2ε logo is produced with \LaTeXe.

# 2   Environments

An *environment* is initiated with the command \begin{*environment*} and is terminated by \end{*environment*}. The allowed values for *environment* are listed in the sections on the various commands.

An environment has the effect that the text within it is treated differently according to the environment parameters. It is possible to alter (temporarily) certain processing features, such as indentation, line width, typeface, and much more. The changes apply only within the environment. For example, with the quote environment,

> *previous text*
> \begin{quote}
> *text1* \small *text2* \bfseries *text3*
> \end{quote}
> *following text*

the left and right margins are increased relative to those of the previous and following texts. In the example, this applies to the three texts *text1*, *text2*, and *text3*. After *text1* comes the command \small, which has the effect of setting the next text in a smaller typeface. After *text2*, there is an additional command \bfseries to switch to bold face type. Both these commands only remain effective up to the \end{quote}.

> The three texts within the quote environment are indented on both sides relative to the previous and following texts. The *text1* appears in the normal typeface, the same one as outside the environment. The *text2* and *text3* appear in a smaller typeface, and *text3* **furthermore appears in bold face.**

After the quote environment has been ended, the following text appears in the same typeface as before.

Most command names may also be used as environment names. In this case the command name is used *without* the preceding \. For example, the command \em switches to an emphatic typeface, usually *italic*, and the corresponding environment \begin{em} will set all the text in *italic* until \end{em} is reached.

An environment without a name can be simulated by bracketing with a {...} pair. The effect of any command within it ends with the closing curly brace.

The user can even create additional environments, as described in Section 7.4.

# .3   Declarations

A *declaration* is a command that changes the values or meanings of certain parameters or commands without immediately printing any text. The

effect of the declaration begins immediately and ends when another declaration of the same type is encountered. However, if the declaration occurs
within an environment or a {...} pair, its range extends only to the corresponding \end command, or to the closing brace }. The commands \em,
\bfseries, and \small mentioned in the previous section are examples
of such non-printing declarations that alter the current typeface.

Some declarations have associated arguments, such as the command
\setlength which assigns a value to a *length parameter* (see Sections 2.4
and 7.2).

Examples:

{\bfseries This text appears in bold face}      The \bfseries
    declaration changes the typeface: **This text appears in bold face**.
    The effect of this declaration ends with the closing brace }.

\setlength{\parindent}{0.5cm} The indentation of the first line of a
    paragraph is set to 0.5 cm. The effect of this declaration ends with
    the next encounter of the command \setlength{\parindent}, or
    at the latest with the \end command that terminates the current
    environment.

\pagenumbering{roman} The page numbering is to be printed in Roman
    numerals.

Some declarations, such as the last example, are global, that is, their
effects are not limited to the current environment. The following declarations are of this nature, the meanings of which are given later:

| | | |
|---|---|---|
| \newcounter | \pagenumbering | \newlength |
| \setcounter | \thispagestyle | \newsavebox |
| \addtocounter | | |

Declarations made with these commands are effective right away and
remain so until they are overridden by a new declaration of the same type.
In the last example above, page numbering will be done in Roman numerals
until countermanded by a new \pagenumbering{arabic} command.

## 2.4    Lengths

### 2.4.1    Fixed lengths

*Lengths* consist of a decimal number with a possible sign in front (+ or −)
followed by a compulsory dimensional unit. Permissible units and their
abbreviated names are:

| | |
|---|---|
| cm | centimeter, |
| mm | millimeter, |
| in | inch (1 in = 2.54 cm), |
| pt | point (1 in = 72.27 pt), |
| bp | big point (1 in = 72 bp), |
| pc | pica (1 pc = 12 pt), |
| dd | didôt point (1157 dd = 1238 pt), |
| cc | cicero (1 cc = 12 dd), |
| em | a font-specific size, the width of the capital M, |
| ex | another font-related size, the height of the letter x. |

Decimal numbers in TEX and LATEX may be written in either the English or European manner, with a *period* or a *comma*: both 12.5cm and 12,5cm are permitted.

Note that 0 is not a legitimate length since the unit specification is missing. To give a zero length it is necessary to write 0pt or 0cm.

Values are assigned to a length parameter by means of the LATEX command \setlength, which is described in Section 7.2 along with other commands for dealing with lengths. Its syntax is:

\setlength{\\*length_command*}{*length_spec*}.

For example, the width of a line of text is specified by the parameter \textwidth, which is normally set to a default value depending on the style and font size. To change the line width to be 12.5 cm, one would give:

\setlength{\textwidth}{12.5cm}.

## 4.2 Rubber lengths

Some parameters expect a *rubber* length. These are lengths that can be stretched or shrunk by a certain amount. The syntax for a rubber length is:

*nominal_value* plus *stretch_value* minus *shrink_value*

where the *nominal_value, stretch_value,* and *shrink_value* are each a length. For example,

\setlength{\parskip}{1ex plus0.5ex minus0.2ex}

means: the extra line spacing between paragraphs, called \parskip, is to be the height of the x in the current font, but it may be increased to 1.5 or reduced to 0.8 times that size.

One special *rubber* length is \fill. This has the natural length of *zero* but can be stretched to any size.

## 2.5    Special characters

### 2.5.1    Spaces and carriage returns

The *space* or *blank* character has some properties different from those of normal characters, some of which have already been mentioned in Section 2.1. During processing, blanks are replaced by rubber lengths (Section 2.4.2) in order to allow the line to fill up to the full line width. As a result, some peculiar effects can occur if one is not aware of the following rules:

- one blank is the same as a thousand, only the first one counts;

- blanks at the beginning of a line are ignored;

- blanks terminating a command name are removed;

- *carriage returns* (a new line) are treated as blanks.

Some of the consequences of these rules are that there may be as many blanks as desired between words or at the beginning of a line (to make the text file more legible) and that a word may come right at the end of a line without the spacing between it and the next word disappearing. To force a space to appear where it would otherwise be ignored, one must give the command \␣ (a \ followed by a blank character, made visible here by the symbol ␣).

Sometimes it is necessary to suppress the space that appears because of the new line. In this case, the line must be ended with the *comment* character % (Section 4.11) before the carriage return.

Two carriage returns in a row produce a blank line, the signal for a new paragraph. As for blank characters, one blank line is the same as a thousand.

### 2.5.2    Quotation marks

The *quotation marks* found on the typewriter " are not used in book printing. Instead different characters are used at the beginning and end, such as 'single quotes' and "double quotes". Single quotes are produced with ' and ', while double quotes are made by typing the respective characters twice: '' for " and '' for ". Furthermore the typewriter character " will also generate the double closing quote ".

### 2.5.3    Hyphens and dashes

In book printing, the character that appears on the typewriter as - comes in various lengths: -, –, —. The smallest of these, the *hyphen*, is used for compound words such as *father-in-law* and for word division at the end of a line; the middle sized one, the *en dash*, is used in ranges of numbers, for example, pages 33–36; and the largest, the *em dash*, is used as punctuation—what is normally called the *dash*. These are generated by typing the hyphen character one, two, or three times, so that - yields -, while -- makes –, and --- produces —. A fourth type of dash is the minus sign −, which is entered in math mode as $-$ (Chapter 5).

## .4  Printing command characters

As mentioned in Section 2.1, the characters # $ ~ _ ^ % { } are interpreted as commands. If they are to be printed as text, the character \ must precede them:

$ = \$     & = \&     % = \%     # = \#     _ = \_     { = \{     } = \}

## .5  The special characters §, †, ‡, ¶, © and £

These special characters do not exist on the computer keyboard. They can however be generated by special commands as follows:

§ = \S     † = \dag     ‡ = \ddag     ¶ = \P     © = \copyright     £ = \pounds

The production of Greek letters and other mathematical symbols is described in Chapter 5.

## .6  Foreign letters

Special letters that exist in European languages other than English can also be generated with TeX. These are:

œ={\oe}   Œ={\OE}   æ={\ae}   Æ={\AE}   å={\aa}   Å ={\AA}   ¡=!`
ø ={\o}   Ø ={\O}   ł ={\l}   Ł ={\L}   ß={\ss}   SS={\SS}   ¿=?`

*Ångstrøm* may be written as {\AA}ngstr{\o}m while *Karlstraße* can be input as Karlstra{\ss}e. The upper case version \SS is new to LaTeX 2ε.

## .7  Accents

In the European languages, there is a multiplicity of *diacritic marks* or *accents*, most of which can be printed with TeX:

ò =\'{o}     ó=\'{o}     ô=\^{o}     ö=\"{o}     õ=\~{o}
ō =\={o}     ȯ=\.{o}     ŏ=\u{o}     ǒ=\v{o}     ő=\H{o}
o͡o=\t{oo}     ǫ=\c{o}     ọ=\d{o}     o̲=\b{o}     o̊=\r{o}

(The last command, \r, is new to LaTeX 2ε.) The *o* above is given merely as an example: any letter may be used. With *i* and *j* it should be pointed out that the dot must first be removed. This is carried out by prefixing these letters with \. The commands \i and \j yield ı and ȷ. In this way ĭ and ĵ are formed by typing \u{\i} and \H{\j}.

The accent commands consisting of a non-letter may also be given without the curly braces:

$$\grave{o}=\backslash`o \quad \acute{o}=\backslash'o \quad \hat{o}=\backslash\char`^o \quad \ddot{o}=\backslash"o \quad \tilde{o}=\backslash\char`~o \quad \bar{o}=\backslash=o \quad \dot{o}=\backslash.o$$

The letter accent commands should always be used with the curly braces. There are other possibilities using TeX notations but since these are not very clear and are often confusing they will not be indicated here.

### 2.5.8  Ligatures

In book printing, certain combinations of letters are not printed as individuals but as a single symbol, a so-called *ligature*. TeX processes the letter combinations ff, fi, fl, ffi, and ffl not as

> ff, fi, fl, ffi, ffl     but rather as     ff, fi, fl, ffi, ffl

Section 3.5.1 describes how one may force TeX to print the letters of such combinations separately. This is sometimes desired for such words as *shelfful*, which looks rather strange when printed with the normal *ff* ligature, *shelfful*.

### 2.5.9  The date

The current date can be placed at any point in the text with the command \today. The standard form for the date is the American style of month, day, year (for example, November 15, 1994). The British form or the date in other languages can be generated with the help of the TeX commands \day, \month, and \year, which return the current values of these parameters as numbers. Examples of how such a new \today command may be made are shown on page 349 in Section C.3.3.

## 2.6  Fragile commands

!

The influence of certain commands is not limited to the place where they appear but may also affect other parts of the document. For example, the sectioning commands, such as \chapter{*heading*}, generate the headings not only at the point where they are issued but also possibly at the top of each of the following pages in a different typeface, and perhaps once again, in yet another typeface, in the table of contents. Such an argument that appears at several places in the document is called a *moving argument*.

Such arguments are literally *shaken up* by the move. (More precisely, they are interpreted prematurely.) If certain commands are included in the moving argument, they can be so distorted that they do not function properly. One speaks figuratively of their *breaking apart*. Such commands are said to be *fragile*, while others that are not so delicate and can withstand the shaking are called *robust*.

Basically all commands that contain optional arguments, such as \begin and \end, are fragile. Fragile commands may still be included in a moving argument if they are preceded by the command \protect, which prevents them from being broken up by the shaking.

A fragile command in a moving argument without the safety of \protect need not be broken up. In fact, a break-up occurs only very rarely. In the very first German edition of this book, it was only the umlauts (the two dots over such letters as ä, ö, and ü) in the section headings that needed a \protect\" to transfer them correctly to the table of contents. (In later versions of LATEX, the accent commands were no longer fragile, and in fact, in LATEX 2$_\varepsilon$, even more have been made robust.)

Fragile commands cannot be properly processed by LATEX and therefore a long string of error messages will appear on the screen. By pressing the return key, the user can try to continue the processing in spite of the incorrect handling of that command. Further error messages may appear at first but eventually, with enough returns, LATEX will usually proceed with the rest of the processing, unless the effect of the broken command is such that further processing is impossible and the program stops.

Only the following commands contain moving arguments:

- all commands that transfer text information to the table of contents; these are the sectioning commands (Section 3.3.3), \addtocontents, \addcontentsline (Section 3.4.3), and \caption (Section 6.6.4);
- the commands \typein and \typeout (Section 8.1.3);
- the commands \markboth and \markright (Section 3.2.1);
- the \thanks commands for the title page (Section 3.3.1);
- @-expressions (Section 4.8.1);
- the optional argument of \bibitem (Section 4.3.6);
- the \begin{letter} command if the command \makelabels has been issued (Section A.1).

It is only necessary to give a \protect command to secure fragile commands when they appear as arguments in one of the above commands. It does not hurt to precede most commands with \protect in a moving argument if their fragility is in doubt. Exceptions to this rule are *length commands* (Section 7.2) and *counter commands* (Section 7.1.4) such as \arabic and \value. These should never have a \protect before them.

# 7 Exercises

As part of a successful teach-yourself course of study, practical exercises are absolutely essential. In addition to the plentiful examples in the text, which the reader should try out, a number of further exercises will also be given in the course of this book, as suggested homework that should definitely be carried out.

All examples and exercises are given for LATEX 2$_\varepsilon$; if you are still using LATEX 2.09, you must use the initial command \documentstyle in place of \documentclass.

**Exercise 2.1:** *This exercise tests the basic operations of running the LATEX program with a short piece of text. A few simple commands are also included. Use the computer editor to produce the following text and store it in a file named* exer.tex.

```
\documentclass{article}
\begin{document}
Today (\today) the rate of exchange between the British
pound and American dollar is \pounds 1 = \$1.63, an
increase of 1\% over yesterday.
\end{document}
```

*Running the LATEX program is dependent on the computer system, but assuming that it is called with the command* latex, *the processing is activated with*

```
latex exer
```

*Note: although the file name is* exer.tex, *only the root name* exer *needs to be given in the call to LATEX.*

*If the processing occurs without any error messages, the* .dvi *file* exer.dvi *has been successfully created and may be further converted for the printer with the help of the printer driver. How this is called also depends on the computer system. The final printed result should look as follows except that your current date will appear:*

Today (November 15, 1994) the rate of exchange between the British pound and American dollar is £1 = $1.63, an increase of 1% over yesterday.

*Note the following points about the commands used:*

- *no blank is necessary after* \today *because the ) suffices to terminate it;*
- *the blank after* \pounds *is optional and it is not printed in the output;*
- *the commands* \$ *and* \% *do not require blanks to terminate them; if blanks are given, they will be printed.*

**Exercise 2.2:** *Take some text of about 3/4 of a page long out of a book or journal article and type it into a LATEX file. Pay attention that the paragraphs are separated by blank lines. Use the same set of commands as in Exercise 2.1, that is, put the text between the commands* \begin{document}...\end{document} *and repeat the procedures for obtaining the printed output.*

*Note: the selected text should not contain any special structures such as block indentation, different typefaces, centered text, enumerations, mathematical formulas, tables, etc. The construction of such structures is explained in the next chapters.*

# 3 Document Layout and Organization

## Document class

The first command in the preamble of a LaTeX file normally determines the global processing format for the entire document. The syntax for this command is:

$\boxed{2\varepsilon}$ \documentclass[*options*]{*class*}

or

$\boxed{2.09}$ \documentstyle[*options*]{*class*}

where the latter is the only possibility under LaTeX 2.09. With LaTeX $2\varepsilon$, the command \documentstyle is provided only for compatibility with older document files.

The possible values of *class*, of which one and only one may be given, are: book, report, article, or letter. (The properties of the letter class are explained in Appendix A.) The basic differences between these classes lie not only in the page layouts, but also in the organization. An article may contain *parts*, *sections*, *subsections*, and so on, while a report can also have *chapters*. A book also has chapters, but treats even and odd pages differently; also, it prints running heads on each page with the chapter and section titles.

## .1 Standard class options

The *options* available allow various modifications to be made to the formatting. They can be grouped as follows.

### Selecting font size

The basic font size is selected with one of the options

$\boxed{2\varepsilon}$ 10pt    11pt    12pt

25

This is the size of the font in which the normal text in the document will be set. The default is 10pt, which means that this is the value assumed if no size option is specified. All other font sizes are relative to this standard size, so that the section titles, footnotes, and so on will all change size automatically if a different basic font size is selected. (Note that in LaTeX 2.09 there is no option 10pt; to select 10 pt as the basic size one specifies no size option.)

### Specifying paper size

LaTeX calculates the text line width and lines per page according to the selected font size and paper mode. It also sets the margins so that the text is centered both horizontally and vertically. In order to do this, it needs to know which paper format is being used. This is specified by one of the following options, all of which exist only for LaTeX $2_\varepsilon$:

| | |
|---|---|
| $\boxed{2\varepsilon}$ `letterpaper` ($11 \times 8.5$ in) | $\boxed{2\varepsilon}$ `a4paper` ($29.7 \times 21$ cm) |
| $\boxed{2\varepsilon}$ `legalpaper` ($14 \times 8.5$ in) | $\boxed{2\varepsilon}$ `a5paper` ($21 \times 14.8$ cm) |
| $\boxed{2\varepsilon}$ `executivepaper` ($10.5 \times 7.25$ in) | $\boxed{2\varepsilon}$ `b5paper` ($25 \times 17.6$ cm) |

The default is `letterpaper`, American letter size paper, $11 \times 8.5$ in.

Normally, the paper format is such that the longer dimension is the vertical one, the so-called *portrait* mode. With the option

$\boxed{2\varepsilon}$ `landscape`

the shorter dimension becomes the vertical one, the *landscape* mode.

### Page formats

The text on the page may be formatted into one or two columns with the options

$\boxed{2\varepsilon}$ `onecolumn`     `twocolumn`

The default is `onecolumn`. In the case of the `twocolumn` option, the separation between the columns as well as the width of any rule between them may be specified by `\columnsep` and `\columnseprule`, described below.

The even and odd numbered pages may be printed differently according to the options

$\boxed{2\varepsilon}$ `oneside`     `twoside`

With `oneside`, all pages are printed the same; however, with `twoside`, the running heads are such that the page number appears on the right on odd pages and on the left on even pages. *It does not force the printer to output double-sided.* The idea is that when these are later printed back-to-back, the page numbers are always on the outside where they are more easily noticed. This is the default for the book class. For article and report, the default is oneside.

With the book class, chapters normally start on a right-hand, odd-numbered page. The options

$\boxed{2\varepsilon}$ openright $\qquad$ $\boxed{2\varepsilon}$ openany

control this feature: with openany a chapter always starts on the next page, but with openright, the default, a blank page may be inserted if necessary.

Normally the title of a book or report will go on a separate page, while for an article, it is placed on the same page as the first text. With the options

$\boxed{2\varepsilon}$ notitlepage $\qquad$ titlepage

this standard behavior may be overruled. See Sections 3.3.1 and 3.3.2.

### Further options

The remaining standard options are:

leqno $\quad$ Equation numbers in displayed formulas will appear on the left instead of the normal right side (Section 5.1).

fleqn $\quad$ Displayed formulas will be set flush left instead of centered (Section 5.1). The amount of indentation may be set with the parameter \mathindent described below.

openbib
$\qquad$ The format of bibliographies may be changed so that segments are set on new lines. By default, the text for each entry is run together.

draft $\quad$ If the LaTeX line-breaking mechanism does not function properly and text must stick out into the right margin, then this is marked with a thick black bar, to make it noticeable.

$\boxed{2\varepsilon}$ final $\quad$ The opposite of draft, and the default. Lines of text that are too wide are not marked in any way.

If multiple options are to be given, they are separated by commas, as for example, \documentclass[11pt,twoside,fleqn]{article}. The order of the options is unimportant. If two conflicting options are specified, say oneside and twoside, it is not obvious which one will be effective. That depends entirely on the definitions in the class file itself, so it would be best to avoid such situations.

### Parameters associated with some options

Some options make use of parameters that have been given certain default values:

`\mathindent`
> specifies the indentation from the left margin for the equation numbers when `fleqn` is selected (Section 5.1);

`\columnsep`
> specifies the space between the two columns for the `twocolumn` option (see Figure F.2 on page 512);

`\columnseprule`
> determines the width of the vertical line between the two columns for the `twocolumn` option. The default is zero width, that is, no vertical rule (see Figure F.2).

The standard values of these parameters may be changed with the LaTeX command `\setlength`. For example, to change `\mathindent` to 2.5 cm, give

> `\setlength{\mathindent}{2.5cm}`

These parameters may be assigned values either in the preamble or at any place in the document. Parameters in the preamble apply to the entire document, whereas those within the text are in effect until the next change or until the end of the environment in which they were made (Section 2.3). In the latter case, the previous values become effective once more.

**Exercise 3.1:** *Take your text file from Exercise 2.2 and change the initial command* `\documentclass{article}` *first to* `\documentclass[11pt]{article}` *and then to* `\documentclass[12pt]{article}` *and print the results of each LaTeX processing. Compare the line breaking of these outputs with that of Exercise 2.2.*
*Note: if there are some improper word divisions, you call tell LaTeX where the correct division should occur with the command* `\-`, *for example,* `man\-u\-script`. *(This is one of the few words that the TeX English word divider does not handle properly.) Additional means of modifying word division are given in Section 3.6.*
*If there are warnings of the sort* `Overfull \hbox` ... *during the LaTeX processing, TeX was not able to break the lines cleanly. In the output, these lines will extend beyond the right margin. The usual cause is that TeX was not able to divide some word, either because it is indivisible or because TeX's word division routines were not adequate. Here again a suggested hyphenation in the text can solve the problem. Other solutions will be given shortly.*

**Exercise 3.2:** *Now employ* `\documentclass[twocolumn]{article}` *in your text file. If you now receive a number of warnings with* `Underfull \hbox` ..., *then these lines will indeed be left and right justified but will have too much empty* *space between the words. Check the output yourself to see whether the word spacing is acceptable. If not, try giving some hyphenation suggestions in the first words of the next line.*

*Note: if you use the classes* book *or* report *instead of* article *in the preceding exercises, you will notice no difference in the outputs. These classes affect the subsequent structural elements of the document. Basically, you should use* article *for short articles (say 10–20 pages) and* report *for longer reports that are to be organized into chapters. The chapters always begin on a new page. The class* book *is available for producing books.*

## .2   Adding features with packages $\boxed{2\varepsilon}$

Although the *class* of the document determines its overall general properties, such as layout and sectioning, it is possible to invoke more specific *packages* that might change the way certain commands behave, or even define totally new commands to add extra features that are not part of the standard LATEX. A number of such packages are provided in the LATEX distribution, or you may obtain some of the hundreds that have been made available by the LATEX user community (Appendix D), or you may even write your own (Appendix C).

A package is nothing more than a set of LATEX (or TEX) commands stored in a file with the extension .sty, although there some special commands that may only appear within them. To invoke a package, simply call

$\boxed{2\varepsilon}$ \usepackage{*package*}

in the preamble, where *package* is the root name of the file. More than one package may be loaded with one call to \usepackage. For example, two packages provided with standard LATEX are stored in files makeidx.sty (Section 8.4) and ifthen (Section 7.3.5). They may be read in together with

\usepackage{makeidx,ifthen}

A package may have options associated with it, which may be selected in the same way as for document classes: by including the option names within square braces. The general syntax is thus:

\usepackage[*opt1,opt2...*]{*package1,package2,...*}

where all the listed options will be applied to all the selected packages. If any of the packages does not understand one of the options, a warning message is output to the monitor.

Just what options are available depends on the package itself. One must read the accompanying description and/or documentation to discover not only its options, but also what the package does and what new commands it defines.

### 3.1.3   Style options ⌐2.09⌐

The \usepackage command does not exist in LATEX 2.09; in fact, it will not
function at all if \documentstyle is issued in place of \documentclass.
In LATEX 2.09, packages were treated in the same way as *style options*:
the file names were added to the list of options in the \documentstyle
command. For this reason, they were called *style option files*, or simply
*style files*, which explains the extension .sty that these files bear. This
extension has been maintained in LATEX 2ε in order that the older style
files may still be employed as packages.

There is a fundamental difference between a true option, which is
programmed within the class or package file, and a package, which is
read in as a file of the same name. In LATEX 2.09, this distinction was never
clear and often led to confusion.

To load the package makeidx with the options 12pt and titlepage
into the class (or 'main style') article in the older LATEX version, one must
write

⌐2.09⌐ \documentstyle[makeidx,12pt,titlepage]{article}

Since packages are handled here as options, it is clear that they themselves
cannot have any further options.

### 3.1.4   Global and local options ⌐2ε⌐

⌐!⌐ One interesting feature about options specified with the \documentclass command is that they also apply to any packages that follow. This means that if
several packages all take the same option, it is only necessary to declare it once in
\documentclass. For example, one might design a package to modify article
for generating a local house style that might do different things for single or
double column text; this package could make use of the class options onecolumn
and twocolumn to achieve this. Or it could elaborate on the draft option to
produce double line spacing, as for a manuscript. Alternatively, several packages
might have language dependent features that could be activated with options like
french or german; it is sufficient to list such options only in \documentclass to
apply it to all packages. Such options are called *global*, for they are passed on to
all subsequent packages automatically.

Global options need not be limited to the standard class options listed in
Section 3.1.1. A warning message is printed only if neither the class nor any of the
packages understand one or more of them. By contrast, any options specified with
\usepackage will be applied only to those packages listed in that one command;
and it is applied to all of them. A warning is printed if one or more of those
packages does not recognize any one of these *local* options.

## 2   Page style

The basic page format is determined by the *page style*. With one exception, this command is normally given in the preamble. Its form is:

>   \pagestyle{*style*}

For the mandatory argument *style*, the following values are available:

plain   The page head is empty, the foot contains the centered page number. This is the default when \pagestyle is not given in the preamble.

empty   Both head and foot are empty; no page numbers are printed.

headings
>   The head contains the page number as well as title information (chapter and section headings) as determined by the document class; the foot is empty. This does not apply to the first page of a chapter.

myheadings
>   The same as headings except that the page titles in the head are not chosen automatically but rather are given explicitly by the commands \markright or \markboth (see below).

The command

>   \thispagestyle{*style*}

functions exactly as \pagestyle except that it affects only the current page. For example, the page numbering may be suppressed for just the current page with the command \thispagestyle{empty}. It is only the *printing* of the page number that is suppressed; the next page will be numbered just as though the command had never been given.

## .1   Heading declarations

For the page styles headings and myheadings, the information appearing in the headline may be given with the declarations

>   \markright{*right_head*}
>   \markboth{*left_head*}{*right_head*}

The declaration \markboth is to be employed with the document class option twoside, with even-numbered pages considered to be on the *left* and odd-numbered pages on the *right*. Furthermore, the page number is printed on the left side of the head for a left page and on the right side for a right page.

For one-sided output, all pages are considered to be right-handed. In this case, the declaration \markright is appropriate. It may also be used with two-sided output to overwrite the *right_head* given in \markboth.

With the page style headings, the standard titles in the page head are the chapter, section, or subsection headings, depending on the document and page style, according to the following scheme:

| Style | | Left Page | Right Page |
|---|---|---|---|
| book, report | one-sided | — | *Chapter* |
| | two-sided | *Chapter* | *Section* |
| article | one-sided | — | *Section* |
| | two-sided | *Section* | *Subsection* |

If there are more than one \section or \subsection on a page, it is the heading of the last one that appears in the page head.

An example of two-sided output with headings is this book itself.

### 3.2.2  Page numbering

The declaration that specifies the style of the page numbering has the form

\pagenumbering{*num_style*}

The allowed values of *num_style* are:

| | |
|---|---|
| arabic | for normal (Arabic) numerals, |
| roman | for lower case Roman numerals, |
| Roman | for upper case Roman numerals, |
| alpha | for lower case letters, |
| Alpha | for upper case letters. |

The standard value is arabic. This declaration resets the page counter to 1. In order to paginate the foreword of a document with Roman numerals and the rest with Arabic numbers beginning with page 1 for chapter 1, one must declare \pagenumbering{roman} at the start of the foreword and then reset the page numbering with \pagenumbering{arabic} immediately after the first \chapter command. (See Section 3.3.5 for an alternative.)

If the pages are to be numbered starting with a value different from 1, this may be achieved with the command

\setcounter{page}{*page_num*}

where *page_num* is the number of the first page.

*Exercise 3.3: Expand your exercise text file so that it fills more than one page of output and include the following preamble:*

```
\documentclass{article}
\pagestyle{myheadings} \markright{Exercises}
\pagenumbering{Roman}
\begin{document}
```

## 2.3  Paragraph spacing

The following parameters affect the appearance of a paragraph and may be given new values with \setlength as explained in Section 7.2:

\parskip
>The distance between paragraphs, expressed in units of ex so that it will automatically change with character font size. This should be a *rubber* length.

\parindent
>The amount of indentation for the first line of a paragraph.

\baselinestretch
>This is a number that magnifies the normal distance between *baselines*, the line on which the letters sit, that is, neglecting the hanging parts of letters such as *g* and *y*. This number is initially 1, for standard line spacing. It may be changed to another number with
>
>$$\renewcommand{\baselinestretch}{factor}$$
>
>where *factor* is any decimal number, such as 1.5 for a 50% increase. This then applies to all font sizes. If this command is given outside the preamble, it does not become effective until another font size has been selected (Section 4.1.2).

These parameters may be set either in the preamble or anywhere in the text of the document. In the latter case, the changes remain in effect until the next change or until the end of the environment in which they were made (Section 2.3).

The true inter-line spacing is contained in the \baselineskip length parameter, which is set automatically whenever a font size declaration is called. For each font size, there is a normal value, which is then multiplied by \baselinestretch to produce \baselineskip. See Section 4.1.2 for more details.

If \baselineskip is changed within a paragraph, the new value determines the inter-line spacing of the whole paragraph. More precisely, it is its value at the end of the paragraph that is effective.

*Exercise 3.4: Add the following to the preamble of your exercise file:*

```
\setlength{\parindent}{0em}
\setlength{\parskip1.5ex plus0.5ex minus 0.5ex}
\renewcommand{\baselinestretch}{1.2}
```

*After processing this exercise, repeat it with another value for the parameter* \baselinestretch, *say 1.5, in order to get a feeling for how it works. Remove these lines from the exercise file afterwards.*

### 3.2.4    Page format

Each page consists of a *head*, the *body* containing the actual text, and a *foot*. The selection of the page style determines what information is to be found in the head and footlines.

LATEX uses default values for the distances between the head, body, and foot, for the upper and left margins, and for the text line width and heights of the head, body, and foot. These formatting lengths are illustrated in Figure 3.1 on the opposite page. They may be changed by declaring new values for them, preferably in the preamble, with the command \setlength (Section 7.2). For example, give

    \setlength{\textwidth}{12.5cm}

to make the text line width to be 12.5 cm.

In LATEX 2.09, an additional parameter \footheight was specified but never used. It has now been removed from LATEX 2$_\varepsilon$.

More detailed diagrams of the page formats for one- and two-column outputs are shown at the end of Appendix F in Figures F.1 and F.2.

In order to calculate the page layout precisely, one must realize that LATEX measures all distances from a point one inch from the top of the paper and one inch from the left edge. Thus the total left margin is \oddsidemargin plus one inch. The LATEX 2$_\varepsilon$ parameters \paperwidth and \paperheight, which include this extra inch, are given their values by the paper size option in the \documentclass command; they are used internally to calculate the margins so that the text is centered. The user may also take advantage of them.

With document class **book** or with the option **twoside**, the bottom edge of the body will always appear at exactly the same position on every page. In the other classes or options, it will vary slightly. In the first two cases, the constant bottom edge is produced by the internal command \flushbottom, whereas the varying bottom is produced by the command \raggedbottom. The user may apply these declarations to change the behavior of the bottom edge at any time, independent of document class and options.

**Exercise 3.5:** *You can change the page format of your text by altering the above parameters. Add to the preamble of your text the following:*

    \setlength{\textwidth}{13cm}   \setlength{\textheight}{20.5cm}

*The upper and left margins of your output will now seem too small. Select new values for* \oddsidemargin *and* \topmargin *to correct this.*
*Note: do not forget the 1 inch margin at the left and top from which additional margins are measured. You must take this into account when you select* \oddsidemargin *and* \topmargin.

\oddsidemargin
  left margin for odd pages,
\evensidemargin
  left margin for even pages,
\topmargin
  upper margin to top of head,
\headheight
  height of head,
\headsep
  distance from the bottom of headline to top of body,
\topskip
  distance from top of body to baseline of first line of text,
\textheight, \textwidth
  height and width of main text,
\footskip
  distance from bottom of body to bottom of foot,

$\boxed{2_\varepsilon}$ \paperwidth, \paperheight
  total width and height of paper as given by paper size option, including all margins,

$\boxed{2.09}$ \footheight, obsolete, has been removed from LaTeX $2_\varepsilon$.

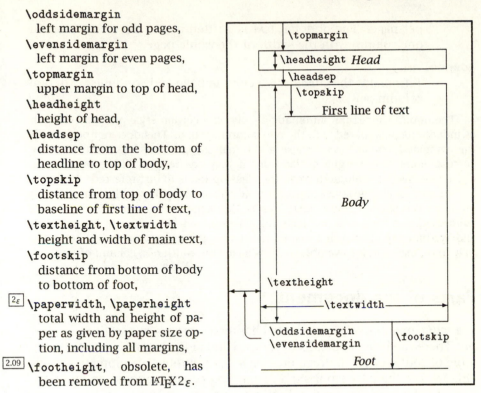

**Figure** 3.1: Page layout parameters

*Exercise 3.6:* *Expand your text so that the output requires more than 2 full pages with the reduced page format. Add* \flushbottom *to the preamble and check that the last line of all pages is at exactly the same location.*

*Exercise 3.7:* *Remove the command* \flushbottom *and select the document class* \documentclass[twoside]{article}. *Now the last lines are at the same location without the* \flushbottom *command. On the other hand, the left margin of the odd pages probably does not agree with the right margin of the even pages. Use the declaration* \evensidemargin *to correct this.*

## 2.5  Single and double column pages

The document class option twocolumn sets the entire document in two columns per page. The default is one column per page. If individual pages are to be output in two or one columns, this may be achieved with the declarations:

\twocolumn[*text*]
        Terminates the current page, starting a new one with *two columns*

per page. The optional *text* is written at the top of the page in one column with the width of the whole page.

`\onecolumn`
Terminates the current two-column page and continues with one column per page.

The option `twocolumn` automatically changes certain style parameters, such as indentation, compared with the one-column format. This does not occur with the command `\twocolumn`. These additional changes must be made with the corresponding `\setlength` declarations if they are desired. If the bulk of the document is in two-column format, the class option is to be preferred.

An additional page style parameter is `\columnwidth`, the width of one column of text. For single column text, this is the same as `\textwidth`, but when `twocolumn` has been selected, LATEX calculates it from the values of `\textwidth` and `\columnsep`. The author should never change this parameter, but he or she may make use of it, for example to draw a rule the width of a column of text.

## 3.3    Parts of the document

Every document is subdivided into chapters, sections, subsections, and so on. There can be an appendix at the end and at the beginning a title page, table of contents, an abstract, etc. LATEX has a number of commands available to free the user from such formatting considerations. In addition, sequential numbering and sub-numbering of headings can take place. Even a table of contents may be generated and printed automatically.

The effects of some sectioning commands depend on the selected document class and not all commands are available in every class.

### 3.3.1    Title page

A title page can be produced either unformatted with the environment

    `\begin{titlepage}` *Title page text* `\end{titlepage}`

or with the commands

    `\title{`*Title text*`}`
    `\author{`*Author names and addresses*`}`
    `\date{`*Date text*`}`

in the prescribed LATEX format.

In the standard LATEX format for the title page, all entries are centered on the lines in which they appear. If the title is too long, it will be broken up automatically. The author may select the break points himself with the `\\` command, that is, by giving `\title{...\\...\\...}`.

If there are several authors, their names may be separated with `\and` from one another, such as `\author{G. Smith \and J. Jones}`. These names will be printed next to each other in one line. The sequence

```
\title{
  How to Write DVI Drivers}

\author{
  Helmut Kopka\thanks{Tel.
    05556--401--451 FRG}\\
  Max--Planck--Institut\\
  f\"ur Aeronomie
\and
  Phillip G. Hardy
  \thanks{Tel.
    319--824--7134 USA}\\
  University\\of Iowa}

\maketitle
```

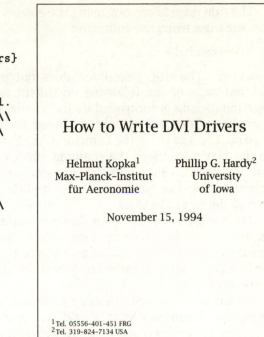

**How to Write DVI Drivers**

Helmut Kopka[1]           Phillip G. Hardy[2]
Max-Planck-Institut          University
  für Aeronomie               of Iowa

November 15, 1994

[1] Tel. 05556-401-451 FRG
[2] Tel. 319-824-7134 USA

**Figure 3.2**: Sample title page and the text that produced it

\author{*Author1*\\*Institute1*\\*Address1*
\and *Author2*\\*Institute2*\\*Address2*}

separately centers the entries, one per line, in each of the sets *Author1, Institute1, Address1* and *Author2, Institute2, Address2* and places the two blocks of centered entries beside each other on the title page.

Instead of printing the author names next to each other, one may position them on top of one another by replacing \and with the \\ command. In this case, the vertical spacing may be adjusted with an optional length specification [*space*] following the \\.

If the command \date is omitted, the current date is printed automatically below the author entries on the title page. On the other hand, the command \date{*Date text*} puts the text *Date text* in place of the current date. Any desired text may be inserted here, including line break commands \\ for more than one line of centered text.

The command

\thanks{*Footnote text*}

may be given at any point in the *title, author*, or *date text*. This puts a marker at that point where the command appears and writes *footnote text* as a footnote on the title page.

The title page is created using the entries in \title, \author, \date, and \thanks when the command

>    \maketitle

is issued.  The title page itself does not possess a page number and the first page of the following document is number 1.  (For book, the page numbering is controlled by the special commands in Section 3.3.5.) A separate title page is only produced for document classes book and report.  For article, the command \maketitle creates a title heading on the first page using the centered entries from the \title, \author, and, if present, \date and \thanks declarations.  If the document class option titlepage has been given, the title appears on a separate page even in the article class.

An example of a title page in the standard LATEX format is shown in Figure 3.2 on the previous page.  Note that the current date appears automatically since the command \date is missing in the definition of the title page. This command may be used to put any desired text in place of the date.

For the unformatted title page produced with the titlepage environment, the commands \title and \author are left out and the entire title page is designed according to the author's specifications within the environment.  To this end he or she may make use of all the structuring commands described in Chapter 4.  In this case the printing of the title page is implemented at the end of the titlepage environment, so the command \maketitle is also left out.

*Exercise 3.8:* *Remove the declarations for changing the page format in Exercises 3.5–3.7. Add to your exercise text a title heading with the title 'Exercises', your name as author, and your address, together with a date entry in the form 'place, date'. To do this, write the following commands after* \begin{document}:

>    \title{Exercises} \author{Your name\\ Your address}
>    \date{Your town, \today} \maketitle

*Make sure that you have selected document class* article. *After printing the document, change the document class command to*

>    \documentclass[titlepage]{article}

*to put the title information on to a title page instead of a title heading.*

*Deactivate these commands by putting the comment character % at the beginning of each of the lines. In this way you avoid getting a title page in the following exercises but you can easily reactivate the commands simply by removing the % characters.*

## 3.3.2   Abstract

The abstract is produced with the command

> \begin{abstract} *Text for the abstract* \end{abstract}

In document class `report`, the abstract appears on a separate page without a page number; in `article`, it comes after the title heading on the first page, unless the document class option `titlepage` has been selected, in which case it is also printed on a separate page. An abstract is not possible in document class `book`.

## 3.3 Sections

The following commands are available for producing automatic, sequential sectioning:

| | | | |
|---|---|---|---|
| \part | \chapter | \subsection | \paragraph |
| | \section | \subsubsection | \subparagraph |

With the exception of \part, these commands form a sectioning hierarchy. In document classes `book` and `report`, the highest sectioning level is \chapter. The chapters are divided into sections using the \section command, which are further subdivided by means of \subsection, and so on. In document class `article`, the hierarchy begins with \section since \chapter is not available.

The syntax of all these commands is

> \sec_command[*short title*]{*title*}   or
> \sec_command*{*title*}

In the first case, the section is given the next number in the sequence, which is then printed together with a heading using the text *title*. The text *short title* becomes the entry in the table of contents (Section 3.4) and the page head (provided that page style `headings` has been selected). If it is absent, *short title* is set equal to the *title*, which should be the normal situation unless *title* is too long to serve for the other entries.

In the second (*-form) case, no section number is printed and no entry in the table of contents is made (however, see Section 3.4.3).

The size of the title heading and the depth of the numbering depend on the position of the sectioning command within the hierarchy. For document class `article`, the \section command generates a single number (say 7), the \subsection command a double number with a period between the two parts (say 7.3), and so on.

In document classes `book` and `report`, the chapter headings are given a single number with the \chapter command, the \section command creates the double number, and so on. Furthermore, the command \chapter always starts a new page and prints **Chapter n** over the chapter title, where **n** is the current chapter number. At this point in the present book, we are in *Chapter 3, Section 3.3, Subsection 3.3.3.*

For each sectioning command there is an internal counter that is incremented by one every time that command is called, and reset to zero on every call to the next higher sectioning command. These counters are not altered by the *-forms, a fact that can lead to difficulties if standard and *-forms of the commands are mixed such that the *-forms are higher in the hierarchy than the standard forms. There are no problems, however, if the *-forms are always lower than the standard forms. The sequence

```
\section ... \subsection ... \subsubsection* ...
```

numbers the headings for \section and \subsection while leaving the headings for \subsubsection without any numbering.

The sectioning command \part is a special case and does not affect the numbering of the other commands.

The automatic numbering of sections means that the numbers might not necessarily be known at the time of writing. The author may be writing them out of their final order, or might later introduce new sections or even remove some. If he or she wants to refer to a section number in the text, a mechanism other than typing in the number explicitly will be needed. The LATEX cross-reference system, described in detail in Section 8.3.1, accomplishes this task with the two basic commands

```
\label{name}    \ref{name}
```

the first of which assigns a keyword *name* to the section number, while the second may be used as reference in the text for printing that number. The keyword *name* may be any combination of letters, numbers, or symbols. For example, in this book the command \label{sec:xref} has been typed in at the start of Section 8.3.1, so that this sentence contains the input text at the start of Section \ref{sec:xref}.

A second referencing command is \pageref for printing the number of the page where the corresponding \label is defined.

The referencing commands may be used in many other situations for labeling items that are numbered automatically, such as figures, tables, equations.

Every sectioning command is assigned a level number such that \section is always level 1, \subsection level 2, ... \subparagraph level 5. In document class article, \part is level 0 while in book and report classes, \part is level −1 and \chapter becomes level 0. Section numbering is carried out down to the level given by the number secnumdepth. This limit is set to 2 for book and report, and to 3 for article. This means that for book and report, the section numbering extends only to the level of \subsection and for article to \subsubsection.

In order to extend (or reduce) the level of the section numbering, it is necessary to change the value of secnumdepth. This is done with the command

```
\setcounter{secnumdepth}{num}
```

(The command \setcounter is explained in Section 7.1.) In article, *num* may take on values from 0 to 5, and in book and report from −1 to 5.

It is possible to change the initial value of a sectioning command within a document with the command

    \setcounter{*sec_name*}{*num*}

where *sec_name* is the name of the sectioning command without the preceding \. This procedure may be useful when individual sections are to be processed by LaTeX as single files. For example,

    \setcounter{chapter}{2}

sets the \chapter counter to 2. The counter will be incremented on the next call to \chapter which then produces **Chapter 3**.

Occasionally it is necessary to change the font size or style in the section headline. This can be done by including the declarations described in Sections 4.1.2–4.1.6 in the section title text. For example,

    \section*{\Large\slshape Larger Slanted Font}

will print the section title 'Larger Slanted Font' in the size \Large and style \slshape. Such deviations from the standard fonts are *not* recommended since the changes affect only the title text itself, and not the preceding numbering.

## 3.4  Appendix

An appendix is introduced with the command \appendix. It has the effect of resetting the section counter for article and the chapter counter for book and report and changing the form of the numbering for these sectioning commands from numerals to capital letters A, B, .... Furthermore, the word 'Chapter' is replaced by 'Appendix' so that subsequent chapter headings are preceded by 'Appendix A', 'Appendix B', etc. The numbering of lower sectioning commands contains the letter in place of the chapter number, for example A.2.1. Alternatively, the appendices may be included in an environment as

    \begin{appendix}
    *appendix text*
    \end{appendix}.

## 3.5  Book structure

To simplify the structuring of a book, the commands

    [2ε] \frontmatter
        *preface, table of contents*
    [2ε] \mainmatter
        *main body of text*
    [2ε] \backmatter
        *bibliography, index, colophon*

are provided in the book class. The \frontmatter command switches page numbering to Roman numerals and suppresses the numbering of chapters; \mainmatter resets the page numbering to 1 with Arabic numbers and reactivates the chapter numbering; this is once again turned off with \backmatter.

*Exercise 3.9:  Insert at the beginning of your exercise text the command \section{Title A} and at some appropriate place near the middle \section{Title B}. Select some suitable text for Title A and Title B. Insert at appropriate places some \subsection commands with reasonable subtitles. Remove the commands included from Exercise 3.3:*

```
\pagestyle{myheadings} \markright{Exercises}
\pagenumbering{Roman}
```

*and print the results.*

*Exercise 3.10:  Include the additional command \chapter{Chapter title} with your own appropriate Chapter title before your first \section command. Change the document class command to \documentclass[twoside]{report} and call the page style command \pagestyle{headings} in the preamble. Note the twofold effect of the sectioning commands in the headings and in the page headlines. Compare the results with the table in Section 3.2.1.*

*Exercise 3.11: Change the chapter command to*

```
\chapter[Short form]{Chapter title}
```

*by putting an abbreviated version of Chapter title for Short form. Now the page head contains the shortened title where the full chapter title previously appeared.*

## 3.4    Table of contents

### 3.4.1    Automatic entries

LATEX can prepare and print a table of contents automatically for the whole document. It will contain the section numbers and corresponding headings as given in the standard form of the sectioning commands, together with the page numbers on which they begin.  The sectioning depth to which entries are made in the table of contents can be set in the preamble with the command

```
\setcounter{tocdepth}{num}
```

The value *num* has exactly the same meaning and effect as it does for the counter secnumdepth described above, by which the maximum level of automatic subsectioning is fixed. By default, the depth to which entries are included in the table of contents is the same as the standard level to which automatic sectioning is done: that is, to level \subsection for book and report and to level \subsubsection for article.

## 4.2 Printing the table of contents

The table of contents is generated and printed with the command

    \tableofcontents

given at the location where the table of contents is to appear, which is normally after the title page and abstract.

This leads to a paradox, for the information in the table of contents is to be printed near the beginning of the document, information that cannot be known until the end. LaTeX solves this problem as follows: the first time the document is processed, no table of contents can be included but instead LaTeX opens a new file with the same name as the document file and with the extension .toc; the entries for the table of contents are written to this file during the rest of the processing.

The next time LaTeX is run on this document, the \tableofcontents command causes the file *document_name*.toc to be read and the table of contents is printed. As the processing continues, the .toc file is updated in case there have been major changes since the previous run. This means that the table of contents that is printed is always the one corresponding to the previous version of the document. For this reason, it may be necessary to run LaTeX twice on the final version.

## 4.3 Additional entries

The *-form sectioning commands are not entered automatically in the table of contents. To insert them, or any other additional entry, the commands

    \addcontentsline{toc}{sec_name}{entry text}
    \addtocontents{toc}{entry_text}

may be used.

With the first command, the entries will conform to the format of the table of contents, whereby section headings are indented more than those for chapter but less than those for subsection. This is determined by the value of the argument *sec_name*, which is the same as one of the sectioning commands without the \ character (for example section). The *entry_text* is inserted in the table of contents along with the page number. If a section number is also to appear, as in the standard form of sectioning commands, *entry_text* must be in the form \protect\numberline{*sec_num*}{*text*}.

The \addtocontents command puts any desired command or text into the .toc file. This could be a formatting command, say \protect\newpage, which takes effect when the table of contents is printed.

## 4.4 Other lists

In addition to the table of contents, lists of figures and tables can also be generated and printed automatically by LaTeX. The commands to produce these lists are

> \listoffigures   reads and/or produces .lof
> \listoftables    reads and/or produces .lot

The entries in these lists are made automatically by the \caption command in the figure and table environments (see Section 6.6.4). Additional entries are made with the same commands as for the table of contents, the general form of which is

> \addcontentsline{*file*}{*format*}{*entry*}
> \addtocontents{*file*}{*entry*}

where *file* stands for one of the three types toc (*table of contents*), lof (*list of figures*), or lot (*list of tables*). The argument *format* is one of the sectioning commands for the table of contents, as described above, or figure for the list of figures, or table for the list of tables. The argument *entry* stands for the text that is to be inserted into the appropriate file.

*Exercise 3.12: In your exercise file, insert after the deactivated title page commands*

> \pagenumbering{roman}
> \tableofcontents \newpage
> \pagenumbering{arabic}

*Process your exercise file* twice *with LATEX and print out the second results. Deactivate the above commands with % before doing the next run.*
*Note: if your section titles contain any commands, they might have to be preceded by the* \protect *command to ensure that they are safely transferred to the corresponding file.*

## 3.5     Fine-tuning text

### 3.5.1     Word and character spacing

The spacing between words and characters is normally set automatically by TEX, which not only makes use of the natural width of the characters but also takes into account alterations for certain character combinations. For example, an A followed by a V does not appear as AV but rather as AV; that is, they are moved together slightly for a more pleasing appearance. Inter-word spacing within one line is uniform, and is chosen so that the right and left ends match exactly with the side margins. This is called left and right *justification*. TEX also attempts to keep the word spacing for different lines as nearly the same as possible.

Words that end with a punctuation mark are given extra spacing, depending on the character: following a period '.' or exclamation mark '!', there is more space than after a comma ','. This corresponds to the rule in English typesetting that there should be extra spacing between sentences. In certain cases, the automatic procedures do not work properly, or it is desirable to override them, as described in the next sections.

### Sentence termination and periods

TEX interprets a period following a lower case letter to be the end of a sentence where additional inter-word spacing is to be inserted. This leads to confusion with abbreviations such as *i. e.*, *Prof. Jones*, or *Phys. Rev.*, where the normal spacing is required. This can be achieved by using the characters ˜ or \␣ instead of the normal blank. (The character ␣ is simply a symbol for the blank which is otherwise invisible.) Both these methods insert the normal inter-word spacing; in addition, ˜ prevents the line from being broken at this point. The above examples should be typed in as `i.˜e.`, `Prof.˜Jones`, and `Phys.\ Rev.`, producing *i. e.*, *Prof. Jones*, and *Phys. Rev.* with the correct spacing and forcing the first two to be all on one line. In the third case, there is nothing wrong with putting *Phys.* and *Rev.* on different lines.

A period following an upper case letter is not interpreted as the end of a sentence, but as an abbreviation. If it really is the end of a sentence, then it is necessary to add `\@` before the period in order to achieve the extra spacing. For example, this sentence ends with NASA. It is typed in as `This sentence ends with NASA\@.`

### French spacing

The additional inter-word spacing between sentences can be switched off with the command `\frenchspacing`, which remains in effect until countermanded with `\nonfrenchspacing`. In this case, the command `\@` is ignored and may be omitted. This paragraph has been printed with `\frenchspacing` turned on, so that all word spacings within one line are the same. It corresponds to the normal rule for non-English typesetting.

### Character combinations "' and '"

A small spacing is produced with the command `\,`. This may be used, for example, to separate the double quotes " and " from the corresponding single quotes ' and ' when they appear together. For example, the text `''\,'Beginning' and 'End'\,''` produces "'Beginning' and 'End'".

### Italic correction

In changing from a sloping type face such as *italic* or *slanted* to a vertical one, the last character may lean too far over into the following spacing, making it appear too small. Extra spacing must be inserted here, depending on the letter (more for a *d* than for an *a*). TEX adds this extra spacing, known as *italic correction*, when the command `\/` is given. This should always be included after the last letter of a sloping type face before switching to a vertical one, for example `{\slshape slanted\/}` spacing for *slanted* spacing. The command may be omitted when the last sloping letter is followed by a period or comma.

The LATEX 2ε font commands \textsl and \textit (Section 4.1.4) automatically add italic corrections, which is another reason to prefer them over the font declarations \slshape, \itshape. For example, instead of {\slshape slanted\/}, one should type \textsl{slanted}. However, it might sometimes be desirable to suppress the italic correction, something that may be accomplished with the command \nocorr at the end of the sloping text.

### Breaking ligatures

The same command \/ may be used to suppress ligatures, that is, letter combinations that are printed as one character. The text shelf\/ful produces *shelfful* instead of the normal *shelfful*. As shown in Section 2.5.8, TEX prints the combinations ff, fi, fl, ffi, and ffl as ligatures. By typing f\/f\/i, the combination *ffi* is produced instead of the ligature *ffi*.

The \/ command may also be used to suppress the reduced spacing between certain letter combinations, such as AV or Te:

    A\/V AV   T\/e Te      instead of      AV   Te

### Inserting arbitrary spacing

Spacing of any desired size may be inserted into the text with the commands

    \hspace{*space*}
    \hspace*{*space*}

where *space* is the length specification for the amount of spacing, for example 1.5cm or 3em. (Recall that one *em* is the width of the letter M in the current type face.)

This command puts blank space of the width *space* at that point in the text where it appears. The standard form (without *) suppresses the spacing if it occurs between two lines, just as normal blanks are removed at the beginning of lines. The *-form, on the other hand, inserts the spacing no matter where it occurs.

The length specification may be negative, in which case the command works as a backspace for overprinting characters with other ones.

A blank before or after the command will also be included:

    \This is\hspace{1cm}1cm          This is      1cm
    \This is \hspace{1cm}1cm         This is      1cm
    \This is \hspace{1cm} 1cm        This is      1cm

The command \hfill is an abbreviation for \hspace{\fill} (see Section 2.4.2). It inserts enough space at that point to force the text on either side to be pushed over to the left and right margins. With Left\hfill Right one produces

Left                                                                    Right

Multiple occurrences of \hfill within one line will each insert the same amount of spacing so that the line becomes left and right justified. For example, the text Left\hfill Center\hfill Right generates

Left                              Center                              Right

If \hfill comes at the beginning of a line, the spacing is suppressed in accordance with the behavior of the standard form for \hspace. If a rubber space is really to be added at the beginning or end of a line, \hspace*{\fill} must be used instead. However, LaTeX also offers a number of commands and environments to simplify most such applications (see Section 4.2.2).

A number of other fixed horizontal spacing commands are available:

> \quad  and  \qquad

The command \quad inserts a horizontal space equal to the current type size, that is, 10 pt for a 10 pt type face, whereas \qquad inserts twice as much.

**Inserting variable ...... and _____ sequences**

Two commands that work exactly the same way as \hfill are

> \dotfill  and  \hrulefill

Instead of inserting empty space, these commands fill the gap with dots or a ruled line, as follows:

Start \dotfill\ Finish\\                                    and
Left \hrulefill\ Center \hrulefill\ Right\\   produce

Start ............................................................ Finish
Left _____ Center _____ Right

Any combination of \hfill, \dotfill, and \hrulefill may be given on one line. If any of these commands appears more than once at one location, the corresponding filling will be printed that many more times than for a single occurrence.

Departure \dotfill\dotfill\dotfill\ 8:30 \hfill\hfill
Arrival \hrulefill\ 11:45\\

Departure ...... ...... ...... 8:30                    Arrival _____ 11:45

## 3.5.2   Line breaking

The breaking up of text into lines is carried out automatically in TeX and LaTeX. However, there are times when a line break must be forced or encouraged, or when a line break is to be suppressed.

### The command \\

A new line with or without additional line spacing can be achieved with the command \\. Its syntax is

> \\ [*space*]
> \\*[*space*]

The optional argument *space* is a length that specifies how much additional line spacing is to be put between the lines. If it is necessary to start a new page, the additional line spacing is not included and the new page begins with the next line of text. The *-form prevents a new page from occurring between the two lines.

With \\*[10cm], the current line is ended and a vertical spacing of 10 cm is inserted before the next line, which is forced to be on the same page as the current line. If a page break is necessary, it will be made before the current line, which is then positioned at the top of the new page together with the 10 cm vertical spacing and the next text line.

The command \newline is identical to \\ without the option *space*. That is, a new line is started with no additional spacing and a page break is possible at that point.

Both commands may be given only within a paragraph, and not between them where they would be meaningless.

### Further line breaking commands

The command \linebreak is used to encourage or force a line break at a certain point in the text. Its form is

> \linebreak[*num*]

where *num* is an optional argument, a whole number between 0 and 4 that specifies how important a line break is. The command recommends a line break, and the higher the number the stronger the recommendation. A value of 0 allows a break where it otherwise would not occur (like in the middle of a word), whereas 4 compels a line break, as does \linebreak without *num*. The difference between this command and \\ or \newline is that the current line will be fully justified, that is, inter-word spacing will be added so that the text fills the line completely. With \\ and \newline, however, the line is filled with empty space after the last word and the inter-word spacing remains normal.

The opposite command

`\nolinebreak[`*num*`]`

discourages a line break at the given position, with *num* specifying the degree of discouragement. Again, `\nolinebreak` without a *num* argument has the same effect as `\nolinebreak[4]`, that is, a line break is absolutely impossible here.

Another way of forcing text to stay together on one line is with the command `\mbox{`*text*`}`. This is convenient for expressions such as 'Voyager-1' to stop a line break at the hyphen.

## 5.3  Paragraph spacing

The normal spacing between paragraphs is set by the length `\parskip` (Section 3.2.3), which may be altered from its original default value with the `\setlength` command:

`\setlength{\parskip}{`*space*`}`

It is possible to add extra vertical spacing of amount *space* between particular paragraphs using the commands

`\vspace{`*space*`}`
`\vspace*{`*space*`}`

The *-form will add the extra space even when a new page occurs, or when the command appears at the top of a new page. The standard form suppresses the extra vertical spacing in these situations.

If these commands are given within a paragraph, the extra space is inserted after the current line, which is right and left justified as usual.

The *space* parameter may even be negative, in order to move the following text higher up the page than where it would normally be printed.

The command `\vfill` is an abbreviation for `\vspace{\fill}` (see Section 2.4.2). This is the equivalent of `\hfill` for vertical spacing, inserting enough blank vertical space to make the top and bottom of the text match up exactly with the upper and lower margins. The comments on multiple occurrences of `\hfill` also apply to `\vfill`. If this command is given at the beginning of a page, its effect is suppressed, just as for the standard form of `\vspace{\fill}`. If a rubber space is to be put at the top of a page, the *-form `\vspace*{\fill}` must be used.

Further commands for increasing the spacing between paragraphs are

`\bigskip`     `\medskip`     `\smallskip`

which add vertical spacing depending on the font size declared in the document class.

Instead of a blank line, the command `\par` may also be used to indicate the end of a paragraph.

### 3.5.4    Paragraph indentation

The amount of paragraph indentation is set with the length \parindent (see Section 3.2.3), which can be changed with the \setlength command:

> \setlength{\parindent}{*space*}

The first line of each paragraph then has blank spacing of width *space* at the left side. If paragraph indentation is to be suppressed for one paragraph, or if it is to be forced where it would otherwise not occur (for example, the first paragraph of a section), this may be accomplished with the commands

> \noindent    and    \indent

which are placed at the beginning of the paragraph that they are to affect.

### 3.5.5    Page breaking

Breaking text into pages occurs automatically in TeX and LaTeX, just as for line breaking. Here again, it may be necessary to interfere with the program's notion of where a break should take place.

#### Normal pages

The commands

> \pagebreak[*num*]
> \nopagebreak[*num*]

are the equivalents of \linebreak and \nolinebreak for page breaking. If \pagebreak appears between two paragraphs, a new page will be forced at that point. If it comes within a paragraph, the new page will be implemented after the current line is completed. This line will be right and left justified as usual.

The command \nopagebreak has the opposite effect: between paragraphs, it prevents a page break from occurring there, and within a paragraph, it stops a page break that might take place at the end of the current line.

Optional numbers between 0 and 4 express the degree of encouragement or discouragement for a page break. The analogy with the command \linebreak goes further: just as the line that is broken will be left and right justified with extra inter-word spacing, so will the broken page be expanded with inter-line spacing to make it top and bottom justified.

The proper command to end a page in the middle, fill it with blank spacing, and go on to a new page is

> \newpage

which is equivalent to \newline with regard to page breaking.

*Exercise 3.13: Place one or two \newpage commands at appropriate spots in your exercise file. In the printout, the rest of the page will be empty. Now remove these commands and insert a \pagebreak command one or two lines after a natural page break. Afterwards, move the command a few lines before the normal break.*

### Pages with figures and tables

If the text contains tables, pictures, or reserved space for figures, these are inserted at the location of the corresponding command, provided that there is enough room for them on the current page. If there is not enough space, the text continues and the figure or table is stored to be put on a following page.

The command

   \clearpage

ends the current page like \newpage and in addition outputs all the pending figures and tables on one or more extra pages. (See also Section 6.6.)

### Two-column pages

If the document class option twocolumn has been chosen, or the command \twocolumn is in effect, then the two commands \pagebreak and \newpage end the current *column* and begin a new one, treating columns as pages. On the other hand, \clearpage and \cleardoublepage (see below) terminate the current page, inserting an empty right column if necessary.

### Two-sided pages

An additional page breaking command is available when the document option twoside has been selected:

   \cleardoublepage

which functions exactly the same as \clearpage (the current page is terminated, all pending figures and tables are output) but in addition, the next text will be put on to an *odd* numbered page. If necessary, an empty page with an even number is printed to achieve this.

### Restricted page breaking

The declaration \samepage limits page breaks to occurring only between paragraphs, before or after displayed formulas or text, before or after a section heading, or between \items (except the first) in a list environment

(Section 4.3). If a page break must occur at some other point in the text, the \pagebreak command is used to allow it explicitly.

This feature actually does not work as well as one might have hoped, and for that reason LATEX 2ε provides some new methods for controlling unwanted page breaks. The \samepage command is retained for compatibility with older documents.

### Controlling page breaks

LATEX 2ε provides the possibility of increasing the height of the current page slightly with commands

> 2ε \enlargethispage{*size*}
>
> 2ε \enlargethispage*{*size*}

which add the length *size* to \textheight for this one page only. Sometimes the difference of a few points is all that is necessary to avoid a bad page break. The *-form of the command also shrinks any inter-line spacing as needed to maximize the amount of text on the page.

### Further tips on page breaking

As mentioned above in Section 3.2.4, in document class book or option twoside the bottom edge of the page body is always the same on every page, but otherwise it may vary. This means that in these two cases extra inter-line spacing will be inserted at appropriate places, such as between paragraphs.

This behavior is regulated by the internal declaration \flushbottom for book and twoside, and by \raggedbottom for all other situations. They are initially set by the internal class and option definitions, but may also be given by the user in the preamble or anywhere else in the text. They remain in effect until countermanded or until the end of the current environment.

It is not normally possible to have more text on a page than is allowed by the selected page length \textheight (Section 3.2.4). However, if it is absolutely necessary to squeeze in one or two extra lines, vertical space must be cleared for them. This can be done with the commands \vspace or \\ with a *negative length* at an appropriate spot. The best places are before and after *displays, enumerations, lists, tables, figures* (see Chapter 4).

A detailed description of the internal rules for page breaking cannot be given here, but it is sufficient to say that TEX issues so-called penalty points (with the command \penalty) at those places where a page break is to be discouraged, with *negative* points indicating an encouragement. Each line of a paragraph is given, say, 10 penalty points (\linepenalty=10), to make it more difficult to break the page within than between paragraphs.

The first and last lines of a paragraph are given 150 penalty points (that is, \clubpenalty=150 and \widowpenalty=150) to discourage (but not to forbid) page breaks that would leave a single line of a paragraph on one page.

As a last resort, one can change the penalty assignments to achieve a desired page break. For example, by setting \clubpenalty=450 it becomes three times more difficult to break the page after the first line of a paragraph compared to normal. Setting the penalty to 10 000 or more makes a page break *absolutely* impossible. Altering the penalty assignments, however, should only be undertaken when all else fails, since this destroys the balance with the rest of the document, and may conjure up even more monstrous page breaks.

# Word division

When a line is to be right and left justified, it often turns out that the break cannot be made between whole words without either shoving the text too close together or inserting huge gaps between the words. It is then necessary to split a word. This fundamental task is performed by TEX, the underlying basis of LATEX, by means of a word-dividing algorithm that works (almost) perfectly for English text, which is more than can be said for most authors. Nevertheless, even it makes mistakes at times which need to be corrected by human intervention.

If normal TEX/LATEX is used for other languages, or if foreign words appear in English text, incorrect hyphenations are very likely to appear. (See Sections 3.6.5, 3.6.6, and D.1 for more discussions about LATEX with other languages.) In these cases too, something must be done to override TEX's hyphenation rules, as described below.

## Manual hyphenation

The simplest way to correct a wrongly divided word is to include a \- command at the right place within the word. The word *manuscript*, for example, will not be hyphenated at all, so if it causes problems with breaking a line, write it as man\-u\-script. This tells TEX to divide the word as necessary either as *man-uscript* or as *manu-script*, and to ignore its normal rules.

The \- command merely makes hyphenation possible at the indicated locations; it does not force it. If the author absolutely insists in dividing a word at a certain point, say between the *u* and *s* in *manuscript*, he can type manu-\linebreak script to achieve this. However, this brute force method is not recommended, because the line break will always occur here even if the text is later changed.

For English text, the spelling of a word remains the same when it is hyphenated, something that is not true in other languages. In German, for example, there is a rule is that if *ck* is split, it becomes *k-k*. TEX allows for such behavior with the general hyphenation command

> \discretionary{*before*}{*after*}{*without*}

where *before* and *after* are the letters (with hyphen) that come on either side of the break if division takes place, and *without* is the normal text with no hyphenation. Thus Boris Becker's name should be typed as

> Boris Be\discretionary{k-}{k}{ck}er

something that one only wants to do in exceptional situations. Incidentally, the \- command is defined as \discretionary{-}{}{}.

## 3.6.2   Hyphenation list

Words that are incorrectly hyphenated and that appear frequently within the document can be put into a *list of exceptions* in the preamble, to avoid laboriously inserting \- every time:

> \hyphenation{*list*}

The *list* consists of a set of words, separated by blanks or new lines, with the allowed division points indicated by hyphens. For example,

> \hyphenation{man-u-script com-pu-ter gym-na-sium
>              coun-try-man re-sus-ci-tate ... }

The list may contain only words with the normal letters *a–z*, with no special characters or accents.

## 3.6.3   Suppressing hyphenation

Another means of avoiding bad word divisions is to turn hyphenation off, at least for a paragraph or two. Actually the command

> \begin{sloppypar} *paragraph text* \end{sloppypar}

does not prevent word division, but does permit larger inter-word spacings without giving a warning message. This means that practically all lines are broken between words. It is also possible to put the command \sloppy in the preamble or in the current environment to reduce the number of word divisions in the whole document or within the environment range. This is recommended when the line width is rather narrow.

When the command \sloppy is in effect, it is possible to undo it temporarily and to turn hyphenation back on with the environment

> \begin{fussypar} *paragraph text* \end{fussypar}

The same effect may be achieved within an environment with the command \fussy.

## .4    Line width and word division

It is appropriate to add some comments here about the effect of the line width on word division.

When TEX reaches the end of a paragraph, it attempts to organize the text into lines of equal width, taking into account the spacing requirements of Section 3.5.1, by breaking the text only between words; that is, without word division. If this fails, it will start looking for break points within the words themselves. Line breaking between words can occur much more easily if the line width is large, or if the average word length is small. Furthermore, for a given line width, the number of word divisions will be fewer if the font size is smaller.

With narrow line widths, right and left justification may not be possible even with word division, in which case TEX will need to insert more inter-word spacing than normally allowed. This can be accomplished with the `sloppypar` environment or `\sloppy` command described above. Justification will be achieved, but at the price of having the words pulled apart by an unacceptable amount. In both cases TEX prints a warning message, either `Overfull \hbox` (justification is impossible and a word will stick out beyond the right margin) or `Underfull \hbox` (word spacing too large). If neither situation is tolerable, the text will have to be adjusted, or suitable break points may be forced with then commands `\linebreak` and `\hfill`.

## .5    More about word division

The information that TEX needs to carry out word division is stored in an internal file `hyphen.tex` containing a list of letter combinations used by the special hyphenation algorithm. This list is made up from statistical studies of the language under consideration. The file also contains a list of exceptions, those words that are incorrectly hyphenated by the algorithm. TEX first looks for a word in the exception list, splitting it according to the pattern it finds there; if it does not find it, it splits it using its algorithm. For other languages, a different list of letter combinations and exceptions must be given.

The list of exceptions is found at the end of the file `hyphen.tex` and consists of the `\hyphenation` command described in the previous section. The entries in this list may be extended with a text editor. In a central computing center, such changes should only be made by the authorized TEX operator. On a PC, the user must consult the TEX installation manual to see where the `hyphen.tex` file is located.

Every time the hyphenation file is altered, a new format file must be generated. This is the main macro definition file for LATEX, stored in a compact format for fast input. See Section D.4 for more information on installing LATEX $2_\varepsilon$.

Incidentally, one may examine the results of TEX's hyphenation algorithm on the screen with the command

> `\showhyphens{`*list of words*`}`

which prints out all the words in the *list of words* with the hyphenations that TEX chooses. For example, giving

> `\showhyphens{interrelations penumbra summation}`

will print to the screen

```
in-ter-re-la-tions penum-bra sum-ma-tion
```

### 3.6.6   Word division with multilingual text

! In TeX versions 2.99 or lower, only one set of letter combinations for hyphenation was allowed in one `plain.fmt` or `lplain.fmt` file. The LaTeX programs using these versions were applicable only for *either* English *or* one other language. It was not possible to mix languages in one document with multiple hyphenation rules.

From TeX version 3.0 on, multiple hyphenation lists may be included in the format, making it possible to switch hyphenation schemes within one document, using a new TeX command `\language`. This command may be used as part of language-specific adaptations to translate certain explicit English words in the output (such as 'Contents'), to simplify accents or punctuation, and to alter the definition of the date command `\today`. More information on multiple languages and `\language` is given in Sections C.3.3 and D.1.4.

# Displayed Text

**4**

There are a variety of ways to display or emphasize the text: changing font style or font size, centering, indentation, marking the paragraphs, and so on. LaTeX supplies us with commands for the most common forms of display.

## Changing font

In typography, a set of letters, numbers, and characters of a certain size and appearance is called a *font*. The standard font in LaTeX for the main body of text is an *upright*, *Roman* one of *medium* weight, in the size specified in the \documentclass or \documentstyle statement at the start. The three possible basic sizes are 10, 11, and 12 pt, depending on the size options 10pt (default), 11pt, and 12pt. (Recall, there are 72.27 points per inch or about 28.45 pt per cm.) The parenthesis characters ( ) extend the full height and depth of the font size.

The differences in the visual appearance of the three standard sizes are greater than would be expected from the ratios of the numbers:

This is an example of the 10 pt font. ( )

And this is the 11 pt font for comparison. ( )

And finally this is a sample of 12 pt font. ( )

## 1 Emphasis

In a typewritten manuscript the simplest way to emphasize text is with underlining. The typesetter will normally transform underlined text into *italics* for the printed version. Switching from standard to *emphasized* text is carried out in LaTeX with the declaration \em or with the command \emph [2ε].

The \em declaration functions as the other font declarations described below: the change of font remains in effect until negated by another appropriate declaration (which can be \em itself), or until the end of the current *environment* (Section 2.2). An environment may also be created with a pair of curly braces {...}. This is the easiest way to *emphasize* short pieces of text, as for example:

```
This is the easiest way to {\em emphasize} short ...
```

A more logical method of *emphasizing* a word or two is provided in LaTeX 2ε with the command \emph:

```
A more logical method of \emph{emphasizing} a word ...
```

Note carefully the difference between the *declaration* that remains in effect until the local environment is ended with the closing curly brace, and the command that operates on an argument enclosed in curly braces. Another more subtle difference is that the command \emph automatically inserts the *italic correction* (see Section 3.5.1), while with the declaration \em one must include it manually.

Both the declaration and the command switch to an emphasizing font. That means, if the current font is upright it switches to *italics, whereas if the text is already slanted, an* upright *font is selected.*

Nested emphasis is possible and is simple to understand:

```
The {\em first}, second, and {\em third font switch}
The {\em first, {\em second, and {\em third font switch}}}
```

both produce 'The *first,* second, and *third font switch*'.

### 4.1.2   Choice of font size

The following declarations are available in LaTeX for changing the font size:

| | | | |
|---|---|---|---|
| \tiny | smallest | \Large | larger |
| \scriptsize | very small | \LARGE | even larger |
| \footnotesize | smaller | \huge | still larger |
| \small | small | \Huge | largest |
| \normalsize | normal | | |
| \large | large | | |

all of which are relative to the standard size selected in the document class option. In this book, the standard size is 10 pt, which is then the size selected with \normalsize.

The font size declarations behave as all other declarations: they make an immediate change that remains in effect until counteracted by another size declaration, or until the current environment comes to an end. If issued within curly braces {..}, the effect of the declaration extends only to the closing brace, as in a nameless environment:

```
normal {\large large \Large larger} normal again
```

normal large larger normal again

In LaTeX 2.09, the font size declarations also reset all the other font attributes (Section 4.1.3) to their defaults, that is, Roman, upright, medium weight. By contrast, in LaTeX $2_\varepsilon$, these attributes remain unchanged. Compare:

| 2.09 | `\sl slanted {\Large larger}` | *slanted* larger |
| 2ε | `\sl slanted {\Large larger}` | *slanted* larger |

If `\documentstyle` is specified in place of `\documentclass`, these size declarations behave as they do in LaTeX 2.09, for compatibility with older documents.

Changing the font size with one of the above commands also automatically changes the inter-line spacing. For every font size, there is a corresponding *natural* line spacing `\baselineskip`. This may be altered at any time. For example, if the natural line spacing is 12 pt, the command `\setlength{\baselineskip}{15pt}` will increase it to 15 pt.

The value of `\baselineskip` that is effective at the end of the paragraph is used to make up the whole paragraph. This means that if there are several changes to `\baselineskip` within a paragraph, only the last value given will be taken into account.

With every change in font size, `\baselineskip` is reset to its natural value for that size. Any previous setting with `\setlength` will be nullified.

In order to create a change in the line spacing that is valid for all font sizes, one must make use of the factor `\baselinestretch`, which has a normal value of 1. The true inter-line spacing is really

> `\baselinestretch`×`\baselineskip`

which maintains the same relative spacing for all font sizes. The user may change this spacing at any time with:

> `\renewcommand{\baselinestretch}{factor}`

where *factor* is any decimal number. A value of 1.5 increases the inter-line spacing (baseline to baseline) by 50% over its natural size for all font sizes.

However, the new value of `\baselinestretch` does not take effect until the next change in font size. In order to implement a new value in the current font size, it is necessary to switch to another size and back again immediately. If the present font size is `\normalsize`, the sequence

> `\small\normalsize`

will do the trick. Any size command may be used in place of `\small`.

Not all font styles are available in every size. If an impossible combination of font size and style is selected, LaTeX answers with a warning and says which typeface will be substituted when printed.

### 4.1.3    Font attributes $\boxed{2_\varepsilon}$

The size of a font is only one of several *attributes* that may be used to describe it. With the New Font Selection Scheme (NFSS), which is an integral part of LaTeX $2_\varepsilon$, it is possible to select fonts strictly by these attributes, as described in Section 8.5. However, for normal usage, there are some declarations and corresponding commands to simplify this procedure.

For the Computer Modern fonts provided with TeX and LaTeX, the following attributes and their values exist:

**Family:** for the general overall style. Traditional typographical families have names like *Baskerville, Bodoni, Times Roman, Helvetica*, and so on. The standard LaTeX $2_\varepsilon$ installation provides three families with declarations

`\rmfamily` to switch (back) to a Roman font;
`\ttfamily` to switch to a `typewriter` font;
`\sffamily` to select a sans serif font.

**Shape:** for the form of the font. The shape declarations available with the standard installation are

`\upshape` to switch (back) to an upright font;
`\itshape` to select an *italic* shape;
`\slshape` to choose a font that is *slanted*;
`\scshape` to switch to CAPS AND SMALL CAPS.

**Series:** for the width and/or weight (boldness) of the font. The declarations possible are

`\mdseries` to switch (back) to medium weight;
`\bfseries` to select a **bold face** font.

These do not exhaust all the possible attribute settings, but they do cover the most standard ones, especially for the Computer Modern fonts. For other fonts, especially PostScript ones, additional attribute values exist. See Section 8.5 for more details.

These declarations are used just like any others, normally enclosed in a pair of curly braces {...}, such as {\scshape Romeo and Juliet} producing ROMEO AND JULIET. For longer sections of text, an environment is preferable:

`\begin{`*font_style*`}` ... *text in new font* ... `\end{`*font_style*`}`

This keeps better track of the beginning and end of the switch-over. For *font_style*, any of the above font commands may be used, leaving off the initial `\`.

Since changing any one attribute leaves the others as they were, all possible combinations may be obtained. (However, this does not mean that a font exists for each possible combination; if not, a substitution will be made.) If we select first a bold series with \bfseries, and then a slanted shape with \slshape, we obtain a bold, slanted font.

```
normal and {\bfseries bold and
    {\slshape slanted} and back} again.
```

produces: normal and **bold and *slanted* and back** again.

Finally, the declaration \normalfont resets all the attributes (except size) back to their defaults: Roman, upright, medium weight. It is often useful to issue this command just to be sure of the font in effect.

## .4  Font commands $\boxed{2\varepsilon}$

For each of the font declarations listed above, there is a corresponding *font command* that sets its argument in a font with the specified attribute.

| | | | |
|---|---|---|---|
| Family: | \textrm{*text*} | \texttt{*text*} | \textsf{*text*} |
| Shape: | \textup{*text*} | \textit{*text*} | \textsl{*text*} |
| | \textsc{*text*} | | |
| Series: | \textmd{*text*} | \textbf{*text*} | |
| Default: | \textnormal{*text*} | | |
| Emphasis: | \emph{*text*} | | |

Note that the \emph command is included here, corresponding to the declaration \em. The argument of \textnormal is set in the standard font selected with \normalfont.

The use of such commands to change the font for short pieces of text, or single words, is much more logical than placing a declaration inside an implied environment. The previous example now becomes

```
normal and \textbf{bold and \textsl{slanted}
    and back} again.
```

to make: normal and **bold and *slanted* and back** again.

As for the \emph command, these font commands automatically add any necessary *italic correction* (Section 3.5.1) when switching between upright and slanted/italic fonts. The correction may be suppressed by including \nocorr where it would otherwise appear, as

```
\textit{some italics\nocorr} without correction
{\slshape italics \nocorr\textup{without} correction}
```

**Reminder:** the font attribute declarations and commands are only available with LaTeX 2$_\varepsilon$, not with version 2.09.

## .5  Old font declarations $\boxed{2.09}$

For compatibility with LaTeX 2.09, the two-letter font declarations (originally part of TeX) have been retained.

| | | | | | |
|---|---|---|---|---|---|
| \rm | Roman | \it | *Italic* | \sc | SMALL CAPS |
| \bf | **Bold face** | \sl | *Slanted* | \sf | Sans Serif |
| \tt | Typewriter | | | | |

These have a different behavior from that of their newer counterparts: they rigidly select a particular font instead of altering only one attribute, albeit retaining the current size. It is as though a \normalfont declaration were issued with them.

{\bf text} equals {\normalfont\bfseries text}

**Note:** In the two releases of NFSS prior to LATEX 2$_\varepsilon$, these two-letter declarations were defined to behave as the newer, longer declarations. To process documents written for those systems, add the package newlfont (Section 8.8.3) in the preamble.

## 4.1.6  Additional fonts

!

It is likely that your computing center or your PC TEX package has even more fonts and sizes than those listed above. Consult the *Local Guide* or the package instructions. If so, they may be made available for use within a LATEX document either by referring to them by name, or by their attributes, if they have been set up for NFSS.

To load a new font by name, the command

\newfont{\\*fnt*}{*name* scaled *factor*}    or
\newfont{\\*fnt*}{*name* at *size*}

is given, which assigns the font to the new command named \\*fnt*. In the first case, *factor* is a number 1000 times the scaling factor that is to be used to magnify or reduce the font from its basic or design size. In the second case, the font is scaled to be of the *size* specified. To install a slanted, sans serif font of size 20.74 pt, as \sss, we load cmssi17 at 20.74pt with

\newfont{\sss}{cmssi17 at 20.74pt}

Now the declaration \sss switches to this font in the same way as \rm and \it change fonts, except that the baseline separation is not altered.

Alternatively, the new font declaration can be made by attributes with (see Section 8.5.4)

\DeclareFixedFont{\sss}{OT1}{cmss}{m}{sl}{20.74}

Indeed, if one wants to use the current encoding and \sffamily without knowing what they are, or without worrying so precisely what size must be stated, it is also possible to give

\DeclareFixedFont{\sss}{\encodingdefault}{\sfdefault}
      {m}{sl}{20}

(The defaults are explained in Section 8.5.3.)

# .7  Character sets and symbols

The character sets that TₑX and LATₑX print are provided with the program implementation. Depending on the version, there are between 400 and 800 font files
for the different typefaces, sizes, and magnifications, each consisting of 128 (in
future 256) single characters or symbols.

The individual character sets are each stored in their own files. The names of
the 75 standard character files are listed in Appendix E, where many of them are
also printed out.

Each symbol within a character set is addressed by means of a number between
0 and 127 (or 255). The command

> \symbol{*num*}

will produce that symbol with the internal identification number *num* in the
current font. The symbol ¿ in the present font has the internal number 62 and can
be printed with the command \symbol{62}. The identification number may also
be given as an *octal* (prefix ') or *hexadecimal* (prefix ") number. Thus the symbol
commands \symbol{28}, \symbol{'34}, and \symbol{"1C} are all identical,
producing 'ø'.

The \symbol command may also be used to generate symbols for which no
other command has been defined: for example, {\tt\symbol{'40} \symbol{'42}
\symbol{'134}} produce ␣ " \.

Section E.6 presents the assignments of the identification numbers with the
characters for the different symbol families.

# ?  Centering and indenting

# .1  Centered text

The environment

> \begin{center} *line 1* \\ *line 2* \\ ... *line n* \end{center}

centers the sections of text that are separated by the \\ command. (An
optional additional line spacing may be inserted with \\[*len*].) If the text
is too long for one line, it is split over several lines using uniform word
spacing, filling the whole line width as best it can, except for the last line.
Word division does not occur.

Within an environment, the command \centering may be used to
center the following text, again with \\ as the line divider. The effect of
the declaration lasts until the end of that environment.

A single line may be centered by typing its text as the argument of the
TₑX command \centerline{*text*}.

# .2  One-sided justification

The environments

> \begin{flushleft} *line 1* \\ *line 2* \\ ... *line 2* \end{flushleft}
> \begin{flushright} *line 1* \\ *line 2* \\ ... *line 2* \end{flushright}

produce text that is left (`flushleft`) or right (`flushright`) justified. If a section of text does not fit on to one line, it is spread over several with fixed word spacing, the same as for the `center` environment. Again, word division does not occur.

The same results may be produced within an environment with the declarations

> `\raggedleft`     replacing the `flushleft`   environment, and
> `\raggedright`   replacing the `flushright` environment.

### 4.2.3   Two-sided indentation

A section of text may be displayed by indenting it by an equal amount on both sides, with the environments

> `\begin{quote}`         *text*     `\end{quote}`
> `\begin{quotation}`   *text*     `\end{quotation}`

Additional vertical spacing is inserted above and below the displayed text to separate it visually from the normal text.

The text to be displayed may be of any length; it can be part of a sentence, a whole paragraph, or several paragraphs.

Paragraphs are separated as usual with an empty line, although no empty lines are needed at the beginning and end of the displayed text since additional vertical spacing is inserted here anyway.

The difference between the above two forms is thus:

> In the `quotation` environment, paragraphs are marked by extra indentation of the first line, whereas in the `quote` environment, they are indicated with more vertical spacing between them.
>
> The present text is produced within the `quotation` environment, while the sample above was done with the `quote` environment.
>
> The `quotation` environment is only really meaningful when the regular text makes use of first-line indentation to show off new paragraphs.

### 4.2.4   Verse indentations

For indenting rhymes, poetry, verses, etc. on both sides, the environment

> \begin{verse} *poem* \end{verse}

is more appropriate.

> Stanzas are separated by blank lines
> while the individual lines of the stanza are divided by \\.

> If a line is too long for the reduced text width, it will be left
> and right justified and continued on the next line, which is
> indented even further.

The above indenting schemes may be nested inside one another. Within a quote environment there may be another quote, quotation, or verse environment. Each time, additional indentations are created on both sides of the text and vertical spacing is added above and below; these quantities however decrease as the depth of nesting increases. A maximum of six such nestings is allowed.

**Exercise 4.1:** *Put some appropriate sections of text in your exercise file into the* quote *and* quotation *environments, that is, enclose these sections within*

> \begin{quote} . . . . . . . \end{quote}      *or*
> \begin{quotation} . . . . . \end{quotation}

*commands.*

**Exercise 4.2:** *Make up a new file with the name* poem.tex *and type your favorite poem in the* verse *environment. Select* 12pt *as the standard font size and italic as the typeface. Put the title of the poem before the* verse *environment in a larger bold typeface, such as* \Large\bfseries. *Include the name of the poet right justified.*
*Note: remember that you may include declarations to change the font style or size within an environment and that these remain in effect only until the end of that environment.*

**Exercise 4.3:** *Make up another file with the name* title.tex. *Do you recall the* titlepage *environment for producing a free-form title page? If not, refer to Section 3.3.1. Create a title page with this environment using font sizes and styles of your choice, centering all the entries.*
*Note: within the* titlepage *environment you may of course make use of the* center *environment, but it is also sufficient to give the* \centering *declaration instead, since this will remain in effect only until the end of the* titlepage *environment.*
*Choose the individual line spacings with the command* \\[len] *using an appropriate value for the spacing len. Remember that vertical spacing before the first line of text must be entered with the \*-form of the command* \vspace\*[len] *(see Section 3.5.3).*
*Experiment with different font sizes and styles for the various parts of the title page, such as title, author's name, address, until you are satisfied with the results.*

*Compare your own title page with that of Exercise 3.8. If your creation appeals to you more, include it in your standard exercise file by replacing the commands* \title, \author, \date, *and* \maketitle *with the* titlepage *environment and your own entries.*

## 4.3    Lists

There are three environments available for producing formatted lists:

| | | |
|---|---|---|
| \begin{itemize} | *list text* | \end{itemize} |
| \begin{enumerate} | *list text* | \end{enumerate} |
| \begin{description} | *list text* | \end{description} |

In each of these environments, the *list text* is indented from the left margin and a label, or marker, is included. What type of label is used depends on which list environment has been selected. The command to produce the label is \item.

### 4.3.1    Sample itemize

- The individual entries are indicated with a black dot, a so-called *bullet*, as the label.

- The text in the entries may be of any length. The label appears at the beginning of the first line of text.

- Successive entries are separated from one another by additional vertical spacing.

The above text was produced as follows:

```
\begin{itemize}
\item The individual entries are indicated with a black dot, a
      so-called \emph{bullet}, as the label.
\item The text in the entries may be of any length. The label
      appears at the beginning of the first line of text.
\item Successive entries are separated from one another by
      additional vertical spacing.
\end{itemize}
```

### 4.3.2    Sample enumerate

1. The labels consist of seqential numbers.

2. The numbering starts at 1 with every call to the enumerate environment.

The above example was generated with the following text:

```
\begin{enumerate}
\item The labels consist of sequential numbers.
\item The numbering starts at 1 with every call to the
      \texttt{enumerate} environment.
\end{enumerate}
```

## 3.3    **Sample** description

**purpose** This environment is appropriate when a number of words or expressions are to be defined.

**example** A keyword is used as the label and the entry contains a clarification or explanation.

**other uses** It may also be used as an author list in a bibliography.

The above sample was created using the following:

```
\begin{description}
\item[purpose] This environment is appropriate when a number of
      words or expressions are to be defined.
\item[example] A keyword is used as the label and the entry
      contains a clarification or explanation.
\item[other uses] It may also be used as an author list in a
      bibliography.
\end{description}
```

The \item[*option*] command contains an optional argument that appears in bold face as the label.

## 3.4    **Nested lists**

The above lists may be included within one another, either mixed or of one type, to a depth of four levels. The type of label used depends on the depth of the nesting. The indentation is always relative to the left margin of the enclosing list. A fourfold nesting of the itemize environment appears as follows:

- The label for the first level is a black dot, a *bullet*.
  - That of the second level is a long dash.
    * That of the third level is an asterisk.
      · And the label for the fourth level is a simple dot.
      · At the same time, the vertical spacing is decreased with increasing depth.
    * Back to the third level.
  - Back to the second level.

- And here we are at the first level of `itemize` once again.

Similarly for the `enumerate` environment, where the style of the numbering changes with the nesting level:

1. The numbering at the first level is with Arabic numerals followed by a period.

    (a) At the second level, it is with lower case letters in parentheses ( ).

        i. The third level is numbered with lower case Roman numerals with a period.

            A. At the fourth level, capital letters are used.

            B. The label style can be changed, as described in the next section.

        ii. Back to the third level.

    (b) Back to the second level.

2. And the first level of `enumerate` again.

An example of a nested list with mixed types:

- The `itemize` label at the first level is a bullet.

    1. The numbering is with Arabic numerals since this is the first level of the `enumerate` environment.

        - This is the third level of the nesting, but the second `itemize` level.

            (a) And this is the fourth level of the overall nesting, but only the second of the `enumerate` environment.

            (b) Thus the numbering is with lower case letters in parentheses ( ).

        - The label at this level is a long dash.

    2. Every list should contain at least two points.

- Blank lines ahead of an `\item` command have no effect.

The above mixed list was produced with the following text:

```
\begin{itemize}
  \item The {\tt itemize} label at the first level is a bullet.
  \begin{enumerate}
    \item The numbering is with Arabic numerals since this is ...
    \begin{itemize}
      \item This is the third level of the nesting, but the ...
      \begin{enumerate}
        \item And this is the fourth level of the overall ...
```

```
    \item Thus the numbering is with lower case letters ...
  \end{enumerate}
  \item The label at this level is a long dash.
\end{itemize}
\item Every list should contain at least two points.
\end{enumerate}

\item Blank lines ahead of an ....
\end{itemize}
```

*Exercise 4.4:* *Produce a nested list using the* itemize *and* enumerate *environ-*
*ments as in the above example, but with a different sequence of these commands.*

*Exercise 4.5:* *Prepare a list of conference participants with their place of residence*
*using the* description *environment, where the name of the participant appears*
*as the argument in the* \item *command.*

*Note: for all three types of lists, any text before the first* \item *command will*
*yield an error message on processing.*

## .5  Changing label style

The labels, or markers, used in the itemize and enumerate environments
can be easily changed by means of the optional argument in the \item
command. With \item[+] the label becomes +, and with \item[2.1:]
it is 2.1:. The optional argument takes precedence over the standard label. For the enumerate environment, this means that the corresponding
counter is *not* automatically incremented and the user must do the numbering manually.

The optional label appears right justified within the area reserved for
the label. The width of this area is the amount of indentation at that level
less the separation between label and text; this means that the left edge
of the label area is flush with the left margin of the enclosing level.

It is also possible to change the standard labels for all or part of
the document. The labels are generated within LaTeX with the internal
commands for itemize

\labelitemi , \labelitemii , \labelitemiii , \labelitemiv

and for enumerate

\labelenumi , \labelenumii , \labelenumiii , \labelenumiv

The endings i, ii, iii, and iv refer to the four possible levels.

These commands may be altered with \renewcommand. For example,
to change the label of the third level of the itemize environment from *
to +, give

```
\renewcommand{\labelitemiii}{+}
```

Similarly the standard labels for the `enumerate` environment may be changed. However, here there is an additional complication that there is a counter for each `enumerate` level, named `enumi`, `enumii`, `enumiii`, and `enumiv`. The value of a counter can be printed using one of the commands `\arabic`, `\roman`, `\Roman`, `\alph`, or `\Alph`, where the style of each command should be obvious from its name. That is, `\Roman{xyz}` prints the current value of the counter `xyz` in upper case Roman numerals, whereas `\alph{xyz}` prints it as a lower case letter (with *a* corresponding to 1 and *z* to 26).

These counters, together with the counter style commands, must be used in the redefinitions of the label commands. For example, to change the second-level label to Arabic numerals followed by '.)', it is necessary to give

> `\renewcommand{\labelenumii}{\arabic{enumii}.)}`

which redefines `\labelenumii` to the value of counter `enumii` printed in Arabic, plus the characters '.)'. In this way, all the numbering levels may be changed. It is even possible to include more than one counter:

`\renewcommand{\labelenumii}{\Alph{enumi}.\arabic{enumii}}`

which will produce for every call to `\item` at level two the value of the counter `enumi` as a capital letter followed by the value of counter `enumii` as a number: that is, in the form A.1, A.2, ..., B.1, B.2, ... and so on.

If the new standard labels are to apply to the whole document, the redefining commands should be included in the preamble. Otherwise, they are valid only within the environment in which they appear.

*Exercise 4.6: Change the standard labels for the `itemize` environment into a long dash — (written `---`) for the first level, to a medium dash – (`--`) for the second level, and to a hyphen - for the third level.*

*Exercise 4.7: Change the standard labels for the `enumerate` environment for the first level to (I), (II), ..., and for the second level to the Roman numerals of the first level followed by the number for the second level in the form I-1:, I-2:, ..., II-1:, II-2:, ....*

The above exercises illustrate that the standard labels, or markings, for the `itemize` and `enumerate` environments may be changed to whatever one wishes. However, such changes should remain the exception, since the standard labels selected by Leslie Lamport can hardly be improved upon, from a typographical point of view. If another set is really required, it should be employed for the entire document.

## 4.3.6   Bibliography

Scientific publications normally include a list of references, or bibliography, containing the names of other works that are referred to within the text by means of a running number. Often the bibliography has not been finalized before the main text is started.

It would be a nuisance to have to go through the whole text and change all the reference numbering every time something was added to the bibliography. Therefore LaTeX contains a device that not only formats the bibliography but also keeps track of its alterations and additions in order to modify the references in the text automatically.

The bibliography is produced with the environment

> \begin{thebibliography}{*sample_label*}
>   *entries*
> \end{thebibliography}

The individual *entries* in the bibliography each begin with the command

> \bibitem[*label*]{*key*} *entry_text*

Without the optional argument *label*, \bibitem produces a running number in square brackets as the label for the reference in the text. With *label*, one can give whatever indicator one wishes, such as an abbreviation of the author's name, or an arbitrary reference number. The mandatory argument *key* is a reference keyword that does not appear in the bibliography but is replaced in the text by the label. The keyword can be made up of any combination of letters, numbers, and symbols except commas.

The actual bibliography information is contained in *entry_text*, such as 'author, title, publisher, year, edition, page numbers,' possibly in various typefaces. The text is indented after the first line by a width equal to that of the *sample_label*, so this should be as large as the longest label in the bibliography. For the standard application with running numbers, *sample_label* should be a dummy number with as many digits as the largest label (for example 99 if there are more than 10 but less than 100 entries).

The citation in the text itself is made with the command

> \cite{*key*}

where *key* is the reference keyword that appears in the \bibitem command. For example, if the bibliography contains the entries

```
\begin{thebibliography}{99}
  \bibitem{lamport} Leslie Lamport. \textsl{\LaTeX\ -- A Document
    Preparation System}.  Addison--Wesley Co., Inc.,
    Reading, MA, 1985
    . . . . . . . .
  \bibitem{knuth} Donald E. Knuth. \textsl{Computers and
    Typesetting Vol.\ A--E}. Addison--Wesley Co., Inc.,
    Reading, MA, 1984--1986
  \bibitem[6a]{knuth:a} Vol A: \textsl{The \TeX book}, 1984
  \bibitem[6b]{knuth:b} Vol B: \textsl{\TeX: The Program.}, 1986
    . . . . . . . .
\end{thebibliography}
```

then the text

```
For additional information about \LaTeX\ and \TeX\ see
\cite{lamport} and \cite{knuth,knuth:a}.
```

will produce: For additional information about LaTeX and TeX see [1] and [6, 6a].

Here `lamport`, `knuth`, and `knuth:a` have been chosen as keywords. The sample label is given as 99 since a two-digit number produces sufficient indentation for the standard form of `\bibitem`. The entry with the keyword `knuth` is the sixth in the list and thus it automatically receives the label [6]; in order for its sub-entries `knuth:a` ... `knuth:e` to be printed as [6a] ... [6e], it is necessary to set their optional *label* arguments to 6a ... 6e.

The results of the `thebibliography` environment are printed as the bibliography at the end of the document. For document classes `book` and `report`, the word **Bibliography** appears as a chapter title at the beginning, whereas for `article` the word **References** is written as a `section` heading. The above sample bibliography appears as:

[1]  Leslie Lamport. *LaTeX – A Document Preparation System*. Addison–Wesley Co., Inc., Reading, MA, 1985

. . . . . . . . .

[6]  Donald E. Knuth. *Computers and Typesetting Vol. A–E.* Addison–Wesley Co., Inc., Reading, MA, 1984–1986

[6a]  Vol A: *The TeXbook*, 1984

[6b]  Vol B: *TeX: The Program.*, 1986

. . . . . . . . .

The actual bibliography style used in this book deviates from the LaTeX standard: the citation in the text is made with the author's name and date of publication. No label at all appears in the bibliography listing. Section C.3.4 describes how such a bibliography style may be achieved.

*Exercise 4.8: Produce a bibliography with the* `thebibliography` *environment, with a label consisting of the first three letters of the author's name followed by the last digits of the year of publication. If the same author has more than one work in a given year, add a running letter to distinguish them, for example knu86c, knu86d. With such labels, it is appropriate to make the reference keywords the same as the labels. The indentation depth should be 1.5 cm.*
*Note: The indentation depth is determined by the argument sample_label in the* `thebibliography` *environment. This is usually a dummy text with the right width. This width can be given precisely with* `\hspace{width}`.

*Exercise 4.9: Copy the* `thebibliography` *environment from the above exercise to the end of your standard exercise file (but ahead of the* `\end{document}` *command). Refer to the entries in the bibliography by inserting* `\cite` *commands into your text. Make sure that the keyword in the* `\cite` *command is written exactly as in the* `\bibitem` *command in the* `thebibliography` *environment.*

Usually the LaTeX installation also contains the program BibTeX, which can produce a bibliography automatically from the \cite (and \nocite) commands by referring to one or more databases of bibliography entries. This is described more fully in Section 8.3.2 and Appendix B. The latter also explains how bibliography databases may be made for application by many users.

# Generalized lists

Lists such as those in the three environments itemize, enumerate, and description can be formed in a quite general way. The type of label and its width, the depth of indentation, spacings for paragraphs and labels, and so on, may be wholly or partially set by the user by means of the list environment:

> \begin{list}{*stnd_lbl*}{*list_decl*} *item_list* \end{list}

Here *item_list* consists of the text for the listed entries, each of which begins with an \item command that generates the corresponding label.

The *stnd_lbl* contains the definition of the label to be produced by the \item command without an argument (see below).

The list parameters described in Section 4.4.2 are set by *list_decl* to whatever new values the user wishes.

## Standard label

The first argument in the list environment defines the *stnd_lbl*, that is, the label that is produced by the \item command when it appears without an argument. In the case of an unchanging label, such as for the itemize environment, this is simply the desired symbol. If this is to be a mathematical symbol, it must be given as $symbol\_name$, enclosed in $ signs. For example, to select ⇒ as the label, *stnd_lbl* must be defined to be $\Rightarrow$.

However, often the label is required to contain a sequential numeration. For this purpose, a counter must be created with the \newcounter{*name*} command, where *name* is its designation. This command must appear before the first application of the counter in a list environment. Suppose a counter named marker has been defined for this use, then the argument *stnd_lbl* could be any of the commands for printing counters described in Section 4.3.5: for example, \arabic{marker} produces a running Arabic number.

Even more complex labels can be made up in this way. If the sequential labels are to be A–I, A–II, ..., *stnd_lbl* is set to A--\Roman{marker}.

Before a counter can function properly within the standard label, it must be associated with that list by including in the *list_decl* the command

\usecounter{*counter*}, where *counter* is the name of the counter to be
assigned (marker in the above example).

!

The standard label is actually generated by the command \makelabel{*label*},
which is called by the \item command. The user can redefine \makelabel with
the aid of the \renewcommand in the list declaration:

> \renewcommand{\makelabel}{*new_definition*}

If the standard label is defined in this manner, the corresponding entry in the
list environment is left blank. This is because \makelabel is the more general command and overrides the other definition. Examples are presented in
Section 7.5.9.

## 4.4.2   List style parameters

There are a number of style parameters used for formatting a list that
are set by LaTeX to certain standard values. These values may be altered
by the user in the *list_decl* for that particular list. The assignment is
made in the usual way with the \setlength command. However, if the
assignment is made outside the list environment, in most cases it will
simply be ignored. This is because there are preset default values for
each parameter at each level that can only be overridden by *list_decl*.

The style parameters are listed below and are also illustrated in Figure 4.1 on the opposite page, which is based on one taken from Lamport
(1985, 1994).

\topsep

> is the vertical spacing in addition to \parskip that is inserted
> between the list and the enclosing text above and below. Its
> default value is set at each list level and cannot be globally
> redefined outside the *list_decl*.

\partopsep

> is the vertical spacing in addition to \topsep + \parskip that
> is inserted above and below the list when a blank line precedes
> the first or follows the last \item entry. It may be redefined
> globally, but only for the first and second levels.

\parsep

> is the vertical spacing between paragraphs of a single \item. Its
> default value is reset at each level, as for \topsep.

\itemsep

> is the vertical spacing in addition to \parsep that is inserted
> between two \item entries. As for \topsep and \parsep, its
> default value is reset at each level and cannot be globally changed.

\leftmargin

> is the distance from the left edge of the current environment
> to the left margin of the list text. There are default values for

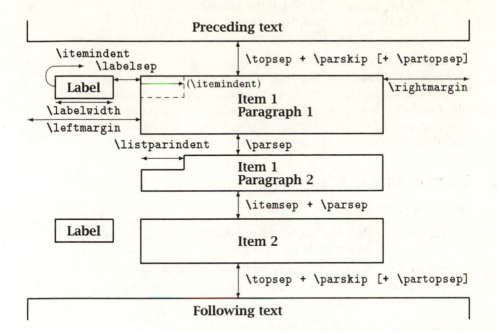

**Figure 4.1**: The list parameters

it at each level that may be globally redefined, as described in Section 4.4.6.

**\rightmargin**
>   is the distance from the right edge of the current environment to the right margin of the list text. Its standard value is 0 pt, which can only be altered in *list_decl*.

**\listparindent**
>   is the indentation depth of the first line of a paragraph within an \item with respect to the left margin of the list text. It is normally set to 0 pt so that no indentation occurs. This can only be changed in *list_decl*.

**\labelwidth**
>   is the width of the box reserved for the label. The text of the label is printed right justified within this space. A new default value may be set globally which then applies to all list levels.

**\labelsep**
>   is the spacing between the label box and the list text. A new value may be assigned globally, but it is only effective at the first level.

`\itemindent`
> is the distance by which the label and the first line of text in an `\item` are indented to the right. It is normally set to 0 pt and so has no effect. This value can only be redefined in *list_decl*.

When changing the vertical spacings from their standard values, it is recommended that a rubber length (Section 2.4.2) be used.

The label created by the `\item` command normally appears right justified within a box of width `\labelwidth`. It is possible to make it left justified, as in the following list of parameters, by putting `\hfill` at the end of the definition of the standard label or in the `\makelabel` command.

## 4.4.3   Example of a user's list

List of Figures:

**Figure 1:**   *Page format with head, body, and foot, showing the meaning of the various elements involved.*

**Figure 2:**   *Format of a general list showing its elements.*

**Figure 3:**   *A demonstration of some of the possibilities for drawing pictures with LATEX.*

This list was produced with the following input:

```
\newcounter{fig}
\begin{list}{\bfseries\upshape Figure \arabic{fig}:}
  {\usecounter{fig}
  \setlength{\labelwidth}{2cm}\setlength{\leftmargin}{2.6cm}
  \setlength{\labelsep}{0.5cm}\setlength{\rightmargin}{1cm}
  \setlength{\parsep}{0.5ex plus0.2ex minus0.1ex}
  \setlength{\itemsep}{0ex plus0.2ex} \slshape}
  \item Page format with head, body, and foot, showing the
        meaning of the various elements involved.
  \item Format of a general list showing its elements.
  \item A demonstration of some of the possibilities for
        drawing pictures with \LaTeX.
\end{list}
```

The command `\newcounter{fig}` sets up the counter `fig`. The standard label is defined to be the word **Figure** in upright, bold face, followed by the running Arabic number, terminated by :. This label is printed for each `\item` command.

The list declaration contains `\usecounter{fig}` as its first command, which makes the counter `fig` operational within the list. The width of the label box (`\labelwidth`) is set to 2.0 cm, the left margin of the list text (`\leftmargin`) to 2.6 cm, the distance between the label and the text (`\labelsep`) to 0.5 cm, and the right edge of the list (`\rightmargin`) is set to be 1 cm from that of the enclosing text.

The vertical spacing between paragraphs within an item (\parsep) is 0.5 ex but can be stretched an extra 0.2 ex or shrunk by 0.1 ex. The additional spacing between items (\itemsep) is 0 ex, stretchable to 0.2 ex.

Standard values are used for all the other list parameters. The last command in the list declaration is \slshape, which sets the list text in a *slanted* typeface.

**Note:** in LaTeX 2ε, if \upshape were not given in the label definition, the text of each \item would also be slanted, as **Figure 1:**. In LaTeX 2.09, the declarations \bf and \sl must be used instead, and a bold, slanted font is not possible.

## 4.4    Lists as new environments

If a particular type of list is employed several times within a document, it can become tiresome typing the same *stnd_lbl* and *list_decl* into the list environment every time. LaTeX offers the possibility of defining a given list as an environment under its own name. This is achieved by means of the \newenvironment command.

For example, the list in the above example can be stored so that it may be called at any time with the name figlist:

```
\newenvironment{figlist}{\begin{list}
    {\bfseries\upshape Figure \arabic{fig}:}
    {\usecounter{fig} ... {0ex plus0.2ex}\slshape}}
    {\end{list}}
```

It can then be called with

```
\begin{figlist} item_list \end{figlist}
```

so that it behaves as a predefined list environment.

**Exercise 4.10:** *Define a new environment with the name* sample *that produces a list in which every call to* \item *prints labels* Sample A, Sample B, *and so on. The labels are to be left justified within a box of width 20mm, and the distance between the label box and the item text is to be 2mm, with a total left margin of 22mm. The right edge of the text is to be moved in 5mm from that of the enclosing text. The extra vertical spacing between two items is to be* 1ex plus0.5ex minus0.4ex *in addition to the normal paragraph spacing. Secondary paragraphs within an item are to be indented by* 1em. *The normal paragraph separation should be* 0ex, *expandable to* 0.5ex.

LaTeX itself makes frequent use of the list environment to define a number of other structures. For example, the quote environment is defined as

```
\newenvironment{quote}{\begin{list}{}
    {setlength{\rightmargin}{\leftmargin}}
    \item[]}{\end{list}}
```

This environment is thus a list in which the value of \rightmargin is set to the current value of \leftmargin which has a default value of 2.5 em. The list itself consists of a single \item call with an *empty* label, a call that is automatically included in the definition of quote with the entry \item[].

In the same way, LATEX defines the quotation and verse environments internally as special list environments. The left margins and the vertical spacings around the structures are left as the standard values for the list environment, and are therefore changed only when the standard values themselves are altered.

Finally, as an example of a possible user-defined special list we offer

\newenvironment{lquote}{\begin{list}{}{}\item[]}{\end{list}}

which creates an lquote environment that does nothing more than indent its enclosed text by the amount \leftmargin, with the right edge flush with that of the normal text, since \rightmargin has the standard value of 0 pt.

## 4.4.5   Trivial lists

LATEX also contains a trivlist environment, with syntax

\begin{trivlist} *enclosed text* \end{trivlist}

in which the arguments *stnd_lbl* and *list_decl* are omitted. This is the same as a list environment for which the label is empty, \leftmargin, \labelwidth, and \itemindent are all assigned the value 0 pt, while \listparindent is set equal to \parindent and \parsep to \parskip.

LATEX uses this environment to create further structures. For example, the call to the center environment generates internally the sequence

\begin{trivlist} \centering \item[] *enclosed text* \end{trivlist}

The environments flushleft and flushright are similarly defined.

## 4.4.6   Nested lists

Lists can be nested within one another with the list environments itemize, enumerate, and description, to a maximum depth of 6. At each level, the new left margin is indented by the amount \leftmargin relative to that of the next higher one.

As mentioned earlier, it is only possible to change the standard values of a limited number of the list parameters with declarations in the preamble. One exception is the indentations of the left margins for the different nesting levels. These are set internally by the parameters \leftmargin$n$, where $n$ stands for i, ii, iii, iv, v, or vi. These values can be changed by the user; for example, by declaring \setlength{\leftmarginiv}{12mm}, the left margin of the fourth level list is shifted 12 mm from that of the third. These declarations must be made *outside* of the list environments and not in the *list_decl*.

At each level of list nesting, the internal macro \@list$n$ ($n$ being i to vi) is called. This sets the value of \leftmargin equal to that of the corresponding \leftmargin$n$, unless \leftmargin is explicitly declared in the list environment. That is, there does not exist a single standard value for \leftmargin externally, but rather 6 different ones. The parameter \leftmargin has meaning only within a list environment.

# 5 Theorem-like declarations

In scientific literature one often has text structures like

**Theorem 1 (Balzano–Weierstrass)** *Every infinite set of bounded points possesses at least one maximum point.*

or

**Axiom 4.1** *The natural numbers form a set S of distinct elements. For any two elements a, b, they are either identical, a = b, or different from one another, a ≠ b.*

Similar structures frequently appear with names such as *Definition, Corollary, Declaration, Lemma,* instead of *Theorem* or *Axiom.* What they have in common is that a keyword and a running number are printed in **bold face** and the corresponding text in *italic.*

Of course, these could be generated by the user by explicitly giving the type styles and appropriate number, but if a new structure of that type is later inserted in the middle of the text, the user would have the tedious job of renumbering all the following occurrences. With the command

\newtheorem{*struct_type*}{*struct_title*}[*in_counter*]

LATEX will keep track of the numbering automatically. Here *struct_type* is the user's arbitrary designation for the structure, while *struct_title* is the word that is printed in bold face followed by the running number (for example, **Theorem**). If the optional argument *in_counter* is missing, the numbering is carried out sequentially throughout the entire document. However, if the name of an existing counter, such as chapter, is given for *in_counter*, the numbering is reset every time that counter is augmented, and both are printed together, as in **Axiom 4.1** above.

The predefined structures are called with the command

\begin{*struct_type*}[*extra_title*]     text     \end{*struct_type*}

which also increments the necessary counter and generates the proper number. The above examples were produced with

```
\newtheorem{theorem}{Theorem} \newtheorem{axiom}{Axiom}[chapter]
. . . . . . . . . . . . . . . . . . . .
\begin{theorem}[Balzano--Weierstrass] Every .... \end{theorem}
\begin{axiom} The natural numbers form .......... \end{axiom}
```

The optional *extra_title* also appears in bold face within parentheses ( ) following the running number.

Occasionally a structure is not numbered on its own but together with another structure. This can be included in the definition with another optional argument

$$\text{\newtheorem}\{\textit{struct\_type}\}[\textit{num\_like}]\{\textit{struct\_name}\}$$

where *num_like* is the name of an existing theorem structure that shares the same counter. Thus by defining \newtheorem{subthrm}[theorem] {Sub-Theorem}, the two structures theorem and subthrm will be numbered as a single series: **Theorem 1**, **Sub-Theorem 2**, **Sub-Theorem 3**, **Theorem 4**, and so on.

## 4.6     Tabulator stops

### 4.6.1     Basics

On a typewriter it is possible to set *tabulator stops* at various positions within a line; then by pressing the tab key the print head or carriage jumps to the next tab location.

A similar possibility exists in LATEX with the tabbing environment

         \begin{tabbing}     *lines*     \end{tabbing}

One can think of the set tab stops as being numbered from left to right. At the beginning of the tabbing environment, no tabs are set, except for the left border, which is called the *zeroth* tab stop. The stops can be set at any spot within a line with the command \=, and a line is terminated by the command \\:

```
Here is the \=first tab stop, followed by\= the second\\
```

sets the first tab stop after the blank following the word *the*, and the second immediately after the word *by*.

After the tab stops have been set in this way, one can jump in the subsequent lines to each of the stops, starting from the left margin, with the command \>. A new line is started with the usual command \\.

Example:

| Type | Quality | Color | Price |
|------|---------|-------|-------|
| Paper | med. | white | low |
| Leather | good | brown | high |
| Card | bad | gray | med. |

```
\begin{tabbing}
Type\qquad\= Quality\quad\=
Color\quad\= Price\\[0.8ex]
Paper     \> med. \> white \> low\\
Leather \> good \> brown \> high\\
Card      \> bad  \> gray  \> med.
\end{tabbing}
```

## 5.2 Sample line

It is often advantageous or even necessary to set the tab stops in a sample line that is not actually printed. It could contain, for example, the widest entries in the various columns that appear later, or the smallest inter-column spacing between stops. The sample line may also contain \hspace commands to force the distance between stops to be a predetermined amount.

To suppress the printing of the sample line, it is terminated with the command \kill in place of \\.

```
\hspace*{3cm}\=sample column \=\hspace{4cm}\= \kill
```

In addition to the left border, the above statement sets three tab stops:

An \hspace command at the beginning of a sample line must be of the *-form, otherwise the inserted spacing will be deleted at the line margin.

## 5.3 Tab stops and the left margin

The left border of each line of the tabbing environment is at first identical with the left margin of the enclosing environment, and is designated the *zeroth* stop. By activating the 'tab key' \> at the start of a line, one sets the following text beginning at the first tab stop. However, the command \+ has the same effect, putting the left border permanently at the first stop, for all subsequent lines. With \+\+ at the beginning or end of a line, all the next lines will start two stops further along. There can be as many \+ commands in all as there are tab stops set on the line.

The command \- has the opposite effect: it shifts the left border for the following lines one stop to the left. It is not possible to set this border to be to the left of the *zeroth* stop.

The effect of the \+ commands may be overridden for a single line by putting \< at the start for each tab to be removed. This line then starts so many tabs to the left of the present border. With the next \\ command, the new line begins at the current left border determined by the total number of \+ and \- commands.

## 5.4 Further tabbing commands

Tab stops can be reset or added in every line. The command \= will add a stop if there have been sufficient \> commands to have jumped to the last stop, otherwise it will reset the next stop.

For example:

| | | |
|---|---|---|
| Old column 1 Old column 2 | | |
| Left column   Middle col | Extra col | |
| New col 1 New col 2 | Old col 3 | |
| Column 1 Column 2 | Column 3 | |

```
Old column 1 \= Old column 2\\
Left column \> Middle col
    \= Extra col\\
New col 1 \= New col 2 \>
    Old col 3\\
Column 1\> Column 2 \> Column 3
\end{tabbing}
```

Occasionally it is desirable to be able to reset the tab stops and then to reuse the original ones later. The command \pushtabs accomplishes this by storing the current tabs and removing them from the active line. All the tab stops can then be set once again. The stored stops can be reactivated with the command \poptabs. The \pushtabs command may be given as many times as needed, but there must be the same number of \poptabs commands within any one tabbing environment.

It is possible to position text on a tab stop with *left_text* \' *right_text*, where *left_text* goes just before the current tab (or left border) with a bit of spacing, while *right_text* starts exactly at the stop. The amount of spacing between the *left_text* and the tab stop is determined by the tabbing parameter \tabbingsep. This may be changed by the user with the \setlength command as usual.

Text may be right justified up against the right border of a line with the command \' *text*. There must not be any more \> or \= commands in the remainder of the line.

The commands \=, \', and \' function as accent commands outside of the tabbing environment (Section 2.5.7). If these accents are actually needed within tabbing, they must be produced with \a=, \a', and \a' instead. For example, to produce ó, ò, or ō inside a tabbing environment, one must give \a'o, \a'o, or \a=o. The command \- also has another meaning outside of the tabbing environment (suggested word division) but since lines are not broken automatically within this environment, there is no need for an alternative form.

Here is an example illustrating all the tabbing commands:

| | | |
|---|---|---|
| Apples: | consumed by: people | |
| | horses | |
| | and  sheep | |
| | reasonably juicy | |
| Grapefruits: a delicacy | | |
| (see also: melons | | |
| | pumpkins) | |
| Horses | feed on | apples |

```
\begin{tabbing}
Grapefruits: \= \kill
Apples: \> consumed by: \= people\+\+\\
horses \\
and \' sheep\-\\
reasonably juicy\-\\
Grapefruits: \> a delicacy\\
\pushtabs
(see also: \= melons\\
 \> pumpkins)\\
\poptabs
Horses \> feed on \> apples
\end{tabbing}
```

## 4.5  Remarks on tabbing

TEX treats the tabbing environment like a normal paragraph, breaking a page if necessary between two lines within the environment. However, the commands \newpage and \clearpage are not allowed within it, and the command \pagebreak is simply ignored. If the user wishes to force a page break within the tabbing environment, there is a trick that he or she may employ: specify a very large inter-line spacing at the end of the line where the break should occur (for example, \\[10cm]). This forces the break and the spacing disappears at the start of the new page.

The line of text is effectively within a { } pair, so that any size or font declarations remain in force only for that one line. The text need not be put explicitly inside a pair of curly braces.

It is not possible to nest tabbing environments within one another.

Beware: the tab jump command \> always moves to the next logical tab stop. This could actually be a move backwards if the previous text is longer than the space available between the last two stops. This is in contrast to the way the tabulator works on a typewriter.

There is no automatic line breaking within the tabbing environment. Each line continues until terminated by a \\ command. The text could extend beyond the right margin of the page. It is up to the user to see that this does not happen.

The commands \hfill, \hrulefill, and \dotfill have no effect inside a tabbing environment, since no *stretching* takes place here.

**Exercise 4.11:** *Generate the following table with the* tabbing *environment.*

```
Project: Total Requirements = $900 000.00
         of which       1995 = $450 000.00
                        1996 = $350 000.00
                        1997 = $100 000.00

         1995 approved: $350 000.00   Deficiency: $100 000.00
         1996           $300 000.00               $150 000.00
         1997           $250 000.00   Surplus:    $150 000.00

         tentative      1996 = $100 000.00 for deficiency 1995
                        1997 = $ 50 000.00                1996
                             + $100 000.00      excess for 1995 in 1996
Commitments             1995 = $100 000.00
                        1996 = $150 000.00               signed: H. André
```

*Hint: the first line in the* tabbing *environment should read*

```
Project: \=Total Requirements\= = \$900\,000.00 \+\\
```

*What is the effect of the* \+ *command at the end of this line? How do you arrange, using these tab stops, for the years 1995, 1996, and 1997 in the second to fourth lines all to be positioned before the second tab stop? Which command should be at the end of the second line just before the terminator* \\?

*Lines one to four and eight to twelve all use the same set of tab stops, although in the eighth line additional stops are set. With \$1\=00\,000.00 one can align the entry \$\>50\,000.00 in the ninth line to match the decimal places of the lines above.*

*Lines 5–7 have their own tab stops. Use the save and recall feature to store the preset tab stops and to bring them back. The left border of lines 5–7 correspond to the first stop of the first group. What command is at the end of the fourth line to ensure that the left border is reset to one stop earlier? How is the left border of the second-to-last line reset?*

*The last line contains 'signed: H. André' right justified. With what* tabbing *command was this produced? Watch out for the accent é in this entry within the* tabbing *environment!*

## 4.7    Boxes

A *box* is a piece of text that TeX treats as a unit, like a single character. A *box* (along with the text within it) can be moved left, right, up, or down. Since the box is a unit, TeX cannot break it up again, even it was originally made up of smaller individual boxes. It is, however, possible to put those smaller boxes together as one pleases when constructing the overall box.

This is exactly what TeX does internally when it carries out the formatting: the individual characters are packed in *character* boxes, which are put together into *line* boxes horizontally with rubber lengths inserted between the words. The *line* boxes are stacked vertically into *paragraph* boxes, again with rubber lengths separating them. These then go into the *page body* box, which with the *head* and *foot* boxes constitutes the *page* box.

LaTeX offers the user a choice of three *box types*: LR boxes, paragraph boxes, and rule boxes. The LR (left–right) box contains material that is ordered horizontally from *left* to *right*. A paragraph box will have its contents made into vertically stacked lines. A rule box is a rectangle filled solidly with black, usually for drawing horizontal and vertical lines.

### 4.7.1    LR boxes

To create boxes containing text in LR (left-to-right) mode the commands

>     \mbox{*text*}   and   \makebox[*width*] [*pos*]{*text*}
>     \fbox{*text*}   and   \framebox[*width*] [*pos*]{*text*}

are available. The two commands at the left produce an LR box with a width exactly equal to that of the *text* given between the braces { }. The \fbox command is the same as \mbox except that the | *text* | is also framed.

With the two commands at the right, the width is predetermined by the optional length argument *width*. The other optional argument *pos* specifies how the text is positioned within the box. With no value given, the *text* is centered. Otherwise *pos* may be

    l  to left-justify the *text*,
    r  to right-justify it,
  $\boxed{2\varepsilon}$ s  to stretch it to fill up the full width.

Thus `\makebox[3.5cm]{centered text}` creates a box of width 3.5 cm in which the text is centered, as       centered text    , filled with white space, while with `\framebox[3.5cm][r]{right justified}` the text is right justified inside a framed box of width 3.5 cm: $\boxed{\qquad\text{right justified}}$. With LATEX$2\varepsilon$, one may also give

    `\framebox[3.5cm][s]{stretched\dotfill text}`

to fill up the box, as $\boxed{\text{stretched}\dots\dots\text{text}}$, in which case some rubber length (Section 2.4.2) or other filler (page 47) must be added where the stretching is to occur.

    If the *text* has a natural width that is larger than that specified in *width*, it will stick out of the box on the left, right, or both sides, depending on the choice of *pos*. For example,

    `\framebox[2mm]{centered}` produces    cen$\boxed{}$ered

    The above application may appear rather silly for `\framebox`, but it can indeed be very useful for `\makebox`. A width specification of 0 pt for `\makebox` can generate a centered, left, or right justified positioning of text in diagrams made with the `picture` environment (see Chapter 6 for examples). It may also be used to cause two pieces of text to overlap, as `\makebox[0pt][l]{/}S` prints a slash through an S, as $\not{S}$.
**Note:** length specifications must always contain a dimensional unit, even when they are zero. Thus `0pt` must be given for the width, not `0`.

    With LATEX$2\varepsilon$, it is also possible to specify the *width* of an LR box relative to its natural dimensions (those produced by the simple `\mbox` command):

  $\boxed{2\varepsilon}$ `\width`  is the natural width of the box,
  $\boxed{2\varepsilon}$ `\height`  is the distance from baseline to top,
  $\boxed{2\varepsilon}$ `\depth`  is the distance from baseline to bottom,
  $\boxed{2\varepsilon}$ `\totalheight`  is `\height` plus `\depth`.

To make a framed box such that the width is six times the total height, containing centered text,

    `\framebox[6\totalheight]{Text}`    $\boxed{\quad\text{Text}\quad}$

**Note:** these special length parameters only have meaning within the *width* specification of an LR box, or within the *height* specification of a paragraph box, as shown below. In any other context, they will produce an error message.

If a set piece of text is to appear in several places within the document, it can be stored by first giving the command

> `\newsavebox{\`*boxname*`}`

to create a box with the name `\`*boxname*. This name must conform to LaTeX command name syntax (letters only) with an inital `\`. The name must not conflict with any existing LaTeX command names. After such a box has been initiated, the commands

> `\sbox{\`*boxname*`}{`*text*`}` or
> `\savebox{\`*boxname*`}[`*width*`][`*pos*`]{`*text*`}`

will store the contents *text* for future use. The optional arguments *width* and *pos* have the same meanings as for `\makebox` and `\framebox`. Now with the command

> `\usebox{\`*boxname*`}`

the stored contents are inserted into the document text wherever desired, as a single unit.

The contents of an LR box may also be stored with the environment

> `2ε` `\begin{lrbox}{`*boxname*`}`
>     *text*
> `\end{lrbox}`

This is equivalent to `\sbox{\`*boxname*`}{`*text*`}`. Its advantage is that it allows text within a user-defined environment (Section 7.4) to be stored for future use with `\usebox`.

## 4.7.2   Vertical shifting of LR boxes

The command

> `\raisebox{`*lift*`}[`*height*`][`*depth*`]{`*text*`}`

produces an `\mbox` with contents *text*, raised above the current baseline by an amount *lift*. The optional arguments tell LaTeX to treat the box as though its extension above the baseline were *height* and that below were *depth*. Without these arguments, the box has its natural size determined by *text* and *lift*. Note that *lift*, *height*, and *depth* are lengths (Section 2.4.1). If *lift* is negative, the box is lowered below the baseline.

For example:

> `Baseline \raisebox{1ex}{high} and \raisebox{-1ex}{low}`
> `and back again`

produces: Baseline $^{\text{high}}$ and $_{\text{low}}$ and back again.

The values for *height* and *depth* can be totally different from the actual ones of the *text*. Their effect is to determine how far away the previous and next lines of text should be from the current line, based on the heights and depths of all the boxes (characters are also boxes) in the line. By raising a box but specifying *height* to be the regular character size, the raised box will overprint the line above, and similarly for *depth* when a box is lowered.

## .3  Parboxes and minipages

Whole paragraphs can be put into separate *vertical* boxes (or *parboxes* in the LaTeX jargon) with the command

> \parbox[*pos*]{*width*}{*text*}

or with the environment

> \begin{minipage}[*pos*]{*width*}  *text*  \end{minipage}

Both produce a vertical box of width *width*, in which the lines of text are stacked on top of each other as in normal paragraph mode.

The optional positioning argument *pos* can take on the values

b    to align the bottom edge of the box with the current baseline,
t    to align the top line of text with the current baseline.

Without any positioning argument, the parbox is centered vertically on the baseline of the external line of text.

The positioning argument is only meaningful when the \parbox command or the minipage environment occurs within a paragraph, for otherwise the current line and its baseline have no meaning. If the parbox is immediately preceded by a blank line, it begins a new paragraph. In this case, the vertical positioning of the parbox is made with reference to the following elements of the paragraph. These could be further parboxes. If the paragraph consists of only a single parbox or minipage, the positioning argument is meaningless and has no effect.

Examples:

```
\parbox{3.5cm}{\sloppy This is a 3.5 cm wide parbox. It is
    vertically centered on the}
\hfill CURRENT LINE \hfill
\parbox{5.5cm}{Narrow pages are hard to format. They usually
    produce many warning messages on the terminal. The command
    {\tt\symbol{92}sloppy} can stop this.}
```

This is a 3.5 cm wide parbox. It is vertically centered on the    CURRENT LINE    Narrow pages are hard to format. They usually produce many warning messages on the terminal. The command \sloppy can stop this.

```
\begin{minipage}[b]{4.3cm}
  The minipage environment creates a vertical box like the parbox
  command. The bottom line of this minipage is aligned with the
\end{minipage}\hfill
\parbox{3.0cm}{middle of this narrow parbox, which in turn is
  aligned with}
\hfill
\begin{minipage}[t]{3.8cm}
  the top line of the right hand minipage. It is recommended that
  the user experiment with the positioning arguments to get used
  to their effects.
\end{minipage}
```

The minipage environment
creates a vertical box like the
parbox command.  The bot-
tom line of this minipage is          middle of this nar-
aligned with the                      row parbox, which in      the top line of the right
                                      turn is aligned with      hand minipage.  It is rec-
                                                                ommended that the user
                                                                experiment with the posi-
                                                                tioning arguments to get
                                                                used to their effects.

In Section 4.7.7 we demonstrate how parboxes can be vertically stacked
in any desired manner relative to one another.

The \parbox command produces a vertical box containing the *text*
just like the minipage environment. However, the latter is more general.
The *text* in a \parbox may not contain any of the centering, list, or other
environments described in Sections 4.2–4.5. These may, on the other
hand, appear within a minipage environment. That is, a minipage can
include centered or indented text, as well as lists and tabbings.

## 4.7.4   Problems with vertical placement

! Vertical positioning of minipages and parboxes can often lead to unexpected
results, which can be explained by showing more graphically how a box is treated
by LaTeX. Suppose we want to place two parboxes of different heights side by side,
aligned on their first lines, and the two together set on the current line of text at
the bottom. The 'obvious' way of doing this is

```
\begin{minipage}[b]{..}
    \parbox[t]{..}{..} \hfill   \parbox[t]{..}{..}
\end{minipage}
```

which does not work, for it produces instead the following results:

Current line   The boxes are made visible here by framing them,   and by marking the baselines (the vertical alignment points) with black dots.   of text.

The reason for this is that each parbox or minipage is treated externally as a single character with its own height and depth above and below the baseline. As far as the outer minipage is concerned, it contains only two 'characters' on the same line, and that line is both the top and bottom one. Thus the bottom line of the outer minipage is indeed aligned with the line of text, but that bottom line is simultaneously the top line. The solution is to add a dummy second line to the outer box, as

```
\parbox[t]{..}{..} \hfill \parbox[t]{..}{..} \\ \mbox{}
```

The dummy line may not be entirely empty, hence the \mbox.

The boxes are made visible here by framing them,   and by marking the baselines (the vertical alignment points) with black dots.

Current line   □   of text.

A similar problem occurs if two boxes are to be aligned with their bottom lines, and the pair aligned at the top with the current line of text. Here there are two possibilities to add a dummy *first* line.

```
\mbox{} \\                       aligns with the very top, or
\mbox{} \\[-\baselineskip]       aligns with the first text line.
```

An example of the first case is shown on page 179. Dummy lines are also needed for the solution of Exercise 4.12 on page 92.

## .5  Paragraph boxes of specific height $\boxed{2\varepsilon}$

In LaTeX $2_\varepsilon$, the syntax of the \parbox command and minipage environment has been extended to include two more optional arguments:

$\boxed{2\varepsilon}$ \parbox[*pos*][*height*][*inner_pos*]{*width*}{*text*}

$\boxed{2\varepsilon}$ \begin{minipage}[*pos*][*height*][*inner_pos*]{*width*}
    text
\end{minipage}

In both cases, *height* is a length specifying the height of the box; the parameters \height, \width, \depth, and \totalheight may be employed within the *height* argument in the same way as in the *width* argument of \makebox and \framebox (page 85).

The optional argument *inner_pos* states how the text is to be positioned *internally*, something that is only meaningful if *height* has been given. Its possible values are:

t   to push the text to the top of the box,
b   to shove it to the bottom,
c   to center it vertically,
s   to stretch it to fill up the whole box.

In the last case, rubber lengths (Section 2.4.2) should be present where the vertical stretching is to take place.

Note the difference between the external positioning argument *pos* and the internal one *inner_pos*: the former states how the box is to be aligned with the surrounding text, while the latter determines how the contents are placed within the box itself.

Example:

```
\begin{minipage}[t][2cm][t]{3cm}
  This is a minipage of height 2~cm with the text
  at the top.
\end{minipage}\hrulefill
\parbox[t][2cm][c]{3cm}{In this parbox, the text
  is centered on the same height.}\hrulefill
\begin{minipage}[t][2cm][b]{3cm}
  In this third paragraph box, the text is at the bottom.
\end{minipage}
```

This is a minipage————                              ————
of  height  2  cm
with the text at the        In this parbox, the
top.                        text is centered on        In this third para-
                            the same height.           graph box, the text
                                                       is at the bottom.

The \hrulefill commands between the boxes show where the baselines are. All three boxes are the same size and differ only in their values of *inner_pos*.

## 4.7.6   Rule boxes

A rule box is a basically a filled-in black rectangle. The syntax for the general command is:

\rule[*lift*]{*width*}{*height*}

which produces a solid rectangle of width *width* and height *height*, raised above the baseline by an amount *lift*. Thus \rule{8mm}{3mm} generates ▬▬. Without the optional argument *lift*, the rectangle is set on the baseline of the current line of text.

The parameters *lift*, *width*, and *height* are all lengths (Section 2.4.1). If *lift* has a negative value, the rectangle is set below the baseline.

It is also possible to have a rule box of zero width. This creates an invisible line with the given *height*. Such a construction is called a *strut* and is used to force a horizontal box to have a desired height or depth that is different from that of its contents. For this purpose, \vspace is inappropriate because it adds additional vertical space to that which is already there.

For example: \fbox{Text} produces Text . In order to print Text ,

one has to tell TeX that the box contents extend above and below the baseline by the desired amounts. This was done with \fbox{\rule[-2mm] {0cm}{6mm}Text}. What this says is that the text to be framed consists of 'an invisible bar beginning 2 mm below the baseline, 6 mm long, followed by the word *Text*.' The vertical bar indeed remains unseen, but it determines the upper and lower edges of the frame.

A rule box with zero height is also allowed, as an invisible horizontal line of given *width*; however, there seems to be no practical use for such a construction since horizontal displacements are readily achieved with the \hspace command.

## .7  Nested boxes

The box commands described above may be nested to any desired level. Including an LR box within a parbox or a minipage causes no obvious conceptual difficulties. The opposite, a parbox within an LR box, is also possible, and is easy to visualize if one keeps in mind that every box is a unit, treated by TeX as a single character of the corresponding size.

> A parbox inside an \fbox command has the effect that the entire parbox is framed. The present structure was made with
>
> \fbox{\fbox{\parbox{10cm}{A parbox...}}}
>
> This is a parbox of width 10 cm inside a framebox inside a second framebox, which thus produces the double framing effect.

Enclosing a parbox inside a \raisebox allows vertical displacements of any desired amount. The two boxes here both have positioning [b], but the one at the right has been produced with:

```
\raisebox{1cm}{\begin{minipage}[b]{2.5cm}
      a b c d e ... x y z\\
      \underline{baseline}
\end{minipage} }
```

a b c d e f g h i
j k l m n o p q r
s t u v w x y z
underline{baseline}

which displaces it upwards by 1 cm.          baseline

A very useful structure is one in which `minipage` environments are positioned relative to one another inside an enclosing `minipage`. The positioning argument of the outside `minipage` can be used to align its contents as a unit with the neighboring text or boxes. An example of this is given in Exercise 4.12.

Finally, vertical boxes such as `\parbox` commands and `minipage` environments may be saved as the *text* in an `\sbox` or `\savebox` command, to be recalled later with `\usebox`, as described in Section 4.7.1.

## 4.7.8   Box style parameters

!

There are two style parameters for the frame boxes `\fbox` and `\framebox` that may be reset by the user:

`\fboxrule`  determines the thickness of the frame lines,

`\fboxsep`  sets the amount of spacing between the frame and enclosed text.

New values are assigned to these length parameters in the usual LaTeX manner with the command `\setlength`: the line thickness for all the following `\framebox` and `\fbox` comands is set to 0.5 mm with `\setlength{\fboxrule}{0.5mm}`.

The range of these settings also obeys the usual rule: if they are found in the preamble then they apply to the entire document; if they are within an environment then they are valid only until the end of that environment.

These parameters do *not* influence the `\framebox` command that is employed within the `picture` environment (Section 6.4.2). Its effects and syntax are much more extensive than those of the normal `\framebox` command.

*Exercise 4.12: How can the following nested structure be generated? (Note: font size is `\footnotesize`)*

The first line of this 3.5 cm wide minipage or parbox is aligned with the first line of the neighboring minipage or parbox.

This 4.5 cm wide minipage or parbox is positioned so that its top line is at the same level as that of the box on the left, while its bottom line is even with that of the box on the right. The naïve notion that this arrangement may be achieved with the positioning arguments set to t, t, and b is incorrect. Why? What would this selection really produce?

The true solution involves the nesting of two of the three structures in an enclosing minipage, which is then separately aligned with the third one.

*Note: there are two variants for the solution, depending on whether the left and middle structures are first enclosed in a minipage, or the middle and right ones. Try to work out both solutions. Incidentally, the third minipage is 3 cm wide.*

*Note: the problems of correctly aligning two side-by-side boxes as a pair on a line of text (Section 4.7.4) arises here once more. It will be necessary to add a dummy line to get the vertical alignment correct.*

*Exercise 4.13: Produce the framed structure shown below and store it with the command* \sbox{\warning}{structure}. *You will first have to create a box named* \warning *with the* \newsavebox{\warning} *command.* *Print this warning at various places in your exercise file by giving* \usebox{\warning}.

> Vertical placement of minipages and parboxes can lead to surprising results which may be corrected by the use of dummy lines.

*Note: the parbox width is 10 cm. There should be no difficulty producing the framed structure if one follows the previous example for the double framed box. Watch out when writing* \sbox{\warning}{structure} *that you have the correct number of closing braces at the end.*

*Next, change the values for the line thickness (*\fboxrule*) and frame spacing (*\fboxsep*) and print your results once more.*

# 3 Tables

With the *box* elements and tabbing environment from the previous sections it would be possible to produce all sorts of framed and unframed tables. However, LaTeX offers the user far more convenient ways to build such complicated structures.

## .1 Constructing tables

The environments tabular, tabular*, and array are the basic tools with which tables and matrices can be constructed. The syntax for these environments is

```
\begin{array}[pos]{cols}          rows  \end{array}
\begin{tabular}[pos]{cols}        rows  \end{tabular}
\begin{tabular*}{width}[pos]{cols}  rows  \end{tabular*}
```

The array environment can only be applied in *mathematical mode* (see Chapter 5). It is described here only because its syntax and the meaning of its arguments are exactly the same as those of the tabular environment. All three environments actually create a minipage. The meaning of the arguments is as follows:

*pos*   Vertical positioning argument (see also the explanation of this argument for parboxes in Section 4.7.3). It can take on the values

     t    the top line of the table is aligned with the baseline of the current external line of text;

     b    the bottom line of the table is aligned with the external baseline;

         with no positioning argument given, the table is centered on the external baseline.

*width* This argument applies only to the `tabular*` environment and determines its overall width. In this case, the *cols* argument must contain the @-expression (see below) `@{\extracolsep{\fill}}` somewhere after the first entry. For the other two environments, the total width is fixed by the textual content.

*cols* The column formatting argument. There must be an entry for every column, as well as possible extra entries for the left and right borders of the table or for the inter-column spacings.

The possible *column formatting symbols* are

l   the column contents are *left* justified;

r   the column contents are *right* justified;

c   the column contents are *centered*;

p{*wth*} the text in this column is set into lines of width *wth*, and the top line is aligned with the other columns. In fact, the text is set in a parbox with the command `\parbox[t]{`*wth*`}{`*column text*`}`;

*{*num*}{*cols*} the *column format* contained in *cols* is reproduced *num* times, so that `*{5}{|c}|` is the same as `|c|c|c|c|c|`.

The available *formatting symbols* for the left and right borders and for the inter-column spacing are

|   draws a vertical line;

||  draws two vertical lines next to each other;

@{*text*} this entry is referred to as an *@-expression*, and inserts *text* in every line of the table between the two columns where it appears.

An @-expression removes the inter-column spacing that is automatically put between each pair of columns. If white space is needed between the inserted text and the next column, this must be explicitly included with `\hspace{ }` within the *text* of the @-expression. If the inter-column spacing between two particular columns is to be something other than the standard, this may be easily achieved by placing `@{\hspace{`*wth*`}}` between the appropriate columns in the formatting argument. This replaces the standard inter-column spacing with the width *wth*.

An `\extracolsep{`*wth*`}` within an @-expression will put extra spacing of amount *wth* between all the following columns, until countermanded by another `\extracolsep` command. In contrast to the standard spacing, this additional spacing is not removed by later @-expressions. In the `tabular*` environment, there must be a command `@{\extracolsep\fill}` somewhere in the column format so that all the subsequent inter-column spacings can stretch out to fill the predefined table width.

If the left or right borders of the table do not consist of a vertical line, spacing is added there of an amount equal to half the normal inter-column spacing. If this spacing is not wanted, it may be suppressed by including an empty @-expression @{} at the beginning or end of the column format.

*rows* contain the actual entries in the table, each horizontal row being terminated with \\. These rows consist of a sequence of column entries separated from each other by the & symbol. Thus each row in the table contains the same number of column entries as in the column definition *cols*. Some entries may be empty. The individual column entries are treated by LATEX as though they were enclosed in braces { }, so that any changes in type style or size are restricted to that one column.

\hline This command may only appear before the first row or immediately after a row termination \\. It draws a horizontal line the full width of the table below the row that was just ended, or at the top of the table if it comes at the beginning.

Two \hline commands together draw two horizontal lines with a little space between them.

\cline{$n - m$} This command draws a horizontal line from the left side of column $n$ to the right side of column $m$. Like \hline, it may only be given just after a row termination \\, and there may be more than one after another. The command \cline{1-3} \cline{5-7} draws two horizontal lines from column 1 to 3 and from column 5 to 7, below the row that was just ended. In each case, the full column widths are underlined.

\multicolumn{*num*}{*col*}{*text*} This command combines the following *num* columns into a single column with their total width including inter-column spacings. The argument *col* contains exactly one of the positioning symbols l, r, or c, with possible @-expressions and vertical lines |. A value of 1 may be given for *num* when the positioning argument is to be changed for that column in one particular row.

In this context, a 'column' starts with a positioning symbol l, r, or c, and includes everything up to but excluding the next one. The first column also includes everything before the first positioning symbol. Thus |c@{}rl| contains three columns: the first is |c@{}, the second r, and the third r|.

The \multicolumn command may only come at the start of a row or right after a column separation symbol &.

\vline This command draws a vertical line with the height of the row at the location where it appears. In this way, vertical lines that do not extend the whole height of the table may be inserted within a column.

Rows may also be terminated with the LATEX 2$_\varepsilon$ commands \tabularnewline, for `tabular` or `array` environments. This is unambiguously a row terminater, while \\ could be ending a line of text within a column entry. (Commands added December 1, 1994.)

Since a table is a vertical box of the same sort as parbox and minipage, it may be positioned horizontally with other boxes or text (see examples in Section 4.7.3). In particular, the table must be enclosed within

> \begin{center} *table* \end{center}

in order to center it on the page.

## 4.8.2   Table style parameters

There are a number of style parameters used in generating tables which LATEX sets to standard values. These may be altered by the user, either globally within the preamble or locally inside an environment. They should not be changed within the `tabular` environment itself.

\tabcolsep  is half the width of the spacing that is inserted between columns in the `tabular` and `tabular*` environments;

\arraycolsep  is the corresponding half inter-column spacing for the `array` environment;

\arrayrulewidth  is the thickness of the vertical and horizontal lines within a table;

\doublerulesep  is the separation between the lines of a double rule.

Changes in these parameters can be made with the \setlength command as usual. For example, to make the line thickness to be 0.5 mm, give \setlength{ \arrayrulewidth}{0.5mm}. Furthermore, the parameter

\arraystretch  can be used to change the distance between the rows of a table. This is a multiplying factor, with a standard value of 1. A value of 1.5 means that the inter-row spacing is increased by 50%. A new value is set by redefining the parameter with the command

> \renewcommand{\arraystretch}{*factor*}

## 4.8.3   Table examples

Creating tables is much easier in practice than it would seem from the above list of formatting possibilities. This is best illustrated with a few examples.

The simplest table consists of a row of columns in which the text entries are either centered or justified to one side. The column widths, the spacing between the columns, and thus the entire width of the table are automatically calculated.

| Position | Club | Games | W | T | L | Goals | Points |
|---:|:---|---:|---:|:---:|---:|:---:|:---:|
| 1 | Amesville Rockets | 33 | 19 | 13 | 1 | 66:31 | 51:15 |
| 2 | Borden Comets | 33 | 18 | 9 | 6 | 65:37 | 45:21 |
| 3 | Clarkson Chargers | 33 | 17 | 7 | 9 | 70:44 | 41:25 |
| 4 | Daysdon Bombers | 33 | 14 | 10 | 9 | 66:50 | 38:28 |
| 5 | Edgartown Devils | 33 | 16 | 6 | 11 | 63:53 | 38:28 |
| 6 | Freeburg Fighters | 33 | 15 | 7 | 11 | 64:47 | 37:29 |
| 7 | Gadsby Tigers | 33 | 15 | 7 | 11 | 52:37 | 37:29 |
| 8 | Harrisville Hotshots | 33 | 12 | 11 | 10 | 62:58 | 35:31 |
| 9 | Idleton Shovers | 33 | 13 | 9 | 11 | 49:51 | 35:31 |
| 10 | Jamestown Hornets | 33 | 11 | 11 | 11 | 48:47 | 33:33 |
| 11 | Kingston Cowboys | 33 | 13 | 6 | 14 | 54:45 | 32:34 |
| 12 | Lonsdale Stompers | 33 | 12 | 8 | 13 | 50:57 | 32:34 |
| 13 | Marsdon Heroes | 33 | 9 | 13 | 11 | 50:42 | 31:35 |
| 14 | Norburg Flames | 33 | 10 | 8 | 15 | 50:68 | 28:38 |
| 15 | Ollison Champions | 33 | 8 | 9 | 16 | 42:49 | 25:41 |
| 16 | Petersville Lancers | 33 | 6 | 8 | 19 | 31:77 | 20:46 |
| 17 | Quincy Giants | 33 | 7 | 5 | 21 | 40:89 | 19:47 |
| 18 | Ralston Regulars | 33 | 3 | 11 | 19 | 37:74 | 17:49 |

The above table is made up of 8 columns, the first of which is right justified, the second left justified, the third centered, the next three right justified again, and the last two centered. The column formatting argument in the `tabular` environment thus appears as

```
{rlcrrrcc}
```

The text to produce this table is

```
\begin{tabular}{rlcrrrcc}
Position & Club & Games & W & T & L & Goals & Points\\[0.5ex]
  1  & Amesville Rockets & 33 & 19 & 13 &  1 & 66:31 & 51:15 \\
  2  & Borden Comets     & 33 & 18 &  9 &  6 & 65:37 & 45:21 \\
... & .....             & .. & .. & .. & .. & ...   &  ...  \\
17  & Quincy Giants     & 33 &  7 &  5 & 21 & 40:89 & 19:47 \\
18  & Ralston Regulars  & 33 &  3 & 11 & 19 & 37:74 & 17:49
\end{tabular}
```

In each row, the individual columns are separated from one another by the symbol & and the row itself is terminated with \\. The [0.5ex] at the end of the first row adds extra vertical spacing between the first two rows. The last row does not need the termination symbol since it is ended automatically by the \end{tabular} command.

The columns may be separated by vertical rules by including the symbol | in the column formatting argument. Changing the first line to

```
\begin{tabular}{r|l||c|rrr|c|c}
```

results in

| Position | Club | Games | W | T | L | Goals | Points |
|---:|---|:---:|:---:|:---:|:---:|:---:|:---:|
| 1 | Amesville Rockets | 33 | 19 | 13 | 1 | 66:31 | 51:15 |
| 2 | Borden Comets | 33 | 18 | 9 | 6 | 65:37 | 45:21 |
| ⋮ | ⋮ |  |  |  |  |  | ⋮ |
| 17 | Quincy Giants | 33 | 7 | 5 | 21 | 40:89 | 19:47 |
| 18 | Ralston Regulars | 33 | 3 | 11 | 19 | 37:74 | 17:49 |

The same symbol | before the first or after the last column format
generates a vertical line on the outside edge of the table. Two symbols ||
produce a double vertical line. Horizontal lines over the whole width of
the table are created with the command \hline. They may only appear
right after a row termination \\ or at the very beginning of the table. Two
such commands \hline\hline draw a double horizontal line.

```
\begin{tabular}{|r|l||c|rrr|c|c|} \hline
Position & Club & Games & W & T & L & Goals & Points\\
\hline\hline
1  & Amesville Rockets & 33 & 19 & 13 &  1 & 66:31 & 51:15 \\
\hline
. . . . . . . . . . . . . . . . . . . . . . . . . . . . . .
18  & Ralston Regulars  & 33 &  3 & 11 & 19 & 37:74 & 17:49 \\
\hline
\end{tabular}
```

The table now appears as

| Position | Club | Games | W | T | L | Goals | Points |
|---:|---|:---:|:---:|:---:|:---:|:---:|:---:|
| 1 | Amesville Rockets | 33 | 19 | 13 | 1 | 66:31 | 51:15 |
| 2 | Borden Comets | 33 | 18 | 9 | 6 | 65:37 | 45:21 |
| ⋮ | ⋮ |  |  |  |  |  | ⋮ |
| 17 | Quincy Giants | 33 | 7 | 5 | 21 | 40:89 | 19:47 |
| 18 | Ralston Regulars | 33 | 3 | 11 | 19 | 37:74 | 17:49 |

In this case, the row termination \\ must be given for the last row too
because of the presence of \hline at the end of the table.

In this example, all rows contain the same entry in the third column,
that is, 33. Such a common entry can be automatically inserted in the
column format as an @-expression of the form @{*text*}, which places *text*
between the neighboring columns. This could be accomplished for our
example by changing the column format to

{rl@{ 33 }rrrcc}   or   {|r|l||@{ 33 }|rrr|c|c|}

so that the text ' 33 ', blanks included, appears between the second and
third columns in every row. This produces the same table with slightly
different row entries: for example, the fourth row would now be given as

```
4  & Daysdon Bombers & 14 & 10 &   9 & 66:50 & 38:28 \\
```

The column format now consists of only 7 column definitions, `rlrrrcc`. The previous third column `c` has been removed, and so each row contains one less column separation symbol `&`. The new third column, the number of games won, begins with the second `&` and is separated from the club name by the contents of `@{ 33 }`, which is entered automatically without any additional `&` symbol.

The last two columns give the relations between goals and points won and lost as a centered entry of the form *m:n*. The colons ':' are only coincidentally ordered exactly over one another since two-digit numbers appear in every case on both sides of the colon. If one entry had been 9:101, the colon would have been shifted slightly to the left as the entire entry was centered.

A vertical alignment of the ':' independent of the number of digits can also be achieved using an @-expression of the form `r@{:}l` in the column format. This means that a colon is placed in every row between a right and a left justified column. The column formatting argument in the example now becomes

```
{rl@{ 33 }rrrr@{:}lr@{:}l}  or
{|r|l||@{ 33 }|rrr|r@{:}l|r@{:}l|}
```

and the row entry is

```
4 & Daysdon Bombers & 14 & 10 &   9 & 66 & 50 & 38 & 28 \\
```

Each of the former `c` columns has been replaced by the two columns in `r@{:}l`. An @-expression inserts its text between the neighboring columns, removing the inter-column spacing that would normally be there. Thus the `r` column is justified flush right with the ':' and the following `l` column flush left.

The same method can be employed when a column consists of numbers with decimal points and a varying number of digits.

The entries for the goal and point relationships are now made up of two columns positioned about the ':' symbol. This causes no problems for entering the number of goals won and lost or for the number of plus and minus points, since each entry has its own column. However, the column headings are the words 'Goals' and 'Points', stretching over two columns each and without the colon. This is accomplished with the `\multicolumn` command, which merges selected columns in a particular row and redefines the column format. The first row of the unframed soccer table is then

```
Position & Club & W & T & L & \multicolumn{2}{c}{Goals}
                             & \multicolumn{2}{c}{Points}\\[0.5ex]
```

Here `\multicolumn{2}{c}{Goals}` means that the next two columns are to be combined into a centered column, containing the text 'Goals'. For the framed table, the new formatting argument in the `\multicolumn` commands must be `{c|}` since the vertical line symbol | was also removed when the old columns were combined. In deciding what belongs to a given column, use the rule that a column 'owns' everything up to but excluding the next r, l, or c.

The table of final results for our soccer league 1994/95 is to have the following title:

```
\begin{tabular}{|r|l||rrr|r@{:}l|r@{:}l||c|}\hline
  \multicolumn{10}{|c|}{\bfseries 1st Regional Soccer League ---
  Final Results 1994/95}\\ \hline
&\itshape Club &\itshape W &\itshape T &\itshape L &
  \multicolumn{2}{c|}{\itshape Goals}
  & \multicolumn{2}{c||}{\itshape Points}
  & \itshape Remarks \\ \hline\hline
```

. . . . . . . . . . . . . . . . . . . . . . . . . . . . . . . . . . .

| 1st Regional Soccer League — Final Results 1994/95 | | | | | | | |
|---|---|---|---|---|---|---|---|
| | *Club* | *W* | *T* | *L* | *Goals* | *Points* | *Remarks* |
| 1 | Amesville Rockets | 19 | 13 | 1 | 66:31 | 51:15 | League Champs |
| 2 | Borden Comets | 18 | 9 | 6 | 65:37 | 45:21 | Trophy Winners |
| 3 | Clarkson Chargers | 17 | 7 | 9 | 70:44 | 41:25 | Candidates |
| 4 | Daysdon Bombers | 14 | 10 | 9 | 66:50 | 38:28 | for |
| 5 | Edgartown Devils | 16 | 6 | 11 | 63:53 | 38:28 | National |
| 6 | Freeburg Fighters | 15 | 7 | 11 | 64:47 | 37:29 | League |
| 7 | Gadsby Tigers | 15 | 7 | 11 | 52:37 | 37:29 | |
| 8 | Harrisville Hotshots | 12 | 11 | 10 | 62:58 | 35:31 | |
| 9 | Idleton Shovers | 13 | 9 | 11 | 49:51 | 35:31 | |
| 10 | Jamestown Hornets | 11 | 11 | 11 | 48:47 | 33:33 | |
| 11 | Kingston Cowboys | 13 | 6 | 14 | 54:45 | 32:34 | Medium Teams |
| 12 | Lonsdale Stompers | 12 | 8 | 13 | 50:57 | 32:34 | |
| 13 | Marsdon Heroes | 9 | 13 | 11 | 50:42 | 31:35 | |
| 14 | Norburg Flames | 10 | 8 | 15 | 50:68 | 28:38 | |
| 15 | Ollison Champions | 8 | 9 | 16 | 42:49 | 25:41 | |
| 16 | Petersville Lancers | 6 | 8 | 19 | 31:77 | 20:46 | Disbanding |
| 17 | Quincy Giants | 7 | 5 | 21 | 40:89 | 19:47 | Demoted |
| 18 | Ralston Regulars | 3 | 11 | 19 | 37:74 | 17:49 | |

The horizontal lines for positions 3–5, 7–14, and 17 were made with the command \cline{1-9} while all the others used \hline:

```
11  & Kingston  Cowboys   & 13 &  6 & 14 & 54&45 & 32&34 &
        Medium Teams \\ \cline{1-9}
```

The last two rows of the table deserve a comment. The remark 'Demoted' is vertically placed in the middle of the two rows. This is accomplished by typing

```
18  & Ralston Regulars  &  3 & 11 & 19 & 37&74 & 17&49
    & \raisebox{1.5ex}[0pt]{Demoted}\\ \hline
```

The `\raisebox` command lifts the text 'Demoted' by 1.5 ex. If the optional argument [Opt] had been left out, this lifting of the box would have increased the total height of the last row by 1.5 ex. This would have resulted in correspondingly more vertical spacing between the horizontal line of row 17 and the text of row 18. This additional spacing is suppressed by the optional argument *height* = [Opt]. (See Section 4.7.2 for a description of the `\raisebox` command.)

Occasionally one wants to increase the vertical spacing between horizontal lines and enclosed text. The soccer table would look better if the heading were thus:

| 1st Regional Soccer League — Final Results 1994/95 | | | | | | |
|---|---|---|---|---|---|---|
| *Club* | *W* | *T* | *L* | *Goals* | *Points* | *Remarks* |

This is done by inserting an invisible vertical rule, a *strut* (Section 4.7.6) into the heading text:

```
\multicolumn{10}{|c|}{\rule[-3mm]{0mm}{8mm}\bfseries 1st
    Regional Soccer League ---  Final Results 1994/95}\\ \hline
```

The included rule has a width of 0 mm, which makes it invisible, extends 3 mm below the baseline, and is 8 mm high. It thus stretches 5 mm (8 − 3) above the baseline. It effectively pushes the horizontal lines away from the baseline in both directions. If a row consists of more than one column, it is sufficient to include a *strut* in only one of them since the size of the whole row is determined by the largest column.

*Exercise 4.14:* Produce your own table for the final results of your favorite team sport in the same manner as for the soccer results above. Watch out that the colons ':' are properly aligned for the goals and points relationships.

*Exercise 4.15:* Generate the following timetable.

| Day | Subj. | 6.15–7.15 pm | Subj. | 7.20–8.20 pm | Subj. | 8.30–9.30 pm |
|---|---|---|---|---|---|---|
| | | Teacher | | Teacher | | Teacher |
| | | Room | | Room | | Room |
| Mon. | UNIX | Dr. Smith | Fortran | Ms. Clarke | Math. | Mr. Mills |
| | | Comp. Ctr | | Hall A | | Hall A |
| Tues. | LaTeX | Miss Baker | Fortran | Ms. Clarke | Math. | Mr. Mills |
| | | Conf. Room | | Conf. Room | | Hall A |
| Wed. | UNIX | Dr. Smith | C | Dr. Jones | ComSci. | Dr. Jones |
| | | Comp. Ctr | | Hall B | | Hall B |
| Fri. | LaTeX | Miss Baker | C++ | Ms. Clarke | canceled | |
| | | Conf. Room | | Conf. Room | | |

The entries 'Day' and 'Subj.' are raised in the same way as 'Demoted' was in the soccer table. To simplify its application, one can introduce a user-defined command with

\newcommand{\rb}[1]{\raisebox{1.5ex}[0pt]{#1}}     *(see Section 7.3.2)*

*so that* \rb{entry} *behaves the same as* {\raisebox{1.5ex}[0pt]{entry}. This can be used, for example, as* \rb{ Mon.} *or* \rb{UNIX} *to elevate the entries by the necessary amount.*

In all the above examples, the entries in the individual columns are each a single line. Some tables contain certain columns with several lines of text that are somewhat separated from the rest of the row:

| **Model** | Description | **Price** |
|---|---|---|
| GXT 1 | **The PC Compatible**: Intel 80386, 1 MB main memory, color graphic card, multi-I/O card, 2 drives 1.2 MB, 17" monitor, keyboard, MS-DOS 6.2, GW Basic | 883.70 |
| GXT 20 | **The XT Compatible**: Data as for GXT, but with Hercules compatible card, 1 drive 1.2 MByte, 1 hard disk 120 MByte unformatted | 1376.40 |
| GAT | **The AT Compatible**: Intel 80486, 1 drive 1.2 MB /720 KB, 8 MByte main memory, 17" monitor, keyboard, Hercules compatible card, hard disk 240 MByte unformatted, Serial/Parallel card, MS-DOS 6.2, GW Basic | 2356.00 |

The above table is made up of three columns, the first left justified, the third right justified. The middle column contains several lines of text with a line width of 8.0 cm. This is generated with the column formatting symbol p{*width*}. The whole column formatting argument in this example is {lp{8.0cm}r}.

```
\begin{tabular}{lp{8.0cm}r}
  \bfseries Model & Description & \bfseries Price \\[1ex]
    GXT 1 &\small{\bfseries  The PC Compatible}: Intel
        80386, 1 MB main memory,color graphic card,
        multi--I/O card, 2 drives 1.2 MB, 17'' monitor,
        keyboard, MS-DOS~6.2, GW Basic & 883.70\\
     . . . . . . . . . . . . . . . . . . . . . . . .
        MS-DOS~6.2, GW Basic & 2356.00
\end{tabular}
```

The text for the middle column is simply typed in, being broken up into lines of width 8.0 cm automatically. The column is separated from the others with the & symbol in the usual way.

**Warning:** the line termination command \\ may not be used within a p column since this would be interpreted as the end of the table row. The line breaking commands \newline and \linebreak are allowed. However, if a line really does need to be broken with \\, the whole column entry must be packed into a \parbox that has the same width as the p column. The column entry may consist of several paragraphs, separated by blank lines.

*Exercise 4.16:* Produce *the following table.*

| Course and Date | Brief Description | Prerequisites |
|---|---|---|
| Introduction to LSEDIT March 14 – 16 | Logging on — explanation of the VMS file system — explanation and intensive application of the VMS editor LSEDIT — user modifications | none |
| Introduction to LATEX March 21 – 25 | Word processors and formatting programs — text and commands — environments — document and page styles — displayed text — math equations — simple user-defined structures | LSEDIT |

The final example describes a blank form produced as a framed table. The difficulty here is to set the heights and widths of the empty boxes, since these are normally determined automatically by the text entries. The example shows how this may be accomplished with the help of *struts* and \hspace commands.

| **Budget Plan 1995–1997** | | | | | |
|---|---|---|---|---|---|
| Project | Nr. ☐☐ | | Name ☐☐☐☐☐☐☐☐☐☐☐ | | |
| Year | 1995 | | 1996 | | 1997 |
| | (GB £) \| US $ | | (GB £) \| US $ | | (GB £) \| US $ |
| Investment Costs | | | | | |
| Operating Costs | | | | | |
| Industrial Contracts | | | | | |
| Signature | | | Authorization | | |

```
\newsavebox{\k}\newsavebox{\kkk}
\sbox{\k}{\framebox[4mm]{\rule{0mm}{3mm}}}
\sbox{\kkk}{\usebox{\k}\usebox{\k}\usebox{\k}}
\begin{tabular} {|l|c|c|c|}\hline
  \multicolumn{4}{|c|}{\rule[-0.3cm]{0mm}{0.8cm}\bfseries
      Budget Plan 1995--1997}\\
  \hline\hline
  \rule[-0.4cm]{0mm}{1cm}Project
    & \multicolumn{3}{l|}{Nr. \usebox{\kkk}\hspace{0.5cm}
  \vline\hspace{0.5cm}Name\usebox{\kkk}\usebox{\kkk}\usebox{\kkk}
    \usebox{\kk}}\\ \hline
  \multicolumn{1}{|r|}{Year} & 1995 & 1996 & 1997 \\
  \cline{2-4}
  & (GB \pounds) \vline\ US \$ & (GB \pounds) \vline\ US \$
```

```
             & (GB \pounds) \vline\ US \$ \\ \hline
     Investment & \hspace{2.5cm}& \hspace{2.5cm}& \hspace{2.5cm} \\
     Costs      & & & \\ \hline
     Operating & & & \\
     Costs      & & & \\ \hline
     Industrial& & & \\
     Contracts & & & \\ \hline
     \multicolumn{4}{|l|}{\rule[-1.2cm]{0mm}{1.5cm}Signature
         \hspace{5cm}\vline~Authorization} \\ \hline
\end{tabular}
```

The first three lines are only indirectly related to the table construction. They arrange for three empty boxes ☐☐☐ to be drawn when the command \usebox{\kkk} is given (see Section 4.7.1).

Except for the command \hspace{2.5cm} to set the column widths of the last three columns and the command \vline to draw a vertical line within a column, this example contains nothing new that was not in the previous examples. It is only necessary to give a brief explanation of the last row in the table:

The command \multicolumn{4}{|l|} merges all four table columns into one, in which the text is set flush with the left margin. This text consists first of a strut \rule[-12mm]{0mm}{15mm} that says the height of the last row begins 12 mm below the baseline and is a total of 15 mm high. Then, beginning at the left margin, comes the word Signature, followed 5 cm later by \vline, a vertical line. The word Authorization is separated from the verical line by a blank space (~).

The above examples clearly illustrate how the column widths and row heights are automatically determined for tables. These sizes, however, may be influenced by *struts* and \hspace commands. In addition, the commands described in Section 4.8.2 permit the *inter-column* and *inter-row* spacings as well as *line thickness* to be altered. For example,

```
\setlength{\tabcolsep}{5mm}
```

inserts 5 mm of spacing before and after every column; that is, it produces an inter-column spacing of 10 mm. Section 4.8.2 gives more information about the use of these *table style* parameters.

## 4.8.4   Floating tables

The tabular environment produces a table at that place in the text where it appears, immediately after the previous text and followed by whatever comes afterwards. This causes no difficulty and is frequently just what one wants when the table fits on the page with the surrounding text. However, if the table is so long that it does not fit on the current page where it is defined, that page is ended and the next begins with the table,

**Primary Energy Consumption**

| Energy Source | 1975 | 1980 | 1986 |
|---|---|---|---|
| Total Consumption | | | |
| (in million tons of BCU[a]) | 347.7 | 390.2 | 385.0 |
| of which (percentages) | | | |
| petroleum | 52.1 | 47.6 | 43.2 |
| bituminous coal | 19.1 | 19.8 | 20.0 |
| brown coal | 9.9 | 10.0 | 8.6 |
| natural gas | 14.2 | 16.5 | 15.1 |
| nuclear energy | 2.0 | 3.7 | 10.1 |
| other[b] | 2.7 | 2.3 | 3.0 |

[a] BCU = Bituminous Coal Unit (1 ton BCU corresponds to the heating equivalent of 1 ton of bituminous coal = 8140 kwh)
[b] Wind, water, solar energy, etc.

*Source:* Energy Balance Study Group, Essen 1987.

followed by the subsequent text. This leads to an undesirable formatting of the current page.

It would be better if the table were inserted into the immediate text position only if there is enough room for it on the present page, otherwise the text should just continue and the table be held in reserve until an appropriate place appears for it, say at the start of the next page. Since tables often are accompanied by headlines and/or captions, these should naturally be moved along with them.

LATEX does offer the possibility to *float* tables (as well as figures), including additional text, in just this manner. This is brought about with the environment

\begin{table} *head_text* *table* *foot_text* \end{table}

where *table* stands for the entire table as defined in a `tabular` environment, *head_text* for whatever text appears above the table, and *foot_text* for that below. Widths, spacing, and positioning of the texts relative to the table are all matters for the user to arrange.

Independently of the enclosed text, everything that appears between \begin{table} and \end{table} is normally placed at the start of the current page. If a table already occupies the top of the page, an attempt is made to place it at the page bottom, if there is enough space for it. Otherwise, it will be placed on the next page, where further tables may be accumulated. The surrounding text is printed as though the table were not there. For further details about floats in general, including automatic sequential numbering, see Section 6.6.

The table at the top of this page was generated within the text at this location with the following (excluding the footnotes, which are described later in Section 4.10.4):

```
\begin{table} {\bfseries Primary Energy Consumption}\\[1ex]
  \begin{tabular*}{118mm}{@{}ll...rr@{}}
  . . . . . . . . . . . . . . . . . . . .
  \end{tabular*}\\[0.5ex]
  \emph{Source:} Energy Balance Study Group, . . .
\end{table}
```

There are a number of formatting parameters that may be used in connection with the `table` environment, which are described together with those for figures in Section 6.6.

*Exercise 4.17: Complete the above text for the table on the previous page (without the footnotes). Pay attention to the following questions (check the explanations for the @-expressions in Section 4.8.1):*

1. *What is the effect of the `@{}` entries at the beginning and end of the formatting definition?*

2. *The `tabular*` environment generates a table with a given width, here 130 mm. What would be the effect of `@{extracolsep{\fill}}` at the beginning of the formatting definition?*

3. *Where in the formatting definition should `@{extracolsep{\fill}}` and the countermanding `@{\hspace{1em}}@{\extracolsep{1em}}` appear in order to format the table as it is printed here? How would the table appear if only `@{\extracolsep{1em}}` were given as countermand?*

## 4.9    Printing source text

Occasionally it is desired to have the text printed exactly as it is typed, unformatted. This is done with the environments

```
\begin{verbatim}    source_text  \end{verbatim}
\begin{verbatim*}   source_text  \end{verbatim*}
```

where *source_text* is printed in a typewriter typeface exactly as it is in the source text, including all blanks and line breaks. Special characters that are normally treated as commands are printed literally as strings of characters. The only exception is the command `\end{verbatim}` itself, which terminates the environment. The printout starts on a new line, as does the normal text following the `verbatim` environment.

The difference between the normal and *-form of the environment is that, in the case of the latter, blanks are printed with the symbol ␣ to make them more visible.

As an example, on page 110 some source text is printed to demonstrate the use of footnotes in forbidden modes. This was done with

```
\begin{verbatim}
  \addtocounter{footnote}{-1}\footnotetext{Small insects}
  \stepcounter{footnote}\footnotetext{Large mammals}
\end{verbatim}
```

Source text may also be printed within a line using the commands

 \verb*c*  *source_text*  *c*
 \verb*\*c* *source_text*  *c*

where *c* is any arbitrary character that does *not* appear in *source_text*. It is used to terminate the literal mode and return to formatting text as usual. There must be no blanks between the \verb or \verb* command and the *c*. Obviously, for the standard form, *c* may not be a *.

Command names in the normal text are printed in this way. For example, to produce '\xyz{ }', the input is \verb=\xyz{ }=. The equals sign = is used here as the delimiting character. The *-form acts the same, but prints out blanks as ␣ as in the verbatim* environment: \xyz{␣}.

The standard LATEX 2ε package shortvrb (page 241) offers a more compact shorthand version of the \verb command.

In contrast to the behavior in the verbatim environment, line breaks may not occur within *source_text*. If the text extends over more than one line, the line break will be treated as a blank (LATEX 2.09), or issues an error message (LATEX 2ε). This message serves to indicate that you just might have forgotten the terminating *c* character.

**Important:** *neither the* verbatim *environment nor the* \verb *command may be used in an argument of any other command!*

*Exercise 4.18: Reproduce some literal lines from this book as source text.*

# 10 Footnotes and marginal notes

## 10.1 Standard footnotes

Footnotes are generated with the command

 \footnote{*footnote_text*}

which comes immediately after the word requiring an explanation in a footnote. The text *footnote_text* appears as a footnote in a smaller typeface at the bottom of the page. The first line of the footnote is indented and is given the same footnote marker as that inserted in the main text. The first footnote on a page is separated from the rest of the page text by means of a short horizontal line.

The standard footnote marker is a small, raised number[1], which is sequentially numbered.

```
... raised number\footnote{The usual method of marking
footnotes in a typewritten ... same page.}, which is ...
```

---

[1] The usual method of marking footnotes in a typewritten manuscript with *, **, etc., could also be done; however, since the page breaks are not known at the time of typing the text, there would be a problem of avoiding duplication of the symbols on the same page.

The footnote numbering is incremented throughout the whole document for the `article` class, whereas it is reset to 1 for each new chapter in the `report` and `book` classes.

The `\footnote` command may only be given within the normal paragraph mode, and not within math or LR modes (Section 1.5.3). In practice, this means it may not appear within an LR box (Section 4.7.1) or a parbox (Section 4.7.3). However, it may be used within a `minipage` environment, in which case the footnote text is printed beneath the minipage and not at the bottom of the actual page.[2]

The `\footnote` command must immediately follow the word that is to receive the note, without any intervening blanks or spacing. A footnote at the end of a sentence can be given after the period, as in the last example above:

```
... of the actual page.\footnote{With nested ... wrong place.}
```

## 4.10.2  Non-standard footnotes

If the user wishes the footnote numbering to be reset to 1 for each `\section` command with the `article` class, this may be achieved with

```
\setcounter{footnote}{0}
```

just before or after a `\section` command.

The internal footnote counter has the name `footnote`. Each call to `\footnote` increments this counter by one and prints the new value in Arabic numbering as the footnote marker. A different style of marker can be implemented with the command

```
\renewcommand{\thefootnote}{\number_style{footnote}}
```

where *number_style* is one of the counter print commands described in Section 4.3.5: `\arabic`, `\roman`, `\Roman`, `\alph`, or `\Alph`. However, for the counter `footnote`, there is an additional counter print command available, `\fnsymbol`, which prints the counter values 1–9 as one of nine symbols:

$$* \quad \dagger \quad \ddagger \quad \S \quad \P \quad \| \quad ** \quad \dagger\dagger \quad \ddagger\ddagger$$

It is up to the user to see that the footnote counter is reset to zero sometime before the tenth `\footnote` call is made.

An optional argument may be added to the `\footnote` command

```
\footnote[num]{footnote_text}
```

---

[2]With nested minipages, the footnote comes after the next `\end{minipage}` command, which could be at the wrong place.

where *num* is a positive integer that is used instead of the value of the footnote counter for the marker. In this case, the footnote counter is not incremented. For example**,

```
\renewcommand{\thefootnote}{\fnsymbol{footnote}}
For example\footnote[7]{The 7th symbol ... marker.},
\renewcommand{\thefootnote}{\arabic{footnote}}
```

where the last line is necessary to restore the footnote marker style to its standard form. Otherwise, all future footnotes would be marked with symbols and not with numbers.

## 10.3 Footnotes in forbidden modes

A footnote marker can be inserted in the text with the command

> \footnotemark[*num*]

even where the \footnote command is normally not allowed, that is, in LR boxes, tables, and math mode. The marker is either the optional argument *num* or, if it is omitted, the incremented value of the footnote counter. The footnote itself is not generated. This must be done external to the forbidden mode with the command

> \footnotetext[*num*]{*footnote_text*}

If the optional argument has been used for the footnote marker, the same *num* must be given as the option for the text command. Similarly, if no option was used for the marker, none may appear with the text. The footnote will be generated with the value of *num* or with that of the footnote counter.

This counter is incremented by a call to \footnotemark without an optional argument. The corresponding \footnotetext command, on the other hand, does not alter the counter.

If there are a number of \footnotemark commands without optional arguments appearing before the next \footnotetext command, it is necessary to adjust the counter with the command

> \addtocounter{\footnote}{*dif*}

where *dif* is a negative number saying how many times the counter must be set back. Then before every \footnotetext command, the counter must be incremented by one. This can be done either with the command \addtocounter, with *dif*=1, or with the command

> \stepcounter{footnote}

which adds 1 to the given counter.

For example: mosquitoes[3] and elephants[4]

---

** The 7th symbol appears as the footnote marker.
[3] Small insects
[4] Large mammals

> For example: \fbox{mosquitoes\footnotemark\ and
>     elephants\footnotemark}

generates the footnote markers [3] and [4]. Now the counter has the value 4. In order for the first \footnotetext outside the framed box to operate with the correct counter value, it must first be decremented by one. The two footnote texts are made with

    \addtocounter{footnote}{-1}\footnotetext{Small insects}
    \stepcounter{footnote}\footnotetext{Large mammals}

immediately following the \fbox{} command. The footnote counter now has the same value as it did on leaving the \fbox.

## 4.10.4  Footnotes in minipages

As mentioned in Section 4.10.1, footnote commands are allowed inside the minipage environment. However, the footnote appears underneath the minipage, not below the main page.

Footnote commands within a minipage[a] have a different marker style. The footnote appears after the next \end{minipage} command.[b] Minipage footnotes make use of a separate counter from that of the main page, called mpfootnote, which counts independently of footnote.

    \begin{minipage}{6cm}
    Footnote commands within
    a minipage\footnote{The
    marker is a raised
    lower-case letter.} have
    a different...
    \end{minipage}

---

[a]The marker is a raised lower-case letter.

[b]This can cause troubles with nested minipages.

> [!]

Footnotes inside tables, that is, within a tabular environment, can normally only be generated with the commands described above: \footnotemark within the table and \footnotetext outside the environment. However, if the tabular environment is enclosed in a minipage, normal \footnote commands may also be used inside the table. The footnote appears below the table where the minipage comes to an end.

*Exercise 4.19: Produce a number of footnotes in your standard exercise file by inserting them where you think fit and by selecting some appropriate footnote text.*

*Exercise 4.20: Redefine the command \thefootnote so that the footnote markers become the symbols illustrated in Section 4.10.2. Add the redefinition to the preamble of your standard exercise file.*

*Exercise 4.21: Complete Exercise 4.17 so that the footnotes [a] and [b] appear as in the table on page 105.*

## 0.5 Footnote style parameters

There are two footnote style parameters that may be changed as needed, either
in the preamble or locally within an environment.

\footnotesep

> The vertical spacing between two footnotes. This is a length that can be
> changed with the \setlength command.

\footnoterule

> The command that draws a horizontal line between the page text and
> the footnotes. It should not add any net vertical spacing. It may be
> changed, for example, by

> > \renewcommand{\footnoterule}
> > {\rule{*wth*}{*hght*}\vspace{-*hght*}}

> A value of 0 cm for the *hght* produces an invisible line of zero thickness.

## 0.6 Marginal notes

Notes in the page margin are produced with the command

> \marginpar{*note_text*}

which puts the text *note_text* into the right-hand margin beginning at the
level of the line where the command is given. The marginal note appearing
here was generated with

> ... The marginal note \marginpar{This\\ is a\\ margin-\\al note}
> appearing here ...

This is a margin- al note

The text is normally enclosed in a parbox of width 1.9 cm (0.75 in).
Such a narrow box causes great difficulties with line breaking, which is
why the lines are manually broken with the \\ command in the above
example. Such a box is far more appropriate for marginal notes in the
form of a single symbol, such as the arrow shown here.

Another common use for the marginal note is to draw attention to
certain text passages by marking them with a vertical bar in the margin.
This is often done to indicate changes in a text, for comparison with
earlier versions after updated single sheets have been redistributed. The
example marking this paragraph was made by including

> \marginpar{\rule[-17.5mm]{1mm}{20mm}}

in the first line.

The width of the marginal note can be changed with a style parameter
described in the next section. The user must watch out that the total page
width does not become too big for the printer.

By default, marginal notes appear in the right-hand margin of the page,
or in the outer margin when the twoside option has been selected. 'Outer'

means the right margin for odd pages, and left for even ones. With the
twocolumn option, they are placed in the outside margins: left for the
left column and right for the right one.

This leads to a problem for marginal markings such as the arrow
illustrated on the previous page.  On this page, it must point in the
⟹ opposite direction.  In fact, its direction depends on which side of the
page it is to appear, and that in turns depends on the page number or
column.  Since these are not known at the time of writing (and may even
change with later revisions) it is necessary to have another solution.  This
is provided by the extended syntax of the \marginpar command

\marginpar [*left_text*] {*right_text*}

This form of the command contains two versions of the marginal text,
*left_text* to go into the left margin, and *right_text* for the right margin,
depending on which one is selected.  Both the arrows on this and the
previous page were generated with the same command

\marginpar[\hfill$\Longrightarrow$]{$\Longleftarrow$}

(The arrow commands are mathematical symbols that are explained fully
in Section 5.3.5.)

Without the \hfill command in the above \marginpar example, the arrow
in the left margin appears as it does at the side of this paragraph, too far over to
the left.  The reason for this is that the \marginpar command sets its contents
flush with the left edge of the narrow margin box, made visible here with a frame.
This left edge is aligned with the main text only when the note is put on the right
side; however, in the left margin, it is displaced from the main text. The \hfill
command has the effect of setting the contents flush with the right edge of the
margin box, which is then properly aligned with the main text.

A similar device was also applied in making the first marginal note in this
section. The actual command that was given to produce it was

\marginpar[\flushright This\\ is a\\ margin-\\al note]
    {This\\ is a\\ margin-\\al note}

Here \flushright (Section 4.2.2) is equivalent to putting an \hfill on each line.

The standard positioning of the marginal notes can be switched with
the command \reversemarginpar. Once this command has been given,
marginal notes will appear in the left margin, or in the 'inner' margin
for the twoside option. This command remains in effect until counter- ⟸
manded by \normalmarginpar. For the twocolumn option, both these
commands are inoperative.

A page break cannot occur within a marginal note.  If the note is near the
bottom of the page and there is not enough room for it, it extends below the
last line of text. In this case, the text in the \marginpar command may include
a \vspace command at the beginning to shove it upwards, or the note must be
split across two pages with two separate \marginpar commands. Such manual
corrections should only be undertaken after the whole document is finished, since
subsequent alterations can upset the conditions under which they were made.

## 0.7 Style parameters for marginal notes

The following style parameters may be changed to redefine how marginal notes appear:

`\marginparwidth`
> determines the width of the margin box;

`\marginparsep`
> sets the separation between the margin box and the edge of the main text;

`\marginparpush`
> is the smallest vertical distance between two marginal notes.

These parameters are all lengths and are assigned new values as usual with the `\setlength` command.

# 11   Comments within text

It is extremely useful to be able to include comments, explanations, reminders, and so forth within the text, to tell the author or some other user later what the purpose of a certain construction was. These comments are not to be formatted with the rest of the text.

In TeX, the single character command % introduces a comment. When this character appears in the text, it and the rest of the line are ignored. If a comment is several lines long, each line must be prefixed with %.

The comment character % is also useful for deactivating commands temporarily. Putting a % character in front of such a command switches off the rest of the line. This is called 'commenting lines out.' Similarly, one may have alternative text versions in the source file, with some commented out, waiting until the author's mind is made up about which version will be used.

Finally, the % character has an important role to play in suppressing implied blanks at the end of a line. This is especially desirable in user definitions where unexpected blanks can creep in between otherwise invisible declarations with arguments. See Section 7.5.8.

**Exercise 4.22:** *Comment out the changes from Exercise 4.20 in your preamble. These commands may be reactivated later by removing the % character.*

# 5 Mathematical Formulas

Mathematics is the soul of TeX. It was because the setting of mathematical formulas is so complicated in normal printing, not to mention on a typewriter, that Donald Knuth invented his text formatting system. On the other hand, the soul of LaTeX is document design. Nevertheless, all the power of TeX's math setting is also available in LaTeX, offering an unbeatable combination. Most, but not all, of what is presented in this chapter really applies to TeX, so that the division between the two becomes difficult to define. We shall therefore refer more often to the commands and environments as belonging to LaTeX, even though many of them equally apply to TeX.

Mathematical formulas are produced by typing special descriptive text. This means that LaTeX must be informed that the *following text* is to be interpreted as a *mathematical formula*, and it must also be told when the *math text* has come to an end and normal text recommences. The processing of *math text* is carried out by switching to *math mode* (Section 1.5.3). Mathematical environments serve this purpose.

## 5.1 Mathematical environments

Mathematical formulas may occur within a line of text, as $(a + b)^2 = a^2 + 2ab + b^2$, or separated from the main text as

$$\int_0^\infty f(x)\, dx \approx \sum_{i=1}^n w_i e^{x_i} f(x_i)$$

These two types are distinguished by referring to them as *text* and *displayed formulas* respectively.

Text formulas, or equations, are generated with the environment

> \begin{math} *formula_text* \end{math}

Since text formulas are often very short, sometimes consisting of only a single character, a shorthand version is available as \( *formula_text* \).

115

If even that is too long, the very short form $formula\_text$ may also be employed. All three forms are effectively the same even though some internal differences may exist: for example, \( is fragile while $ is robust.

The contents of the formula, *formula_text*, consist of math constructs, which are described in the following sections.

Displayed formulas, or equations, are produced in the environments

\begin{displaymath}   *formula_text*   \end{displaymath}
\begin{equation}      *formula_text*   \end{equation}

The difference between these two is that the `equation` environment automatically adds a sequential equation number. The `displaymath` environment may be given with the shorthand form \[ *formula_text* \].

By default displayed formulas are centered horizontally with the equation number, if it is present, set flush with the right margin. By selecting the document class option `fleqn` (Section 3.1.1), the formulas are set left justified with an adjustable indentation. This option remains valid for the entire document whereas the amount of indentation may be changed at will with \setlength{\mathindent}{*indent*}, where *indent* is a length specification. Moreover, the document class option `leqno` sets the equation numbers flush with the left margin throughout the whole document.

Finally, multi-line formulas can be created with the environments

\begin{eqnarray}    *formula_text*   \end{eqnarray}
\begin{eqnarray*}   *formula_text*   \end{eqnarray*}

where the standard form adds a sequential equation number for each line and the *-form is without equation numbers.

## 5.2    Main elements of math mode

### 5.2.1    Constants and variables

Numbers that appear within formulas are called *constants*, whereas *simple variables* are represented by single letters. The universal practice in mathematical typesetting is to put constants in Roman typeface and variables in *italics*. LATEX adheres to this rule automatically in math mode. Blanks are totally ignored and are included in the source text simply to improve the appearance for the writer. Spacing between constants, variables, and operators like $+$, $-$, $=$ are set automatically by LATEX. For example \$z=2a+3y\$, \$  z  =  2 a  +  3 y \$ both produce $z = 2a + 3y$.

Mathematical symbols that are available on the keyboard are

$$+ \quad - \quad = \quad < \quad > \quad / \quad : \quad ! \quad ' \quad | \quad [ \quad ] \quad ( \quad )$$

all of which may be used directly in formulas. The curly braces { } serve the purpose of logically combining parts of the formula and therefore cannot act as printable characters. To include braces in a formula, the same commands \{ and \} are used as in normal text.

$M(s) < M(t) < |M| = m$          `$M(s)<M(t)<|M| = m$`
$y'' = c\{f[y', y(x)] + g(x)\}$          `$y'' = c\{f[y',y(x)] + g(x)\}$`

**Preparation:** *Create a new LATEX file with the name* `math.tex` *containing at first only the commands* \documentclass{article}, \begin{document}, *and* \end {document}.

**Exercise 5.1:** *Produce the following text with your math exercise file: 'The derivative of the indirect function $f[g(x)]$ is $\{f[g(x)]\}' = f'[g(x)]g'(x)$. For the second derivative of the product of $f(x)$ and $g(x)$ one has $[f(x)g(x)]'' = f''(x)g(x) + 2f'(x)g'(x) + f(x)g''(x)$.'*
*Note: higher derivatives are made with multiple ' symbols:* `$y'''$` *yields $y'''$.*

## .2   Exponents and indices

Mathematical formulas often contain exponents and indices, characters that are either raised or lowered relative to the main line of the formula, and printed in a smaller typeface. Although their mathematical meanings are different, superscripts and subscripts are typographically the same things as exponents and indices, respectively. It is even possible that exponents themselves have exponents or indices, and so on. These are produced by multiple applications of the raising and lowering operations.

LATEX and TEX make it possible to create any combination of exponents and indices with the correct type size in a simple manner: the character command ^ sets the next character as an exponent (raised), while the character command _ sets it as an index (lowered).

$x^2$  `x^2`     $a_n$  `a_n`     $x_i^n$  `x^n_i`

When exponents and indices occur together, their order is unimportant. The last example above could also have been given as `x_i^n`.

If the exponent or index contains more than one character, the group of characters must be enclosed in braces { }:

$x^{2n}$  `x^{2n}`     $x_{2y}$  `x_{2y}`     $A_{i,j,k}^{-n!2}$  `A_{i,j,k}^{-n!2}`

Multiple raisings and lowerings are generated by applying ^ and _ to the exponents and indices:

$x^{y^2}$  `x^{y^2}`     $x^{y_1}$  `x^{y_1}`
$A_{j_{n,m}}^{x_i^2}$     `A^{x_i^2}_{j^{2n}_{n,m}}`

**Note:** The raising and lowering commands ^ and _ are only permitted in math mode.

### 5.2.3   Fractions

Short fractions, especially within a text formula, are best represented using the slash character /, as in $(n+m)/2$ for $(n + m)/2$. For more complicated fractions, the command

\frac{*numerator*}{*denominator*}

is employed to write the *numerator* on top of the *denominator* with a horizontal fraction line of the right width between them.

$$\frac{1}{x + y}$$    \[ \frac{1}{x+y} \]

$$\frac{a^2 - b^2}{a + b} = a - b$$    \[ \frac{a^2 - b^2}{a+b} = a-b \]

Fractions may be nested to any depth within one another.

$$\frac{\frac{a}{x-y} + \frac{b}{x+y}}{1 + \frac{a-b}{a+b}}$$    \[ \frac{\frac{a}{x-y} + \frac{b}{x+y}}
{1 + \frac{a-b}{a+b}}   \]

LATEX sets fractions within fractions in a smaller typeface. Section 5.5.2 describes how the automatic type sizes may be overridden if LATEX's choice is unsuitable.

### 5.2.4   Roots

Roots are printed with the command

\sqrt[*n*]{*arg*}

as in the example: $\sqrt[3]{8} = 2$ produces $\sqrt[3]{8} = 2$. If the optional argument $n$ is omitted, the square root is generated: $\sqrt{a}$ yields $\sqrt{a}$.

The size and length of the root sign are automatically fitted to *arg*:
$\sqrt{x^2 + y^2 + 2xy} = x+y$    $\sqrt{x^2 + y^2 + 2xy} = x + y$, or

$$\sqrt[n]{\frac{x^n - y^n}{1 + u^{2n}}}$$    \[ \sqrt[n]{\frac{x^n - y^n}{1 + u^{2n}}} \]

Roots may be nested inside one another to any depth:

$$\sqrt[3]{-q + \sqrt{q^2 + p^3}}$$    \[ \sqrt[3]{-q + \sqrt{q^2 + p^3}} \]

## .5 Sums and integrals

Summation and integral signs are made with the two commands \sum and \int, which may appear in two different sizes depending on whether they occur in a text or displayed formula.

Sums and integrals very often possess upper and lower limits. These are printed with the exponent and index commands ^ and _. The positioning of the limits also depends on whether the formula is in text or displayed.

In a text formula \sum_{i=1}^n and \int_a^b produce $\sum_{i=1}^n$ and $\int_a^b$, whereas in a displayed formula they appear as at the left below:

$$\sum_{i=1}^n \int_a^b$$

Some authors prefer the limits for the integral also to be placed above and below the integral sign, the same as for summation. This is achieved with the command \limits immediately following the integral sign: \int\limits_{x=0}^{x=1}

$$\int\limits_{x=0}^{x=1}$$

The rest of the formula text coming before and after the sum and integral signs is correctly aligned with them.

$$2 \sum_{i=1}^n a_i \int_a^b f_i(x)g_i(x)\,dx$$

```
\[ 2\sum_{i=1}^n a_i \int^b_a
       f_i(x)g_i(x)\,dx \]
```

In integrals such as $\int y\,dx$ and $\int f(z)\,dz$, there should be a little extra spacing between the differential operators $dx$ and $dz$ and the integrands preceding them. Inserting a blank will not achieve this since blanks are totally ignored in math mode: $\int y dx$ produces $\int ydx$. One may get around this problem by employing the small spacing command \, mentioned in Section 3.5.1. Thus $\int y\,dx$ and $\int f(z)\,dz$ yield the desired results $\int y\,dx$ and $\int f(z)\,dz$. More spacing commands for mathematical formulas are described in Section 5.5.1.

## .6 Continuation dots—ellipsis

Formulas occasionally contain a row of dots ..., meaning *and so on*. Simply typing a period three times in a row produces an undesirable result: ..., that is, the dots are too close together. Therefore LATEX provides several commands

| \ldots | ... | *low dots* | \cdots | $\cdots$ | *center dots* |
| \vdots | $\vdots$ | *vertical dots* | \ddots | $\ddots$ | *diagonal dots* |

to space the dots correctly. The difference between the first two commands is best illustrated by the examples $a_0, a_1, \ldots, a_n$ and $a_0 + a_1 + \cdots + a_n$, which are produced with $a_0,a_1,\ldots,a_n$ for the first and $a_0 + a_1 + \cdots + a_n$ for the second.

The command \ldots is also available in normal text mode, whereas the other three are only allowed in math mode. In text mode, the command \dots may be used in place of \ldots with the same effect.

*Exercise 5.2: Generate the following output:*
The reduced cubic equation $y^3 + 3py + 2q = 0$ has one real and two complex solutions when $D = q^2 + p^3 > 0$. These are given by Cardan's formula as

$$y_1 = u + v, \quad y_2 = -\frac{u+v}{2} + \frac{i}{2}\sqrt{3}(u - v), \quad y_3 = -\frac{u+v}{2} - \frac{i}{2}\sqrt{3}(u - v)$$

where

$$u = \sqrt[3]{-q + \sqrt{q^2 + p^3}}, \qquad v = \sqrt[3]{-q - \sqrt{q^2 + p^3}}$$

*Note: the spacings between the parts of the displayed equations are made with the spacing commands \quad and \qquad.*

*Exercise 5.3: Select the option* fleqn *in the document class command and include the specification* \setlength{\mathindent}{2cm} *in the preamble. Redo the three y equations above, each as a separate displayed formula, using the* equation *environment instead of* displaymath *or* \[...\] *brackets.*

*Exercise 5.4: Create the following text:*
Each of the measurements $x_1 < x_2 < \cdots < x_r$ occurs $p_1, p_2, \ldots, p_r$ times. The mean value and standard deviation are then

$$x = \frac{1}{n}\sum_{i=1}^{r} p_i x_i, \qquad s = \sqrt{\frac{1}{n}\sum_{i=1}^{r} p_i(x_i - x)^2}$$

where $n = p_1 + p_2 + \cdots + p_r$.

*Exercise 5.5: Although this equation looks very complicated, it should not present any great difficulties:*

$$\int \frac{\sqrt{(ax+b)^3}}{x}\,dx = \frac{2\sqrt{(ax+b)^3}}{3} + 2b\sqrt{ax+b} + b^2 \int \frac{dx}{x\sqrt{ax+b}}$$

*The same applies to* $\int_{-1}^{8}(dx/\sqrt[3]{x}) = \frac{3}{2}(8^{2/3} + 1^{2/3}) = 15/2$.

## 5.3     Mathematical symbols

There is a very wide range of symbols used in mathematical text, of which only a few are directly available from the keyboard. LaTeX provides almost every imaginable mathematical symbol that is commonly used. They are called with the symbol name prefixed with the command character \. The names themselves are derived from their mathematical meanings.

## .1  Greek letters

Lower case letters

| | | | | | | | |
|---|---|---|---|---|---|---|---|
| $\alpha$ | \alpha | $\theta$ | \theta | $o$ | o | $\tau$ | \tau |
| $\beta$ | \beta | $\vartheta$ | \vartheta | $\pi$ | \pi | $\upsilon$ | \upsilon |
| $\gamma$ | \gamma | $\iota$ | \iota | $\varpi$ | \varpi | $\phi$ | \phi |
| $\delta$ | \delta | $\kappa$ | \kappa | $\rho$ | \rho | $\varphi$ | \varphi |
| $\epsilon$ | \epsilon | $\lambda$ | \lambda | $\varrho$ | \varrho | $\chi$ | \chi |
| $\varepsilon$ | \varepsilon | $\mu$ | \mu | $\sigma$ | \sigma | $\psi$ | \psi |
| $\zeta$ | \zeta | $\nu$ | \nu | $\varsigma$ | \varsigma | $\omega$ | \omega |
| $\eta$ | \eta | $\xi$ | \xi | | | | |

Upper case letters

| | | | | | | | |
|---|---|---|---|---|---|---|---|
| $\Gamma$ | \Gamma | $\Lambda$ | \Lambda | $\Sigma$ | \Sigma | $\Psi$ | \Psi |
| $\Delta$ | \Delta | $\Xi$ | \Xi | $\Upsilon$ | \Upsilon | $\Omega$ | \Omega |
| $\Theta$ | \Theta | $\Pi$ | \Pi | $\Phi$ | \Phi | | |

The Greek letters are made simply by putting the command character \ before the name of the letter. Upper case (capital) letters are distinguished by capitalizing the first letter of the name. Greek letters that do not appear in the above list are identical with some corresponding Latin letter. For example, upper case $\rho$ is the same as Latin P and so needs no special symbol.

The upper case Greek letters are normally set in Roman (upright) type within a mathematical formula. If they need to be in italics, this can be brought about with the *math font style command* \mathnormal [2ε] : $\mathnormal{\Gamma\Pi\Phi}$ appears as $\Gamma\Pi\Phi$. (This replaces the math font style *declaration* \mit [2.09] which is used in LaTeX 2.09 as $\mit \Gamma\Pi\Phi$.)

Greek letters may only be used in math mode. If they are needed in normal text, the command must be enclosed in $...$ signs.

## .2  Calligraphic letters

The following 26 *calligraphic* letters may also be used in math formulas

$$\mathcal{A,B,C,D,E,F,G,H,I,J,K,L,M,N,O,P,Q,R,S,T,U,V,W,X,Y,Z}$$

These are called with the font style command \mathcal [2ε] :

    $\mathcal{A, B, C,...,Z}$

(or with the equivalent declaration \cal [2.09] ).

### 5.3.3    Binary operators

Two mathematical quantities combined with one another to make a new quantity are said to be joined by a *binary operation*. The symbols that are available for use as binary operators are

| | | | | | | | |
|---|---|---|---|---|---|---|---|
| ± | \pm | ∩ | \cap | ∘ | \circ | ○ | \bigcirc |
| ∓ | \mp | ∪ | \cup | • | \bullet | □ | \Box |
| × | \times | ⊎ | \uplus | ◇ | \diamond | ◊ | \Diamond |
| ÷ | \div | ⊓ | \sqcap | ◁ | \lhd | △ | \bigtriangleup |
| · | \cdot | ⊔ | \sqcup | ▷ | \rhd | ▽ | \bigtriangledown |
| * | \ast | ∨ | \vee | ⊴ | \unlhd | ◁ | \triangleleft |
| ⋆ | \star | ∧ | \wedge | ⊵ | \unrhd | ▷ | \triangleright |
| † | \dagger | ⊕ | \oplus | ⊘ | \oslash | \ | \setminus |
| ‡ | \ddagger | ⊖ | \ominus | ⊙ | \odot | ≀ | \wr |
| ⅠⅠ | \amalg | ⊗ | \otimes | | | | |

**Note:** the symbols whose names are underlined in the above and following tables are only available in LaTeX 2$_\varepsilon$ if the package latexsym has been loaded (Section 8.8.3).

### 5.3.4    Relations and their negations

When two mathematical quantities are compared, they are connected by a *relation*. The different types of relational symbols for the various comparisons are

| | | | | | | | | | |
|---|---|---|---|---|---|---|---|---|---|
| ≤ | \le | \leq | ≥ | \ge | \geq | ≠ | \neq | ~ | \sim |
| ≪ | \ll | | ≫ | \gg | | ≐ | \doteq | ≃ | \simeq |
| ⊂ | \subset | | ⊃ | \supset | | ≈ | \approx | ≍ | \asymp |
| ⊆ | \subseteq | | ⊇ | \supseteq | | ≅ | \cong | ⌣ | \smile |
| ⊏ | \sqsubset | | ⊐ | \sqsupset | | ≡ | \equiv | ⌢ | \frown |
| ⊑ | \sqsubseteq | | ⊒ | \sqsupseteq | | ∝ | \propto | ⋈ | \bowtie |
| ∈ | \in | | ∋ | \ni | | ≺ | \prec | ≻ | \succ |
| ⊢ | \vdash | | ⊣ | \dashv | | ≼ | \preceq | ≽ | \succeq |
| ⊨ | \models | | ⊥ | \perp | | ‖ | \parallel \| | | \mid | |

A number of the above symbols may be called by more than one name. For example, ≤ may be produced with either \le or \leq.

The opposite, or negated, meaning of the relation is indicated in mathematics with a slash / through the symbol: = and ≠ mean *equals* and *not equals*. For ≠ there is a special command \neq. However, in general one may put a slash through most of the above symbols by prefixing its name with \not. Thus \not\in yields ∉. The same is true for the keyboard characters: \not=, \not>, and \not< produce ≠, ≯, and ≮.

The following symbols may be negated in this manner. Note that the last two, \not\in and \notin are not exactly the same: ∉ and ∉. The latter form is the preferred one.

| ⊀ | \not< | ⊁ | \not> | ≠ | \not= |
| ⪯̸ | \not\le | ⪰̸ | \not\ge | ≢ | \not\equiv |
| ⊀ | \not\prec | ⊁ | \not\succ | ≁ | \not\sim |
| ⪯̸ | \not\preceq | ⪰̸ | \not\succeq | ≄ | \not\simeq |
| ⊄ | \not\subset | ⊅ | \not\supset | ≉ | \not\approx |
| ⊈ | \not\subseteq | ⊉ | \not\supseteq | ≇ | \not\cong |
| ⋢ | \not\sqsubseteq | ⋣ | \not\sqsupseteq | ≭ | \not\asymp |
| ∉ | \not\in | ∉ | \notin | | |

## 5.5   Arrows and pointers

Mathematical manuscripts often contain arrow symbols, also called *pointers.* The following multitude of arrow symbols are available:

| ← | \leftarrow \gets | ⟵ | \longleftarrow | ↑ | \uparrow |
| ⇐ | \Leftarrow | ⟸ | \Longleftarrow | ⇑ | \Uparrow |
| → | \rightarrow \to | ⟶ | \longrightarrow | ↓ | \downarrow |
| ⇒ | \Rightarrow | ⟹ | \Longrightarrow | ⇓ | \Downarrow |
| ↔ | \leftrightarrow | ⟷ | \longleftrightarrow | ↕ | \updownarrow |
| ⇔ | \Leftrightarrow | ⟺ | \Longleftrightarrow | ⇕ | \Updownarrow |
| ↦ | \mapsto | ⟼ | \longmapsto | ↗ | \nearrow |
| ↩ | \hookleftarrow | ↪ | \hookrightarrow | ↘ | \searrow |
| ↼ | \leftharpoonup | ⇀ | \rightharpoonup | ↙ | \swarrow |
| ↽ | \leftharpoondown | ⇁ | \rightharpoondown | ↖ | \nwarrow |
| ⇌ | \rightleftharpoons | ⤳ | \leadsto | | |

Here again the symbols → and ← may also be referred to under the names \to and \gets. Furthermore, the command \Longleftrightarrow may be substituted by \iff, although the latter ( ⟺ ) has a little more spacing on either side than the former (⟺).

## 5.6   Various other symbols

LATEX by no means contains all possible symbols that may appear in mathematical texts. However, the following symbols are additional ones that LATEX does make available. (There are a few repetitions from the previous tables in order to group related symbols together.)

| ℵ | \aleph | ′ | \prime | ∀ | \forall | □ | \Box |
| ℏ | \hbar | ∅ | \emptyset | ∃ | \exists | ◊ | \Diamond |
| ι | \imath | ∇ | \nabla | ¬ | \neg | △ | \triangle |
| ȷ | \jmath | √ | \surd | ♭ | \flat | ♣ | \clubsuit |
| ℓ | \ell | ∂ | \partial | ♮ | \natural | ♦ | \diamondsuit |
| ℘ | \wp | ⊤ | \top | ♯ | \sharp | ♥ | \heartsuit |
| ℜ | \Re | ⊥ | \bot | ∥ | \| | ♠ | \spadesuit |
| ℑ | \Im | ⊢ | \vdash | ∠ | \angle | ⋈ | \Join |
| ℧ | \mho | ⊣ | \dashv | \ | \backslash | ∞ | \infty |

## 5.3.7    Symbols with two sizes

The following symbols are printed in different sizes depending on whether they appear in text or displayed formulas:

| | | | | | | | | |
|---|---|---|---|---|---|---|---|---|
| $\Sigma$ | $\sum$ | \sum | $\cap$ | $\bigcap$ | \bigcap | $\odot$ | $\bigodot$ | \bigodot |
| $\int$ | $\int$ | \int | $\cup$ | $\bigcup$ | \bigcup | $\otimes$ | $\bigotimes$ | \bigotimes |
| $\oint$ | $\oint$ | \oint | $\sqcup$ | $\bigsqcup$ | \bigsqcup | $\oplus$ | $\bigoplus$ | \bigoplus |
| $\Pi$ | $\prod$ | \prod | $\vee$ | $\bigvee$ | \bigvee | $\uplus$ | $\biguplus$ | \biguplus |
| $\amalg$ | $\coprod$ | \coprod | $\wedge$ | $\bigwedge$ | \bigwedge | | | |

The symbols \int and \sum have already been introduced in Section 5.2.5. There it was shown how these symbols may take on upper and lower limits; in the same way, all the above symbols may also be assigned upper and lower limits using the shifting commands ^ and _. The positioning of the limits varies for some symbols depending on whether they occur in text or displayed formulas. As indicated in Section 5.2.5, the command \limits forces the limits to be written above and below the symbol where they would otherwise be placed beside it. Similarly the complementary command \nolimits sets them beside the symbol when the standard positioning is above and below.

$$\oint_0^\infty \quad \oint\limits_0^\infty \qquad\qquad \text{\[ \oint^\infty_0 \quad \oint\limits^\infty_0 \qquad \]}$$

$$\prod_{\nu=0}^n \quad \prod{}_{\nu=0}^n \qquad\qquad \text{\[ \prod^n_{\nu=0} \quad \prod\nolimits^n_{\nu=0} \]}$$

## 5.3.8    Function names

The universal standard for mathematical formulas is to set variable names in *italics* but the names of functions in Roman. If one were simply to write the function names *sin* or *log* in math mode, LaTeX would interpret these as variables s i n and l o g and write them as $sin$ and $log$. In order to tell LaTeX that a function name is wanted, it is necessary to prefix the name with the command character \. The following functions are recognized by LaTeX:

| | | | | | | |
|---|---|---|---|---|---|---|
| \arccos | \cosh | \det | \inf | \limsup | \Pr | \tan |
| \arcsin | \cot | \dim | \ker | \ln | \sec | \tanh |
| \arctan | \coth | \exp | \lg | \log | \sin | |
| \arg | \csc | \gcd | \lim | \max | \sinh | |
| \cos | \deg | \hom | \liminf | \min | \sup | |

Some of these functions may also appear with limits attached to them. This is easily achieved by means of the $\lim_{x\to\infty}$ in text formulas and index command coming after the name $\displaystyle\lim_{x\to\infty}$ in displayed formulas of the function: `\lim_{x\to\infty}`.

In all, the following function names may take on a limit with the lowering (index) command _:

> `\det`  `\gcd`  `\inf`  `\lim`  `\liminf`  `\limsup`  `\max`  `\min`
> `\Pr`  `\sup`

Finally, there are the function commands `\bmod` and `\pmod{arg}`, both of which produce the function *mod* in one of two forms:

> `$ a \bmod b $`  $\qquad$ $a \bmod b$ $\qquad$ or as
> `$ y \pmod{a+b} $`  $\quad$ $y \pmod{a+b}$.

## 3.9  Mathematical accents

The following mathematical accents are available within math mode:

> $\hat{a}$ `\hat{a}`  $\breve{a}$ `\breve{a}`  $\grave{a}$ `\grave{a}`  $\bar{a}$ `\bar{a}`
> $\check{a}$ `\check{a}`  $\acute{a}$ `\acute{a}`  $\tilde{a}$ `\tilde{a}`  $\vec{a}$ `\vec{a}`
> $\dot{a}$ `\dot{a}`  $\ddot{a}$ `\ddot{a}`

The letters $i$ and $j$ should be printed without their dots when they are given an accent. To accomplish this, type the symbols `\imath` and `\jmath` instead of the letters, as in

> `$\vec{\imath} + \tilde{\jmath}$:`  $\qquad$ $\vec{\imath} + \tilde{\jmath}$

There are wider versions of `\hat` and `\tilde` available with the names `\widehat` and `\widetilde`. In this way, these accents may be placed over parts of a formula:

> $\widehat{1-x} = \widehat{-y}$  `$\widehat{1-x}=\widehat{-y}$`
> $\widetilde{xyz}$  $\qquad$ `$\widetilde{xyz}$`

**Exercise 5.6:** *The union of two sets $A$ and $B$ is the set of all elements that are in at least one of the two sets, and is designated as $A \cup B$. This operation is commutative $A \cup B = B \cup A$ and associative $(A \cup B) \cup C = A \cup (B \cup C)$. If $A \subseteq B$, then $A \cup B = B$. It then follows that $A \cup A = A$, $A \cup \{\emptyset\} = A$ and $J \cup A = J$.*

**Exercise 5.7:** *Applying l'Hôpital's rule, one has*

$$\lim_{x\to 0}\frac{\ln\sin\pi x}{\ln\sin x} = \lim_{x\to 0}\frac{\pi\frac{\cos\pi x}{\sin\pi x}}{\frac{\cos x}{\sin x}} = \lim_{x\to 0}\frac{\pi\tan x}{\tan\pi x} = \lim_{x\to 0}\frac{\pi/\cos^2 x}{\pi/\cos^2\pi x} = \lim_{x\to 0}\frac{\cos^2\pi x}{\cos^2 x} = 1$$

**Exercise 5.8:** *The gamma function $\Gamma(x)$ is defined as*

$$\Gamma(x) \equiv \lim_{n\to\infty}\prod_{v=0}^{n-1}\frac{n!\,n^{x-1}}{x+v} = \lim_{n\to\infty}\frac{n!\,n^{x-1}}{x(x+1)(x+2)\cdots(x+n-1)} \equiv \int_0^\infty e^{-t}t^{x-1}\,dt$$

*The integral definition is valid only for $x > 0$ (2nd Euler integral).*

**Exercise 5.9:** *Remove the option* `fleqn` *from the document class command in Exercise 5.3 and redo the output.*

**Exercise 5.10:**
$$\alpha \vec{x} = \vec{x}\alpha, \qquad \alpha\beta\vec{x} = \beta\alpha\vec{x}, \qquad (\alpha + \beta)\vec{x} = \alpha\vec{x} + \beta\vec{x}, \qquad \alpha(\vec{x} + \vec{y}) = \alpha\vec{x} + \alpha\vec{y}.$$
$$\vec{x}\vec{y} = \vec{y}\vec{x} \text{ but } \vec{x} \times \vec{y} = -\vec{y} \times \vec{x}, \quad \vec{x}\vec{y} = 0 \text{ for } \vec{x} \perp \vec{y}, \quad \vec{x} \times \vec{y} = 0, \text{ for } \vec{x} \parallel \vec{y}.$$

**Exercise 5.11:** *Reproduce Equations 5.1 and 5.2 from the next section.*

## 5.4     Additional elements

The math elements described in the previous sections already permit the construction of very complex formulas, such as

$$\lim_{x \to 0} \frac{\sqrt{1+x} - 1}{x} = \lim_{x \to 0} \frac{(\sqrt{1+x} - 1)(\sqrt{1+x} + 1)}{x(\sqrt{1+x} + 1)} = \lim_{x \to 0} \frac{1}{\sqrt{1+x} + 1} = \frac{1}{2} \qquad (5.1)$$

$$\frac{\partial^2 U}{\partial x^2} + \frac{\partial^2 U}{\partial y^2} = 0 \quad \Longrightarrow \quad U_M = \frac{1}{4\pi} \oint_\Sigma \frac{1}{r} \frac{\partial U}{\partial n} ds - \frac{1}{4\pi} \oint_\Sigma \frac{\partial \frac{1}{r}}{\partial n} U ds \qquad (5.2)$$

$$I(z) = \sin(\frac{\pi}{2}z^2) \sum_{n=0}^{\infty} \frac{(-1)^n \pi^{2n}}{1 \cdot 3 \cdots (4n+1)} z^{4n+1} - \cos(\frac{\pi}{2}z^2) \sum_{n=0}^{\infty} \frac{(-1)^n \pi^{2n+1}}{1 \cdot 3 \cdots (4n+3)} z^{4n+3}$$
$$(5.3)$$

By reading the formulas from left to right there should be no difficulty in reconstructing the text that produced them. For example, the last equation is generated with

```
\begin{equation}
I(z) = \sin( \frac{\pi}{2} z^2 ) \sum_{n=0}^\infty
    \frac{ (-1)^n \pi^{2n} }{1 \cdot 3 \cdots (4n+1) } z^{4n+1}
   -\cos( \frac{\pi}{2} z^2 ) \sum_{n=0}^\infty
    \frac{ (-1)^n \pi^{2n+1} }{ 1 \cdot 3 \cdots (4n+3) } z^{4n+3}
\end{equation}
```

The above examples were made using the `equation` environment instead of the `displaymath` environment or its abbreviated form `\[...\]`, which has the effect of adding the equation numbers automatically. In the document classes `book` and `report`, equations are sequentially numbered within the chapter, the number being preceded by the chapter number and set within parentheses ( ), as illustrated above. For document class `article`, the equations are numbered sequentially throughout the entire document.

By default the equation number appears right justified and vertically centered with the equation. If there is not enough room for it on the same line, it is printed right justified below the equation. If the document class option `leqno` has been selected, the equation numbers are set left justified for the entire document.

The automatic numbering of equations means that the author may not know at the time of writing just what the equation number is. The LATEX cross-reference system described in Section 8.3.1 has already been explained for referring to section numbers (Section 3.3.3) and may also be used for equation numbers. By including a command `\label{`*name*`}` within the `equation` environment, one can print the unknown equation number in the text with the command `\ref{`*name*`}`, where *name* is a keyword consisting of any combination of letters, numbers, or symbols.

Examining Equation 5.3 more closely, one notices that the two parenthesis pairs ( ) in cos() and sin() could stand to be somewhat larger. Furthermore, this equation just fills the line width, and if it were any longer, it would have to be broken at some appropriate spot and the parts positioned in a meaningful way relative to one another. None of the math elements described so far can accomplish these requirements.

Even something so simple as including some normal text within a formula has not yet been mentioned. The rest of this section addresses these problems.

Finally, there are times when one is not happy with the sizes that TEX has chosen, as for example in the last integral of Equation 5.2 where $\partial \dfrac{1}{r}$ would be more desirable than $\partial \frac{1}{r}$. This and other formatting aids, such as adjusting horizontal spacing between parts of formulas, are dealt with in Section 5.5.

## .1 Automatic sizing of bracket symbols

Mathematics often contains bracketing symbols, usually in pairs that enclose part of the formula. When printed, these bracket symbols should be the same size as the included partial formula. LATEX provides a pair of commands

> `\left`*lbrack*    *sub_form*  `\right`*rbrack*

to accomplish this. The command `\left` is placed immediately before the opening (left hand) bracket symbol *lbrack* while `\right` comes just before the closing (right hand) symbol *rbrack*.

$$\left[ \int + \int \right]_{x=0}^{x=1}$$

`\[ \left[ \int + \int \right]_{x=0}^{x=1} \]`
The pair of brackets [ ] is adjusted to the size of the enclosed formula, as are the raised exponent and lowered index as well.

The commands `\left` and `\right` must appear as a pair. For every `\left` command there must be a corresponding `\right` command somewhere afterwards. The pairs may be nested. The first `\left` is paired with the last \right; the following \left with the second last \right, and so on. There must be the same number of \right as \left commands in a nesting.

The corresponding bracket symbols *lbrack* and *rbrack* may be perfectly arbitrary and do not need to be a logical pair.

$$\vec{x} + \vec{y} + \vec{z} = \left( \begin{array}{c} a \\ b \end{array} \right[ \quad$$

```
This set of brackets is admittedly unusual but permissible.
\[ \vec{x} + \vec{y} + \vec{z} =
        \left( ... \right[ \]
```

Sometimes a formula contains only a single opening or closing bracket without a corresponding counterpart. However, the \left ... \right commands must still be given as a pair, but with a period '.' as an *invisible* bracket symbol.

$$y = \left\{ \begin{array}{rcl} -1 & : & x < 0 \\ 0 & : & x = 0 \\ +1 & : & x > 0 \end{array} \right.$$

```
\[  y = \left\{ \begin{array}
                 {r@{\quad:\quad}l}
        -1 & x<0 \\ 0 & x=0 \\ +1 & x>0
        \end{array} \right.      \]
```

The array environment in the above example is described in Section 4.8.1 and produces a table in math mode.

The \left ... \right commands may be applied to a total of 22 different symbols. These are

| ( | ( | ) | ) | ⌊ | \lfloor | ⌋ | \rfloor |
|---|---|---|---|---|---------|---|---------|
| [ | [ | ] | ] | ⌈ | \lceil | ⌉ | \rceil |
| { | \{ | } | \} | ⟨ | \langle | ⟩ | \rangle |
| \| | \| | ‖ | \| | ↑ | \uparrow | ⇑ | \Uparrow |
| / | / | \ | \backslash | ↓ | \downarrow | ⇓ | \Downarrow |
| | | | | | ↕ | \updownarrow | ⇕ | \Updownarrow |

For example, \left| ... \right| produces two vertical bars adjusted in height to contain the enclosed formula text.

*Exercise 5.12:* *In Equation 5.3, generate* $\cos\left(\frac{\pi}{2}z^2\right)$ *and* $\sin\left(\frac{\pi}{2}z^2\right)$ *instead of* $\cos(\frac{\pi}{2}z^2)$ *and* $\sin(\frac{\pi}{2}z^2)$.

## 5.4.2　Ordinary text within a formula

It is often necessary to include some *normal* text within a formula, for example single words such as *and, or, if*, and so on. In this case one must switch to LR mode (Sections 1.5.3 and 4.7.1) while staying in math mode. This is carried out with the command \mbox{*normal text*} given inside the formula, together with horizontal spacing commands such as \quad or \hspace. For example:

$$X_n = X_k \qquad \text{if and only if} \qquad Y_n = Y_k \quad \text{and} \quad Z_n = Z_k$$

```
\[  X_n = X_k \qquad\mbox{if and only if}\qquad
    Y_n = Y_k \quad\mbox{and}\quad Z_n = Z_k          \]
```

In order to set a longer piece of text beside a displayed formula, as in some of the above examples, it is more appropriate to put both the formula and the text in their own parboxes or minipages, placed side by side with the proper vertical positioning.

On the other hand, if letters from text fonts are required as mathematical symbols, they should be entered with the LATEX 2ε *math alphabet commands*:

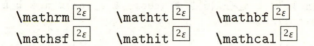

We have already met \mathcal in Section 5.3.2 on calligraphic letters. All these commands function the same way: they set their argument in the corresponding font.

$B^0(x)$   $T^i_j$      `$\mathbf{B}^0(x)$ \quad $\mathsf{T}^i_j$`

The command \mathnormal in Section 5.3.1 also belongs to this group. The difference between it and \mathit is that it sets its argument in the regular *math* italic font, while the latter uses the normal *text* italic. The letters are the same, but the spacing is different.

`$\mathnormal{differ} \ne \mathit{differ}$`
*differ* ≠ *differ*

All the math alphabet commands set their text in math mode, which means that spaces are ignored as usual. This is not the case for text placed in an \mbox.

In LATEX 2.09, the same effect is achieved by placing the two-letter font declarations within a nameless environment, even in math mode. The first of the above examples is given as `${\bf B}^0(x)$`.

## .3  Matrices and fields

$$
\begin{array}{cccc}
a_{11} & a_{12} & \cdots & a_{1n} \\
\vdots & \vdots & \ddots & \vdots \\
a_{n1} & a_{n2} & \cdots & a_{nn}
\end{array}
$$

Structures like the one at the left are the basis for matrices, determinants, system of equations, and so on. They will all be referred to here as *fields*.

Fields are produced by means of the `array` environment, whose syntax and construction are described in Section 4.8.1 on tables. The `array` environment generates a table in math mode, that is, the column entries are interpreted as formula text. For example:

$$a_{11}x_1 + a_{12}x_2 + \cdots + a_{1n}x_n = b_1$$
$$a_{22}x_1 + a_{22}x_2 + \cdots + a_{2n}x_n = b_2$$
$$\cdots\cdots\cdots\cdots\cdots\cdots\cdots\cdots\cdots\cdots\cdots\cdots$$
$$a_{n1}x_1 + a_{n2}x_2 + \cdots + a_{nn}x_n = b_n$$

```
\[ \begin{array}{*{3}{c@{\:+\:}}c@{\;=\;}c}
     a_{11}x_1 & a_{12}x_2 & \cdots & a_{1n}x_n & b_1 \\
     a_{22}x_1 & a_{22}x_2 & \cdots & a_{2n}x_n & b_2 \\
     \multicolumn{5}{c}{\dotfill}                    \\
     a_{n1}x_1 & a_{n2}x_2 & \cdots & a_{nn}x_n & b_n
   \end{array}     \]
```

As a reminder of the table construction elements (Section 4.8.1): @{t} inserts the contents of $t$ between the adjacent columns.  In the above example, this is \:+\: and \;+\;.  The commands \: and \; have not yet been introduced but they produce small horizontal spacing in math mode (Section 5.5.1). *{3}{c@{\:+\:}} is an abbreviation for three repetitions of the column definition c@{\:+\:}.  c defines the column to be one of centered text. \multicolumn{5}{c} says that the next 5 columns are to be merged and replaced by one with centered text. \dotfill fills the column with dots.  The above system of equations could be produced somewhat more simply with

```
\begin{array}{c@{\:+\:}c@{\:+\cdots+\;}c@{\;=\;}c}
```

It is possible to nest array environments:

$$\left( \left| \begin{array}{cc} x_{11} & x_{12} \\ x_{21} & x_{22} \end{array} \right| \atop \begin{array}{c} y \\ z \end{array} \right)$$

```
\[ \left( \begin{array}{c}
     left| \begin{array}{cc}
       x_{11} & x_{12} \\ x_{21} & x_{22}
       \end{array} \right| \\
     x \\ y \end{array} \right)      \]
```

The outermost field consists of one column with centered text (c). The first entry in this column is also a field, with two centered columns. This field is surrounded left and right by vertical lines with adjusted sizes.

The array environment is structurally the same as a vertical box. This means that it is treated as a single character within the surrounding environment, so that it may be coupled with other symbols and construction elements.

$$\sum_{p_1<p_2<\cdots<p_{n-k}}^{(1,2,\ldots,n)} \Delta_{\begin{array}{l} p_1p_2\cdots p_{n-k} \\ p_1p_2\cdots p_{n-k} \end{array}} \sum_{q_1<q_2<\cdots q_k} \left| \begin{array}{cccc} a_{q_1q_1} & a_{q_1q_2} & \cdots & a_{q_1q_k} \\ a_{q_2q_1} & a_{q_2q_2} & \cdots & a_{q_2q_k} \\ \cdots & \cdots & \cdots & \cdots \\ a_{q_kq_1} & a_{q_kq_2} & \cdots & a_{q_kq_k} \end{array} \right|$$

```
\[ \sum_{p_1<p_2<\cdots<p_{n-k}}^{(1,2,\ldots,n)}
   \Delta_{\begin{array}{l}
        p_1p_2\cdots p_{n-k} \\ p_1p_2\cdots p_{n-k}
```

```
            \end{array}}
\sum_{q_1<q_2<\cdots q_k} \left| \begin{array}{llcl}
        a_{q_1q_1} & a_{q_1q_2} & \cdots & a_{q_1q_k} \\
        a_{q_2q_1} & a_{q_2q_2} & \cdots & a_{q_2q_k} \\
            \multicolumn{4}{c}\dotfill\\
        a_{q_kq_1} & a_{q_kq_2} & \cdots & a_{q_kq_k}
            \end{array} \right|        \]
```

In this example, an array environment is used as an index on the $\Delta$. However, the indices appear too large with respect to the rest of the formula. Section 5.4.6 presents a better solution for field indices.

As for all table environments, an optional vertical positioning parameter b or t may be included with the array environment. The syntax and results are described in Sections 4.7.3 and 4.8.1. This argument is included only if the field is to be positioned vertically relative to its top or bottom line rather than its center.

$$x - \begin{array}{c} a_1 \\ \vdots \\ a_n \end{array} - u - v \quad \begin{array}{cl} 10 \\ 12 \\ -120 \end{array}$$

```
\[ x - \begin{array}{c}
    a_1 \\ \vdots \\ a_n \end{array}
  - \begin{array}[t]{cl}
    u - v & 10\\
    u + v & \begin{array}[b]{r}
        12\\-120  \end{array}
    \end{array}                    \]
```

We suggest to the reader that he or she try to deduce how the various fields are structured with the help of the generating text on the right.

*Exercise 5.13:* The solution for the system of equations

$$F(x,y) = 0 \quad \text{and} \quad \begin{vmatrix} F''_{xx} & F''_{xy} & F'_x \\ F''_{yx} & F''_{yy} & F'_y \\ F'_x & F'_y & 0 \end{vmatrix} = 0$$

yields the coordinates for the possible inflection points of $F(x,y) = 0$.
*Note: the above displayed formula consists of two sub-formulas, between which the word 'and' plus extra spacing of amount \quad are inserted. Instead of enclosing the array environment within size-adjusted vertical lines with \left|...\right|, one may use a formatting argument {|...|} (Section 4.8.1) to produce the vertical lines. Such a structure is called a* determinant *in mathematics.*

*Exercise 5.14:* The shortest distance between two straight lines represented by the equations

$$\frac{x - x_1}{l_1} = \frac{y - y_1}{m_1} = \frac{z - z_1}{n_1} \quad \text{and} \quad \frac{x - x_2}{l_2} = \frac{y - y_2}{m_2} = \frac{z - z_2}{n_2}$$

is given by the expression

$$\frac{\pm \begin{vmatrix} x_1 - x_2 & y_1 - y_2 & z_1 - z_2 \\ l_1 & m_1 & n_1 \\ l_2 & m_2 & n_2 \end{vmatrix}}{\sqrt{\begin{vmatrix} l_1 & m_1 \\ l_2 & m_2 \end{vmatrix}^2 + \begin{vmatrix} m_1 & n_1 \\ m_2 & n_2 \end{vmatrix}^2 + \begin{vmatrix} n_1 & l_1 \\ n_2 & l_2 \end{vmatrix}^2}}$$

If the numerator is zero, the two lines meet somewhere.
*Note: it is not recommended using {|cc|} in the formatting argument of the three determinants in the denominator under the root sign.   Here the* `\left|`*...*`\right|` *pair should be applied. Try out both possibilities for yourself and compare the results.*

**Exercise 5.15:** *Laurent expansion: using* $c_n = \frac{1}{2\pi i} \oint (\zeta - a)^{-n-1} f(\zeta)\, d\zeta$*, for every function* $f(z)$ *the following representation is valid* $(n = 0, \pm 1, \pm 2, \dots)$

$$f(x) = \sum_{n=-\infty}^{+\infty} c_n (z-a)^n = \begin{cases} c_0 + c_1(z-a) + c_2(z-a)^2 + \cdots + c_n(z-a)^n + \cdots \\ \qquad + c_{-1}(z-a)^{-1} + c_{-2}(z-a)^{-2} + \cdots \\ \qquad\qquad + c_{-n}(z-a)^{-n} + \cdots \end{cases}$$

*Tip: the right-hand side of the equation can be created with an* `array` *environment consisting of only one column. What is its formatting argument?*

## 5.4.4   Lines above and below formulas

The commands

> `\overline{`*sub_form*`}`   and   `\underline{`*sub_form*`}`

can be used to draw lines over or under a formula or sub-formula.  The may be nested to any desired level:

$$\overline{a^2 + xy + \overline{\overline{z}}}$$
```
\[  \overline{\overline{a}^2 + \underline{xy}
        + \overline{\overline{z}}}        \]
```

The command `\underline` may also be employed in normal text mode to underline text, whereas `\overline` is allowed only in math mode.
Exactly analogous to these are the two commands

> `\overbrace{`*sub_form*`}`   and   `\underbrace{`*sub_form*`}`

which put horizontal curly braces above or below the sub-formula.

$$\overbrace{a + \underbrace{b+c} + d}$$
```
\overbrace{a + \underbrace{b+c} + d}
```

In displayed formulas, these commands may have exponents or indices attached to them. The (raised) exponent is set above the *overbrace* while the (lowered) index is placed below the *underbrace*.

$$\underbrace{a + b + \cdots + \overbrace{y}^{123} + z}_{\alpha\beta\gamma}$$

```
\[ \underbrace{a + \overbrace{b + \cdots +
   y}^{123} + z}_{\alpha\beta\gamma}  \]
```

**Exercise 5.16:** The total number of permutations of $n$ elements taken $m$ at a time (symbol $P_n^m$) is

$$P_n^m = \prod_{i=0}^{m-1}(n-i) = \underbrace{n(n-1)(n-2)\dots(n-m+1)}_{\text{total of } m \text{ factors}} = \frac{n!}{(n-m)!}$$

## 4.5  Stacked symbols

The command

> `\stackrel{upper_sym}{lower_sym}`

places the symbol *upper_sym* centered on top of *lower_sym*, whereby the symbol on top is set in a smaller typeface.

$\vec{x} \stackrel{\text{def}}{=} (x_1,\dots x_n)$   `$ \vec{x} \stackrel{\mathrm{def}}{=} (x_1,...$`

$A \stackrel{\alpha'}{\longrightarrow} B \stackrel{\beta'}{\longleftarrow} C$   `$ A \stackrel{\alpha'}{\longrightarrow} B ... $`

By making use of math font size commands (Section 5.5.2) it is possible to construct new symbols with this command. For example, some authors prefer to have the \le symbol appear as $\stackrel{<}{=}$ instead of $\le$. This is achieved by combining $<$ and $=$ with `$\stackrel{\textstyle<}{=}$`. If the command \textstyle were omitted, the symbol would be printed as $\stackrel{<}{=}$.

## 4.6  Additional T<sub>E</sub>X commands for math

The T<sub>E</sub>X math commands \atop and \choose are useful additions to the set of commands and may be applied within any LAT<sub>E</sub>X document. (In fact, all T<sub>E</sub>X math commands except \eqalign, \eqalignno, and \leqaligno may be used in a LAT<sub>E</sub>X manuscript.) Their syntax is

> {*top* \atop *bottom*}
> {*top* \choose *bottom*}

Both commands produce a structure that looks like a fraction without the dividing line. With the \choose command, this structure is also enclosed within round brackets (in mathematics this is called a *binomial coefficient*).

$$\binom{n+1}{k} = \binom{n}{k} + \binom{n}{k-1}$$

```
\[ {n+1 \choose k} =
   {n \choose k} + {n \choose k-1} \]
```

$$\prod_{j\geq0}\left(\sum_{k\geq0} a_{jk}z^k\right) = \sum_{n\geq0} z^n \left(\sum_{\substack{k_0,k_1,\ldots\geq0\\k_0+k_1+\cdots=0}} a_{0k_0}a_{1k_1}\cdots\right)$$

```
\[ \prod_{j\ge0}\left( \sum_{k\ge0} a_{jk}z^k \right) =
   \sum_{n\ge0} z^n \left(\sum_{k_0,k_1\ldots\ge0 \atop
      k_0+k_1+\cdots=0} a_{0k_0} a_{1k_1}\ldots \right)      \]
```

Similar structures can be generated with the LATEX environments

```
\begin{array}{c}    upper_line \\    lower_line  \end{array}                (atop)
\left(\begin{array}{c} upper \\    lower  \end{array}\right)    (choose)
```

The difference between these `array` structures and those of the TEX commands is that the former are always printed in the size and style of normal text formulas, whereas the latter will have varying sizes depending on where they appear within the formula.

For comparison

$$\Delta_{\substack{p_1p_2\cdots p_{n-k}\\p_1p_2\cdots p_{n-k}}}$$     The index field is produced using `\atop`

$$\Delta \quad \begin{array}{c} p_1p_2\cdots p_{n-k} \\ p_1p_2\cdots p_{n-k} \end{array}$$     The index field is produced using `\array`

The above TEX commands may also be employed to produce small matrices within text formulas, such as $\left(\begin{smallmatrix}1&0\\0&1\end{smallmatrix}\right)$ or $\left(\begin{smallmatrix}a&b&c\\l&m&n\end{smallmatrix}\right)$. Here the first matrix was typed in with

```
${1\,,0\choose0\,,1}$
```

and the second with

```
$\left({a\atop l}{b\atop m}{c\atop n}\right)$
```

## 5.4.7   Multi-line equations

A multi-line equation is one that is developed over several lines in which the relation symbols (for example, $=$ or $\leq$) in each line are all vertically aligned with each other. For this purpose, the environments

```
\begin{eqnarray}  line_1\\  ...  \\ line_n end{eqnarray}
\begin{eqnarray*} line_1\\  ...  \\ line_n end{eqnarray*}
```

are used to set several lines of formulas or equations in displayed math mode. The individual lines of the equation or formula are separated from one another by `\\`. Each entry line has the form

*left_formula* & *mid_formula* & *right_formula* \\

When printed, all the *left_formula*s appear right justified in a left column, the *right_formula*s left justified in a right column, and the *mid_formula*s centered in between. The column separation character & designates the various parts of the formula. Normally the *mid_formula* is a single math character, the relation operator mentioned above. The individual lines thus have the same behavior as they would in a \begin{array}{rcl} ...\end{array} environment.

The difference between the array and eqnarray environments is that in the latter the lines are set as displayed formulas. This means that for those symbols listed in Section 5.3.7 the larger form will be selected, and that the numerator and denominator of fractions will be in normal size. On the other hand, for the array environment the column entries will be set as text formulas, the smaller form of these symbols will be chosen and the parts of the fraction will appear in a smaller type size.

The standard form of the eqnarray environment adds an automatic sequential equation number, which is missing in the *-form. To suppress the equation number for a single line in the standard form, add the command \nonumber just before the line termination \\.

The equation numbers may be referred to in the text with the command \ref{*name*} once the keyword *name* has been assigned to the equation number with the \label{*name*} command somewhere in the line of the equation. See Section 8.3.1 for more details.

Examples:

$$
\begin{aligned}
(x+y)(x-y) &= x^2 - xy + xy - y^2 \\
&= x^2 - y^2 \\
(x+y)^2 &= x^2 + 2xy + y^2
\end{aligned}
$$

$$(5.4)$$
$$(5.5)$$

```
\begin{eqnarray}
     (x+y)(x-y) & = & x^2-xy+xy-y^2 \nonumber\\
                & = & x^2 - y^2 \\
     (x+y)^2    & = & x^2 + 2xy + y^2
\end{eqnarray}
```

$$
\begin{aligned}
x_n u_1 + \cdots + x_{n+t-1} u_t &= x_n u_1 + (ax_n + c)u_2 + \cdots \\
&\quad + \left(a^{t-1}x_n + c(a^{t-2} + \cdots + 1)\right)u_t \\
&= (u_1 + au_2 + \cdots + a^{t-1}u_t)x_n + h(u_1, \ldots, u_t)
\end{aligned}
$$

```
\begin{eqnarray*}
x_nu_1 + \cdots + x_{n+t-1}u_t & = & x_nu_1 + (ax_n + c)u_2 +
                                      \cdots\\
    &  & + \left(a^{t-1}x_n + c(a^{t-2} + \cdots+1)\right)u_t\\
    & = & (u_1 + au_2 + \cdots + a^{t-1}u_t)x_n + h(u_1,\ldots,u_t)
\end{eqnarray*}
```

The lower example requires some explanation. In the second line there is a \left( ... \right) pair for the automatic sizing of the (). Such a pair may only appear within a single line; that is, it may *not* be broken by a line terminator \\! If automatic bracket sizing is to occur in a multi-line equation, it may only be found within a single line.

If bracket pairs must appear on different lines, one can try using the construction \left( ... \right. \\ \left. ... \right). In the first line, the \left( is paired with the *invisible* bracket \right., while the second begins with the invisible \left. which is paired with the closing \right). However, this will only work satisfactorily if both parts of the equation have roughly the same height so that the two automatic sizings yield much the same results. Section 5.5.3 describes how to select bracket sizes manually in the event that the automatic method fails.

The + sign at the beginning of the second line also requires a remark. The signs + and − have two meanings in mathematics: between two math quantities they act as a coupling (*binary operator*), but coming before a math symbol they serve as a sign designation (positive or negative). LATEX stresses this difference by inserting different spacing in the two cases (for example, compare $+b$ with $a + b$).

$$y \;=\; a+b+c+d$$
$$+e+f+g$$
$$+h+i+j$$

If a long formula is broken into several lines and one of them begins with + or −, LATEX regards it as a sign designation and moves it closer to the next character.

The solution is to introduce an *invisible* character of *zero* width at the beginning of such a line. This may be the empty structure {}. Compare the effects of && +e+f+g and &&{}+h+i+j in the above equation.

Since the extra spacing is always inserted between + and an opening parenthesis (, it was not necessary to give the empty structure {} at the beginning of the second line of the eqnarray* example above.

Occasionally it is better to break long multi-line equations as follows:

$$w + x + y + z =$$
$$a + b + c + d + e + f +$$
$$g + h + i + j + k + l$$

that is, the second and subsequent lines are not aligned with the equals sign but are left justified with a certain indentation from the beginning of the first line.

```
\begin{eqnarray*}
\lefteqn{w+x+y+z = } \\
  & & a+b+c+d+e+f+   \\
  & & g+h+i+j+k+l
\end{eqnarray*}
```

The command \lefteqn{w+x+y+z =} \\ in the first line has the effect that the contents of the argument are indeed printed out, but that LATEX considers them to have *zero* width. The left-hand column then contains only inter-column spacing, which produces the indentation for the rest of the lines.

The indentation depth may be altered by inserting \hspace{*depth*} between the \lefteqn{...} and the line termination \\. A positive value for *depth* increases the indentation, a negative value decreases it.

*Exercise 5.17:* The following equations are to be broken as shown:

$$\arcsin x \quad = \quad -\arcsin(-x) = \frac{\pi}{2} - \arccos x = \left[\arccos \sqrt{1 - x^2}\right]$$

$$= \quad \arctan \frac{x}{\sqrt{1 - x^2}} = \left[\operatorname{arccot} \frac{\sqrt{1 - x^2}}{x}\right] \tag{5.6}$$

$$f(x + h, y + k) = f(x, y) + \left\{ \frac{\partial f(x, y)}{\partial x} h + \frac{\partial f(x, y)}{\partial y} k \right\}$$

$$+ \frac{1}{2} \left\{ \frac{\partial^2 f(x, y)}{\partial x^2} h^2 + 2 \frac{\partial^2 f(x, y)}{\partial x \partial y} kh + \frac{\partial^2 f(x, y)}{\partial y^2} k^2 \right\} \tag{5.7}$$

$$+ \frac{1}{6} \{\cdots\} + \cdots + \frac{1}{n!} \{\cdots\} + R_n$$

*Note on possible error messages:*

Long formulas with many sets of logical brackets, especially deeply nested ones, will almost always contain errors at first. The cause is often brackets that have been incorrectly ordered or overlooked.

If LATEX produces error messages during formula processing, which the beginner is not able to interpret correctly (error messages are described in detail in Chapter 9), he or she should check the bracket pairing very carefully for the formula text. Some text editors can do the search for the matching bracket, which greatly simplifies the task.

If the error is not found in this way, one can try pressing the return key at the error message in order to proceed with the processing. The resulting printout can indicate where things may have gone wrong.

*Exercise 5.18:* The `eqnarray` environment inserts additional spacing where the column separation character `&` appears. This is undesirable when an equation is to be broken aligned on $+$ or $-$ within a long summation. For example:
The inverse function of the polynomial expansion $y = f(x) = ax + bx^2 + cx^3 + dx^4 + ex^5 + fx^6 + \cdots$  ($a \neq 0$) begins with the elements

$$x = \varphi(y) = \frac{1}{a} y \quad - \quad \frac{b}{a^3} y^2 + \frac{1}{a^5} (2b^2 - ac) y^3$$

$$+ \quad \frac{1}{a^7} (5abc - z^2 d - fb^3) y^4$$

$$+ \quad \frac{1}{a^9} (6a^2 bd + 3a^2 c^2 + 14b^4 - a^3 e - 21ab^2 c) y^5$$

$$+ \quad \frac{1}{a^{11}} (7a^3 be + 7a^3 cd + 84ab^3 c - a^4 f -$$

$$28a^2 b^2 d - 28a^2 bc^2 - 43b^5) y^6 + \cdots$$

Select a value for the declaration `\arraycolsep` (Section 4.8.2) such that the distance between the $+$ and $-$ and the break points are as near as possible to those in the rest of the formula.

## 5.4.8   Framed or side-by-side formulas

Displayed formulas or equations may be put into vertical boxes of appropriate width, that is, in a `\parbox` command or `minipage` environment. Within the vertical box, the formulas are horizontally centered or left justified with indentation `\mathindent` according to the selected document class option.

Vertical boxes may be positioned relative to one another just like single characters (Sections 4.7.3 and 4.7.7). In this way the user may place displayed formulas or equations side by side.

$$\begin{aligned}\alpha &= f(z) & (5.8)\\ \beta &= f(z^2) & (5.9)\\ \gamma &= f(z^3) & (5.10)\end{aligned}$$

$$\begin{aligned}x &= \alpha^2 - \beta^2\\ y &= 2\alpha\beta\end{aligned}$$

The left-hand set of equations is set in a `\parbox` of width 4 cm, the right-hand set in one of width 2.5 cm, while this text is inside a `minipage` of width 4.5 cm.

```
\parbox{4cm}{\begin{eqnarray} \alpha &=& f(z)...\end{eqnarray}}
\hfill  \parbox{2.5cm}{\begin{eqnarray*}
   x &=& \alpha^2 - \beta^2\\ y &=& 2\alpha\beta \end{eqnarray*}}
\hfill  \begin{minipage}{4.5cm} The left-hand ... \end{minipage}
```

The application of vertical boxes can also be useful when equation numbers are placed in an unconventional manner. The `eqnarray` environment generates an equation number for every line, which may be suppressed with `\nonumber`. To add a vertically centered equation number to a set of equations, for example,

$$\begin{aligned}P(x) &= a_0 + a_1 x + a_2 x^2 + \cdots + a_n x^n\\ P(-x) &= a_0 - a_1 x + a_2 x^2 - \cdots + (-1)^n a_n x^n\end{aligned} \qquad (5.11)$$

the following text may be given:

```
\parbox{10cm}{\begin{eqnarray*} ... \end{eqnarray*}} \hfill
\parbox{1cm}{\begin{eqnarray}\end{eqnarray}}
```

The actual set of equations is produced here in the `eqnarray*` environment, within a vertical box of width 10 cm, followed by an empty `eqnarray` environment in a box of width 1 cm that generates the equation number. Both boxes are vertically aligned along their center lines.

Emphasizing formulas by framing requires no new construction elements. It is sufficient to put them into an `\fbox` (Section 4.7.7). Text formulas $\boxed{a+b}$ are simply framed with `\fbox{$a+b$}`.

To frame a displayed formula, it is necessary to put it first into a `\parbox` or `minipage` environment of sufficient width, and to pack the whole thing into an `\fbox`. (See, however, Section 5.5.6.)

$$\boxed{\int_0^\infty f(x)\,dx \approx \sum_{i=1}^n w_i e^{x_i} f(x_i)}$$

is produced with

```
\fbox{\parbox{5cm}{\[ \int^\infty_0 f(x)\,dx \approx ..... \] }}
```

## 4.9    Chemical formulas and bold face in math formulas

In mathematics it is sometimes necessary to set individual characters or parts of the formula in bold face. This can be achieved simply with the math typeface command \mathbf $\boxed{2\varepsilon}$ that we met in Section 5.4.2:

    $\mathbf{S^{-1}TS = dg(\omega_1,\ldots,\omega_n) = \Lambda}$

produces   $\mathbf{S^{-1}TS = dg(\omega_1,\ldots,\omega_n) = \Lambda}$

In this example, the entire formula has been set as the argument of \mathbf so that everything should be set in bold face. In fact, only numbers, lower and upper case Latin letters, and upper case Greek letters are set in **bold Roman** with \mathbf. Lower case Greek letters and other math symbols appear in the normal *math* font.

If only part of the formula is to be set in bold face, that part must be given as the argument of the \mathbf command.

    $\mathbf{2\sqrt{x}/y} = z$     $\mathbf{2\sqrt{x}}/y = z$

The math font style command \boldmath will set all characters in bold face, with the following exceptions:

- raised and lowered symbols (exponents and indices)
- the characters  + : ; ! ? ( ) [ ]
- symbols that exist in two sizes (Section 5.3.7)

The \boldmath declaration may not appear in math mode. It must be called before switching to math mode or within a parbox or minipage. The countercommand \unboldmath resets the math fonts back to the normal ones.

$$\oint_C V\,d\tau = \oint_\Sigma \nabla \times V\,d\sigma$$

    \boldmath \[ \oint\limits_C V\,d\tau =
    \oint\limits_\Sigma\nabla\times
    V\,d\sigma \] \unboldmath

If \boldmath has been turned on outside the math mode, it may be temporarily turned off inside with \mbox{\unboldmath$...$} to set part of the formula in normal math fonts.

    \boldmath\( P = \mbox{\unboldmath$m$}b\)\unboldmath

yields:  $P = mb$. Similarly, \boldmath can be temporarily turned on within math mode with the structure \mbox{\boldmath$...$}:  $W_r = \int M\,d\varphi = r^2 m\omega^2/2$

    \( W_r = \int\mbox{\boldmath$M\,d\varphi$} = ... \)

**Chemical Formulas** are normally set in Roman type, not in italics as for mathematical formulas. This may be brought about by setting the formula as the argument of the font command \mathrm $\boxed{2\varepsilon}$:

$\mathrm{Fe_2^{2+}Cr_20_4}$    $Fe_2^{2+}Cr_2O_4$.

!

If one looks very carefully one can see that the indices for Cr and O are not quite as low as that for Fe. Section 7.3.4 describes in Example 5 on page 192 how chemical formulas may be generated more easily and this weakness eliminated.

In LaTeX 2.09, the font *commands* \mathbf and \mathrm must be replaced by *declarations* \bf and \rm, as illustrated in Section 5.4.2.

## 5.5    Fine-tuning mathematics

The mathematical elements that have been presented so far should be sufficient to produce almost all formulas that would appear in normal manuscripts, as long as the author adheres to certain generally accepted rules of style that pertain to printing mathematics. Authors who so far have only worked with typewriter manuscripts may find that some of the spacings selected by TeX between characters are too narrow. In fact, TeX knows more about mathematical typesetting than most authors. Before going to a great deal of effort to alter the appearance of an equation by means of the formatting tools listed in this section, an author should first examine similar formulas in the printed literature. Otherwise, it might happen that the hand-polished formulas in the LaTeX document are later reset by the professional printer so as to appear exactly as they do under standard TeX.

### 5.5.1    Horizontal spacing

Even though TeX has a thorough knowledge of the rules of mathematical typesetting, it cannot hope to understand the mathematical meaning. For example, $y\,dx$ normally means the joining of the variable $y$ with the differential operator $dx$, and this joining is designated by a small space between the two. However, TeX removes the blank in the entry y dx and prints $ydx$, the product of three variables $y$, $d$, and $x$. At this point, LaTeX needs some fine-tuning assistance.

Small amounts of horizontal spacing can be added in math mode with the commands

| | | |
|---|---|---|
| \, | small space | = 3/18 of a quad |
| \: | medium space | = 4/18 of a quad |
| \; | large space | = 5/18 of a quad |
| \! | negative space | = −3/18 of a quad |

In the following examples, the third column contains the results without the additional horizontal spacing command.

| | | |
|---|---|---|
| `$\sqrt{2}\,x$` | $\sqrt{2}\,x$ | $\sqrt{2}x$ |
| `$\sqrt{\,\log x}$` | $\sqrt{\log x}$ | $\sqrt{\log x}$ |
| `$0\left(1/\sqrt{n}\,\right)$` | $O\,(1/\sqrt{n}\,)$ | $O\,(1/\sqrt{n})$ |
| `$[\,0,1)$` | $[\,0,1)$ | $[0,1)$ |
| `$\log n\,(\log\log n)^2$` | $\log n\,(\log\log n)^2$ | $\log n(\log\log n)^2$ |
| `$x^2\!/2$` | $x^2/2$ | $x^2/2$ |
| `$n/\!\log n$` | $n/\log n$ | $n/\log n$ |
| `$\Gamma_{\!2}+\Delta^{\!2}$` | $\Gamma_2+\Delta^2$ | $\Gamma_2+\Delta^2$ |
| `$R_i{}^j{}_{\!kl}$` | $R_i{}^j{}_{kl}$ | $R_i{}^j{}_{kl}$ |
| `$\int_0^x\!\int_0^y dF(u,v)$` | $\int_0^x\int_0^y dF(u,v)$ | $\int_0^x\int_0^y dF(u,v)$ |
| `\[ \int\!\!\!\!\int_D dx\,dy \]` | $\iint_D dx\,dy$ | $\iint_D dxdy$ |

Note: in the third last example R_i{}^j is so constructed that an invisible character of zero width comes after the index of $R_i$, and it is this dummy character that receives the following exponent. The result is $R_i{}^j$, instead of $R_i^j$ which is produced by R_i^j.

There are no hard and fast rules for applying the math spacing commands. Some candidates are the differential operator mentioned earlier, small root signs in text formulas followed by a variable, the dividing sign /, and multiple integral signs. The above examples illustrate many suitable situations.

## 5.2   Selecting font size in formulas

It is possible to alter the font sizes that TeX selects for the various parts of the formula. First we must explain what sizes are available in math mode and what TeX's selection rules are.

In math mode there are four font sizes that may be chosen, their actual sizes being relative to the basic font size of the document class:

| | | |
|---|---|---|
| `\displaystyle` | $D$ | Normal size for displayed formulas |
| `\textstyle` | $T$ | Normal size for text formulas |
| `\scriptstyle` | $S$ | Normal size for first sub-, superscript |
| `\scriptscriptstyle` | $SS$ | Normal size for later sub-, superscripts |

From now on we shall make use of the symbolic abbreviations $D$, $T$, $S$, and $SS$. When math mode is switched on, the active font size becomes $D$ for displayed and $T$ for text formulas. Their only difference lies in those symbols that appear in two sizes, plus the corresponding style of those superscripts and subscripts (Section 5.3.7). The larger symbols belong to $D$, the smaller to $T$.

Starting from these base sizes, various math elements will be set in other sizes. Once another size has been chosen for an element, it remains the active size within that element.

The table below shows the selection rules:

| Active size | Fractions upper | lower | Super-, subscripts |
|---|---|---|---|
| $D$ | $T$ | $T$ | $S$ |
| $T$ | $S$ | $S$ | $S$ |
| $S$ | $SS$ | $SS$ | $SS$ |
| $SS$ | $SS$ | $SS$ | $SS$ |

If the active size is $D$, size $T$ is selected for both parts of the fraction. That is, for both numerator and denominator $T$ becomes the active size. If they in turn contain further fractions, these will be set in $S$. If the active size is $D$ or $T$, superscripts and subscripts (exponents and indices) appear in $S$; within them $S$ is the active size and any fractions or shiftings inside them will be set in $SS$.

The TEX elements { \atop } and { \choose } are treated as fractions.

The active font size inside an array environment is $T$.

The smallest available math font size is $SS$. Once it has been reached, no further reduction is possible, so that all subsequent superscripts and subscripts appear in $SS$ as well.

From the table one easily sees that

```
\[ a_0 + \frac{1}{a_1 + \frac{1}{a_2
      + \frac{1}{a_3 + \frac{1}{a_4}}}} \]
```

$$a_0 + \cfrac{1}{a_1 + \cfrac{1}{a_2 + \cfrac{1}{a_3 + \frac{1}{a_4}}}}$$

must appear as shown at the right.

Such a math structure, called a *continued fraction*, is normally printed as

$$a_0 + \cfrac{1}{a_1 + \cfrac{1}{a_2 + \cfrac{1}{a_3 + \cfrac{1}{a_4}}}}$$

```
\[ a_0 + \frac{1}{\displaystyle a_1
      + \frac{1}{\displaystyle a_2
      + \frac{1}{\displaystyle a_3
      + \frac{1}{a_4}}}}
\]
```

By explicitly giving the font size within each element, one makes that size active rather than relying on the internally selected size. In this example, $D$ is chosen for each denominator. Thus the next fraction acts as though it were outermost. The \displaystyle command may be omitted in the last fraction. (Why?)

The selection table allows one to predict precisely which math font size will be applied at any part of the formula so that an explicit specification may be made if necessary. The effects of such a choice may also be calculated for the following math elements.

The examples below show on the right-hand side how the formulas appear without explicitly specifying the math font size.

$$\frac{\dfrac{a}{x-y}+\dfrac{b}{x+y}}{1+\dfrac{a-b}{a+b}}$$

```
\[ \frac{\displaystyle\frac{a}{x-y}
              +\frac{b}{x+y}}
   {\displaystyle 1+\frac{a-b}{a+b}} \]
```

$$\frac{a}{x-y}+\frac{b}{x+y}$$
over
$$1+\frac{a-b}{a+b}$$

$$e^{-\frac{x_i-x_j}{n^i+n^j}}$$

```
\[   e^{\textstyle -
        \frac{x_i-x_j}{n^i+n^j}}   \]
```

$$e^{-\frac{x_i-x_j}{n^i+n^j}}$$

$$\begin{pmatrix} \binom{ab}{cd} & \dfrac{e+f}{g-h} \\ 0 & \left|\genfrac{}{}{0pt}{}{ij}{kl}\right| \end{pmatrix}$$

```
\[ \left(\begin{array}{cc}
\displaystyle{ab\choose cd} &
\displaystyle\frac{e+f}{g-h}\\
0 & \displaystyle \left|
   {ij\atop kl} \right|
\end{array}\right)         \]
```

$$\begin{pmatrix} \binom{ab}{cd} & \dfrac{e+f}{g-h} \\ 0 & \left|\genfrac{}{}{0pt}{}{ij}{kl}\right| \end{pmatrix}$$

If an explicit size specification is to be given frequently within a document—say within every entry in an array environment—then considerable writing effort may be avoided by adding to the preamble

```
\newcommand{\D}{\displaystyle}\newcommand{\T}{\textstyle}...
```

In this way the size command may be given simply by typing \D or \T, etc.

The rest of this section is unimportant for practical applications. The math font size selection rules given above are in fact a simplification. For those readers who wish to know the exact details, we now present the complete description.

For each of the four math font sizes $D, T, S, SS$ there is a modified version $D'$, $T', S', SS'$. The difference is that with $D$, $T, S, SS$ the superscripts (exponents) are somewhat higher than they are with $D'$, $T', S', SS'$. Compare carefully the positions of the exponent 2 above and below the line: $\dfrac{x^2}{x^2}$. Otherwise the primed and unprimed font sizes are identical. The true selection rules are given in the table at the right.

| Active size | Fractions upper | Fractions lower | Super-scripts | Sub-scripts |
|---|---|---|---|---|
| $D$ | $T$ | $T'$ | $S$ | $S'$ |
| $D'$ | $T'$ | $T'$ | $S'$ | $S'$ |
| $T$ | $S$ | $S'$ | $S$ | $S'$ |
| $T'$ | $S'$ | $S'$ | $S'$ | $S'$ |
| $S, SS$ | $SS$ | $SS'$ | $SS$ | $SS'$ |
| $S', SS'$ | $SS'$ | $SS'$ | $SS'$ | $SS'$ |

When the font size is explicitly stated within a numerator or superscript, the unprimed version is selected; and in the denominators and subscripts, the primed fonts.

## 5.3 Manual sizing of bracket symbols

The \left ... \right commands preceding one of the 22 bracket symbols listed in Section 5.4.1 adjust the symbol size automatically according to the height of the enclosed formula text. However, it is possible to select a size explicitly by placing before the bracket symbol one of the TeX commands \big, \Big, \bigg, or \Bigg.

In contrast to the \left ... \right pairs, the explicit bracket size commands do not have to be contained within one line of a multi-line formula. The opening and closing brackets may appear on different lines. This applies also to the commands described in the next paragraph.

!

Another two sets of bracket size commands exist with the names \bigl ...\Biggl and \bigr...\Biggr. These cause the following bracket symbol to be treated internally as an opening or closing bracket. The practical difference between these and the normal commands is insignificant for LaTeX.

Further bracket size commands are \bigm...\Biggm. With them, the following bracket symbol acts like a relation operator in that larger horizontal spacing is inserted between it and the neighboring parts of the formula.

$$\big[(a+b)\big|(c+d)\big]$$

```
\[ \big[ (a+b) \big| (c+d) \big] \]
\[ \bigl[ (a+b) \bigl| (c+d) \bigr] \]
\[ \bigm[ (a+b) \bigm| (c+d) \bigm] \]
```

$$\bigl[(a+b)\bigl|(c+d)\bigr]$$

$$\bigm[(a+b)\bigm|(c+d)\bigm]$$

## 5.5.4   Math style parameters

!

The mathematical style parameters listed below are set to standard values by LaTeX. The user may alter them at any time with the \setlength command in the usual manner.

\arraycolsep
>           Half the width of the inter-column spacing for the array environment (see also Section 4.8.2).

\jot        Extra vertical spacing that appears between the rows of multi-line equations in the eqnarray and eqnarray* environments.

\mathindent
>           The amount of indentation for math formulas when the document class option fleqn has been selected.

`\abovedisplayskip`
> The vertical spacing above displayed formulas when the left side of the formula is closer to the left margin than the end of the preceding line of text. Such a formula is designated *long*.

`\belowdisplayskip`
> The vertical spacing inserted below a *long* displayed formula.

`\abovedisplayshortskip`
> Vertical spacing added above a *short* displayed formula. This is one in which the left edge is to the right of the end of the preceding line of text.

`\belowdisplayshortskip`
> Vertical spacing inserted after a *short* displayed formula.

`\topsep`
> The above four spacings are not used with the document class option `fleqn` where instead `\topset` is inserted above and below displayed formulas (see Section 4.4.2).

All the above parameters, except `\jot`, should be rubber lengths (Section 2.4.2).

## 5.5 Some further advice

Sometimes authors desire horizontal and vertical alignments of their formulas that just cannot be achieved using the means described so far. They should consider placing their formulas inside horizontal or vertical boxes which may then be positioned wherever they please.

Similarly the `array` environment together with explicit size declarations and the table construction and style elements from Sections 4.8.1 and 4.8.2 should be able to accomplish just about any horizontal and vertical alignment.

**Exercise 5.19:** *Generate this continued fraction. Note: in contrast to the example on page 142, the 1 here in the numerator appears left justified. Hint: do you remember the command \hfill?*

**Exercise 5.20:** *Produce the following set of equations with the* `array` *environment.*

$$\sin 2\alpha = 2\sin\alpha\cos\alpha, \qquad \cos 2\alpha = \cos^2\alpha - \sin^2\alpha$$
$$\sin 3\alpha = 3\sin\alpha - 4\sin^3\alpha \qquad \cos 3\alpha = 3\cos^3\alpha - 3\cos\alpha$$
$$\sin 4\alpha = 8\cos^3\alpha\sin\alpha - 4\cos\alpha\sin\alpha \qquad \cos 4\alpha = 8\cos^4\alpha - 8\cos^2\alpha + 1$$

*Hint: recall that* `@{...}` *expressions in the formatting field of the* `array` *environment can be used to insert horizontal spacing and/or mathematical text between the columns (see the first example in Section 5.4.3).*

*Exercise 5.21:* Create the following output with the `array` environment.

| Equations for the tangential plane and surface normal | | |
|---|---|---|
| Equation for the surface | Tangential plane | Surface normal |
| $F(x,y,z)=0$ | $\dfrac{\partial F}{\partial x}(X-x)+\dfrac{\partial F}{\partial y}(Y-y)$ $+\dfrac{\partial F}{\partial z}(Z-z)=0$ | $\dfrac{X-x}{\dfrac{\partial F}{\partial x}}=\dfrac{Y-y}{\dfrac{\partial F}{\partial y}}=\dfrac{Z-z}{\dfrac{\partial F}{\partial z}}$ |
| $z=f(x,y)$ | $Z-z=p(X-x)+q(Y-y)$ | $\dfrac{X-x}{p}=\dfrac{Y-y}{q}=\dfrac{Z-z}{-1}$ |
| $x=x(u,v)$ $y=y(u,v)$ $z=z(u,v)$ | $\begin{vmatrix} X-x & Y-y & Z-z \\ \dfrac{\partial x}{\partial u} & \dfrac{\partial y}{\partial u} & \dfrac{\partial z}{\partial u} \\ \dfrac{\partial x}{\partial v} & \dfrac{\partial y}{\partial v} & \dfrac{\partial z}{\partial v} \end{vmatrix}=0$ | $\dfrac{X-x}{\begin{vmatrix}\frac{\partial y}{\partial u}&\frac{\partial z}{\partial u}\\\frac{\partial y}{\partial v}&\frac{\partial z}{\partial v}\end{vmatrix}}=\dfrac{Y-y}{\begin{vmatrix}\frac{\partial z}{\partial u}&\frac{\partial x}{\partial u}\\\frac{\partial z}{\partial v}&\frac{\partial x}{\partial v}\end{vmatrix}}$ $=\dfrac{Z-z}{\begin{vmatrix}\frac{\partial x}{\partial u}&\frac{\partial y}{\partial u}\\\frac{\partial x}{\partial v}&\frac{\partial y}{\partial v}\end{vmatrix}}$ |
| $r=r(u,v)$ | $(R-r)(r_1\times r_2)=0$ or $(R-r)N=0$ | $R=r+\lambda(r_1\times r_2)$ or $R=r+\lambda N$ |

In this Table $x$, $y$, $z$ and $r$ are the coordinates and the radius vector of a fixed point $M$ on the curve; $X$, $Y$, $Z$ and $R$ are the coordinates and radius vector of a point on the tangential plane or surface normal with reference to $M$; furthermore $p=\frac{\partial z}{\partial x}, q=\frac{\partial z}{\partial y}$ and $r_1=\partial r/\partial u, r_2=\partial r/\partial v$.

*Note: If you succeed with your output for this mathematical table you should have no more problems in future with positioning formulas and their parts!*
  *Hints for the solution:*

1. *Define abbreviations such as* `\D` *for* `\displaystyle` *and* `\bm` *for* `\boldmath` *and possibly even* `\ba` *and* `\ea` *for* `\begin{array}` *and* `\end{array}`.

2. *Build the table in stages. Start with the head and only proceed further when it looks reasonable. Watch out that normal text within the* `array` *environment must be included inside an* `\mbox`.

3. *Continue with the first mathematical row. Here the first entry in the second column is also an* `array` *environment that is aligned with the rest of the row by means of the* `[t]` *positioning argument. Do not forget to activate the size* `\D` *at the necessary places in the inner structures. Insert a possible strut (Section 4.7.6) to generate the right distance from the head. The distance to the next row can be adjusted with a length specification added to the row terminating command* `\\[..]`.

4. *After this row has been successfully accomplished, the next should pose no difficulties.*

5. *In the third mathematical row, both the first column and the left side of the second column consist of* `array` *environments. The third column contains*

*three fractions whose denominators may be produced either with* array *or with the TEX* {... \atop...} *command; the fractions themselves are placed in two rows with another* array *environment.*

6. *The second and third columns of the last mathematical row again contain* array *environments. Some of the sub-formulas in this row appear in* \boldmath. *Recall that this command may only be invoked within text mode, that is, within an* \mbox.

7. *In the last row, all three columns of the outer* array *environment are merged together and the text is set within a parbox of appropriate width:*

$$\texttt{\textbackslash multicolumn\{3\}\{|c|\}\{\textbackslash parbox\{..\}\{......\}\}}$$

## 5.6  Framed displayed formulas

In Section 5.4.8 we showed one method for framing a displayed formula, by putting it first into a \parbox or minipage of suitable width and then into an \fbox to produce the frame itself. The problem here is to find a reasonable width without a lot of trial and error.

However, there is another method that makes use of the math font size commands of Section 5.5.2 and does not require a width specification for framing displayed formulas (this method was suggested by Günter Green from the University of Kiel, Germany):

```
\begin{displaymath}    or    \begin{equation}
    \fbox{$ \displaystyle formula_text $}
\end{displaymath}    or    \end{equation}
```

The framed equation in the example on page 138 would now appear as

$$\boxed{\int_0^\infty f(x)\,dx \approx \sum_{i=1}^n w_i e^{x_i} f(x_i)} \tag{5.12}$$

and is produced with

```
\begin{equation}
    \fbox{$ \displaystyle \int^\infty_0 f(x)\,dx \approx ... $}
\end{equation}
```

Since the equation environment was invoked here, an automatic equation number is added at the extreme right of the line while the frame encloses only the actual equation. By the previous method, the equation number would also be inside the box. In contrast to the example on page 138, the frame now hugs the equation more tightly. The user may alter this behavior by changing the parameter \fboxsep (Section 4.7.8). Similarly, the line thickness of the frame can be set with \fboxrule.

In the same way the array environment can be applied to frame multi-line formulas or sets of equations:

```
\begin{displaymath}     or     \begin{equation}
    \fbox{$ \begin{array}{rcl} formula_text \end{array} $}
\end{displaymath}       or     \end{equation}
```

Since math font size commands are used fairly intensively in this application, it is advisable to follow the suggestion on page 143 regarding a redefinition of the command names.

### 5.5.7   What else?

The mathematical construction elements presented in this chapter, along with the formatting adjustments (fine-tuning), should be sufficient to fulfill even the most exotic of authors' wishes regarding mathematical composition.  The extra suggestions in Section 5.5.5 especially permit practically any desirable positioning and ordering of formulas: it is just a question of enough applied experience to be able to take advantage of the myriad of possibilities that are offered.

If certain symbols are required that are not available under LaTeX, one can try to create them from existing symbols with overprinting, raising, lowering, etc.  The use of such combined symbols can be simplified by defining a new command with \newcommand and storing the definition in a separate file for general use.

If there are configuration requirements that cannot be met within the capabilities of LaTeX, there is always the possibility of resorting to original TeX commands.  However, we wish to point out that any of the TeX construction elements that go beyond those of LaTeX demand a very thorough knowledge of the workings of TeX, something that cannot be expected of the majority of users.

A more suitable but still wearisome solution for completely flexible designing is the set of commands described in the next chapter for constructing pictures.

If the author insists on his individual formula format, it is most likely that were he to submit his manuscript to a scientific and technical publishing house, his formulas would deviate so much from international standards that the publisher would reset them in a form similar to that chosen by LaTeX.

The occasional request to alter the style of equation numbering is on the other hand often justified.  An example that illustrates how to accomplish this is presented in Section 7.3.4 and can serve as a model for other such demands.

# Pictures

**6**

It is possible to create *simple* pictures and diagrams with LaTeX. The building blocks from which pictures are constructed are text, straight lines of various inclinations, arrows, circles, ovals, and segments thereof, which may be placed wherever the user wishes within the picture.

## Picture size and position

The picture building blocks can only be put in place once a *coordinate system* has been established for that picture. This consists of a *reference point* or *origin*, and two mutually perpendicular *coordinate axes*, as well as a *length unit* for the coordinates. The origin is the lower left corner of the picture and the axes are its lower and left edges. These edges are referred to as the *x-axis* (lower) and *y-axis* (left).

Once the unit of length (UL) has been specified, every point within the picture area can be uniquely referred to with two decimal numbers: the first is the number of length units along the x-axis, the second the number along the y-axis.

149

The unit length is selected with the command

`\setlength{\unitlength}{`*length*`}`

In the left-hand example on the previous page, the unit length was set to a value of 1.5 cm with the command `\setlength{\unitlength}{1.5cm}`. The point (1.8,1.4) then lies 1.8 times the unit length (= 2.7 cm) to the right, and 1.4 times (= 2.1 cm) above the origin.

The coordinate numbers are generally positive, meaning that the point lies to the right and above the reference point. Since this point is the lower left corner of the picture, all other points should be more to the right and higher than it. However, negative values are also possible. A negative x value (a negative number for the first member of a coordinate pair) defines a point *left* of the origin, while a negative y value (the second member of the pair is negative) specifies a point below the reference point.

This is illustrated in the right-hand example on the previous page. The unit of length is given as 1 cm so that the numbers in the coordinate pairs are the distances in cm from the origin.

The unit of length is normally set to a convenient size such as 1 cm, 1 mm, or 1 in and the picture is built up accordingly. Once it has been completed, it is possible to rescale the whole thing simply by changing the value of the length unit. A picture that was originally designed with `\unitlength` set to 1 cm can be enlarged by a factor 1.2 by redefining its length unit to be 1.2 cm.

## 6.2    The picture environment

Pictures are constructed within the `picture` environment whose syntax is

`\begin{picture}`(*x_dimen*,*y_dimen*)
    *picture_commands*
`\end{picture}`

where (*x_dimen*,*y_dimen*) is a pair of numbers that specifies the size (dimensions) of the picture in the *x-direction* (horizontal) and *y-direction* (vertical). This pair of numbers is enclosed in *round* parentheses! The unit of length is that previously selected by `\unitlength`.

`\setlength{\unitlength}{1.5cm}`
`\begin{picture}`(4,5) ... ... ... `\end{picture}`

produces a picture that is 4 length units wide and 5 units high. Since the length unit has been set to 1.5 cm, the actual size is 6 cm wide and 7.5 cm high.

*Picture commands* are those commands described below that are used to produce and position the individual picture elements. These are the only commands that are allowed within the picture environment, other than font style and size declarations (Section 4.1) and the line thickness commands \thicklines and \thinlines. These last determine which of the two available line thicknesses will become current for drawing lines: one may switch back and forth as one pleases. Initially *thin* lines are active.

The value of the parameter \unitlength must not be altered within the picture environment, for it must remain the same for the entire picture. It may, however, be changed between pictures.

If the \unitlength specification together with the picture environment are enclosed within another environment, such as \begin{center} ... \end{center}, then that value of \unitlength is valid only until the end of the environment. A picture environment without a preceding \unitlength command uses the standard value of 1 pt.

## The positioning commands

Picture elements are generated and positioned by means of the two commands \put and \multiput, which have the syntaxes:

\put(*x_coord*,*y_coord*){*pic_elem*}
\multiput(*x_coord*,*y_coord*)(*x_incr*,*y_incr*){*num*}{*pic_elem*}

The *pic_elem* is one of the picture element commands described in the next section. The arguments (*x_coord*,*y_coord*) are the *placement coordinates*, designating the location of the picture element within the picture coordinate system, in units of \unitlength. If this is 1 cm, then (2.5,3.6) means that the element is to be positioned 2.5 cm to the right and 3.6 cm above the lower left corner of the picture.

The \multiput command generates the same picture element *num* times, moving it by (*x_incr*,*y_incr*) each time. Thus the element is drawn repeatedly at

(*x_coord*, *y_coord*), (*x_coord* + *x_incr*, *y_coord* + *y_incr*),
(*x_coord* + 2*x_incr*, *y_coord* + 2*y_incr*), ... up to
(*x_coord* + [*num* − 1]*x_incr*, *y_coord* + [*num* − 1]*y_incr*)

The coordinate pair (*x_coord*, *y_coord*) is incremented by (*x_incr*, *y_incr*) for each successive placement. The values of the incrementing pair may be positive or negative.

Thus \multiput(2.5,3.6)(0.5,-0.6){5}{*pic_elem*} produces the *pic_elem* a total of five times, first at the location (2.5,3.6) and then at (3.0,3.0), (3.5,2.4), (4.0,1.8), and finally (4.5,1.2).

Note that the numbers for the *coordinate* and *increment* pairs are given in round parentheses ( , ) and that the two numbers within each pair are separated by a comma. The *num* and *pic_elem* entries, on the other hand, are enclosed in curly brackets { } as usual.

**Warning:** since it is the comma that separates the two numbers in a coordinate pair, it may *not* be used in place of a decimal point. *For coordinate entries, decimal numbers must be written with a period, not a comma.*

## 6.4    Picture element commands

### 6.4.1    Text within pictures

The simplest picture element of all is a piece of text, positioned at the desired location within the picture. This is accomplished by putting text in place of *pic_elem* in the \put or \multiput command.

An arrow

(1.8,1.2)

The arrow points to the location (1.8,1.2). The command \put(1.8,1.2){An arrow} inserts the text 'An arrow' so that its lower left corner is at the specified position.

The text as picture element may also be packed into a \parbox or a minipage environment, and the reference point for the coordinate entry in the \put command depends on the positioning arguments of the vertical box:

\parbox[b]{..}{..}
Reference point is the lower left corner of the last line in the parbox

\parbox{32mm}{...}
For a standard parbox, the reference point is the vertical center of the left edge.

\parbox[t]{..}{..}
Reference point is the lower left corner of the top line in the parbox

*Exercise 6.1: Produce a picture 100 mm wide and 50 mm high with \unitlength equal to 1 mm. Place the given texts at the following locations: (0,0) 'The First Picture', (90,47) 'upper left', (70,40) 'somewhere upper right', and put a parbox of width 60 mm at (25,25) containing* 'A separate exercise file with the name picture.tex *should be created for the exercises in this Chapter.'*

*Exercise 6.2:  Repeat the picture processing with a value of 1.5 mm for* \unitlength, *and with positioning arguments t and b for the parbox.*

### 6.4.2    Picture boxes—rectangles

The box commands \framebox, \makebox, and \savebox (Section 4.7.1) are available in the picture environment but with an extended syntax. In addition, there is another box command \dashbox:

```
\makebox(x_dimen,y_dimen)[pos]{text}
\framebox(x_dimen,y_dimen)[pos]{text}
\dashbox{dash_dimen}(x_dimen,y_dimen)[pos]{text}
```

The *dimensional* pair ($x\_dimen$, $y\_dimen$) defines the width and height of the rectangular box in units of \unitlength. The positioning argument *pos* determines how the *text* is located within the box. It may take on values:

[t]  *top* - The input text appears—centered horizontally—*below* the *upper* edge of the box.

[b]  *bottom* – The input text appears—centered horizontally—*above* the *lower* edge of the box.

[l]  *left* – The input text *begins*—centered vertically—at the *left* edge of the box.

[r]  *right* – The input text *ends*—centered vertically—at the *right* edge of the box.

$\boxed{2\varepsilon}$ [s]  *stretch* – The input text is stretched horizontally to fill up the box, and centered vertically.

*Without* the optional argument *pos*, the input text is centered vertically and horizontally within the box.

These positional values may be combined two at a time:

[tl]  *top left* – The text appears at the *upper left.*

[tr]  *top right* – The text appears at the *upper right.*

[bl]  *bottom left* – The text appears at the *lower left.*

[br]  *bottom right* – The text appears at the *lower right.*

The order of the values is unimportant: tl has the same effect as lt.
These box commands are to be used as *pic_elem* in the placement commands \put and \multiput. The box is so placed that its lower left corner is at the position given by the coordinate pair in the placement command.

```
\put(1.5,1.2){\framebox(2.5,1.2){center}}
```

The arrow indicates the point (1.5,1.2) which is the position of the lower left corner of the rectangle with width 2.5 units and height 1.2 units. The text 'center' is centered both horizontally and vertically. UL = 0.8 cm.

The effect of the text positioning argument is made clear with the following examples (UL = 1 cm):

```
\put(0.0,1.95){\framebox(2,1.0)
          [t]{top center}}
\put(3.0,1.95){\framebox(2,0.8)
          [lb]{bot. left}}
\put(3.0,3.2){\framebox(2,0.6)
          [r]{center right}}
\put(2.0,0.3){\framebox(2,0.6)
          [s]{stretch\hfill center}}
```

The picture element \makebox is exactly the same as the \framebox command but without the rectangular frame. It is most often employed with the dimensional pair (0,0) in order to place text at a desired location. (See Section 4.7.1 for the effect of *zero* width boxes on the enclosed text.)

```
\put(3,1.6){\makebox(0,0){center center}}
\put(2,0.5){\makebox(0,0)[tr]{top right}}
\put(4,1.0){\makebox(0,0)[b]{bot center}}
\put(2,2.8){\makebox(0,0)[l]{flush left}}
```

The combination [lb] positions the text in exactly the same way as simply typing the text in as *pic_elem* without a box, as shown in Section 6.4.1.

The picture element \dashbox also produces a framed box, but with a *dashed* line around it. The additional argument *dash_dimen* specifies the dash length.

```
\put(1.0,0.75){\dashbox{0.2}(4,1){dashed frame}}
```

A dashed frame looks best when both the height and width are a multiple of the dash length.

Even in the above picture box commands, the entered *text* may be put into a vertical box (\parbox or minipage). Since vertical boxes themselves possess an optional positioning argument b or t, which must not conflict with that of the picture box, the following rule must be observed:

> If a picture box command contains the positioning argument b or t, then the same value must be applied to the enclosed vertical box. If the picture box command has no positioning argument or only r or l, then the vertical box must be used in the standard (no argument) form.

The positioning argument of a picture box has the same effect on the enclosed vertical box as it does on a line of text, in that the whole box is treated as a single unit.

*Exercise 6.3:* *Reproduce the organization table below with the boxes and included text but without the horizontal and vertical lines and arrows. These will be part of the next exercise.*

*Hint: first draw the boxes on a piece of squared paper so that the edges of the boxes lie on the printed rules. Select the unit of length to be the rule spacing of the paper. Take as the origin the lower left corner of an imaginary frame surrounding the entire diagram.*

*Note: you will soon be able to generate your own squared paper with whatever rule spacing you wish!*

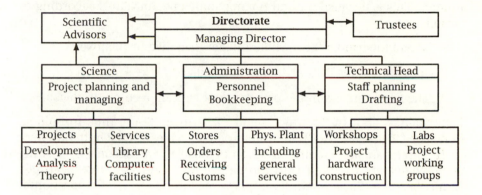

## 6.3  Straight lines

In the `picture` environment, LaTeX can draw straight lines of any length, horizontally and vertically as well as at a limited number of angles. The syntax for this picture element reads

$\line(\Delta x, \Delta y)\{length\}$

For horizontal and vertical lines, *length* specifies how long the line is to be in length units. For lines at an angle, it has a somewhat more complicated meaning, as is explained below. The line begins at that spot given by the placement coordinates in the \put or \multiput command.

```
\thicklines
\put(0,0){\line(1,0){6}}
\put(0,0){\line(0,1){1}}
\put(6,0){\line(0,1){0.5}}
```

The angle at which the line is drawn is given by the *slope pair* $(\Delta x, \Delta y)$. The slope pair $(1,0)$, in which $\Delta x = 1$ and $\Delta y = 0$, produces a *horizontal* line, while the pair $(0,1)$ leads to a *vertical* line. This is illustrated in the above example.

In general $(\Delta x, \Delta y)$ has the following meaning:

Beginning at a point A on the line and moving a distance $\Delta x$ in the x direction (horizontally), $\Delta y$ is the distance one must move in the y direction (vertically) in order to rejoin the line.

By specifying a slope pair $(\Delta x, \Delta y)$, a line is drawn at just that angle to fulfill the above conditions.

As mentioned already, the number of different slopes available is limited. This is because $\Delta x$ and $\Delta y$ may only take on values according to certain rules:

1. The number must be a whole integer (negative or positive).

2. Only the values $0, 1, \ldots, 6$ are allowed.

3. The two numbers in the pair may not contain a common divisor.

Pairs such as $(3.5, 1.2)$ (rule 1) and $(7,0)$ (rule 2) are thus forbidden. Similarly $(2,2)$ and $(3,6)$ are invalid pairs by rule 3, since both numbers in the first pair are divisible by 2, and those in the second by 3. The same angles are achieved with the pairs $(1,1)$ and $(1,2)$ respectively. In all there are 25 allowed slope pairs, including $(1,0)$ for horizontal and $(0,1)$ for vertical lines, as one can verify by writing down all the possibilities.

In addition, the numbers in the slope pair may be positive or negative, for example, $(0,-1)$, $(-2,-5)$. A negative $\Delta x$ in the above diagram means motion to the left, and a negative $\Delta y$ is for motion downwards. Thus `\put(2,3){\line(0,-1){2.5}}` draws a line starting at point (2,3) and going 2.5 length units vertically downwards.

For lines at an angle, the argument *length* determines the projected distance along the x-axis. This is made clearer with the help of the diagram on the left.
        `\put(1.0,2.75){\line(2,-1){3.5}}`
If one draws dashed lines straight down from the two end points, then that part of the x-axis between them is the projection of the line on to the x-axis.

Sloping lines must have a minimum length of about 10 pt or 3.5 mm, otherwise no line is drawn. This restriction does not apply if the `pict2e` package is included (Section 6.5.6).

## 6.4.4    Arrows

The *arrow* picture element is made with the command

$$\verb|\vector|(\Delta x,\Delta y)\{\textit{length}\}$$

which functions exactly the same as the `\line` command as far as the arguments and their limitations are concerned. The command draws a line from the placement location given in the `\put` or `\multiput` command and places an arrow head at the end.

Just as for lines, arrows too must have a length of at least 10 pt or 3.5 mm. Rules 1–3 apply to $\Delta x$ and $\Delta y$ as well, with the further restriction that the allowed numbers are limited to 0, 1, ..., 4. This makes a total of 13 possible angles for arrows, not counting changes in sign.

```
\begin{picture}(5,2)\thicklines
  \put(5,0){\vector(-1,0){5}}
  \put(0,0){\vector(1,1){2}}
  \put(2,2){\vector(3,-2){3}}
\end{picture}
```

*Exercise 6.4:* *Complete the diagram in Exercise 6.3 by including the missing horizontal and vertical lines and arrows.*

*Exercise 6.5:* *Produce a sheet of graph paper 6.5 × 9 inches with a grid separation of 0.1 in. It is only necessary to have two* `\multiput` *commands to achieve this. Overlay the grid with a second one with the same overall size but with a grid separation of 0.5 in and line thickness given by* `\thicklines`.

*Exercise 6.6:* *Generate the figure at the right. The corner points are (0,5), (0,10), (5,15), (10,15), (15,10), (15,5), (10,0), and (5,0) and the length unit is 0.1 inch.*

## .5 Circles

The *circle* picture element is produced with the commands

```
\circle{diameter}
\circle*{diameter}
```

With the *-form of the command, a solid filled-in circle is printed rather than just an outline as for the standard form. Only certain sizes are available so LaTeX selects the one closest to the specified *diameter* entry. (The `pict2e` package of Section 6.5.6 allows any diameter.)

```
\begin{picture}(3,1.6)
  \put(1,1){\circle*{0.2}}
  \put(1,1){\circle{1.2}}
  \put(1,1){\vector(0,1){0.6}}
  \put(2.5,1){\circle*{0.5}}
\end{picture}
```

The placement location in the corresponding \put command refers to the center of the circle.

## 6.4.6    Ovals and rounded corners

The term *oval* is used here to mean a rectangle whose corners have been replaced by quarter circles; the largest possible radius is chosen for the circles such that the sides join together smoothly.   The command to produce them is

    \oval(x_dimen,y_dimen)[part]

The placement location in the corresponding \put command refers to the center of the oval.

    \put(3.0,0.75){\oval(4.0,1.5)}

Here we have set the values x_dimen=4.0 UL and y_dimen=1.5 UL, whereby the unit length UL has been selected to be 0.8 cm. The center of the oval is at the placement coordinates in the \put command, at (3.0,0.75).

The optional argument *part* takes on values t, b, l, or r, for making half ovals.

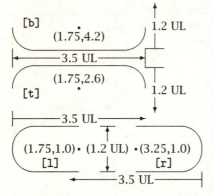

    \put(1.75,4.2){\oval(3.5,1.2)[b]}
    \put(1.75,2.6){\oval(3.5,1.2)[t]}
    \put(1.75,1.0){\oval(3.5,1.2)[l]}
    \put(3.25,1.2){\oval(3.5,1.2)[r]}

The width and height specifications for half ovals are always those of the *entire* figure even though only part of it is being drawn. Similarly, the placement coordinates in the corresponding \put command refer to the center of the complete oval. (Unit length here is UL = 1 cm.)

The argument *part* may also be one of the combinations tl, tr, bl, or br to generate a quarter oval. The order of the two letters is unimportant, so that lt, rt, lb, and rb are equally valid.

    \put(2.0,2.5){\oval(3.0,1.0)[tl]}
    \put(2.5,2.5){\oval(3.0,1.0)[tr]}
    \put(1.0,1.5){\oval(1.0,2.0)[bl]}
    \put(3.5,1.5){\oval(1.0,2.0)[br]}

Once again the size specifications refer to the *entire* oval and not just to the part that is drawn, and the placement coordinates in the \put command refer to the center of the complete oval.

Quarter and half circles may also be drawn as partial ovals with equal width and height, but only up to a certain size. The following examples demonstrate that sections of circles are possible up to a size of about 1.5 cm.

```
\put(2.0,1.0){\oval(4.0,4.0)[t]}
\put(2.0,1.0){\oval(1.5,1.5)[t]}

\put(0.75,0.75){\oval(1.5,1.5)[bl]}
\put(1.75,0.0){\oval(1.5,1.5)[tl]}
\put(2.25,0.0){\oval(1.5,1.5)[tr]}
\put(3.25,0.75){\oval(1.5,1.5)[br]}
```

Sections of ovals may be combined with other picture elements. The placement coordinates in the \put command, however, require some serious consideration to get them positioned properly.

```
\put(0.5,2.5){\oval(1.0,1.0)[t]}
\put(0.0,2.5){\vector(0,-1){2.5}}
\put(1.0,2.5){\vector(0,-1){1.5}}
\put(0.5,2.5){\circle*{0.1}}

\put(2.5,0.5){\line(0,1){2.5}}
\put(2.75,0.5){\oval(0.5,0.5)[bl]}
\put(2.75,0.25){\vector(1,0){1.25}}
```

In all the above examples, the centers of the ovals have been marked with a black dot to indicate where they are. They are not normally a part of the \oval picture element.

*Exercise 6.7:* *Although the object pictured below is no longer very relevant in the post-Cold-War era, it does make an excellent exercise for the* picture *environment. Hint: sizing and positioning can be worked out best by overlaying the illustration with transparent graph paper.*

UL=1 mm

### 6.4.7  Vertically stacked text

It is sometimes necessary to write text vertically in a diagram, as in the example here at the right. This is carried out with the command

$\backslash$shortstack$[pos]\{col\}$

The positioning argument can take on values l, r, or c. The standard is c for centered. The command is similar to a tabular environment with only one column. The text is entered as *col*, each row being separated from the next by $\backslash\backslash$.

The \shortstack command is most frequently implemented for placing single letters on top of one another, even though longer pieces of text may also be vertically stacked. The individual rows are separated from each other with the smallest possible vertical spacing. This means that rows without any letters that stick up or down (like *h* and *y*) will be placed closer to their neighbors than rows with such letters.

This
spacing
leaves
some
room
for
help

Not
really
the
best
for words
at all

Single
characters
place much
better
than
words

L
e
t
t
e
r
s

b
e
s
t

(1.0,0.5)    (3.0,0.5)    (5.0,0.5)         (8.0,0.8)  (9.0,1.2)

The placement coordinates of the corresponding \put command refer to the lower left corner of an imaginary box that contains the vertically stacked text. The first of the above texts is left justified, the second centered, and the third right justified. The last two on the right are centered. They were entered with

```
\put(1.0,0.5){\shortstack[l]{This\\spacing\\leaves\\some\\ ...}}
\put(3.0,0.5){\shortstack{Not\\really\\the\\best\\ ...}}
\put(5.0,0.5){\shortstack[r]{Single\\characters\\ ... }}
\put(8.0,0.8){\shortstack{L\\e\\t\\t\\e\\r\\s}}
\put(9.0,1.2){\shortstack{b\\e\\s\\t}}
```

The \shortstack command may also be used outside of the picture environment within normal text. One possible application is for marginal notes, as in Section 4.10.6.

### 6.4.8  Framed text

⚠

The \framebox command generates a frame of a predetermined size in which text may be inserted at various positions (Section 6.4.2). In text mode, there is the command \fbox for drawing a frame around text that fits it exactly (Section 4.7.1). This command is also available in the picture environment.

The amount of spacing between the box frame and the enclosed text is given by the parameter \fboxsep. The placement of an \fbox by means of the \put command occurs in an unexpected manner, as shown below:

```
\begin{picture}(5,2)
\setlength{\fboxsep}{0.25cm}
\put(0,0){\framebox(5,2){}}
\put(1,1){\fbox{fitted frame}}
\end{picture}
```

The additional frame spacing is often unwanted in a diagram, especially if the frame surrounds a picture object rather than text. In this case, the command

    \frame{*pic_elem*}

is used instead. The placement coordinate of the \put command then refers to the lower left corner as usual.

```
\put(0.0,0.5){\frame{TEXT}}
\put(1.5,0.0){\frame{\shortstack{W\\O\\R\\D}}}
```

The contents of the \frame command can be any of the previous picture elements, and need not be merely text. However, in many cases the output comes out wrong.

```
\put(0,0){\frame{\vector(1,1){1.0}}}
\put(2,0){\frame{\circle{1.0}}}
```

The first example produces the correct result, while the second has failed. In such cases, one can try putting the picture object inside a \makebox of suitable size and positioning as argument for the \frame command. However, it would then make more sense to use the \framebox command itself in place of \frame {\makebox...}.

## .9   Curved lines

Curved lines may be drawn in the picture environment with the commands

    \bezier{*num*}$(x_1,y_1)(x_2,y_2)(x_3,y_3)$

    $\boxed{2\varepsilon}$ \qbezier[*num*]$(x_1,y_1)(x_2,y_2)(x_3,y_3)$

which draw a quadratic *Bézier* curve from point $(x_1,y_1)$ to $(x_3,y_3)$ with $(x_2,y_2)$ as the extra Bézier point. The curve is actually drawn as $num + 1$ dots. The only difference between \bezier and \qbezier is that, for the latter, the number of points *num* is an optional argument; if it is omitted, its value will be calculated to produce a solid-looking line. The \bezier command is retained only for compatibility with older LATEX 2.09 documents.

The meaning of the extra point can be illustrated with the example at the right. The input is

```
\begin{picture}(40,20)
\qbezier(0,0)(20,20)(40,10)
\end{picture}
```

The curve is drawn from (0,0) to (40,10) such that the tangents at the endpoints (the dotted lines) intersect at the extra Bézier point (20,20). Another way of stating this is that, as one moves from the first to the third point, one begins by heading directly towards the second point, and on arrival at the destination, one is moving directly away from that second point again. The dotted lines in the above example, which are not drawn by the \bezier functions, illustrate this.

A dotted curve may be drawn by specifying the number of points *num*; some experimentation may be required to get just the right effect.

**Note:** the \bezier command is not an integral part of LATEX 2.09, but is contained in an extra file bezier.sty which must be read in by including bezier in the list of options to \documentstyle. In LATEX 2ε, an empty file of the same name is provided for compatibility.

## 6.5     Further picture commands and examples

### 6.5.1     Line thickness

There is a choice of two line thicknesses for the picture elements \circle, \oval, and \vector, as well as for sloping lines. These may be selected with

> \thicklines   or   \thinlines

Each of these declarations remains in effect until countermanded by a call to the other one, or until the end of the environment in which it was invoked. Initially, \thinlines is in effect.

The thickness of the horizontal and vertical lines may be set with the declaration

> \linethickness{*thickness*}

to any desired size. The argument *thickness* is a positive length specification. With \linethickness{1.5mm}, all subsequent horizontal and vertical lines will have a thickness of 1.5 mm. If the pict2e package is included (Section 6.5.6), this command applies to sloping lines as well.

Since frame boxes are constructed out of horizontal and vertical lines, the command \linethickness also affects the \framebox and \dashbox commands.

.2   **Nested pictures**

The *pic_elem* of a \put or \multiput command may be another picture
environment. The syntax for such a multiple picture is

\put(*x_coord*,*y_coord*){\setlength{\unitlength}{*ul*}
                \begin{picture}(*x_dim*,*y_dim*)
                ... *sub_pic* ... \end{picture} }

The positioning coordinates within the inner picture environment refer
to its origin, that is, to its lower left corner; this in turn is located at the
placement coordinates of the \put command in the outer picture. A
different value of \unitlength *ul* may be selected for the inner picture;
however, if no new value is set, the same value of \unitlength is used
as in the outer environment.

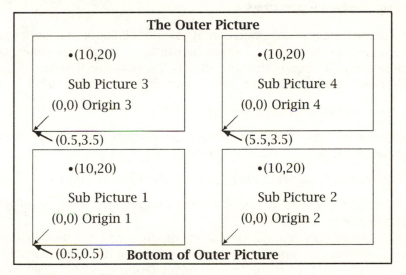

```
\begin{picture}(10.0,6.6)
\thicklines\put(0,0){\framebox(10.0,6.6){}}
 \put(5.0,6.3){\makebox(0,0){\bfseries The Outer Picture}}
 \thinlines
 \put(.5,.5){\setlength{\unitlength}{1mm}\begin{picture}(50,25)
 \put(0,0){\framebox(50,25){Sub Picture 1}}
 \put(10,20){\circle*{1}} \put(10,20){\makebox(0,0)[l]{(10,20)}}
 \put(4,4){\vector(-1,-1){4}}
 \put(5,5){\makebox(0,0)[lb]{(0,0) Origin 1}} \end{picture}}
\put(5.5,0.5){   ...   Sub Picture 2   ...   }
\put(0.5,3.5){   ...   Sub Picture 3   ...   }
\put(5.5,3.5){   ...   Sub Picture 4   ...   }
\put(5,0.1){\makebox(0,0)[b]
      {\bfseries Bottom of Outer Picture}}
\end{picture}
```

The unit length has been set to UL = 1 cm in the outer picture, which is 10 cm wide and 6.6 cm high. Its picture elements consist of a frame with thick lines, the same size as the picture itself, two pieces of text 'The Outer Picture' and 'The Bottom Edge of the Outer Picture', and four sub-pictures, each with a unit length of UL = 1 mm and size 50 × 25 mm. The objects inside the sub-pictures are positioned relative to their respective origins. The • symbol in each of the sub-pictures has the same coordinates (10,20) in every case.

By nesting pictures it is possible to simplify the relative positioning of certain individual objects that logically belong to each other, thus considerably reducing placement errors. This is especially true if \unitlength can be set to a different value within a calling \put command.

### 6.5.3    Saving parts of pictures

It is possible to store a combination of picture elements as a sub-picture under a certain name, and to recall the whole set as often as one wants without having to reissue the individual commands every time.

First each sub-picture must have a name reserved for it with

\newsavebox{\sub_pic_name}

which creates a box with the name \sub_pic_name for storing the picture. Afterwards, the sub-picture is saved with

\savebox{\sub_pic_name}(x_dim,y_dim)[pos]{sub_pic}

where the arguments (x_dimen,y_dimen) and pos have the same meaning as for \makebox in Section 6.4.2.

If the picture commands sub_pic are simply a piece of text, this command is exactly the same as the \makebox command except that the text is not printed but stored under the name \sub_pic_name. The sub_pic may be set down anywhere within the main picture as a separate picture element.

\usebox{\sub_pic_name}

```
\newsavebox{\sub}
\savebox{\sub}(2,1)[br]{\small Sub-Pic}
....
\put(0.7,0.0){\frame{\usebox{\sub}}}
\put(3.0,1.0){\frame{\usebox{\sub}}}
```

This example may not seem very practical, since the \savebox and \usebox commands could have been replaced by a \framebox together with \multiput to achieve the same result with even less effort. However, the main advantage of these two commands is not for multiple setting of text, but rather for more complex sub_pic compositions.

It should be pointed out that a \savebox command may be given outside of the picture environment, and even within the preamble. Such a sub-picture is then available in all picture environments throughout the document. However, if a \savebox is defined within an environment, it keeps its contents only until that environment comes to an end.

The picture elements inside a \savebox will be sized according to the value of \unitlength in effect at the time that the box is constructed. It will not be rescaled by a later change in \unitlength.

```
\newsavebox{\testcon}
\savebox{\testcon}(0,0){%
  \thicklines
  \put(0,0.5) {\line(-2,-1){1.0}}
  \put(0,0.5) {\line(2,-1) {1.0}}
  \put(0,-0.5){\line(-2,1) {1.0}}
  \put(0,-0.5){\line(2,1)  {1.0}}
  \put(0,0.5) {\makebox(0,0)[b]
    {\put(0,0){\line(0,1){0.5}}}}
  \put(1.0,0) {\line(1,0){1.0}}
  \put(-1.0,0){\line(-1,0){1.0}}
\put(-1.1,0.1){\makebox(0,0)[br]{no}}
\put(1.1,0.1){\makebox(0,0)[bl]{yes}}
```

This defines the symbol for conditional branching that is frequently used in flow diagrams for computer programs

+ denotes the reference point for the symbol \testcon.

In the above \savebox command, the argument (0,0) defines a box of zero height and width, whose center becomes the reference point for the placement coordinates in the \put commands. Since we want the middle of the diamond to be that reference point, the vertical line going out of the top of the diamond must appear as having no height, otherwise its presence will displace the center of the whole figure away from the center of the diamond. For this reason, that vertical line (\line(0,1){0.5}) is placed in a \makebox of zero size. As a result, the reference point for the symbol as a whole (in external \put commands) is where the + sign is.

The symbol \testcon may now very simply be combined with other picture elements.

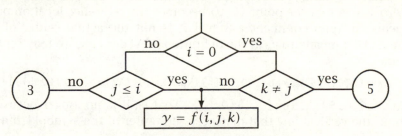

```
\begin{picture}(10,3)  \thicklines
\put(5,2){\usebox{\testcon}\makebox(0,0){$i=0$}}
\put(3,1){\usebox{\testcon}\makebox(0,0){$j\le i$}}
\put(7,1){\usebox{\testcon}\makebox(0,0){$k\neq j$}}
\put(0.5,1){\circle{1.0}\makebox(0,0){3}}
```

```
\put(9.5,1){\circle{1.0}\makebox(0,0){5}}
\put(5,1){\vector(0,-1){0.5}\circle*{0.1}}
\put(3.5,0){\framebox(3,0.5){$y = f(i,j,k)$}}
\end{picture}
```

As shown in this example, it is possible to include more than one picture object in a \put command. Here both the \usebox{\testcon} command for the symbol and a \makebox(0,0) command for the contained text are set together. Similarly, the \circle{1.0} commands are placed with their centered numbers 3 and 5 each with one \put command. Lastly, the \vector and \circle commands are set together. When multiple objects are included in one \put command, there must be *no blanks* between the picture element commands.

A \savebox command can also be used to store an entire picture environment. In this case the arguments (*x_dim, y_dim*) and [*pos*] are omitted since the size specifications appear in the picture environment itself. The syntax is

\savebox{\\*pic_name*}{\begin{picture}(*x_dim,y_dim*)

. . . . . . . . .

\end{picture} }

If such saved pictures are to be used only as sub-pictures, (*x_dim, y_dim*) may be readily set to (0,0) since this establishes a relative positioning with respect to the sub-picture. The scaling of the stored picture will be done according to the outer picture environment. The sample symbol \testcon could have been stored as

\savebox{\testcon}{\begin{picture}(0,0) ...

\end{picture} }

where ... stands for the same set of commands defining \testcon on the previous page, starting with the command \thicklines and ending with the last }.

Another advantage of storing sub-pictures as a picture environment of zero size is that the point (0,0) becomes the reference location point for external \put commands even if it is not the actual center of the symbol. This means that, in the definition of \testcon, we may replace the line

\put(0,0.5){\makebox(0,0)[b]{\put(0,0){\line(0,1){0.5}}}}

by \put(0,0.5){\line(0,1){0.5}}. That is, it is no longer necessary to 'hide' the vertical line that displaces the center of the symbol from the point (0,0).

*Exercise 6.8: The following symbols often appear in flow diagrams for computer programs. Generate the given boxes and store them as symbols under the corresponding name. Combine simpler symbols together to make more complex ones. Note the relative coordinates of the connection and reference points.*

Note:
the + sign denotes the reference point, or origin, for the whole symbol, while (+) indicates a reference point for a sub-symbol relative to +. UL = 1.8 mm.

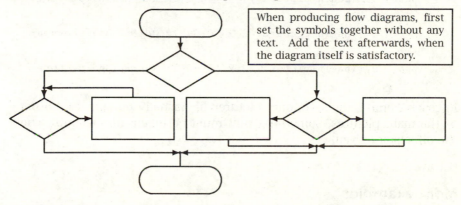

*Make use of the above symbols to compose the picture below.*

When producing flow diagrams, first set the symbols together without any text. Add the text afterwards, when the diagram itself is satisfactory.

## 6.4   Extended syntax of the picture environment

The generalized syntax of the picture environment contains a further coordinate pair as an optional argument

$$\verb|\begin{picture}| (x\_dimen, y\_dimen)(x\_offset, y\_offset)$$
$$picture\_commands \ \verb|\end{picture}|$$

In this form, $(x\_offset, y\_offset)$ specifies the coordinates of the lower left corner. This means that for all \put commands in the environment, the amounts $x\_offset$ and $y\_offset$ are effectively subtracted from the placement coordinates, so that the entire picture is shifted by $x\_offset$ to the *left* and by $y\_offset$ *downwards*.

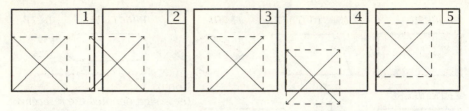

Here we have five main pictures each consisting of a frame with thick lines, 3 UL wide and 3 UL high (UL=7.2 mm). In each of these frames, a sub-picture has been added with \put(0,0), a dashed box 2 × 2 UL with two diagonal lines, which is identical in each case except for the offsets.

1. \put(0,0){\begin{picture}(2,2)(0,0)     *sub_pic* \end{picture}

2. \put(0,0){\begin{picture}(2,2)(0.5,0)  *sub_pic* \end{picture}

3. \put(0,0){\begin{picture}(2,2)(-0.5,0) *sub_pic* \end{picture}

4. \put(0,0){\begin{picture}(2,2)(0,0.5)  *sub_pic* \end{picture}

5. \put(0,0){\begin{picture}(2,2)(0,-0.5) *sub_pic* \end{picture}

In cases 2 and 4, the secondary pictures lie partially outside the borders of the main pictures, something that must be taken into account when the offsets are given.

## 6.5.5   More examples

So far the picture elements have been illustrated with very detailed examples. However, the \multiput command has been somewhat neglected so that it is worthwhile giving some extra examples of its usage. (The \multiput command is described in Section 6.3.)

```
\multiput(0,0)(1,2){7}{\circle*{1}}
\multiput(8,0)(2,0){10}{\begin{picture}(0,0)
         \multiput(0,0)(1,2){7}{\circle*{1}}
                  \end{picture}}
```

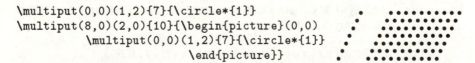

The first \multiput command produces 7 dots with a diameter of 1 mm, beginning at (0,0) with each successive point shifted 1 mm to the right and 2 mm upwards. The second \multiput command then generates 10 sub-pictures, each one 2 mm to the right of the previous one. The sub-pictures themselves are the 7 points produced by the first \multiput command.

**Example: Grid Network**

```
\setlength{\unitlength}{0.1in}
\begin{picture}(20,30)
\linethickness{0.25mm}
   \multiput(0,0)(10,0){3}{\line(0,1){30}}
   \multiput(0,0)(0,10){4}{\line(1,0){20}}
\linethickness{0.15mm}
   \multiput(5,0)(10,0){2}{\line(0,1){30}}
   \multiput(0,5)(0,10){3}{\line(1,0){20}}
\linethickness{0.075mm}
   \multiput(1,0)(1,0){19}{\line(0,1){30}}
   \multiput(0,1)(0,1){29}{\line(1,0){20}}
\end{picture}
```

First, 3 vertical lines of thickness 0.25 mm and length 30 UL, and 4 horizontal lines of the same thickness and length 20 UL are drawn starting at (0,0) each with a spacing of 10 UL. Then another 2 vertical and 3 horizontal lines of thickness 0.15 mm are drawn beginning at (5,0) and (0,5). Finally, 19 vertical and 29 horizontal lines of 0.075 mm thickness are drawn at 1 UL separations.

**IC Symbol**

```
\newcounter{ic} \setlength{\unitlength}{1mm}
\begin{picture}(25,40) \thicklines \scriptsize
\put(5,0){\framebox(15,40){}} \thinlines
\multiput(5,37.5)(0,-5){8}{\oval(8,3)[l]%
\stepcounter{ic}\makebox(0,0)[r]{\arabic{ic}\,\,}}
\put(20,2.5){\oval(8,3)[r]%
\stepcounter{ic}\makebox(0,0)[l]{\,\,\arabic{ic}}}
\multiput(20,7.5)(0,5){7}{\oval(8,3)[r]%
\stepcounter{ic}\makebox(0,0)[l]{\,\arabic{ic}}}
\put(6.5,38.5){\circle*{1}}
\end{picture}
```

Both \multiput commands in this example contain two picture objects: a semi-oval and text in the form of an automatic counter. The first \multiput command generates the left side, from top to bottom, the second the right side from bottom to top. The command \newcounter{ic} establishes a new counter with the name ic, which is then incremented by \stepcounter{ic} and printed as an Arabic number with \arabic{ic}. (In the above sample source text, each of the \multiput command lines has been continued on to a second line; in fact, the commands must be typed in without blanks or carriage returns in order to avoid horizontal shifts in the picture!)

**Exercise 6.9:** *Using the cm ruler at the right as a model, generate both a vertical and a horizontal ruler of 10 cm lengths.*

**Exercise 6.10:** *Improve your graph paper from Exercise 6.5 by making every 5th* *and 10th line thicker as in the grid network shown above. Number the 10th lines along the outer edge.*

## 6.5.6   Extension packages $\boxed{2_\varepsilon}$

Two new packages that enhance the `picture` environment are available in the standard LaTeX $2_\varepsilon$ installation.

### Removing some restrictions

The restrictions on lengths and angles for sloping lines and arrows can be removed by making use of features in the printer driver. The package `pict2e` activates these capabilities for certain drivers. The results may not be truly device-independent, but should work for the most popular ones that do support such drawing possibilities.

With this package, the circles may also be drawn with any radius, being no longer limited to those available in the special circle font.

Include this package as usual with `\usepackage{graphpap}` in the preamble.

**Note:** at the time of writing this package is not yet available, hence no details on possible options or driver selection can be given here.

### Graph paper

The package `graphpap` adds a new command for drawing gridded paper:

$\boxed{2_\varepsilon}$ `\graphpaper[`*num*`](`*x*,*y*`)(`*lx*,*ly*`)`

which places a grid with its lower left corner at $(x, y)$, which is *lx* units wide and *ly* units high. Grid lines are drawn for every *num* units, with every fifth one thicker and labeled. If *num* is not specified, it is assumed to be 10. All arguments must be integers, not decimal fractions.

For example, `\graphpaper(50,50)(200,100)` produces

## 5.7  General recommendations

With practice, every user develops his or her own style for using the
`picture` environment. We would like to mention some suggestions by
Leslie Lamport, with which we fully agree, and to add a few of our own.

1. Graph paper of various grid sizes is extremely useful for sketch-
   ing and positioning the individual picture elements. With the grid
   network example, or the `\graphpaper` command, the user may produce graph paper in any desired grid size which may be copied in
   sufficient quantity for future sketches.

2. The smallest grid separation should be taken as the size of the unit
   length. This avoids decimal fractions in the placement entries.

3. If the picture contains no sloping lines, the placement coordinates
   for the picture elements may be read directly from the graph paper.
   The reference points of the individual objects should be at a grid
   point and not between them.

4. For sloping lines, there is only a limited number of possible slopes
   (Section 6.4.3). When a permissible slope is specified, the end points
   of the line should be at grid points. The same applies to arrows (Section 6.4.4). (This does not apply if the `pict2e` package is included.)

5. Pictures should be constructed out of sub-pictures, or even out of
   sub-sub-pictures (Section 6.5.2). This simplifies the positioning of
   basic picture elements by making them relative to the sub-picture.

6. Sub-pictures that are frequently used should be stored in a `\savebox`
   and collected together in one or more separate files. In this way,
   one can build up a library of symbols over the years. Such symbols
   should be documented with respect to their names, reference and
   connection points, and made available to other users.

⚠ Small errors in the `picture` environment can have devastating effects. If a
totally nonsensical result appears, there is no reason to panic. For example, if
the picture was designed for a unit length of 1 cm but no `\unitlength` has
been set, LaTeX takes a value of 1 pt as its default and the picture shrinks to
almost a point with any contained text being printed illegibly all on the same spot.
The unexpected appearance of picture elements outside of the main picture area
results from incorrect placement specifications, possibly due to a wrong sign or
a neglected decimal point.

⚠ Sometimes small errors in horizontal positioning occur, especially when several picture elements are placed with a single `\put` or `\multiput` command. This
could be caused by blanks included between the picture commands. Such blanks
are interpreted as picture elements themselves and thus shift the next symbol a
little to the right. Thus there should be no blanks or carriage returns (new lines)
between element commands. If the error persists, try changing the sequence of

the elements within the placement command. If that still does not work, use a
\put or \multiput command for each separate element.

## 6.6    Floating tables and figures

The picture environment produces a diagram at that point in the text
where it is typed in, coming between the previous and following texts.
This presents no problems, and is often desirable, as long as there is
sufficient room for it on the current page. However, if the figure (or table
for that matter) is so high that it no longer fits on the current page, that
page is terminated and the figure (or table) is placed at the top of the next
page. This means that the current page is badly formatted.

It would be better if there were a mechanism that would place the
figure or table on the current page if there is enough room for it, but
otherwise continue with the following text, holding the table or figure
in reserve until a suitable location becomes available. Since tables and
figures are often accompanied by headlines or captions, these should be
moved with them.

Such a mechanism has already been introduced in Section 4.8.4 for
tables. Here a complete description of the *float* procedures will be given.

### 6.6.1    Float placement

LaTeX does make it possible to *float* figures and tables, together with their
headlines and captions, in the manner mentioned above. This is invoked
with the environments

> \begin{figure}[*where*]   *figure*   \end{figure}
> \begin{figure*}[*where*]  *figure*   \end{figure*}
> \begin{table}[*where*]    *table*    \end{table}
> \begin{table*}[*where*]   *table*    \end{table*}

The *-forms apply only to the two column page format and insert the
figure or table across both columns instead of the normal single column.
They function exactly the same as the standard forms when the page
format is single column.

In the above syntax, *figure* and *table* are the texts for the contents of
the float, either in picture or tabular environments, together with a
possible \caption command, as described later in Section 6.6.4.

The argument *where* specifies the allowed locations for the figure or
table. There are several possibilities so that *where* consists of from zero
to four letters with the following meanings:

  h *here*: the float may appear at that point in the text where the
    environment is typed in; this is not permitted for the *-form;

t *top*: the float may appear at the top of the current page, provided there is enough room for both it and the previous text; if this is not the case, it is added at the top of the next page; the subsequent text continues on the current page until the next normal page break; (for two column format, read *column* in place of *page*);

b *bottom*: the float may be placed at the bottom of the page; the subsequent text continues until the room left on the current page is just enough for the float; if there is already insufficient room, the float will be put at the bottom of the next page; this is not permitted for the *-form;

p *page*: the float may be put on a special page (or column) containing only figures and/or tables;

$\boxed{2\varepsilon}$ ! used together with any combination of the other letters, suspends all the spacing and number restrictions described in Section 6.6.3.

The argument values may be combined to allow several possibilities. If none is given, LaTeX assumes the standard combination tbp.

The placement arguments permit certain possibilities for locating the float, but the actual insertion takes place *at the earliest possible point* in accordance with the following rules:

- no float appears on a page prior to that where it is defined;

- figures and tables are output in the order in which they were defined in the text, so that no float appears before a previously defined float of the same type; figures and tables may, however, be mixed in their output sequence; in two-column format, the double column *-floats may also appear out of sequence;

- floats will be located only at one of the allowed positions given by the placement argument *where*; without an argument, the standard combination tbp is used;

- unless the ! is included in *where*, the positioning obeys the limitations of the style parameters described in Section 6.6.3;

- for the combination ht, the argument h takes priority; the float is inserted at the point of its definition even if there is enough room for it at the top of the page.

When any of the commands \clearpage, \cleardoublepage, or \end{document} is given, all floats that have not yet been output will be printed on a separate page or column regardless of their placement arguments.

## 6.6.2   Postponing floats

Sometimes it is desired that floats do not appear on a certain page, for example at the top of a title page. (LaTeX automatically corrects that case.) However, there are other occasions where a float should be suppressed temporarily. One might want it at the top of a page, but not before the start of the section that refers to it. The command

$\boxed{2_\varepsilon}$ \suppressfloats[*loc*]

sees to it that *for the current page only* no further floats of the specified placement *loc* should appear. If the optional *loc* is omitted, all floats are suppressed; otherwise *loc* may be either t or b, but not both.

Note that \suppressfloats does not suppress all floats for the current page, but only *further* ones that come between the issuing of this command and the end of the page. Thus it is possible for floats from a previous section still to appear on the page.

The command \suppressfloats and the location parameter !, which are both new to LaTeX $2_\varepsilon$, are attempts to give the author more control over the sometimes capricious actions of float placement.

## 6.6.3   Style parameters for floats

$\boxed{!}$ There are a number of style parameters that influence the placement of floats, which may be altered by the user as desired.

topnumber
> The maximum number of floats that may appear at the top of a page.

bottomnumber
> The maximum number of floats that may appear at the bottom of a page.

totalnumber
> The maximum number of floats that may appear on any page regardless of position.

dbltopnumber
> The same as topnumber but for floats that extend over both columns in two-column page format.

The above parameters are all *counters* and may be reset to new values with the command \setcounter{*ctr*}{*num*}, where *ctr* is the name of the counter and *num* the new value that it is to take on.

\topfraction
> A decimal number that specifies what fraction of the page may be used for floats at the top.

\bottomfraction
> A decimal number that specifies what fraction of the page may be used for floats at the bottom.

\textfraction

> The fraction of a page that must be filled with text. This is a minimum, so that the fraction available for floats, whether top or bottom, can never be more than 1−\textfraction.

\floatpagefraction

> The smallest fraction of a float page that is to be filled with floats before a new page is called.

\dbltopfraction

> The same as \topfraction but for double column floats in two-column page format.

\dblfloatpagefraction

> The same as \floatpagefraction but for double column floats in two-column page format.

These style parameters are altered with \renewcommand{*cmd*}{*frac*} where *cmd* stands for the parameter name and *frac* for the new decimal value, which in every case must be less than 1.

\floatsep

> The vertical spacing between floats appearing either at the top or at the bottom of a page.

\textfloatsep

> The vertical spacing between floats and text, for both top and bottom floats.

\intextsep

> The vertical spacing above and below a float that appears in the middle of a text page with the h placement argument.

\dblfloatsep

> The same as \floatsep but for double column floats in two-column page format.

\dbltextfloatsep

> The same as \textfloatsep but for double column floats in two-column page format.

This group of style declarations are rubber lengths that may be changed with the \setlength command (Section 2.4.2).

[2ε] \topfigrule

> A command that is executed after a float at the top of a page. It may be used to add a rule to separate the float from the main text. Whatever it adds must have zero height.

[2ε] \botfigrule

> Similar to \topfigrule, but is executed before a float that appears at the bottom of a page.

[2ε] \dblfigrule

> Similar to \topfigrule, but for double column floats.

These three commands normally do nothing, but they may be redefined if necessary. For example, to add a rule of thickness 0.4 pt below a top float,

```
\renewcommand{\topfigrule}{\vspace*{-3pt}
  \rule{\columnwidth}{0.4pt}\vspace{2.6pt} }
```

Because of the negative argument in \vspace*, the total vertical spacing is zero, as required.

All the one-column style parameters also function within the two-column page format, but they apply only to floats that fill up one column.

If the style parameters are set to new values within the preamble, they apply from the first page onwards. However, if they are changed within a document, they do not take effect until the next page.

## 6.6.4   Float captions

A figure caption or table title is produced with the command

\caption[*short_title*]{*caption_text*}

inside the figure or table environment. The *caption_text* is the text that is printed with the float and may be fairly long. The *short_title* is optional and is the text that appears in the list of figures or tables (Section 3.4.4). If it is missing, it is set equal to *caption_text*. The *short_title* should be given if the *caption_text* is longer than about 300 characters, or if it is more than one line long.

In the table environment, the \caption command generates a title of the form 'Table *n*: *caption_text*', and in the figure environment 'Figure *n*: *caption_text*', where *n* is a sequential number that is automatically incremented. In document class article, the figures and tables are numbered from 1 through to the end of the document. For the report and book classes, they are numbered within each chapter in the form *c.n*, where *c* is the current chapter number and *n* is the sequential number reset to 1 at the start of each chapter. Figures and tables are numbered independently of one another.

The \caption command may be omitted if numbering is unwanted, since any text included in the *float* environment will accompany the contents. The advantages of \caption over simple text are the automatic numbering and entries in the lists of figures and tables. However, a manual entry in these lists may be made as described in Section 3.4.4 using

\addcontentsline   and   \addtocontents

A *title*, or *headline*, is produced with \caption when the command comes at the beginning of the material in the *float* environment: the number and text are printed above the table or figure. A *caption* is added below the object if the command comes after all the other float commands. In other words, the \caption is just another item within the float and whether its text appears at the top (as *title*) or below (as *caption*) depends on how the user places it.

**Table 6.1**: Computer Center Budget for 1995

| Nr. | Item | 51505 | 52201 | 53998 | Total |
|---|---|---|---|---|---|
| 1.1 | Maintenance | 130 000 | | 15 000 | 145 000 |
| 1.2 | Network costs | 5 000 | | 23 000 | 28 000 |
| 1.3 | Repairs | 25 000 | 6 000 | | 31 000 |
| 1.4 | Expendables | | 68 000 | | 68 000 |
| 1. | Total | 160 000 | 74 000 | 38 000 | 272 000 |

The *caption_text* will be centered if it is shorter than one line, otherwise it is set as a normal paragraph. The total width may be adjusted to that of the table or figure by placing the command inside a parbox or minipage. For example,

`\parbox{`*width*`}{\caption{`*caption_text*`}}`

The following examples contain further examples of how text, table, and picture commands may be combined in floats.

## 6.5  Float examples

The first two tables are produced with the following texts:

```
\begin{table} \caption{Computer Center Budget for 1995}
   \begin{tabular}{|l|l||r|r|r|r|} ... ...   \end{tabular}
\end{table}
```

(This text was typed in before the last paragraph of the previous section. The second table is entered here in the current text.)

```
\begin{table}
   \caption{\textbf{Estimates for 1996} {\em A continuation...}}
   \begin{tabular}{|l|l||r|r|r|r|} ... ... ...  \end{tabular}
\end{table}
```

Because the placement argument is missing from the `table` environments, the standard values `tbp` are used. The first was placed at the top of this page because it was typed in early enough (during the last section) that there was still room for it there. Then the command `\suppressfloats` (Section 6.6.2) was issued to prevent any more floats appearing on the same page. The second table is therefore forced to float to the top of the next page.

Narrow figures or tables may be set beside each other, as shown in the following example (which appears at the bottom of the following page).

```
\begin{figure}[b]
\unitlength1cm
```

**Table 6.2: Estimates for 1996.** *A continuation of the previous budget is no longer practical since, with the installation of the new computing system in 1995, the operating conditions have been completely overhauled.*

| Nr. | Item | 51505 | 52201 | 53998 | Total |
|-----|------|-------|-------|-------|-------|
| 1.1 | Maintenance | 240 000 | | | 240 000 |
| 1.2 | Line costs | 12 000 | 8 000 | 36 000 | 56 000 |
| 1.3 | Training | | | 50 000 | 50 000 |
| 1.4 | Expansion | 80 000 | 3 000 | | 83 000 |
| 1.5 | Expendables | | 42 000 | | 42 000 |
| 1. | Total | 332 000 | 53 000 | 86 000 | 471 000 |

```
\begin{minipage}[t]{5.0cm}
\begin{picture}(5.0,2.5) ... ... \end{picture}\par
\caption{Left}
\end{minipage}
\hfill
\begin{minipage}[t]{6.0cm}
\begin{picture}(6.0,3.0) ... ... \end{picture}\par
\caption{Right}
\end{minipage}
\end{figure}
```

The two figures along with their captions are each set in a `minipage` environment of widths 5 and 6 cm. The minipages are separated from one another by an \hfill space. The positioning argument t has the effect that the minipages are aligned along their first lines (Section 4.7.3). The entire structure within the `figure` environment floats as a single entity.

The question might now arise as to why, since the two figures have unequal heights and are supposedly aligned vertically along their top lines, their bottom edges are at the same level. The explanation is that a `picture` environment establishes an LR box (Section 4.7.1) to contain all the picture commands, and that is viewed by LaTeX as a single line of

Figure 6.1: Left　　　　　　　　　Figure 6.2: Right

output text with the baseline at the bottom edge of the picture. In both minipages, the picture environment is the first entry and is therefore the first logical line of text. It is these baselines that are taken for the vertical alignment of the minipages.

If the two pictures were to be aligned along their top edges, it would be necessary to include a dummy first line (Section 4.7.4) in each minipage before the picture environments. This could be something like \mbox{}, for example.

The application of box commands within a float permits completely free positioning. If the caption text is to appear, say, beside the table or figure, instead of above or below it, the objects may be put into minipages or parboxes with suitable alignment arguments. Here is an example:

```
\begin{table}[b]
  \centerline{\bfseries Results and Seat Distribution of the...}
  \mbox{\small
  \begin{minipage}[b]{7.7cm}
    \begin{minipage}[t]{4.4cm}
      \mbox{}\\ \unitlength0.75cm
      \begin{picture}(5.75,5.0) ... ... ... \end{picture}
    \end{minipage} \hfill
    \parbox[t]{3.2cm}{\makebox[0cm]{}\\{\bfseries Seat ...} ...}
  \end{minipage}
  \hspace{-3cm}
  \begin{minipage}[b]{7cm}
    \parbox[b]{2.5cm}{{\bfseries Results:}\\ General Election...}
    \hfill
    \begin{tabular}[b]{|l||r|r|} ... ... \end{tabular}
  \end{minipage} }
\end{table}
```

Here the vertical boxes are nested inside one another. The left side, consisting of graphics and a title at the upper right, is contained in a minipage of width 7.7 cm, in which the picture is in another minipage of width 4.4 cm while the text is in a parbox of width 3.2 cm. Both are aligned with the top lines. A dummy line

**Results and Seat Distribution of the 1994 General Election**

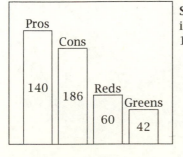

**Seat Distribution**
in the Assembly of
1994–1998

**Results:**
1994 General
Election

| Party | Votes | % |
|---|---|---|
| Pros | 15 031 287 | 37.7 |
| Cons | 12 637 418 | 31.7 |
| Reds | 6 499 210 | 16.3 |
| Greens | 4 486 514 | 11.3 |
| Others | 1 201 078 | 3.0 |

containing \mbox{} (Section 4.7.4) is added before the first picture to provide a top line with which the second parbox can be aligned.

The right-hand side consists of a minipage of width 7 cm, shifted to the left by 3 cm, aligned with the left-hand minipage along the bottom lines. It contains a parbox of width 2.5 cm for the text as well as a table, which is automatically a vertical box. Both of these are aligned with the bottom lines.

## 6.6.6   References to figures and tables in text

The automatic numbering of tables and figures has the consequence that the author does not know the numbers at the time of writing. Since he or she would like to be able to refer to these objects by number, as 'see Figure 3' or 'Table 5 illustrates', another means of referencing must be found. It is not sufficient to keep track of the number of \caption calls that have been made, since the document may not be written in the order in which it finally appears, and new figures or tables may be inserted during revision, or some removed.

These problems are solved with the LaTeX cross-reference system, described in more detail in Section 8.3.1. The basic commands are

\label{*name*}     \ref{*name*}

which assign a keyword *name* to the figure or table number that may be used as reference in the text. The keyword *name* may be any combination of letters, numbers, or symbols. The assignment is made with the \label command given anywhere within the caption text of the \caption command; in the main text, the command \ref inserts the number that is associated with its keyword.

This is best shown with an example. The budget table on page 177 was actually written as

\caption{\label{budget95} Computer Center ... }

so that Table \ref{budget95} produces 'Table 6.1' when used in the main text.

There is a second referencing command \pageref to generate the page number where the referenced object is to be found. For example, a few lines up, the input text on page \pageref{budget95} was used to create the text '... on page 177'.

# User Customization

**7**

LaTeX allows the user to define his or her own commands and environments. However, since these make extensive use of the LaTeX counters and lengths, we will first present a more detailed discussion of these objects and how they may be manipulated.

## Counters

### .1  LaTeX counters

LaTeX manages a number of counters by giving them initial values at the start and by changing these values when certain commands are called. Most of these counters have the same name as the commands that alter them:

| part | chapter | paragraph | figure | enumi |
|------|---------|-----------|--------|-------|
| | section | subparagraph | table | enumii |
| | subsection | page | footnote | enumiii |
| | subsubsection | equation | mpfootnote | enumiv |

The meanings of most of these counters are obvious from their names and need no further explanation. The counters `enumi` ... `enumiv` refer to the four levels of the `enumerate` environment (Sections 4.3.4 and 4.3.5), while the counter `mpfootnote` controls the footnote numbering within the `minipage` environment (Section 4.10.4).

In addition to these counters, there may be further counters created by the `\newtheorem` command, having the same name as the *struct_type* argument (Section 4.5). For the two examples of the `\newtheorem` command on page 79, this book also contains the counters `theorem` and `axiom`.

The value of a counter is an integer number, usually non-negative. A command may output several numbers at once: the current `\subsection` command outputs 7.1.1, in which case more than one counter is addressed

181

at a time. For example, the \subsection command increments the value of the subsection counter by one, and prints the values of the chapter, section, and subsection counters, separated by periods. At the same time, this command sets the counter subsubsection to zero without it actually appearing.

## 7.1.2   User-defined counters

The user may create new counters with the command

\newcounter{*counter_name*}[*in_counter*]

where *counter_name* is the name of the newly established counter. This may be any combination of letters that is not already the name of an existing counter. Thus none of the names of the LaTeX counters listed above may be used as *counter_name* nor any name of a previously defined user counter. The optional argument *in_counter* is the name of another counter that already exists (LaTeX or user defined) and has the effect that the newly defined counter is reset to zero whenever *in_counter* is incremented by one of the commands \stepcounter or \refstepcounter (see below).

When a counter has been created with \newcounter, its initial value is zero.

The \newcounter command may not appear in any file that is read in with the \include command (Section 8.1.2). It is therefore best to put all \newcounter commands into the preamble.

## 7.1.3   Changing counter values

Every counter, whether LaTeX or user defined, can have its value altered with the following commands:

\setcounter{*counter*}{*num*}
>   This command is self-explanatory: the specified *counter* is assigned the integer value *num*.

\addtocounter{*counter*}{*num*}
>   With this command, the value of the *counter* is increased by the integer *num*, which may be positive or negative.

\stepcounter{*counter*}
>   The value of the *counter* is increased by one, and at the same time all its sub-counters (that is, those that have this counter as their *in_counter*) are reset to zero (see above).

\refstepcounter{*counter*}
>   This command has the same effect as \stepcounter but also makes *counter* the current counter for the cross-referencing command \label (see Section 8.3.1).

This last command may be applied, for example, within the `figure` or `table` environments when the `\caption` command is missing and yet there is to be a reference in the text to the figure or table number using the `\ref` command. Then `\refstepcounter{figure}` or `\refstepcounter {table}` is given within that float environment to bring the corresponding counter to the right value and to allow that value to be assigned a keyword with the `\label` command (Section 8.3.1).

The value of a counter may be treated as a number with the command

> `\value{`*counter*`}`

which does not change the value at all. This command is mostly used in connection with `\setcounter` or `\addtocounter`. For example, if the user-defined counter mypage has been created, it may be set to the same value as the page counter page by giving `\setcounter{mypage}{\value {page}}`.

Normally the `\protect` command, which prevents fragile commands from being broken up during transport, may also be included in front of robust commands without any harm being done. The `\value` is the exception to this rule. It may never be preceded by the `\protect` command.

## .4    Printing counter values

The numerical value in a counter can be printed with the commands

> | `\arabic{`*counter*`}` | as an Arabic number, |
> | `\Roman{`*counter*`}` | as a capital Roman numeral, |
> | `\roman{`*counter*`}` | as a lower case Roman numeral, |
> | `\alph{`*counter*`}` | as a lower case letter, |
> | `\Alph{`*counter*`}` | as a capital letter, |
> | `\fnsymbol{`*counter*`}` | as a footnote symbol. |

For the commands `\alph` and `\Alph`, the numbers 1...26 correspond to the letters *a...z* and A...Z. It is up to the user to ensure that the counter value lies within this range. For `\fnsymbol`, the numbers 1...9 are output as the symbols   * † ‡ § ¶ ‖ ** †† ‡‡. Here again, the user must take care that the counter does not reach a value of 10 or more.

For some of the counters commands of the form

> `\the`*counter*

are also available, consisting of `\the` immediately followed by the name of the counter, such as `\thepage`. This type of command is often identical to `\arabic{`*counter*`}`, but may sometimes be composed of several counter commands. In the document classes book and report, for example, the command `\thesection` is defined in terms of both the chapter and section numbers: \arabic{chapter}.\arabic{section}. Here is the result of printing \thesection at this point: 7.1.

The automatic printing of counter values such as the page, equation, or sectioning numbers is accomplished by means of calls to the appropriate \the*counter* commands. If a different format for some automatic numbering is desired, say alphabetical equation numbers, the definition of the corresponding \the*counter* command can be altered using the methods described in Section 7.3.

*Exercise 7.1:* *Take your standard* exercise.tex *file and print out the final values of the LaTeX counters with* \arabic{counter} *commands at the end. Change some the values with the* \setcounter *and* \addtocounter *commands and print the values out once more.*

## 7.2    Lengths

It has been constantly pointed out in all the descriptions of the length parameters such as \parskip or \textwidth that new values may be assigned with the \setlength command.  Some of these parameters expect rubber length values that may stretch or shrink. These are mainly parameters that produce vertical spacing.  The types of length units, both fixed and rubber, are described in detail in Section 2.4.  This will not be repeated here, but rather additional commands for assigning and handling lengths are discussed in this section.

The standard LaTeX method for assigning a value to a length parameter is with the command

> \setlength{\\*length_cmd*}{*length_spec*}

where *length_spec* may be a length specification (with units) or another length parameter.  In the latter case, \\*length_cmd* takes on the current value of that other parameter.  Thus with \setlength{\rightmargin}{\leftmargin} the right-hand margin in a list environment is set to the same value as that of the left-hand margin.

Lengths may be increased with

> \addtolength{\\*length_cmd*}{*length_spec*}

which adds *length_spec* to the value of the length parameter \\*length_cmd*. A negative value for *length_spec* decreases \\*length_cmd* by that amount. Once again, another length parameter may be used for *length_spec*, with or without a preceding minus sign, and its value will be added or subtracted. A decimal number just before a length parameter multiplies its value by that quantity: 0.5\textwidth means half the width of the text column and 2\parskip twice the inter-paragraph spacing.

With the command

> \settowidth{\\*length_cmd*}{*text*}

the length parameter \\*length_cmd* is set equal the natural length of a piece of text set in LR mode (normal left-to-right).

Similarly the commands

> [2ε] \settoheight{\\*length_cmd*}{*text*}
> [2ε] \settodepth{\\*length_cmd*}{*text*}

set the \\*length_cmd* equal to the height and depth of the *text* above and below the baseline, respectively.

Finally, the command

> \stretch{*decimal_num*}

yields a rubber length that is *decimal_num* times as stretchable as \fill (Section 2.4.2).

A user-defined length parameter is created with

> \newlength{\\*new_len_cmd*}

which establishes \\*new_len_cmd* as a length with a value of 0pt. All the above commands may be used to manipulate its value further.

The command

> \addvspace{*length_spec*}

inserts extra vertical spacing of the amount *length_spec* at that point where it appears. If more than one such command is given, the total inserted spacing will be that of the largest argument and not the sum of them all. This command may only be given *between* paragraphs. Its application for user-defined commands and environments lies in the generation of structures that should behave like paragraphs.

## 3   User-defined commands

New commands may be defined or redefined under LaTeX with the commands

> [2ε] \newcommand   {\\*com_name*}[*narg*][*opt*]{*def*}
> [2ε] \renewcommand{\\*com_name*}[*narg*][*opt*]{*def*}

or

> [2.09] \newcommand   {\\*com_name*}[*narg*]{*def*}
> [2.09] \renewcommand{\\*com_name*}[*narg*]{*def*}

The first version is used to define a command \\*com_name* that does not yet exist. Its name may be any combination of letters that do not form the name of another command. The second version redefines an already existing command \\*com_name*. In both cases, an error message is printed if the incorrect variant is called. The first optional argument *narg* is a number between 1 and 9 specifying how many arguments the new or altered command is to have. In LaTeX 2ε, a second optional argument *opt* gives the default value for an optional argument that the new command may take. The actual definition of the command is contained in the text *def*.

## 7.3.1   Commands without arguments

We will first illustrate the use of the \newcommand without the optional argument [*narg*]. This form is applied when a fixed combination of LaTeX or user commands is to be repeated frequently as a command with its own name. For example, the structure $x_1, \ldots, x_n$, called an x-vector, often occurs in mathematical formulas and is formed in math mode with x_1,\ldots,x_n. Typing

> \newcommand{\xvec}{x_1,\ldots,x_n}

creates a new command named \xvec that may be called and used just like any other command. When called, it inserts the sequence of text and commands, in this case x_1,\ldots,x_n, into the current text exactly as if one had typed it oneself. In fact, this is precisely what happens: when \xvec is called, it is its definition that goes into the LaTeX processing.

Since the new command \xvec contains a math command (the subscript command _), it may only be called within math mode. Thus $\xvec$ is required to produce $x_1, \ldots, x_n$ in text mode. It might therefore seem a good idea to include the switching to math mode in the definition itself, as

> \newcommand{\xvec}{$x_1,\ldots,x_n$}

Now \xvec yields $x_1, \ldots, x_n$. However, this command may only be applied in text and never in math mode. There is a trick to enable the command to be called in both modes: define it as

> 〔2ε〕 \newcommand{\xvec}{\ensuremath{x_1,\ldots,x_n}}

Now both \xvec and $\xvec$ are allowed, both with the same result.

(In LaTeX 2.09, the command \ensuremath does not exist. Instead, one must use \mbox{$...$}. In text mode, the \mbox is ignored, but in math mode, it temporarily switches to text mode, from which the $ signs activate math mode. The two methods do not produce identical results, and \ensuremath is to be preferred in LaTeX 2ε.)

The above text mode example was actually written as \xvec{}, since TeX treats it as a command without arguments, terminating its name with the first non-letter that it finds. If this character is a blank, it only ends the command name and does not insert inter-word spacing (Section 2.1). Thus \xvec and ... produces '$x_1, \ldots, x_n$ and ...' without any spacing between. This problem is solved by adding a space command \␣ or the empty structure {} after the command name, in this case as \xvec\␣ or \xvec{}.

It would also have been possible to include the blank in the definition of \xvec, as {\ensuremath{x_1,\ldots,x_n} }. Now the blank following the command name is still removed, but the command itself inserts one to make up for it. However, this is not recommended practice since this 'programmed' blank will always be present, even when some punctuation or other symbol directly follows the command.

The different versions of the above example were all illustrated with the command \newcommand, although in fact this command may only be used once to initiate a user-defined command that does not already exist. Once \xvec has been created, a revised definition can only be given with the command \renewcommand. This was indeed done with the second and subsequent definitions of \xvec.

Following this example, the user may employ \newcommand (or alternatively \renewcommand) to combine any set of commands and text to form a command under a new name that may then be called whenever necessary. In this way, a considerable amount of typing can be avoided and the possibility of error reduced, especially for complex mathematical structures.

If it is not known whether or not a command with the chosen name already exists, one may use instead

$\boxed{2_\varepsilon}$ \providecommand{\com_name}[narg][opt]{def}

which has the same syntax as \newcommand and \renewcommand. The difference is that if the command already exists, the new definition will be ignored. The opposite effect (overwriting the current definition of a command without knowing if it already exists) can be achieved by first calling \providecommand to ensure the command exists, and then issuing the true definition with \renewcommand. However, this should be done only with great care!

*Exercise 7.2: Define the commands* \iint, \iiint, *and* \idotsint, *to make the multiple integrals shown at the right as displayed formulas, or as the following text formulas:* $\iint, \iiint, \int \cdots \int$
$$\iint \quad \iiint \quad \int \cdots \int$$

*Exercise 7.3: Change the* \thechapter, \thesection, *and* \thesubsection *commands so that for the document classes* book *and* report *the chapter numbering is done with capital letters, such as B, the section numbering with capital Roman numerals after the chapter letter, in the form B–III, and the sub-section numbering with lower case Roman numerals following a comma: B–III,v.*
*Hint: the original versions of these commands in* book *and* report *are defined as*

```
\newcommand{\thechapter}{\arabic{chapter}}
\newcommand{\thesection}{\thechapter.\arabic{section}}
\newcommand{\thesubsection}{\thesection.\arabic{subsection}}
```

*Now apply* \renewcommand *to make the required changes.*

## 7.3.2  Commands with arguments

In addition to the structure $x_1, \ldots, x_n$, there are the equivalent vectors $y_1, \ldots, y_n$ and $z_1, \ldots, z_n$ in mathematics. It would be possible to define commands \yvec and \zvec following the pattern for \xvec. However, it is also possible to define a generalized vector command and to specify the variable part as an argument. In the present example, the variable part is the letter $x$, $y$, or $z$. A command with *one* variable part is created with the optional argument [1]. For example,

```
\newcommand{\avec}[1]{\ensuremath{#1_1,\ldots,#1_n}}
```

defines the general vector command \avec{*arg*}. Calling \avec{x} yields $x_1, \ldots, x_n$ while invoking \avec{y} prints out $y_1, \ldots, y_n$. The character #1 in the command definition is a dummy argument representing the text of *arg* that replaces all occurrences of #1 when the command is called. By imagining an x or a y at each location of the #1 in the definition, the desired structures in each case can be recognized.

The digit 1 in the dummy argument #1 seems at first to be rather pointless. In fact, for a command with only one argument it really has no meaning. However, its function becomes more obvious for commands with *multiple* arguments. Let us say, for example, that we want a command to generate structures such as not only $u_1, \ldots, u_n$ but also $v_1, \ldots, v_m$. This requires two arguments, one to specify the letter $u$, $v$, etc., and a second to determine the last subscript $n$, $m$, and so on. Such a command is created with

```
\newcommand{\anvec}[2]{\ensuremath{#1_1,\ldots,#1_#2}}
```

and invoked as \anvec{u}{n} for $u_1, \ldots, u_n$ and as \anvec{v}{m} for $u_1, \ldots, u_m$. The optional argument [2] for \newcommand says that the command being defined contains two arguments; in the definition part, #1 is replaced by the first argument and #2 by the second. By imagining u or v in place of #1 and n or m where #2 stands, one can see how the command \anvec{*arg1*}{*arg2*} operates.

This pattern may be carried on for even more arguments. With

```
\newcommand{\subvec}[3]{\ensuremath{#1_#2,\ldots,#1_#3}}
```

a command \subvec is defined with three arguments. It should be clear from the definition that calling \subvec{a}{i}{j} produces $a_i, \ldots, a_j$.

A command argument that consists of only a single character need not be put into curly brackets { } but may be given directly. If it is the first argument, it must be separated from the command name with a blank, as usual. Thus the sequence `\subvec aik` is the same as `\subvec{a}{i}{k}`, and `\subvec x1n` produces the same structure $x_1, \ldots, x_n$ as our first user-defined example `\xvec`.

Arguments must be enclosed in curly brackets { } when they contain more than one character, since the brackets indicate that the contents are to be treated as a unit. Thus `\subvec{A}{ij}{lk}` prints out $A_i j, \ldots, A_l k$. The three replacement arguments are `A` for `#1`, `ij` for `#2`, and `lk` for `#3`.

Why does `\subvec{A}{ij}{lk}` produce $A_i j, \ldots, A_l k$ and not the expected result $A_{ij}, \ldots, A_{lk}$? The answer is that, although the arguments within curly brackets are set as units into the definition text, the brackets themselves are not. Here, the command text after replacement looks like `\ensuremath{A_ij,\ldots,A_lk}` so that only the first characters following the subscript symbols _ are actually lowered. In order for both letters to be lowered, they must be seen as a unit within the command text, that is as `$A_{ij},\ldots,A_{lk}$`. This may be achieved with the `\subvec` command by including an extra set of brackets in the arguments: `\subvec{A}{{ij}}{{lk}}`. A better solution, however, is to put the brackets in the definition to begin with:

```
\renewcommand{\subvec}[3]{\ensuremath{#1_{#2},\ldots,#1_{#3}}}
```

which will always produce the desired result with only a single set of brackets per argument: `\subvec{A}{ij}{lk}` prints $A_{ij}, \ldots, A_{lk}$.

## .3   Commands with an optional argument $\boxed{2\varepsilon}$

As we have seen, many LaTeX commands may take *optional* arguments, including the command `\newcommand` itself. In LaTeX $2_\varepsilon$, it is also possible to define user commands with one optional argument. The advantage of this is that, although an argument is provided, in most applications it will usually take some standard value that need not be given explicitly.

As an example, the user-defined vector command `\subvec` in the last section has three arguments, for the letter and for the first and last subscripts. However, it may be that the letter is normally `x`, so it makes sense to include it as an optional argument, which is to be specified only for a different letter. This is accomplished with

```
\renewcommand{\subvec}[3][x]{\ensuremath{#1_{#2},\ldots,#1_{#3}}}
```

The difference between this and the previous definition is the addition of `[x]` after the `[3]` argument. This states that the *first* of the 3 arguments is to be optional, and its standard value is `x`. Now `\subvec{i}{j}` prints $x_i, \ldots, x_j$ while `\subvec[a]{1}{n}` produces $a_1, \ldots, a_n$.

There may only be one optional argument in the user-defined command, and it must always be the first one, the `#1` in the definition.

## .4   Additional examples of user-defined commands

In the above explanation of user-defined commands, a very simple case of a vector structure was taken as an example. We would now like to demonstrate some more complex situations, in which counters, lengths, and even some special TEX commands are applied.

**Example 1:** In Section 5.4.6, the TEX commands \atop and \choose were presented as useful mathematical commands even for LATEX applications. Unfortunately, the syntax of these commands deviates considerably from that of the similar LATEX command \frac. However,

```
\newcommand{\latop}[2]{#1\atop\#2}        and
\newcommand{\lchoose}[2]{#1\choose\#2}
```

define two commands \latop and \lchoose that yield the same results with a syntax like that of LATEX: \latop{*upper*}{*lower*}.

**Example 2:** The command \defbox{*sample_text*} is to set a box width equal to the length of the text *sample_text*. A subsequent call to the command \textbox{*text*} centers *text* within a frame with the same width as *sample_text*.

```
\newlength{\wdth}
\newcommand{\defbox}[1]{\settowidth{\wdth}{#1}}
\newcommand{\textbox}[1]{\framebox[\wdth]{#1}}
```

First, a new length parameter \wdth is created, then \defbox is defined so that \wdth is set equal to the length of its argument (Section 7.2), and finally \textbox makes a framed box of that same width containing its argument, centered. (Do not call the length parameter \width, for this already exists, Section 4.7.5.)

```
as wide as this text\\
\defbox{as wide as this text}\textbox{}\\
\textbox{text}\\
\textbox{longer text}
```

as wide as this text

| text |
|---|
| longer text |

**Example 3:** A footnote command \myftnote is to be created that behaves as the normal command \footnote{*text*} in putting *text* into a footnote, but instead of using numbers as the marker, it should take the symbols * † ‡ § ¶ ‖ ** †† ‡‡ one after the other, starting again with the symbol * on each new page. First a new counter must be established that will be reset to zero every time the page counter is incremented. This is done with (see Section 7.1.2)

```
\newcounter{myfn}[page]
```

making a user-defined counter myfn that is set to zero every time the page counter is incremented. Next the command

```
\renewcommand{\thefootnote}{\fnsymbol{footnote}}
```

redefines the footnote marker to be that symbol in the sequence given by the counter footnote (Sections 4.10.2 and 7.1.4). Now the actual new footnote command can be constructed with

```
\newcommand{\myftnote}[1]{\setcounter{footnote}{\value{myfn}}%
    \footnote{#1}\stepcounter{myfn}}
```

yielding the desired results.* The user-defined command \myftnote possesses one argument, which is passed to the LaTeX \footnote command after the LaTeX counter footnote has been set equal to the value of the user counter myfn. Once the command \footnote has been executed, the counter myfn is then incremented by one with \stepcounter{myfn}. This counter, however, is reset to zero whenever the page counter is incremented, that is, whenever a new page begins.

The footnote on the previous page was generated with the command \myftnote as described. It is now used here[†] and again here[‡], demonstrating how the symbols have been reset on a new page.

**Example 4:** A command \alpheqn is to be set up so that once it has been called, the subsequent equations will all have the same number but be followed by letters *a, b, . . .* , separated by a hyphen '-' from the number. The command \reseteqn restores the numbering scheme to its original style. Thus a sequence of equation numbers could be 4, 5, 6-a, 6-b, 7.

```
\newcounter{saveeqn}%
\newcommand{\alpheqn}{\setcounter{saveeqn}{\value{equation}}%
\stepcounter{saveeqn}\setcounter{equation}{0}%
\renewcommand{\theequation}
       {\mbox{\arabic{saveeqn}-\alph{equation}}}}%
\newcommand{\reseteqn}{\setcounter{equation}{\value{saveeqn}}%
\renewcommand{\theequation}{\arabic{equation}}}%
```

The example should be easy to comprehend with the help of the commands and counters in Section 7.1. The current value of counter equation is saved in the counter saveeqn and then incremented, while equation itself is set to zero. The form of the equation marker, \theequation, is redefined using these two counters. The equation numbering routines will operate on equation as usual, leaving saveeqn unchanged. The resetting command \reseteqn puts the value of saveeqn back into equation and restores the definition of \theequation.

This example is only appropriate for the document class article. For report and book, the definition of \theequation is

```
\arabic{chapter}.\arabic{equation}
```

The necessary modifications are left as an exercise for the reader.

The \mbox command in the first \renewcommand{\theequation} defining the combined equation number is necessary because the result will be printed

---

*The % sign at the end of the first line is there to prevent the implied blank at the end from being interpreted as part of the command (Section 4.11). It is often necessary to split command definitions over several lines to improve readability.

[†]another footnote

[‡]and yet another footnote

in *math mode*, where the hyphen '-' is interpreted as a binary operator (minus sign) with extra spacing between it and its two 'operands', \arabic{saveeqn} and \alph{equation}. Thus $6 - a$ would be output instead of 6-a. The \mbox command causes a temporary switch out of math into LR mode.

**Example 5:** Finally we give an example making use of some very fundamental TEX commands, which therefore cannot be fully explained here. Nevertheless, it could be useful to someone who needs to write text containing many chemical formulas.

In Section 5.4.9 it was pointed out that the indices in the chemical formula $Fe_2^{2+}Cr_2O_4$ are not all at the same level, and that relatively short formulas are awkward to set within text mode. The user-defined command

```
\newlength{\fntxvi} \newlength{\fntxvii}
\newcommand{\chemical}[1]
{{\fontencoding{OMS}\fontfamily{cmsy}\selectfont
  \fntxvi\the\fontdimen16\font
  \fntxvii\the\fontdimen17\font
  \fontdimen16\font=3pt\fontdimen17\font=3pt
  $\mathrm{#1}$
  \fontencoding{OMS}\fontfamily{cmys}\selectfont
  \fontdimen16\font=\fntxvi \fontdimen17\font=\fntxvii}}
```

can remove these minor problems. Now \chemical{Fe_2^{2+}Cr_20_4} produces the correct form $Fe_2^{2+}Cr_2O_4$.

Explanation: the TEX commands \fontdimen*n* describe certain properties of the character fonts, such that $n = 16$ and $n = 17$ determine the positions of indices (subscripts). The commands in the lines ending with \selectfont (described in Section 8.5.1) make the mathematical symbol font current with its internal designation stored in the TEX command \font. All indices in math formulas of the current size (here 10 pt) are to be lowered uniformly by 3.0 pt. See the hints in Exercise 7.7 for other sizes. Since changes in \fontdimen are always *global* (they are not restored to their previous values on exit from a true or implicit environment) it is necessary to save the current values first, and then reset them manually.

**Exercise 7.4:** *Define LATEX commands* \lbrack *and* \lbrace *in the same manner as in Example 1 for* \latop *and* \lchoose *corresponding to the TEX commands* \brack *and* \brace*. These TEX commands behave as* \choose *from Section 5.4.6 except that they enclose their contents in square brackets [*\lbrack*] or curly braces {*\lbrace*}.*

**Exercise 7.5:** *Generalize Example 4 with a command* \vareqn{num}{type} *to make the subsequent equation numbers have the value num followed by a running number in square brackets printed as* \alph ... \Roman*, as given by the argument type. For example,* 33[A], 33[B], *would result from calling* \vareqn{33}{\Alph}*.*

*Exercise 7.6:* Generalize the integral commands in Exercise 7.2 to include an argument to represent the area of integration set centered below the entire symbol. Thus \iint{(D)}, \iiint{V}, and \idotsint{G} should produce:

 Hint: the second command can be made simply with a subscript on the middle integral (but see \limits in Section 5.2.5). For the other two, negative horizontal shifting of the subscripted symbol is needed using \hspace{-..}.

*Exercise 7.7:* The value of 3 pt for the subscripts in chemical formulas in Example 5 above is appropriate for a font size of 10 pt. For 11 and 12 pt, values of 3.3 and 3.6 pt would be more suitable. Extend the command \chemical so that this value is an optional argument with a standard value of 3 pt. This means that for 12 pt font size, it would be called as \chemical[3.6pt]{...}.

## .5   Conditional text

Practiced TeX users will be familiar with the conditional commands that are available, both for TeX and LaTeX. However, their usage is not always straightforward and often requires extensive knowledge of TeX's deeper principles. Leslie Lamport has provided a package named ifthen, which has been extended by David Carlisle for LaTeX$2\varepsilon$, which not only simplifies their application, but also gives them a LaTeX syntax.

   The package is loaded as usual with the command

$\boxed{2\varepsilon}$ \usepackage{ifthen}

in the preamble, or by specifying it as an 'option' in \documentstyle, as

$\boxed{2.09}$ \documentstyle[..,ifthen,..]{...}

It then makes available the two commands \ifthenelse and \whiledo, which have the following syntaxes:

       \ifthenelse{*test*}{*then_text*}{*else_text*}
       \whiledo{*test*}{*do_text*}

In both cases, *test* is a logical statement (explained below); in the first command, if it evaluates to ⟨*true*⟩ *then_text* is inserted into the text, otherwise *else_text* is.  In the second command, the *do_text* is inserted (executed) as long as *test* evaluates to ⟨*true*⟩. (The *do_text* must alter the inputs to *test* or it will never stop!) The texts may also contain commands, or even define or redefine commands.

   There are four types of basic logical statements which may be combined to form more complicated ones.

### Testing numbers

To compare two numbers or commands that evaluate to numbers, simply put one of the relational operators <, =, or > between them, which stand for *less than*, *equals*, and *greater than*, respectively.   The value of a counter may be tested by putting its name as the argument of the \value command. Examples:

```
\newcommand{\three}{3}
\ifthenelse {\three = 3} {O.K.} {What?}
\ifthenelse {\value{page} < 100 }
   {Page xx} {Page xxx}
```

The first case prints 'O.K.' since \three is equal to 3; in the second case *Page xx* is printed if the current page number is less than 100, else *Page xxx*. (The blanks above are added for clarity, since spaces between arguments are always ignored.)

Whether a number is even or odd can be tested with \isodd $\boxed{2\varepsilon}$

```
\ifthenelse {\isodd{\value{page}}
   {odd} {even}
```

### Testing text

To test if two commands evaluate to the same piece of text, or if a command is defined as a certain *string* of text, use

```
\equal{string1}{string2}
```

where *string1* and *string2* are texts or commands that reduce to text. For example, with

```
\ifthenelse {\equal{\name}{Fred}} {Fredrick} {??}
```

the text Fredrick is inserted if \name has been defined to be Fred (with \newcommand), otherwise two question marks are printed.

### Testing lengths

Another logical statement compares two lengths.

$\boxed{2\varepsilon}$ \lengthtest{*relation*}

where *relation* consists of two lengths or length commands separated by a relational operator <, =, or >. For example,

```
\newlength{\horiz} \newlength{\vert}
\newlength{\min}
. . . . . .
\ifthenelse {\lengthtest{\horiz > \vert}}
   {\setlength{\min}{\vert}} {\setlength{\min}{\horiz}
```

sets \min to be the smaller of \horiz and \vert.

**Testing switches**

A *boolean switch* is a parameter that is either ⟨*true*⟩ or ⟨*false*⟩, also called a *flag*. Three commands exist to handle them:

| 2ε | `\newboolean{`*string*`}` | creates a new switch |
| 2ε | `\setboolean{`*string*`}{`*value*`}` | assigns a value `true` or `false` |
| 2ε | `\boolean{`*string*`}` | tests its value |

The last of these is used as *test* in `\ifthenelse` and `\whiledo`.

There are a number of internal LATEX switches that may also be tested (but never reset!). The most useful of these are `@twoside` and `@twocolumn` for checking if two-side or two-column modes are active. Since they contain the character `@`, they may only be used inside a class or package file (Appendix C).

**Combining logical statements**

Any of the above logical statements may be combined to form a more complex statement by means of the logical operators

`\and`     `\or`     `\not`     `\(`     `\)`

which should be straightforward to anyone familiar with boolean logic. For example, to set `\textwidth` to 10 cm if two-column mode is active or if `\paperwidth` is greater than 15 cm and the page counter is below 100,

```
\ifthenelse {\lengthtest{\textwidth > 10cm} \or
      \( \lengthtest{\paperwidth > 15cm} \and
        \value{page} < 100 \) }
      {\setlength{\textwidth}{10cm}} {}
```

will accomplish this.

Such conditionals are fairly complicated, and they are most appropriate for defining new commands that may have alternative actions, or for including in package and class files (Appendix C).

A relatively simple example: suppose one is uncertain whether British or American spelling is wanted by the publisher. One can write the document with both included in the text, with a switch in the preamble to make the final selection.

```
\newboolean{US}
\setboolean{US}{true} %For American spelling
%\setboolean{US}{false} %For British spelling
\newcommand{\spell}[2]{\ifthenelse{\boolean{US}}{#1}{#2}}
```

Now `\spell` is a command that prints its first or second argument according to the setting of the flag US. Thus in the text one may write

> ... the \spell{color}{colour} of music ...

which will yield American spelling if \setboolean{US}{true} has been specified, otherwise the British version. In fact, different sections of the work could have different spelling simply by changing the value of the switch at the appropriate point. (This book was written in this way, which was a good thing, because the editor did change his mind about spelling style after the manuscript was finished.)

As an example of \whiledo: one wishes to write some text $n$ times, where both the text and $n$ are to be variable.

```
\newcounter{mycount}
\newcommand{\replicate}[2]{\setcounter{mycount}{#1}
    \whiledo{\value{mycount}>0}{#2\addtocounter{mycount}{-1}}}
```

Now \replicate{30}{?} will print 30 question marks.

## 7.4     User-defined environments

Environments may be created or changed with the commands

[2ε] \newenvironment   {env_name}[narg][opt]{beg_def}{end_def}
[2ε] \renewenvironment{env_name}[narg][opt]{beg_def}{end_def}

or

[2.09] \newenvironment   {env_name}[narg]{beg_def}{end_def}
[2.09] \renewenvironment{env_name}[narg]{beg_def}{end_def}

where the arguments have the following meanings:

env_name: the name of the environment; for \newenvironment, it may not be the same as any existing environment or command name, whether LATEX or user-defined. For \renewenvironment, on the other hand, there must already be an environment bearing this name. Any changes to LATEX environments should only be undertaken if the user has a thorough knowledge of the internal workings of LATEX.

narg: a number between 1 and 9 that states how many arguments the environment is to have; if the optional argument narg is omitted, the environment is to have no arguments.

[2ε] opt: the default text for the first argument (#1) if it is to be optional; this behaves the same as for \(re)newcommand (page 185).

beg_def: the initial text to be inserted when \begin{env_name} is called; if this text contains entries of the form #n, with $n = 1, \ldots, narg$, then when the the environment is started with the call

\begin{*env_name*}{*arg_1*}...{*arg_n*}...

each occurrence of #*n* within *beg_def* is replaced by the text of the argument *arg_n*.

*end_def:* the *final* text that is inserted when \end{*env_name*} is called; here the dummy arguments #*n* are not allowed since they are only to appear in the *beg_def* text.

## .1 Environments without arguments

Just as for user-defined commands, environments without the optional argument *narg* will be illustrated first. A user-defined environment named sitquote is created with

```
\newenvironment{sitquote}{\begin{quote}\small
    \itshape}{\end{quote}}
```

> *which sets the text appearing between* \begin{sitquote} text \end {sitquote} *in the typeface* \small\itshape, *and indented on both sides from the main margins, as demonstrated here.*

In this case, *beg_def* consists of the command sequence \begin{quote} \small\itshape while *end_def* is simply \end{quote}. Now the call

\begin{sitquote} *text* \end{sitquote}    is the same as
\begin{quote}\small\itshape *text* \end{quote}

which produces the desired result.

This example does not appear to be very practical since the same effect can be achieved with less typing by adding \small\itshape at the beginning of the quote environment. However, if such a structure were to occur very often within a document, this new environment would be useful in saving some typing and reducing the chance of writing the command sequence \small\itshape incorrectly.

Let us expand the previous example somewhat as follows:

```
\newcounter{com}
\newenvironment{comment}
{\noindent\slshape Comment:\begin{quote}\small\itshape}
{\stepcounter{com}\hfill}(\arabic{com})\end{quote}}
```

where now *beg_def* contains the text and commands

\noindent\slshape Comment:\begin{quote}\small\itshape

and *end_def* is

\stepcounter{com}\hfill(\arabic{com})\end{quote}

where com is a user counter created by the \newcounter command. Now since the command \begin{comment} inserts the text *beg_def* at the start of the environment and \end{comment} the text *end_def* at the finish, it should be clear that

```
\begin{comment} This is a comment.
    Comments should ...
    ... in round parentheses.
\end{comment}
```

will generate the following type of structure:

*Comment:*

> *This is a comment. Comments should be preceded by the word Comment: the text being in a small, italic typeface, indented on both sides from the main margins. Each comment receives a running comment number at the lower right in round parentheses.* (1)

The reader should examine the sequence of commands with the replacement text of this example to see precisely what the effect of this environment is. Two weaknesses should become apparent: what would happen if \begin{comment} were called in the middle of a line of text without a blank line before, and what would take place if the last line of the comment text were so long that there was no more room for the running comment number on the same line?

The following revision removes these two problems:

```
\renewenvironment{comment}
{\begin{sloppypar}\noindent\slshape Comment
    \begin{quote}\small\itshape}
{\stepcounter{com}\hspace*{\fill}(\arabic{com})\end{quote}
    \end{sloppypar}}
```

With the \begin{sloppypar} command, the call to the environment always starts a new paragraph in which no *overfull* line can occur upon line breaking. If the comment number does not fit on the last line of text, a new line begins with the number right justified because of the command \hspace*{\fill}. Again the reader should examine carefully just what is inserted into the processing between the \begin{comment} and the \end{comment}.

## 7.4.2   Environments with arguments

Passing arguments over to an environment is carried out exactly as for commands. As an example, the comment environment will be modified so that the name of the person making the comment is added after the word *Comment:*, and this name will be an argument when the environment is invoked.

```
\renewenvironment{comment}[1]
{\begin{sloppypar}\noindent\slshape Comment: #1
      \begin{quote}\small\itshape}
{\stepcounter{com}\hspace*{\fill}(\arabic{com})%
      \end{quote}\end{sloppypar}}
```

The text

```
\begin{comment}{Helmut Kopka} This is a modified ...
   ... environment argument \end{comment}
```

now produces

*Comment: Helmut Kopka*

> *This is a modified comment. Comments should be preceded by the word Comment:, followed by the name of the commenter, with the text of the comment being in a small, italic typeface, indented on both sides from the main margins. Each comment receives a running comment number at the lower right in round parentheses. The name of the commenter is transferred as an environment argument.* (2)

This example will now be modified once again by interchanging the comment number and the name of the commenter. Placing the running number after the word *Comment:* is no problem, for it is simply necessary to insert those commands from {*end_def*} at the location of the #1 dummy argument. However, putting the symbol #1 where the comment number used to be will produce an error message during the LaTeX processing since this violates the syntax of the \newenvironment command: '*No dummy arguments shall appear within the {end_def}*.' If the dummy argument comes after \begin{quote}, the name will be printed at the wrong place, at the beginning of the comment text.

There is a trick to solve this problem:

```
\newsavebox{\comname}
\renewenvironment{\comment}[1]
{\begin{sloppypar}\noindent\stepcounter{com}\slshape
   Comment \arabic{com}\sbox{\comname}{#1}
   \begin{quote}\small\it}
{\hspace*{\fill}\usebox{\comname}\end{quote}\end{sloppypar}}
```

The commands \newsavebox, \sbox, and \usebox are all described in Section 4.7.1. Here \comname is the name of a box that has been created with \newsavebox, in which the first argument, the commenter's name, is stored. With this new definition, a comment now appears as follows:

*Comment 3*

> *In this form, every comment is assigned a sequential number after the word Comment. The comment text appears as before, while the name of the commenter is entered as the environment argument and is placed at the right of the last line.* Helmut Kopka

The implementation of more than one argument for environments is the same as for commands and needs no further explanation.

### 7.4.3   Environments with an optional argument $\boxed{2\varepsilon}$

Similarly, environments may be defined with an optional argument, just as commands. To take our last example once more, if we feel that most comments will be made by Helmut Kopka, we could alter the first line of the definition to

```
\renewenvironment{comment}[1][Helmut Kopka]{..}{..}
```

Now it is only necessary to specify the name of the commenter if it is someone else. With

```
\begin{comment}[Patrick W. Daly]More than ...
   ... appropriate.\end{comment}
```

we obtain

*Comment 4*

> *More than one person may want to make a comment, but perhaps one person makes more than others do. An optional argument for the name is then appropriate.*                    *Patrick W. Daly*

**Exercise 7.8:** *Extend the definition of the comment environment so that a page break cannot occur either between the heading 'Comment n' and the comment text or between the comment text and the commenter's name.*
*Hint: the solution can be achieved either with the* samepage *environment or with the* \nopagebreak *command.*

**Exercise 7.9:** *Create a new environment making use of the* minipage *environment, to be named* varpage *and possessing one argument that is a sample text to determine the width of the minipage. The call*

```
\begin{varbox}{'As wide as this sample text'}
. . . . . . . . . . . . . . . . . . . . . .\end{varbox}
```

*should pack the enclosed text into a minipage that has a width equal to that of the text 'As wide as this sample text'.*
*Hint: a user-defined length parameter must first be established, say* \varwidth. *See Section 7.2 for details on assigning lengths to text widths.*

**Exercise 7.10:** *Generate an environment named* varlist *with two arguments that behaves as a generalization of the sample list in Section 4.4.3. The first argument is to be the item word that is printed on each call to* \item; *the second is the numbering style of the item numeration. For example, with the call*

```
\begin{varlist}{Sample}{\Alph} . . . . . \end{varlist}
```

*every* \item *command within the environment should produce the sequence 'Sample A', 'Sample B', . . . . The indentation should be 1 cm larger than the width of the item word, which itself should be left-justified within the label box.*
*Hint: once again a user-defined length, say* \itemwidth, *is necessary for this solution. After the length of the item word has been stored with* \settowidth, *the indentation may be set with*

```
\setlength{\leftmargin}{\itemwidth}
```

*to be equal to the width of the item word, and then with*

```
\addtolength{\leftmargin}{1cm}
```

*to be 1 cm larger. Length assignments for* `\labelwidth` *and* `\labelsep` *may be similarly set to appropriate values.*
*All further details may be obtained from Section 4.4.*

# 5    Some comments on user-defined structures

This section contains some general remarks on the creation and use of user-defined LaTeX structures. They are not strict rules but merely reflect ideas that we have obtained through our own experiences. Every user will develop his or her own methods of application according to personal requirements.

## 5.1    Saving user-defined structures

The creation of user-defined structures can save the user a great deal of work. Frequently used commands and/or text should be stored individually with the `\newsavebox`, `\newcommand`, or `\newenvironment` definitions written to a separate file. This file may then be read in with the `\input` command and made available in any other document file.

   With time, a very large number of such stored structures may accumulate. To put them all into a *single* file will slow down the processing and may make it difficult to keep track of the contents and command names. It is therefore recommended that the user structures be sorted according to areas of application and stored in a number of *separate* files.

## 5.2    Abbreviating structures

A simple application of user-defined commands is to shorten the names of LaTeX structures. For example, with

```
\newcommand{\be}{\begin{enumerate}}
\newcommand{\ee}{\end{enumerate}}
```

it is sufficient to write `\be` to start the LaTeX environment `enumerate`, and `\ee` to end it.

   Such abbreviations can avoid a considerable amount of writing, but they are not so suitable for a large collection of stored commands since it is easy to forget the meaning behind the command name. The author of LaTeX, Leslie Lamport, has deliberately selected names that clearly indicate the function of the command or environment. Such unambiguous, unabridged names are easier to remember than unclear, arbitrary abbreviations. Nevertheless, some abbreviations may be practical within a single document, provided they do not become too numerous. It is a question of the individual user's style and his or her typing capabilities.

### 7.5.3    Identical command and counter names

In the previous examples a number of counters were introduced for application to specific commands or environments, such as `myfn` for the command `\myfootnote` on page 190, or `com` for the environment `comment` on page 197. In these cases, the counter and the corresponding command or environment were given different names. This was not necessary: *counters may have a name that is identical to that of a command or environment.* LaTeX knows from the context whether the name refers to a counter or to a command/environment.

The different names were chosen in the examples in order to avoid confusion for the beginner. In fact, it is reasonable to give a counter the same name as the command or environment with which it is coupled, a practice that LaTeX itself constantly employs (Section 7.1.1). In the above-mentioned examples, the counters could just as easily have been named `myfootnote` and `comment` to emphasize their interdependence with the command and environment of the same names.

### 7.5.4    Range of user definitions

User structures that are defined within the preamble are valid for the entire document. Command and environment definitions that are made inside an environment remain in effect only until its end. Even their names are unknown to LaTeX outside the environment in which they were defined. Thus if they are to be defined once again in another environment, it is `\newcommand` or `\newenvironment` that must be used and not the `\renew` versions.

For command and environment names that have been globally defined, that is, in the preamble, all further new definitions of these names must be made with the `\renew` version. However, these subsequent definitions will apply only locally within the environment in which they are declared; outside, the previous global definitions will be valid once more.

The same applies to structure definitions within nested environments. A definition in the outer environment is effective within all inner ones, but a new definition must be made at the deeper levels with `\renewcommand` or `\renewenvironment`. On leaving the inner environment, the new definition will no longer be operative, but rather the old one will be re-established.

**Warning:** structures that have been created with `\newsavebox` or with

\newcounter are globally defined. If they are given within an environment, their definitions remain effective even outside that environment. Similarly \setcounter functions globally, although \savebox does not.

## 5.5 Order of definitions

User-defined structures may be nested within one another. If one user definition contains another user-defined structure, it is often the case that the inner one has already been defined. However, this is not necessary. *User definitions may contain other user structures that are defined afterwards.* What is important is that the other structure is defined before the first command is invoked.

For example, a normal sequence of definitions would be

```
\newcommand{\A}{defa}
\newcommand{\B}{defb}
\newcommand{\C}{\A \B}
```

where \C is defined in terms of \A and \B. However, it is also permissible to write

```
\newcommand{\C}{\A \B}
```
*normal text, but without calling* \C
```
\newcommand{\B}{defb}
\newcommand{\A}{defa}
```
*further text with any number of calls to* \A, \B *and* \C

## 5.6 Transferring arguments

The dummy arguments in a command or environment definition may be used as arguments for other commands within that definition. For example, if the commands \A and \B each take one argument, the command definition

```
\newcommand{\C}[3]{\A{#1}#2\B{#3}}
```

is a permissible one. Here the first and third arguments of \C are transferred to the commands \A and \B, and only the second argument enters the definition directly. All combinations of direct and transferred arguments are allowed. Here is a more concrete example:

```
\newcommand{\sumvec}[4]{\anvec{#3}{#4} = #1_1+#2_1,\ldots
    ,#1_#4+#2_#4}
```

The call $\sumvec xyzn$ produces $z_1,\ldots,z_n = x_1 + y_1,\ldots,x_n + y_n$, where \anvec is the command defined in Section 7.3.2.

## 7.5.7    Nested definitions

!

User definitions may be nested inside one another. A structure such as

> `\newcommand{\`*outer*`}{{\newcommand{\`*inner*`}...}}`

is permissible. The command that is defined with the name {\\*inner*} is valid and known only within the command {\\*outer*}, according to the remarks on the range of definitions on page 202. Although the TeX macros make copious use of nested command definitions to limit the lifetime of temporary commands, it is not recommended to nest LaTeX definitions excessively since it is too easy to lose track of the bracketing. A forgotten bracket pair will produce an error message on the *second* call to the outer command, since the inner definition still exists as a leftover from the first call. Nevertheless, here is an example:

```
\newcommand{\twentylove}
  {{\newcommand{\fivelove}
     {{{\newcommand{\onelove}
         {I love \LaTeX!}%
          \onelove\ \onelove\ \onelove\ \onelove\ \onelove}}}
      \fivelove\\ \fivelove\\ \fivelove\\ \fivelove}}
```

The entry `My opinion of \LaTeX:\\ \twentylove` now produces:

My opinion of LaTeX:

I love LaTeX! I love LaTeX! I love LaTeX! I love LaTeX! I love LaTeX!
I love LaTeX! I love LaTeX! I love LaTeX! I love LaTeX! I love LaTeX!
I love LaTeX! I love LaTeX! I love LaTeX! I love LaTeX! I love LaTeX!
I love LaTeX! I love LaTeX! I love LaTeX! I love LaTeX! I love LaTeX!

Indenting the lines of the definition, as shown above, can help to keep track of the nesting levels; each line of the same level starts in the same column, ignoring braces.

!

If both the *inner* and *outer* definitions are to be provided with arguments, the symbols for the inner and outer dummy arguments must be distinguished. The symbols for the *inner* definition are `##1` ... `##9`, while those for the *outer* one are the normal `#1` ... `#9`. For example:

```
\newcommand{\thing}[1]{{\newcommand{\color}[2]{The ##1 is ##2.}
  \color{#1}{red} \color{#1}{green} \color{#1}{blue}}}
```

The entry `The colors of the objects are\\`
  `\thing{dress}\\ \thing{book}\\ \thing{car}`    produces
The colors of the objects are

The dress is red. The dress is green. The dress is blue.
The book is red. The book is green. The book is blue.
The car is red. The car is green. The car is blue.

The separate definition and calling as in Section 7.5.5 is easier to follow and would be:

```
\newcommand{\thing[1]}{\color{#1}{red} \color{#1}{green}
                       \color{#1}{blue}}
\newcommand{\color}[2]{The #1 is #2.}
```

## 5.8 Unwanted spacing

Occasionally user-defined structures generate spacing where none was expected, or more spacing than was desired. This is almost always due to blanks or new lines in the definition, included only to improve the legibility of the source text but interpreted as spacing when the structure is invoked.

For example, if the % character had been left out of the first line of the \myftnote definition on page 190, a line feed would have been added to the command text at that point, and converted into a blank. This blank would be inserted between the previous word which should receive the footnote marker and the call to the \footnote command that actually generates the marker, with the result that it would be displaced from that word (for example, wrong * instead of right*).

At this point we should like to remind the reader that many LaTeX commands are *invisible*, in that they do not produce any text at that point where they are called. If such an invisible command is given separated by blanks from the surrounding text, it is possible that two blanks will appear.

```
For example \rule{0pt}{0pt} produces
```

'For example  produces' the inter-word spacing twice. Invisible commands without arguments do not present this problem since the trailing blank acts solely as a command name terminator and disappears. Furthermore, the following LaTeX commands and environments always remove the subsequent blanks even when arguments are present.

```
\pagebreak      \linebreak      \label    \glossary   \vspace   figure
\nopagebreak    \nolinebreak    \index    \marginpar            table
```

## 5.9 Two final examples

The normal description environment (Section 4.3.3) sets the label in bold face, and indents all lines following the first one by a fixed amount. For describing command names in computer code, it might be more desirable to print the labels in typewriter font (\texttt command or \ttfamily declaration) and to have the subsequent lines indented by the amount of the longest label. Let us define a new environment ttscript for this purpose that is invoked thus:

```
\begin{ttscript}{sample_text}  list_text   \end{ttscript}
```

The text of the argument *sample_text* determines the left indentation as its width with the font command \texttt. The *list_text* consists of \item[*label_text*] commands followed by the corresponding explanatory text, every line of which is indented from the left margin by the width of *sample_text*. The *label_text* appears printed with \texttt left-justified within the label box. The ttscript environment is defined as

```
\newenvironment{ttscript}[1]{%
  \begin{list}{}{%
```

```
\settowidth{\labelwidth}{\texttt{#1}}
\setlength{\leftmargin}{\labelwidth}
\addtolength{\leftmargin}{\labelsep}
\setlength{\parsep}{0.5ex plus0.2ex minus0.2ex}
\setlength{\itemsep}{0.3ex}
\renewcommand{\makelabel}[1]{\texttt{##1\hfill}}}}
{\end{list}}
```

which may be easily adapted to other font styles for the label text, renamed, and stored as a user-defined structure for general applications.

The first seven lines of the above definition should not present any problems in understanding. The environment definition contains one argument that is transferred to

```
\settowidth{\labelwidth}{\texttt{#1}}
```

in order to set the width of the label. The left margin is then set with

```
\setlength{\leftmargin}{\labelwidth}
```

to be the same as the width of the label \labelwidth, and finally

```
\addtolength{\leftmargin}{\labelsep}
```

increments the left margin by the amount of the label separation \labelsep.

The sixth and seventh lines set \parsep and \itemsep to appropriate values that may be changed as needed by the user. Other list parameters may also be included if desired.

The last line redefining the \makelabel command needs some further explanation. This command was briefly described in Section 4.4.1. It is valid only within the list environment and is used by each call to \item to form the actual label. Its normal argument is the *optional* argument to the \item command. With the above redefinition, that label is now set with the font command \texttt, followed by \hfill to left justify the whole within the label box. Because of the nesting of the redefinition within the definition of the ttscript environment, it is necessary for the dummy argument to be given as ##1 instead of #1, as explained in the previous section.

As an example, by giving the text

```
\begin{ttscript}{description}
\item[list] environments are useful for . . .
\item[enumerate] environments number . . .
\item[itemize] environments mark the . . .
\item[description] environments label . . .
\end{ttscript}
```

we can generate the following description of the LaTeX listing environments:

list          environments are useful for generating lists in which the various items are set off from one another for greater clarity;

enumerate     environments number their items consecutively, starting at 1;

itemize       environments mark the various items with a distinguishing symbol, often a bullet •;

`description` environments label the items with some text in bold face type, for greater stress.

*Exercise 7.11: Generalize the `ttscript` environment into a universal `varscript` environment with two arguments such that the second one determines the font style of the item text.*

User-defined commands and environments may contain up to 9 arguments. The more arguments a structure possesses, the more flexible it is. On the other hand, the calls to the commands become more complex and awkward, since not only the number but also the sequence of arguments must be strictly maintained.

The sample user-defined environment `figlist` on page 77 in Section 4.4.4 contains no arguments. When it is called, every `\item` command produces **Figure 1:**, **Figure 2:**, etc. The text is indented 2.6 cm from the left and 2 cm from the right margin of the surrounding text. Additional list parameters like `\labelsep`, `\parsep`, and `\itemsep` are set to fixed values in the list declaration. However, with the definition

```
\newcounter{itemnum} \newlength{\addnum}
\newenvironment{genlist}[8]
  {\begin{list}{\textbf{#1 \arabic{itemnum}:}}
    {\usecounter{itemnum}
    \settowidth{\labelwidth}{\textbf{#1}}
    \settowidth{\addnum}{\textbf{\ \arabic{itemnum}: }}
    \addtolength{\labelwidth}{\addnum}
    \setlength{\labelsep}{#2}
    \setlength{\leftmargin}{\labelwidth}
    \addtolength{\leftmargin}{\labelsep}
    \setlength{\rightmargin}{#3}
    \setlength{\listparindent}{#4}
    \setlength{\parsep}{#5}
    \setlength{\itemsep}{#6}
    \setlength{\topsep}{#7}#8}}
  {\end{list}}
```

a generalized list is created in which the first argument determines the uniform item name printed with every `\item` command together with the sequential number. The left indentation is set to the width of the item name plus the size of `\labelsep`, given as the second argument. The next five arguments determine the lengths of various list parameters. The last argument specifies the font declaration for the text within the environment. The syntax for this new environment is

```
\begin{genlist}{itemname}{labelsep}{rightmargin}{listparindent}
  {parsep}{itemsep}{topsep}{fontstyle}
\item text
  ... ...
\item text
\end{genlist}
```

and the call

```
\begin{genlist}{Sample}{4mm}{1cm}{0pt}{1ex plus0.5ex}
    {0pt}{0pt}{\slshape}
  \item no value
  \item The enclosed coupon is worth a value of \$2.00 towards
        the purchase of your next order.
\end{genlist}
```

produces

**Sample 1:**   *no value*

**Sample 2:**   *The enclosed coupon is worth a value of $2.00 towards the*
                *purchase of your next order.*

In this example, the length entries must be given with their units. It is also possible to include the units directly in the definition so that only pure numbers need to be given in the call. Similarly the rubber length in the vertical spacing could be generated by an algorithm within the definition:

```
\setlength{\parsep}{#5ex plus0.3#5ex minus0.5#5ex}
```

which expects a pure number as the fifth argument. If this entry were 2, `\parsep` would be set equal to `2ex plus0.6ex minus1ex`. Once again, there is a trade-off between simplified entries and the complexity of remembering what they mean, especially if the various length arguments all have different dimensions and algorithms.

# Advanced Features

**8**

This chapter describes those features of LaTeX that justify the name 'document preparation system', whereas previous chapters have concentrated more on text processing. The term *advanced* is perhaps misleading, since these features are essential for producing large, complex documents in an efficient manner. The subjects included here are the splitting of a document into several files, selective processing of part of a document, cross-references to sections, figures, and equations, automated production of bibliographies, indices, and glossaries, handling different sets of fonts, and preparing presentation material.

## Processing parts of a document

As often pointed out, a LaTeX document consists of a preamble and the actual text part. Short documents, such as those that a beginner might have, are written to a single file by means of a text editor, and might be corrected after the first trial printing. As the user gathers experience and confidence, the LaTeX documents will rapidly expand in length until one is faced with the task of producing an entire book of more than a hundred pages.

Such long documents could theoretically be kept in one file, although that would make the whole operation increasingly clumsy. The file editor functions less efficiently on longer files and the LaTeX processing takes correspondingly more time. A better idea is to split the work into several files which LaTeX then merges during the processing.

### .1 The \input command

The contents of another file may be read into a LaTeX document with the command

\input{*filename*}

where the name of the other file is *filename*.tex. It is only necessary to specify the root name of the other file, leaving off the extension .tex. During the LaTeX processing, the text contained in this second file is read in at that location in the first file where the command is given.

The result of the \input command is the same as if the contents of the file *filename*.tex had been typed into the document file at that position. The command may be given anywhere in the document, either in the preamble or within the text part.

Since the \input command may be given in the preamble, it is possible to put the whole preamble text itself into a separate file. The actual LaTeX processing file could even be reduced to simply \begin{document} ... \end{document} with a number of \input commands.  A preamble file makes sense if one has a series of documents all of the same type requiring a common preamble.  This also simplifies any later change to the specifications that must be made in *all* the documents.  Different preamble files may be prepared for various types of processing and may then be selected with \input{*proc_type*}.

A file that is read in by means of the \input command may also contain further \input commands. The nesting depth is limited only by the capacities of the computer.

In order to obtain a listing of all extra files read in, give the command

$\boxed{2\varepsilon}$ \listfiles

in the preamble. The list appears both on the computer monitor and in the transcript file, at the end of the processing run. The version numbers and any other loading information are also printed. This provides a check as to which files have been input. See Section C.2.9 for more details.

*Exercise 8.1: Put the preamble of your standard exercise file* exercise.tex *into a separate file* preamble.tex.  *Split the text part into three files* exer1.tex, exer2.tex, *and* exer3.tex. *What should the main file now contain to ensure that LaTeX processes the whole exercise text?*

## 8.1.2   The \include command

Splitting the document into several files may be practical for writing and editing, but when the files are merged with the \input commands, it is still the entire document that is processed. Even if only one file contains a small correction, all files will be read in and processed once again.  It would therefore be desirable to be able to reprocess only the one corrected file.

One rough-and-ready method is to write a temporary main file containing only the preamble (which may be read in) and an \input command to read in that specific file. The disadvantage is that all automatic numbering of page numbers, sections, figures, equations, etc. will start from 1, since all the information from the previous files will be missing. Furthermore, all cross-references from other files will be absent.

A much better method is to employ the LaTeX command

> \include{*filename*}

which is only allowed within the text part of the document, together with

> \includeonly{*file_list*}

in the preamble, containing a list *file_list* of those files that are to be read in. The file names are separated by commas and the extension .tex is left off.

If *filename* is in the *file_list*, or if \includeonly is missing from the preamble, the command \include{*filename*} is identical to

> \clearpage \input{*filename*} \clearpage

However, if *filename* is not contained within the *file_list*, \include is equivalent to \clearpage and the file contents are not read in.

The command \include is less general than the \input command, since it always begins a new page. The document must therefore be split into files at those points where a new page occurs, such as between chapters. Another limitation is that \include commands may not be nested: they may only appear in the main processing file. However, an \input command may be given within a file that is \included.

The great advantage of the \include command is that the additional information about page, section, and equation numbers will be supplied by the \includeonly command so that the selective processing takes place with the correct values of these counters. Cross-reference information from the other files is also available so that the \ref and \pageref commands (Section 8.3.1) yield the correct results. All these values will have been determined during a previous processing of the entire document.

If the changes in the file that is being selectively processed lead to an increase or reduction in the number of pages, the following files will also have to be reprocessed to correct their page numbers. The same is true if sections are added or removed, or if the number of equations, footnotes, figures, etc. is altered.

For example, suppose *file_3* ends on page 17, but after the selective processing it now extends to page 22. The following *file_4* still begins on page 18, and all further files also have their original starting page numbers. If *file_4* is now selectively processed, it will receive the correct number for its first page, 23, based on the stored information in the revised *file_3*. So far so good. However, if instead *file_6* were to be selectively processed right after *file_3*, it would receive its starting page number from *file_5*, which has not yet been corrected and would be in error by 5. The same applies to all other structure counters. Their correct values can only be guaranteed when the files have been reprocessed in their proper order.

In spite of these restrictions, the \include command is extremely useful for large documents, saving considerable computation time. Longer documents are normally written and edited in many stages. The \include command permits one to reprocess selective alterations in a short time, even if the numbering systems temporarily go awry. This can be repaired later on with a complete reprocessing of the entire document, by deactivating the \includeonly command in the preamble.

A file that is read in with \include may not contain any \newcounter declarations. This is not much of a restriction, since they should normally be given in the preamble.

Each chapter of this book was written to a separate file with names gtl1.tex, gtl2.tex, .... The processing file itself contains the text

```
\documentclass{book}
 .  .  .  .  .  .  .  .  .  .  .  .  .  .
  \includeonly{...}
\begin{document}
  \frontmatter \include{toc}
  \mainmatter
  \include{gtl1} . . . \include{gtl7} . . .
  \backmatter \printindex
\end{document}
```

where the file toc.tex contains simply

```
\setcounter{page}{7}
\tableofcontents \listoftables \listoffigures
```

By making the appropriate entry in the \includeonly command, it is possible to process the various chapters selectively: for example, by giving \includeonly{toc,gtl3} one processes the table of contents and Chapter 3.

### 8.1.3　Terminal input and output

There are times when it is desirable that LaTeX write a message to the computer terminal during processing. This can be achieved with the command

```
\typeout{message}
```

where *message* stands for the text that is to appear on the screen. This text is written when the LaTeX processing reaches this command. At the same time, the message is written to the .log file (Section 8.9).

If *message* contains a user-defined command, it will be interpreted and its translation appears on the screen. The same thing applies to

LaTeX commands. This could have dire consequences if the commands, either user or LaTeX, are not really printable. To print the command name literally, add the command \protect in front of it.

The command

\typein[\com_name]{message}

also writes the *message* text to the terminal, but then it waits for the user to enter a line of text from the keyboard, terminated by a carriage return. If the optional argument \com_name is missing, the line of text is inserted directly into the processing. In this way, one could, for example, reuse the same text for a letter for several addressees, entering the name each time from the keyboard. Suppose the text contains

Dear \typein{Name:}\\ ...

then what appears on the screen is

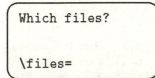

Name:

\@typein=

At this point, one enters the name of the recipient. If on successive processings 'George', 'Fred', and 'Mary' are entered, the result will be a set of identical letters differing only in their salutations as 'Dear George', 'Dear Fred', and 'Dear Mary'.

If the \typein command contains the optional argument \com_name, this is treated the same as

\typeout{message} \newcommand{\com_name}{entered definition}

In this case the definition is stored under the command name \com_name interactively and may be invoked and executed in the rest of the document like any other LaTeX command.

With some experience in LaTeX methodology, it soon becomes obvious that *interactive* processing with the \typein command can be very practical. For example, if the preamble contains

\typein[\files]{Which files?}
\includeonly{\files}

the following appears on the terminal screen:

Which files?

\files=

and LaTeX waits for the user to type in the names of one or more files (separated by commas) to be processed. This avoids having to modify the main processing file with an editor every time.

This book was produced with precisely this addition to the main file shown on the previous page.

A similar procedure may be employed when a form letter is to be sent to various recipients. One can enter the name and address and even the salutation interactively. Complete forms may be processed by LATEX in this way, with the entries being made from the keyboard. All the order forms in the authors' institute are produced in this manner, for example.

**Warning:** the \typein command may not be used as the argument of another LATEX command! It may, however, be given in environments such as minipage.

*Exercise 8.2: Change the main file from Exercise 8.1 so that the files* exer1.tex, exer2.tex, *and* exer3.tex *may be read in with the* \include *command. Arrange that you can determine interactively which of the files is to be processed.*

*Exercise 8.3: Generate output of the form*

## Certificate
# Olympic Spring Games
# Walterville 1992

### Finger Wrestling

| | | | | |
|---|---|---|---|---|
| **Gold** | A. T. Glitter | AUR | 7999.9 | Points |
| **Silver** | S. Lining | ARG | 7777.7 | Points |
| **Bronze** | H. D. Tarnish | CUP | 7250.0 | Points |

*so that the following enquiries appear on the screen one after the other*

| Message | Command= | Input |
|---|---|---|
| Sport: | \@typein= | Finger Wrestling |
| Unit: | \unit    = | Points |
| Gold: | \@typein= | A. T. Glitter |
| Country: | \@typein= | AUR |
| Value: | \@typein= | 7999.9 |
| Silver: | \@typein= | S. Lining |
| . . . | . . .    = | . . . |

*and the appropriate entries are made interactively. The third column contains the answers necessary to produce the above sample output. Repeat the program with different entries. Let your imagination run wild.*

## 8.2    Including TEX commands in LATEX

The rapid increase in TEX applications is primarily due to the availability of LATEX, something that many users are unaware of. They consider LATEX to be a separate executable program, an alternative to TEX. In reality, LATEX is merely an interface between the user and the TEX processing program that simplifies the TEX operation enormously. It *translates* the input logical structures into functional TEX commands and executes them through internal calls to TEX.

Thus it is possible to give pure TEX commands within LATEX. This applies to all the TEX primitive commands as a matter of course. In addition to the roughly 300 primitive TEX commands, there are another 600 or so macros defined in the Plain TEX format. The formal difference between running LATEX and Plain TEX is that the format file `latex.fmt` (or `lplain.fmt` for LATEX 2.09) is loaded instead of the original TEX format file `plain.fmt`. However, since the LATEX formats contain most, but not all, of the macro definitions in Plain TEX, the majority of the TEX macros may also be invoked within LATEX.

Those TEX macros that are not permissible in LATEX are listed in Section F.3. These are the only TEX commands that may not be used or that function differently in LATEX.

Notwithstanding the possibility of employing (Plain) TEX commands in a LATEX document, it is recommended to stay with the high-level commands wherever possible. This is the best guarantee for portability and durability. However, since many refined features (or tricks) can only be realized at the TEX level, it would be foolish to ban such practices altogether. See Section C.1.4 for a further discussion on coding guidelines, and Section C.2.12 for some useful TEX commands.

# In-text references

In a longer text, one often wants to refer to other chapters, sections, tables, and figures, or to pages where some other description has been given. There is also a need to produce an index register which is also a reference to certain keywords throughout the document. In the days before electronic text processing, such cross-references and index registers meant an enormous amount of extra work for the author or secretary. Today the computer can alleviate much of this burden.

In the old days, referring to earlier parts of the text by page number was tedious but feasible. Referencing future parts that had not yet been written had to be limited to section numbers since the page numbers were not yet known, or space had to be left for the page number to be entered at a later date.

The production of a book is usually a progressive and constantly shifting process. The manuscript may not necessarily be written in the order in which it is to appear, and even once the initial draft version is finished, there will be major changes due to new considerations by the author or to knowledgeable advice from reviewers. Revisions, deletions, and insertions of entire sections or even chapters are commonplace, not to mention possible reordering of parts of the text.

LATEX relegates all the problems associated with such major alterations to the past. No matter what changes the author makes, the information necessary for the cross-references and index register is stored for use at any point in the text.

### 8.3.1   Cross-references

As already pointed out in several places, the command

> \label{*marker*}

is used to set a marker at that point in the text where it appears, which may be referred to at other places. The handle identifying the marker is the text *marker*, which may be any combination of letters, numbers, and characters (except those special symbols representing single character commands: \ # $ % & ˜ ˆ _ { } ).

The page number on which the \label command was issued can be printed with

> \pageref{*marker*}

at any point earlier or later in the document.

If the \label command is given after a sectioning command, or within an equation, eqnarray, or enumerate environment, or inside the argument of a \caption within the figure or table environments, the command

> \ref{*marker*}

prints that number of the section, equation, figure, table, or enumeration that was current when *marker* was defined, and in the correct format. For enumerate, the same number is printed as is generated by the \item command where the \label appeared. Reference may also be made to theorem-like structures created by a \newtheorem command if the \label is given within the text of that theorem command. For example, a \label with marker text bo-wei was issued in the text of the Bolzano–Weierstrass theorem on page 79:

> \begin{theorem}[Balzano--Weierstrass]
>                 \label{bo-wei}...\end{theorem}

so that the input text

> Theorem˜\ref{bo-wei} on page˜\pageref{bo-wei}

generates the output 'Theorem 1 on page 79'. Similarly, the input text

> for Table˜\ref{budget95} on page˜\pageref{budget95},
> see also Section˜\ref{sec:figref}

produces 'for Table 6.1 on page 177, see also Section 6.6.6', since that section contains the marker \label{sec:figref}.

The marker command \label may be given within the argument of a sectioning command, but may also be issued anywhere within the text of that section. The number printed by the corresponding \ref will be that of the innermost section where the \label appeared. To avoid possible confusion, it is recommended to place the \label immediately after the sectioning command to which it is to refer.

A list of all label markers, their translations, and page numbers may be produced by processing the file lablst.tex, provided with the LaTeX installation.

It is useful to know how the cross-referencing information is managed. What the \label command actually does is to write the marker text together with the current value of the appropriate counter(s) and the current page number to an auxiliary file with the root name of the document file plus the extension .aux. The \ref and \pageref commands obtain their information from this .aux file, which is read in at the beginning by the \begin{document} command. The same situation as for the table of contents (Section 3.4.2) also applies here: on the first run, the .aux file does not exist so that no cross-reference information can be output; instead the information is gathered and written to a new .aux file at the end of the run. A warning message is printed at the end if the auxiliary information has changed and a new run is necessary.

## .2    References to the bibliography

The creation of a bibliography and references (citations) to it have already been described in Section 4.3.6 and are demonstrated on page 356, but are repeated here to complete the discussion on cross-referencing. The bibliography is produced as follows:

```
\begin{thebibliography}{sample_label}
  \bibitem[label_1]{key_1} entry_text_1
  \bibitem[label_2]{key_2} entry_text_2

  . . . . . . . . . . . . . . . . . . .
\end{thebibliography}
```

The meaning of the arguments is explained in Section 4.3.6 and will not be repeated here, except for the reference key. This marker *key* plays the same role as *marker* for the \label command. Again, any combination of letters, numbers, and characters is allowed, except commas in this case. Reference is made in the text to the bibliography entry with

```
\cite[extra]{key}
```

which sets the corresponding \bibitem label in square brackets. The input text

```
For additional information about \LaTeX\ and \TeX\
see~\cite{lamport} and \cite{knuth,knuth:a}.
```

together with the sample bibliography in Section 4.3.6 produces as output:

For additional information about LaTeX and TeX see [1] and [6, 6a].

The reference markers `lamport`, `knuth`, and `knuth:a` are translated into the corresponding citation labels from the bibliography.

If the optional argument *extra* is included in the `\cite` command, this text is added after the label(s) but still inside the square brackets.

```
The creation of a bibliographic database is described in
\cite[Appendix B]{lamport}, while the program \BibTeX\
itself is explained in \cite[pages 74, 75]{lamport}.
```

The creation of a bibliographic database is described in [1, Appendix B], while the program BibTeX itself is explained in [1, pages 74, 75].

The `thebibliography` environment allows the author to set up a bibliography with `\bibitem` commands for the individual entries. There is a separate program BibTeX that will generate the bibliography automatically by searching one or more bibliographic databases for the *key* markers given in the `\cite` commands. The keys must of course agree with those in the databases.

Entries to which no reference is made in the text may be included in the bibliography. This is achieved by putting

$$\texttt{\textbackslash nocite\{} key\_i, key\_j, \dots \}$$

anywhere in the text, where *key_i, key_j, ...* are the keywords for the extra entries. The bibliography itself is now generated with the command

$$\texttt{\textbackslash bibliography\{} database\_a, database\_b, \dots \}$$

where *database_a, database_b, ...* are the root names of the files containing the bibliographic databases to be searched. The extension for these files is `.bib`. An example of the use of BibTeX is shown on page 356.

Appendix B describes how bibliographic databases may be set up and how the program BibTeX may be used properly. Basically, BibTeX must be called as a separate program with the root name of the document file after the first run on LaTeX. Afterwards, LaTeX must be run again *at least twice*, the first time to set up the bibliography and to define the relationships between keywords and labels, the second time to insert the label text in place of the keys in the `\cite` commands. BibTeX need only be run again later if new references are added or old ones removed by means of their keywords.

## 8.3.3   Index register

LaTeX does not produce an index register automatically as it does a table of contents, but it does offer the author assistance is setting up an index of keywords and page numbers.

An index register is produced with the environment

`\begin{theindex}` *index entries* `\end{theindex}`

which switches to a two-column page format with a running head *INDEX*. The first page of the index register carries the heading **Index** in the same size as a chapter heading for the `book` and `report` document classes, and as a section heading for the `article` class. (More precisely, the actual word printed is contained in the command `\indexname` which may be redefined for other languages.) The individual entries are made with commands

`\item`  `\subitem`  `\subsubitem`  and  `\indexspace`

followed by the keywords and their page numbers. For example,

| | |
|---|---|
| commands, 18 | `\item commands, 18` |
|   as environments, 42 | `\subitem as environments, 42` |
|   arguments, 19, 101 | `\subitem arguments, 19, 101` |
|     multiple, 103, 104 | `\subsubitem multiple, 103, 104` |
|     replacement symbol, 20 | `\subsubitem replacement symbol, 20` |
|   used as arguments for sec- | `\subitem used as arguments for` |
|     tioning commands, 41, 42 |    `sectioning commands, 41, 42` |
| | `\indexspace` |
| displayed text, 21–32 | `\item displayed text, 21--32` |

If the text entry is too long for one line, it is broken and continued on the next line, indented deeper than all other lines, as in the above example 'used as argument for sectioning commands, 41, 42'. The command `\indexspace` leaves a blank line in the index register.

The `theindex` environment only sets up a suitable format for the index register. The entries themselves, as well as their page numbers, must be entered by hand. However, LaTeX can be of some help in determining the page numbers.

It is possible to issue the command

`\index{`*index entry*`}`

anywhere in the text, where *index entry* is any desired text, but should be the entry that is later made in the index. It may contain any combination of letters, numbers, and symbols *including even command characters and blanks*. This means that even commands may be included in the *index entry*, such as `\index{\section}`, `\index{\[}`, or `\index{%}`. Even the one command that may otherwise never be used as an argument `\verb` may be included. However, if *index entry* does contain a command, `\index` may not be used as an argument of another command. One other restriction is that if an opening curly brace is in *index entry*, the closing partner must also be present. Thus `\index{\{}` is not allowed, but `\index{\{\}}` is.

All the `\index` commands are ignored by LaTeX unless the preamble contains the command

```
\makeindex
```

which activates the \index commands and opens a file with the root name of the document file plus the extension .idx. Now the \index commands write *index_entry* and the current page number to this file in the form

```
\indexentry{index_entry}{pagenumber}
```

In the simplest situation, the .idx file may be output to offer the user a list of the index entries and corresponding page numbers. With this list, he or she could make the entries into theindex environment in the fashion shown earlier. This should be the very last task undertaken after the document has reached its final form, since otherwise the page numbers could change with every minor revision.

! In the LaTeX installation, there is the file idx.tex which can improve the readability of the .idx files. By processing the idx.tex file (that is, calling latex idx), the user is prompted for the name of the .idx file to list:

```
*******************************
* Enter idx file's first Name. *
*******************************
\filename=
```

After the root name of the .idx file has been entered from the keyboard, a two-column page format is output containing the *index_entry* texts listed under page headings of the form **Page n**. No further information is obtained through such a formatted listing, but it is far easier to work with than a straightforward output of the .idx file alone.

Even if the \index commands have no effect without the \makeindex command in the preamble, it is a good idea to include them in the text from the initial development of the document. The \makeindex command can be included later when the final version of the document is ready. Finally the theindex environment with the entries from the .idx or idx.dvi files can be organized. This is still a tedious job requiring much patience and power of concentration, since the \item, \subitem, and \subsubitem entries must be alphabetically ordered and the .idx listing only offers them in the sequence in which they appear in the document.

However, there is a better way! There are programs available that will produce theindex environments from the data in the .idx file just as BibTeX produces thebibliography environments. One such tool is described in the next section.

! The LaTeX installation also contains the package showidx, which prints the index entries from the \index commands as marginal notes, beginning at the top of the page on which they occur. This is useful for going through a preliminary version of the document to check that all index entries are really on the proper page or whether additional entries have to be made. The package is loaded with the \usepackage command, or by adding it to the option list of \documentstyle.

If showidx is used, it is a good idea to increase the width of the marginal note box with the declaration \marginparwidth (Section 4.10.7) in the preamble. Unfortunately, the present book format is not suitable for such a demonstration.

## .4   Glossary

A 'glossary' is a special index of terms and phrases alphabetically ordered together with their explanations. To help set up a glossary, LATEX offers the commands

> \makeglossary         in the preamble and
> \glossary{*glossary_entry*}     in the text part

which function just like the commands for making up an index register. The entries are written to a file with extension .glo after the command \makeglossary has been given in the preamble. The form of these file entries from each \glossary command is

> \glossaryentry{*glossary_entry*}{*pagenumber*}

The information the .glo file can be used to establish a glossary. However, there is no equivalent to the theindex environment for a glossary, but a recommended structure is the description environment (Section 4.3.3) or a special list environment (Section 4.4).

## MakeIndex—a keyword processor

The tiresome drudgery of making up the theindex environment for an index register can be dispensed with if the program MakeIndex is available. This program was written by Pehong Chen with the support of Leslie Lamport. We will give only an abbreviated description of its use here. More details are in the documentation accompanying the program package.

The program MakeIndex processes the .idx file, producing as output another file with the root name of the document and the extension .ind, containing the complete theindex environment. The program is called by

> makeindex *root_name*.idx   or simply   makeindex *root_name*

A subsequent LATEX processing outputs the index at the location of the \printindex command, which together with the \see command, is defined in the package file makeidx.sty. Thus the production of an index register in this way requires the package file makeidx to be loaded with the \usepackage command.

The MakeIndex program expects the \index entries to be of one of the three forms:

> \index{*main_entry*}
> \index{*main_entry*!*sub_entry*}
> \index{*main_entry*!*sub_entry*!*sub_sub_entry*}

The individual main and sub-entries may contain any combination of characters with the exceptions of !, @, and |. The exclamation point is the divider between the various entry fields. If the \index command contains only a main entry, this will become the text for an \item command. The main entries will be in alphabetical order.

If the \index command contains a main and a sub-entry, the text *sub_entry* will be assigned to a \subitem command underneath the corresponding *main_entry*. The texts for the \subitem will also be in alphabetical order. Similarly the text of a *sub_sub_entry* will appear following a \subsubitem command, alphabetically ordered, below the appropriate *sub_entry* text.

The main and sub-entries may also contain special characters and even LATEX commands that are to be neglected during alphabetization. This is indicated by an entry of the form *lex_entry@print_entry*, in which *lex_entry* is used for the alphabetical ordering while *print_entry* is the actual text to be output. For example, in the index register in this book, which was generated with MakeIndex, all the command names appear as source text and are ordered without the preceding \ character. These entries were made in the text as \index{put@\verb=\put=}

An entry may be terminated with the character sequences |( or |) to designate the beginning and end of a range of page numbers. For example,

> \index{picture!commands|(}   on page 150
> \index{picture!commands|)}   on page 162

produces the sub-entry 'commands' to the main entry 'picture' with page numbers given as 150–162.

Instead of having the page number printed after the entry, a reference may be made to another index entry. For example, with

> \index{space|see{blank}}

the entry 'space, *see* blank' is made in the index. (More precisely, it is the text stored in the command \seename that is printed in place of *see*; this may be changed for other languages.)

The three characters !, @, and | therefore have special functions for the MakeIndex program. In order to print these characters literally as text without their functions, the *quote* character " must precede them. For example, "! represents a literal exclamation point and not the entry divider.

The quote character itself is thus a fourth special symbol and must be entered literally as "". However, there is a special rule in MakeIndex syntax that says a quote character preceded by a backslash will be interpreted as part of a command: thus \" may be used to put a German umlaut in an entry (as in \index{Knappen, J\"org}). This special rule can lead to

additional problems at times: in this book the index entry \! had to be
typed as "\"!.

It is possible to specify varying fonts for the page number. For example,
in the index register of this book, page numbers are set in bold face to
indicate the page where a command is defined or first explained. This is
achieved with an entry of the form

```
\index{blank}       on page 11, and
\index{blank|bb}    on page 20
```

which in the second case puts the page number for this entry as the
argument of a command \bb. The line in the theindex environment
becomes

```
\item blank, 11, \bb{20}
```

The procedure will only be effective once the command \bb has been defined with \newcommand{\bb}[1]{\textbf{#1}} in the preamble. Note:
the vertical bar in the \index entry is not a typing error, but must replace
the backslash as the LATEX command symbol under these circumstances.

Other page number styles may be defined, say

```
\newcommand{\ii}[1]{\textit{#1}}      and
\newcommand{\zz}[1]{\textsl{#1}}
```

for italic and slanted fonts. These will be specified by terminating the
entry in the \index command with |ii or |zz.

The alphabetical ordering of MakeIndex normally follows the standard
ASCII code, first *symbols*, then *digits*, and finally *letters*, where upper case
comes before lower case. Blanks are included as symbols. There are a
number of options that allow these rules to be changed. How the options
are invoked when the program is called depends on the computer type,
but we assume here a hyphen preceding the option letter, as in

```
makeindex -g -l  root_name
```

The most important options are:

-l      Letter ordering: blanks are ignored when sorting;

-c      Compress blanks: multiple and leading blanks are removed as
        they are in normal LATEX;

-g      German ordering: following the German rules in which *symbols*
        precede *letters* (*lower* before *upper* case) which precede *numbers*;
        the sequences "a, "o, "u, and "s (the codes for *ä, ö, ü,* and *ß* in
        the usual LATEX adaptions for German) are treated as though they
        were ae, oe, ue, and ss, which is standard German practice;

-s      Style specification: allows the name of a index formatting file to
        be included to redefine the functioning of MakeIndex.

The -s option reads in an index style file containing commands to define both the input and output of the MakeIndex program. For example, it is possible to change the special symbols !, @, |, and " so that different characters execute their functions and they themselves revert to being pure text.

The style-defining file consists of a list of pairs in the form *keyword attribute*. The attribute is either one character in single quotes (for example, 'z'), or a character string in double quotes (for example, "a string"). The most important keywords, together with their default definitions, are:

quote    '"' defines the quote symbol;

level    '!' defines the entry separation symbol;

actual   '@' defines the lexical switch symbol;

encap    '|' defines the dummy command symbol for page formatting.

There are many more keywords for defining complicated output structures. These are described in the documentation that should be included with the MakeIndex program package.

The file `makeindex.tex` contains a short manual by Leslie Lamport (but without mentioning style definitions).

## 8.5    The New Font Selection Scheme (NFSS) $\boxed{2_\varepsilon}$

When TeX and LaTeX were originally invented, the fonts available for them were very limited in number.  For this reason, LaTeX 2.09 had a very inflexible system of defining the fonts that were to be used, since it was not obvious that one might want to change them.  The association between the high-level font commands such as \large and \bf and the external font name that is ultimately selected was rigidly fixed in the file `lfonts.tex` which went into making up the `lplain` format.

Today there are many additional fonts available, some of which should be used alongside the standard CM fonts, and others that should replace them altogether. For example, the Cyrillic fonts of Section E.7 should be added parallel to the Latin fonts, but to make them operate automatically under the LaTeX size commands was a complex procedure. (We know: we have done it!) Similarly, installing PostScript fonts involved calling intricate interface macros, which admittedly were provided with the PostScript driver package, but which represented an enormous effort on the part of some LaTeX programmer.

Another problem with LaTeX 2.09 was the behavior of the font style and size commands (Sections 4.1.5 and 4.1.2).  Each of the font declarations \rm, \bf, \sc, \sl, \it, \sf, and \tt activates a particular font, depending on the currently selected size. Each of these declarations is mutually exclusive. Thus the combination \bf\it is exactly the same as \it. There is no way to select a bold italic font in this scheme. Furthermore, every size declaration from \tiny to \Huge automatically switches to \rm, so that \bf\large does *not* produce a bold large font as one might expect. Finally, the use of declarations rather than commands with arguments violates the basic philosophy of LaTeX. That is, to emphasize a *single* word, it makes more sense to type \emph{single} than {\em single\/}. (Experienced LaTeX users may deny this, but that is only because they have deeply rooted habits.)

In 1989 Frank Mittelbach and Rainer Schöpf proposed a New Font Selection Scheme (NFSS) for LaTeX and a preliminary test package was ready in early 1990. A second release (NFSS2) was published mid-1993 with many substantial changes. With the official release of LaTeX $2_\varepsilon$ in June 1994, NFSS has become firmly entrenched in the new standard. The new font declarations and commands are described in Sections 4.1.3 and 4.1.4. Here we explain the system in more detail, presenting some of the lower-level font selection commands.

## .1   Font attributes under NFSS

According to the NFSS scheme, every character set can be classified by five attributes called *encoding*, *family*, *series*, *shape*, and *size*, which may be selected with the commands

> \fontencoding{*encode*} \fontfamily{*fam*} \fontseries{*wt_wth*}
> \fontshape{*form*}  and  \fontsize{*sz*}{*line_sp*}

The *encode* attribute was new to the second release of NFSS. It specifies the layout of the characters within the font. Possible values for it are listed in Table 8.1. It is unlikely that one would want to change encoding within a document, except to activate Cyrillic fonts perhaps. This feature is more for LaTeX programmers to install new fonts on the system.

**Table 8.1**: The NFSS encoding schemes

| Encoding | Description | Sample Font | Page |
|---|---|---|---|
| OT1 | Original text fonts from Knuth | cmr10 | 406 |
| OT2 | Univ. Washington Cyrillic fonts | wncyr10 | 410 |
| T1 | The Cork (DC) fonts | dcr10 | 421 |
| OML | TeX math letter fonts | cmmi10 | 408 |
| OMS | TeX math symbol fonts | cmsy10 | 410 |
| OMX | TeX math extended fonts | cmex10 | 409 |
| U | Unknown coding | — | — |

The argument *fam* in \fontfamily denotes a set of basic properties of the font, or origin.  For the Computer Modern fonts, all the serif fonts listed in Section E.3.1 belong to the family cmr. The family cmss includes all the sans serif fonts from Section E.3.2 while cmtt contains the typewriter fonts of Section E.3.3.  A number of special decorative fonts in Section E.4 are the only members of their families. Table 8.3 on the opposite page lists the CM fonts according to the family and other attributes.

**Note:** The font attribute *family* has no relationship to the primitive TEX concept of the same name.  A TEX family consists of three fonts of different sizes for use in math formulas as normal characters, and first- and second-level indices.

The argument *wt_wth* in \fontseries designates the *weight* (=*bold-ness*) and *width* of the characters. These are specified by 1 to 4 letters as shown in Table 8.2.

Table **8.2**: The NFSS *series* attributes

| Weight class | | Width class | | |
|---|---|---|---|---|
| Ultralight | ul | Ultracondensed | 50% | uc |
| Extralight | el | Extracondensed | 62.5% | ec |
| Light | l | Condensed | 75% | c |
| Semilight | sl | Semicondensed | 87.5% | sc |
| Medium (normal) | m | Medium | 100% | m |
| Semibold | sb | Semiexpanded | 112.5% | sx |
| Bold | b | Expanded | 125% | x |
| Extrabold | eb | Extraexpanded | 150% | ex |
| Ultrabold | ub | Ultraexpanded | 200% | ux |

The argument for \fontseries{*wt_wth*} consists of the letter or letters for the weight, followed by those for the width. Thus ebsc indicates weight *extrabold* and width *semicondensed* while bx means weight *bold* and width *expanded*. The letter m is omitted when combined with any non-normal weight or width; if both are to be normal, it is sufficient to give m alone.

In \fontshape, the argument *form* is one of the letter combinations n, it, sl, or sc for selecting normal (or upright), italic, slanted, or small caps.

The \fontsize attribute command takes two arguments, the first *sz* being the point size of the font (without the dimension pt explicitly given) and the second *line_sp* being the vertical spacing from one baseline to the next.  The second argument becomes the new value of \baselineskip (Section 3.2.3). For example, \fontsize{12}{15} selects a font size of

12 pt with inter-line spacing of 15 pt. (The second argument may be given a dimension, such as 15pt, but pt is assumed if no dimension is stated.)

Once all five attributes have been set, the font itself is selected with the command \selectfont. The new feature here is that the various attributes are independent of one another. Changing one of them does not alter the others. For example, if the selection

```
\fontfamily{cmr} \fontseries{bx} \fontshape{n} \fontsize{12}{15}
```

has been made for an upright, bold, expanded, Roman font of size 12 pt and inter-line spacing 15 pt, then when \fontfamily{cmss} is later selected for a sans serif font, the attributes weight and width bx, form n, and size 12(15pt) remain in effect when the next \selectfont is issued.

Alternatively, all attributes but the size may be specified and the font activated immediately with the command

$$\usefont\{code\}\{family\}\{series\}\{shape\}$$

The following table (by F. Mittelbach and R. Schöpf) lists the classification of the Computer Modern character sets according to the attributes \fontfamily, \fontseries, and \fontshape. That there are so many attribute combinations without a corresponding CM font may appear to be a weakness in the NFSS system, but it must be recalled that it is designed for the future. It may also be employed with the PostScript fonts, which are becoming ever more popular, to exploit their complete variability.

**Table 8.3**: Attributes of the Computer Modern fonts

| series | shape(s) | Examples of external names |
|--------|----------|----------------------------|
| *Computer Modern Roman* — (\fontfamily{cmr}) | | |
| m | n, it, sl, sc, u | cmr10, cmti10, cmsl10, cmcsc10, cmu10 |
| bx | n, it, sl | cmbx10, cmbxti10, cmbxsl10 |
| b | n | cmb10 |
| *Computer Modern Sans Serif* — (\fontfamily{cmss}) | | |
| m | n, sl | cmss10, cmssi10 |
| bx | n | cmssbx10 |
| sbc | n | cmssdc10 |
| *Computer Modern Typewriter* — (\fontfamily{cmtt}) | | |
| m | n, it, sl, sc | cmtt10, cmitt10, cmsltt10, cmtcsc10 |

Formally it is possible to set any combination of attributes; however, there may not exist any font matching all the attributes selected. If that is the case, then when \selectfont is called, LaTeX issues a warning stating which font has been activated in its place. The font size attribute of the \fontsize command may normally take on values of 5, 6, 7, 8, 9, 10, 10.95, 12, 14.4, 17.28, 20.74, and 24.88, but other values may also be added. The second argument, the inter-line spacing, may take on any value since it is not something intrinsic to the font itself.

With the \begin{document} command, LaTeX sets the five attributes to certain preset default values. These are normally standard encoding OT1, family cmr, medium series m, normal shape n, and the base size selected. The user may change these initial values within the preamble, or they might be set differently by a special option, say when a PostScript font has been selected.

## 8.5.2    Simplified font selection

The attribute commands \fontencoding, \fontfamily, \fontseries, \fontshape, and \fontsize, together with the command \selectfont, are the basic tools in the New Font Selection Scheme. The user need not employ these commands directly, but rather may make use of the higher-level declarations presented in Sections 4.1.2 and 4.1.3. In fact, a font declaration like \itshape is defined as \fontshape{it}\selectfont.

The high-level commands to select font sizes are:

| | | | | | |
|---|---|---|---|---|---|
| \tiny | (5pt) | \normalsize | (10pt) | \LARGE | (17.28pt) |
| \scriptsize | (7pt) | \large | (12pt) | \huge | (20.74pt) |
| \footnotesize | (8pt) | \Large | (14.4pt) | \Huge | (24.88pt) |
| \small | (9pt) | | | | |

The sizes listed for the commands are those when 10pt (the default) has been selected as the basic size option in the \documentclass command; for 11pt and 12pt, they will all scale accordingly.

The family declarations and their standard family attribute values are:

\rmfamily (cmr)     \sffamily (cmss)     \ttfamily (cmtt)

which are the three Computer Modern families, Roman, Sans Serif, and Typewriter (Section E.2).

The series declarations and their initial attribute values are:

\mdseries (m)          \bfseries (bx)

meaning that only a medium and a bold extended series are provided as standard.

Finally, the shape declarations and their attribute values are:

| | | | |
|---|---|---|---|
| \upshape | (n) | \itshape | (it) |
| \slshape | (sl) | \scshape | (sc) |

to select upright, *slanted*, *italic*, and SMALL CAPS.

Note that there are no high-level declarations for the encoding attributes. This is because there is normally no need to change encoding within a document. An exception might be to use Cyrillic fonts (coding OT2), in which case one could define

```
\newcommand{\cyr}{\fontencoding{OT2}\selectfont}
\newcommand{\lat}{\fontencoding{OT1}\selectfont}
```

to be able to switch back and forth more conveniently.

The family, shape, and series attributes may be reset to their standard values at any time with the `\normalfont` command, which also activates that font in the current size.

For each of the above font attribute declarations there is also a corresponding font command (Section 4.1.4) that sets its argument in that font. Thus `\textit{text}` is almost the same as `{\itshape text}`, the only difference being that the command also contains the *italic correction* automatically. The complete list of such commands is:

| | | | | |
|---|---|---|---|---|
| **Family:** | `\textrm` | `\textsf` | `\texttt` | |
| **Series:** | `\textmd` | `\textbf` | | |
| **Shape:** | `\textup` | `\textit` | `\textsl` | `\textsc` |
| **Other:** | `\emph` | `\textnormal` | | |

The `\emph` command is described in Section 4.1.1; `\textnormal` sets its argument in `\normalfont`.

## 5.3   Default attribute values

The font attribute declarations in the previous section do not set their attribute values explicitly, but rather do so by means of certain default commands. Thus the true definition of `\itshape` is

```
\fontshape{\itdefault}\selectfont
```

The default commands available are

| | | | |
|---|---|---|---|
| **Family:** | `\rmdefault` | `\sfdefault` | `\ttdefault` |
| **Series:** | `\mddefault` | `\bfdefault` | |
| **Shape:** | `\updefault` | `\itdefault` | `\sldefault`   `\scdefault` |

It is also necessary to define the standard attributes chosen when the command `\normalfont` is issued. These are contained in the four defaults

```
\encodingdefault \familydefault \seriesdefault
\shapedefault
```

All this may sound like a complicated route linking the high-level commands to a particular font. However, it does provide flexibility and modularity. The author only needs to know that three families, two series, and four shapes are available, and does not care what they really are. A programmer defines these with the defaults at a lower level.

An example of how all the standard fonts may be replaced by PostScript ones, by simply redefining the three family defaults, is shown on page 236. Such redefinitions are much simpler than trying to alter the font declarations themselves, including \normalfont. Those definitions are in fact much more complex than implied here, whereas the default commands really are as simple as indicated.

## 8.5.4   Defining font commands

!

There are a number of commands available for defining new font declarations and commands. These are intended mainly for LaTeX package programmers but may be used in a normal document as well.

[2ε] \DeclareFixedFont{\*cmd*}{*code*}{*family*}{*series*}{*shape*}{*size*}

defines \*cmd* to be a declaration that selects the font of the specified attributes. It is rigidly fixed in all attributes. This is equivalent to \newfont except that the font is determined by attributes and not by name.

[2ε] \DeclareTextFontCommand{\*cmd*}{*font_specs*}

defines \*cmd* to be a font *command* that sets its argument according to *font_specs*. This command is used internally to define all the font commands like \textbf, which is defined with *font_specs* as \bfseries.

[2ε] \DeclareOldFontCommand{\*cmd*}{*text_specs*}{*math_specs*}

defines \*cmd* to be a font *declaration* that may be used in math mode in the manner of LaTeX 2.09: as a declaration, not a command. It is useful for defining commands to be compatible with the old version, but should be avoided. For example, \it is defined with

        \DeclareOldFontCommand{\it}{\normalfont\itshape}{\mathit}

## 8.5.5   Mathematical alphabets

The font that has been activated for text processing does *not* influence the characters and their fonts in math mode, since special mathematical symbol fonts are used for this purpose. If a formula is to appear in bold face, the command \boldmath (Section 5.4.9) must be issued, which remains in effect until it is countermanded by \unboldmath. Both of these declarations must be made outside of math mode.

These commands may still be employed in the same way under NFSS. However, the internal math font selection command is

```
\mathversion{vers_name}
```

in which the argument *vers_name* currently takes on values `normal` and `bold`. The declarations `\unboldmath` and `\boldmath` are defined in terms of this command. It is planned that special package files will become available to allow additional sets of math symbols.

On the other hand, mathematical alphabet commands may be issued within math mode itself, to set letters as symbols in particular fonts (Section 5.4.2):

```
\mathrm \mathcal \mathnormal \mathbf \mathsf \mathit \mathtt
```

These are all *commands* operating on arguments rather than *declarations*, unlike the LaTeX 2.09 equivalents.

New math font alphabets may be defined by the user. For example, to define a slanted math font `\mathsl`, give

```
\DeclareMathAlphabet{\mathsl}{OT1}{cmr}{m}{sl}
```

which means that the new math font command `\mathsl` selects that font in family `cmr` with weight `m` and shape `sl`, which, with the normal font definitions, is font `cmsl` in the appropriate size. However, this font will be selected in *all* math versions, whereas it would be more suitable if a bold font were selected when `\mathversion{bold}` is in effect. This is accomplished by adding to the definition of `\mathsl`

```
\SetMathAlphabet{\mathsl}{bold}{OT1}{cmr}{bx}{sl}
```

which redefines `\mathsl` exceptionally for math version `bold` to be a font with weight `bx`. For the normal font definitions, this is `cmbxsl` in the current size.

New math versions can be created with

```
\DeclareMathVersion{vers_name}
```

and the fonts belonging to it are determined by issuing `\Set...` commands for each math alphabet or symbol font.

## 5.6 Mathematical symbol fonts

Mathematical symbols must be defined in a totally different manner from text characters: they bear a command name (like `\alpha`), may come from various fonts, behave differently depending on type, and can appear in different sizes. Under LaTeX 2.09, the symbol names were fixed to the Computer Modern math fonts, but NFSS offers more flexibility for additional (or replacement) symbol fonts.

A symbol font name is declared with the command

```
[2ε] \DeclareSymbolFont{sym_fnt_name}{code}{family}{series}{shape}
```

which associates the name *sym_fnt_name* with the given set of attributes. This name is not a command, but rather an internal designation for use in defining symbols. The selected font is valid for all versions, but if a different font is to be associated with the same name under other versions,

[2ε] `\SetSymbolFont{`*sym_fnt_name*`}{`*version*`}{`*code*`}{`*family*`}{`*series*`}{`*shape*`}`

may be used to redefine *sym_fnt_name* for that one version.

The standard LATEX setup declares

```
\DeclareSymbolFont{operators}{OT1}{cmr}{m}{n}
\DeclareSymbolFont{letters}{OML}{cmm}{m}{it}
\DeclareSymbolFont{symbols}{OMS}{cmsy}{m}{n}
\DeclareSymbolFont{largesymbols}{OMX}{cmex}{m}{n}
```

the sequence of which is important for reasons that are built deeply into TEX itself.

Once the symbol font names have been defined, they may be used to construct math alphabets and various types of symbols.

[2ε] `\DeclareSymbolFontAlphabet{\`*math_alph*`}{`*sym_fnt_name*`}`

defines `\`*math_alph* to be a math alphabet based on the font with the internal name *sym_fnt_name*. This command is to be preferred over `\DeclareMathAlphabet` if a symbol font exists with the proper attributes for the math alphabet.

The primary command for defining symbols is

[2ε] `\DeclareMathSymbol{\`*symbol*`}{`*type*`}{`*sym_fnt_name*`}{`*pos*`}`

which makes `\`*symbol* print the symbol in position *pos* of font *sym_fnt_name*. The *pos* is a number, in decimal (10), octal (′12) or hexadecimal ("0A) representation. The *type* specifies the functionality of the symbol and is one of

| | |
|---|---|
| `\mathord` | an ordinary symbol |
| `\mathop` | a large operator like $\sum$ |
| `\mathbin` | a binary operator like $\times$ |
| `\mathrel` | a relational operator like $\geq$ |
| `\mathopen` | an opening bracket like { |
| `\mathclose` | a closing bracket like } |
| `\mathpunct` | punctuation |
| `\mathalpha` | an alphabetic character |

Math alphabet commands operate only on the symbols of type `\mathalpha`; other types always produce the same symbol, for a given math version, within all math alphabets.

The sizes have not been specified in any of the above math declarations. This is because there are normally four different sizes available, depending on the math style, as explained in Section 5.5.2. However, these sizes must somehow be specified. This is done with

[2ε] `\DeclareMathSizes{`*text*`}{`*math_text*`}{`*script*`}{`*sscript*`}`

where the four arguments are numbers giving a point size. When the normal text font is size *text* pt, `\textstyle` will be in *math_text* size, `\scriptstyle` in *script*, and `\scriptscriptstyle` in *sscript* size. For example,

```
\DeclareMathSizes{10}{10}{7}{5}
```

All the `\Declare...` and `\Set...` commands may only be called in the preamble.

## 5.7 Addressing the attribute values

In some programming situations, it is necessary to make use of the current values of the attributes without knowing what they are. These are stored in the internal commands

| | | |
|---|---|---|
| `\f@encoding` | `\f@shape` | `\tf@size` |
| `\f@family` | `\f@size` | `\sf@size` |
| `\f@series` | `\f@baselineskip` | `\ssf@size` |

The values of these commands should never be changed directly. However, they may be used to test if they possess a certain value. Since they all contain the character @ in their names, they may only be used in class or package files, and not in the main document file (Appendix C).

## 5.8 Defining fonts under NFSS

Under NFSS, fonts are specified within a document by giving the attributes required and then calling `\selectfont`. How is the set of font attributes then associated with a particular external font name such as those found in Appendix E? This is done by means of *font definition commands* which are usually stored in files with extensions `.def` and `.fd`.

First the declaration

$2\varepsilon$ `\DeclareFontEncoding{`*code*`}{`*text_set*`}{`*math_set*`}`

sets up a new encoding attribute named *code*; whenever a text font of this encoding is selected, *text_set* is executed in order to redefine accent commands or other things that are coding-dependent; similarly *math_set* is called for every math alphabet of this encoding. It is possible to define default *text_set* and *math_set* with

$2\varepsilon$ `\DeclareFontEncodingDefaults{`*text_set*`}{`*math_set*`}`

This allows general text and math mode settings to be declared with this command, while more specialized ones, which are executed afterwards, appear in `\DeclareFontEncoding`.

If no font can be found for the specified attributes,

$2\varepsilon$ `\DeclareFontSubstitution{`*code*`}{`*family*`}{`*series*`}{`*shape*`}`

declares the values of the attributes that should be substituted; substitutions are made in order of *shape*, *series*, then *family*; the encoding is never substituted. If even this fails to find a valid font, then

[2ε] \DeclareErrorFont{*code*}{*family*}{*series*}{*shape*}{*size*}

determines which font is to be used as a last resort.

A new family with a specified encoding scheme is established with

[2ε] \DeclareFontFamily{*code*}{*family*}{*option*}

where *option* is a set of commands that may be executed every time a font of this family and encoding is selected.

The main font-defining declaration that associates external font names with font attributes is

[2ε] \DeclareFontShape{*code*}{*family*}{*series*}{*shape*}
　　　　　{*font_def*}{*option*}

where *option* is additional commands that are executed when one of these fonts is selected.

The *font_def* contains a series of size/font associations, each consisting of a size part, a function, an optional argument, and a font argument. For example,

```
\DeclareFontShape{OT1}{cmr}{m}{n}
  {  <5> <6> <7> <8> <9> <10> <12> gen * cmr
     <10.95> cmr10
     <14.4>  cmr12
     <17.28> <20.74> <24.88> cmr17}{}
```

states that the medium series, normal shape members of the cmr family are to be represented by external fonts cmr5 ... cmr12 for sizes 5–12 pt, by cmr10 scaled to 10.95 pt for sizes near 11 pt, and so on. If the specified size is not present, the nearest size within certain limits is taken instead.

The size part consists of one or more numbers in angle brackets, representing point sizes. The brackets may also contain ranges, as <-10> means all sizes up to, but excluding, 10 pt, <10-14> means 10 pt to less than 14 pt, and <24-> indicates 24 pt and higher. The possible functions are:

**(empty)** (as in the second, third, and fourth lines above) load the named font scaled to the requested point size; if an optional argument in square brackets precedes the font name, it acts as an additional scaling factor;

　　<11> [.95] cmr10　　would load cmr10 scaled to 95% of 11 pt;

**gen** * (as in the first line above) generates the font name by adding the point size to the font argument;

　　<12> gen * cmr　　loads cmr12;

**sub** * substitutes a different font whose attributes are given in the font argument as *fam*/*ser*/*shp*;

> `<-> sub * cmtt/m/n`    this is best used when there is no font of the required attributes; a message is output to the monitor and to the transcript file;

**subf** * is like the empty function, but issues a warning that an explicit substitute font has been loaded;

**fixed** * load the specified font at its normal size, ignoring the size part; if an optional argument is given, it is the point size to which the font is scaled, as in

> `<10> fixed * [11] cmr12`    which loads `cmr12` at 11 pt when 10 pt is requested.

All the above functions may be preceded by an s (for silent) to suppress messages to the monitor screen. Thus silent `sub *` is `ssub *`, and silent empty is `s *`.

As another example, consider the definition of bold, italic, typewriter, for which there is no font in the Computer Modern collection:

> `\DeclareFontShape{OT1}{cmtt}{bx}{it}{`
> `<-> ssub * cmtt/m/it }{}`

This substitutes (silently) for all sizes (`<->`) the medium italic typewriter attributes. Which fonts those are is determined by a `\DeclareFontShape` command with those attributes.

The font definition commands may be issued in a package file, or even in the document itself. However, the normal procedure is to store each of the `\DeclareFontEncoding` commands in a file named *code*`enc.def` (for example, `OT1enc.def` for the OT1 encoding), and to place the commands `\DeclareFontFamily` and `\DeclareFontShape` in a file whose name consists of the encoding and family designations plus the extension `.fd`. For example, the shape specifications for encoding `OT1` and family `cmr` are to be found in `OT1cmr.fd`. When a coding and family combination that is not already defined is selected, LATEX tries to find the appropriate `.fd` file for input. It is therefore not necessary to input such files explicitly, for they are loaded automatically as required.

However, it is important that the encoding be declared beforehand. If it is not already known in the current format, `\DeclareFontEncoding` must be issued, either explicitly, or by loading the *code*`enc.def` file. One way of doing this is to invoke the provided package `fontenc`, as for example

> `\usepackage[OT2,T1]{fontenc}`

where the desired codings are listed as options in square brackets, the last of which is made current.

The normal user will never need to worry about such problems. However, LATEX programmers will find things considerably easier for them.

For example, to install PostScript fonts under NFSS is almost trivial. The common PostScript fonts are already defined as separate families in .fd files of their own; for example OT1ptm.fd associates PostScript Times Roman fonts to a family named ptm. A package to activate these fonts is supplied under the name times.sty containing essentially the lines

```
\renewcommand{\rmdefault}{ptm}
\renewcommand{\sfdefault}{phv}
\renewcommand{\ttdefault}{pcr}
```

This makes Times Roman ptm the default Roman family, invoked with the command \rmfamily, Helvetica phv the default sans serif family (called by \sffamily), and Courier pcr the default typewriter family (activated by \ttfamily).

Another two examples of the usefulness of NFSS are the Cyrillic fonts of the University of Washington (Section E.7) and the extended DC fonts with the Cork encoding (Section E.10.3). Both of these may be activated within a document simply by selecting another encoding, OT2 for Cyrillic, T1 for the DC fonts. (These encodings must first be declared, for example with the fontenc package as illustrated on the previous page.)

## 8.5.9    Encoding commands

! In LATEX, special characters and accents are addressed by means of commands, such as \O to print the Scandinavian letter Ø. The position of this character in the font tables depends on the encoding (character 31 in OT1 and 216 in T1), so that it is necessary to redefine all such symbol commands when the encoding is altered. This is carried out with the help of certain *encoding commands*, which normally appear in the *code*enc.def file along with the \DeclareFontEncoding command.

To define a command that functions differently in the various encodings,

$\boxed{2\varepsilon}$ \ProvideTextCommand{\\*cmd*}{*code*}[*narg*][*opt*]{*def*}

$\boxed{2\varepsilon}$ \DeclareTextCommand{\\*cmd*}{*code*}[*narg*][*opt*]{*def*}

are available and behave just like \providecommand and \newcommand except \\*cmd* has the definition *def* only when the encoding *code* is active. Thus \\*cmd* may have different definitions for each encoding.

$\boxed{2\varepsilon}$ \DeclareTextSymbol{\\*cmd*}{*code*}{*pos*}

defines \\*cmd* to print the character in the font position *pos* when encoding *code* is active.

$\boxed{2\varepsilon}$ \DeclareTextAccent{\\*cmd*}{*code*}{*pos*}

defines \\*cmd* to be an accent command, using the character in font position *pos* as the accent symbol, when encoding *code* is active.

$\boxed{2\varepsilon}$ \DeclareTextComposite{\\*cmd*}{*code*}{*letter*}{*pos*}

$\boxed{2\varepsilon}$ \DeclareTextCompositeCommand{\\*cmd*}{*code*}{*letter*}{*def*} define the action of command \\*cmd* followed by the single *letter* either to print the character in font position *pos* or to execute the definition *def.* These declarations are most useful with the T1 encoding, where many accented letters are separate symbols on their own (Section E.10.3). Thus \\'{e} in OT1 prints an acute accent (character 19) over the letter *e*, while in T1, it prints the single character in position 233. This behavior is achieved with

```
\DeclareTextAccent{\'}{OT1}{19}
\DeclareTextComposite{\'}{T1}{e}{233}
```

The command must already have been defined for the encoding, either with \\DeclareTextAccent or with \\DeclareTextCommand; in the latter case, it must be defined to take a single argument.

All of the above definition commands create new commands for a specific encoding. If the defined commands are invoked in some other encoding, an error message is issued. Default definitions may be provided for all unspecified encodings with

> [2ε] \\DeclareTextCommandDefault{\\*cmd*}[*narg*][*opt*]{*def*}
> [2ε] \\ProvideTextCommandDefault{\\*cmd*}[*narg*][*opt*]{*def*}
> [2ε] \\DeclareTextAccentDefault{\\*cmd*}{*code*}
> [2ε] \\DeclareTextSymbolDefault{\\*cmd*}{*code*}

where the first two create a default definition that applies to all unspecified encodings, while the second two declare which encoding is to be taken as the default.

**Note:** \\DeclareTextCompositeCommand, the \\Provide... and default commands were added in the LaTeX 2ε version from December 1, 1994. Any file that uses them should therefore contain \\NeedsTeXFormat{LaTeX2e}[1994/12/01].

# 6   Input encoding [2ε]

Depending on the computer system, it is possible to type many of the special symbols of Sections 2.5.5–2.5.7 directly into the input file and have them appear on the monitor screen during the preparation of the LaTeX file with a text editor. Some TeX installations can actually translate these special characters into the corresponding command. Unfortunately, there is no standard coding for such special characters, so that such files become system dependent. For example, the special letter Æ is character 198 in the ISO-Latin1 coding scheme, but 146 in the IBM PC extended system.

The inputenc package can solve this problem of system dependency. It is invoked as

> \\usepackage[*code*]{inputenc}

which defines the input character codes from 128–255 according to the coding scheme *code*. Possible values for *code* are ascii (all extended characters are undefined and thus ignored) and latin1 for the ISO-Latin1 scheme.

The coding information is obtained from a file named *code*.def, which contains a list of commands

> \DeclareInputText{*pos*}{*text*}    or
> \DeclareInputMath{*pos*}{*math*}

which assign *text* or *math* coding to the character *pos*. For example, `latin1.def` contains

> \DeclareInputText{198}{\AE}

to translate the input character 198 to the LaTeX command \AE.

This means that it is possible to produce *the rôle of the æther* with the input the rôle of the æther (rather than with The r\^{o}le of the {\ae}ther), even though the same text might appear quite differently when inspected on another computer.

## 8.7  Alternatives for special symbols $\boxed{2_\varepsilon}$

$\boxed{!}$   If one inspects the font layout schemes for the CM (page 406) and DC (page 421) fonts, one sees that there are a number of symbols that cannot be printed directly with regular commands.  For example, ¡ and ¿ are produced as ligatures of the input texts !' and ?', as are many other special symbols. Others may have their own commands that are only valid in math mode.

A possible problem with symbols produced by ligature combinations is that some special fonts may not support them, even though they contain the symbols in the right location.

Any symbol may be addressed directly by the \symbol command with the layout position number as argument, but the character that is actually produced will depend on the font encoding. A number of special \text.. commands are available (from December 1, 1994) to print all these symbols independently of the current encoding.

| Command | Symbol | Replaces |
|---|---|---|
| *Ligatures* | | |
| \textemdash | — | --- |
| \textendash | – | -- |
| \textexclamdown | ¡ | !' |
| \textquestiondown | ¿ | ?' |
| \textquotedblleft | " | '' |
| \textquotedblright | " | '' |
| \textquoteleft | ' | ' |
| \textquoteright | ' | ' |
| *Math symbols* | | |
| \textbullet | • | $\bullet$ |
| \textperiodcentered | · | $\cdot$ |
| *Miscellaneous* | | |
| \textvisiblespace | ␣ | \verb*+ + |

To these can also be added

> \textcompworkmark for an invisible character to break ligatures
> \textcircled{*char*} to circle a character, as Ⓧ.

# 8 Additional standard files

The basic LaTeX format contains most of the fundamental features that one needs for producing regular documents. However, there are many additional features that are indispensible for certain applications, and may be included by means of the \usepackage command (Section 3.1.2). Hundreds of such packages have been written by various users and made available over computer networks (Section D.5); others have been developed by members of the LaTeX3 Project Team and are offered parallel to the standard installation; finally, a number are part of that installation itself.

## 8.1 Special documents

The standard installation includes a number of special 'documents', files with the .tex extension. These are:

small.tex $\boxed{2.09}$ a short sample document in LaTeX 2.09;

sample.tex $\boxed{2.09}$ a longer sample document in LaTeX 2.09;

small2e.tex $\boxed{2\varepsilon}$ a short sample document in LaTeX $2\varepsilon$;

sample2e.tex $\boxed{2\varepsilon}$ a longer sample document in LaTeX $2\varepsilon$;

lablst.tex (Section 8.3.1) for printing out all the cross-reference labels, with translations and page numbers; it asks interactively the name of the document that is to be so listed;

idx.tex (Section 8.3.3) lists all the \index entries for a document, ordered in two columns, by page; it asks interactively the name of the document that is to be so listed;

testpage.tex to test the positioning of the text on a page; this is more a test of the printer driver, to make sure that the margins are correct and that the scaling comes out properly; in LaTeX 2.09, this file is for American letter paper only, while for LaTeX $2\varepsilon$, one is asked interactively for the desired paper size;

nfssfont.tex $\boxed{2\varepsilon}$ is a document to print out a font table, sample text, and various other tests; it asks for the name of the font interactively; the command \help prints out a list of commands that can be given;

docstrip.tex $\boxed{2\varepsilon}$ (Section D.3.1) this is more a program than a document; it is the basic tool for unpacking operating files from their documented source files; it not only removes comments, but also includes alternative coding depending on various options.

## 8.8.2    Extra classes $\boxed{2\varepsilon}$

In addition to the standard classes that have already been discussed (book, report, article, letter) the standard installation also contains

proc for producing camera-ready copy of conference proceedings; it is a variant of the two-column article class; it contains one extra command: \copyrightspace, which leaves blank space at the bottom of the first column for typing in a copyright notice; (in LaTeX 2.09, this is a style option to the article style, and may also be used as such in LaTeX $2_\varepsilon$, but only in compatibility mode);

slides (Section 8.10) the former SliTeX of LaTeX 2.09, for producing presentation material;

ltxdoc (Section D.3.2) to produce the documentation of class and package files.

## 8.8.3    Standard packages

Those packages that are part of the standard installation of LaTeX should be considered universal, in that one can expect them always to be available. The other packages, even those of the LaTeX3 Team, are optional.

The standard packages, some of which have been described elsewhere, are:

alltt enables the alltt environment which is much like verbatim except that \, {, and } behave as normal; this means that commands included in the text are executed and not printed literally;

bezier $\boxed{2.09}$ (Section 6.4.9) provides the possibility of drawing quadratic curves in the picture environment; this feature is now internal to LaTeX $2_\varepsilon$, but a dummy package file is available for compatibility with older documents;

doc $\boxed{2\varepsilon}$ (Section D.3.2) provides many special features for documenting LaTeX packages;

exscale $\boxed{2\varepsilon}$ allows the mathematical symbols that appear in different sizes to scale with the font size option given in the \documentclass command; normally the size of these symbols is fixed, independent of the basic size of the text;

fontenc $\boxed{2\varepsilon}$ (Section 8.5.8, page 235) declares font encodings by loading their .def files; the names of the encodings are listed as options;

`graphpap` $\boxed{2\varepsilon}$ (Section 6.5.6) provides the command \graphpaper which produces coordinate grids in the `picture` environment;

`ifthen` (Section 7.3.5) allows text or command definitions depending on the state of various conditionals; one may test the state of a boolean switch, the value of a counter or length, or the text definition of a command;

`inputenc` $\boxed{2\varepsilon}$ (Section 8.6) allows a LaTeX document file to be prepared with a system-dependent input encoding scheme for special characters;

`latexsym` $\boxed{2\varepsilon}$ loads the 11 special LaTeX symbols in the `lasy` fonts (Section E.5.2), which are no longer internal to LaTeX $2_\varepsilon$; this file is automatically read in in compatibility mode;

`makeidx` (Section 8.4) provides the commands that may be used with the MakeIndex program to generate a keyword index;

`newlfont` $\boxed{2\varepsilon}$ redefines the two-letter font declarations to behave as they did in the first release of NFSS; the font declarations change only one attribute; that is, \bf is like \bfseries, and so on;

`oldlfont` $\boxed{2\varepsilon}$ defines the two-letter font declarations, such as \bf, to behave as they do in LaTeX 2.09, in both text and math mode; these declarations are no longer internal to LaTeX $2_\varepsilon$, but they are provided by all the standard classes; the contents of this package are included in compatibility mode;

`pict2e` $\boxed{2\varepsilon}$ (Section 6.5.6) enhances some of the `picture` environment commands by removing the restrictions on line lengths, thicknesses, slopes, and circle radius; makes use of driver-dependent features;

`showidx` (Section 8.3.3) makes the \index entries visible by printing them as marginal notes;

`shortvrb` $\boxed{2\varepsilon}$ provides \MakeShortVerb and \DeleteShortVerb, which may be used to designate (and remove) a certain character as being equivalent to \verb for printing source text. The character, preceded by a backslash, is given as an argument to these commands. Thus after issuing
    \MakeShortVerb{\|}
|\cmd{}| is equivalent to \verb|\cmd{}|, producing \cmd{};

`syntonly` $\boxed{2\varepsilon}$ provides the command \syntaxonly which, when given in the preamble, suppresses all output to the .dvi file, but continues to issue errors and warnings; the job runs about four times faster than normal; this is used to check the processing when output is not immediately needed;

`T1enc` $\boxed{2\varepsilon}$ makes the DC font encoding (Section E.10.3) the standard;

`tracefnt` $\boxed{2\varepsilon}$ is a diagnostic tool for checking NFSS font selections; the options given with \usepackage control its action:

`errorshow` suppresses all warnings and information messages to the monitor, which are still sent to the transcript file; only error messages are printed to the monitor;

`warningshow` prints warnings and error messages on the monitor; this behavior is much the same as when the package is not used at all;

`infoshow` (default option) sends font selection information to the monitor, which is normally only written to the transcript file;

`debugshow` writes considerably more information to the transcript file about every change of font; can produce a very large transcript;

`pausing` turns all warnings into error messages so that processing temporarily stops, awaiting user response;

`loading` shows the loading of external fonts.

### 8.8.4   Accessory software

On the network servers where LaTeX can be found (Section D.5), there are a number of parallel directories offering even more accessory packages than those in the standard installation.  These all have a semi-official status. Some of them are described later in Appendix D on extensions to the standard.

**amslatex** is a set of packages supported by the American Mathematical Society for advanced mathematical typesetting.

**babel** provides support for multilingual LaTeX, described in Section D.1.3.

**graphics** makes packages available for including, rotating, manipulating foreign figures and diagrams, color.

**mfnfss** provides packages for installing extra METAFONT (bit-map) fonts with NFSS (see examples below).

**psnfss** provides packages for installing certain PostScript type 1 fonts with NFSS, as illustrated in Section D.2.1.

**tools** is a set of useful packages written by members of the LATEX3 Project Team, described in Section D.3.

Most of the above packages come with full documentation, making use of the documented source code technique described in Section D.3.2. The source file is processed under LATEX to obtain the manual and/or detailed explanation of the coding, while an installation file is run to extract various files (.sty, .fd, and so on) from the source file.

## 8.5    Contributed packages

The LATEX3 Project Team members are not the only ones who have written class and package files for LATEX. On the network servers (Section D.5) there are hundreds of private packages that have been made public. A number of the most useful are described in *The LATEX Companion* (Goosens *et al.*, 1994). To date, most of these were written for LATEX 2.09, but will function quite happily under LATEX 2ε. It is expected that the authors will update them to the new version soon.

The ability to write one's own classes and packages (explained in more detail in Appendix C) is one of the great strengths of LATEX. Rather than expecting the originators to anticipate *everything* that might be required of the text processor, the real users can establish their specialist needs, find the solutions, and make them readily available for others. The basic program is not overloaded with applications that are used extensively only by a limited number of people; furthermore, it is those users with the practical experience who produce the new extensions.

## 8.9    The various LATEX files

A number of different files are used during the LATEX processing: some are read in while others are created to store information for the next run. They all consist of two parts:

*root_name.extension*

For every LATEX document, there is a *main* file, whose root name is used when the program LATEX is called. It normally possesses the extension .tex, as do any other files that it might read in with \input or \include commands. (If they have a different extension, it must be given explicitly.)

The other files that are created during a LATEX processing run normally have the same root name as the main file but a variety of different extensions, depending on their functions. If the main file contains \include commands, there will be additional files created having the same root names as the included .tex files but with the extension .aux.

Some of these files are created with every LATEX run, whereas others appear only when certain LATEX commands have been issued, such as \tableofcontents or

\makeindex. The .aux files as well as those produced by special LATEX commands may be suppressed by including the command

> \nofiles

in the preamble. This command is useful if a document is being constantly corrected and reprocessed, so that the information in the special files is not yet finalized and may therefore be dispensed with. Files created at the TEX level of processing will always be generated.

Other extensions describe files that contain formatting information, or additional instructions (coding), or databases. The root part of these file names is not associated with any document file. An example of this type is the `article.cls` file that defines the `article` class.

The rest of this section contains a list of the LATEX file extensions with a short description of the role they play in the LATEX processing.

.aux  This is the auxiliary file written by LATEX, containing information for cross-references as well as some commands necessary for the table of contents and other lists. There will be one .aux file created (or recreated) for the main file, in addition to one for every file read in by an \include command.

When a document is processed by LATEX for the first time, there is no .aux file and the cross-referencing commands cannot function. The message
> No file *main_name*.aux.
is written to the terminal in this case. The .aux files are read in by the command \begin{document}. As they are read in, their names appear on the terminal screen in the form
> (*main_name*.aux)(*sub1_name*.aux) ...
New .aux files are written for every LATEX processing run. The new .aux file for the main file begins with the \begin{document} command, whereas those for the \included files are initiated by the corresponding \include command, and are closed when the .tex file is fully read in. The main .aux file is closed by the \end{document} command.

The auxiliary .aux files may be suppressed by issuing \nofiles in the preamble.

.bbl  This file is not created by LATEX, but by the program BibTEX. It has the same root name as the main file. BibTEX actually only reads the .aux file for its information. The .bbl file is read into the next LATEX processing run by the command \bibliography and produces the list of literature references.

.bib  Bibliographic databases have the extension .bib. BibTEX reads them to extract the information it needs to generate the .bbl file. The root name describes the database and not (necessarily) any text file. The database name is included in the text by means of the \bibliography command.

.blg  This is the transcript file from a BibTEX run. The root name is the same as that of the input file.

.bst  This is a *bibliography style file* that is used as input to BibTEX to determine the format of the bibliography. The name of the .bst file is included in the text by means of the \bibliographystyle command.

.cfg $\boxed{2\varepsilon}$ Some classes permit local *configurations* for paper size or other requirements by putting specifications into a .cfg file of the same root name as the class. The ltxdoc class (Section D.3.2) is one of these.

.clo $\boxed{2\varepsilon}$ This is a *class option* file in LaTeX $2\varepsilon$, containing the coding for certain options that might apply to more than one class. There is no special command to input them.

.cls $\boxed{2\varepsilon}$ This is a *class* file in LaTeX $2\varepsilon$, defining the overall format of the document. It is read in by the \documentclass command. A .cls file may also be input from another one with the \LoadClass command.

.def $\boxed{2\varepsilon}$ Additional definition files of various types carry the .def extension. Examples are T1enc.def (to define the T1 encoding) and latex209.def (for compatibility mode between LaTeX $2\varepsilon$ and 2.09).

.drv $\boxed{2\varepsilon}$ As an alternative to processing a .dtx file directly to obtain the documentation, a *driver* .drv file may be processed instead. It is normally extracted from the .dtx file by means of DocStrip. The advantage is that the user may edit the driver as needed for different page sizes, or different requirements, such as manual only or with coding explained. (In earlier versions, this was the *only* way to print the documentation.)

.dtx $\boxed{2\varepsilon}$ These are documented source files for the LaTeX $2\varepsilon$ installation. If a .dtx file is processed directly, the documentation is printed. This is an explanatory manual and/or a detailed description of the coding. The class, package, .ltx, .fd or other file(s) are extracted by processing the .dtx file with DocStrip (Section D.3.1).

.dvi This is the TeX output file, containing the processed text in a format that is independent of the output printer, hence a 'device-independent' file. It too is generated by every TeX process run and cannot be suppressed by \nofiles. The message

> Output written on *main_name*.dvi(*n* pages, *m* bytes).

is written to the terminal when this file is closed.

When certain errors occur, the .dvi file is not written, in which case the terminal message is

> No pages of output

The .dvi file must be further processed by a *printer driver* program that converts it into the special commands for the desired output device (printer).

.fd $\boxed{2\varepsilon}$ Files containing the NFSS commands associating external font names with font attributes (Section 8.5.8) are *font definition files*. The root names consist of the encoding and family designations, such as OT1cmr.fd. When a font of a given family is requested for the first time, the corresponding .fd file is automatically read in, if it exists.

.fdd ⌊2ε⌋ Documented sources for .fd files have the extension .fdd, and are nothing more than a special type of .dtx file. They may be processed for the documentation, or have the .fd files extracted by DocStrip.

.fmt This extension belongs to a TEX *format* file that has been created with the special program initex (Section 1.2.1). Format files contain all the basic instructions in a compact coding for quick loading. LATEX is nothing less than TEX run with the format latex.fmt ⌊2ε⌋ or lplain.fmt ⌊2.09⌋. (Plain TEX uses the format file plain.fmt.)

.glo This file is only generated when the command \makeglossary exists in the preamble. It has the same root name as the main file and contains only \glossaryentry commands that have been produced by \glossary commands in the source text. This file will be suppressed in spite of the presence of \makeglossary if the command \nofiles is issued in the preamble.

.gls This file is the glossary equivalent of the .ind file. It too is generated by the MakeIndex program, but with the .glo file as input. The input and output extensions must be explicitly given. There are no standard LATEX commands to read in the .gls file. The doc package uses it to record a change history.

.idx This file is only generated when the command \makeindex exists in the preamble. It has the same root name as the main file and contains only \indexentry commands that have been produced by \index commands in the source text. This file will be suppressed in spite of the presence of \makeindex if the command \nofiles is issued in the preamble.

.ilg This is the transcript file from a MakeIndex run. The root name is the same as that of the input file.

.ind This file is generated by the MakeIndex program, with the .idx file as input. It is read in by the \printindex command which is defined by the makeidx package. It contains a theindex environment, built up from the entries in the input file.

.ins ⌊2ε⌋ To facilitate the DocStrip run on a .dtx file, the necessary commands (and options) are put into an *installation* file. The extraction is then accomplished simply by processing (with TEX or LATEX) the appropriate .ins file.

.ist This is an *index style file*, containing style settings for MakeIndex. The root name reflects the style and has no relationship to any text file. For the doc package, the files gind.ist and gglo.ist are provided for specialized index formatting.

.lis This is an alternative to .log on some systems.

.lof This file contains the information for the list of figures. It behaves exactly like the .toc file except that it is opened by the command \listoffigures instead of by \tableofcontents.

.log  This file contains the protocol of the TᴇX processing run, that is, all the messages that were sent to the terminal during the run as well as additional information that can be of use to TᴇX experts when errors occur. This file is always generated, even when \nofiles has been issued. The message

> `Transcript written on` *main_name*`.log.`

is written to the terminal when this file is closed.

.lot  This file contains the information for the list of tables. It behaves exactly like the .toc file except that it is opened by the command \listoftables instead of by \tableofcontents.

.ltx  [2ε] Certain files that are inputs to the initex program bear the extension .ltx in LATᴇX 2ε. They form the basis for generating the format `latex.fmt`. The main such file is named `latex.ltx`.

.sty  This is a *package* file in LATᴇX 2ε, to be loaded with \usepackage. A package contains additional LATᴇX commands to define new features or alter existing ones. It should not contain any printable text. It may be input by another package with the command \RequirePackage.

In LATᴇX 2.09, the .sty files are *main style* files (equivalent to classes) as well as *style option* files (packages). The two have quite different properties although they both have the same extension. They are read in by the \documentstyle command.

.tex  The file containing the user's source text should have the extension .tex. For every LATᴇX document there is at least one .tex file. If there is only one .tex file, it is also the *main* file that determines the root name of all the others. If there are \input or \include commands within the source text, there are other files belonging to the document with different root names but all with the extension .tex. The main file is the one whose name appears when the program LATᴇX is called. It contains the highest level \input commands and is the only file that may have \include commands.

.toc  This file contains the information for the table of contents. The command \tableofcontents reads in the .toc file, if it exists, and then outputs the table of contents. At the same time, a new .toc file is opened where all the contents information for the current processing run is written. This .toc file is closed by the \end{document} command, so that if the LATᴇX run is interrupted before completion, the .toc file is lost.

A .toc file is only generated if the document contains a \tableofcontents command and if the \nofiles command has not been issued. It has the same root name as the main file.

# 10  Presentation material (S‌ʟɪTᴇX)

LATᴇX 2.09 provided a parallel version of itself called S‌ʟɪTᴇX for producing presentation material such as colored slides or viewgraphs. This special variant makes use of a different set of fonts that is more appropriate for projection than the regular book style of letters. However, this required another TEX *format* (Section 1.2.1) since the older LATEX version programs its whole set of fonts explicitly into the format file. The name *SLITEX* was used to distinguish it from regular LATEX. Running SLITEX rather than LATEX meant invoking the TEX program with the `splain` instead of the `lplain` format.

Under LATEX2ε, with the New Font Selection Scheme, there is no longer any problem in replacing all the fonts within the one LATEX format. Since SLITEX has ceased to be something similar to, but separate from, LATEX, there is no further need for a distinguishing name. Instead, we refer to the class `slides` for generating presentation material. This class may be selected with regular LATEX2ε just like any other class, whereas with LATEX 2.09, the `slides` style could only be chosen with SLITEX, and in fact was the only style that it would accept.

We will use the word *SLITEX* only to refer to the LATEX 2.09 version, which has some important differences from the LATEX2ε `slides` class.

### 8.10.1  The `slides` class

By *presentation material*, we mean slides or viewgraphs that are to be projected before an audience. One could of course make up the text for such sheets with the normal LATEX commands, but there would be problems getting the font size right, arranging overlays, making sure that the text does not change pages unexpectedly, and the question of whether book-style fonts are suitable for projection. The LATEX class `slides` attempts to solve these.

A different set of fonts is used by this class, ones in which the lower case letters are relatively larger than in the normal fonts, and with a much bigger base size. This has the effect of limiting the amount of text that fits on one page/slide, but this is in fact very good practice for presentation material. The text really should be restricted to keywords and abbreviated sentences. A full page of normal text projected on to a screen will not be read by the audience.

Slides should also make use of color. On this point, SLITEX is rather out of date. When LATEX was first created in the mid-1980s, there were no reasonably priced color printers available. Instead, a system of *color layers* was used, whereby the text for each color was printed separately (in black and white) to be later copied in color to transparencies that would then be superimposed. Today there are better methods to produce colored slides directly. Although color support is not part of the LATEX2ε kernel, there is a `color` package that does provide color commands for certain drivers (Section D.3.3). This package may be used everywhere in LATEX2ε, not just with the `slides` class.

Even without the color feature, the `slides` class is useful for producing black-and-white viewgraphs with the special fonts and the other advantages that it offers. Most of the formatting commands of regular LATEX may be used, except for the page breaking and sectioning commands. The special features that are unique to `slides` are described in the next sections.

The color layer commands are no longer provided in LATEX $2_\varepsilon$, except in the compatibility mode.

## 0.2  The slide environments

The source file for producing slides is structured much the same as that for a normal document, except that it is the `slides` class that is invoked as

2ε `\documentclass{slides}`
    *preamble text*
  `\begin{document}`
    *slide text*
  `\end{document}`

If true colors are wanted (not color layers in black and white), the `color` package can be added in the preamble as for example

2ε `\usepackage[dvips]{color}`

Since this package is not specific to the `slides` class, it is described in Section D.3.3 and not here.

The preamble may contain global specifications, such as to change the paper size or select page style, as usual. It may not contain any printable material.

Any text that appears after `\begin{document}` but before the special slide environments described below is output to an unnumbered *leading page* that comes before any slides. This may serve as a cover page for the slides.

There are three environments available for organizing different parts of a slide: the main *slide* itself, possible *overlays*, and additional *notes* to the slide.

### Slides

A slide or viewgraph is created by means of the environment

2ε `\begin{slide}`  *text and commands*  `\end{slide}`

The contents of a `slide` environment may be any text that one pleases. Note that the `slides` class makes use of its own set of character fonts.

The standard font in the normal size is roughly equivalent to the LaTeX sans serif font \sffamily in the size \LARGE. All the regular font commands and declarations of Section 4.1 are available, along with the other display and list environments of Chapter 4. However, there can be no page breaks within the environment, for the entire text is expected to fit on one page (slide or viewgraph). The successive slide environments will be numbered consecutively. If the page should overflow, a warning message is printed.

Any color commands from the color package may be employed, if that package has been loaded. The colors are then output directly, and not as layers as for the older SliTeX.

### Overlays

An *overlay* is an addition to a slide that can be laid on top of it to fill in certain gaps. The idea is to create suspense during a presentation, by filling in some key words a few minutes later, or to be able to replace some text by alternatives.

The slides class generates overlays with the overlay environment, which functions exactly the same as the slide environment, except that the numbering is done as a sub-number of the last slide. Thus the overlays following slide 6 are numbered 6-a, 6-b, and so on.

$\boxed{2\varepsilon}$ \begin{overlay}   *text and commands*   \end{overlay}

The slide environment for a viewgraph that is to have overlays must come before the overlay environments that go with it. Both the slide and overlay should contain identical texts, except that certain parts are printed in 'invisible' ink by means of the two declarations

\invisible   and   \visible

These two commands function just like font declarations. They may be set within curly braces {} to limit their range, or used to apply to the whole environment. Normally, in the slide, a few words might be made invisible, while in the corresponding overlay, \invisible is declared at the start and only those words that were blanked out in the slide are made visible. This may be seen in the sample on page 253.

One application for overlays is to present alternative text. One might, for example, show a table of cost estimates, with the figures on an overlay. By exchanging this overlay for another, new numbers that can be achieved by certain procedural changes may be fitted into the same table.

### Notes

During a presentation, it is often necessary to refer to a list of keywords or other notes between the actual projected slides. The slides class has the note environment for producing such reminders for the speaker.

\begin{note}  *text*  \end{note}

Like the overlays, notes are sub-numbered with respect to the previous slide, but with numbers instead of letters. Following slide 4, notes are numbered 4-1, 4-2, and so on.

## 0.3  Further features

### Page styles

The LATEX command \pagestyle{*style*} may also be used with the slides class. The following styles are available:

plain    All slides, overlays, and notes have their number at the lower right corner.

headings

The same as plain except that if the clock option is selected (see below), a time marker is printed in the lower left corner of the notes. This is the default page style.

(The distinction between headings and plain is greater in SʟɪTᴇX, where alignment markers are drawn for the former.)

empty    The sheets are printed with no page numbers (or alignment markers).

In normal LATEX, the command \pagestyle is issued in the preamble and is valid for the whole document. Individual pages may be given a different style by means of the \thispagestyle command which remains in effect for only one page. This command should not be employed within one of the environments, but rather a new \pagestyle command may be given *outside* of the slide, overlay, and note environments.

### Timing notes

The option clock can be selected with \documentclass; it activates two additional commands:

2ε \settime{*secs*}
2ε \addtime{*secs*}

and prints the time in minutes at the bottom of each note. In this way, the notes contain a reminder of how far advanced the presentation should be at that point. The value of the time marker is set and incremented with the above two commands, which take a number in seconds as argument. The initial value of the timer is 0.

### Selective slide processing

If the slide file possesses very many slide environments, it is possible that the user may want to alter only a small number of them, without having to output the complete set once again. This may be accomplished with the command

{*slide_list*}

in the preamble. The *slide_list* stands for a list of slide numbers in ascending order, for example, 2,5,9-12,15, specifying the slides, or range of slides, that are to be processed.

Non-existent slide numbers may also appear in the *slide_list*. If the slide file contains, say, 20 slides, the command \onlyslides{1,18-999} will allow only slides 1 and 18–20 to be processed. Any overlays that belong to these slides will also be output.

Finally, the command

{*note_list*}

in the preamble limits the notes that are output to those listed in *note_list*. Supposing that slide 5 has three note environments associated with it, \onlynotes{5} arranges that only the note pages 5-1, 5-2, and 5-3 are printed.

The \onlyslides and \onlynotes commands function similarly to the command \includeonly described in Section 8.1.2. An interactive means of selecting slides and notes to process may be set up exactly as illustrated in Section 8.1.3 with the \typein command:

```
\typein[\slides]{Which slides to do?}
\onlyslides{\slides}
```

During processing, the message 'Which slides to do?' is typed to the screen, and the user replies with the desired slide numbers. A similar scheme may be set up for \onlynotes.

### A sample slide file

An example of input text with the slides class, with a leading page, overlay, and note, and using the clock option, is given here. The four-page result is shown on the opposite page.

```
\documentclass[a4paper,clock]{slides}
\begin{document}
\begin{center}\Large\bfseries
Sample Viewgraphs
\end{center}

\begin{slide}
```

**The Leading Page**

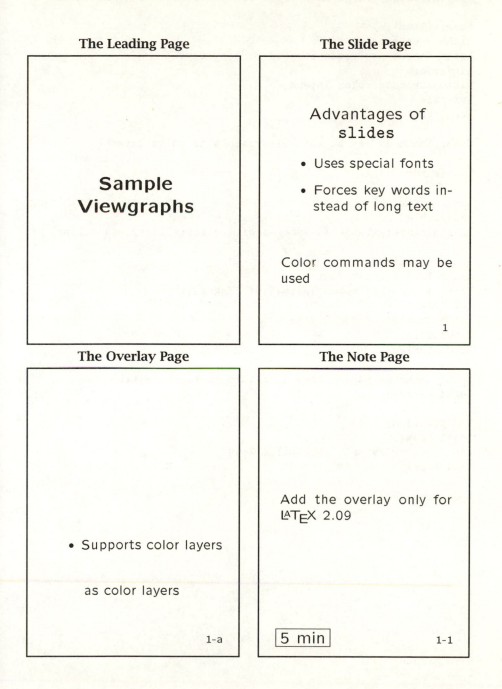

Sample
Viewgraphs

**The Slide Page**

Advantages of
slides

- Uses special fonts
- Forces key words in-
  stead of long text

Color commands may be
used

1

**The Overlay Page**

- Supports color layers

as color layers

1-a

**The Note Page**

Add the overlay only for
LATEX 2.09

5 min     1-1

```
\begin{center}\large Advantages of \texttt{slides}\end{center}

\begin{itemize}
\item Uses special fonts
\item Forces key words instead of long text
\invisible
\item Supports color layers
\visible
\end{itemize}

Color commands may be used {\invisible as color layers}

\end{slide}

\begin{overlay}
\invisible
\begin{center}\large Advantages of \texttt{slides}\end{center}

\begin{itemize}
\item Uses special fonts
\item Forces key words instead of long text
\visible
\item Supports color layers
\invisible
\end{itemize}

Color commands may be used {\visible as color layers}
\end{overlay}

\addtime{300}
\begin{note}
Add the overlay only for \LaTeX~2.09
\end{note}

\end{document}
```

# Error Messages

Errors are bound to be made at times during the preparation of a long LaTeX document. The mistakes can be of various kinds, from simple typing errors for command names to forgetting that some commands must be paired or to an incorrect syntax for a complicated command.

Errors during the LaTeX processing produce a list of messages on the terminal screen, which appear totally incomprehensible to the beginner. Even the advanced user can have difficulty figuring out a particular error message. However, these messages contain information about fundamental structures that can aid an experienced TeX programmer to see much deeper into the heart of the problem.

In addition, the error messages contain useful information even for the beginner. It is the purpose of this chapter to explain some of these messages that can be of assistance to non-programmers.

## Basic structure of error messages

Error messages have two sources: those from LaTeX and those from the underlying TeX program. The LaTeX messages are often followed by TeX messages since LaTeX operates at a higher level.

## .1  TeX error messages

We start with a simple error as an example.

```
\documentclass{article}
\begin{document}
The last words appear in \txetbf{bold face}.
\end{document}
```

Here the command \textbf has been mistakenly typed as \txetbf. During the processing, LaTeX assumes that the user wants to invoke a TeX command \txetbf. Since LaTeX does not know the TeX commands, it passes this text on to TEX, which then decides that there is no such command in its repertoire. The following error message is written to the screen:

```
! Undefined control sequence.
1.3 The last words appear in \txetbf
                               {bold face}.
?
```

The program stops at this point and waits for a response from the user. This message can be understood even by beginners. It consists of an error indicator that starts with an exclamation point !. Here the indicator is: ! Undefined control sequence, meaning that an *unknown command name* (control sequence) was the cause of the error. Next comes a *pair of text lines*, the *first* of which is prefixed with 1.3, meaning that the error occurred in 'line 3' of the input text. The error itself was encountered at the last symbol printed in this *upper* line. The *lower* line shows the continuation of the input line being processed when the error was found, here the words {bold face}. Before continuing, TEX waits for a reaction from the user, as indicated by the question mark in the last line of the message.

Entering another ? and carriage return as response produces the following information:

```
Type <return> to proceed, S to scroll future error messages,
R to run without stopping, Q to run quietly,
I to insert something, E to edit your file,
1 or ... or 9 to ignore next 1 to 9 tokens of input,
H for help, X to quit
?
```

This is a list of the possible user responses:

1. ⟨*return*⟩: simply typing the return key tells TEX to continue processing after making an attempt to handle the error according to some preprogrammed rules. In the case of an unknown command name, the error treatment is to ignore it.

2. S *scroll mode*: TEX continues the processing, writing further error messages to the screen as they are encountered, but without stopping for a user response. This is as though ⟨*return*⟩ were pressed after all subsequent errors.

3. R *run mode*: TEX continues processing as with S, but does not even stop as it would in *scroll mode* if the file named in an \input or \include command is missing.

4. Q *quiet mode*: the same as with R except that no further error messages are printed to the screen. They are, however, written to the .log file.

5. I *insert*: the mistake can be corrected by inserting the proper text. TeX puts the line of text entered from the keyboard into the processing in place of the error and then continues. Such a correction applies only to the processing: the original text in the .tex file is unchanged and must be altered with an editor. Typing in I\stop brings the program to a halt with the current page in the .dvi file.

6. 1 ...: entering a number less than 100 will delete that many characters and commands from the subsequent text. The program then stops to await further response from the user.

7. H *help*: an extended account of the problem is printed to the screen, which is more informative than the brief error indicator and which may contain tips for relieving the error.

8. X *exit*: The TeX processing is halted at this point. The current page does *not* appear in the .dvi file.

9. E *edit*: The process is halted as with X and a message is printed saying on which line of which file the error occurred. For some implementations, the editor may actually be called automatically, going directly to the faulty line.

The above response letters may be typed in either in capitals or in lower case. The response does not take effect until after ⟨*return*⟩ is pressed.

Typing H or h for *help* on the previous sample error message produces the text:

```
The control sequence at the end of the top line
of your error message was never \def'ed. If you have
misspelled it (e.g., '\hobx'), type 'I' and the correct
spelling (e.g., 'I\hbox'). Otherwise just continue
and I'll forget about whatever was undefined.

?
```

The error is described in more detail: the command name at the end of the upper line is unknown; if this is simply a typing error, enter the proper text with the I response, in this case I\textbf. Otherwise, press ⟨*return*⟩ and the faulty command will be ignored. The line of text will be processed as though it had been The last word appears in bold face. Of course, no bold face can actually appear.

The basic structure of a TeX error message is summarized as:

*Every error message begins with an error indicator, marked by a ! at the beginning of the first line. The indicator text is a brief description of the problem. Following are one or more lines of input text. The last symbol of the first of these lines is the one that has caused TeX to stop and print the error message. The last line contains the text or commands that are the next to be processed. TₑX waits for a response from the user. If that response is the typing of an H for help, a more detailed description, with possible tips, is printed to the screen, and TₑX waits for a further response.*

## 9.1.2   LaTeX error messages

One of the major differences between LaTeX 2.09 and LaTeX 2ε is the appearance of their error messages.  While the older version prints many lines of incomprehensible text in order to show the deep, internal coding that underlies the error, the newer one prints only that line of text where the actual error presumably occurred.  In the next section we will show samples of error messages from LaTeX 2.09, but otherwise all examples are from LaTeX 2ε, release <1994/06/01>.

As an example of a text with a LaTeX error, we take

```
\documentclass{article}
\begin{document}
\begin{qoute}\slshape
  Text indented at both ends
\end{quote}
\end{document}
```

Here the call \begin{quote} was incorrectly typed as qoute. The LaTeX processing writes the error message:

```
! LaTeX Error: Environment qoute undefined.

See the LaTeX manual or LaTeX Companion for explanation.
Type  H <return>  for immediate help.
 ...


1.3 \begin{qoute}
                  \slshape
?
```

The first line of this message states that LaTeX itself discovered this error, with a brief error indicator, in this case Environment qoute undefined. All LaTeX error messages begin with a line like this, followed by a reference to the LaTeX manuals for detailed explanation (which is also to be found in Section 9.3 of this book). The third line of text is a reminder that the response H ⟨*return*⟩ will also type additional clarification.

The line of three dots ... indicates that there are more lines of internal coding that have been suppressed. In LaTeX 2.09, these internal lines are actually printed, and even in LaTeX 2ε, it is possible to choose to have them appear. See Section 9.1.3.

The next pair of lines shows just where the processing was halted when the error was detected.  As for TₑX messages, the current input line of text is broken at the error, with the processed part on the first line, here \begin{qoute}, and the remainder on the next line. Here this remainder is \slshape. The line indicator 1.3 (small letter L, not number one) shows on which line (3) of the input file the error was found.

LaTeX now awaits a response from the user. Typing H ⟨return⟩ yields the additional information:

```
Your command was ignored.
Type I <command> <return> to replace it with another command,
or  <return>  to continue without it.
?
```

This means the last command in the upper line of the pair beginning with 1.3 has not been read into the processing. The mistake may thus be corrected *for the current process run only* with I\begin{quote} ⟨return⟩. The misspelling will still be in the text file, though, and needs to be removed by an editor run later.

However, if the processing is continued by simply pressing ⟨return⟩, then \begin{qoute} is ignored, as though this text were not in the source file. This leads directly to another error when the command \end{quote} is encountered, since now the matching \begin{quote} command is missing. The actual text of this second error message is:

```
! LaTeX Error: \begin{document} ended by \end{quote}.

See the LaTeX manual or LaTeX Companion for explanation.
Type  H <return>  for immediate help.
 ...

1.5 \end{quote}

?
```

The message again contains the standard LaTeX announcement, with error indicator, in the first line, followed by a reference to the manuals, and an invitation to type H for help. The error indicator in this case is

    \begin{document} ended by \end{qoute}.

This arises because when LaTeX encountered \end{quote}, it checked the name of the current environment. Since \begin{quote} was missing, the matching \begin command is the \begin{document} statement, producing a mismatched \begin...\end pair.

The last pair of lines again shows just how far the processing had occurred before the error was detected. In this case, the whole of the current line has already been taken in, so the remainder line is blank.

The response H ⟨return⟩ at this point leads to the same message as for the first error. A correction with an I entry will not do any good since the missing \begin{quote} can no longer be inserted ahead of the environment text. Entering I\begin{quote} will replace the \end{quote} with \begin{quote}, but that does not solve the real problem. The best response now is to type ⟨*return*⟩ so that the command \end{quote} is ignored and the processing continues.

Now both the faulty \begin{qoute} and correct \end{quote} commands are removed and the processing takes place as if the quote environment had never been in the source text at this point.

If the typing error qoute had been made in the \end instead of in the \begin command, the error message would have been:

```
! LaTeX Error: \begin{quote} on input line 3 ended by \end{qoute}

See the LaTeX manual or LaTeX Companion for explanation.
Type  H <return>  for immediate help.
 ...

1.5 \end{qoute}

?
```

The previous explanations should be enough for the reader to understand what is now being said. The error indicator here is

```
\begin{quote} on input line 3 ended by \end{qoute}
```

and the last pair of lines indicate that the problem is in line 5 and that the troublesome command is \end{qoute}. The obvious thing to do now, and the H message encourages this conclusion, is to make a correction with I\end{quote}. However, now a new message appears on the screen:

```
! Extra \endgroup.
<recently read> \endgroup
1.5 \end{qoute}

?
```

With the exception of the last pair beginning with 1.5, this makes no sense at all. The error indicator ! Extra \endgroup is seemingly meaningless. That this is a TeX error message and not a LaTeX one is hardly any compensation.

The frustrated user is not really to blame. The response was perfectly reasonable even if it was wrong.  Only experience could say that the best action at that point was to have just pressed ⟨*return*⟩. The quote environment is closed off anyway, although any special actions associated with \end{quote} would be left off.

The help message at this point is

```
Things are pretty mixed up, but I think the worst is over.
```

This is at least encouraging, and the reader should not lose heart. The best thing is to just keep on pressing ⟨return⟩ to get through the run.

We give here two recommendations for choosing a response, one specific and one general. The specific one is:

> If a false environment name appears in a \begin command, the proper correction of the error is
>
> I\begin{*right_name*}
>
> If the misspelling has occurred in the \end command, the best way to handle this mistake is just to press ⟨return⟩. The environment will be closed and any local declarations or definitions will be terminated. However, if there are any commands to be executed or text to be printed by the \end command, these will be missing.

The general recommendation is

> If the user knows how to correct the error with the help of the error message, this should be done with
>
> I *correction*
>
> Otherwise, one may give ⟨return⟩ and wait and see what happens. Even if more peculiar (TEX) error messages appear, one can keep on pressing ⟨return⟩ until the processing is finally at an end. The following print-out should indicate where the mistake was.

Instead of continually pressing ⟨return⟩, one may also enter S, R, or Q and ⟨return⟩ to speed up the error treatment (Section 9.1.1). Here, as with the simple ⟨return⟩ entry, the faulty commands are not just ignored. TEX attempts to treat them by making assumptions about what the user wanted to do at this spot. Only when this is no longer possible will TEX ignore the command completely. For example, if the indicator reads

\begin{*environment*} ended by \end{*environment*}

there was at least a \begin command with a valid environment name earlier. It could be assumed that the name of the environment in the \end command is wrong. LATEX thus tries to execute this command using the name of the current environment.

## .3    Error messages from LATEX 2.09

For comparison, we show the equivalent error messages from LATEX 2.09, after replacing \documentclass with \documentstyle in the sample input on page 258. The first message reads

```
LaTeX error.   See LaTeX manual for explanation.
                Type  H <return>  for immediate help.
! Environment qoute undefined.
\@latexerr ...diate help.}\errmessage {#1}

1.3 \begin{qoute}

?
```

The major difference here is that the error indicator appears in the third
line by itself, and not as part of the LaTeX error announcement in the first
line. The other difference is the strange text in the fourth line that begins
with \@latexerr .... This is actually part of the internal command that
produced the message, and should be simply ignored.

The second error message, which follows when ⟨return⟩ is pressed
without any corrective text, is more radically different from that for
LaTeX 2ε:

```
LaTeX error.   See LaTeX manual for explanation.
                Type  H <return>  for immediate help.
! \begin{document} ended by \end{quote}.
\@latexerr ...diate help.}\errmessage {#1}

\@checkend ...urrenvir \else \@badend {#1}
                                            \fi
\end ...me end#1\endcsname \@checkend {#1}
                                           \expandafter ...
1.5 \end{quote}

?
```

The extra pairs of line between the \@latexerr... and 1.5... show the
internal decoding of the \end command, something that is of no interest
or use to the regular LaTeX user. They only serve to confuse. If you are
still using LaTeX 2.09 and are presented with such error messages, you
should just ignore these lines altogether. Otherwise, the error indicators,
the input lines beginning with 1.n, the help messages, and the responses
are to be interpreted and employed as for LaTeX 2ε.

Sometimes it is desirable to look deeper behind the error message, especially
for practiced TeXperts who know how to interpret them. In this case, LaTeX 2ε can
be made to output the missing lines of coding by setting

> \setcounter{errorcontextlines}{*num*}

where *num* is the number of levels a macro will be decoded on an error. By default,
*num* = −1 for LaTeX 2ε, while for LaTeX 2.09 it is equal to 5. The knowledgeable
user can set it to 5 or more to gain this extra insight.

## .4    Error messages from TₑX macros

The majority of TₑX commands and practically all the LATₑX commands are so-called TₑX macros. These are combinations of primitive commands grouped together under a new command name, by which they may be called as a unit. TₑX macros are structures similar to those that may be defined by the LATₑX command \newcommand. Up to 9 arguments may be passed to them, just as for LATₑX commands. However, the corresponding TₑX commands for generating macros are more general than \newcommand.

In fact, of the approximately 900 Plain TₑX commands available, only 300 are primitives, or fundamental commands. The remaining 600 are macros. If an error occurs within a macro, the other commands within it may also be affected.

Here is an example for clarification. The command \centerline is a macro defined as

```
\def\centerline#1{\@@line{\hss#1\hss}}
```

in which \@@line is itself a macro while \hss is a TₑX primitive, a rubber length that can be infinitely stretched or shrunk. To avoid leading the reader into the murky depths of TₑX commands, we will simply point out that the above macro definition is more or less equivalent to the LATₑX command sequence

```
\newcommand{\centerline}[1]{\makebox[\textwidth][c]{#1}}
```

Now take the following sample source text

```
\documentclass{article}
\begin{document}
\centerline{This is an \invalid command}
\end{document}
```

in which a \ has been placed before the word invalid, making a false command named \invalid. During the LATₑX processing, the following TₑX error message appears:

```
! Undefined control sequence.
<argument> This is an \invalid
                                command
l.3 ...erline{This is an \invalid command}

?
```

This TₑX message is now a bit more understandable. The error indicator is the same as for the example in Section 9.1.1

```
! Undefined control sequence.
```

The following pair of lines claim that the error was recognized after the 'command' \invalid was processed, and that the next piece of text to be read in is the word command. As the same time, the <argument> at the beginning of the upper line says that this text is the argument of some other command.

The next pair of lines are familiar: the error occurred in line 3 of the input text, after the entire line, command and argument, had been read in for processing.

## 9.2    Some sample errors

### 9.2.1    Error propagation

The example with the incorrect \begin{qoute} environment showed that a simple response with the ⟨return⟩ key led to a second error message in spite of the fact that the \end{quote} command that produced it was correct. That one wrongly corrected error leads to further errors is more often the rule than the exception.

Let us look at the source text

```
\documentclass{article}
\begin{document}
\begin{itemie}
  \item This is the first point in the list
  \item And here comes the second
\end{itemize}
\end{document}
```

The only mistake in this text is the misspelled environment name itemie in place of itemize. The LaTeX processing first produces the same error message as for the incorrect quote environment earlier:

```
! LaTeX Error: Environment itemie undefined.

See the LaTeX manual or LaTeX Companion for explanation.
Type  H <return>  for immediate help.
 ...

1.3 \begin{itemie}

?
```

At this point, the user response I \begin{itemize} alleviates the error and the processing proceeds correctly.  However, if ⟨return⟩ is entered, a new error messages arises:

```
! LaTeX Error: Lonely \item--perhaps a missing list environment.
```

```
See the LaTeX manual or LaTeX Companion for explanation.
Type  H <return>  for immediate help.
 ...


1.4   \item T
             his is the first point in the list
?
```

What has happened here is that without the \begin command, the \item has been issued outside of a list environment, where it is rather meaningless. (Actually, it does have a meaning here: it prints an error message!) It is now too late to try to insert the missing start of the itemize environment. Typing H ⟨*return*⟩ for help yields

```
Try typing  <return>  to proceed.
If that doesn't work, type  X <return>  to quit.
?
```

Following this advice and pressing ⟨*return*⟩, one obtains the same error message once again, but this time on line 5, for the second \item command. Perservering further and pressing ⟨*return*⟩ once again, one is presented with

```
! LaTeX Error: \begin{document} ended by \end{itemize}.

See the LaTeX manual or LaTeX Companion for explanation.
Type  H <return>  for immediate help.
 ...


1.6 \end{itemize}


?
```

The itemize environment has now come to its end, but since it was never properly started, LaTeX complains about a mismatch of \begin and \end commands. Now at last, typing another ⟨*return*⟩ leads to a proper continuation of the processing. Of course the itemized text will be incorrectly formatted, but the rest of the document will not be affected.

In this example, a single mistake in the source text generated three further error messages. This is by no means unusual. Some LaTeX errors can produce hundreds of such successive errors. It is even possible that the chain of errors never ceases and that the processing never advances. In this case, there is nothing else to do but to terminate the program. This should be done with the entry I\stop after the next error message. It may be necessary to give it several times before it takes effect. If this does not work, that is, if the same message appears every time, then the response X ⟨*return*⟩ will halt the program immediately.

It is better to stop the program with I\stop than with X, since then the output will include the last page being processed. This can be of assistance in trying to deduce what the source of the error was.

The final lesson of this section is simply: *even when faced with a host of error messages, don't panic! Continue to press the return key to advance the processing.*

Pressing S ⟨*return*⟩ instead will produce the same set of error messages on the screen but without waiting for a user response in between (Section 9.1.1).

## 9.2.2  Typical serious errors

Occasionally it may happpen that a user forgets to include one of the commands \documentclass or \begin{document}, or the entire preamble. The last can easily occur when a LaTeX file is to be read in with \input or \include, but is mistakenly entered directly with the LaTeX program call. If a file with the text

```
This file has no preamble.
```

is put directly into the LaTeX processing, the following message appears on the screen:

```
! LaTeX Error: Missing \begin{document}.

See the LaTeX manual or LaTeX Companion for explanation.
Type  H <return>  for immediate help.
 ...

1.1 T
     his file has no preamble.
?
```

with the accompanying help message after typing H ⟨*return*⟩:

```
You're in trouble here.  Try typing  <return>  to proceed.
If that doesn't work, type  X <return>  to quit.
?
```

One sees from the error message that LaTeX has discovered a mistake on reading the very first letter of the text. The help message is also not very encouraging. There is no point trying to continue the processing with ⟨*return*⟩. Rather one should stop it with X or E right away, since nothing useful can be achieved here.

Even when the above example file contains the environment

```
\begin{document}
    This file has no preamble.
\end{document}
```

it is not possible to carry out a proper processing. The TeX error message now printed is

```
! LaTeX Error: The font size command \normalsize is not defined:
there is probably something wrong with the class file.

See the LaTeX manual or LaTeX Companion for explanation.
Type  H <return>  for immediate help.
 ...

1.1 \begin{document}

?
```

The error indicator is rather peculiar since the command \normalsize never appears in the input. Only the last two lines of this message are easily understood. They state that the error was recognized on line 1 after \begin{document} was read in. The fact that this is the text of the first line is enough to show that no meaningful processing can take place, since the mandatory \documentclass command that must precede it is missing.

Here again there is no choice but to halt the program with X or E, since a continuation of the processing would be meaningless.

(The reason for the strange error indicator is that many formatting parameters are initiated by the \begin{document} statement, including the standard font. It is here that \normalfont is called internally, and that command must be defined in the class file, which is missing. Other initiating commands are defined in the LaTeX format itself, and so they do not cause this error.)

If the name of the document class is wrongly typed, say as

> \documentclass{fred}

the following message appears:

```
! LaTeX Error: File 'fred.cls' not found.

Type X to quit or <RETURN> to proceed,
or enter new name. (Default extension: cls)

Enter file name:
```

This message should be fairly clear: the program is looking for a file with the name fred.cls but cannot find it, so would the user be so kind as to enter an alternative name. If the new name has the same extension as that requested (.cls), it need not be explicitly given. In this case, the name of any standard LaTeX class, such as article, report, book, or letter, may be typed in, as well as that of any additional classes that you might have access to. Of course, it should be the class for which the document was written.

This same error message is printed whenever a file is to be read in that cannot be found on the system. The issuing command may be \input,

\include, or \usepackage. If the file sought really does exist, perhaps it is not located where TEX is looking for files. Usually there is a system parameter set by the installation to point TEX to its files. If your file is somewhere else, you can trying entering its full name, with directory or path designations.

If LATEX is asking for a file that you know does not exist, or which is totally unknown to you, you will want to halt the processing right away or tell LATEX to skip the silly file. At this point, you have a problem. LATEX insists on a valid file name. Typing X ⟨*return*⟩ only produces the message once again, this time stating that it cannot find the file x.*ext*. Some installations provide a dummy file named null.tex, while one of the extension packages available (Section D.3.4) offers a set of files named after the standard response letters x.tex, e.tex, r.tex, h.tex, s.tex to emulate the responses to normal error messages.

**Emergency stop:** sometimes one reaches a situation where the program cannot be halted after an error, even with I\stop or X. In such a case, one has to apply the operating system's program interrupt. Details from the computer center or PC manuals.

## 9.2.3   Mathematical errors

Surprisingly few errors occur as a result of incorrect application of mathematical formula commands themselves, even for a user with only a little experience. More often, the errors in mathematical formulas are fiddly ones such as forgetting a closing brace } or neglecting to switch back to text mode. Another type of common error is to use a symbol in text mode that may only appear in math mode. We will point out a few typical examples here.

One wants to produce the text: 'The price is $3.50 and the order number is type_sample', and types in as source text:

```
The price is $3.50 and the order number is type_sample.
```

This text contains two errors, such that the first cancels the second one: the $ sign is the math mode switch for generating formulas within text (Section 5.1). The proper way to write a true dollar sign in text is as \$. Instead, in the sample text, the $ alone switches to math mode, setting everything that follows as a formula. However, the closing switch-back $ is missing, something that TEX will first notice at the end of the current paragraph.

```
! Missing $ inserted.
<inserted text>
                $
1.53

?
```

If ⟨*return*⟩ is simply pressed as a response, TEX inserts a $ at this point. For our sample text, this would be at the end of the text before the blank line. This means that the text from the first $ to the end of the paragraph will be set as a text formula:

The price is $3.50 and the order number is type_s ample.$

This output should show the user right away what went wrong. Near the end of the line, there is a letter s printed as an index. This is the second error in the example. The underbar character _ is only permitted in math mode and should have been typed here as \_. However, after the first $ had switched (incorrectly) into math mode, the _ sign became allowed, with the result that the following letter s was lowered.

If we now correct the text by replacing the $ sign with \$, then the _ symbol is no longer in math mode, producing the error message:

```
! Missing $ inserted.
<inserted text>
                $
1.5 ...$3.50 and the order number is type_
                                    sample.
?
```

Pressing ⟨*return*⟩ here tells TEX to recover from the error by inserting the apparently missing $ sign at this point before the math command _. The processing continues, and at some place before the end of the current paragraph, TEX will notice again that the closing $ is not present. The same error message is printed as in the first case. The processing goes on with another ⟨*return*⟩ response, with the result:

The price is $3.50 and the order number is type$_s ample.$

In all three cases, asking for more help with H would type to the screen:

```
I've inserted a begin-math/end-math symbol since I think
you left one out. Proceed, with fingers crossed.
```

The last sentence above is just what we recommend for mathematical error messages: *keep on pressing ⟨return⟩ or S to get through to the end of the processing, and then look at the printed output to find the mistake.*

## 2.4  Errors from multi-file texts

If the document text is split over many files that are to be read in with \input or \include commands, the line number in the error message refers to the file currently being read. A response with E ⟨*return*⟩ will call the editor program and open that file, going to the indicated line where the error was recognized. With the other responses, the editor has to be called separately, with the faulty file explicitly named.

It is possible to determine which file was being processed at the time of the error by examining the processing messages or the .log file. As the files are opened for reading, TEX writes an opening parenthesis ( and the name of the file to the terminal screen and to the .log file. When the file is closed, a closing parenthesis ) is printed. Output page numbers are similarly written to both the screen and .log file in square brackets. For example, if the screen contains the processing messages

```
..(sumfile.tex [1] [2] [3] (part1.tex [4] [5]) (part2.tex [6] [7]
! Undefined control sequence
1.999 \finish
?
```

this can be interpreted as follows: a file sumfile.tex was being read, and after pages 1, 2, and 3 had been output, the file part1.tex was read in with an \input or \include command inside the file sumfile.tex. Pages 4 and 5 were output and part1.tex was closed, after which another file part2.tex was opened for input. An error was discovered in line 999 of this file. If this error is corrected from the keyboard, or if the processing is otherwise continued, the screen messages proceed as

```
[8] [9]) [10]
! Too many }'s
1.217 \em sample}
```

The closing parenthesis after page 9 indicates that the file part2.tex has been closed. The next error is on page 10 in the main file sumfile.tex, since there is no closing ) for it. The error was discovered on line 217 of this file.

## 9.3     List of LATEX error messages

The LATEX error messages are listed here, divided into general, package, or font error messages. Within each group, they are ordered alphabetically according to the error indicators. A description of the possible causes and solutions is also given.

Many messages are new to LATEX 2$\varepsilon$, while others have a slightly altered text from the 2.09 version. All messages in LATEX 2$\varepsilon$ are preceded by the words ! LaTeX Error:, while in 2.09 the error identifier is prefixed only by the exclamation point and appears on the third line. If these are the only differences between the two texts, the 2.09 version is not shown.

The usual icons are used to indicate messages that are exclusive to one version or the other.

## 3.1    General LaTeX error messages

The following error messages are those not involving font selection or definition, nor any of the special features for LaTeX programming class and package files (Appendix C).

! LaTeX Error: ... undefined.

The argument of a \renewcommand or \renewenvironment has not been previously defined. The corresponding \new... command should be used instead.

! LaTeX Error: \< in mid line.

The command \< in a tabbing environment occurred in the middle of a line. This command may only appear at the beginning of a line (Section 4.6.3).

! LaTeX Error: Bad \line or \vector argument.

The first argument of a \line or \vector command specifies the angle of the line or arrow. This message states that the selected angle entries are invalid. See Sections 6.4.3 and 6.4.4.

! Bad use of \\.     (LaTeX 2.09)

2.09 (This message has been replaced by There's no line here to end in LaTeX 2ε.)

! LaTeX Error: Bad math environment delimiter.

LaTeX has encountered a math switch command in the wrong mode: either a \[ or \( command in math mode or the corresponding \] or \) in normal text mode. Either the math switches have been improperly paired or some braces {...} are incorrect.

! LaTeX Error: \begin{...} on input line ... ended by \end{...}.
! \begin{...} ended by \end{...}.     (LaTeX 2.09)

LaTeX has encountered an \end command without a corresponding \begin of the same name. This may be due to a typing mistake in the name of the environment, or to the omission of a previous \end command. A good way to avoid this error is always to enter the \end command immediately after the \begin, inserting the actual environment text with the editor in between the two. This is especially useful for long, nested environments. It also reduces the risk of typing the environment name incorrectly in the \end command.

! LaTeX Error: Can be used only in preamble.

Many commands may only be called within the preamble.    These include \documentclass, \usepackage, \nofiles, \includeonly, \makeindex, \makeglossary, and several others. Certain commands that only have meaning within class or package files, such as \ProvidesClass and \ProvidesPackage (Section C.2.1), as well as many \Declare.. and \Set.. commands are also only allowed in the preamble. If one of these commands is issued after \begin{document}, this message is printed.

```
! LaTeX Error: Command ... invalid in math mode.
```

[2ε] A command has been issued in math mode that only makes sense in text mode, such as \item or \circle. The LaTeX 2ε font commands \itshape, \bfseries, and so on, also produce this error in math mode, since the math alphabet commands \mathit, \mathbf should be used instead.

```
! LaTeX Error: Command ... already defined.
! Command name ... already used.    (LaTeX 2.09)
```

The user has tried to redefine an existing structure with one of \newenvironment, \newcommand, \newtheorem, \newsavebox, \newfont, \newlength, \newcounter, or \DeclareMathAlphabet. Either a different name must be selected or, in the case of commands and environments, the \renew... version must be employed. (Note that when an environment named sample is defined, the commands \sample and \endsample are also created.)

```
! LaTeX Error: Command ... undefined in encoding ....
```

[2ε] The specified command has been defined with \DeclareTextCommand for a certain NFSS encoding (say OT1) but was executed while another encoding (for example T1) for which there is no definition was active.

```
! LaTeX Error: Counter too large.
```

A counter that is to be printed as a letter contains a value greater than 26.

```
! LaTeX Error: Environment ... undefined.
```

LaTeX has encountered a \begin command with an unknown environment name. This is probably due to a typing mistake. It may be corrected during the processing with the response I followed by the correct name. (This does not alter the source file, where the error remains.)

```
! LaTeX Error: File '...' not found
Type X to quit or <RETURN> to proceed,
or enter new name. (Default extension: ...)
Enter file name:.
```

[2ε] A file is to be loaded with one of the inputting commands, but it cannot be found. You may type a new file name, or quit, or proceed without it.

If the file name has been given correctly, and it does exist, maybe it is not located where LATEX looks for files. Make sure that it is in one of the right directories. The user is offered a chance to type in an alternative, or correctly typed, name via the keyboard. Type in the file name, with optional extension, and press ⟨*return*⟩. LATEX proposes a default extension that is the same as that requested. There is no default for the main part of the file name.

`! LaTeX Error: Float(s) lost.`

A `figure` or `table` environment or a `\marginpar` command was given within a vertical box (`\parbox` or `minipage` environment), or these structures were issued within a LATEX command that uses vertical boxes internally, such as a footnote. This error is first recognized by LATEX when a page is output so that the actual cause could be many lines earlier in the text. A number of tables, figures, or marginal notes may have been lost as a result, but certainly not the one that triggered the problem.

`! LaTeX Error: Illegal character in array arg.`

A `tabular` or `array` environment contains an unknown column formatting character (see Section 4.8.1) or the formatting entry in the second argument of a `\multicolumn` command is wrong.

`! LaTeX Error: \include cannot be nested.`

⌐2ε⌐ An attempt has been made to call `\include` from a file that has already been read in by an `\include` command. All `\include` commands must be issued in the main file (Section 8.1.2).

`! LaTeX Error: LaTeX2e command ... in LaTeX 2.09 document.`

⌐2ε⌐ This error occurs if a LATEX 2ε command is used in compatibility mode, that is, if the document uses `\documentstyle` instead of `\documentclass`. Some of these are `\LaTeXe`, `\usepackage`, `\ensuremath`, the `lrbox` environment, as well as the new syntax for adding an optional argument with `\newcommand` and `\newenvironment`. The reason that these are forbidden in compatibility mode is so that the author can be sure that the document conforms to LATEX 2.09 if it is to be sent to other installations that only have the older version.

`! LaTeX Error: Lonely \item--perhaps a missing list environment.`

An `\item` command has been given outside of a list environment (Section 4.3). Either the environment name has been misspelled in the `\begin` command and not corrected by keyboard entry, or the `\begin` command has been forgotten.

! LaTeX Error: Missing @-exp in array arg.

The column formatting argument of a `tabular` or `array` environment
contains a @ symbol without the necessary following text in curly braces
{ } that must go with it (Section 4.8.1 for @-expressions), or the same
thing occurs in the second argument of a `\multicolumn` command.

! LaTeX Error: Missing begin{document}.

Either the `\begin{document}` command has been forgotten or there is
printable text inside the preamble of the document. In the latter case,
there could be a declaration with incorrect syntax, such as a command
argument without curly braces { } or a command name without the
backslash `\`.

! LaTeX Error: Missing p-arg in array arg.

The column formatting argument of a `tabular` or `array` environment
contains a p symbol without the necessary width specification that must
go with it (Section 4.8.1), or the same thing occurs in the second argument
of a `\multicolumn` command.

! LaTeX Error: No counter '...' defined.
! No such counter.     (LaTeX 2.09)

A `\setcounter` or `\addtocounter` command was called that referred
to a counter name that does not exist. Most likely the name was typed
incorrectly. If this error occurs while an `.aux` file is being read and if
the name of the counter is indeed correct, the defining `\newcounter`
command was probably given outside of the preamble. Therefore it is
highly recommended always to give the `\newcounter` commands inside
the preamble. (If the other LaTeX counter commands are used with an
undefined counter name, a long list of funny TeX error messages appears.)

! No theorem environment '...' defined.     (LaTeX 2.09)

[2.09] (In LaTeX 2$_\varepsilon$, this message is replaced by No counter defined.)
A `\newtheorem` command has been given with an optional argument
naming another theorem-like declaration that shares the same counter,
but this other theorem does not exist (Section 4.5). Either the name of the
other theorem has been misspelled or it has not been previously defined.

! LaTeX Error: No \title given.

[2$_\varepsilon$] The `\maketitle` command has been given before `\title` has been declared.

! LaTeX Error: Not in outer par mode.

A `figure` or `table` environment or a `\marginpar` command was given within math mode or inside a vertical box (\parbox or minipage environment). In the first case, the math switch-back command was probably forgotten.

! LaTeX Error: Page height already too large.

2ε The command \enlargethispage is trying to extend the vertical size of the page, which LaTeX already considers too large.

! LaTeX Error: \pushtabs and \poptabs don't match.

The number of \poptabs commands in a tabbing environment does not agree with the number of previous \pushtabs given (Section 4.6.4).

! LaTeX Error: Something's wrong--perhaps a missing \item.

The most likely cause of this error is that the text in a list environment (list, itemize, enumerate, or description) does not begin with an \item command. It will also occur if thebibliography environment is given without the argument {*sample_label*} (Section 4.3.6).

! LaTeX Error: Suggested extra height (...) dangerously large.

2ε The command \enlargethispage is trying to extend the vertical size of the page more than LaTeX considers reasonable.

! LaTeX Error: Tab overflow.

The last \= command in a tabbing environment exceeded the maximum number of tab stops allowed by LaTeX.

! LaTeX Error: There's no line here to end.
! Bad use of \\.     (LaTeX 2.09)

The command \newline or \\ has been issued after a \par or blank line where it makes no sense. If additional vertical space is to be inserted here, this should be done with a \vspace command.

! LaTeX Error: This may be a LaTeX bug.

This message states that LaTeX is fully confused. This could be the result of a previous error after which the user response was to press ⟨*return*⟩. In this case, the processing should be brought to a halt with I\stop or X or E and the earlier error corrected. It is also possible, although unlikely, that there is a bug in the LaTeX program itself. If this is the first error message in the processing, and the text seems otherwise to be satisfactory, the file should be saved and submitted to the computing center for further investigation.

`! LaTeX Error: Too deeply nested.`

Too many list environments (description, itemize, enumerate, or list) have been nested inside one another.  The maximum depth of such nesting is dependent on the installation but should always be at least four.

`! LaTeX Error: Too many columns in eqnarray environment.`

$2_\varepsilon$ The eqnarray environment may only have three columns per line. You may have forgotten to start a new row with \\, or have placed an extra & in the line.

`! LaTeX Error: Too many unprocessed floats.`

This error may occur if there are too many \marginpar commands on one page. However, it is more likely that LaTeX is retaining more figure and table floats than it can hold. This happens if too many such float objects have been given before they can be output (Section 6.6). In this case, the last figure or table should be added later in the text. Another cause could be that the figure or table cannot be located on a normal text page, but rather on a special float page at the end of the text or after a \clearpage or \cleardoublepage command. Since the output sequence of figures and tables will be the same as that with which they were input, one such float can block the entire queue. A \clearpage or \cleardoublepage command can free the blockage.

`! LaTeX Error: Undefined tab position.`

A \>, \+, \-, or \< command in a tabbing environment has tried to move to a tabulator stop that does not exist (Section 4.6).

`! LaTeX Error: \verb ended by end of line.`

$2_\varepsilon$ The text of an in-line verbatim command \verb+...+ extends over more than one line of text.  This is permissible in LaTeX 2.09, but in LaTeX $2_\varepsilon$, it is forbidden in order to catch a common error: the missing terminating character.  Make sure that the entire text between the initial and terminating characters is all on one input line.

`! LaTeX Error: \verb illegal in command argument.`

$2_\varepsilon$ The \verb command may not be used in the argument of any other command, except \index and \glossary.  It may not be used within section titles or footnotes, for example.

## .2   LaTeX package errors

The special programming commands for handling class and package files
(Appendix C) have their own set of error messages. If one of these features
issues a serious error, there is often little the user can do about it other
than report the problem to the author of the file. On the other hand,
some errors are due to the improper use of the file or of the options that
it provides.

Often classes and packages contain their own error or warning messages with text and meanings that are peculiar to them. These are indicated as such, along with the name of the class or package that issued
them. For example, the package mypack could print the error

```
Package mypack Error: cannot mix options 'good'
(mypack)              and 'bad'.
```

A help message should also be available when H is typed. Obviously,
such error (and warning) messages cannot be explained here, since they
depend entirely on the package in question.

```
! LaTeX Error: \LoadClass in package file.
```

[2ε] A package file has called \LoadClass, which it is not allowed to do. A
class file can only be loaded from another class file.

```
! LaTeX Error: Option clash for package ....
```

[2ε] The specified package has been requested a second time with a different
set of options. A package file will only be loaded once and a second
attempt will be ignored. Thus, if two \usepackage or \RequirePackage
commands load the same package with different options, there is a conflict. Try to arrange for a consistent set. Typing H for help after this
message will print out the two sets of options.

```
! LaTeX Error: \RequirePackage or \LoadClass in Options Section.
```

[2ε] These two commands may not appear in the definition of a class or
package option made with the \DeclareOption command. Instead, the
option should set some flag or other indicator that is later tested before
calling the command in question.

```
! LaTeX Error: This file needs format '...' but this is '...'.
```

[2ε] The \NeedsTeXFormat command specifies a different format from the
one being used. The *format* is the pre-stored set of instructions that
determine what type of TeX is being run. For LaTeX 2ε, the format name
specified must be LaTeX2e. This file cannot be processed at all with the
current format in use.

```
! LaTeX Error: Two \documentclass or \documentstyle commands.
```

2ε A document may contain only one \documentclass or \documentstyle command. If you can only see one in the main document file, check that other files being loaded do not contain an offending second one.

```
! LaTeX Error: Two \LoadClass commands.
```

2ε The class file contains more than one \LoadClass command, something that is not allowed. The class file has been improperly written.

```
! LaTeX Error: Unknown option '...' for package '...'.
```

2ε An option has been specified with \usepackage but it is not defined for that package. Check the instructions for the package or look for a misprint.

```
! LaTeX Error: \usepackage before \documentclass.
```

2ε The \usepackage command may not appear before \documentclass. A class file must be loaded before any packages.

### 9.3.3 LaTeX font errors

The following error messages occur when defining or selecting fonts with the New Font Selection Scheme (Section 8.5). Some of these messages indicate that the fonts have not been properly set up, in which case the font description files may be corrupted or contain mistakes. In either case, the system manager must see that a proper set of files are installed.

```
! LaTeX Error: ... allowed only in math mode.
```

2ε A math alphabet command such as \mathbf has been used in text mode. Perhaps a $ has been forgotten.

```
! LaTeX Error: Command '...' not defined as a math alphabet.
```

2ε The name of a non-existent math alphabet has been specified in one of the \Set.. or \Declare.. commands that take a math alphabet name as argument. The math alphabet name must be declared with the command \DeclareMathVersion before it may be used.

```
! LaTeX Error: Command ... not provided in base LaTeX2e.
```

2ε A number of symbols that were part of the basic LaTeX 2.09, but not in TeX, are no longer automatically included in LaTeX 2ε. Add the package latexsym to include them.

```
! LaTeX Error: \DeclareTextComposite used on inappropriate
                command ....
```

[2ε] \DeclareTextComposite (Section 8.5.9) is used to redefine an existing accenting command to print a single character for a certain encoding. If the accenting command does not already exist, this message is issued.

```
! LaTeX Error: Encoding scheme '...' unknown.
```

[2ε] A font declaration or selection command that refers to a non-existent encoding scheme has been issued.  There is probably a typing error involved here.

```
! LaTeX Error: Font family '...+...' unknown.
```

[2ε] A \DeclareFontShape command has been issued for a font encoding and family combination that has not been previously declared by means of a \DeclareFontFamily command (Section 8.5.8).

```
! LaTeX Error: Font ... not found.
```

[2ε] The font with the specified attributes could not be found, nor could an adequate substitution be made. The font defined by \DeclareErrorFont is used instead.

```
! LaTeX Error: Math alphabet identifier ... is undefined
                in math version '...'.
```

[2ε] A math alphabet (Section 8.5.5 that has not been defined for the current math version has been invoked.  This means that the alphabet has been created by \DeclareMathAlphabet with an empty shape attribute, but no \SetMathAlphabet declaration has been given to define it for the selected math version.

```
! LaTeX Error: Math version '...' is not defined.
```

[2ε] The name of a non-existent math version has been specified in one of the \Set... or \Declare... commands that take a math version name as argument. The version name must be declared with \DeclareMathVersion before it may be used.

```
! LaTeX Error: *** NFSS release 1 command ... found
                *** Recovery not possible. Use ....
```

[2ε] A command from the first version of NFSS has been used, which is no longer valid. Use the suggested replacement command instead.

```
! LaTeX Error: Not a command name: '...'.
```

[2ε] The first argument of \DeclareMathAccent must be a command name, like \acute. Most likely the backslash \ character has been forgotten.

```
! LaTeX Error: Symbol font '...' not defined.
```

²ε The name of a non-existent symbol font has been specified in one of the \Set.. or \Declare.. commands that take a symbol font name as argument. The font name must be declared with \DeclareSymbolFont before it may be used as a symbol font.

```
! LaTeX Error: The font size command \normalsize is not defined:
                there is probably something wrong with class file.
```

²ε It is necessary for class files to define \normalsize, the basic size of standard text in the document. This is a change from the practice in LaTeX 2.09. If the class file does not do this, if it only defines \@normalsize, then it must be repaired. This message also appears if \documentclass is missing, for an empty class file is clearly a faulty one.

```
! LaTeX Error: This NFSS system isn't set up properly.
```

²ε Something is wrong with the font descriptions in the .fd files, or there is no valid font declared by \DeclareErrorFont. This is a serious problem, to be reported to the system manager.

```
! LaTeX Error: Too many math alphabets used in version ....
```

²ε There is a limit of 16 math alphabets possible, a number set by TeX itself. Any additional math alphabet definitions are ignored.

```
! LaTeX Error: Unknown symbol font '...'.
```

²ε The name of a non-existent symbol font has been used as argument to the command \DeclareSymbolFontAlphabet. The font name must first be declared with \DeclareSymbolFont before it may be used.

## 9.4     TeX error messages

This section contains a list of some of the most common TeX error messages, ordered alphabetically according to the error indicator, together with a brief description of the possible cause. Each one begins with an exclamation point only. Since these messages are generated by TeX, there is no difference between LaTeX 2.09 and LaTeX 2ε.

```
! Counter too large.
```

As a TeX error, this message refers to a footnote marked either with letters or symbols in which the counter has exceeded a value of 26 or 9. It may also occur if there are too many \thanks commands on a title page.

`! Double subscript.`

A mathematical formula contains two subscripts for the same variable, for example, `x_2_3` or `x_{2}_{3}`. The proper way to produce $x_{2_3}$ is with `x_{2_3}` or `x_{2_{3}}` (Section 5.2.2).

`! Double superscript.`

A mathematical formula contains two superscripts for the same variable, for example, `x^2^3` or `x^{2}^{3}`. The proper way to produce $x^{2^3}$ is with `x^{2^3}` or `x^{2^{3}}` (Section 5.2.2).

`! Extra alignment tab has been changed to \cr.`

A line in a `tabular` or `array` environment contains more & commands than there are columns defined. The error is probably due to a forgotten `\\` at the end of the previous line.

`! Extra }, or forgotten $.`

In math mode, either an opening brace { has been left off or an extra closing brace } has been included by mistake. Another possibility is that a math mode switch command such as $, \[, or \( has been forgotten.

`! Font ... not loaded: Not enough room left.`

The text processing requires more character fonts to be loaded than TEX can handle owing to memory limitations. If certain parts of the document need different fonts, you can try to split it up and to process the parts separately.

`! I can't find file '...'.`

This message has actually been replaced by the LATEX $2_\varepsilon$ equivalent `File ... not found`, and functions much the same way. The specified file is to be read in but it cannot be found in the directories being searched. The user has an opportunity to type in an alternative (or the correctly spelled) name. After printing the error indicator, TEX asks for the name of another file to read:

  `Please type another input file name:`

and then waits for you to enter the new name and to press ⟨*return*⟩. Unlike for the LATEX $2_\varepsilon$ message, the default file extension is always `.tex` and not the extension requested.

`! Illegal parameter number in definition of ....`

This error message is probably due to a `\newcommand`, `\newenvironment`, `\renewcommand`, or `\renewenvironment` command in which the substitution character # has been applied incorrectly. This character may appear within the defining text only in the form #$n$, where $n$ is a number between 1 and the number of arguments specified in the command. Otherwise the character # may only appear in the definition as \#. This error may also arise if the substitution character is applied within the last argument {*end_def*} (Section 7.4).

`! Illegal unit of measure (pt inserted).`

If this error message comes right after another error with the message

`! Missing number, treated as zero.`

the problem lies with this previous error (see below). Otherwise, the mistake is that TEX expects a length specification at this point but has only been given a number without a length unit. This occurs most often when a length is to be set to zero and 0 has been typed in instead of 0mm or 0pt. If this is the case, then responding with ⟨*return*⟩ produces the right result since for a zero value any unit specification is all right. This error may also occur if a length specification has been completely forgotten.

`! Misplaced alignment tab character &.`

The single character command & has been given in normal text outside of the `tabular` and `array` environments. Possibly the intention was to print &, in which case \& should be typed. This may still be achieved during the processing by responding with I\& to the error message.

`! Missing control sequence inserted.`

This error is most likely caused by a \newcommand, \renewcommand, \newlength, or \newsavebox command in which the backslash \ is missing from the first argument. Pressing ⟨*return*⟩ as response will complete the processing correctly since TEX assumes a backslash is missing and inserts it.

`! Missing number, treated as zero.`

This error is most likely due to a LATEX command that expects a number or length as argument, which is missing. It may also occur when a command that takes an optional argument is followed by text beginning with [. Finally another cause can be a \protect command preceding a length or \value command.

`! Missing { inserted.`
`! Missing } inserted.`

TEX is totally confused when either of these error indicators is written. The line number printed will probably not be where the source of the error is to be found, which is a missing opening or closing brace. If the error is not obvious, continue the processing by pressing ⟨*return*⟩ and try to deduce where it might be from the printed output.

`! Missing $ inserted.`

Most likely a symbol or command that may only appear in math mode was used in normal text. Recall that all those commands described in Chapter 5 are only allowed in math mode unless otherwise stated. If an \mbox command is inserted within a math formula, its argument has temporarily exited from math to normal text mode. The message may also occur if a blank line appears within a math formula, signalling a new paragraph and the end of the formula without the necessary $ sign.

`! Not a letter.`

The word list in a \hyphenation command contains a character that is not recognized as a letter, such as an accent command like \'{e}. Such words can only be hyphenated by explicitly inserting the hyphenation possibilities (Sections 3.6.1 and 3.6.2).

`! Paragraph ended before ... was complete.`

The argument of a command contains a blank line or a \par command, something that is not allowed. Probably a closing brace } has been omitted.

`! \scriptfont ... is undefined (character ...).`
`! \scriptscriptfont ... is undefined (character ...).`
`! \textfont ... is undefined (character ...).`

These messages arise in LaTeX 2.09 when a math formula makes use of symbols in a font which was not designed for math mode, such as \sf (sans serif). Such character fonts must be made available with the command \load{*size*}{*style*}, for example \load{\normalsize}{\sf}. If such a formula is to appear in a footnote, it is necessary to give \load {\footnotesize}{\sf} beforehand. In LaTeX 2$_\varepsilon$, this problem does not arise with the math alphabet commands such as \mathsf.

`! TeX capacity exceeded, sorry [...].`

TeX sets up various storage buffers in the computer memory to carry out the text processing. This message appears when one of these buffers is full and can no longer be used. The name of the buffer and its maximum size are printed in the square brackets of the error indicator. With this message, the TeX processing is terminated. The source of this problem is hardly ever due to insufficient memory, no matter how much complicated text is being processed, but rather to an error in the text itself. The methods described in Section 9.6 may be applied to try to detect the true error.

The following descriptions of the various buffers should help to decide whether the storage capacity allotted to TeX really is too small and to explain what one might do to correct this.

buffer size The problem here can be that the text in the argument of a sectioning, \caption, \addcontentsline, or \addtocontents command is too long. The message then normally appears when the \end{document} command is processed, but may also arise at one of \tableofcontents, \listoffigures, of \listoftables. The way to avoid this is to use the optional argument for the short form of the heading text (Sections 3.3.3 and 6.6.4). Indeed, such a long entry in the table of contents is a nuisance anyway and should be shortened. After the correction has been made in the source text, the previous LaTeX .aux file must be deleted before reprocessing.

This problem can occur on a PC if a word processing program has been used to generate the source text instead of a text editor. Some of these programs put an entire paragraph into a single line even though the text on the screen is broken up into lines.

exception dictionary The list of hyphenation exceptions that have been entered with the \hyphenation commands has become too large. Words used less frequently should be removed and their possible word divisions indicated explicitly with the \- command.

hash size The source file contains too many command definitions or uses too many cross-reference markers. This does not mean that the source text really needs all these commands, for it may be that the user has developed a large collection of private commands that are stored in a single file and read into every document, whether they are all applicable or not.

input stack size An overflow of this buffer is probably due to a mistake in a command definition. For example, the command defined with

```
\newcommand{\com}{One more \com}
```

produces One more {One more {...One more \com}...}} going on for ever, since it continually calls itself. Actually, it does not go on for ever, but only until this buffer is full.

main memory size This buffer contains the text for the page currently being processed. It also overflows if a recursively defined command has been called. However, the more usual reasons are: (1) a large number of very complicated commands have been defined on one page; (2) there are too many \index or \glossary commands on one page; (3) the page itself is too complex to fit all within the allotted buffer space.

The solution to the first two situations is clear: reduce the number of command definitions and/or \index and \glossary commands on that page. In the third case, the cause might be a long tabbing, tabular, array, or picture environment, or a stuck float (figure or table) waiting for an output command.

To find out whether the memory overflow is really due to an overly complex page, add the command \clearpage just before the spot where the overflow occurs. If the error message no longer appears on the next processing run, then this page was indeed too complicated for TeX. However, if the overflow still persists, the error is probably a mistake in the source text. If necessary, it may have to be located with the method explained in Section 9.6.

If the page really is too complex for the TᴇX processing, it must be simplified. However, first recall that the entire last paragraph is processed before that page is output, even if the page break occurs near the beginning of the paragraph. Introducing a \newpage may solve the problem and should be tried out before attempting a tedious restructuring of the text. If the error is due to a stuck figure or table, it might be alleviated by moving the float object to later in the text, or by changing the positioning argument (Section 6.6.1). If the whole text is not yet complete, one can try giving \clearpage for now in order to clear the blocked floats and then decide on a better ordering when the text is finalized.

pool size Most likely there are too many command definitions and/or labels, or their names are too long. Try shortening the names. This error may also occur if a closing right brace } has been forgotten in the argument of a counter command such as \setcounter or in a \newenvironment or \newtheorem command.

save size This buffer overflows when commands, environments, and the range of declarations are nested too deeply. For example, if the argument of a \multiput command contains a picture environment, which in turn possesses a \footnotesize declaration with another \multiput command, and so on. Such a nesting must be simplified, unless the real problem is a forgotten closing brace } that merely makes the structure appear so complex.

`! Text line contains an invalid character.`

The source text contains a strange symbol that TᴇX does not recognize. This could be a problem with the editor itself, that it is inserting extra characters. If an examination of the source file does not reveal the strange symbol, consult the computing center for help.

`! Undefined control sequence.`

Every TᴇX user encounters this error message on his screen at some point. It is usually the result of an incorrectly typed command name. It may be amended during the processing by responding with I and the proper name of the command, plus ⟨return⟩. This does not alter the source file, which must be corrected separately after the LATᴇX run. If the command name has been entered correctly in a LATᴇX command, it may be that it was issued in an improper environment where it is not allowed (that is, not defined there).

`! Use of ... doesn't match its definition.`

If '...' is the name of a LATᴇX command, it is likely that one of the picture commands from Sections 6.3 and 6.4 has been called with the wrong syntax for its arguments. If the name is \@array, there is a faulty @-expression (Section 4.8.1) in a tabular or array environment. Possibly a fragile command was given in the @-expression without the \protect command preceding it.

```
! You can't use 'macro parameter #' in ... mode.
```

The special symbol # has been used in normal text. Probably there should have been a \# in order to print # itself. This can be corrected during the processing with the response I\# and ⟨return⟩.


## 9.5    Warnings

TEX and LATEX errors both bring the processing run to a temporary stop and wait for a reaction from the user, or they may halt the program completely. Warnings, on the other hand, merely inform the user that the processed output may contain some faults that he or she might want to correct. Warnings appear on the screen along with the page number where they occur, without the program coming to a stop. They are also written to the .log file where they may be examined after the LATEX processing and possible printing. Warnings may be issued either by LATEX or by TEX itself.


### 9.5.1    General LATEX warnings

LATEX warnings are indicated by the words 'LaTeX Warning:' at their start, followed by the warning message itself.

```
LaTeX Warning: Citation '...' on page ... undefined on
                input line ....
```

The keyword in a \cite command has not yet been defined with a corresponding \bibitem command (Sections 4.3.6 and 8.3.2).

```
LaTeX Warning: Citation '... ' undefined on input line ....
```

The keyword in a \nocite command has not yet been defined.

```
LaTeX Warning: Command ... has changed.
                Check if current package is valid.
```

The \CheckCommand statement is used to test if a given command has a certain definition. This warning is issued if the test fails. This is used to be sure that a given package is doing what the programmer thinks it is doing.

LaTeX Warning: Float too large for page by ..pt on input line ...

[2ε] A float (`figure` or `table` environment) is too big to fit on the page. It will be printed anyway, but will extend beyond the normal page margins.

LaTeX Warning: 'h' float specifier changed to 'ht'.

[2ε] The float placement specifier 'h' for 'here' (Section 6.6.1) does not really mean exactly at the location of the float environment. It will be placed 'here' only if there is enough room remaining on the page for it, otherwise it appears at the top of the next available page. This message is a reminder of this fact.

LaTeX Warning: inputting '...' instead of obsolete '...'.

[2ε] Some packages written for LaTeX 2.09 explicitly input certain files, such as `article.sty`, that have a new equivalent with a different name (in this case `article.cls`). Dummy files with the old names that issue this message and input the right file are provided.

LaTeX Warning: Label '...' multiply defined.

Two \label or \bibitem commands have defined markers with the same name (Sections 8.3.1 and 8.3.2). Even after the correction has been made, this message will be printed once more to the screen since the information that led to it is to be found in the .aux file from the last processing run. On the run after that, it should be gone.

LaTeX Warning: Label(s) may have changed.
              Rerun to get cross-references right.

The printed outputs from the \ref, \pageref, and \cite commands may be incorrect since their values have been altered during the processing. LaTeX must be run once more so that the right values are used.

LaTeX Warning: Marginpar on page ... moved.

A marginal note on the given page has been shifted downwards to prevent it from being too close to another one. This means that it will not be beside the line of text where the \marginpar command was actually given.

LaTeX Warning: No \author given.

[2ε] The \maketitle command has been issued without a previous \author command. Unlike a missing \title command, this is not an error, but merely peculiar. The warning is printed just in case you did mean to specify an author.

LaTeX Warning: Optional argument of \twocolumn too tall on page..

[2ε] The \twocolumn command (Section 3.2.5) starts a new page and switches to two-column formatting. The text in the optional argument is printed in one wide column above the double column text. If that text is too large to fit onto one page, this warning is printed.

```
LaTeX Warning: Oval too small on input line ....
```

The size specified for an \oval command is too small for LaTeX to find an appropriate quarter circle for it.

```
LaTeX Warning: Reference '...' on page ... undefined on
                input line ....
```

The marker name in a \ref or \pageref command has not been defined by a \label command in the previous processing run (Section 8.3.1). If this message does not disappear on the next run, the corresponding \label command is missing.

```
LaTeX Warning: Text page ... contains only floats.
```

$\boxed{2_\varepsilon}$ This message points out that the float style parameters (Section 6.6.3) have excluded any regular text from appearing on the specified page. This is not necessarily bad, but you might want to check that page visually.

```
LaTeX Warning: There were multiply-defined labels.
```

$\boxed{2_\varepsilon}$ This message is printed at the end of the LaTeX run if there were any \label or \bibitem commands that used the same marker name more than once. A warning is also printed near the beginning of the run for each repeated marker name.

```
LaTeX Warning: There were undefined references.
```

$\boxed{2_\varepsilon}$ This message is printed at the end of the LaTeX run if there were any \ref or \pageref commands whose markers had not been defined during a previous run. A warning is also printed earlier for each undefined marker used.

## 9.5.2    LaTeX package warnings

The class and package warnings are those that check the names and versions of the loaded files against those requested, or the use of options, or whether the filecontents environment has written some text to a file. The commands involved are described in Section C.2.9.

Classes and packages can also issue their own warnings which are peculiar to them. These cannot be listed here, since they depend entirely on the class or package itself.

```
LaTeX Warning: File '...' already exists on the system.
                Not generating it from this source.
```

[2ε] The `filecontents` environment is *not* extracting text from the main file because it has discovered a file of the same name already on the system.

```
LaTeX Warning: Unused global option(s):.
```

[2ε] Options specified in the `\documentclass` statement are *global*, meaning they can apply to the class and/or to any following packages. However, if no class or package recognizes any of these options, this warning is printed, followed by a list of the unused options.

```
LaTeX Warning: Writing file '...'.
```

[2ε] The `filecontents` environment (Section C.2.9) is extracting text out of the main file and writing it to a file of the given name.

```
LaTeX Warning: You have requested class/package '...',
                but the class/package provides '...'.
```

[2ε] The name of the class or package as given by its internal identifying command `\ProvidesClass` or `\ProvidesPackage` does not agree with the file that was read in with `\usepackage` or `\RequirePackage`.

```
LaTeX Warning: You have requested, on input line ..., version
                '...' of class/package ...,
                but only version '...' is available.
```

[2ε] The date of a class or package file, as given by its internal identifying command `\ProvidesClass` or `\ProvidesPackage`, is earlier than that asked for by the `\usepackage` or `\RequirePackage` command. The class or package may not have all the features that the inputting file expects.

```
LaTeX Warning: You have requested release '...' of LaTeX,
                but only release '...' is available.
```

[2ε] The date of your LaTeX version is earlier than that specified for some input file in a `\NeedsTeXFormat` command (Section C.2.1). Your LaTeX may not provide all the features needed by that file.

## 5.3 LaTeX font warnings

Font warnings are those involving the NFSS commands (Section 8.5). They are indicated by the text: `LaTeX Font Warning:` plus the warning text.

```
LaTeX Font Warning: Command ... invalid in math mode.
```

[2ε] A command that should only appear in text mode has been given in math mode. The command is simply ignored. The commands \mathversion, \boldmath, \unboldmath, and \em lead to this message. There are other commands that produce an *error* message with the same text.

```
LaTeX Font Warning:  Command \tracingfonts not provided.
(Font)               Use the 'tracefnt' package.
(Font)               Command found: on input line ....
```

[2ε] The font tracing diagnostic tool \tracingfonts may only be used if the tracefnt package (page 242) has been loaded. Otherwise, this command is ignored.

```
LaTeX Font Warning:  Encoding '...' has changed to '...' for
(Font)               symbol font '...' in the math version '...'.
```

[2ε] To make use of the specified symbol font in the given math version, it was necessary to change the font encoding temporarily.

```
LaTeX Font Warning:  Font shape '...'in size <...> not available
(Font)               size <...> substituted.
```

[2ε] No font has been defined for the size and shape requested, so a substitute size is used instead.

```
LaTeX Font Warning:  Font shape '...' undefined
(Font)               using '...' instead.
```

[2ε] The shape attribute that has been requested is unknown, or has not been defined, so a substitute shape will be used instead.

```
LaTeX Font Warning:  *** NFSS release 1 command ... found
(Font)               *** Update by using release 2 command ....
(Font)               *** Recovery is probably possible.
```

[2ε] A command from the first version of NFSS has been used, which is no longer valid. However, LaTeX will try to insert the newer equivalent and proceed with it.

## 9.5.4   TeX warnings

A TeX warning is recognized by the fact that it is not an error message (not prefixed with !) and that the processing is not halted. The most common TeX warnings are:

```
Overfull \hbox ....
```

TeX could not break this line in a reasonable way so part of it will extend into the right margin. The rest of the information in the message can be of assistance.

For example, with the complete warning message

```
Overfull \hbox (17.2122pt too wide) in paragraph at lines 4--6
[]\OT1/cmr/m/n/10 If T[]X can-not find an ap-pro-pri-ate
 spot to di-vide a word at the end of the line, as right
 here aaaaaaaaaaaaaaaaaaaaaaaaaa
```

one knows that the line is about 17.2 pt (6 mm) too long and extends this amount into the right-hand margin. The line is part of the paragraph in lines 4 to 6. The font used is designated by its attributes `\OT1\cmr\m\n\10`. The text of the problem line is `If ... ... right here aaaaaaaaaaaaaaaaaaaaaaaaaa`. Possible word divisions are shown with hyphens, such as `di-vide`. The last word cannot be divided, which is the cause of the problem.

A way around this is to include some suggested hyphenations with the `\-` command, such as `aaaaaaaaa\-aaaaaaaaaaaaaa`. Similarly, a `\linebreak` command before the problem word, or setting the whole paragraph in a `sloppypar` environment, will get rid of this warning message.

If a badly broken line extends only a tiny bit into the right margin, say 1 pt or less, in most cases this will hardly be noticed and may be left as it is. A sample output should be printed just to verify the appearance.

```
Overfull \vbox ....
```

This warning occurs very rarely. TₑX could not break the page properly so that the text extends beyond the bottom of the page. More often TₑX sets less text on a page than too much. Thus this warning arises only when the page contains a very large vertical box, higher than the value of `\textheight`, such as a long table.

```
Underfull \hbox ....
```

This is the opposite of the `Overfull \hbox` warning. It appears when TₑX has filled a line right and left justified, but with so much inter-word spacing that it considers the appearance to be undesirable. This is often the result of a `sloppypar` environment, a `\sloppy` declaration, or a `\linebreak` command. It may also come about after an inappropriate application of a `\\` or `\newline` command, such as two `\\` commands one after the other. The additional information in the warning message contains the text of the badly formatted line plus an evaluation of the 'badness' of the word spacing.

If in the example of the `Overfull \hbox` a `\linebreak` is included in the text at the spot `...`, as `right\linebreak here`, then the warning becomes

```
Underfull \hbox (badness 5504) in paragraph at lines 4--6
[]\OT1/cmr/m/n/10 If T[]X can-not find an ap-pro-pri-ate
 spot to di-vide a word at the end of the line, as right
```

which states that the paragraph in lines 4 to 6 contains an output line in which the inter-word spacing may be unacceptably wide. The text of this line reads `If ... ...,` `as right` and is set in the font `\OT1/cmr/m/n/10`. The evaluation `badness 5504` is TeX's estimate of how unacceptable the spacing is: *the smaller this number the better.*

In order to appreciate the magnitude of this 'badness', it is necessary to know how it is calculated. All inter-word spacings have a basic size and optimal amounts by which they may be stretched or shrunk. For each output line, the sum of the actual word spacings as well as those of the ideal stretches and shrinkages are found. The value of the 'badness' is then

$$\text{badness} = 100 \times (\text{actual shrinkage}/\text{optimal shrinkage})^3 \quad \text{or}$$
$$\text{badness} = 100 \times (\text{actual stretch}/\text{optimal stretch})^3$$

where 'actual shrinkage' and 'actual stretch' are the sums of the additional or subtracted spacings to make the line justified at both ends.

Normally TeX tolerates an over-stretching of the word spacings up to a value of badness = 200, which corresponds to a factor of 1.26 between the true and ideal stretch values. Within the `sloppypar` environment or after a `\sloppy` declaration, lines may be infinitely stretched. An `Underfull \hbox` warning appears when the badness exceeds a value of 1000, which means the stretching has reached a value 2.15 times its ideal. The badness value is limited to 10000 if the above formula yields a number greater than this.

In practice, a value of badness < 2000 can be tolerated even though it will be noticeable that the spacing is not ideal. A sample printing should be examined to see how bad it looks.

`Underfull \vbox ....`

The page has been broken with head and foot justified, but TeX judges the amount of inter-paragraph spacing to be possibly unacceptable. The `badness` number here corresponds to the quantity with the same name from the `Underfull \hbox` warning.

# 9.6     Search for stubborn errors

At some point or another you will encounter an error message for which you cannot identify any cause, try as you may. For such devious errors, we recommend the following search strategy:

1. Copy the file twice into a *previous* and a *working* copy (in addition to the original, which remains untouched during this search).

2. In the working copy, find the outermost environment where the error occurred and remove one or more inner environments. If there are no inner environments, shorten the remaining text. Process the file with LaTeX once more.

3. If the error still occurs, copy the shortened working copy to the previous copy and repeat step 2. If the outer environment in step 2 is \begin{document} ... \end{document}, the shortening may be carried out by simply inserting \end{document} at some earlier point.

4. If the error is no longer in the shortened working copy, copy the previous copy back to the working copy. The error is still present in this version. Remove less of the text than last time and repeat steps 2 to 4.

5. If in this way the error is found to be in the next innermost environment, repeat the procedure for this environment with steps 2 to 4.

With this strategy, the error may be localized to one command or to the innermost environment with only a small remaining structure. If the error still cannot be identified in spite of its being precisely localized, seek help from a more experienced colleague or from the computing center. However, it is normally possible to recognize the mistake once the position of the error has been found.

It does happen that even though the error has been corrected, the same error message appears on the next LaTeX process run. This is because of the internal transfer in information through the LaTeX auxiliary files, which are always one run behind on the current situation. For example, if there is a mistake in one of the sectioning commands, then after it has been eliminated, the faulty entry still exists in the .toc file. If the document contains the \tableofcontents command, LaTeX will read in that .toc file on the next run, and issue the error message once more, since a new .toc file is only created after a successful processing.

In this case, the .toc file should also be edited and the error removed. If that is not possible, the file should be erased and the corrected source file processed *twice* with LaTeX. If the error was in \caption, \addcontentsline, or \addtocontents, the same applies to the corresponding .lof or .lot file.

Occasionally the .aux file itself must be erased to prevent an error in it from being repeated even after the .tex file has been repaired. Here one must be careful that the command \nofiles has not been given in the preamble, for then a corrected .aux file will not be generated after a further LaTeX process run.

# A Letters

In addition to the three standard LaTeX document classes, there is a fourth one named `letter` for formatting correspondence. As provided, the file `letter.cls` is intended for private letters without any frills such as letterheads or business reference codes. However, this can be changed by the local LaTeX expert.

We first present the standard LaTeX `letter` class, and then demonstrate how a house style can be written using our own institute style as an example. As always, it is highly recommended that each of these modifications be given its own file name so that `letter.cls` refers only to the provided LaTeX version.

## 1 The LaTeX `letter` class

The `letter` document class is meant for writing letters. A single input file may contain the text for more than one letter and addressee, all from the same sender. Address labels may also be printed automatically if one wishes. Most of the normal LaTeX commands function as usual within the `letter` class. One exception, however, is the sectioning commands, which will lead to the error message `! Undefined control sequence` when issued. It actually makes little sense to try to divide a letter up into chapters, sections, etc. On the other hand, there are a number of special commands that may be applied only within this style.

The source text for a letter begins as for every LaTeX document with

> `\documentclass[`*options*`]{letter}`

in which all the options listed in Section 3.1 may be given for *options* except for `twocolumn` and `titlepage` which hardly make any sense within a letter. The option `twoside` is allowed in LaTeX $2_\varepsilon$, but not in LaTeX 2.09.

Every letter must contain the name and address of the sender, which are set for all the letters in one file by including the commands

295

```
\address{sender_address}
\signature{sender_name}   or   \name{sender_name}
```

in the preamble. The *sender_address* normally consists of several lines, separated by \\ commands, as in the example

```
\address{Max-Planck-Institut f\"ur Aeronomie\\
        Postfach 20\\
        D--37189 Katlenburg--Lindau\\Germany}
```

The entry in the \name command will be used in the return address in the letterhead, if such has been programmed. The entry in the \signature command will be printed at the end of the letter below the space left blank for the writer's signature. If \signature has not been specified, the \name entry is inserted here instead. This allows a more formal \name to be used for the return address and a different form, perhaps with multiple lines, for the signature, as in

```
\name{Prof.\ M.\ Ostmann}
\signature{Martin Ostmann\\Project Leader}
```

When the above commands are issued in the preamble, they remain valid for all the letters in the document, except for those letters that contain new versions of these commands. Thus one letter might have a different \signature from the others. The range of these entries extends only to the end of the environment in which they were called (see Section 7.5.4).

Two other sender entries are possible in standard LaTeX letter class. They are intended to be employed in local modifications for a house style. The idea is that if \address is *not* called, the preprogrammed company letterhead which might also contain the sender's room and/or telephone number is generated. Thus the commands

```
\location{room_number}   and   \telephone{tel_number}
```

are provided. As letter.cls is delivered, the entries *room_number* and *tel_number* are printed at the bottom of the first page *only if* \address *is not issued*.

The preamble may also contain the \pagestyle command with the usual entries plain, empty, or headings. The first is the default, putting the page number centered at the bottom of all pages after the first. The headings page style adds the recipient's name, the date, and page number in a line at the top of all pages after the first.

After the preamble commands, the actual text begins as in all LaTeX files with the command \begin{document}. The text consists of one or more letters, each enclosed in a letter environment with the syntax:

```
\begin{letter}{recipient} text of letter \end{letter}
```

where *recipient* stands for the name *and* address of the addressee, divided into several lines separated by \\ commands.

```
\begin{letter}{Mr Donald J. Burns\\
               Ontario Institute of Physics\\
               41 Adelaide St.\\
               London, Ontario\\Canada N4R 3X5}
```

The *text of letter* normally begins with the command \opening and ends with \closing, between which the body of the letter appears, mixed with whatever LaTeX commands are desired. The syntax of these two commands is

\opening{*dear*}
\closing{*regards*}

where *dear* is the salutation, such as Dear Mr Tibs, and *regards* stands for the terminating text, for example Yours sincerely,. The \opening command could also contain other text, for example a subject entry line, with the true salutation as part of the following body text.

LaTeX places the *sender's* name and address in the upper right corner of the first page with the current date set right justified below it. Then the *recipient's* name and address appear at the left margin, followed by the *salutation* and the body of the letter. The letter ends with the *terminating text* and the sender's *name* or *signature* left justified from the center of the line with sufficient vertical space between them for the handwritten signature.

After the \closing, a number of other commands may appear as part of the letter. One is \cc to produce a copy distribution list:

\cc{*name1* \\ *name2* \\ ... }

The text 'cc:' (or more correctly, the text defined in \ccname) is printed at the left margin, followed by an indented list of names of the copy recipients.

The second additional command is \encl for making a list of enclosures:

\encl{*enclosure1* \\ *enclosure2* \\ ... }

The word 'encl:' (actually the text in \enclname) is printed at the left margin and then the list of enclosures.

Finally, the command \ps may be used to add a postscript after the signature. The command itself does not generate any text, nor does it take an argument. The postscript text is everything located between the \ps and \end{letter} commands.

Normally the letter is dated automatically with the current date. However, if it is desired that the letter be back-dated, or that the date be otherwise fixed in the text, it may be set with

\date{*date_text*}

A sample letter produced with the standard `letter` class.

---

Max–Planck–Institut für Aeronomie
Postfach 20
D-37189 Katlenburg–Lindau
Germany

January 8, 1995

TEXproof Ltd
P. O. Box 123
9876 Wordtown
Textland

Dear Sir;

We are most pleased to be able to answer your request for information about the use of LaTeX for general text processing at a scientific institute.

1. After some initial trepidation on the part of the secretarial staff, which was mainly due to the first experience with a computer in any form, the system is now fully accepted and appreciated.

2. Much to the surprise of many secretaries, they find that they are able to set the most complicated mathematical formulas in a reasonably short time without difficulties. The same applies to the production of detailed tables.

3. Creating cross-references and index registers no longer causes horror, even when the boss is well known for demanding constant changes.

4. Finally, the high quality appearance of the output has assisted in winning acceptance for LaTeX in our house.

An additional positive note is the ability to write business letters readily, making use of the `letter` class provided with LaTeX. In our institute, we have designed a special version to print our own letterhead, saving the need to have special letter paper printed.

Yours truly,


Patrick W. Daly

encl: Listing of our `mpletter.cls`
        Sample output

cc: H. Kopka
     B. Wand

in which case *date_text* appears where the current date would be placed.

A letter file may contain any number of `letter` environments, one per letter. As stated already, when \address, \name, and \signature have been specified in the preamble, they remain in force for all the letters in the file. It is possible to alter any one or more of these sender entries by reissuing the command within one of the letters, *before* the \opening command, but then this change is valid solely for that letter. If both \name and \signature have been declared, it is the latter that is printed below the signature space.

The first page contains no page number. Subsequent pages have either a centered page number at the bottom (default) or a heading line with recipient, date, and page number at the top (page style `headings`).

The sample letter on the facing page was generated with the following source text.

```
\documentclass[a4paper,11pt]{letter}
\name{Dr P. W. Daly}
\address{Max--Planck--Institut f\"ur Aeronomie\\
        Postfach 20\\
        D-37189 Katlenburg--Lindau\\Germany}
\signature{Patrick W. Daly}
\date{January 8, 1995}
\begin{document}
\begin{letter}{\TeX proof Ltd\\P.\,O. Box 123\\
            9876 Wordtown\\Textland}
\opening{Dear Sir;}
We are most pleased to be able to answer your request for
information about the use of \LaTeX{} for general text processing
at a scientific institute.
\begin{enumerate}
  \item
  After some initial trepidation on the part of the secretarial
  . . . . . . . . . . . . . . . . . . . . . . . . . . . . . . . . .
  in winning acceptance for \LaTeX{} in our house.
\end{enumerate}
An additional positive note is the ability to write business
  . . . . . . . . . . . . . . . . . . . . . . . . . . . . . . . .
special paper printed.
\closing{Yours truly,}
\encl{Listing of our \texttt{mpletter.cls}\\Sample output}
\cc{H. Kopka\\B. Wand}
\end{letter}
\end{document}
```

By adding the command \makelabels in the preamble, the user can print out address stickers after all the letters have been output. The entries for the addresses are taken from the recipients' names and addresses in the argument to the `letter` environment. The standard LATEX `letter` class is designed for a page of labels $4\frac{1}{4} \times 2$ inches, ordered in two columns. This could be altered for other formats. An address sticker without a corresponding letter may be printed by including an *empty* `letter` environment of the form

> \begin{letter}{*recipient*}\end{letter}

## A.2    A house letter style

The sample letter above demonstrates the possibilities of the standard LaTeX `letter` class. The height and width of the text may easily be altered with appropriate declarations in the preamble. The use of explicit English words and date style is no problem for other languages since they are all contained in special commands that can be redefined. (This actually only applies to LaTeX versions after December 1, 1991, for before then the English words were explicitly used.)

The `letter` class has been designed so that if the `\address` command is omitted, a company letterhead will be printed instead. This presupposes that the file has been reprogrammed at the local installation for this purpose. Each employee using this house letter style will have certain personal entries to make, such as his or her room and/or telephone number. These commands have been provided for in the standard `letter` class.

We have such a house letter style at our institute which we will illustrate here. However, it was found necessary to add some more personal entries, such as 'Our Ref.', 'Your Ref.', and electronic mail codes. In addition, a command to print out 'Subject:' has also been added.

To distinguish our local house style from that of standard LaTeX, we have named it `mpletter`. It contains most of the features of `letter`, since it in fact reads in that class file and then makes its alterations and additions. The `\address` command is not necessary, since all letters are printed with the institute letterhead, including its address. The recipient's name and address are taken from the argument of the `letter` environment and are vertically centered in the space provided in the letterhead.

The writer's name and telephone extension are entered with

> \name{*author*}   and   \telephone{*ext_number*}

which, if given in the preamble, apply to all the letters in the file. If different letters have other authors, these commands must be made in the appropriate `letter` environment *before* the `\opening` command. New entry commands specific to `mpletter` are

> \yref{*your_code*}
> \ymail{*your_date*}
> \myref{*our_code*}
> \subject{*subj_text*}

# MAX–PLANCK–INSTITUT FÜR AERONOMIE

Postfach 20
Katlenburg–Lindau
GERMANY

---

MPI für Aeronomie, Postfach 20, D–37189 Katlenburg–Lindau

Dr P. W. Daly
Tel.: 05556-401-279
INTERNET:
daly @ linmpi.gwdg.de

Mr George Murphy
35 Waterville Rd.
Centertown, Middlesex
United Kingdom

May 10, 1995

---

*Your Ref.:* GFM/sdf     *Your letter from:* April 28, 1995     *Our Ref.:* PWD/sib

*Subject:* LaTeX information

Dear George,

Thank you for your inquiry about the latest version of the LaTeX installation and additional packages. As you may know, there was a major update last year with the release of LaTeX2ε on June 1, 1994, which became the official standard at the time. It is intended that updates be issued every six months, in June and December, with absolutely urgent fixes coming out as patches when necessary.

I am sending you a copy of the current version of the entire LaTeX package on an MS-DOS floppy disk, as you requested. In a separate directory named `bibtex` you will find the special bibliography formatting style files mentioned in 'A Guide to LaTeX'. I hope you will find these of use.

Do not hesitate to get in touch with me again if you have any further questions about the installation or running of the package.

Regards,

Patrick W. Daly

encl: 1 diskette with LaTeX package

cc: H. Kopka

---

| Telephone | 05556–401–1 | Bank | | Train Station |
|---|---|---|---|---|
| Telefax | 05556–401–240 | Kreis–Sparkasse Northeim | | Northeim |
| Telex | 9 65 527 aerli | 41 104 449 (BLZ 262 500 01) | | (Han.) |

which produce the words

   *Your Ref.:,    Your letter of:,    Our Ref.:,    Subject:*

properly positioned under the letterhead together with the corresponding text argument. If any of these commands are missing, their text will not appear in the letter.

    Since ours is a German institute, there is an option german that translates all these words into their German equivalents. The entry commands have the same names, however.

    As in the standard letter class, the current date is printed automatically, but may be changed to any desired text with the command

    \date{*date_text*}

if one wishes to back-date a letter or to fix the dating within the letter file itself. This is often handy if one only keeps electronic copies of the letters for the record. Otherwise, when a hard copy is run off months later, it will appear with the new current date and not with the original one.

    The entry *author* that is given as the argument to the \name command appears in the letterhead as the name of the sender. It will also appear below the space left for the signature, unless it is overridden by the \signature command that specifies an alternative form of the name for this purpose.

    The sample letter on the previous page has been generated with our house style, using the following source text.

```
\documentclass[12pt]{mpletter}
\name{Dr P. W. Daly} \signature{Patrick W. Daly}
\myref{PWD/sib}
\date{May 10, 1995}
\subject{\LaTeX{} information}
\telephone{279} \internet{daly}
\ymail{April 28, 1995} \yref{GFM/sdf}
\begin{document}
\begin{letter}{%
Mr George Murphy\\35 Waterville Rd.\\
Centertown, Middlesex\\United Kingdom}
\opening{Dear George,}
Thank you for your inquiry about the latest version of the
\LaTeX{} installation and additional packages.  As you may know,
. . . . . . . . . . . . . . . . . . . . . . . . . . . . . . . .
Do not hesitate to get in touch with me again if you have any
further questions about the installation or running of the
package.

\closing{Regards,}
\encl{1 diskette with \LaTeX{} package}
\cc{H. Kopka}
```

```
\end{letter}
\end{document}
```

The first page of our institute letter appears as shown, without a page number. If the text must continue beyond one page, the next page will have the heading

## MAX–PLANCK–INSTITUT FÜR AERONOMIE

*To Mr George Murphy*          *May 10, 1995*          *Page 2*

The addressee's name that appears in this heading is taken from the first line of the *recipient* argument in the \begin{letter}. This argument is split up by the LATEX processing so that the first line is contained in the command \toname, and the rest of the lines in \toaddress. The words 'To' and 'Page' are in the standard commands \headtoname and \pagename, and may be changed by an appropriate language adaptation option as shown in Section C.3.3.

# 3    A model letter customization

Adapting the letter.cls class file to the requirements of a company style should present few difficulties to an experienced LATEX programmer. Even a normal user may be able to make the necessary changes with the help of the example in this section.

We present here the class file mpletter.cls that was used to produce the sample letter on page 301. It makes heavy use of the LATEX programming features described in Appendix C. In order to understand it, one should be familiar with Section C.2. It will not be necessary to make any changes to the file letter.cls itself, since all modifications are in a separate class file that inputs the original.

The new class file is to be called mpletter.cls. It begins by specifying the TEX format that it requires, and by identifying itself.

```
\NeedsTeXFormat{LaTeX2e}
\ProvidesClass{mpletter}
```

It will be necessary to execute conditionals, so we will need the ifthen package described in Section 7.3.5. We will want a flag to decide if the letter is to be in German or not, determined by an option. Create the flag and define the option german to set it.

```
\RequirePackage{ifthen}
\newboolean{@german}
\setboolean{@german}{false}
\DeclareOption{german}{\setboolean{@german}{true}}
```

All other options that are valid in the standard letter class will also be accepted here, so simply pass them on to that class with the default option. Then process all options before loading letter itself with the a4paper option. We only have A4 paper in our institute.

```
\DeclareOption*{\PassOptionsToClass{\CurrentOption}{letter}}
\ProcessOptions
\LoadClass[a4paper]{letter}
```

This completes the preliminaries. So far, we have read in the standard letter class, along with the package ifthen, and defined a new option that is not present in the original class. Otherwise, all options and functions are unchanged, so far.

We now define the new 'name' commands to contain language-sensitive text, such as 'Subject', which are not provided for in the basic class. The actual definitions will be executed by two commands \englishnames and \germannames.

```
\newcommand{\englishnames}{%
 \newcommand{\yrefname}{\textsl{Your Ref.}}
 \newcommand{\ymailname}{\textsl{Your letter from}}
 \newcommand{\myrefname}{\textsl{Our Ref.}}
 \newcommand{\subjectname}{\textsl{Subject}}
 \newcommand{\telephonename}{Telephone}
 \newcommand{\stationname}{Train Station}
 \newcommand{\germanname}{GERMANY}
 \newcommand{\telcode}{[49]-5556-401}
 \newcommand{\postcode}{D--37189}
}

\newcommand{\germannames}{%
 . . . . . . . . . . . . . . . . . . . . . .
 \newcommand{\telcode}{(05556) 401}
 \newcommand{\postcode}{37189}
}

\ifthenelse{\boolean{@german}}
  {\RequirePackage{german}\germannames}{\englishnames}
```

The last lines test whether the flag @german has been set (by the option german), and if so, the package german is loaded, and the German names are defined, otherwise the English names. The package german already translates the standard names commands \toname, \headtoname, and \pagename, so they are not included in \germannames.

Having settled the language problem, we now attack those commands for entering extra information in the header. Each of these stores its text argument in an internal command for future use. First the internal storage commands must be created.

```
\newcommand{\@yref}{}      \newcommand{\@ymail}{}
\newcommand{\@myref}{}      \newcommand{\@subject}{}
\newcommand{\@internet}{}
```

```
\newcommand{\yref}[1]{\renewcommand{\@yref}{\yrefname: #1}}
\newcommand{\ymail}[1]{\renewcommand{\@ymail}{\ymailname: #1}}
\newcommand{\myref}[1]{\renewcommand{\@myref}{\myrefname: #1}}
\newcommand{\subject}[1]{\renewcommand{\@subject}
                          {\subjectname: #1}}
\newcommand{\internet}[1]{\renewcommand{\@internet}{#1}}
\newcommand{\INTERNET}{@linmpi.gwgd.de}
```

Set the dimensions of the text on the page and its margins. These numbers are appropriate for A4 paper (which does make the a4paper option superfluous).

```
\setlength{\textheight}{215mm}   \setlength{\textwidth}{160mm}
\setlength{\oddsidemargin}{0pt} \setlength{\evensidemargin}{0pt}
\setlength{\topmargin}{-20pt}    \setlength{\headheight}{12pt}
\setlength{\headsep}{35pt}
```

The next step is to define some fixed fonts that are needed for the letterhead. We refer to the fonts with their explicit NFSS attributes; in this case they are all Computer Modern sans serif fonts in various sizes. These fonts will not change if totally different families are used for the body of the letter.

```
\DeclareFixedFont{\xviisf}{OT1}{cmss}{m}{n}{17}
\DeclareFixedFont{\xsf}{OT1}{cmss}{m}{n}{10}
\DeclareFixedFont{\viiisf}{OT1}{cmss}{m}{n}{8}
```

The letterhead itself is divided into two fields, the left one containing the institute name in large letters, the right one the address in a smaller font. Below the first horizontal line, the left field displays the name and address of the recipient, positioned to fit in the window of an envelope, and the right one has the personal data of the letter writer, name, extension, computer address. The widths of these fields are established.

```
\newlength{\leftfield}     \setlength{\leftfield}{117mm}
\newlength{\rightfield}    \setlength{\rightfield}{43mm}
```

The total width of these two fields equals 160 mm, which is the same as \textwidth.

Next, we place the institute name and address in several saved boxes.

```
\newsavebox{\FIRM}         \newsavebox{\firmaddress}
\newsavebox{\firm}         \newsavebox{\firmreturn}

\sbox{\FIRM}
  {\parbox[t]{\leftfield}
      {\xviisf MAX--PLANCK--INSTITUT F\"UR AERONOMIE}}

\sbox{\firm}
  {\xsf MAX--PLANCK--INSTITUT F\"UR AERONOMIE}
```

```
\sbox{\firmreturn}
  {\viiisf\underline{MPI f\"ur Aeronomie, Postfach 20,
                     \postcode{} Katlenburg--Lindau}}

\sbox{\firmaddress}
  {\parbox[t]{\rightfield}{\viiisf\baselineskip10pt
    POSTFACH 20\\Max--Planck--Stra\{\ss}e 2\\
    \postcode{} Katlenburg--Lindau\\\germanname}}
```

Using these boxes as building blocks, we put together the actual head and
foot of the letterhead page in two further save boxes.

```
\newsavebox{\firmhead}    \newsavebox{\firmfoot}

\sbox{\firmhead}
  {\parbox{\textwidth}{\usebox{\FIRM}\raisebox{6pt}
    {\usebox{\firmaddress}}\\[3pt] \rule{\textwidth}{1pt}}}

\sbox{\firmfoot}
  {\parbox{\textwidth}{\rule{\textwidth}{0.6pt}\\[5pt]
    \viiisf\setlength{\baselineskip}{12pt}%
    \begin{tabular}[t]{@{}ll}
      \underline{\telephonename}  & \telcode-1\\
      \underline{Telefax}         & \telcode-240\\
      \underline{Telex}           & 9\,65\,527 aerli
    \end{tabular}\hfill
    \begin{tabular}[t]{l}
      \underline{Bank}\\
      Kreis--Sparkasse Northeim\\
      41\,104\,449 (BLZ 262\,500\,01)
    \end{tabular}\hfill
    \begin{tabular}[t]{l@{}}
      \underline{\stationname}\\
      Northeim\\
      (Han.)
    \end{tabular} }}
```

The box \firmhead is fairly clear: it is a \parbox of width \textwidth
containing the boxes \FIRM and \firmaddress side by side, with a line
below. The foot \firmfoot is also a \parbox of the same width, but
containing three columns of general institute information, set in tabular
environments.

It now remains to have the head and foot boxes placed on the first
page. In the letter class, there is a special page style named firstpage
that is always invoked for the first page of a letter. This must be redefined.

```
\renewcommand{\ps@firstpage}
  {\setlength{\headheight}{41pt}\setlength{\headsep}{25pt}%
  \renewcommand{\@oddhead}{\usebox{\firmhead}}%
```

```
\renewcommand{\@oddfoot}{\raisebox{-20pt}[0pt]
                           {\usebox{\firmfoot}}}%
\renewcommand{\@evenhead}{}\renewcommand{\@evenfoot}{}}
```

This page style must (re)define the commands \@oddhead and \@oddfoot, which are always inserted at the top and bottom of odd pages, to place our special \firmhead and \firmfoot. The even pages are unimportant, since the first page is always odd. It is necessary to enlarge \headheight and \headsep to allow the big boxes to fit in.

Subsequent pages are set with the headings or plain page styles. We want to modify the former to include the firm address once more.

```
\renewcommand{\ps@headings}
  {\setlength{\headheight}{41pt}%
   \renewcommand{\@oddhead}
     {\parbox{\textwidth}{\usebox{\firm}\\[5pt]
        \slshape \headtoname{} \toname\hfill\@date\hfill
                                    \pagename{} \thepage\\
        \rule[3pt]{\textwidth}{1pt}}}
   \renewcommand{\@oddfoot}{}
   \renewcommand{\@evenhead}{\@oddhead}
   \renewcommand{\@evenfoot}{\@oddfoot}
```

One small problem remains: the first time one of these page style commands is executed, the head and foot commands may not yet exist, causing \renewcommand to complain. We ensure that they are there at the start by predefining them with \providecommand (Section 7.3.1).

```
\providecommand{\@evenhead}{}\providecommand{\@oddhead}{}
\providecommand{\@evenfoot}{}\providecommand{\@oddfoot}{}
```

Now make headings the active page style.

```
\pagestyle{headings}
```

There is only one last thing to do, and that is to redefine the opening command that prints the recipient's address and the salution. We add a bit more, including the personal data of the sender, as well as the reference information. The address goes in the left field, the personal data to the right. The references go in a line below the rule, followed by the subject line. These entries are tested first, and are only included if they are not blank. Several stored entry commands used here are part of the standard letter class, such as \toname and \toaddress. The \@date entry is either \today or whatever text was stored with \date.

```
\renewcommand{\opening}[1]{\thispagestyle{firstpage}%
  \parbox[t]{\leftfield}
    {\usebox{\firmreturn}\\
      \parbox[b][3.5cm][c]{\leftfield}{\toname\\\toaddress}}%
  \parbox[t]{\rightfield}
    {\fromname
```

```
      \ifthenelse{\equal{\telephonenum}{}}
         {}{\\ Tel.: \telcode-\telephonenum}
      \ifthenelse{\equal{\@internet}{}}
         {}{\\{\viiisf E-mail: \@internet\INTERNET}}
      \\[5mm] \@date}
\par
\rule{\textwidth}{0.6pt}
\makebox[\leftfield][l]
   {\ifthenelse{\equal{\@yref}{}}
      {\@ymail}{\@yref\hfill\@ymail\hfill}}
\@myref\par
\ifthenelse{\equal{\@subject}{}}
   {}{\@subject\par}
\vspace{2\parskip} #1 \par\nobreak}
```

The result of this formatting can be seen on page 301. It should be possible to modify the coding as needed for other organizations without too much difficulty.

The field for the recipient's name and address has been positioned so that it will appear in the address window of an envelope when properly folded. The smaller return address will also be visible through this window. The printing of extra address stickers is thus superfluous.

*As an exercise, the user should design a document class* `pletter` *for writing personal letters. With the tips for formatting company letters, it should not be difficult to add a letterhead of the form*

# Sheila Joan McDonald

Tel.: 234-9871
31 Maple Drive
Willowtown

*Hint: The name has been printed with the font* `cmdunh10 scaled \magstep4`*, declared with* `\newfont`*. Such a* `pletter` *class must remain in the personal directories of the user at a computer center. It would be rather embarrassing if everyone made use of the same personal letterhead.*

# Bibliographic Databases

In scientific publications, a bibliography or list of references is standard procedure. We have already described in Sections 4.3.6 and 8.3.2 how a bibliography can be formatted with the thebibliography environment and how its entries are referred to within the text. Often authors find that they are constantly referring to the same publications in most of their own papers. Similarly, researchers working in the same field will frequently be referring to the same set of papers. This means that many of the entries in the thebibliography environment will be repeated from one work to the next, or even among co-workers at one institute.

It would be very useful if the bibliographic entries could be stored in one database file once and for all to be available for all documents with a list of reference in that field. Such a database system is possible with the BIBTEX program supplied with the LATEX package. The information about the various publications is stored in one or more files with the extension .bib. For each publication there is a *key* that identifies it, and which may be used in the text document to refer to it. Such a file is called a *bibliographic database*.

## The BIBTEX program

BIBTEX is an auxiliary program to LATEX that automatically constructs a bibliography for a LATEX document by searching one or more databases. To this end, the LATEX file must contain the command

> \bibliography{*database1, database2, ...*}

at that point in the text where the bibliography is to appear. Here the argument *database1, database2, ...* is a list of root names, separated by commas, of the bibliographic database files that are to be searched. The extension .bib is not explicitly written.

Reference can be made to a publication in one of the databases at any place in the text with the command

    \cite{*key*}

as is explained in Section 8.3.2. The *key* is the database identifier for that publication, which of course the user must know beforehand. After the first LaTeX processing, the BibTeX program must be run. How this is called depends on the computer installation (see the *Local Guide*), but it is often with the operating command bibtex plus the root name of the LaTeX file. Supposing this root name is comets, the call

    bibtex comets

produces a new file with the name comets.bbl, containing the extracted information for those publications for which there was a \cite reference, packaged in a thebibliography environment to be input into the document on the next LaTeX run.

  Occasionally the bibliography is to include publications that were *not* referenced in the text. These may be added with the command

    \nocite{*key*}

given anywhere within the main document. It produces no text at all but simply informs BibTeX that this reference is also to be put into the bibliography. With \nocite{*}, *every* entry in all the databases will be included, something that is useful when producing a list of all entries and their keys. (\*\*Does not work for BibTeX version 0.98 and earlier.\*\*)

  After running BibTeX to make up the .bbl file, it is necessary to process LaTeX *at least twice* to establish both the bibliography and the in-text reference labels. The bibliography will be printed where the \bibliography command is issued; it in fact inputs the .bbl file.

  The style of the bibliography may be selected with the declaration

    \bibliographystyle{*style*}

which may be issued anywhere after the preamble. The *style* argument can take on one of the following values:

plain   The entries in the bibliography are ordered alphabetically; each is assigned a running number in square brackets as the in-text reference marker, printed where the \cite commands are issued.

unsrt   The entries are ordered according to their first references by the \cite and \nocite commands. The entry for the first \cite receives the number 1, that of the next \cite with a different key the number 2, and so on. The markings and listings are otherwise the same as for plain.

alpha   The ordering in the bibliography is the same as for plain but the markers are an abbreviation of the author's name plus year of publication. A reference to Smith (1987) would appear as [Smi87] instead.

abbrv   The ordering and marking are the same as for plain, but the
bibliographic listing is shortened by abbreviating first names,
months, and journal names.

There may be other styles available on your computer. In particular,
those for author–year citations, as described in Section B.3.1, deviate a
great deal from those of the standard LATEX package. Bibliography styles
are contained in files with the extension .bst.

The next section describes the bibliographic databases for use with
the program BIBTEX version 0.99. There are a number of new features over
version 0.98, which are indicated with a double asterisk **. Databases
(.bib files) that worked under the older version will still function under
0.99. However, the bibliography style files (.bst) operate with one version
or the other and may not be mixed. To find out what version you have,
look at the first line of output from the BIBTEX run, either on the screen or
in the .blg protocol file.

# 2  Creating a bibliographic database

Creating a bibliographic database might seem like more work than typing
up a list of references with the thebibliography environment; the great
advantage is that the entries need to be included in the database once
and only once and are then available for all future publications. Even
if a different bibliography style is demanded in later works, all the information is already on hand in the database for BIBTEX to write a new
thebibliography environment in another format. In fact, our experience
finds that even for a single document, it is simpler to make an entry into
the database than to adhere to the very precise and fiddly requirements of
a literature list, especially regarding punctuation and positioning of the
authors' initials. The data bank entry procedes very quickly and easily if
one has a generalized template, as illustrated in Section B.2.6.

The entries in a bibliographic database are of the form

```
@BOOK{knuth:86a,
   AUTHOR = "Donald E. Knuth",
   TITLE = {The \TeX{}book},
   EDITION = "third",
   PUBLISHER = "Addison--Wesley",
   ADDRESS = {Reading, Massachusetts},
   YEAR = 1986  }
```

The first word, prefixed with @, determines the *entry_type*, as explained
in the next section. The *entry_type* is followed by the reference information
for that entry enclosed in curly braces { }. The very first entry is the *key*
for the whole reference by which it is referred to in the \cite command.

In the above example this is knuth:86a. The *key* may be any combination of letters, numerals, and symbols, except commas. The actual reference information is then entered in various *fields*, separated from one another by commas. Each *field* consists of a *field_name*, an = sign, with optional spaces on either side, and the *field text*. The *field_names* shown above are AUTHOR, TITLE, PUBLISHER, ADDRESS, and YEAR. The *field text* must be enclosed either in curly braces or in double quotation marks. However, if the text consists solely of a number, as for YEAR above, the braces or quotation marks may be left off.

For each entry type, certain fields are *required*, others are *optional*, and the rest are *ignored*. These are listed with the descriptions of the various entry types below. If a required field is omitted, an error message will occur during the BIBTEX run. Optional fields will have their information included in the bibliography if they are present, but they need not be there. Ignored fields are useful for including extra information in the database that will not be output, such as a comment or an abstract of the paper. Ignored fields might also be ones that are used by other database programs.

The general syntax for entries in the bibliographic database reads

> @*entry_type*{*key*,
>     *field_name* = {*field text*},
>     . . . .
>     *field_name* = {*field text*} }

The names of the *entry_types* as well as the *field_names* may be written in capitals or lower case letters, or in a combination of both. Thus @BOOK, @book, and @bOOk are all acceptable variations.

The outermost pair of braces for the entire entry may be either curly braces { }, as illustrated, or parentheses ( ). In the latter case, the general syntax reads

> @*entry_type*(*key*, . . . . . . )

However, the *field text* may only be enclosed within curly braces {. . .} or double quotation marks ". . ." as shown in the example above.

## B.2.1   The entry types

The following is a list of the standard entry types in alphabetical order, with a brief description of the types of works for which they are applicable, together with the required and optional fields that they take. The meanings of the fields are explained in the next section.

@article Entry for an article from a journal or magazine.
　　　*required fields*　author, title, journal, year.
　　　*optional fields*　volume, number, pages, month, note.

@book  Entry for a book with a definite publisher.
>  *required fields*   author or editor, title, publisher, year.
>  *optional fields*   volume or number, series, address, edition, month, note.

@booklet Entry for a printed and bound work without the name of a publisher or sponsoring organization.
>  *required fields*   title.
>  *optional fields*   author, howpublished, address, month, year, note.

@conference Is the same as @inproceedings below.

@inbook Entry for a part (chapter, section, certain pages) of a book.
>  *required fields*   author or editor, title, chapter and/or pages, publisher, year.
>  *optional fields*   volume or number, series, type, address, edition, month, note.

@incollection Entry for part of a book that has its own title.
>  *required fields*   author, title, booktitle, publisher, year.
>  *optional fields*   editor, volume or number, series, type, chapter, pages, address, edition, month, note.

@inproceedings Entry for an article in conference proceedings.
>  *required fields*   author, title, booktitle, year.
>  *optional fields*   editor, volume or number, series, pages, address, month, organization, publisher, note.

@manual Entry for technical documentation.
>  *required fields*   title.
>  *optional fields*   author, organization, address, edition, month, year, note.

@mastersthesis Entry for a Master's thesis.
>  *required fields*   author, title, school, year.
>  *optional fields*   type, address, month, note.

@misc Entry for a work that does not fit under any of the others.
>  *required fields*   none.
>  *optional fields*   author, title, howpublished, month, year, note.

@phdthesis Entry for a PhD thesis.
>  *required fields*   author, title, school, year.
>  *optional fields*   type, address, month, note.

@proceedings Entry for conference proceedings.
> *required fields*   `title, year.`
> *optional fields*   `editor, volume or number, series, address,`
> `month, organization, publisher, note.`

@techreport Entry for a report published by a school or other institution, usually as part of a series.
> *required fields*   `author, title, institution, year.`
> *optional fields*   `type, number, address, month, note.`

@unpublished Entry for an unpublished work with an author and title.
> *required fields*   `author, title, note.`
> *optional fields*   `month, year.`

Each entry type may also have the optional fields `key` and `crossref`. The former provides additional information for alphabetizing the entries, especially when the author information is missing. The author information is normally found in the `author` field but may also be in the `editor` or even `organization` fields. This `key` field has nothing to do with the *key* for identifying the entry in the \cite command. The `crossref` field gives the *key* for another entry in the database that shares many of the information fields, as illustrated in Section B.2.3.

## B.2.2   The fields

The fields that may be used within a bibliographic entry are listed below together with their meanings. They are always given in the form:

> *field_name* = {*field text*}   or
> *field_name* = "*field text*"

address
> The address of the publisher or other institution.  For major publishing houses, it is sufficient to give just the city. For smaller publishers, giving the full address is recommended.

annote An annotation that may be used by non-standard bibliography styles to produce an annotated bibliography. The standard BɪʙTᴇX styles ignore it.

author The name(s) of the author(s) as described in Section B.2.4.

booktitle
> The title of a book when only part of it is being cited.   See Section B.2.4 for special considerations on capitalization.

chapter
> A chapter or section number.

crossref
: The key of another entry in the database that shares many of the same field entries. See Section B.2.3.

edition
: The edition of a book, usually written in full and capitalized, as 'Second'. The standard styles will change it to lower case as necessary.

editor
: The name(s) of the editor(s) in the form described in Section B.2.4. If there is also an `author` field, then this gives the editor of the book or collection in which the citation appears.

howpublished
: States anything unusual about the method of publishing. Should be capitalized. Example: 'Privately published'.

institution
: The name of the sponsoring institution for a technical report.

journal
: The name of a journal or magazine. Abbreviations are provided for the most common ones (see Section B.2.5).

key
: An addition for alphabetizing purposes when the author information is missing. This is not the same as the *key* for identifying the entry to a `\cite` command.

month
: The month in which the work was published or, if unpublished, when it was written. Abbreviations exist in the form of the first three letters of the (English) names.

note
: Any additional information that should be added. Capitalize the first letter.

number
: The number of a journal, magazine, technical report, or work in a series. Journals are usually identified by volume and number; technical reports are issued a number by the institution; books in series sometimes have a number given to them.

organization
: The sponsoring organization for a conference or a manual.

pages
: A page number or a range of pages, in the form `32,41,58` or `87--101` or `68+`. The last form indicates page 68 and following pages. A single hyphen given for a range will be converted by the standard styles to the double hyphen to produce a dash, as '87-101'.

publisher
: The publisher's name.

school  The name of the academic institution where a thesis was written.

series  The name of a series or set of books. When citing a book from a series, the `title` field gives the name of the book itself while the optional `series` specifies the title of whole set.

title   The title of the work, obeying the capitalization rules listed in Section B.2.4.

type    The type of technical report, for example, 'Research Note'.

volume  The volume number of a journal or multi-volume book.

year    The year in which the work was published or, if unpublished, in which it was written. It should normally consist of four numerals, such as 1993.

Additional field names may be included, which B<small>IB</small>T<small>E</small>X will simply ignore. For example, to add the abstract of an article in the database,

    abstract = {*text of an abstract*}

This can be of use in other applications as well as for database management.

## B.2.3    Cross-referencing fields

**This section applies only to B<small>IB</small>T<small>E</small>X version 0.99 and later.**
If many entries in the bibliographic database share a common set of field information, such as for a number of works all appearing in the same conference proceedings, it is possible to refer to another entry containing that common set with the `crossref` field. For example,

```
@INPROCEEDINGS{xyz-1,
  crossref = {xyz-proceedings},
  author = {J. S. Jones},
  title = {The First Results from the {Appleville Experiment}},
  pages = {34--38}  }
. . . . . . . . . . . . .
@PROCEEDINGS{xyz-proceedings,
  editor = {C. H. Kelvin},
  title = {Proceedings of the First Conference on the
            {Appleville Experiment}},
  booktitle = {Proceedings of the First Conference on the
            {Appleville Experiment}}
  year = 1991    }
```

The first entry, with key xyz-1, is to obtain all its missing fields from the second entry, by means of the `crossref` field referring to the entry with key `xyz-proceedings`. The missing fields are `editor`, `booktitle`, and `year`, those that are common to all articles in the conference proceedings. Note that `booktitle` is an ignored field for `@PROCEEDINGS` but needs to be included here since it is required for `@INPROCEEDINGS`.

If an entry is referred to by two or more other entries, then it too will be included in the bibliography, even though its key never appeared as the argument of a `\cite` or `\nocite` command.

In order for this system to function properly, the entry that is referred to must appear in the database(s) *after* all those that refer to it. It is therefore recommended to put all such referenced entries at the end of the database. Cross-references may not be nested.

## .4  Special field formats

There are some special rules for entering the texts to the fields `author`, `editor`, `title`, and `booktitle`. BιвTεX will process names, putting surnames first, abbreviating given names with initials, and so on, according to the instructions in the style file. Thus it is important that the program knows what is a given name and what a surname. Similarly for titles, capitalization may change depending on style and/or entry type, so BιвTεX must know what words are always capitalized.

### Names

The names in the `author` and `editor` fields may be typed in either in the form {*Given Names Surname*} or as {*Surname, Given Names*}. That is, BιвTεX assumes that if there is no comma the last capitalized name is the surname, or family name; otherwise what comes before the comma is taken to be the surname. Thus the name texts `"John George Harrison"` and `"Harrison, John George"` are equivalent for Mr J. G. Harrison. However, if a person has a double surname, without a separating hyphen, the second form must be employed, or the double name must be enclosed in braces, as

> `"San Martino, Maria"`   or   `"Maria {San Martino}"`

for Ms M. San Martino.

Auxiliary words to a surname that are not capitalized, such as *von* or *de*, may be entered in either form:

> `"Richard von Mannheim"`   or   `"von Mannheim, Richard"`
> `"Walter de la Maire"`   or   `"de la Maire, Walter"`

Anything enclosed in braces will be treated as a single item, something that is used in ambiguous cases, or when the name contains a comma or the word *and*. An example is

```
"{Harvey and Sons, Ltd}"
```

A *Junior* added to a name creates its own complications. If a comma appears between the name and the *Jr*, then the text should be written as

```
"Ford, Jr, Henry"
```

However, if there is no comma, then the *Jr* must be treated as part of a double surname:

```
"{Filmore Jr}, Charles"   or   "Charles {Filmore Jr}"
```

**BibTeX 0.99 and later.** Accents within a name formed with a backslash command should be enclosed in braces *with the backslash as the first character after the opening brace.* In this way, the alphabetization and the formation of labels with the alpha bibliography style will function properly. For example,

```
author = "Kurt G{\"o}del",
year = 1931
```

will produce the label [Göd31] as desired. The accent text must not be enclosed any deeper than shown here. (In all versions of BibTeX, accents may be put into the name text for printing in the bibliography. What is new here is the treatment of labels and alphabetization.)

**BibTeX 0.99 and later.** Hyphenated first names are properly abbreviated. Thus "Jean-Paul Sartre" becomes 'J.-P. Sartre'. (In earlier versions, the result is 'J. Sartre'.)

If an author or editor field is to contain more than one name, the names are separated by the word and. For example,

```
author = "Helmut Kopka and Daly, Patrick William"  or
AUTHOR = {Peter C. Barnes and Tolman, Paul and Mary Smith}
```

If the and is actually part of the name, the whole name must be enclosed in braces, as pointed out above.

If the author list is too long to type in all the names, it may be terminated with and others. This will be converted to the form of *et al.* prescribed in the style file.

## Titles

The capitalization of the title depends on the bibliography style: usually book titles are capitalized while article titles are not. The text in the fields title and booktitle should be written in the capitalized form so that BibTeX can change to lower case as required.

The general rules for capitalizing titles in English state that the first word of the title, the first word after a colon, and all other words are capitalized except articles and unstressed prepositions and conjunctions. For example:

```
title="The Right Way to Learn: A Short-Cut to a Successful Life"
```

Words that are always to be capitalized, such as proper nouns, must be enclosed in braces. It is sufficient to enclose only the letter that must be capitalized. The two following examples are equivalent:

```
title = "The {Giotto} Mission to Comet {Halley}"  or
TITLE = {The {G}iotto Mission to Comet {H}alley}
```

## .5 Abbreviations

It is always possible to use an abbreviation in the field text in place of actual text. Some abbreviations, such as the names of the months and some standard journal names, are already available, and the user is free to define new ones for his or her personal use.

The name of an abbreviation consists of any combination of letters, numbers, and symbols except

```
" # % ' ( ) , = { }
```

An abbreviation is defined with the command

```
@string{abbrev_name = {text}}       or
@string(abbrev_name = {text})
```

where *abbrev_name* stands for the name of the abbreviation and *text* is the replacement text. For example, if the abbreviation

```
@string{JGR = {Journal of Geophysical Research}}
```

has been defined, the following two field statements are identical:

```
journal = JGR
journal = {Journal of Geophysical Research}
```

The name of the abbreviation is *not* enclosed in braces or double quotes, otherwise the name itself will be interpreted literally as the field text. In both the @string command and the name of the abbreviation, the case of the letters is unimportant. The above abbreviation could just as well be defined as

```
@STRING{jgr = {Journal of Geophysical Research}  or even
@StrinG{jGr = {Journal of Geophysical Research}
```

and it may be referred to in the fields as JGR, JGr, JgR, Jgr, jGR, jGr, jgR, or jgr.

**BiBTeX 0.99 and later.** Abbreviations may be concatenated with the symbol # between them. Thus after giving

```
@string{yrbk = {Institute Yearbook}}
```

this abbreviation may be combined with other abbreviations and text, as in

```
title = "Max-Planck~" # yrbk # 1993
```

to produce 'Max-Planck Institute Yearbook 1993'.

Standard abbreviations exist for the months of the year, the names consisting of the first three letters of the name, as `jan`, `feb`, etc. Further predefined abbreviations are available for some standard journal names, but the user will have to inquire about these at the computing center, or consult the *Local Guide*, since these will be dependent on the installation.

The `@string` commands may be issued anywhere in the database between two bibliographic entries, but must already be defined before they are used. Therefore, it makes most sense to insert all the abbreviation definitions at the beginning of the database file.

## B.2.6   Using a template

Typing in the text for bibliographic entries into a database might seem to be rather complicated since there are so many things to remember, such as which fields are required and which are optional, what their formats are, and so on. One way to simplify this task is to make up *templates* for the most common entry types that you use. A template is basically a complete entry with all the fields left blank. It is stored in a separate file on its own, to be inserted into the database file whenever a new entry of that type is to be made. Then the field texts are written in.

An appropriate template for the entry type `@article` could be

```
@ARTICLE{<key>,
    AUTHOR  = {},
    TITLE   = {},
    YEAR    = {},
    JOURNAL = {},
        VOLUME  = {},
        NUMBER  = {},
        MONTH   = {},
        PAGES   = {}
}
```

in which the `<key>` is a reminder that the key word is to go here, the required fields come first and are indented relative to the entry type name, and the optional fields are further indented. The field `note` is not included since it is less commonly used and since it may be included in all entry types.

Finally, we mention that BⁱʙTₑX has been written by Oren Patashnik, Stanford University, in close association with Leslie Lamport. The BⁱʙTₑX installation should contain the two files `btxdoc.tex` and `btxhak.tex` for additional information about BibTeX. In particular, `btxhak.tex` contains instructions for writing bibliographic style files. Both these files are to be processed with LaTeX and output in the usual way for document files.

# 3 BibTeX extensions

## 3.1 Author–year bibliography styles

The bibliography style used in this book, as well as in many of the journals of the natural sciences, is completely different from that provided by LaTeX. In this style, reference is made to other published works by citing the author's name and year of publication. Furthermore, the citation may be either parenthetical [*Jones et al.*, 1990] or textual, as shown by *Jones et al.* [1990]. There may be some variations within this style: for example, in this book parentheses are used in place of square brackets and the name is left in normal type.

Standard LaTeX produces a citation as a running number within square brackets [10], and will permit a comment to be added [10, page 188], but does not recognize textual citations. The numbers are considered to be labels which are then listed in the bibliography itself beside the corresponding literature references. The author–year bibliography contains no labels since the correspondence between citation and reference is clear from the list of authors and year.

There are in fact a number of non-standard author–year bibliographic styles available, all of which require some document package file to redesign the `thebibliography` environment and to be able to interpret the revised `\bibitem` command.

The simplest of these, by Oren Patashnik, the originator of BibTeX, are called `apalike.bst` and `apalike.sty`. This style gives the `\bibitem` command an optional argument containing the author and year, as

    \bibitem[Jones et al., 1990]{jone90}

The `\cite` command operates as normal, which means that only parenthetical citations are possible. There are at least 8 `.bst` styles that conform to this scheme.

Another set of LaTeX and BibTeX styles are named `newapa.sty` and `newapa.bst`, written by Stephen N. Spence with modifications by Young U. Ryu, latest version dated June 1991. This is a very flexible system, allowing parenthetical and textual citations, with full or abbreviated author lists. The form of the `\bibitem` command is

    \bibitem[\protect\citeauthoryear{Jones, Smith, and Harris}
        {Jones et al.}{1990}]{jone90}

The special command \citeauthoryear in the optional argument to \bibitem transfers the full author list, an abbreviated list, and the year, as three separate items over to the LaTeX document. This command is defined in the corresponding .sty package file. A large number of variations on the \cite command are provided in order to print all combinations of lists and year, textual and parenthetical. A number of other bibliography styles, noticeably the chicago family, also make use of this command.

With newapa itself, it is also possible to change the punctuation of the citations easily, say from (Jones & Smith: 1990, pages 60-65) to [Jones and Smith, 1990: pages 60-65]. This is done with a \citepunct command that sets the various punctuations as one wishes.

There is also an astronomy family of bibliographic styles, with at least 7 members. These all make use of a special command \astroncite which is really identical to \citeauthoryear, except that it only takes two arguments, the short author list and year. They require the package file astronomy.sty.

Another set of author-year bibliographic styles belong to the harvard family. They use a command \harvarditem which replaces \bibitem but functions the same as \citeauthoryear. The package file harvard.sty, written by Peter Williams and Thorsten Schnier, is required for their use. This package has been updated for LaTeX $2_\varepsilon$, and now includes many new flexible features for customizing the citations. It has become a very powerful package, and should be considered ahead of any of the others mentioned above.

Finally, there are some styles that use a command \citename within the optional argument of \bibitem. However, the syntax is not the same as that of the others, and in our opinion is not so appropriate for the complete spectrum of citation possibilities.

A general purpose package has been written by Patrick W. Daly to accept *all* of the above author-year formats of \bibitem as well as numerical citation schemes. This package, named natbib.sty, actually takes as its native form for author-year an optional argument in which the year is in parentheses,

```
\bibitem[Jones et~al.(1990)]{jone90}
```

and defines all the other author-year commands in terms of this format. It is also possible to associate the type of braces and punctuation marks used, as well as any other special features required, with the name of the .bst file such that they are invoked by calling the \bibliographystyle command. Thus all documents making use of the same bibliography style will have the correct citation punctuation without any further action on the part of the author. Even the choice of numerical or author-year style is made automatically. The package has been updated for LaTeX $2_\varepsilon$, and contains the same functionality as harvard.sty, so that it can be recommended as a universal package for all bibliographic styles.

A simplified version of `natbib.sty` is given in Section C.3.4, together with a basic author–year bibliography style.

All of the styles mentioned here, including `natbib.sty`, are available from the CTAN file servers listed in Section D.5, either in the BibTeX or LaTeX contributed directories.

## .2 Customizing bibliography styles

It seems that every journal and publishing house has its own set of rules for formatting bibliographies. The differences are really minor, such as whether to use commas or colons here, or to put volume numbers in bold or italic typeface. Nevertheless, in spite of this triviality, the rules are rigid for each house.

Standard LaTeX provides only four bibliography styles, and their differences have more to do with sorting and labeling than with such fussy details. It is possible to design one's own .bst file, by modifying existing ones; however, this requires a knowledge of the peculiar BibTeX programming language, something that puzzles even experienced LaTeX users. There are some 50 .bst files in the BibTeX directories of the TeX file servers, and probably many more in contributed LaTeX directories. Each is designed for a specific journal and there is no guarantee that it would be accepted by another one. What is a user to do if his or her publisher demands a certain format that just is not to be found? How can one seek a given format anyway among those offered?

Some help can be found in the `custom-bib` package written by Patrick W. Daly, available in the contributed LaTeX directories of the file servers. The heart of this package is a generic (or master) bibliography style `genbst.mbs` containing alternative coding for a multitude of different bibliographic features or options. It is processed with the DocStrip program which is capable of including alternative coding according to selected options (see Section D.3.1).

Because of the large number of options that are offered, a menu-guided interface is provided, called `makebst.tex`. When processed under TeX or LaTeX, this 'program' first asks which .mbs file is to be read, and then interactively constructs a DocStrip batch job to produce the selected bibliographic features according to menu information contained in the .mbs file itself. This means that there could be a number of .mbs files to choose from, each one explaining its set of options to the user via `makebst`.

Another .mbs file provided is called `babel.mbs` which is much the same as `genbst.mbs` except that multi-language support is also available.

Some of the features provided by the supplied generic bibliographic style file are:

- numerical or author–year citations; in the latter case, one may also choose which \bibitem style is to be used;

- order of references: by citation order, alphabetical by all authors, alphabetic by author–year label;

- format of authors' names: first name plus surname, initials plus surname, surname plus initials, reversed initials only for first author;

- number of author names to include before giving *et al.*;

- position of date, parentheses or brackets around the year;

- format of volume and number for journals;

- capitalization of article titles as sentence or title style;

- whether to use the word *and* or an ampersand &;

- whether to abbreviate *editor, volume, chapter,* etc.;

- first and last page numbers or only first;

- and much more.

# C $\quad$ LaTeX Programming

One of the major improvements in LaTeX $2_\varepsilon$ is the support for class and package writers, or more simply, for LaTeX programmers. Most users will not really appreciate the other changes from LaTeX 2.09, seeing only some extra font commands, a \documentclass declaration at the start, and the \usepackage command to load what used to be *option files*. There are some additional extras here and there, but generally, they will feel that the new version has not brought them anything truly new. However, the LaTeX programmer who has written those option files, or who has tried to install new font schemes, certainly will appreciate the NFSS and the new class and package control features. Gradually these contributed extensions to the basic LaTeX installation will become so dependent on LaTeX $2_\varepsilon$ that any user who wants to take advantage of them will have no choice but to update his or her system.

The New Font Selection Scheme is described in Section 8.5. In this appendix, we present the special commands that were designed for class and package files, with several examples of useful packages.

## Class and package files

### .1 $\quad$ Style files in LaTeX 2.09

The concept of class and package files is new to LaTeX $2_\varepsilon$, replacing those of *main style* and *style option* files of LaTeX 2.09. In that system, one had to select the main style with

2.09 \documentstyle[*option_list*]{*style*}

This loaded a file named *style*.sty that defined the overall format for the type of document wanted. The major styles were article, report, and book, just like the most important classes in LaTeX $2_\varepsilon$. Somewhere in the style file there would be the command \@options which processes the options in the *option_list* as follows:

1. if a command \ds@*option* exists, it is executed; otherwise, the option name is put into a second list;

2. after the *option_list* is exhausted, the second list is taken and for each entry the file *option*.sty is input.

This procedure allows options to be internally defined in the style file, or to be stored in a separate style option file with the same name as that option, and the extension .sty. The idea is that the coding for some options is independent of the main style, so it could be stored external to the style files.

That may have been the original philosophy behind the concept of option files; what developed out of it is a multitude of additional 'options' written by hosts of contributers. LaTeX is programmable, so anyone could add on valuable extra features, store them in a file, and read them into other documents. With network servers, these additions became widely distributed and used. Since many of them tinker with internal LaTeX commands, they cannot be simply read in by an \input command in the preamble, but rather need to be given the .sty extension so that they can be included as a pseudo-option under point 2 above. They are not really options at all, but extended coding or extra features.

Another difficulty arose in writing new main styles. If one needed an article-like style for a certain journal, or a book-like style for a certain publisher, one could take the existing article.sty or book.sty files as a basis and make new ones with the necessary modifications, but these would not be immune to future updates to the originals. Sometimes these updates were vital to be consistent with changes to LaTeX itself. Alternatively, one could simply write an 'option' to contain the modifications, or even a new main style that input the original. However, these would not be true main styles with their own option lists.

## C.1.2   The LaTeX $2_\varepsilon$ concept

The wealth of contributed LaTeX programming was probably never anticipated by Leslie Lamport when he released LaTeX. It is now a fact of life, and indeed one of the great strengths of the system. LaTeX $2_\varepsilon$ not only accommodates such 'foreign' extensions, it actually supports and encourages them, as witnessed by the copious presentations of such packages in *The LaTeX Companion* (Goosens *et al.*, 1994).

And this is the way it should be. The extensions have been written by people who needed them, who realized that LaTeX was missing something vital for them. On the other hand, to add all of them to the basic LaTeX installation would overload it with features that 90% of the users would never require. The philosophy now is that LaTeX provides a fundamental core, or kernel, which is extended first by the standard class files, and then by the myriad of contributed packages and other classes.

It is the role of the LaTeX Team to establish guidelines for programming, to ensure that packages do not clash needlessly with the kernel, or with each other, and to provide a basis of stability so that useful packages continue to operate through further updates to the kernel and the standard classes. This security factor was missing in LaTeX 2.09, where programmers were really left on their own to 'hack' as they felt best, and not to do true programming. The new features of LaTeX $2_\varepsilon$ for class and package control, together with a set of programming tools, should offer an enhanced degree of reliability and durability, both among packages and against future updates of the kernel.

## 1.3   Levels of commands

There are a number of levels of commands with varying degrees of security for the future:

**user commands** (highest level) described in this and the other manuals, consisting of lower case letters, such as \texttt, are part of the LaTeX external definition to be supported for ever;

**class and package commands** with longish names of mixed upper and lower cases (like \NeedsTeXFormat) are intended mainly for programmers, and are also guaranteed; most are preamble-only commands, but there is otherwise no real restriction to class and package files;

**internal LaTeX commands** containing the character @ in their names can only be used in class and package files; they are not guaranteed for ever, although many of them are indispensable for special effects; a programmer makes use of them at the risk that some day his package may become obsolete;

**low level TeX commands** also have names with lower case letters, and no @; they should be safe against future evolution of LaTeX, but even this is not absolutely certain; they should be avoided where possible, as explained below;

**internal private commands** are those used within a contributed class or package file; it is recommended that they all be prefixed with some upper case letters representing the package name and @ in order to avoid clashes with other packages; for example, \SK@cite, from the showkeys package.

A question that confronts LaTeX programmers is to what extent the internal LaTeX commands may be used in class and package files. There is always a danger that such commands may vanish in later versions, since they have never been documented in the official books (Lamport, 1985,

1994; Goosens *et al.*, 1994). Like the TeX commands discussed in the next section, their use cannot be forbidden, but one must be aware that a certain degree of risk will accompany them.

The guidelines issued by the LATEX Team strongly recommend employing the high-level LATEX commands whenever possible.

- Use \newcommand and \renewcommand instead of \def; if one of the TeX defining commands must be used, because a template is required, or because it must be \gdef or \xdef, issue a dummy \newcommand beforehand to test for a name clash. If it is uncertain whether the command name already exists, and it is truly unimportant, issue a dummy \providecommand followed by \renewcommand. The ability to define commands with one optional argument at the high level removes one reason for wanting to reach down to the lower ones.

- Use \newenvironment and \renewenvironment instead of defining \\*myenv* and \end*myenv*.

- Assign values to lengths and glues (rubber lengths) with \setlength, rather than by simply equating.

- Avoid the TeX box commands \setbox, \hbox, and \vbox; use instead \sbox, \mbox, \parbox and the like. With the extra optional arguments in LATEX $2_\varepsilon$, the need for the TeX equivalents is greatly diminished, and the LATEX versions are far more transparent. Moreover, the LATEX boxes will function properly with the color package, while the others are unpredictable.

- Issue error and warning messages with \PackageError and \PackageWarning rather than with \@latexerr or \@warning; the former also inform the user of the source of the message, instead of labeling them all as LATEX messages.

- There is no suggestion that one should exclusively use the \ifthenelse command from the ifthen package (Section 7.3.5) in place of the TeX conditionals. It seems that this package is offered to simplify employing conditionals, in a manner more consistent with LATEX syntax. All the examples in this book make use of it rather than trying to explain the TeX versions.

Adhering to these and similar rules will help ensure that a package will remain fit through future extensions of the LATEX kernel.

## C.1.4    TeX commands

Why should primitive TeX commands be shunned? To define commands with \def rather than \newcommand must be just as good, and is often unavoidable. Is there really a chance that it might be removed from a future LaTeX3? The primitives are the building blocks on which all flavors of LaTeX are constructed. Surely they must remain!

This is not really the point. The primitive TeX commands form the bedrock of any format, and anything defined with them will always do exactly what the programmer expected. However, the equivalent LaTeX tools could actually do more as time goes on. The \newcommand checks for name clashes with existing commands, for example. It might even be possible that a debugging device that keeps track of all redefinitions will be added later; any commands defined with \def would be excluded from such a scheme. Even now in LaTeX 2ε, there is something like this to keep track of all files input with middle and high-level commands.

Another example of how low-level programming can go astray is the case of robust commands in LaTeX 2ε. Many commands are intrinsically fragile, meaning that they are prematurely interpreted when used as arguments of other commands, but they may be made robust by prefixing them with \protect. In LaTeX 2.09, several fragile commands were defined in a robust manner by including the \protect in the definition, as for the LaTeX logo command:

```
\def\LaTeX{\protect\p@LaTeX}
\def\p@LaTeX{...}
```

The true definition is in the internal \p@LaTeX, not the external \LaTeX. Since that definition for the logo actually possessed many flaws, several packages have included an improved version. Those that simply redefined \LaTeX itself made the command fragile; those that were cleverer only redefined \p@LaTeX, with the result that they are totally left behind in LaTeX 2ε, where commands are made robust in a completely different (and much better) manner. (Incidentally, the internal definition of the LaTeX logo has also been greatly improved.)

In spite of the desirability of employing only official LaTeX commands, there are many occasions when either the internal LaTeX commands or the TeX primitives just must be used. The risk of future incompatibility must be taken in order to have a workable package now. However, one should not take this risk lightly, where a high-level equivalent is available.

## 2  Programming commands of LaTeX 2ε

All the commands described in this section are new to LaTeX 2ε. They are not essential to class and package files, but they do extend their usefulness and guarantee that they are employed properly.

## C.2.1    File identification

Three commands test that the external environment in which the class or package has been inserted is correct. The first of these is

> [2ε] \NeedsTeXFormat{*format*}[*version*]

The first statement in a class or package should be the declaration of the TeX format needed. Although there are existing formats with other names, only the one named LaTeX2e actually recognizes this statement. All others will immediately issue the error message

```
! Undefined control sequence.
l.1 \NeedsTeXFormat
                   {LaTeX2e}
```

which all by itself is fairly informative.

What is perhaps of more use within LaTeX2ε is the optional *version* argument, which must contain the date of issue in the form yyyy/mm/dd. If a package is making use of features that were introduced in a certain version, its date should be given, so that if it is used with an earlier version of LaTeX2ε, a warning is printed. For example, the command \DeclareRobustCommand did not exist in the preliminary test release of LaTeX2ε, but was first introduced with the official release of June 1, 1994. Thus any package containing this command should begin with

> \NeedsTeXFormat{LaTeX2e}[1994/06/01]

The form of the date is important, including the zeros and slashes.

This declaration is not limited to class and package files: it may also be issued at the start of the document itself to ensure that it is processed with the right LaTeX. It must, however, be given in the preamble.

The next two commands identify the class or package file itself:

> [2ε] \ProvidesClass{*class*}[*version*]
> [2ε] \ProvidesPackage{*package*}[*version*]

In both cases, the *version* consists of three parts: date, version number, and additional information. The date is in the same format as above, while the version number can be any designation without blanks, and the additional information is text with or without blanks. An example is

\ProvidesPackage{shortpag}[1995/03/24 v1.4 (F. Barnes)]

Only the date part is actually checked by LaTeX against the date specified in the calling \usepackage command. The version number and additional information are printed out if \listfiles has been requested. However, the above format is necessary for the \GetFileInfo command in the doc package (Section D.3.2).

Both the \documentclass and \usepackage commands (as well as \LoadClass and \RequirePackage) may take an optional argument to specify the earliest acceptable release date for the class/package. For example, with

\documentclass[12pt]{article}[1995/01/01]

if the article class file loaded contains

\ProvidesClass{article}[1994/07/13 v1.2u
    Standard LaTeX document class]

a warning message is printed. The same procedure applies to the commands \usepackage and \ProvidesPackage.

This system of version checking allows a document to insist that suitable versions of the class and package files are loaded. It assumes, however, that all later versions are fully compatible with earlier ones.

There is a further identifying command for general files, those to be loaded with \input.

[2ε] \ProvidesFile{*file_name*}[*version*]

There is no checking of the name or version in this case, but both pieces of information will be printed by \listfiles.

## 2.2  Loading further classes and packages

In the main document file, classes are read in by means of the initializing \documentclass command, and packages with \usepackage. Within class and package files, the commands

[2ε] \LoadClass[*options*]{*class*}[*version*]
[2ε] \RequirePackage[*options*]{*packages*}[*version*]

must be used instead. The first allows one class file to load another, with selected options, if desired; the second permits class and package files to load other packages. Only one \LoadClass command may appear within any class file; it may not be called from a package file. Neither command may be invoked in the document file. The *packages* argument may be a list of several package names, separated by commas.

How the optional *version* arguments interact with the corresponding \Provides.. command has been explained in the previous section; how the *options* argument is treated is described below.

## 2.3  Processing options

Both classes and packages may take on options which are defined with

⌜2ε⌝ \DeclareOption{*option*}{*code*}

where *option* is the name of the option and *code* is the set of instructions
that it is to execute. Internally, a command named \ds@*option* is created.
Often the code does nothing more than set flags, or input an option
file. (\RequirePackage may *not* be used within the option code!) Two
examples from article.cls are

```
\DeclareOption{fleqn}{\input{fleqn.clo}}
\DeclareOption{openbib}{\setboolean{\@openbib}{true}}
```

A default option is defined with \DeclareOption*, which takes no option
name, specifying the code to be executed for all requested options that
are undefined.

There are two special commands that may be used only within the
*code* of the default option definition:

\CurrentOption contains the name of the option being processed;

\OptionNotUsed declares \CurrentOption to be unprocessed.

For example, to have a class file emulate LATEX 2.09 behavior where all
undefined options load a .sty file of the same name, define

```
\DeclareOption*{\InputIfFileExists{\CurrentOption.sty}%
                {}{\OptionNotUsed}}
```

which first checks if there is a .sty file of the requested name, and if not
declares the option to be unused. Requested options that have not been
used (processed) are listed in a warning message.

The options are then processed with the commands

⌜2ε⌝ \ExecuteOptions{*option_list*}

⌜2ε⌝ \ProcessOptions

⌜2ε⌝ \ProcessOptions*

where \ExecuteOptions calls the \ds@*option* commands for those options in *option_list*. This is normally done to establish certain options as
being present by default. \ProcessOptions executes all the requested
options *in the order in which they were defined* and then erases them.
Options are therefore executed only once by this command. The starred
version is similar, except that the options are executed *in the order requested*. For compatibility with LATEX 2.09 styles, the command \@options
is maintained as another name for \ProcessOptions*.

It is also possible to specify options for a class or package file with

⌜2ε⌝ \PassOptionsToClass{*options*}{*class_name*}

⌜2ε⌝ \PassOptionsToPackage{*options*}{*package_name*}

where *options* is a list of valid options recognized by the specified class or package file. These commands may be used within the definition of other options. The most common use is to pass default options on to another class, as for example,

`\DeclareOption*{\PassOptionsToClass{\CurrentOption}{article}}`

The class or package named must later be loaded with `\LoadClass` or `\RequirePackage`.

If the default options of class and package files have not been altered by `\DeclareOption*`, the standard procedure for handling options that have been requested but are undefined is

- all options requested in the `\documentclass` statement are designated *global*; they are considered to apply to all subsequent packages, but not to classes loaded with `\LoadClass`; if they are not defined in the main class, no error or warning is issued;

- all options requested with other commands, including `\LoadClass` and the `\PassOptionsTo..`, are *local*; if they are not defined in that class or package, an error is issued;

- after all packages have been read in, if there are any global options that have not been used (undefined in all packages), a warning is issued;

- options, global and local, are executed in the order in which they are defined (unless `\ProcessOptions*` has been called).

## 2.4   Deferred processing

Sometimes, to achieve certain special effects or to avoid possible conflicts with other packages, it is desirable to have some commands executed at the end of the package or class, or at the beginning or end of the document. This can be accomplished with

2ε `\AtEndOfClass{`*cmds*`}`

2ε `\AtEndOfPackage{`*cmds*`}`

2ε `\AtBeginDocument{`*cmds*`}`

2ε `\AtEndDocument{`*cmds*`}`

The first two store away *cmds* to be carried out when the class or package comes to an end. They can be used by local configuration files that are read in at the beginning, but contain modifications that should be made at the end so that they are not overwritten by the defaults. The last two declarations store away the *cmds* to be executed with `\begin{document}` and `\end{document}` respectively. All of these may be issued more than once, in which case the *cmds* are processed in the order in which they were issued.

The *cmds* stored with \AtBeginDocument are inserted into the processing stream effectively within the preamble, but after the command \begin{document} has done almost everything else that it does. Thus the *cmds* may be considered to be part of the main body but preamble-only commands are also allowed.

## C.2.5  Robust commands

In Section 7.3 we showed how new commands may be defined with \newcommand, redefined with \renewcommand, and provisionally created with \providecommand. Two other defining commands, with exactly the same syntax, also exist.

$\boxed{2\varepsilon}$ \DeclareRobustCommand{\\com_name} [narg] [opt] {def}

is used to define or redefine a command named \com_name such that it is *robust*, meaning it may be used in the argument of another command without a \protect before it. If the command already exists, a message is written to the transcript file, and the old definition is overwritten.

The other command checks the current definition of \com_name.

$\boxed{2\varepsilon}$ \CheckCommand{\\com_name} [narg] [opt] {def}

issues a warning message if the definition is not the same as *def*, with the same number of arguments, and so on. This is used to ensure that the state of the system is as one expects, and that no previously loaded packages have altered some important definition.

Both \DeclareRobustCommand and \CheckCommand may be called at any point in the document.

## C.2.6  Commands with short arguments

Normally, the arguments to user-defined commands are allowed to contain new paragraphs, with the \par command or with a blank line. In TEX jargon, these commands are said to be 'long'. This is not the standard behavior for commands created with the TEX \def command, where the arguments must be short in order to act as a test for forgotten closing braces.

As of December 1, 1994, LATEX 2ε provides starred versions of all the defining commands:

```
\newcommand*            \renewcommand*
\newenvironment*        \renewenvironment*
\providecommand*
\DeclareRobustCommand*  \CheckCommand*
```

which create user-defined commands with 'short' arguments in the same way as does \def.

It is recommended that one should almost always take the *-version of these defining commands, unless there is some very good reason to expect that the possible arguments may be 'long', that is, contain new paragraphs. Long arguments should be the exception, not the rule.

## 2.7  Issuing errors and warnings

Classes and packages may be programmed to issue their own error messages and warnings.  This is useful so that one knows which file is responsible for the message.

Error messages are generated with

[2ε] \ClassError{*class_name*}{*error_text*}{*help*}

[2ε] \PackageError{*package_name*}{*error_text*}{*help*}

where *error_text* is the message printed to the monitor and to the transcript file, and *help* is additional text printed after the user responds with H. If the texts contain command names that are to be printed literally, they must be preceded by \protect; spaces are generated with \space, and new lines with \MessageBreak. For example,

```
\PackageError{ghost}{%
    The \protect\textwidth\space is too large\MessageBreak
    for the paper you have selected}
    {Use a smaller width.}
```

produces the error message

```
! Package ghost Error: The \textwidth is too large
(ghost)                     for the paper you have selected.

See the ghost package documentation for explanation.
Type  H <return>  for immediate help.
```

Typing H ⟨*return*⟩ produces

```
Use a smaller width.
```

after which LATEX halts again to wait for a response as described in Section 9.1.

Warnings may also be issued from classes and packages in a similar way. The difference is that there is no *help* text, and the processing does not stop for a response.  The line number of the input file where the warning occurred may be optionally included.

[2ε] \ClassWarning{*class_name*}{*warning_text*}

[2ε] \ClassWarningNoLine{*class_name*}{*warning_text*}

[2ε] \PackageWarning{*package_name*}{*warning_text*}

[2ε] \PackageWarningNoLine{*package_name*}{*warning_text*}

For example, with the warning

```
\PackageWarning{ghost}
   {This text is haunted}
```

one obtains the message

```
Package ghost Warning: This text is haunted on input line 20.
```

and the processing continues. Warnings may be split into several lines with the \MessageBreak command, just like error texts.

Two last commands of this type are

[2ε] \ClassInfo{*class_name*}{*info_text*}

[2ε] \PackageInfo{*package_name*}{*info_text*}

which write their texts only to the transcript file, and not to the monitor. They are otherwise just like the corresponding NoLine warnings.

## C.2.8    Inputting files

Files other than classes and packages may also be input, in which case it is often desirable to make sure that they exist beforehand. Or, alternative actions might be taken depending on the existence of a certain file. These goals are met with

[2ε] \IfFileExists{*file_name*}{*true*}{*false*}

[2ε] \InputIfFileExists{*file_name*}{*true*}{*false*}

Both these commands test for the presence of the specified *file_name* in the area that LᴬTᴇX is looking for files, and execute *true* if it is found, otherwise *false*. In addition, \InputIfFileExists reads in that file after executing *true*.

These commands are not restricted to the preamble, nor to class or package files. In fact, the regular \input command is defined in terms of them.

Many special classes make use of these commands to read in a local configuration file. For example, the class ltxdoc contains

```
\InputIfFileExists{ltxdoc.cfg}
   {\typeout{Local config file ltxdoc.cfg used}}
   {}
```

just before \ProcessOptions is called. This allows one to have a local configuration that might specify

```
    \PassOptionsToClass{a4paper}{article}
```

for a European installation, without altering the files that are processed with the ltxdoc class.

## 2.9   Checking files

Although not really part of programming, two new features of LATEX 2$_\varepsilon$ to keep track of files used are described here. The first of these, already mentioned in Section 8.1.1, is the command

[2$_\varepsilon$] `\listfiles`

which may be given in the preamble, even before `\documentclass`. It causes a list of all input files to be printed at the end of the processing, along with their version and release data. In this way, one has a record of just which files were included, something that may be of use when deciding to send a document file to another installation for processing there. Since any non-standard files may also have to be included, these may be more readily identified from such a listing.

For example, the simple document file

```
\documentclass{article}
\usepackage{ifthen}
\listfiles
\begin{document}
  \input{mymacros}
    This is \te.
\end{document}
```

produces the listing

```
*File List*
article.cls 1994/07/13 v1.2u Standard LaTeX document class
 size10.clo 1994/07/13 v1.2u Standard LaTeX file (size option)
 ifthen.sty 1994/05/27 v1.0i Standard LaTeX ifthen package (DPC)
mymacros.tex
 **********
```

In this case, the local file `mymacros.tex` contains no version information because it is missing a `\ProvidesFile` command.

What should one do if a local file, such as `mymacros.tex` above, is needed for the processing of a document file that is to be sent elsewhere? One could send it along with the main file, but that requires giving the recipient more instructions on what to do. Or, its contents could simply be included in the main file, for shipping purposes. For a package file, this is not so easy, since internal commands containing the @ sign would cause trouble, and the options would not be handled properly. LATEX 2$_\varepsilon$ now provides the environment

[2$_\varepsilon$] `\begin{filecontents}{`*file_name*`}`
     *file contents*
   `\end{filecontents}`

which may only appear at the very beginning of the document, before the \documentclass command. It tests to see if there is a file on the system with the name *file_name*, and if not, it writes its contents literally to a file of that name. This may be a package file that is subsequently input with \usepackage. In this way, the missing non-standard files can be ported together with the main document file.

If we extend the above simple example by including at the very start

```
\begin{filecontents}{mymacros}
\newcommand{\te}{the end}
\end{filecontents}
```

the newly written file mymacros.tex contains

```
%% LaTeX2e file 'mymacros'
%% generated by the 'filecontents' environment
%% from source 'mydoc' on 1994/09/27.
%%
\newcommand{\te}{the end}
```

Note that the filecontents environment adds some comment lines to explain where the new file came from. If this is undesirable, the filecontents* environment may be used instead.

## C.2.10 Compatibility mode

In order that older documents that were written for LaTeX 2.09 may still be processed under LaTeX $2_\varepsilon$, there is the *compatibility* mode which is initiated with the \documentstyle command in place of \documentclass. The entire document file should then conform to the older standard, avoiding all of the new features of LaTeX $2_\varepsilon$.

However, compatibility mode will still load the newer class files, rather than the older style files, which may no longer be on the system. It looks first for a file with extension .cls, and only if that does not exist will it try to load the .sty file. This is to accommodate older, non-standard, style files that can still function as classes.

Since the standard classes, like article, exist as .cls files, they will be loaded even by \documentstyle, but must function like their obsolete .sty counterparts. There are very many differences, such as how the margins and text dimensions are set. Nevertheless, the output in compatibility mode must be the same as if it had been processed by LaTeX 2.09 with article.sty. To accomplish this, compatibility mode sets the boolean switch (Section 7.3.5) @compatibility to ⟨*true*⟩, so that any class or package may test for the mode. The form of the test is

```
\ifthenelse{\boolean{@compatibility}}{true}{false}
```

where *true* represents the commands that are to apply only in compatibility mode, and *false* those in the normal, LaTeX $2_\varepsilon$ native mode.

For all the standard class files, dummy .sty files, such as `article.sty`, also exist, which do nothing more than issue a warning and load the class file. This is for compatibility with older packages which loaded these files explicitly.

## C.2.11  Useful internal commands

Notwithstanding the guidelines in Section C.1.3 that recommend avoiding internal LaTeX commands, there are a number that are fairly fundamental, and indeed form many of the building blocks of the LaTeX kernel and many standard packages. Since they are still internal commands, they are not guaranteed for all future updates. However, if they were to vanish, many of the interesting extension packages provided by the LaTeX Team itself would have to be drastically overhauled. We merely present them briefly here for the sake of the bolder user. They all exist in both LaTeX2ε and 2.09.

```
\@namedef{cmd}{def}
\@nameuse{cmd}
```

define and execute a command named \cmd, where the backslash is not included in the command name. This name may contain any characters, even those normally forbidden in command names.

```
\@ifundefined{cmd}{true}{false}
```

executes *true* if the command \cmd does not exist, else *false*. Again, the backslash is not included in *cmd*, and any characters may appear in the command name. This test is often used to define commands conditionally, a task that has been taken over by \providecommand. It may also be employed to determine whether the main class is `article`-like or not: `\@ifundefined{chapter}{..}{..}` tests for the existence of the \chapter command.

```
\@ifnextchar char{true}{false}
```

tests if the next character is *char*, and if so, executes *true*, else *false*. This command is traditionally used to define commands with optional arguments, where *char* is [. The new extended syntax of \newcommand offers a high-level means of achieving this.

```
\@ifstar{true}{false}
```

tests if the next character is a star *, and if so, executes *true*, else *false*. It is used to define starred forms of commands and environments, something that still cannot be done at the high level.

```
\@for \obj := \list \do {cmds}
```

where \\*list* is a command that is defined to be a list of elements separated by commas, and \\*obj* is successively set equal to each of these elements while the code *cmds* is executed once for each element. For example,

```
\newcommand{\set}{start,middle,end}
\@for \xx := \set \do {This is the \xx. }
```

prints 'This is the start. This is the middle. This is the end.'

## C.2.12  Useful TEX commands

!

Many of the most sophisticated features of LATEX and its packages can only be programmed with the help of Plain TEX commands.  These are described not only in *The TEXbook* (Knuth, 1984), but also in the excellent reference manual by Eijkhout (1992), *TEX by Topic, a TEXnician's Reference*.

We do not intend this book to a manual for TEX; nevertheless, there are a few common TEX commands that appear in many packages, and even in the examples to follow.  A brief description of what they do will aid the understanding of these codings.  A true TEXpert or TEXnician can skip this section altogether.

>   \def\\*cmd*#1#2..{*definition*}

is the standard defining command in TEX.  It is the equivalent of \newcommand except that there is no check for name clashes, and the arguments are specified differently.  For example, the command \Exp to write scientific notation can be defined as

>   \def\Exp#1#2{\ensuremath{#1\times10^{#2}}}    or as
>   \newcommand{\Exp}[2]{\ensuremath{#1\times10^{#2}}}

In both cases, \Exp{1.1}{4} produces $1.1 \times 10^4$.  However, \def can go further: it can put the arguments in a template, such as

>   \def\Exp#1(#2){\ensuremath{#1\times10^{#2}}}

to allow the more convenient notation \Exp1.1(4), something that cannot be produced with \newcommand. The \def command is often used when a command is to be defined without knowing (or caring) whether its name already exists, or when a template is needed.  Commands with optional arguments have actually been defined with a template.

>   \gdef      \edef      \xdef

are variations on \def: the first makes a *global* definition, valid even outside the current environment or {..} bracketing; the second is an *expanded* definition, such that any commands in it have their meanings and not the command itself inserted in the definition; the last is a combination of the other two, expanded and global.

>   \noexpand      \expandafter

control the expansion of commands in definitions and execution. Any commands in the definition part of \edef are expanded (their meanings inserted) unless they have \noexpand before them. The opposite is achieved with \expandafter, which jumps over the following command, expands the next one, and then executes the one skipped. This is very deep TEXnology, and is best illustrated by an example with the \Exp command defined above.

>   \newcommand{\mynums}{1.1(4)} \expandafter\Exp\mynums

is identical to \Exp1.1(4), whereas \Exp\mynums is not; \mynums is expanded to 1.1(4) *before* \Exp is executed.

> \let\\*cmd_a* = \\*cmd_b*   or   \let\\*cmd_a*\\*cmd_b*

makes \\*cmd_a* take on the *current* meaning of \\*cmd_b*. This is often employed to save the current meaning of a command before redefining it, possibly using the older meaning too.

> \relax

does absolutely nothing, but it is often inserted in places where something should be but nothing is wanted.

> \if*cond true_code* \else *false_code* \fi

is the form of a TEX conditional. There are too many variations on the condition *cond* to explain here, but one common application is the equivalent of the LATEX boolean switch commands:

```
\newif\if flag        = \newboolean{flag}
\flagtrue             = \setboolean{flag}{true}
\flagfalse            = \setboolean{flag}{false}
\if flag ..\else..\fi = \ifthenelse{\boolean{flag}}{..}{..}
```

For those who are used to it, the TEX form is more compact, but does not conform to the general LATEX style of doing things.

> \ifcase *num text_0* \or *text_1* \or ... \fi

executes one of the *text_num* according to the value of *num*.

> \endinput

terminates the current file being input. This is not really necessary, but it is considered good programming to end all files this way. The main document file does not need it since \end{document} has the same effect.

# Sample packages

We present here some demonstration packages to illustrate the programming commands of the previous section. These packages are not trivial but are all useful in their own right.

## 1  Modifying the text size

The standard LATEX classes set the text size parameters \textwidth and \textheight according to the size option specified in \documentclass, such as a4paper or legalpaper. They also adjust the margins so that the text is centered both horizontally and vertically. The value of \textwidth is restricted, however, so that there are at most 60–70 characters per line, this being considered optimal by the rules of typography.

Often one wants to ignore this limitation and use the paper to its maximum extent. Only with trial and error can one find a good combination of parameter values that fits a certain paper size. It would be nice to have a package to do this for us.

The fullpage package presented here uses the values of \paperwidth and \paperheight, which have been set according to the paper size option, to produce a margin of one inch on all sides. It even considers what the page style is so that room for head and foot lines may be taken into account. Optionally, it may set an even narrower margin of 1.5 cm.

Before proceeding, it might be useful to review the page format parameters shown in the figures on pages 35 and 511.

The package file begins by stating that it needs LATEX $2_\varepsilon$ and by identifying itself. The package information contains the date in prescribed form, the version number, and additionally the initials of the author. The ifthen package is then loaded since conditionals will be required.

```
\NeedsTeXFormat{LaTeX2e}
\ProvidesPackage{fullpage}[1994/02/15 1.0 (PWD)]
\RequirePackage{ifthen}
```

Next the options are prepared. These are to be in and cm for margins of 1 in and 1.5 cm respectively (1 cm is really too narrow). A special length is used to store the margin value. This is a private, internal command, conforming to the convention mentioned on page 327.

```
\newlength{\FP@margin}
\DeclareOption{in}{\setlength{\FP@margin}{1in}}
\DeclareOption{cm}{\setlength{\FP@margin}{1.5cm}}
```

Furthermore, the four standard page styles are also to be option names. They will set two internal boolean switches and the page style.

```
\newboolean{FP@plain}
\newboolean{FP@empty}
\DeclareOption{plain}{\setboolean{FP@plain}{true}
                      \setboolean{FP@empty}{false}
                      \pagestyle{plain}}
\DeclareOption{empty}{\setboolean{FP@plain}{true}
                      \setboolean{FP@empty}{true}
                      \pagestyle{empty}}
\DeclareOption{headings}{\setboolean{FP@plain}{false}
                         \setboolean{FP@empty}{false}
                         \pagestyle{headings}}
\DeclareOption{myheadings}{\setboolean{FP@plain}{false}
                           \setboolean{FP@empty}{false}
                           \pagestyle{myheadings}}
```

Finally, the default set of options is executed, and then the selected options are processed, in this case, in the order specified. The reason for this is that if more than one page style has been given, the last one should dominate.

```
\ExecuteOptions{in,plain}
\ProcessOptions*
```

Now the calculation can begin. First, for plain and empty, there are no headlines, so set the relevant parameters to zero. This is when FP@plain is ⟨true⟩. Then set the space reserved for the footline to zero for the empty page style (FP@empty is ⟨true⟩). For headings and myheadings, this space is maintained since these styles normally have a plain page (with footline) on the first page.

```
\ifthenelse{\boolean{FP@plain}}
   {\setlength{\headheight}{0pt}
     \setlength{\headsep}{0pt}}{}
\ifthenelse{\boolean{FP@empty}}
   {\setlength{\footskip}{0pt}}{}
```

With all the margins and headline and footline spacings set, the actual calculation can be made. Recall that the driver program leaves a 1 inch margin at the left and above, which must be subtracted from \topmargin and \oddsidemargin.

```
\setlength{\textwidth}{\paperwidth}
\addtolength{\textwidth}{-2\FP@margin}
\setlength{\oddsidemargin}{\FP@margin}
\addtolength{\oddsidemargin}{-1in}
\setlength{\evensidemargin}{\oddsidemargin}

\setlength{\textheight}{\paperheight}
\addtolength{\textheight}{-\headheight}
\addtolength{\textheight}{-\headsep}
\addtolength{\textheight}{-\footskip}
\addtolength{\textheight}{-2\FP@margin}
\setlength{\topmargin}{\FP@margin}
\addtolength{\topmargin}{-1in}
```

Remember that \paperheight and \paperwidth are set to the full dimensions of the paper by the paper size option. If this is wrongly specified, of course, the final result will be incorrect.

This completes the coding for the package file fullpage.sty. An example of how it might be invoked is

```
\documentclass[a4paper,12pt]{article}
\usepackage[headings]{fullpage}
```
      . . . . . .

## .2  Redesigning the head and footlines

Something that is often demanded by LaTeX users is the possibility of altering the head and footlines that appear on each page. Standard LaTeX does provide a limited number of *page styles* (Section 3.2) but these are not always sufficient. The most flexible of them is the `myheadings` page style which allows the author to determine the text of the running heads with \markright and \markboth. However, the general format, including font style and placement of the page number, is still fixed by LATEX.

We show here an example of how the headline can be modified for the documentation of large projects requiring particular information in the page headline. Apart from a short version of the title and the section and page numbers, they might demand the document serial number, date, and version number. It would be useful to have a generalized documentation page style that allows these entries to be specified outside of the page style definition itself.

Since this coding is only feasible for the `article` class, we will create a new class, called `dochead`, that inputs `article.cls` and then defines a new page style. Actually this class could contain many other special features of which our new page style is only one.

Again we start by declaring the TEX version that we need, and identifying the class file.

```
\NeedsTeXFormat{LaTeX2e}
\ProvidesClass{dochead}[1994/09/28 1.0 (PWD)]
```

This class has no new options of its own, passing any specified ones on to the underlying `article` class. However, it selects options 12pt and a4paper automatically itself.

```
\DeclareOption*{\PassOptionsToClass{\CurrentOption}{article}}
\ProcessOptions
\LoadClass[12pt,a4paper]{article}
```

Now come the commands that are used to enter the four pieces of information for the headline: short title, date, serial number, and version. Each of these commands stores its argument in an internal \DH@ command, each of which is initially set to be empty. Finally, the entering commands are declared to be allowed only in the preamble, since it would be disastrous if they were called after the main text had started.

```
\newcommand{\DocTitle}[1]   {\renewcommand{\DH@title}{#1}}
\newcommand{\DocDate}[1]    {\renewcommand{\DH@date}{#1}}
\newcommand{\DocNumber}[1]  {\renewcommand{\DH@number}{#1}}
\newcommand{\DocVersion}[1] {\renewcommand{\DH@version}{#1}}
\newcommand{\DH@title}{}     \newcommand{\DH@date}{}
\newcommand{\DH@number}{}    \newcommand{\DH@version}{}
\@onlypreamble{\DocTitle}    \@onlypreamble{\DocDate}
\@onlypreamble{\DocNumber}   \@onlypreamble{\DocVersion}
```

The \@onlypreamble command is an internal LATEX one.

We now define the new page style, dochead, which means we must create a command \ps@dochead, to be executed by \pagestyle{dochead}. What this command must do is redefine the four internals \@oddhead,

`\@evenhead`, `\@oddfoot`, and `\@evenfoot`. We make the footlines empty, and the even and odd headlines identical. That headline is to be a mini-page, the full width of the page, containing a table with the relevant document information.

```
\newcommand{\ps@dochead}{%
  \renewcommand{\@oddhead}{%
    \begin{minipage}{\textwidth}\normalfont
      \begin{tabular*}{\textwidth}{@{}l@{\extracolsep{\fill}}%
          l@{\extracolsep{0pt}:~}l@{}}%
      \DH@number       & Version & \DH@version  \\
      \DH@title        & Section & \thesection  \\
      Date:~\DH@date   & Page    & \thepage
      \end{tabular*}\vspace{0.5ex} \rule{\textwidth}{0.6pt}%
    \end{minipage}}
  \renewcommand{\@evenhead}{\@oddhead}
  \renewcommand{\@oddfoot}{}
  \renewcommand{\@evenfoot}{}
}
\pagestyle{dochead}
```

The last line activates the new page style.

It is also necessary to increase the size of `\headheight` and `\headsep` because our headline is much higher than normal. We pick a height of 3.5 times a regular line.

```
\setlength{\headheight}{3.5\baselineskip}
\setlength{\headsep}{3em}
```

We now add a further refinement. Such documentation normally wants the pages to be numbered within the sections. Therefore, we want to redefine the command `\thepage` which prints the page number from the page counter (Section 7.1.4), and we need to modify the `\section` command to start a new page and to reset the page counter. This is done by storing the current definition of `\section` and then redefining it.

```
\let\DH@section=\section
\renewcommand{\thepage}{\thesection-\arabic{page}}
\renewcommand{\section}{\newpage\setcounter{page}{1}\DH@section}
```

Notice that the new `\section` command calls the old one stored in the internal command `\DH@section`.

If the above is stored in a file named `dochead.cls`, the following main text could be used to invoke it:

```
\documentclass{dochead}
\DocTitle{Spacecraft Cleanliness}
\DocNumber{ESA--XY--123}
\DocDate{1995 Feb 26}
\DocVersion{3.1}
\begin{document}
```

. . . . . . . . . . . . .

The headline on the fourth page of Section 3 would then appear as below.

| | |
|---|---|
| ESA–XY–123 | Version: 3.1 |
| Spacecraft Cleanliness | Section: 3 |
| Date: 1995 Feb 26 | Page    : 3-4 |

With this example as a model, it should not be difficult to create similar headlines for other applications with different entries.

## C.3.3    Adapting LAT<sub>E</sub>X to another language

Standard LAT<sub>E</sub>X is designed for the English language since English words appear automatically in many situations, such as 'Abstract' or 'Contents'. Accented letters from other languages are indeed possible to print, but are too complicated for long sections of text. Finally, the hyphenation patterns are set up for English word division. Therefore, if LAT<sub>E</sub>X is to be applied to another language, there are three types of alterations that need to be made. In order of increasing complexity, they are

1. replace explicit English words by their translations,

2. define simplifying commands for accents or special punctuation,

3. change the hyphenation patterns.

Section D.1.3 deals with these aspects for multilingual LAT<sub>E</sub>X. Here we restrict ourselves to making a package that functions with *one* non-English language and English itself.

Point 3 is discussed in Sections D.1.4 and D.4. If the T<sub>E</sub>X version is earlier than 3.0, only one set of hyphenation patterns may be saved and no true language switching is possible.

Point 1 can best be realized with relatively recent versions of LAT<sub>E</sub>X. Originally words such as 'Abstract' and 'Contents' were included explicitly in the commands that produced these special sections. In Europe, a modified version of LAT<sub>E</sub>X was set up by J. Schrod from Darmstadt, following suggestions by H. Partl of the Technical University of Vienna, in which all explicit English words are replaced by commands of the form `\abstractname` and `\contentsname`. It thus becomes easy for a language adaptation simply to change the definitions of these naming commands rather than to redefine the entire `\abstract` or `\tableofcontents` commands. These naming commands have been part of the official LAT<sub>E</sub>X since the release of December 1, 1991.

### Adaptation to Esperanto

We take as a sample language to demonstrate the principles of LAT<sub>E</sub>X adaption the international language Esperanto. All three problems listed above apply to it; the solutions are not trivial but not nearly as complex as they are for French and German. Furthermore, by selecting *la internacia lingvo* no linguistic grouping is at a special advantage, and that is the basic philosophy of Esperanto.

There are two Esperanto packages available, one named `espo.sty` which is unsigned, undated, and fairly basic, and another, `esperant.sty`, by Jörg Knappen, University of Mainz, Germany, dated December 10, 1991. The author gives credit to the former as well as to `german.sty`. (There is a third one, also called `esperant.sty`, which is part of the `babel` system described in Section D.1.3.)

Esperanto uses an alphabet of 28 letters: the normal 26 letters of the Latin alphabet without *q*, *w*, *x*, or *y*, but with special letters *ĉ*, *ĝ*, *ħ*, *ĵ*, *ŝ*, and *ŭ*, corresponding to English *ch*, *j*, German *ch*, French *j*, English *sh* and *w*. The accented letters are considered to be separate characters, not just decorated letters as in French or as a replacement for another letter combination as in German. The circumflex accent is generated in LaTeX with the command \^, and the breve accent with \u. There are some complications because the circumflex should be positioned slightly differently for *h*, and the dot should be left off for *j*. Furthermore, *ŭ* is typed in as \u{u} with 5 keystrokes. To simplify all this for the user, the Esperanto styles have made a new one-character command ^ to work for all special letters. Thus ^c ^g ^h ^j ^s ^u are typed in to produce *ĉ* *ĝ* *ħ* *ĵ* *ŝ* *ŭ*.

However, it is not sufficient just to make ^ into an active (command) character and to define it to be \^, as was done in the earlier version. Not only should this command be made robust (Section 2.6), but there are also questions of hyphenation within words containing ^, of switching between languages, and most importantly, the translation of English titles by means of naming commands.

We present here a LaTeX $2_\varepsilon$ adaptation of Jörg Knappen's `esperant.sty` which addresses all these problems. The original was meant to run both under Plain TeX and as a LaTeX 2.09 style option. It uses a fair amount of TeX trickery which we will not explain fully here, only mentioning what the final result should be.

As a package file, it begins with the usual identifications.

```
\NeedsTeXFormat{LaTeX2e}[1994/06/01]
\ProvidesPackage{esperant}
     [1994/06/08 1.1a2e Daly's adaption of Knappen's]
```

This is a minimal adaptation to LaTeX $2_\varepsilon$, so no options are defined. We go right to the main part, where the first item is a TeX trick to allow hyphenation within words with accents. This works by adding a dummy word break with no line breaks allowed.

```
\newcommand{\allowhyphens}{\penalty\@M \hskip\z@skip}
```

The second item is to add the ^ character to certain special lists that are necessary for `verbatim` outputting of source text. Do not expect an exact explanation but just accept the fact that it works.

```
\begingroup
  \def\do{\noexpand\do\noexpand}%
  \xdef\dospecials{\dospecials\do\^}%
  \def\@makeother{\noexpand\@makeother\noexpand}%
  \xdef\@sanitize{\@sanitize\@makeother\^}%
\endgroup
```

Thirdly, two commands are defined to switch the functioning of the circumflex character ^ between its normal role as a superscript operator, and being 'active', that is, a single character command.

```
\newcommand{\modifiedhaton}{\catcode`\^\active}
\newcommand{\modifiedhatoff}{\catcode`\^7 }
```

The circumflex command is now defined, first by making it active, and then defining it as a robust command with one argument. In math mode (`\ifmmode`) the normal superscript function `\sp` is called, otherwise the argument is checked for special cases before proceeding. For U and u, it prints the breve accent; for j, it uses the dotless variant; for h, it calls an overlapping function.

```
\modifiedhaton
\DeclareRobustCommand{^}[1]{\ifmmode\sp{#1}
      \else\ifx#1u\u u\allowhyphens
\else\ifx#1U\u U\allowhyphens
      \else\ifx#1h{h\llap{\^{}}}\allowhyphens
      \else\ifx#1j{\^\j}\allowhyphens
      \else\ifx#1|\discretionary{-}{}{}\allowhyphens
      \else{\^{#1}}\allowhyphens
\fi\fi\fi\fi\fi\fi}
\modifiedhatoff
```

Note that there is an additional function for ^ here: ^| inserts a discretionary hyphen, a suggested word division, in such a way that the rest of the word may still be hyphenated automatically. Normally in TEX, word division may occur *only* at discretionary hyphens if any are present.

The fourth point establishes three commands for defining the date in Esperanto, in American, and in British English. A little Esperanto grammar is necessary to explain the two commands \hodiau and \hodiaun: the word for *today* is *hodiaŭ*, as in *Hodiaŭ estas la 15a de novembro, 1994*, but frequently the date must appear in the accusative to express time-when or as the date of a letter (*la 15an de novembro, 1994*). Both possibilities are provided for.

Rather than redefine \today explicitly, a number of redefining commands are created to allow one to switch between Esperanto, American, and British English. The latter two are defined by \providecommand just in case they have already been defined by a previous package.

```
\newcommand{\dateesperanto}{\renewcommand{\today}
  {la \number\day -an de \ifcase\month\or
  januaro\or februaro\or marto\or aprilo\or majo\or junio\or
  julio\or a\u{u}gusto\or septembro\or oktobro\or novembro\or
  decembro\fi,\space \number\year}%
 \let\hodiaun=\today}
\newcommand{\hodiau}{la \number\day -a de \ifcase\month\or
  januaro\or februaro\or marto\or aprilo\or majo\or junio\or
  julio\or a\u{u}gusto\or septembro\or oktobro\or novembro\or
  decembro\fi,\space \number\year}

\providecommand{\dateUSenglish}{\renewcommand{\today}{%
  \ifcase\month\or January\or February\or March\or April\or
  May\or June\or July\or August\or September\or October\or
  November\or December\fi \space \number\day, \number\year}}

\providecommand{\dateenglish}{\renewcommand{\today}{%
  \ifcase\day\or 1st\or 2nd\or 3rd\or 4th\or 5th\or 6th\or 7th\or
  8th\or 9th\or 10th\or 11th\or 12th\or 13th\or 14th\or 15th\or
  16th\or 17th\or 18th\or 19th\or 20th\or 21st\or 22nd\or
  23rd\or 24th\or 25th\or 26th\or 27th\or 28th\or 29th\or
  30th\or 31st\fi~\ifcase\month\or
  January\or February\or March\or April\or May\or June\or
  July\or August\or September\or October\or November\or
  December\fi \space \number\year}}
```

Next, the section titles, or captions, are to be translated according to
the naming commands of IAT<sub>E</sub>X or L<sup>A</sup>T<sub>E</sub>X versions later than December 1,
1991. As for the date definitions, these are not done directly but rather
with the commands \captionsesperanto and \captionsenglish which
carry out the translations. (Note, the two sets of captions are listed here
side by side but they really come one after the other.) The definitions
are carried out with the T<sub>E</sub>X \def because we do not care if these names
already exist or not.

```
\def\captionsesperanto{%                \def\captionsenglish{%
\def\contentsname{Enhavo}%              \def\contentsname{Contents}%
\def\listfigurename{Listo              \def\listfigurename{List
   de figuroj}%                           of Figures}%
\def\listtablename{Listo               \def\listtablename{List
   de tabeloj}%                           of Tables}%
\def\abstractname{Resumo}%             \def\abstractname{Abstract}%
\def\partname{Parto}%                  \def\partname{Part}%
\def\chaptername{\^Capitro}%           \def\chaptername{Chapter}%
\def\prefacename{%                     \def\prefacename{Preface}%
   Anta\u{u}parolo}%
\def\appendixname{Apendico}%           \def\appendixname{Appendix}%
\def\refname{Cita\^{\j}oj}%            \def\refname{References}%
```

```
\def\bibname{Bibliografio}%          \def\bibname{Bibliography}%
\def\indexname{Indekso}%             \def\indexname{Index}%
\def\figurename{Figuro}%             \def\figurename{Figure}%
\def\tablename{Tabelo}%              \def\tablename{Table}%
\def\pagename{Pa\^go}%               \def\pagename{Page}%
\def\seename{vidu}%                  \def\seename{see}%
\def\alsoname{vidu anka\u{u}}%       \def\alsoname{see also}%
\def\notesname{Rimarkoj}%            \def\notesname{Notes}%
\def\enclname{Aldono(j)}%            \def\enclname{encl}%
\def\ccname{Kopie al}%               \def\ccname{cc}%
\def\headtoname{Al}%                 \def\headtoname{To}%
\def\subjectname{Temo}%              \def\subjectname{Subject}%
}                                    }
```

These names appear only in certain classes, and some of them are non-standard. For example, \refname is used only in article class, being replaced by \bibname in book and report classes, and \abstractname is used only in article and report classes. The names \pagename, \enclname, \ccname, and \headtoname appear only in letter class, while \seename is for the makeidx package. The rest are non-standard for special applications or modifications: \prefacename, \notesname, \alsoname (for makeidx) and \subjectname (for letter).

As was pointed out above, the accented letters in Esperanto are considered to be separate letters. This means that when items are listed by letter, they must appear as 'A B C Ĉ ...' or as 'a b c ĉ ...'. To provide for this, two new counter styles are defined, \Esper and \esper, analogous to \Alph and \alph.

```
\newcommand{\esper}[1]{\@esper{\value{#1}}}
\newcommand{\Esper}[1]{\@Esper{\value{#1}}}
\newcommand{\@esper}[1]{\ifcase#1\or a\or b\or c\or \^c\or d\else
    \@iesper{#1}\fi}
\newcommand{\@iesper}[1]{\ifcase#1\or \or \or \or \or \or
    \or e\or f\or g\or \^g\or h\or h\llap\^{}\or i\or j\or \^\j\or
    k \or l\or m\or n\or o\or p\or r\or s\or \^s\or t\or u\or
    \u{u}\or v \or z\else\@ctrerr\fi}
\newcommand{\@Esper}[1]{\ifcase#1\or A\or B\or C\or \^C\or D\else
    \@Iesper{#1}\fi}
\newcommand{\@Iesper}[1]{\ifcase#1\or \or \or \or \or \or E\or
    F\or G\or \^G\or H \or \^H\or I\or J\or \^J\or K\or L\or M\or
    N\or O\or P\or R\or S\or \^S\or T\or U\or \u{U}\or V\or
    Z\else\@ctrerr\fi}
```

The next part defines some language counters to keep track of the current language. This only works for TEX versions later than 3.0, where setting \language to a number activates the hyphenation patterns stored under that language number. Here one assumes that English hyphenations have been stored as language 0, while Esperanto patterns are under language 1. (The `babel` system in Section D.1.3 uses a safer means of assigning and selecting language numbers.) The command `\selectlanguage` turns on the chosen language by invoking the date and caption defining commands.

```
\newcounter{USenglish}    \setcounter{USenglish}{0}
\newcounter{esperanto}    \setcounter{esperanto}{1}
\newcounter{english}      \setcounter{english}{0}

\providecommand{\selectlanguage}{}
\renewcommand{\selectlanguage}[1]{%
  \ifcase \value{#1}%
  \dateUSenglish  \captionsenglish    \or
  \dateesperanto  \captionsesperanto \or
  \dateenglish    \captionsenglish    \fi
  \language=\value{#1}}
```

Finally, switches for turning Esperanto on and off are defined, and used to turn it on at the beginning of the document.

```
\newcommand{\EsperantoOff}{\modifiedhatoff}
\newcommand{\EsperantoOn}{\modifiedhaton}
\AtBeginDocument{\EsperantoOn\selectlanguage{esperanto}}
```

## B.4 Author–year citations

In Section B.3.1 we point out that standard LaTeX cannot handle the bibliography styles in which citations are made by means of author and year instead of by number. Here we present both a package and a bibliography style that can solve this problem.

### The package file

We name the package `authyear`. It is a very simplified version of the generalized package for author-year citations, `natbib`, written by Patrick W. Daly, but it does demonstrate the most important features.

In the author-year citation system, we need both parenthetical and textual citations. We distinguish between the two by means of the optional note argument to the `\cite` command. Supposing we have as an entry in the `thebibliography`

```
\bibitem[{\it Jones et~al.}(1990)]{jone90}
Jones, F. B., Smith, T. E., and Harris, R. E. ...
```

`jone90` is the keyword for the `\cite` command and its label, or raw translation, is `{\it Jones et~al.}(1990)`. In this case, the parentheses around the year in the label act as delimiters to allow a separation of authors from year. How these are then treated depends on how \cite is used:

\cite{jone90}                 yields    *Jones et al.* [1990]
\cite[]{jone90}               yields    [*Jones et al.*, 1990]
\cite[page~30]{jone90}        yields    [*Jones et al.*, 1990, page 30]

The type of brackets around the citation can be selected to be round parentheses or square brackets; the punctuation between citations may be a comma or semi-colon.

The package file begins as usual by identifying itself. It also needs the ifthen package, which is loaded right away.

```
\NeedsTeXFormat{LaTeX2e}[1994/06/01]
\ProvidesPackage{authyear}[1994/09/17 2.0 (PWD)]

\RequirePackage{ifthen}
```

We now prepare and execute the options. These will set various commands that store the punctuation and bracket types. Since the storage commands are not private internal commands, they may be redefined by the user at any time. However, the standard options provide the normal situations. The storage commands are created, options defined to set them, default options round and colon selected, and then the specified options processed.

```
\newcommand{\citebegin}{} \newcommand{\citeend}{}
\newcommand{\citesep}{}
\newcommand{\auyrsep}{,}

\DeclareOption{round}{\renewcommand{\citebegin}{(}
                      \renewcommand{\citeend}{)}}
\DeclareOption{square}{\renewcommand{\citebegin}{[}
                       \renewcommand{\citeend}{]}}
\DeclareOption{comma}{\renewcommand{\citesep}{,}}
\DeclareOption{colon}{\renewcommand{\citesep}{;}}
\ExecuteOptions{round,colon}
\ProcessOptions
```

The internal command \AY@cite prints the actual citation, after it has been formatted by the other commands that come below. Its first argument is the formatted citation(s), and the second is the optional argument to \cite, the optional note. If this note is missing, #2 is a period (see \cite below) and the citation is printed without enclosing it in brackets (textual citation); otherwise, it is wrapped in brackets, with the note enclosed (parenthetical citation).

```
\newcommand{\AY@cite}[2]
   {\ifthenelse{\equal{.}{#2}}
    {#1}
    {\citebegin#1%
```

```
\ifthenelse{\equal{#2}{}}
  {}
  {, #2}%
\citeend}}
```

The really heavy work is done by \cite. Much of what happens here is internal LaTeX wizardry, based on the definition of \cite in LaTeX $2_\varepsilon$. The new \cite command takes two arguments, the first being the optional note. However, the presence of a note is to be used to indicate a parenthetical citation. The note may in fact be empty, for a parenthetical citation without a note. To accommodate this, the default value for the optional (first) argument is a period. This indicates that \cite was invoked with no optional argument at all, not even an empty one.

The main argument (#2) is a list of citation keys. These must be processed one by one with \@for \do, setting \@citeb successively to each key in the list. The line with \@iden in it removes any leading blanks from \@citeb; then an entry is made in the auxiliary file for BibTeX; a test is done to see if the key has a translation (stored in \b@\@citeb), and a warning is printed if does not. At this point, the new features appear: the command \AY@parse is called to interpret the key, putting the author part into \AY@author and the year into \AY@year; these are put together, with the year in brackets for a textual citation (argument #1=.). Finally, the citation printing command \AY@cite is called with the list of translated citations as the first argument, and the optional argument of \cite as the second argument. Note that \AY@sep is added before each citation in the list; this is initially empty, but becomes \citesep after the first citation in the list. This adds the comma or semi-colon between the citations.

```
\newcommand{\AY@sep}{}

\renewcommand{\cite}[2][.]{%
  \renewcommand{\AY@sep}{}%
  \AY@cite{\@for\@citeb:=#2\do
    {\edef\@citeb{\expandafter\@iden\@citeb}%
      \ifthenelse{\boolean{@filesw}}
        {\immediate\write\@auxout{\string\citation{\@citeb}}}
        {}%
      \@ifundefined{b@\@citeb}
      {\AY@sep{\reset@font\bfseries ?}\G@refundefinedtrue
       \@latex@warning
         {Citation '\@citeb' on page \thepage \space undefined}}
      {\AY@parse{\@citeb}%
        \ifthenelse{\equal{.}{#1}}
          {\AY@sep{\AY@author} \citebegin\AY@year
           \renewcommand{\AY@sep}{\citeend\citesep\ }}
          {\AY@sep{\AY@author}\auyrsep\ \AY@year
           \renewcommand{\AY@sep}{\citesep\ }}}}% ends \do
  \ifthenelse{\equal{.}{#1}}
```

```
    {\citeend}
    {}%
  }{#1}}
```

The command that parses the citation key translation into author and year takes as argument the key involved. The expansion (translation) is used as argument to \AY@split. An additional dummy () must be added here just in case the translation does not contain any year in parentheses. The \let\protect= is special treatment for robust commands, to prevent them from being expanded at this point and wreaking havoc.

```
\newcommand{\AY@parse}[1]{{\let\protect=\@unexpandable@protect
    \xdef\@tempa{\@nameuse{b@#1}}%
    \expandafter\AY@split\@tempa()@}}
```

```
\def\AY@split#1(#2)#3@{\gdef\AY@author{#1}\gdef\AY@year{#2}}
```

That completes the redefinition of \cite and its accompanying internal commands. We now need to fix up the thebibliography environment. Unfortunately, this means redefining the whole environment, since there is no convenient internal command to modify. Also, we need to know whether we are in an article-like class, with a \chapter command, or not, because this determines whether the list of references is under a \chapter* or \section*.

```
\@ifundefined{chapter}
  {\newcommand{\AY@bibsect}{\section*{\refname
    \@mkboth{\uppercase{\refname}}{\uppercase{\refname}}}}}
  {\newcommand{\AY@bibsect}{\chapter*{\bibname
    \@mkboth{\uppercase{\bibname}}{\uppercase{\bibname}}}}}
```

```
\providecommand{\refname}{References}
\providecommand{\bibname}{Bibliography}
```

Now we redefine the thebibliography environment such that labels are not printed, the first line is flush left, with all following lines indented by 1em. We also make use of the \AY@bibsect command created above.

```
\renewenvironment{thebibliography}[1]
{\AY@bibsect
  \setlength{\parindent}{0pt}\list{}
  {\setlength{\leftmargin}{1em}%
   \setlength{\itemindent}{-\leftmargin}}
  \ifthenelse{\boolean{@openbib}}
    {\renewcommand\newblock{\newline}}
    {\renewcommand\newblock{\hskip .11em plus.33em minus.07em}}
  \sloppy\clubpenalty4000\widowpenalty4000
  \frenchspacing}
{\renewcommand{\@noitemerr}{\@latex@warning
    {Empty 'thebibliography' environment}}%
  \endlist\vspace{-\lastskip}}}
```

One last thing to do is to stop the \bibitem command from printing its label. Here we just need to alter an internal command to ignore its argument.

```
\renewcommand{\@biblabel}[1]{\hfill}
```

**The bibliography style file**

This completes the package file authyear.sty. However, it only works if the \bibitem commands in the thebibliography environment have the form shown at the beginning of this section. This may be done by hand, or by BIBTEX, but only if there is a bibliography style (.bst) file of the right format. Such a style file is not in the standard BIBTEX package, but the alpha.bst file can be changed slightly to do the job. We shall simply list the necessary coding to make this possible without explanation, since BIBTEX uses a language all of its own.

Copy the file alpha.bst to a new file named authyear.bst and look for the text FUNCTION {output.bibitem}. The fifth line of this function reads "]{" write$; replace it with ")]{" write$, that is, add a closing parenthesis before the closing bracket.

Next, find FUNCTION {format.date} and add extra.label * before the last closing brace of the function. Thus the last three lines now appear as

```
  if$
  extra.label *
}
```

Now look for the text FUNCTION {format.lab.names}. Replace the text of this function (everything up to the FUNCTION {author.key.label}) with

```
FUNCTION {format.lab.names}
{ 's :=
  s #1 "{vv~}{ll}" format.name$
  s num.names$ duplicate$
  #2 >
    { pop$ " et~al." * }
    { #2 <
        'skip$
        { s #2 "{ff }{vv }{ll}{ jj}" format.name$ "others" =
            { " et~al." * }
            { " and " * s #2 "{vv~}{ll}" format.name$ * }
          if$
        }
      if$
    }
  if$
}
```

Finally, look for FUNCTION {calc.label} and find the line containing duplicate$. Add emphasize "(" * after it. In the next line, change #2 to #4. These and the neighboring lines should then appear as

```
if$
duplicate$
emphasize "(" *
year field.or.null purify$ #-1 #4 substring$
*
'label :=
```

(The emphasize above means that the authors in the citations, not the references, will be in italics. If this is not desired, leave it out.)

Note: this new bibliography style will work only for BibTeX versions 0.99 or later.

To demonstrate how this may be used, suppose there is an entry in the bibliography data file mylit.bib (see Section B.2)

```
@ARTICLE{jone90,
    AUTHOR = {Fred B. Jones and
              Thomas Elwood Smith and
              Richard E. Harris},
    TITLE = {Activity in the Night-Side Ionosphere},
    YEAR = {1990},
    JOURNAL = {J. Geophys. Res.},
    VOLUME = {101},
    PAGES = {1234-1254} }
```

If the LaTeX file now contains the lines

```
\documentclass{article}
\usepackage[square]{authyear}
\begin{document}
. . . as shown by \cite{jone90}, it is possible . . .
. . . has been measured \cite[]{jone90}. This is  . . .
\bibliographystyle{authyear}
\bibliography{mylit}
\end{document}
```

the resulting output will be

... as shown by *Jones et al.* [1990], it is possible ...
... has been measured [*Jones et al.*, 1990]. This is ...

## References

Fred B. Jones, Thomas Elwood Smith, and Richard E. Harris. Activity in the night-side ionosphere. *J. Geophys. Res.*, 101:1234-1254, 1990.

# LATEX Extensions

One of the reasons for the great popularity of LATEX is that it can be reprogrammed: if some feature is missing from the basic installation (the kernel) it is possible for a knowledgeable user to add it by writing a package. Under the LATEX 2.09 regime, hundreds of packages (then called *style options*) were made public by means of computer file servers. Many of these are still compatible with LATEX 2ε, while others are being converted, and more are being written.

It is not the intention of this book to go much beyond the standard LATEX packages; a description of *some* of the many contributed packages is to be found in *The LATEX Companion* by Goosens *et al.* (1994). Instead, we outline only some few extensions for multilingual LATEX, PostScript fonts, importing graphics and using color. We then describe some advanced features of the basic installation, like integrated documentation of packages, some semi-official extensions, and finally how LATEX 2ε is installed.

All LATEX packages described in this appendix may be obtained from the sources listed in Section D.5.

## 1 International LATEX

In the original version of LATEX, there are several English words such as 'Figure' and 'Bibliography' included explicitly in certain commands. This in fact violates the rules of good programming which forbid doing anything explicitly. In Europe, LATEX users quickly made customizations for their particular languages. The adaptation for German, `german.sty`, is a set of macros from many contributors collected together by H. Partl of the Technical University of Vienna, and has become the standard for the German-speaking TEX Users Group (DANTE). It contains some facilities for other languages, including French and English. More details are given in the next section.

The key to `german.sty` is the fact that the standard LATEX document styles (classes) have been altered so that explicit English words in the output are replaced by command names. These names have become standardized among European users for application to all languages. The modified LᴬTᴇX version by J. Schrod from Darmstadt was known as IᴌᴬTᴇX, for International LᴬTᴇX. These names and their standard English values are to be found on page 349.

As of December 1, 1991, these naming features became part of the LᴬTᴇX standard. They represent good programming practice, since they allow even English-speaking users to change certain titles easily, for example 'Abstract' into 'Summary' or 'Contents' into 'Table of Contents'.

Another important tool for multilingual usage is the TᴇX \language counter which allows more than one set of hyphenation patterns to be stored in the format with initex (Section D.4). Different patterns are activated by setting \language to the appropriate number. This is only possible with TᴇX version 3.0 or greater.

### D.1.1   The file `german.sty`

At the 6th Meeting of German TᴇX Users in October 1987, a standard set of TᴇX and LᴬTᴇX commands was agreed upon for application to the German language. The package `german.sty` was set up by H. Partl of the Technical University of Vienna, and extended by many other workers. The latest version is 2.4a, dated April 12, 1992, and is maintained by Bernd Raichle of the University of Stuttgart. A modification of it, called `german3.sty`, possesses the same functionality, but works only with fonts of the Cork, or T1, encoding (Section E.10.2). Its latest version is 1.0c, from April 8, 1992, and is maintained by Rainer Schöpf.

It is not our purpose to present and explain the entire `german.sty` file, since the explanation of `esperant.sty` in Section C.3.3 contains all the basic elements of a general language adaptation. In fact, `esperant.sty` is derived from `german.sty` and may be considered a miniature variant of it. In this appendix, we illustrate the additional commands that it contains specifically for German. In the next section, we do the same for the package `french.sty`.

Since `german.sty` was the inspiration for International LᴬTᴇX and for the `babel` multilingual system, it does deserve this extra attention at this point.

The original, minimal adaptation for German before `german.sty` existed consists of three commands:

```
\catcode'\"=\active \def"{\"} \def\3{\ss}
```

which make the double quote " a command (active), define it to be the umlaut accent (\"), and define \3 to be the German double *s*, or *eszet*, ß. These were meant only to simplify the typing of German texts.

**The double quote command symbol**

The modern `german.sty` elaborates the definition of the double quote command so that:

- the umlaut in Computer Modern fonts is positioned closer to the letter than it is in normal LaTeX, compare ö (`"o`) with ö (`\"o`);

- the double quote may be used in `\verb` commands and `verbatim` environments;

- hyphenations are allowed in the whole word in which the umlaut appears;

- the *eszet* may be printed with `"s`; the older form `\3` is kept for consistency with earlier texts, but is not encouraged.

The double quote symbol is also employed for other special functions in German, in particular for word division:

`"ck` The German rules of hyphenation require that when *ck* is divided, it becomes *k-k*. This is achieved by typing `"ck`, for example `Dru"cker`.

`"mm` Another rule states that when two words are joined together, there may only be at most two doubled letters (for example, *Schwimm + Meister = Schwimmeister*), but when they are divided again, the missing third letter must be reinserted (*Schwimm-meister*). This is entered in the text as `Schwi"mmeister`. Other double-triple letter possibilities also exist.

`"-` Suggested hyphenations are typed in with `"-`, which permits further automatic hyphenations within the word, something that the normal TeX command `\-` does not allow.

`"|` Finally, ligatures may be broken with `"|` where they are not appropriate, such as between joined words (*Auf + Lage = Auflage* `auf"|lage` and not *Auflage*).

**Quotation marks**

Instead of the English 'inverted commas', German uses „Gänsefüßchen", or ‚goose-feet' for double and single quotation marks. The commands to produce these are `\glqq` for German left quote quote, the opening double quote („), `\grqq` ("), `\glq` (‚), and `\grq` ('). The two double quote commands may be abbreviated as `"'` and `"'`.

Provision is made for the French «guillemets» which are typed in with commands `\flqq` and `\frqq`. These may be abbreviated to `"<` and `">`. Single ‹guillemets› may also be generated with commands `\flq` and `\frq`. Both of these often appear in German texts.

### Captions and dates

The name commands of International LATEX are activated for German in a manner analogous to Esperanto on page 349, that is, with the command \captionsgerman. They may be switched back with \captionsenglish; a command \captionsfrench is also available in german.sty, although a better French adaptation is achieved with french.sty (Section D.1.2).

The \today command to print out the current date may be redefined with the declarations \dategerman, \dateaustrian, \dateUSenglish, \dateenglish, and \datefrench. The definitions of the two English variants are the same as those on page 349. Depending on the language chosen, \today produces 'November 15, 1994', '15th November 1994', „15. November 1994", or «15 novembre 1994». The Austrian date differs from the German one only in the name of the first month of the year: *Jänner* instead of *Januar*.

### Language selection

With german.sty it is possible to select the French and English languages as well by means of a \selectlanguage command, which takes as its argument one of german, french, english, USenglish, or austrian. This command activates the hyphenation patterns by setting \language to the corresponding value.

## D.1.2   The file french.sty

The French style file french.sty was originally initiated independently of german.sty by a number of people writing documents in French. It was then enlarged and secured by Bernard Gaulle who offered his work to the French-speaking TEX Users Group (GUTenberg). The current version is 3.32, dated August 9, 1994.

We present here an overview of *some* of the special commands available in this French style for both TEX and LATEX. As for the German example, the purpose is to show the nature of the customizations necessary and the complexity of the problem.

Whereas the main concerns of german.sty are to simplify the umlaut accent and to accommodate the German hyphenation rules, french.sty has no special accent commands but does consider French punctuation and abbreviations. The alterations may be grouped into five different categories, each of which has a pair of commands to activate and deactivate the whole group. The overall command \french calls all five activating commands.

## Hyphenations

With the command \frenchhyphenation, TEX switches over to the French word division patterns which were loaded into the format by initex. This means that words are divided according to French rules. With the counter-manding \nofrenchhyphenation, it switches back to the standard set, language 0, which is normally English.

## Captions and date

The command \frenchtranslation calls \captionsfrench to redefine all the name commands in International LⁱᵀEX. It also sets \today to be the French version, shown above. There are a number of additional name commands, especially for letters that are not present in standard LⁱᵀEX. There is also a \resume command parallel to \abstract since many French papers require a summary (a *résumé*) both in French and English.

   The command \nofrenchtranslation deactivates the French trans-lations.

## Punctuation

The rules of French typography require that extra spacing be inserted before the 'double punctuation marks ! ? ; :'. This spacing is less than the usual inter-word spacing; the source text should contain a full space before these characters (but see \untypedspaces below), which is re-duced automatically when the command \frenchtypography has been given: this paragraph is being set with this command in effect! Is this not obvious? The TEX command \frenchspacing is also activated so that the spacing after the end of a sentence remains the same as that between words.

   The only quotation marks allowed in French are the *guillemets* which are printed here as « guillemets » as they appear with TEX and now as « guillemets » with LⁱᵀEX. They are produced with << and >>, and are some-what different from those generated by \flqq and \frqq in german.sty («German»). They automatically include extra spacing around the enclosed text. Quoted text may also be put into the environment guillemets. The opening guillemets are added at the start of every paragraph within the quotation.

   There are a number of sub-options also available, some of which are:

\untypedspaces Inserts the extra space before ! ? ; : even if it has been omitted in the source text (for the benefit of non-French typists).

\noTeXdots Changes the \ldots and \dots commands to print the ellipsis in the French manner (...) as three closely spaced periods instead of in the English way (. . . ).

\todayguillemets Paragraphs within a second-level quotation, or in the guillemets environment, have an opening « preceding them, the same as the first-level paragraphs: this is the modern style and is the default.

\ancientguillemets The paragraphs within a second-level quotation are started with closing (») instead of opening («) guillemets; this is an old-fashioned practice in French.

\noenglishquote Turns the single quote characters ' and ' into grave and acute accents ` and ´.

\noenglishdoublequotes Turns the double quote characters '' and '' into the « guillemets ».

\idotless Produces a dotless *i* for accents *î* and *ï*.

The command \nofrenchtypography switches the special punctuation and any sub-options off.

### Layout

With the command \frenchlayout, several changes are made in the LᴬTₑX formats. These are

- All paragraphs are indented, even the first one in a section, which LᴬTₑX normally does not indent.

- The \item labels in the itemize environment are made into dashes at every level, as illustrated here.

- The sectioning counters are reset after a new part has been started.

- A new environment order is defined like enumerate but numbers its items as 1° 2° 3° ....

These format changes may be removed with the \nofrenchlayout command.

### Abbreviations

A number of new commands are defined when \frenchmacros is issued to help in printing certain common French abbreviations.

\ier To print the masculine 1$^{er}$ with 1\ier.

\iere To print the feminine 1$^{re}$ with 1\iere.

\ieme To print other ordinal numbers, such as 3$^{e}$ with 3\ieme.

\at To print the « a enroulé » (@).

\bv To print the « barre verticale » with the \tt font (|).

\chap To print the « chapeau » or « circonflexe » (^).

\boi To print the « barre oblique inversée » (backslash) with the \tt font (\).

\tilde To print the tilde (˜).

\Numero To print N°.

\degres To print the degree sign °.

\fup{x} To raise and reduce $x$, as M\fup{me} for M$^{\text{me}}$.

\primo \secundo \tertio \quatro To print 1°, 2°, 3°, and 4°. When followed by a closing parenthesis, for example \tertio), they print 3°).

\quando=$n$ To print any number in the above form, for example: \quando={10} for 10°.

\minMAJ{oe} To print œ or Œ following the automatic case selection in the table of contents and page head. Other arguments are possible, such as ae and i.

These special commands may be turned off with the \nofrenchmacros declaration.

### Language selection

The routines in french.sty also provide the possibility to switch back to English, with the command \english. The companion file english.sty contains the caption names in English as well as the relevant switching commands.

Extra languages that make use of an existing set of hyphenation patterns may be defined with \NouveauLangage[*num*]{*lang*}. This command then creates a new command \*lang* which switches to *lang* by setting the counter \language to *num*. A command \*lang*TeX is also executed, which must be separately defined, to activate any other special features of this language.

## .1.3  Multilingual LATEX—the babel system

One problem with both german.sty and french.sty is that, although they allow further languages to be added, they do so in incompatible ways. It is therefore not possible to make use of both these style files within one document.

The babel system has been developed by Johannes Braams at the Dutch PTT Research Laboratories. Its main purpose is to provide a standard means of switching languages with a flexible method for loading the hyphenation patterns. It has been written to work with both TEX (versions 2.x and 3.x) and LATEX (international and English only).

On page 346, we listed the three main requirements for a language adaptation: translation of the explicit English titles, special commands to simplify certain features of that language, and selection of the appropriate hyphenation patterns. To these `babel` adds removal of the special commands and testing for the current language. The language-specific files must conform to the `babel` selection command structure. The concept of 'dialects' is also included, that is, two 'languages' that share a common set of hyphenation patterns. Examples are German and Austrian as well as British and US English, which only differ in the form of the dates (see page 360).

At present, the `babel` package contains style files for the following languages:

> Esperanto,
> Dutch, English, German,
> French, Italian, Portuguese, Spanish, Catalan, Galician,
> Danish, Norwegian, Swedish,
> Finnish, Hungarian,
> Czech, Slovak, Romanian, Croatian, Slovene,
> Russian (planned), Polish,
> Turkish,
> Bahasa.

These package files are delivered with the installation. The hyphenation patterns for the various languages must be obtained from another source, however. For most of these files, there are no special commands for accents or punctuation: they only redefine the naming commands for International LATEX.

The `german.sty` file has been a great inspiration for `babel`. However, since the command `\selectlanguage` is employed slightly differently, it was necessary to create a new `germanb.sty` for `babel` applications, which contains the same set of special commands, but with a few `babel` additions. Similarly, the `babel` French file had to be named `francais.sty` to distinguish it from `french.sty`.

### The `babel` files

The `babel` installation provides the following files for its implementation:

`babel.def` contains some of the basic macros for running `babel`, and must be loaded by the first language file read in; the remaining macros are either already in the format itself (loaded from `hyphen.cfg`) or read in from `switch.def`; `babel.def` determines which is the case and reacts accordingly;

`switch.def` contains the additional `babel` macros, to be read in if these macros are not already stored in the LaTeX format;

`hyphen.cfg` contains the same macro definitions as in `switch.def`, plus some more that are to be run by initex; if this file is available during the creation of the LaTeX 2$_\varepsilon$ format (Section D.4), these macros are built into that format and file `switch.def` is not necessary at run time;

`babel.sty` is a master package that loads the language files specified as options;

`language.dat` contains a list of languages and the file names of their hyphenation patterns; this file is read in by `hyphen.cfg` during the initex run; it is the only file that may (must!) be edited for the particular installation (Section D.1.4);

`esperant.sty...` the language-specific files.

## Invoking `babel`

Under LaTeX 2$_\varepsilon$, there are two ways to initiate `babel` in a document: either load the language-specific packages, as

```
\usepackage{english,esperant}
```

or load the package `babel` with the desired languages as options:

```
\usepackage[english,esperanto]{babel}
```

Alternatively, the language names may be used as global options, something that is recommended if there are other packages that take the languages as options, as

```
\documentclass[english,esperanto]{article}
\usepackage{babel,varioref}
```

In all cases, the last named language is the one that is immediately active.

Calling the languages as options is more flexible, because the package names are limited to the file names available:

| | | | |
|---|---|---|---|
| bahasa | english | italian | russian |
| catalan | esperant | magyar | slovak |
| croatian | finnish | norsk | slovene |
| czech | francais | polish | spanish |
| danish | galician | portuges | swedish |
| dutch | germanb | romanian | turkish |

These file names are truncated to 8 letters to be compatible with all operating systems. On the other hand, the options use the full name of the language, and recognize several variations for the same package:

| | | | |
|---|---|---|---|
| american | dutch | germanb | romanian |
| austrian | english | hungarian | russian |
| bahasa | esperanto | italian | spanish |
| brazil | finnish | magyar | slovak |
| catalan | francais | norsk | slovene |
| croatian | french | nynorsk | swedish |
| czech | galician | polish | turkish |
| danish | german | portuges | |

If the `babel` package is loaded, all it does is read in the specified language packages; they in turn read in `babel.def` and possibly `switch.def` (if its macros are not already in the format).

### Language switching commands

The normal user needs to know very little about the `babel` internal operations. The only new commands that are needed are:

> `\selectlanguage{`*language*`}`     and
> `\iflanguage{`*language*`}{`*yes_text*`}{`*no_text*`}`

The first switches *language* to being the current language, and the second executes *yes_text* if *language* is current otherwise *no_text*.

The user must of course also know what language-specific commands are made available by this selection. However, that is not really part of `babel` itself, which is primarily a standardized switching mechanism.

### Contents of a language-specific file

Although the normal user does not need to know anything about how the switching mechanism functions, we will outline it here for the interested user.

Two additional internal `babel` commands are:

> `\addlanguage{`*lang_num*`}`   and
> `\adddialect{`*lang_num_1*`}{`*lang_num_2*`}`

where *lang_num* is an internal language number for specifying the set of hyphenation patterns. The command `\addlanguage` sets its argument equal to the next available language number. The form of *lang_num* used in `babel` is `\l@`*language*; for example, `\l@english`. This command is executed on those language names listed in `language.dat` during the initex run. The command `\adddialect` sets the first argument equal to the second so that the two languages make use of the same set of hyphenation patterns. For example, in `english.sty` there is the command `\adddialect{\l@american}{\l@english}`.

A language-specific file must contain four command definitions:

\captions*lang* to redefine the naming commands like \tablename;
\date*lang* to define \today;
\extras*lang* to define any language-specific commands;
\noextras*lang* to remove the language-specific commands.

If the language *lang* is not one of those with prestored hyphenation patterns in the current format file (that is, if \l@*lang* is undefined), it is set to be a 'dialect' of language number 0.

Finally, the language-specific file calls \selectlanguage{*lang*} to activate that language. This is accomplished by

- calling \language\l@*lang* to select the set of hyphenation patterns,

- invoking \originalTeX in order to remove any existing language-specific commands,

- activating \captions*lang*, \date*lang*, and \extras*lang* to invoke the language-specific names, date, and commands,

- redefining \originalTeX to be \noextras*lang* so that the next language switch will remove those features specific to *lang*.

## 1.4   Use of the \language command

As has been mentioned before, with TeX version 3.0 and later it is possible to store more than one set of hyphenation patterns in the format file. The counter \language is used to switch between them by setting it to a different number.

However, there is no standard to dictate which languages belong to which numbers. The packages esperant in Section C.3.3 and german in Section D.1.1 assume a certain ordering, but might function incorrectly at other installations. The babel system invokes a much more reliable procedure, which is also used by the french package.

The file language.dat, which is read in during the creation of the format, contains a list of languages to add as well as the names of the files with their hyphenation patterns. For example, if language.dat contains

```
english    hyphen.tex
germanb    ghyphen.tex
francais   fhyphen.tex
```

then the hyphenation patterns in hyphen.tex, ghyphen.tex, and fhyphen.tex are loaded under languages 0, 1, and 2 respectively, and \l@english, \l@germanb, and \l@francais are defined as numbers 0, 1, and 2 for use with the \selectlanguage command. Thus the language francais is directly linked to the French hyphenations. At a French institution, this might be language 1 rather than 2, but that is irrelevant. The point is that the numbers are stored in the format and are addressable through standard names.

Such a format can be generated by making the file hyphen.cfg available during the initex run (Section D.4). The only file that needs to be tailored to the local installation is language.dat.

## D.2     LᴬTEX and PostScript

The introduction of PostScript as a printing and plotting language has established a new standard for ready-to-print files that is very flexible and still portable by electronic transfer to other institutions. A number of DVI driver programs exist to translate the .dvi output of TEX into this versatile output format. The most popular of these is called dvips, a non-commercial program by Tomas Rokicki, available on the CTAN file servers (Section D.5).

PostScript can offer many additional features to LᴬTEX, such as the importation of external graphics, color, scaling, and rotating. The dvips installation includes a number of packages for implementing these. However, they are applicable only to the one driver; other programs make use of different packages and commands. As part of the official extensions to LᴬTEX 2$_\varepsilon$, a standard set of commands has been developed for these functions, with the driver-specific coding hidden away in .def files. In this way, the high-level user commands remain fairly uniform for all drivers, and one only has to specify the driver as an option to the graphics or color packages.

Since these features are not necessarily restricted to PostScript, we explain them later in Section D.3.3.

### D.2.1     Invoking PostScript fonts

Using a PostScript driver for the output of a LᴬTEX document means that the many PostScript fonts may also be exploited, especially now that NFSS is fully part of LᴬTEX 2$_\varepsilon$.

A collection of packages can be obtained to simplify the selection of these fonts. They are to be found in the directory psnfss on the CTAN servers (see the diagram on page 388). They contain the package files as well as the necessary font definition .fd files for the 35 standard PostScript fonts, plus a number of other commercially available fonts. The packages are actually quite simple; for example, the times.sty file contains only three lines, which are listed on page 236. All these packages do is redefine the three font families, \rmdefault, \sfdefault, and \ttdefault.

The packages for the 35 standard fonts, and the three assignments that they make, are listed in Table D.1 opposite. (The 35 fonts include italic and bold variants of these.)

**Table D.1**: The `psnfss` packages and their fonts

| Package | \rmfamily | \sffamily | \ttfamily |
|---------|-----------|-----------|-----------|
| times.sty | TimesRoman | Helvetica | Courier |
| palatino.sty | Palatino | Helvetica | Courier |
| newcent.sty | NewCenturySchoolbook | AvantGarde | Courier |
| bookman.sty | Bookman | AvantGarde | Courier |
| avant.sty | | AvantGarde | |
| helvet.sty | | Helvetica | |

What is missing from the `psnfss` collection are the necessary font metric `.tfm` files. These are located on CTAN in the directory `font/metrics`, with a sub-directory for each font. For example, the TimesRoman font metrics are in sub-directory `ptm`.

These fonts make use of TEX's *virtual font* mechanism, which means that what TEX sees are actually artificial fonts that do not really exist. Since TEX only reads the `.tfm` files, it is perfectly happy. What the driver then does is to read a `.vf` file instead of the pixel `.pk` or `.pxl` files. The instructions in the virtual font file tell the driver how to create each character: they may be drawn, taken from other fonts, or distorted. This is how PostScript slanted and small caps fonts are emulated, for such fonts do not exist in the 'raw' form.

Even the font layout can be redesigned with virtual fonts. The raw PostScript fonts have an encoding scheme that conforms to that of neither the CM nor the DC layouts (Sections E.6 and E.10.3), but the virtual fonts do. In particular, the Computer Modern fonts contain upper case Greek letters in the first 11 slots (Layout 1 on page 406) which are to be found in the PostScript symbol font only. The virtual font `ptmr` conforms to this by taking its characters from both the raw TimesRoman and Symbol fonts.

One must obtain all the `.tfm` and `.vf` files from the metric directory for the fonts to be printed properly.

# 3   Further LATEX accessories

## 3.1   The DocStrip utility

That the TEX program can be used as a programming as well as a text formatting language can be exploited to provide a number of utility 'programs' to manipulate files. Such programs are immediately portable: if you have TEX, you can run them. One example of such a program is the DocStrip utility by Frank Mittelbach which removes comment lines from files.

At first sight one might ask why anyone would want to do such a thing, since comments are ignored anyway. In the original release of LATEX, Leslie Lamport provided all the support files with copious comments, which are many times longer than the coding itself. In those days, storage space and speed were at a premium, so for working purposes he provided the same files without the comments. The commented versions could be stored off-line, for reference. Mittelbach's idea was to create a program to simplify the decommenting of files for compact storage and fast loading.

Out of this simple concept came two additional features that extended the application of DocStrip: alternative lines of coding could be selectively suppressed or included depending on options chosen at processing time; and multiple files, or modules, could be input to form a single output file. This means that one source file can be the home of several different LATEX packages, and that a package file can be constructed out of many different components. In fact, the main LATEX $2_\varepsilon$ generation file `latex.ltx` is built up out of over 30 individual files, while the standard class files, with much common coding, are all extracted from the one file `classes.dtx` along with their option files.

It is with the integrated documentation system of Section D.3.2 that DocStrip finds one of its most important applications today. However, it has other uses as well, such as with the generic bibliographic style files presented in Section B.3.2. It has become something like the C preprocessor and `makefile` utility of Unix, but running under TEX to make it fully portable to all systems.

### Running interactively

The simplest way of running DocStrip on a file is to invoke it with TEX (or LATEX, but TEX is faster), as

```
tex docstrip
```

which produces the response

```
****************************************************************
* This program converts documented macro-files into fast *
* loadable files by stripping off (nearly) all comments! *
****************************************************************
*********************************************************
* First type the extension of your input file(s):   *
\infileext=
*********************************************************
```

One replies by entering the input extension (usually `.dtx`); then one is asked in turn for the output extension, the options wanted, and finally, for the root name of the file(s) to be processed. Execution follows.

There are some limitations to this method, since the input and output files have the same root name, differing only in the extension, and initial and final comments added to the output are fixed. The more flexible means of running the utility is with a batch job.

## Running as a batch job

A DocStrip batch job is a file containing instructions for the utility. For example, suppose the `fullpage` package illustrated in Section C.3.1 is put into a documented source file called `fullpage.dtx`, and the true package file `fullpage.sty` is to be extracted with the option `package`; the batch file, named `fullpage.ins`, could look like

```
\def\batchfile{fullpage.ins}
\input docstrip

\preamble
This is a stripped version of the original file.
\endpreamble

\postamble
This is the end of the stripped file.
\endpostamble

\generateFile{fullpage.sty}{f}{\from{fullpage.dtx}{package}}
```

The first two lines are vital: `\batchfile` is defined as the name of the file containing the instructions; then `docstrip.tex` is loaded (the `\input` command must be written *exactly* as shown here), reads in and executes the specified file *and stops!* The remaining lines of instructions have already been processed when DocStrip read in the `\batchfile`. In fact, they could be in a different file altogether from that containing the first two lines; the only requirement is that `\batchfile` must be defined to be precisely that file containing the instructions.

The commands `\preamble` and `\postamble` allow one to include explanatory comments at the beginning and end.

The main command is `\generateFile` which specifies the output file name as its first argument. The second argument is either `t` or `f` to tell DocStrip whether it should issue a warning if a file with the output name already exists. With `f` for ⟨*false*⟩, no warning is given. The third argument contains one or more `\from` commands, whose two arguments are the input file name and its option(s) for alternative coding.

The created `fullpage.sty` files now contains

```
%% This is file 'fullpage.sty', generated
%% on <1994/10/15> with the docstrip utility (2.2h).
%%
%% The original source files were:
%%
%% fullpage.dtx  (with options: 'package')
```

```
%% This is a stripped version of the original file.
\NeedsTeXFormat{LaTeX2e}
. . . . . . . . . . . . . . . . . . . .
\addtolength{\topmargin}{-1in}
%% This is the end of stripped file.
```

It is possible to have a master batch job to process individual ones, in which case the master must input them with \batchinput, and not with \input.

### Rules for removing lines

The \generateFile command causes the input file(s) to be transferred to the output file, line by line, according to the following rules:

1. any lines beginning with a *single* % sign are removed;

2. any lines beginning with two % signs are retained;

3. any line beginning with %<opt> (or %<+opt>) will have the rest of its text transferred if opt is one of the selected options; otherwise it is removed;

4. any line beginning with %<!opt> (or %<-opt>) will have the rest of its text transferred if opt is *not* one of the selected options; otherwise it is removed;

5. all lines between %<*opt> and %</opt> are retained or removed depending on whether opt is a selected option or not.

Options can be combined logically, negated, and grouped:

```
a&b        (a and b);
a|b        (a or b);
!a         (not a);
(a|b)&c (c and one of a or b)
```

For more information on DocStrip, see the documentation which can be obtained by processing docstrip.dtx with LᴬTEX.

## D.3.2  Documenting LᴬTEX coding

The documenting of software products is extremely important: it provides on the one hand a manual for the user, and on the other details about the coding for the programmer. The original LᴬTEX styles, as well as the basic latex.tex file, were heavily commented by Leslie Lamport, but only with straightforward normal text. It was Frank Mittelbach's doc package that first allowed sophisticated, integrated documentation of the source codes.

By *integrated* documentation, we mean that the descriptions and the coding are to be found merged together in a single source file. Thus two processes are necessary, one to extract the actual coding on its own (the DocStrip utility of Section D.3.1) and another to print the documentation (the doc package). The basic idea behind this package is that the comments are in fact regular LATEX text, with some extra features to allow automatic indexing and to track the record of evolution of the program. The coding itself appears in a special type of verbatim environment.

The documentation is produced by running a special driver file through LATEX. Such a driver for a source file named fullpage.dtx would be, in its simplest form,

```
\documentclass{article}
\usepackage{doc}
\begin{document}
  \DocInput{fullpage.dtx}
\end{document}
```

The \DocInput command reads in the specified file, but it first alters the function of the % character from 'comment' to 'do nothing'. This means all comment lines in fullpage.dtx become real text to be processed!

Originally, the source files were given the extension .doc, and they were nothing more than a .sty file with the special doc package commands. One could rename the file to .sty and use it as the package file itself. With the introduction of the LATEX $2_\varepsilon$ standard, both doc.sty and DocStrip have become part of the basic installation, no longer optional extensions. Now the source files are labeled .dtx and they behave as the documentation driver file. This means that one only has to process them under LATEX to obtain the documentation. The package .sty file must be extracted with DocStrip before it can be used.

We describe some of the extra features that the doc package makes available for the 'comments' in the .dtx files, illustrated by an example, the source file fullpage.dtx for the fullpage package presented in Section C.3.1. As usual, a more complete manual can be acquired by processing doc.dtx.

## The description part

The documentation consists of two parts: the *description*, which is a manual for the end user, and the *coding*, a detailed explanation of how the software works, including the lines of code themselves. It is possible to suppress the coding part and to print only the description by issuing

```
\OnlyDescription
```

in the preamble.

Special commands for the description part are:

```
\DescribeMacro{\macro_name}
\DescribeEnvironment{env_name}
```

which are placed at the start of the text that illustrates a new high-level command (macro) or environment. These commands do two things: they place the macro or environment name in a marginal note at that location (for easy reference when reading) and they insert an entry in the index.

Because documentation needs to use the \verb command frequently for printing source text, some abbreviations are provided with

```
\MakeShortVerb{\c}   and   \DeleteShortVerb{\c}
```

which first turn the character *c* into shorthand for \verb*c*, and then re-store its normal use. For example, after \MakeShortVerb{\|}, |\mycom| prints \mycom. (These commands can be made available for any document by loading the package shortvrb, which is actually extracted from the doc package.)

If the comment character % has been deactivated, how can one put comments into the documentation text? One way is to make use of the TᴇX conditional \iffalse to form a block, or *meta* comment, as

```
% \iffalse
%       These lines are ignored even when the
%       percent character is inactive
% \fi
```

The other method is to use ^^A in place of %, a special doc feature.

The description part is terminated with

```
\StopEventually{final text}
```

where *final text* is to appear at the very end of the article; if only the description part is printed, *final text* is printed immediately and the documentation is ended.

### The coding part

The coding part should normally contain the more specialized material that is of no interest to the everyday user. The special commands that may be used here are

```
\begin{macro}{\macro_name} text and code \end{macro}
\begin{environment}{env_name} text and code \end{environment}
```

both of which again insert a marginal note and make an entry in the index. They also organize any \changes commands, as explained below.

The most important environment in the coding part is macrocode, which prints its contents as in verbatim, optionally with a code line number. The form of this environment is somewhat special:

␣␣␣␣`\begin{macrocode}`
*lines of code*
␣␣␣␣`\end{macrocode}`

The four spaces before the `\end{macrocode}` absolutely must be present; those before the `\begin` are not necessary, but it is good to insert them for symmetry. This environment also counts all the backslashes within it for a checksum test, and makes an index entry for every command name that it finds. So it is something more than a mere `verbatim` environment!

The coding part is brought to an end with

   `\Finale`

which carries out the checksum test and prints the stored *final text* from `\StopEventually`. There may actually be more text following it, which is only printed when both description and coding parts are output.

### Index of macros and record of changes

The `doc` package makes automatic entries into an index by means of the two `\Describexxx` commands and the two environments presented above. As well, all commands that appear in the coding are indexed. However, the indexing is turned on only if one of

   `\CodelineIndex`     or     `\PageIndex`

is given in the preamble. The first references the indexed commands to the number of the code line where they appear, the second to the page number. In the second case, the code lines are not numbered, unless the declaration `\CodelineNumbered` is also issued.

Since not all commands in the coding really need to be indexed, especially those that are part of standard LATEX and TEX, the command

   `\DoNotIndex{`*list of command names*`}`

is given, often repeatedly, near the beginning, to exempt the listed commands from being indexed.

The automatic indexing of all the commands in the code slows down the processing considerably. Once the index `.idx` file has been produced, future runs do not need to repeat this effort (unless there have been changes to the code). The command

   `\DisableCrossrefs`

will suppress this indexing, but it may be countermanded by an earlier `\EnableCrossrefs` which neutralizes the disabling command.

The text of the index is generated from the `.idx` data file by the MakeIndex program (Section 8.4), which must be run with the special indexing style `gind.ist` as

```
makeindex -s gind.ist filename
```

The indexing style file gind.ist can be extracted from doc.dtx.
To print the index, the command

```
\PrintIndex
```

is placed where it should appear.  Often this is part of the *final text* in
\StopEventually.  An up-to-date index can only appear after MakeIndex
has been run between two LATEX processings.
   A record of changes to the software can be made by inserting

```
\changes{version}{date}{text}
```

throughout the documentation, in both the description and coding parts.
To form the change history list, the command

```
\RecordChanges
```

must be placed in the preamble.  This enables the change entries to be
placed in a glossary file, which is then processed by MakeIndex as

```
makeindex -s gglo.ist -o filename.gls filename.glo
```

(The indexing style file gglo.ist is also extracted from doc.dtx.)  The
change history is then printed in the documentation where

```
\PrintChanges
```

is located, again often as part of *final text*.  The texts of the \changes
commands are ordered, first by version number, then by the name of the
macro or environment in which they appear.


## Integrity tests

If the source file is to be sent over electronic networks, there is a danger
that it might be corrupted or truncated.  Two tests are possible to check
for this.  By placing

```
\CheckSum{num}
```

near the start of the documentation (before the coding anyway), all the
backslashes in the macrocode environments will be added up, and the
total compared with the number *num* by the \Finale command.  If
*num*=0, the true total will be printed on the monitor; otherwise, if the
sum does not agree with *num*, an error is printed, with the two values.
   The other test checks that the character set has not been corrupted by
passing through computer systems with different character codes.

```
\CharacterTable
{Upper-case     \A\B\C\D\E\F\G\H. . .
 . . . . .
 . . . . .    Tilde    \~}
```

The argument must agree exactly with that expected by doc (except for inactive % signs and multiple spaces). It should be copied from the doc.sty or doc.dtx files.

### Obtaining the file information

A new feature in the LATEX 2$_\varepsilon$ version of doc is the command

> \GetFileInfo{*filename*}

which defines \filename, \filedate, \fileversion, and \fileinfo from the optional release information to be found in the \Provides*xxx* command identifying the specified file (Section C.2.1). The idea is that the .dtx file should contain this information once, and only once, but it needs to be known to print it in the title of the article. These \file*xxx* commands may be used for this purpose. The release information must conform to the sequence *date*, blank, *version*, blank, *text*.

### The ltxdoc class

A special class called ltxdoc is provided to assist running the doc package. It invokes the article class with the doc package, and then issues commands

> \AtBeginDocument{\MakeShortVerb{\|}}
> \CodelineNumbered
> \DisableCrossrefs

and defines a number of other useful commands for aiding the documentation. See the description by processing ltxdoc.dtx. It also provides for local configuration: if ltxdoc.cfg exists, it is read in. This can pass paper size or other formatting options to article, issue \OnlyDescription by means of \AtBeginDocument, and so on.

### A sample .dtx file

To illustrate these features, we show part of the source file fullpage.dtx. The initial lines ensure that all the files that can be extracted from it (the package .sty and the documentation driver .drv) receive their proper identifying commands. The date and version information appears only once, but is transferred to both extracted files.

```
% \iffalse        (This is a meta-comment)
%% Copyright (C) 1994 Patrick W. Daly
\NeedsTeXFormat{LaTeX2e}
%<*dtx>
\ProvidesFile          {fullpage.dtx}
%</dtx>
```

```
%<package>\ProvidesPackage{fullpage}
%<driver>\ProvidesFile{fullpage.drv}
% \fi
%\ProvidesFile{fullpage}
                    [1994/02/15 1.0 (PWD)]
```

It is the last `\ProvidesFile{fullpage}` that enables the proper functioning of `\GetFileInfo`; the first one is only a dummy to absorb the
information line when the .dtx file is read directly.

Next, the driver part is given. This is what LATEX sees when it processes
the file directly.

```
%\iffalse
%<*driver>
\documentclass[a4paper,11pt]{article}
\usepackage{doc}
\EnableCrossrefs
\RecordChanges
\CodelineIndex
\begin{document}
   \DocInput{fullpage.dtx}
\end{document}
%</driver>
%\fi
```

Now the checksum and list of commands that are not to be indexed
are given, followed by the start of the article.

```
% \CheckSum{73}
% \DoNotIndex{\addtolength,\boolean,\ExecuteOptions,\ifthenelse}
% \DoNotIndex{\newboolean,\newlength,\ProcessOptions}
% \DoNotIndex{\RequirePackage,\setboolean,\setlength}
% \changes{1.0}{1994 Feb 15}{Initial version}
%
% \GetFileInfo{fullpage}
% \title{\bfseries A Package to Set Margins to Full Page}
% \author{Patrick W. Daly}
% \date{This paper describes package \texttt{\filename}\\
%       version \fileversion, from \filedate}
% \maketitle
% \MakeShortVerb{\|}
%
% \section{Purpose}
% To set a uniform margin of one inch or 1.5~cm on all four
% . . . . . .
```

We advance to the end of the description and start of the coding part.

```
% \StopEventually{\PrintIndex\PrintChanges}
%
% \section{The Coding}
```

```
% The first thing is to read in the \texttt{ifthen} package,
% if it is not already there.
%     \begin{macrocode}
%<*package>
\RequirePackage{ifthen}
%     \end{macrocode}
%
% \begin{macro}{\DeclareOption}
% \begin{macro}{\FP@margin}
% Define the options with help of the length |\FP@margin|. The
% options |in| and |cm| select the actual margin size.
%     \begin{macrocode}
\newlength{\FP@margin}
\DeclareOption{in}{\setlength{\FP@margin}{1in}}
\DeclareOption{cm}{\setlength{\FP@margin}{1.5cm}}
%     \end{macrocode}
% \end{macro}
```

The end of the file finishes the coding and calls `\Finale`.

. . . . . . . .

```
\setlength{\topmargin}{\FP@margin}
\addtolength{\topmargin}{-1in}
%</package>
%     \end{macrocode}
% \end{macro}\end{macro}
% \Finale
```

## 3.3 Graphics and color

As mentioned in Section D.2, the advent of PostScript drivers for TEX offers the opportunity to expand the capabilities of LATEX to include a number of very useful features, such as the importation, scaling, and rotation of external graphics files, and color. Since each of these drivers tends to have its own packages and user interface commands, the resulting LATEX document file becomes tied to one particular driver.

The `graphics` and `color` packages present a unified set of commands for all drivers, with the specialized coding located in certain `.def` files which are loaded by options to these packages. Thus one only needs to change the option to switch to another driver; the main text remains unchanged.

The commands that they define are the building blocks for other packages that provide a more comfortable (to some) syntax for these functions. As long as these other packages are based on `graphics` and `color`, they should be equally compatible with all the supported drivers.

These packages are to be found on the CTAN servers in the directory `graphics` (diagram on page 388). They are provided by Sebastian Rahtz and David Carlisle.

The drivers that are currently supported (end of 1994) are

```
dvi2ps          dvipsone        dviwindo        textures
dvialw          dvitops         emtex
dvilaser        dvitps          oztex
dvips           dviwin          pubps
```

but only `dvips` and `dvipsone` have full, tested functionality. Many of the others have importation possible, but may never have anything more than that. The situation is still under development, so that one should consult the current documentation for the latest status.

There are two packages available, the more fundamental `graphics`, and the extended `graphicx` one, which calls and makes use of the macros in the first. The separate `color` package provides the color macros. All three are loaded with one of the driver names as an option, as

> `\usepackage[dvips]{graphics,color}`

Local configurations may be added by means of the files `graphics.cfg` and `color.cfg` which are read in if present.

In addition to the driver names, there are some other options that may be invoked when the package `graphics` is loaded:

> `draft` (countered by `final`) leaves space but does not import;
> `hidescale` leaves blank space where scaling should be;
> `hiderotate` leaves blank space where rotation should be.

These might be used for a draft version, especially if the previewing driver does not support the graphics functions. Similarly, the `color` package also recognizes the option

> `monochrome`

to convert all color commands to black and white, again for proofing purposes.

### Importing external graphics

The problem is to have a graphics file produced by some other program included in the document, most likely as a figure. It may be necessary to scale it or to rotate it by 90°. One wants to do by computer what used to be done with scissors and glue.

The basic command is

> `\includegraphics[`*llx,lly*`][`*urx,ury*`]{`*file_name*`}`

where *llx, lly* are the coordinates of the lower left corner, and *urx, ury* those of the upper right corner of the *bounding box* containing the part of the picture that is to be included. In other words, they say where the scissors are to be applied. Units may be specified (like [3cm, 2in]) but if they are omitted, big points (bp, 72 per inch) are assumed. If only one optional argument is given, it is the upper right corner, and the lower left is assumed to be [0,0].

If no bounding box coordinates are given, the driver will obtain them some other way, depending on the type of graphics file. For example, for the very common *encapsulated PostScript* files with extension .eps, the bounding box information is extracted from the graphics file itself.

With \includegraphics*, the figure is clipped, so that only the contents of the specified frame are included.

### Scaling

The graphics file is transferred in its original size. In order to scale it, there are two commands available:

> \scalebox{*h_scale*}[*v_scale*]{*text*}

which applies horizontal and vertical scale factors to the contents *text*; if *v_scale* is omitted, it is the same as *h_scale*;

> \resizebox{*h_length*}{*v_length*}{*text*}

adjusts the figure to fit into the specified horizontal and vertical sizes; if either length is given as !, the one scale factor is used for both dimensions. A starred form allows *v_length* to refer to the height + depth of the box, rather than just to the height. In both cases, the contents *text* may be an \includegraphics command.

### Reflection

The contents of a box may be reflected horizontally with

> \reflectbox{*text*}

### Rotation

Rotation of a box about the left-hand end of its baseline is done with

> \rotatebox{*angle*}{*text*}

where *angle* is in degrees, and the rotation is counter-clockwise.

### The graphicx package

If one selects the graphicx rather than the graphics package, a different interface is available for both importing and rotation.

> \includegraphics[bb=*llx lly urx ury*,angle=*angle*,width=*h_length*,
>    height=*v_length*,scale=*factor*,clip=*true/false*,
>    draft=*true/false*]{*file_name*}

The order of the key values is unimportant, and not all need be present. Most of them should be self-explanatory, except that `clip=` is the same as ⟨*true*⟩, and `draft` means that the file is not really imported, but space is left for it. A starred version is available, which inserts a ⟨*true*⟩ value for `clip`.

The `\rotatebox` is similarly redefined with key values.

### The `rotating` package

The `rotating` package by Sebastian Rahtz and Leonor Barroca tries to make the interface for rotation somewhat simpler. It defines

> \begin{sideways} *text* \end{sideways}
> \begin{turn}{*angle*} *text* \end{turn}
> \begin{rotate}{*angle*} *text* \end{rotate}
> \turnbox{*angle*}{*text*}

where `sideways` rotates *text* by 90°, `turn` by an arbitrary angle. The environment `rotate` and command `turnbox` are equivalent: they rotate but in a box of zero size, so that the contents overlap the surroundings.

### The `epsfig` package

Sebastian Rahtz has provided a package `epsfig` that not only updates the earlier (2.09) version, but also re-implements Rokicki's `epsf` package by means of the `graphics` commands. This is helpful for users who are accustomed to those syntaxes. For `epsf`, this is

> \epsfysize=*y_size*   or   \epsfxsize=*x_size*
> \epsf[*llx lly urx ury*]{*file_name*}

If the bounding box coordinates are omitted, they are taken from the imported file itself.

The `epsfig` package also defines an importing command that makes use of keywords to enter its parameters:

\epsfig{file=*file_name*,height=*ht*,width=*wd*,clip=,silent=,
    rotate=*angle*,bbllx=*llx*,bblly=*lly*,bburx=*urx*,bbury=*ury*}

For compatibility with some older versions, there is a `\psfig` command which is synonymous with the above. The `epsfig` package automatically invokes the `dvips` driver as default.

The variety of rotation and importing commands only shows that a standard syntax has yet to crystallize; however, the basis of all these is still the `graphics` package, so that they should all work with other drivers. Or at least, they will not cause the drivers to crash.

## Colors

Colors are specified either by a defined name, or by the form

[*model*]{*specs*}

where *model* is one of rgb (red, green, blue), cmyk (cyan, magenta, yellow, black), gray, or named. The *specs* is a list of numbers from 0 to 1 giving the strengths of the components in the model. Thus [rgb]{1,0,0} defines red, [cmyk]{0,0,1,0} yellow. The gray model takes only one number. The named model is used for drivers that recognize colors by their internal names, such as dvips which knows 68 colors. Look into dvips.def to see what names are available.

A color can be defined with

\definecolor{*name*}{*model*}{*specs*}

and then the *name* may be used in all the following color commands. Certain colors are automatically predefined for all drivers: red, green, blue, yellow, cyan, magenta, black, white.

In the following color commands, *col_spec* is either the name of a defined color, like {blue}, or [*model*]{*spec*}, like [rgb]{0,1,0}.

\pagecolor *col_spec* sets the background color for the current and following pages;

\color *col_spec* is a declaration to switch to setting text in the given color;

\textcolor *col_spec*{*text*}  sets the text of its argument in the given color;

\colorbox *col_spec*{*text*}  sets its argument in a box with the given color as background;

\fcolorbox *col_spec1col_spec2*{*text*}  is like \colorbox, with a frame of *col_spec1* around a box of background color *col_spec2*; the two specifications must either both be names, or use the same model, which is given only once;

\normalcolor switches to the color that was active at the end of the preamble. Thus placing a \color command in the preamble can change the standard color for the whole document.  This is the equivalent to \normalfont for font selection.

## .4  Further useful packages

The members of the LATEX3 Team, as individuals, have written a number of packages that they collectively make available in a special directory called `tools` (see the diagram on page 388). Many of these originate from the days of LᴬTᴇX 2.09 and have now been updated for LᴬTᴇX 2$_\varepsilon$.

We describe here briefly what some of these packages do; a detailed explanation of each one can be obtained by processing the corresponding `.dtx` file with LᴬTᴇX.

`array` is a new implementation of the `tabular` and `array` environments (Section 4.8.1) of standard LᴬTᴇX, with additional features. In addition to the column definition p{*wth*}, which is equivalent to \parbox[t]{*wth*}, there are also m{*wth*} (like \parbox{*wth*}) and b{*wth*} (like \parbox[b]{*wth*}), all of which define the column width to be *wth* wide, but with the vertical alignment on the top, center, and bottom lines, respectively. It is also possible to insert declarations at the start and end of a column with >{*decl*} and <{*decl*}, which can be used to include a font declaration automatically in all rows of a column, or to switch into and out of math mode. It is also possible to define one's own column types.

`dcolumn` requires the `array` package, allows decimal point alignment in the `tabular` tables.

`delarray` requires the `array` package, permits large bracketing symbols to be put around `array` environments, for making matrices of various sorts.

`hhline` requires the `array` package, allows more flexibility in putting horizontal rules in tables.

`longtable` (does not require the `array` package but will recognize its features) enables one to make tables that extend over several pages, with breaks occurring automatically.

`tabularx` defines a `tabularx` environment which is like `tabular*`, a table of desired width, except that it is the column widths that expand and not the inter-column spacing.

`afterpage` permits coding to be saved and inserted at the end of the current page.

`enumerate` re-implements the `enumerate` environment so that an optional argument can determine the style of the numbers printed with each \item.

`fileerr.dtx`, when unpacked, produces a set of small files that may be used to reply to TᴇX when a file is not found; this makes the responses similar to those to error messages; the files are named h.tex, e.tex, s.tex, and x.tex; thus, replying x⟨*return*⟩ loads the last one, which terminates the input.

`fontsmpl` a package to print out a sample of a desired font.

`ftnright` puts footnotes in the right-hand column in two-column mode.

`indentfirst` indents the first paragraph of sections, which normally are not indented.

`layout` defines the command `\layout` which drawns a diagram of the current page format, with the values of the parameters printed.

`multicol` introduces the environment `multicols` which is an extension of the `\twocolumn` command, setting its text into the specified number of columns without starting a new page, either at the beginning or end, and balancing all the columns to the same height.

`showkeys` prints out all the cross-reference keys defined by `\label` and `\bibitem` and used by `\ref`, `\pageref`, and `\cite`; these are marginal and interlinear notes for a draft only, to check the cross-referencing.

`somedefs` allows only selected commands to be defined in a package, depending on options in `\usepackage`.

`theorem` extensions to the `\newtheorem` command for more flexible 'theorem-like' environments.

`varioref` defines `\vref` and `\vpageref` commands, analogous to `\ref` and `\pageref`, which check if the referenced object is only one page away, and if so, prints text like 'on the previous page'; the actual text printed can alternate between two variants.

`verbatim` a re-implementation of the `verbatim` environment that prevents memory overflow for long texts; also defines a command `\verbatiminput` to input a file and print its contents literally, as well as a `comment` environment for a block comment in the source text.

`xr` a package to allow `\ref` to cross-reference `\label` commands from other documents.

`xspace` a device to fix the problem of command names swallowing up the blank that follows them; thus the command `\PS` defined as

```
\newcommand{\PS}{\PostScript\xspace}
```

may be used as a `\PS file` without having to terminate the `\PS` command with `\␣` or `{}`.

## D.4     Installing LᴬTEX 2ε

The set of files delivered for installing LᴬTEX 2ε contain some instructions, both general and specific to certain operating systems. The latter bear the extension .txt and the name of the TEX supplier, such as emtex.txt or oztex.txt, while the general instructions are in a file install.txt. These instructions should be read carefully before proceeding.

The files needed come in either packed or unpacked form. The packed files consist of a large number of .dtx files, the integrated source and documentation files. These are unpacked by running initex on the batch job file unpack.ins. This generates the necessary .cls, .sty, .clo, and other files. It also constructs the fundamental file latex.ltx which is needed to produce the format file.

If your set of files contains latex.ltx then they are already unpacked. This is convenient because the unpacking can take from 5 minutes to 3 hours, depending on the computer. On the other hand, it takes much less time to transfer the packed files over networks.

The next step should be to run initex on the latex.ltx file to produce the LᴬTEX 2ε format latex. However, before doing that, there are a number of configuration aspects to be considered. At several points during the processing, certain files are read in, but if a file of the same name but extension .cfg exists, it is loaded instead. It is this device that permits one to configure the final format for local conditions or desires. The possible configuration files are:

texsys.cfg offers the possibility of adding some very machine-specific adjustments for older versions of TEX or for some peculiarities of the TEX installation; information is to be found in the specific .txt file, or in ltdirchk.dtx;

fonttext.cfg is loaded in place of fonttext.ltx if it is present; this defines the fonts that are to be available for processing text; details can be found in fontdef.dtx;

fontmath.cfg is loaded in place of fontmath.ltx if it is present; this is the equivalent of fonttext.cfg for math fonts;

preload.cfg is loaded in place of preload.ltx if it is present; this determines which fonts are preloaded into the format; a number of other preload files may be extracted from preload.dtx, any one of which may be renamed to .cfg to be implemented;

hyphen.cfg is loaded in place of hyphen.ltx if it is present; this specifies the hyphenation patterns and their assignments; by default, the patterns in hyphen.tex are loaded into language 0; the babel system provides such a configuration file (Section D.1.4).

Once any configuration files have been set up and located where TeX can read them, initex may be run on `latex.ltx` to generate the format file `latex.fmt`. This file must be placed where format files are read, the other class, option, and package files where TeX reads its files. Finally the LaTeX processing command must be defined to call TeX with the `latex` format, for example, as

```
tex &latex
```

**Note:** the LaTeX 2.09 format is called `lplain`; thus the name of the format itself reveals the version of LaTeX being activated.

## .1 Updating LaTeX

It is planned to update LaTeX twice a year, in June and December. At these times, a new `latex.ltx` must be obtained or generated from the new `.dtx` files. Any urgent changes that are to be made in between will take place by means of patches in an `ltpatch.ltx` file, which is read in by `latex.ltx`. In this way, one only needs to obtain the patch file and to regenerate the format file from the existing `latex.ltx`.

## 5 Sources for LaTeX files

The easiest way to obtain the extended LaTeX software is via one of the network servers supported by various educational institutions. They also provide the most up-to-date standard LaTeX installation, TeX extensions, programs for running TeX (and thus LaTeX) on various PCs, collections of drivers for different printers, hyphenation patterns for other languages, etc. Such a server is a treasure trove for the dedicated TeX and LaTeX user.

There are three main network servers for TeX and LaTeX located in the United States, Great Britain, and Germany, forming the Comprehensive TeX Archive Network, CTAN. They are not only kept up to date but also regularly exchange contributions among themselves. They are all Unix machines, reachable under the *File Transfer Protocol* (FTP).

| Country | IP address | IP number |
|---------|------------|-----------|
| USA | `pip.shsu.edu` | 192.92.115.10 |
| UK | `ftp.tex.ac.uk` | 134.151.79.32 |
| Germany | `ftp.dante.de` | 129.206.100.192 |

To make the connection, simply type `ftp` *address*; after a few seconds, you may log on with

```
user anonymous
```

giving as password your own FTP address, although any text at all will be accepted. The host computer now answers with the prompt

**Figure D.1**: Partial directory tree of CTAN servers

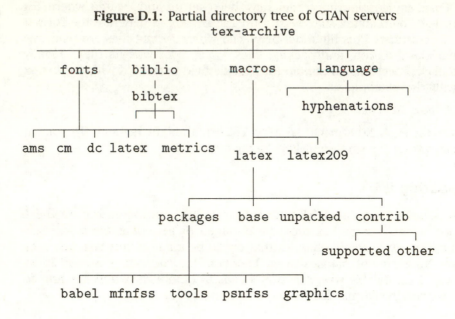

```
ftp>
```
to signal that it is ready to receive FTP commands. The session is terminated with the command `exit` or `quit`.

A listing of the directory is obtained with `dir`, although it mostly
contains more sub-directories, the names of which indicate what they
might hold. The file `INDEX` offers a brief description of the purpose of
each sub-direc-tory. Sub-directories specific to LᴬTₑX are to be found in
the sub-direc-tory `macros/latex`.

The directory structure is the same for all three servers. A sketch of
the main parts of the directory tree is presented in Figure D.1.

The latest version of the LᴬTₑX package may be found under the sub-
directories `base` or `unpacked`, where in the latter the files are already
unpacked and `latex.ltx` is ready. The LᴬTₑX extensions and general style
files that have been contributed by other users are located in the sub-
directory `contrib/supported`, with each contribution in a sub-direc-tory
of its own. Extensions offered by the LᴬTₑX3 Team are to be found in
`packages`, which include `babel`, `graphics`, `tools`, and so on.

To copy a file to the home computer, the FTP command

    get *filename.extension*

is given. To copy several files at once, the command `mget` is issued instead,
with * as a wildcard character in the file specification.

Many files have been compressed with special packing programs and
must therefore be transferred as binary rather than ASCII files. This is

done by typing the FTP command `binary` at some point before issuing the `get` or `mget` command. For text files, it is necessary to switch back to ASCII, since ASCII files will usually not be transferred correctly in binary mode.

In addition, the complete contents of any directory may be transferred in one of the archiving/compression systems, by moving to the directory just above it and giving

| | | |
|---|---|---|
| get | *directory_name*`.tar` | for Unix tape archive format |
| get | *directory_name*`.tar.Z` | for Unix `tar`, compressed |
| get | *directory_name*`.tar.gz` | for Unix `tar`, GNU zip |
| get | *directory_name*`.zip` | for zip compression |
| get | *directory_name*`.zoo` | for zoo archiving |

For example, `get tools.zip` will transfer the entire `tools` directory as a zip file. Naturally, the recipient must have the appropriate programs to unpack the file on his or her own machine.

## 5.1   TeX organizations

There are a number of organizations dedicated to disseminating the TeX and LATEX ideas and programs. These user groups will also provide the necessary files for those who are not on a network.

We have obtained these addresses from a listing on the CTAN file servers and have checked a number of them. But of course, they are all subject to change without notice.

**TUG** (International Users Group)

Christina Thiele, President
Patricia Monohon, Executive Director
TeX Users Group
P.O. Box 869
Santa Barbara, CA 93102-0869 USA

Tel:  [+1] 805-963-1338
FAX: [+1] 805-963-8358
Email: `tug@tug.org`

**CsTUG** (Czech and Slovak Republics)
   Dr. Karel Horák, President
   Československé sdružení uživatelů
   TeXu
   CsTUG, c/o MÚK UK
   Sokolovská 83
   CS-186 00 Praha 8, Czechoslovakia
   Email: `horakk@earn.cvut.cz`

**CyrTUG** (Russia)
   Irina Makhovaya, Executive Director
   Associaciia Pol'zovateleĭ
   Kirillicheskogo TeX'a

Mir Publishers
2, Pervyĭ Rizhskiĭ Pereulok
Moscow 129820, Russia
Tel:  [+95] 286-0622, 286-1777
FAX: [+95] 288-9522
Email: `cyrtug@mir.msk.su`

**DANTE** (German-speaking)
   Joachim Lammarsch, President
   Deutschsprachige
   Anwendervereinigung TeX e.V.
   Postfach 101840
   D-69008 Heidelberg, Germany

Tel:  [+49] 6221 29766
FAX: [+49] 6221 167906
Email: dante@vm.urz.
        uni-heidelberg.de

**Estonian User Group**
Enn Saar, Tartu
Astrophysical Observatory, Toravere
EE 2444 Estonia
Email: saar@aai.ee

**GUST**  (Poland)
Hanna Kołodziejska, President
Polska Grupa Użytkowników
Systemu TeX
Instytut Badań Systemowych PAN
ul. Newelska 6
PL-01-447 Warszawa, Poland
Email: gust@camk.edu.pl

**GUTenberg**  (French-speaking)
Michel Goossens, President
Groupe francophone des Utilisateurs
de TeX
Association GUTenberg
BP 10
F-93220 Gagny principal
Tel:  [+33] 1 44 32 37 96
FAX: [+33] 1 44 32 20 80
Email: gut@irisa.fr

**ITALIC**  (Irish)
Not a user group yet. Public
discussion list: ITALIC-L on
listserver
listserv@irlearn.ucd.ie.

**Nordic TeX Users Group**
(Scandinavian countries)
Dag Langmyhr
Chair, Nordic TeX Users Group
Department of Informatics
P.O. Box 1080 Blindern

University of Oslo
N-0316 Oslo, Norway
Tel:  [+47] 22 85 24 50
FAX: [+47] 22 85 24 01
Email: dag@ifi.uio.no

**NTG**  (Dutch-speaking)
Johannes Braams, Chair
Nederlandstalige TeX
Gebruikersgroep
Postbus 394
NL-1740 AJ Schagen
The Netherlands,
Email: ntg@nic.surfnet.nl

**Spanish TUG**  (no formal group)
Electronic mail discussion list:
spanish-tex@eunet.es. Send
subscription requests to
listserv@eunet.es.
Julio Sanchez
GMV SA
Isaac Newton 11  PTM Tres Cantos
E-28760 Madrid, Spain
Email: jsanchez@gmv.es

**TeXCeH**  (Slovenian User Group)
(part of larger group, Informatica)
Vladimir Batagelj
Jadranska 19
61111 Ljubljana
Slovenia
Email: texceh@uni-lj.si

**UK TUG**  (United Kingdom)
C. A. Rowley, Chairman
UK TeX Users' Group
For information:
J. Fine
203 Coldhams Lane
Cambridge CB1 3HY, England
Email:
uktug-enquiries@tex.ac.uk

# E Computer Modern Fonts

When Donald E. Knuth invented the TEX program, he also provided it with an extensive set of character sets, or fonts, which he named *Computer Modern*, rather than relying on the fonts available on any given printer. At that time, the printer fonts were not so good, and certainly were not uniform. With the supplied fonts, TEX could produce identical, high-quality results on all printers.

LATEX, of course, has inherited these fonts, so that they have almost become a trademark for documents produced by TEX or LATEX. This is not really necessary, for LATEX need not be married to any particular set of fonts, especially now with the New Font Selection Scheme (Section 8.5) which simplifies font installation enormously. The main fonts used in this book, for example, are Lucida Bright and Lucida Sans, designed by Bigelow & Holmes, whereas the typewriter font used is Knuth's Computer Modern Typewriter.

Nevertheless, the Computer Modern fonts still play a major role for most TEX/LATEX users, and deserve a detailed description. Even though one only specifies font attributes under NFSS, ultimately those attribute combinations are linked to a particular existing font name, as shown in Section 8.5.8. For the standard installation, those names come from the collection described in the rest of this appendix.

## 1 Introduction

Typography is the study and classification of typefaces, something that goes back to Gutenberg's invention of *movable type* (not of the printing press, which was invented by the Chinese) five and a half centuries ago. Since that time, many families of fonts have been created, bearing classical names like Baskerville, Garamond, Univers, and so on. Each member of such a family has the same overall design, or basic look, but vary by being slanted, italic, bold, or thin; and of course, they come in different sizes.

Font families are classified according to certain criteria that often determine to what use they will be put.

**Serif fonts:** are those that have little horizontal lines, or *serifs*, at their edges, to guide the eye better. Experience has shown these to be best for general reading, and so they are regularly used for the main body of text. The NFSS terminology refers to these as *Roman* fonts.

**Sans serif fonts:** are those that are lacking any serifs. Such fonts with their starker appearance are often employed for titling or headlining. Compare sans serif with regular text.

**Fixed fonts:** are those with a uniform letter width, something that has evolved from the typewriter and has been carried over to computer listings. Classically, such fonts have no business in book printing, where *proportional* fonts (the letter *i* is narrower than *m*) have always dominated.

**Decorative fonts:** are ones that stand out because of some unusual characteristic. They are intended to catch attention and to attract the eye. Such families are not complete, with a full range of shapes and widths, and are employed mostly by advertising.

**Mathematical fonts:** are collections of special symbols needed for mathematical works. Their further classification cannot be compared to that of text fonts at all.

A book designer must decide what kinds of typeface families are needed. He or she might decide on a Roman (serifed) font for the main body, a sans serif one for headlines, and then, if it is a book containing computer code, select a fixed font for setting those parts. Finally, symbol fonts will be needed if the work contains mathematical sections.

The Computer Modern set of fonts provides all these classes of families. However, since they were produced before the NFSS attribute system of classification was established, the CM font nomenclature does not conform perfectly with this scheme. The NFSS system frees the user from having to think about the CM font names, for specifying the attributes is sufficient. Of course, the NFSS installation must provide the font description .fd files which translate any set of attributes into a real font name, or into some acceptable substitute.

## E.2 · Classification of the basic TeX fonts

Any particular font can be used in LaTeX either by addressing it directly by name with the \newfont command (Section 4.1.6) or by its attributes with \usefont (Section 8.5.1) or \DeclareFixedFont (Section 8.5.4).

All the TEX font file names begin with the letters cm, which stands for 'Computer Modern', followed by one to four letters describing the style of font, and finally one or two digits specifying the design size in points. This is the root name of the font which must be given in the \newfont command. The full syntax of this root name is thus:

cmxxnn   xx = style, nn = design size

The extension for the basic font file is .tfm, which stands for 'TEX font metric'.

The .tfm files do not contain the information for producing the symbols, but rather only the sizes of the characters, such as width, height, and depth. For slanted fonts, they also possess the 'italic correction' (Section 3.5.1) for each letter. Furthermore, they specify for which letter combinations a different spacing is required, such as AV instead of AV, or for which a ligature is available. Finally, the .tfm contains information about the slope of the characters (zero for an unslanted font), the standard word spacing and its stretch and shrinkage (Section 9.5.4), the width of the em and quad spacings, and the spacings at the end of a sentence. Mathematical and symbol fonts require even more information which is also included in their .tfm files.

The general syntax for the \newfont command is

\newfont{\fnt}{root_name scaled factor}

where root_name is the external root name of the font file, and factor is the scaling factor times 1000 by which the font should be magnified. The new command \fnt is a declaration that activates the specified font until the end of the current environment, or until a new font command is issued. As far as LATEX is concerned, factor may take on any value, since the numbers in the .tfm file are simply multiplied by this factor during the processing.

The same effect may be achieved with

\DeclareFixedFont{\fnt}{code}{fam}{ser}{size}

which defines \fnt automatically to be the appropriate font, with necessary scaling if needed.

Here we will present the CM fonts by name, indicating how they fit into the NFSS attribute pattern. They are organized as follows:

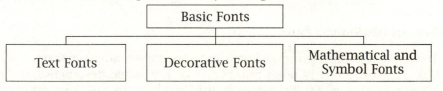

## 3   Text fonts

The fonts that are used for setting straightforward text are divided into three families, all of which possess the encoding OT1.

## E.3.1    Roman family

The Roman family of fonts are those with serifs and proportional spacing. These are the fonts used for setting the main bulk of any text.

The cmr family, encoding OT1

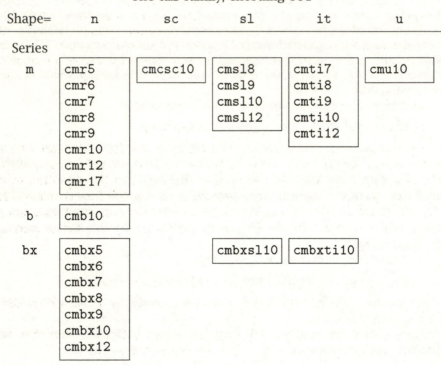

| Shape= | n | sc | sl | it | u |
|--------|---|-----|-----|-----|---|
| Series | | | | | |
| m | cmr5<br>cmr6<br>cmr7<br>cmr8<br>cmr9<br>cmr10<br>cmr12<br>cmr17 | cmcsc10 | cms18<br>cms19<br>cms110<br>cms112 | cmti7<br>cmti8<br>cmti9<br>cmti10<br>cmti12 | cmu10 |
| b | cmb10 | | | | |
| bx | cmbx5<br>cmbx6<br>cmbx7<br>cmbx8<br>cmbx9<br>cmbx10<br>cmbx12 | | cmbxsl10 | cmbxti10 | |

### The upright Roman fonts

The upright Roman group of fonts includes the standard character sets that are most used in book printing.  The font style designation is the letter r, so that all the file names in this family begin with cmr, followed by the design size in points. The design sizes range from 8 to 17 pt. The font cmscs10 is also assigned to this family with the shape sc. Here csc stands for *capital and small caps*, since the upper case letters in this font are the same as those in cmr10 while the lower case letters are smaller capitals of a size between those in cmr7 and cmr8.

cmr10

ABCDEFGHIJKLMNOPQRSTUVWXYZ ÆŒØ @#$%&
abcedfghijklmnopqrstuvwxyz ﬀﬁﬂﬃﬄ æœøßɪȷ 0123456789
ΓΔΘΛΞΠΣΥΦΨΩ ˋˊˇ˘ˉ ˚ ˆ˙¨˝˜ ̧ ̦,;:?¡!'''""----*+/=()[]

cmcsc10

ABCDEFGHIJKLMNOPQRSTUVWXYZ ÆŒØ @#$%&
ABCEDFGHIJKLMNOPQRSTUVWXYZ ↑↓'¡¿ÆŒØSSIJ 0123456789
ΓΔΘΛΞΠΣΥΦΨΩ ˋˊˇ˘ˉ ˚ ˆ˙¨˝˜ ̧ ̦,;:>?<!'''""----*+/=()[]

By examining the cmcsc10 font carefully and comparing it with cmr10, one notices that the lower case letters are all the same height (between that of cmr7 and cmr8) but are somewhat wider with greater spacing between the letters. Also, the ligatures have been replaced by other symbols.

cmu10

ABCDEFGHIJKLMNOPQRSTUVWXYZ ÆŒØ @#£%&
abcedfghijklmnopqrstuvwxyz ﬀﬁﬂﬃﬄ æœøßɪȷ 0123456789
ΓΔΘΛΞΠΣΥΦΨΩ ˋˊˇ˘ˉ ˚ ˆ˙¨˝˜ ̧ ̦,;:?¡!'''""----*+/=()[]

The font cmu10 is actually an italic font with zero inclination. This makes it an upright font with italic shape. It occupies a special shape attribute u in the NFSS scheme.

## The slanted fonts

The characters in this group are derived from those in the upright Roman ones by giving them a slope equal to 1/6; that is, they are inclined to the right by a sixth of their height. The *slanted* fonts are provided in 4 design sizes between 8 and 12 pt. The font style designation is sl, so that all members have names beginning with cmsl, followed by the design size specification 8, 9, 10, or 12. These fonts are assigned the shape specification sl.

cmsl10

*ABCDEFGHIJKLMNOPQRSTUVWXYZ ÆŒØ @#$%&*
*abcedfghijklmnopqrstuvwxyz ﬀﬁﬂﬃﬄ æœøßɪȷ 0123456789*
*ΓΔΘΛΞΠΣΥΦΨΩ* ˋˊˇ˘ˉ ˚ ˆ˙¨˝˜ ̧ ̦,;:?¡!'''""----*+/=()[]

## The italic fonts

The italic group of fonts contain characters that differ in their basic form from those of the upright and slanted Roman fonts. The inclination has a value of 1/4, even stronger than that for the slanted ones. The shape attribute is designated it, while the font style indication is ti for *text italic*. Thus the font names begin with cmti, followed by the design size specification. Five sizes are available from 7 to 12 pt. (The mathematical character fonts belong to a separate italic family with the style designation mi for *math italic*.)

cmti10

---

*ABCDEFGHIJKLMNOPQRSTUVWXYZ ÆŒØ @#£%&*
*abcedfghijklmnopqrstuvwxyz ff fi fl ffi ffl  æœøßıȷ 0123456789*
*ΓΔΘΛΞΠΣΥΦΨΩ* `´˘¯˚ ^'"˝˜ ¸.,;:¿?¡!'°'""- – —*+/=( )[ ]

---

## The bold font series

This set of fonts contains the Roman characters once more but in a bold face form, with thicker lines.  The font style designation is bx for *bold extended*, since these letters are somewhat wider than the corresponding Roman ones of the same height. This is also the NFSS series specification for them. Seven design sizes are offered between 5 and 12 pt, with names cmbx5 ... cmbx12. A slanted and an italic bold font are also available in the design size 10 pt, with names cmbxsl10 and cmbxti10.

The design size 10pt contains in addition a font cmb10, which is a bold face with the same widths as the normal Roman characters. The series designation of this font is b, normal bold.

cmbx10

---

**ABCDEFGHIJKLMNOPQRSTUVWXYZ ÆŒØ @#$%&**
**abcedfghijklmnopqrstuvwxyz ff fi fl ffi ffl æœøßıȷ 0123456789**
**ΓΔΘΛΞΠΣΥΦΨΩ** `´˘¯˚ ^'"˝˜ ¸.,;:¿?¡!'°'""- – —*+/=( )[ ]

---

cmbxsl10

---

*ABCDEFGHIJKLMNOPQRSTUVWXYZ ÆŒØ @#$%&*
*abcedfghijklmnopqrstuvwxyz ff fi fl ffi ffl æœøßıȷ 0123456789*
*ΓΔΘΛΞΠΣΥΦΨΩ* `´˘¯˚ ^'"˝˜ ¸.,;:¿?¡!'°'""- – —*+/=( )[ ]

---

cmbxti10

---

*ABCDEFGHIJKLMNOPQRSTUVWXYZ ÆŒØ @#£%&*
*abcedfghijklmnopqrstuvwxyz ff fi fl ffi ffl æœøßıȷ 0123456789*
*ΓΔΘΛΞΠΣΥΦΨΩ* `´˘¯˚ ^'"˝˜ ¸.,;:¿?¡!'°'""- – —*+/=( )[ ]

---

cmb10

---

**ABCDEFGHIJKLMNOPQRSTUVWXYZ ÆŒØ @#$%&**
**abcedfghijklmnopqrstuvwxyz ff fi fl ffi ffl æœøßıȷ 0123456789**
**ΓΔΘΛΞΠΣΥΦΨΩ** `´˘¯˚ ^'"˝˜ ¸.,;:¿?¡!'°'""- – —*+/=( )[ ]

## 3.2 Sans serif family

All the sans serif fonts have the style designation ss in their names, so they begin with cmss. This is also the name of the NFSS family.

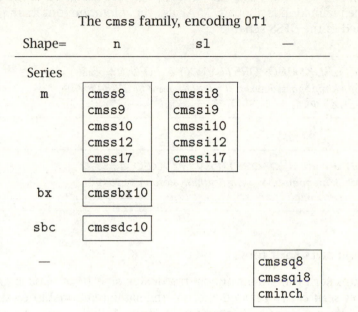

The cmss family, encoding OT1

| Shape= | n | sl | — |
|--------|---|-----|---|
| **Series** | | | |
| m | cmss8 cmss9 cmss10 cmss12 cmss17 | cmssi8 cmssi9 cmssi10 cmssi12 cmssi17 | |
| bx | cmssbx10 | | |
| sbc | cmssdc10 | | |
| — | | | cmssq8 cmssqi8 cminch |

**The upright sans serif fonts**

Five upright sans serif fonts are available in design sizes from 8 to 17 pt, with names cmss5 ... cmss17. An additional font cmssq8 is called *sans serif quotation*, in which the lower case letters are proportionally larger than usual. This font is not classified within the standard NFSS attribute scheme.

cmss10

ABCDEFGHIJKLMNOPQRSTUVWXYZ ÆŒØ @#$%&
abcedfghijklmnopqrstuvwxyz ff fi fl ffi ffl æœøßıȷ 0123456789
ΓΔΘΛΞΠΣΥΦΨΩ ˋ´ˇ˘¯˚˙^¨""„ ‚.,:;¿?¡!'' ""-‐—*+/=()[]

cmssq8

ABCDEFGHIJKLMNOPQRSTUVWXYZ ÆŒØ @#$%&
abcdefghijklmnopqrstuvwxyz ff fi fl ffi ffl æœøßıȷ 0123456789
ΓΔΘΛΞΠΣΥΦΨΩ ˋ´ˇ˘¯˚˙^¨""„ ‚.,:;¿?¡!'' ""-‐—*+/=()[]

## The slanted sans serif fonts

The slanted sans serifs fonts correspond exactly in size and number to the upright ones. The style designation is `ssi` and `ssqi`, where the i stands for *inclined*, not *italic*. For this reason, they are assigned to the attribute `sl`. The inclination is about 1/5. Again, the *quotation* font `cmssqi8` is not included in the NFSS scheme.

cmssi10

*ABCDEFGHIJKLMNOPQRSTUVWXYZ ÆŒØ @#$%&*
*abcedfghijklmnopqrstuvwxyz ff fi fl ffi ffl æœøßıj 0123456789*
*ΓΔΘΛΞΠΣΥΦΨΩ ` ´ ˇ ˘ ¯ ˚ ˆ ˙ ¨ ˝ ˜ ‚ -.,;:¿?¡!'"""---—*+/=( )[]*

cmssqi8

*ABCDEFGHIJKLMNOPQRSTUVWXYZ ÆŒØ @#$%&*
*abcedfghijklmnopqrstuvwxyz ff fi fl ffi ffl æœøßıj 0123456789*
*ΓΔΘΛΞΠΣΥΦΨΩ ` ´ ˇ ˘ ¯ ˚ ˆ ˙ ¨ ˝ ˜ ‚ -.,;:¿?¡!'"""---—*+/=( )[]*

## The bold sans serif fonts

Bold sans serif fonts exist only in the design size 10 pt. One is `cmssbx10` for *sans serif bold extended* and has the same relationship to `cmss10` as `cmbx10` does to `cmr10`. A second bold font is called `cmssdc` for *sans serif demibold condensed*.

cmssbx10

**ABCDEFGHIJKLMNOPQRSTUVWXYZ ÆŒØ @#$%&**
**abcedfghijklmnopqrstuvwxyz ff fi fl ffi ffl æœøßıj 0123456789**
**ΓΔΘΛΞΠΣΥΦΨΩ ` ´ ˇ ˘ ¯ ˚ ˆ ˙ ¨ ˝ ˜ ‚ -.,;:¿?¡!'"""---—*+/=( )[]**

cmssdc10

**ABCDEFGHIJKLMNOPQRSTUVWXYZ ÆŒØ @#$%&**
**abcedfghijklmnopqrstuvwxyz ff fi fl ffi ffl æœøßıj 0123456789**
**ΓΔΘΛΞΠΣΥΦΨΩ ` ´ ˇ ˘ ¯ ˚ ˆ ˙ ¨ ˝ ˜ ‚ -.,;:¿?¡!'"""---—*+/=( )[]**

## The font `cminch`

The font `cminch` contains only the upper case letters and the numerals 0, 1, ..., 9, and no other symbols. The characters are all 1 inch high. The font name is an exception since it does not contain the numbers specifying its design size. In this case, `inch` stands for both the font style and size. This font too has no classification within NFSS.

cminch

## 3.3 Typewriter family

For fixed fonts, every character has the same width. Even the spacing between words is the same as a character width, with no stretch or shrinkage. However, just as for all TeX fonts, the amount of spacing between words does *not* depend on the number of blanks typed in. The standard fixed fonts, which have a typewriter style of character, are:

The cmtt family, encoding OT1

| Shape= | n | sc | sl | it | — |
|--------|---|-----|-----|-----|---|
| **Series** | | | | | |
| m | cmtt8<br>cmtt9<br>cmtt10<br>cmtt12 | cmtcsc10 | cmsltt10 | cmitt10 | |
| — | | | | cmtex8<br>cmtex9<br>cmtex10<br>cmvtt10 | |

### Upright typewriter fonts

The upright typewriter fonts are available in four design sizes from 8 to 12 pt. The style designation code is tt for *typewriter type*. The root file names are thus cmtt8 ... cmtt12.

```
ABCDEFGHIJKLMNOPQRSTUVWXYZ ÆŒØ @#$%& ΓΔΘΛΞΠΣΤΦΨΩ
abcedfghijklmnopqrstuvwxyz æœø ßıɉ¡¿ ()[]{}\|/↑↓
0123456789 -+*<=> ˌ-⊔.,:;!?'ʹˆˇ˜ˊˋ˗˗˗˗ˉˉ˙ˈ˝˝
```

## Caps and small caps

The font cmtcsc10, *typewriter capitals and small caps*, produces upper case letters in 10 pt typewriter font, while the lower case letters are printed as 8 pt typewriter capitals.

```
ABCDEFGHIJKLMNOPQRSTUVWXYZ ÆŒØ @#$%& ΓΔΘΛΞΠΣΤΦΨΩ
ABCEDFGHIJKLMNOPQRSTUVWXYZ ÆŒØ SSIɈ¡¿()[]{}\|/↑↓
0123456789 -+*<=> ˌ-⊔.,:;!?'ʹˆˇ˜ˊˋ˗˗˗˗ˉˉ˙ˈ˝˝
```

## Sloping typewriter fonts

There are two sloping typewriter fonts in the design size 10 pt only. The font cmsltt10, *slanted typewriter type*, is the same as the upright tt font with a slope of 1/6. On the other hand, the cmitt10 font, *italic typewriter type*, makes use of characters with an italic design and a slope of 1/4.

```
ABCDEFGHIJKLMNOPQRSTUVWXYZ ÆŒØ @#$%& ΓΔΘΛΞΠΣΤΦΨΩ
abcedfghijklmnopqrstuvwxyz æœø ßıɉ¡¿ ()[]{}\|/↑↓
0123456789 -+*<=> ˌ-⊔.,:;!?'ʹˆˇ˜ˊˋ˗˗˗˗ˉˉ˙ˈ˝˝
```

```
ABCDEFGHIJKLMNOPQRSTUVWXYZ ÆŒØ @#£%& ΓΔΘΛΞΠΣΤΦΨΩ
abcedfghijklmnopqrstuvwxyz æœø ßıɉ¡¿ ()[]{}\|/↑↓
0123456789 -+*<=> ˌ-⊔.,:;!?'ʹˆˇ˜ˊˋ˗˗˗˗ˉˉ˙ˈ˝˝
```

## Mathematical typewriter fonts

The letters and numerals in the math typewriter fonts are the same as in the corresponding upright tt fonts. All the other characters are replaced by special mathematical symbols.

These character sets are available in design sizes 8, 9, and 10 pt, with root names cmtex8, cmtex9, and cmtex10 for *typewriter extension*.

These fonts do not fit into the NFSS scheme. In fact, they are rather peculiar entities, being a typewriter version of the math fonts cmex. They have never had any function in any version of LaTeX.

cmtex10

---

·↓αβ∧¬∈πλγδ↑±⊕ω∂⊂⊃∩∪∀∃⊗π←→≠◇≤≥≡∨ !"#$%&'()*+,-./0123456789:;<=>?
@ABCDEFGHIJKLMNOPQRSTUVWXYZ[\]^_'abcefghijklmnopqrstuvwxyz{|}~ʃ

---

### Variable typewriter

Another peculiar font that has no position within the NFSS attribute system is cmvtt10, which is a font with typewriter shaped characters, but with variable spacing.

cmvtt10

---

ABCDEFGHIJKLMNOPQRSTUVWXYZ ÆŒØ @#$%&
abcedfghijklmnopqrstuvwxyz ff fi fl ffi ffl æœøßıȷ 0123456789
ΓΔΘΛΞΠΣΥΦΨΩ `´˜¯˘˙ˆ¨˝ˇ¸˛,-.,;:¿?¡!''""--—*+/=()[]

---

# Decorative families

Three families of decorative or special fonts are available in a single design size and limited attributes.

Miscellaneous families, encoding OT1, series m

| | Shape= | n | it |
|---|---|---|---|
| Family | Name | | |
| cmfr | Funny | cmff10 | cmfi10 |
| cmfib | Fibonacci | cmfib8 | |
| cmdh | Dunhill | cmdunh10 | |

cmfr *Funny Roman*, consists of two fonts, cmff10 with negative inclination −0.1, that is, it leans to the left rather than to the right, and cmfi10 with a positive inclination 0.1. The lower case letters are also higher than normal.

cmfib *Fibonacci*, has been derived from the Fibonacci series of numbers. It is strictly speaking a non-extended bold font, but has been classified with the medium series attribute anyway.

cmdunh *Dunhill*, in which the lower case letters have the same height as for 10 pt, but the capitals, the numerals, and the ascenders for b, d, f, h, k, and l are all exaggerated in height.

# E.5 Mathematical and symbol fonts

Mathematical and symbol fonts contain special characters that are needed in math formulas. In addition, the special symbols that are employed in the LATEX picture environment, such as sloping lines and arrow heads, are also to be found in LATEX symbol fonts. Finally, some special logo fonts are also included here.

## E.5.1 Mathematical families

The mathematical fonts possess encoding schemes that bear no relationship to those of normal text fonts. For this reason, each one has its own encoding and family specification.

Mathematical families

| Encoding= | OML | OMS | OMX |
|---|---|---|---|
| Family= | cmm | cmsy | cmex |
| Shape= | it | n | n |

| Series | | | |
|---|---|---|---|
| m | cmmi5 | cmsy5 | cmex10 |
| | cmmi6 | cmsy6 | |
| | cmmi7 | cmsy7 | |
| | cmmi8 | cmsy8 | |
| | cmmi9 | cmsy9 | |
| | cmmi10 | cmsy10 | |
| | cmmi12 | | |
| b | cmmib10 | cmsyb10 | |

## Mathematical text fonts

These fonts contain the Latin and Greek letters, in upper and lower case, plus a number of extra symbols. Since variable names are set in *italics* within formulas, these are basically italic fonts, with the font style designation mi for *mathematical italic* to distinguish them from normal italic. The fonts come in seven design sizes from 5 to 12 pt. In design size 10 pt, there is also a *mathematical italic bold* mib font.

cmmi10

$\Gamma\Delta\Theta\Lambda\Xi\Pi\Sigma\Upsilon\Phi\Psi\Omega\alpha\beta\gamma\delta\epsilon\zeta\eta\theta\iota\kappa\lambda\mu\nu\xi\pi\rho\sigma\tau\upsilon\phi\chi\psi\omega\varepsilon\vartheta\varpi\varrho\varsigma\varphi\leftharpoonup\leftharpoondown\rightharpoonup\rightharpoondown\lhd\rhd\lhd$
$0123456789.,</>\star\partial ABCDEFGHIJKLMNOPQRSTUVWXYZ$
$\flat\natural\sharp\smile\frown\ell abcdefghijklmnopqrstuvwxyz\imath\jmath\wp\vec{}\frown$

cmmib10

$\Gamma\Delta\Theta\Lambda\Xi\Pi\Sigma\Upsilon\Phi\Psi\Omega\alpha\beta\gamma\delta\epsilon\zeta\eta\theta\iota\kappa\lambda\mu\nu\xi\pi\rho\sigma\tau\upsilon\phi\chi\psi\omega\varepsilon\vartheta\varpi\varrho\varsigma\varphi\leftharpoonup\leftharpoondown\rightharpoonup\rightharpoondown$
$\rhd\lhd 0123456789.,</>\star\partial ABCDEFGHIJKLMNOPQRSTUVWXYZ$
$\flat\natural\sharp\smile\frown\ell abcdefghijklmnopqrstuvwxyz\imath\jmath\wp\vec{}\frown$

## Mathematical symbols

These symbol fonts provide the rest of the math symbols for formulas, except for those that appear in variable sizes. The font style code is sy for *symbol*. Six design sizes are available from 5 to 10 pt. An additional *bold symbol* cmbsy10 font exists in design size 10 pt. The root names of these symbol fonts read cmsy5 ... cmsy10.

cmsy10

─·×∗÷◇±∓⊕⊖⊗⊘⊙○∘•≍≡⊆⊇≤≥≼≽∼≈⊂⊃≪≫≺≻
←→↑↓↔↗↘≃⇐⇒⇑⇕⇔↖↙∝∞∈∋△▽/∣∀∃¬∅ℜℑ⊤⊥
ℵ𝒜𝐵𝒞𝒟𝐸𝐹𝒢𝐻𝐼𝒥𝒦𝐿𝑀𝒩𝒪𝒫𝒬𝑅𝒮𝒯𝒰𝒱𝒲𝒳𝒴𝒵∪∩⊎∧∨
⊢⊣⊔⊓{}⟨⟩‖∥↕↨\≀√∐∇∫∮∪∩⊏⊐⊒§†‡¶♣◇♡♠

cmbsy10

─·×∗÷◇±∓⊕⊖⊗⊘⊙○∘•≍≡⊆⊇≤≥≼≽∼≈⊂⊃≪≫≺≻
←→↑↓↔↗↘≃⇐⇒⇑⇕⇔↖↙∝∞∈∋△▽/∣∀∃¬∅ℜℑ⊤⊥
ℵ𝒜𝐵𝒞𝒟𝐸𝐹𝒢𝐻𝐼𝒥𝒦𝐿𝑀𝒩𝒪𝒫𝒬𝑅𝒮𝒯𝒰𝒱𝒲𝒳𝒴𝒵∪∩⊎∧∨
⊢⊣⊔⊓{}⟨⟩‖∥↕↨\≀√∐∇∫∮∪∩⊏⊐⊒§†‡¶♣◇♡♠

## Variable sized symbols

Those symbols that come in various sizes for automatic scaling to the rest of the formula are contained in the font `cmex10`, *extension*, which is provided only in the design size 10 pt.

cmex10

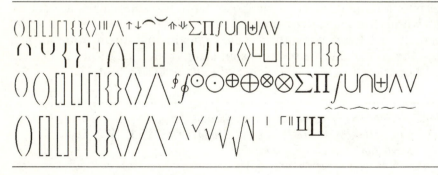

## E.5.2   Additional character fonts

The 75 character fonts presented in the previous sections are the standard ones provided by the TEX implementation. Additional fonts may be obtained from commercial or from public domain sources. You should ask your computing center what other fonts are available on your machine or consult the *Local Guide*.

The LATEX package contains some additional fonts with a few very special symbols and the construction elements for the `picture` environment, such as sloping lines and arrow heads.

Finally, some logo character fonts are often included in the TEX implementation that Donald E. Knuth employs in his *The TEXbook* (Knuth, 1984) and *The METAFONTbook* (Knuth, 1986b).

### The LᴬTEX lasy fonts

As an extension of the cmsy fonts for mathematical symbols, LᴬTEX provides some additional symbols in six design sizes from 5 to 10 pt. The root names of these font files are lasy5 ... lasy10. They each contain the 15 symbols: ⟨⟩ ˌ ˅ ◁ ⊴ ▷ ⊵ ℧ ⋈ □ ◇ ⇝ ⊏ ⊐.

In LᴬTEX 2ε, these fonts are not defined unless the package latexsym is used.

### Fonts for making pictures

The special picture elements for use in the LᴬTEX picture environment are stored in fonts named line10, lcircle10, linew10, and lcirclew10. The first two are used for lines, ovals, and circles when \thinlines (Section 6.5.1) is in effect. The sloping lines and arrow heads (Sections 6.4.3 and 6.4.4) are to be found in line10 while the circles and oval segments (Sections 6.4.5 and 6.4.6) are in lcircle10. The second pair of fonts with the added w contain thicker lines, for use when \thicklines has been issued.

### Logo fonts

The fonts logo8, logo9, logo10, logosl10, and logobf10 contain only the 7 letters A, E, F, M, N, O, and T, for generating the logos

METAFONT    *METAFONT*    **METAFONT**

# Character assignments within a font

With the exception of cminch, all standard TEX fonts consist of 128 characters, assigned internally to the numbers 0 through 127. The layout of the characters within the fonts is illustrated in the following tables. These are based on the octal system, with the corresponding decimal number written beside each symbol.

Font Layout 1 presents the character assignments for the Roman font cmr10, which is the true OT1 encoding scheme representative of the majority of the fonts in that the same symbols, in different styles perhaps, occupy the same locations. The *text italic* fonts differ only slightly. The *caps–small caps* font cmcsc10 deviates much more since the ligatures are missing. The typewriter fonts exhibit extreme discrepancies from the OT1 standard ordering of Layout 1. Finally, the mathematical and symbol fonts have completely different assignments since their contents do not correspond with those of text fonts. All these deviant font patterns are illustrated in Layouts 2 to 8.

**Note:** Future fonts for TeX 3.0 will contain 256 characters. They conform to the T1 assignments presented in Section E.10.3.

|      | 0 | 1 | 2 | 3 | 4 | 5 | 6 | 7 |
|------|---|---|---|---|---|---|---|---|
| '00x | Γ 0 | Δ 1 | Θ 2 | Λ 3 | Ξ 4 | Π 5 | Σ 6 | Υ 7 |
| '01x | Φ 8 | Ψ 9 | Ω 10 | ff 11 | fi 12 | fl 13 | ffi 14 | ffl 15 |
| '02x | ı 16 | J 17 | ` 18 | ´ 19 | ˇ 20 | ˘ 21 | ¯ 22 | ˚ 23 |
| '03x | ¸ 24 | ß 25 | æ 26 | œ 27 | ø 28 | Æ 29 | Œ 30 | Ø 31 |
| '04x | ´ 32 | ! 33 | ” 34 | # 35 | $ 36 | % 37 | & 38 | ’ 39 |
| '05x | ( 40 | ) 41 | * 42 | + 43 | , 44 | - 45 | . 46 | / 47 |
| '06x | 0 48 | 1 49 | 2 50 | 3 51 | 4 52 | 5 53 | 6 54 | 7 55 |
| '07x | 8 56 | 9 57 | : 58 | ; 59 | ¡ 60 | = 61 | ¿ 62 | ? 63 |
| '10x | @ 64 | A 65 | B 66 | C 67 | D 68 | E 69 | F 70 | G 71 |
| '11x | H 72 | I 73 | J 74 | K 75 | L 76 | M 77 | N 78 | O 79 |
| '12x | P 80 | Q 81 | R 82 | S 83 | T 84 | U 85 | V 86 | W 87 |
| '13x | X 88 | Y 89 | Z 90 | [ 91 | " 92 | ] 93 | ^ 94 | . 95 |
| '14x | ` 96 | a 97 | b 98 | c 99 | d 100 | e 101 | f 102 | g 103 |
| '15x | h 104 | i 105 | j 106 | k 107 | l 108 | m 109 | n 110 | o 111 |
| '16x | p 112 | q 113 | r 114 | s 115 | t 116 | u 117 | v 118 | w 119 |
| '17x | x 120 | y 121 | z 122 | – 123 | — 124 | ” 125 | ˜ 126 | ¨ 127 |

**Font Layout 1:** The character font `cmr10`. This is the standard assignment of the characters to their numerical values. Non-standard assignments are presented in the following layouts.

|      | 0 | 1 | 2 | 3 | 4 | 5 | 6 | 7 |
|------|---|---|---|---|---|---|---|---|
| '00x | Γ 0 | Δ 1 | Θ 2 | Λ 3 | Ξ 4 | Π 5 | Σ 6 | Υ 7 |
| '01x | Φ 8 | Ψ 9 | Ω 10 | ↑ 11 | ↓ 12 | ' 13 | ¡ 14 | ¿ 15 |
| '02x | I 16 | J 17 | ` 18 | ´ 19 | ˇ 20 | ˘ 21 | ¯ 22 | ˚ 23 |
| '03x | ¸ 24 | SS 25 | Æ 26 | Œ 27 | Ø 28 | Æ 29 | Œ 30 | Ø 31 |
| '04x | ´ 32 | ! 33 | ” 34 | # 35 | $ 36 | % 37 | & 38 | ’ 39 |
| '05x | ( 40 | ) 41 | * 42 | + 43 | , 44 | - 45 | . 46 | / 47 |
| '06x | 0 48 | 1 49 | 2 50 | 3 51 | 4 52 | 5 53 | 6 54 | 7 55 |
| '07x | 8 56 | 9 57 | : 58 | ; 59 | < 60 | = 61 | > 62 | ? 63 |
| '10x | @ 64 | A 65 | B 66 | C 67 | D 68 | E 69 | F 70 | G 71 |
| '11x | H 72 | I 73 | J 74 | K 75 | L 76 | M 77 | N 78 | O 79 |
| '12x | P 80 | Q 81 | R 82 | S 83 | T 84 | U 85 | V 86 | W 87 |
| '13x | X 88 | Y 89 | Z 90 | [ 91 | " 92 | ] 93 | ^ 94 | . 95 |
| '14x | ` 96 | A 97 | B 98 | C 99 | D 100 | E 101 | F 102 | G 103 |
| '15x | H 104 | I 105 | J 106 | K 107 | L 108 | M 109 | N 110 | O 111 |
| '16x | P 112 | Q 113 | R 114 | S 115 | T 116 | U 117 | V 118 | W 119 |
| '17x | X 120 | Y 121 | Z 122 | – 123 | — 124 | ” 125 | ˜ 126 | ¨ 127 |

**Font Layout 2:** The character font `cmcsc10`. The differences from Layout 1 are symbols 11–15, 25, 60, and 62. The ligatures that normally appear in 11–15 have been replaced by some extra symbols.

|      | 0 | 1 | 2 | 3 | 4 | 5 | 6 | 7 |
|------|---|---|---|---|---|---|---|---|
| '00x | Γ 0 | Δ 1 | Θ 2 | Λ 3 | Ξ 4 | Π 5 | Σ 6 | Υ 7 |
| '01x | Φ 8 | Ψ 9 | Ω 10 | ff 11 | fi 12 | fl 13 | ffi 14 | ffl 15 |
| '02x | ı 16 | ȷ 17 | ` 18 | ´ 19 | ˇ 20 | ˘ 21 | ¯ 22 | ˚ 23 |
| '03x | ¸ 24 | ß 25 | æ 26 | œ 27 | ø 28 | Æ 29 | Œ 30 | Ø 31 |
| '04x | ˝ 32 | ! 33 | ” 34 | # 35 | £ 36 | % 37 | & 38 | ’ 39 |
| '05x | ( 40 | ) 41 | * 42 | + 43 | , 44 | - 45 | . 46 | / 47 |
| '06x | 0 48 | 1 49 | 2 50 | 3 51 | 4 52 | 5 53 | 6 54 | 7 55 |
| '07x | 8 56 | 9 57 | : 58 | ; 59 | ¡ 60 | = 61 | ¿ 62 | ? 63 |
| '10x | @ 64 | A 65 | B 66 | C 67 | D 68 | E 69 | F 70 | G 71 |
| '11x | H 72 | I 73 | J 74 | K 75 | L 76 | M 77 | N 78 | O 79 |
| '12x | P 80 | Q 81 | R 82 | S 83 | T 84 | U 85 | V 86 | W 87 |
| '13x | X 88 | Y 89 | Z 90 | [ 91 | “ 92 | ] 93 | ^ 94 | . 95 |
| '14x | ‘ 96 | a 97 | b 98 | c 99 | d 100 | e 101 | f 102 | g 103 |
| '15x | h 104 | i 105 | j 106 | k 107 | l 108 | m 109 | n 110 | o 111 |
| '16x | p 112 | q 113 | r 114 | s 115 | t 116 | u 117 | v 118 | w 119 |
| '17x | x 120 | y 121 | z 122 | – 123 | — 124 | ″ 125 | ~ 126 | ¨ 127 |

**Font Layout 3:** The character font `cmti10`. The differences from Layout 1 are symbols 36 (£ instead of $) and 38 (& instead of &). All other *text italic* fonts have the same pattern.

|      | 0 | 1 | 2 | 3 | 4 | 5 | 6 | 7 |
|------|---|---|---|---|---|---|---|---|
| '00x | Γ 0 | Δ 1 | Θ 2 | Λ 3 | Ξ 4 | Π 5 | Σ 6 | Υ 7 |
| '01x | Φ 8 | Ψ 9 | Ω 10 | ↑ 11 | ↓ 12 | ' 13 | ı 14 | ¿ 15 |
| '02x | ı 16 | J 17 | ` 18 | ´ 19 | ˇ 20 | ¯ 21 | ¯ 22 | . 23 |
| '03x | ¸ 24 | ß 25 | æ 26 | œ 27 | ø 28 | Æ 29 | Œ 30 | Ø 31 |
| '04x | ⊔ 32 | ! 33 | " 34 | # 35 | $ 36 | % 37 | & 38 | ' 39 |
| '05x | ( 40 | ) 41 | * 42 | + 43 | , 44 | - 45 | . 46 | / 47 |
| '06x | 0 48 | 1 49 | 2 50 | 3 51 | 4 52 | 5 53 | 6 54 | 7 55 |
| '07x | 8 56 | 9 57 | : 58 | ; 59 | < 60 | = 61 | > 62 | ? 63 |
| '10x | @ 64 | A 65 | B 66 | C 67 | D 68 | E 69 | F 70 | G 71 |
| '11x | H 72 | I 73 | J 74 | K 75 | L 76 | M 77 | N 78 | O 79 |
| '12x | P 80 | Q 81 | R 82 | S 83 | T 84 | U 85 | V 86 | W 87 |
| '13x | X 88 | Y 89 | Z 90 | [ 91 | \ 92 | ] 93 | ^ 94 | _ 95 |
| '14x | ‘ 96 | a 97 | b 98 | c 99 | d 100 | e 101 | f 102 | g 103 |
| '15x | h 104 | i 105 | j 106 | k 107 | l 108 | m 109 | n 110 | o 111 |
| '16x | p 112 | q 113 | r 114 | s 115 | t 116 | u 117 | v 118 | w 119 |
| '17x | x 120 | y 121 | z 122 | { 123 | | 124 | } 125 | ~ 126 | ¨ 127 |

**Font Layout 4:** The character font `cmtt10`. All `tt` fonts are set up with the same pattern, except for `cmvtt10` which corresponds to Layout 1. The differences lie in symbols 11–15, 60, 62, 92, 123, 124, and 125. Furthermore, the italic typewriter fonts `cmit` replace symbols 36 and 38 with £ and &, as in all italic fonts. The font `cmtcsc10` contains smaller capitals in positions 97–122.

| | 0 | 1 | 2 | 3 | 4 | 5 | 6 | 7 |
|---|---|---|---|---|---|---|---|---|
| '00x | · 0 | ↓ 1 | α 2 | β 3 | ∧ 4 | ¬ 5 | ∈ 6 | π 7 |
| '01x | λ 8 | γ 9 | δ 10 | ↑ 11 | ± 12 | ⊕ 13 | ∞ 14 | ∂ 15 |
| '02x | ⊂ 16 | ⊃ 17 | ∩ 18 | ∪ 19 | ∀ 20 | ∃ 21 | ⊗ 22 | ↔ 23 |
| '03x | ← 24 | → 25 | ≠ 26 | ◇ 27 | ≤ 28 | ≥ 29 | ≡ 30 | ∨ 31 |
| '04x |  32 | ! 33 | " 34 | # 35 | $ 36 | % 37 | & 38 | ' 39 |
| '05x | ( 40 | ) 41 | * 42 | + 43 | , 44 | − 45 | . 46 | / 47 |
| '06x | 0 48 | 1 49 | 2 50 | 3 51 | 4 52 | 5 53 | 6 54 | 7 55 |
| '07x | 8 56 | 9 57 | : 58 | ; 59 | < 60 | = 61 | > 62 | ? 63 |
| '10x | @ 64 | A 65 | B 66 | C 67 | D 68 | E 69 | F 70 | G 71 |
| '11x | H 72 | I 73 | J 74 | K 75 | L 76 | M 77 | N 78 | O 79 |
| '12x | P 80 | Q 81 | R 82 | S 83 | T 84 | U 85 | V 86 | W 87 |
| '13x | X 88 | Y 89 | Z 90 | [ 91 | \ 92 | ] 93 | ^ 94 | _ 95 |
| '14x | ' 96 | a 97 | b 98 | c 99 | d 100 | e 101 | f 102 | g 103 |
| '15x | h 104 | i 105 | j 106 | k 107 | l 108 | m 109 | n 110 | o 111 |
| '16x | p 112 | q 113 | r 114 | s 115 | t 116 | u 117 | v 118 | w 119 |
| '17x | x 120 | y 121 | z 122 | { 123 | | 124 | } 125 | ~ 126 | ∫ 127 |

**Font Layout 5:** The font `cmtex10`. The differences from Layout 4 are in positions 0–31 and 127, which here contain special math symbols.

| | 0 | 1 | 2 | 3 | 4 | 5 | 6 | 7 |
|---|---|---|---|---|---|---|---|---|
| '00x | $\Gamma$ 0 | $\Delta$ 1 | $\Theta$ 2 | $\Lambda$ 3 | $\Xi$ 4 | $\Pi$ 5 | $\Sigma$ 6 | $\Upsilon$ 7 |
| '01x | $\Phi$ 8 | $\Psi$ 9 | $\Omega$ 10 | $\alpha$ 11 | $\beta$ 12 | $\gamma$ 13 | $\delta$ 14 | $\epsilon$ 15 |
| '02x | $\zeta$ 16 | $\eta$ 17 | $\theta$ 18 | $\iota$ 19 | $\kappa$ 20 | $\lambda$ 21 | $\mu$ 22 | $\nu$ 23 |
| '03x | $\xi$ 24 | $\pi$ 25 | $\rho$ 26 | $\sigma$ 27 | $\tau$ 28 | $\upsilon$ 29 | $\phi$ 30 | $\chi$ 31 |
| '04x | $\psi$ 32 | $\omega$ 33 | $\varepsilon$ 34 | $\vartheta$ 35 | $\varpi$ 36 | $\varrho$ 37 | $\varsigma$ 38 | $\varphi$ 39 |
| '05x | ↼ 40 | ↽ 41 | ⇀ 42 | ⇁ 43 | ⌐ 44 | ⌐ 45 | ▷ 46 | ◁ 47 |
| '06x | 0 48 | 1 49 | 2 50 | 3 51 | 4 52 | 5 53 | 6 54 | 7 55 |
| '07x | 8 56 | 9 57 | . 58 | , 59 | < 60 | / 61 | > 62 | ⋆ 63 |
| '10x | $\partial$ 64 | $A$ 65 | $B$ 66 | $C$ 67 | $D$ 68 | $E$ 69 | $F$ 70 | $G$ 71 |
| '11x | $H$ 72 | $I$ 73 | $J$ 74 | $K$ 75 | $L$ 76 | $M$ 77 | $N$ 78 | $O$ 79 |
| '12x | $P$ 80 | $Q$ 81 | $R$ 82 | $S$ 83 | $T$ 84 | $U$ 85 | $V$ 86 | $W$ 87 |
| '13x | $X$ 88 | $Y$ 89 | $Z$ 90 | ♭ 91 | ♮ 92 | ♯ 93 | ⌣ 94 | ⌢ 95 |
| '14x | $\ell$ 96 | $a$ 97 | $b$ 98 | $c$ 99 | $d$ 100 | $e$ 101 | $f$ 102 | $g$ 103 |
| '15x | $h$ 104 | $i$ 105 | $j$ 106 | $k$ 107 | $l$ 108 | $m$ 109 | $n$ 110 | $o$ 111 |
| '16x | $p$ 112 | $q$ 113 | $r$ 114 | $s$ 115 | $t$ 116 | $u$ 117 | $v$ 118 | $w$ 119 |
| '17x | $x$ 120 | $y$ 121 | $z$ 122 | $\imath$ 123 | $\jmath$ 124 | $\wp$ 125 | ⃗ 126 | ⌢ 127 |

**Font Layout 6:** The font `cmmi10`. The `cmmi` family of fonts, including `cmmib10`, contain lower case Greek letters in positions 11–39 and a number of math symbols in 40–47, 60–64, and 123–127.

| | 0 | 1 | 2 | 3 | 4 | 5 | 6 | 7 |
|---|---|---|---|---|---|---|---|---|
| '00x | ( 0 | ) 1 | [ 2 | ] 3 | ⌊ 4 | ⌋ 5 | ⌈ 6 | ⌉ 7 |
| '01x | { 8 | } 9 | ⟨ 10 | ⟩ 11 | ∣ 12 | ∥ 13 | / 14 | \ 15 |
| '02x | ( 16 | ) 17 | ( 18 | ) 19 | [ 20 | ] 21 | ⌊ 22 | ⌋ 23 |
| '03x | ⌈ 24 | ⌉ 25 | { 26 | } 27 | ⟨ 28 | ⟩ 29 | / 30 | \ 31 |
| '04x | ( 32 | ) 33 | [ 34 | ] 35 | ⌊ 36 | ⌋ 37 | ⌈ 38 | ⌉ 39 |
| '05x | { 40 | } 41 | ⟨ 42 | ⟩ 43 | / 44 | \ 45 | / 46 | \ 47 |
| '06x | ( 48 | ) 49 | ⌈ 50 | ⌉ 51 | ⌊ 52 | ⌋ 53 | ∣ 54 | ∣ 55 |
| '07x | ⎧ 56 | ⎫ 57 | ⎩ 58 | ⎭ 59 | { 60 | } 61 | ▪ 62 | ∣ 63 |
| '10x | \ 64 | / 65 | ∣ 66 | ∣ 67 | ⟨ 68 | ⟩ 69 | ⊔ 70 | ⊔ 71 |
| '11x | ∮ 72 | ∮ 73 | ⊙ 74 | ⊙ 75 | ⊕ 76 | ⊕ 77 | ⊗ 78 | ⊗ 79 |
| '12x | Σ 80 | Π 81 | ∫ 82 | ∪ 83 | ∩ 84 | ⊎ 85 | ∧ 86 | ∨ 87 |
| '13x | Σ 88 | Π 89 | ∫ 90 | ∪ 91 | ∩ 92 | ⊎ 93 | ∧ 94 | ∨ 95 |
| '14x | ⨆ 96 | ⨆ 97 | ⌢ 98 | ⌢ 99 | ⌢ 100 | ∼ 101 | ∼ 102 | ∼ 103 |
| '15x | ⌈ 104 | ⌉ 105 | ⌊ 106 | ⌋ 107 | ⌈ 108 | ⌉ 109 | { 110 | } 111 |
| '16x | √ 112 | √ 113 | √ 114 | √ 115 | √ 116 | ∣ 117 | ⌈ 118 | ∥ 119 |
| '17x | ↑ 120 | ↓ 121 | ⌢ 122 | ⌣ 123 | ⌢ 124 | ⌣ 125 | ⇑ 126 | ⇓ 127 |

**Font Layout 7:** The font `cmex10`, containing the mathematical symbols that appear in varying sizes.

| | 0 | 1 | 2 | 3 | 4 | 5 | 6 | 7 |
|---|---|---|---|---|---|---|---|---|
| '00x | − 0 | · 1 | × 2 | ∗ 3 | ÷ 4 | ⋄ 5 | ± 6 | ∓ 7 |
| '01x | ⊕ 8 | ⊖ 9 | ⊗ 10 | ⊘ 11 | ⊙ 12 | ◯ 13 | ∘ 14 | • 15 |
| '02x | ≍ 16 | ≡ 17 | ⊆ 18 | ⊇ 19 | ≤ 20 | ≥ 21 | ≼ 22 | ≽ 23 |
| '03x | ∼ 24 | ≈ 25 | ⊂ 26 | ⊃ 27 | ≪ 28 | ≫ 29 | ≺ 30 | ≻ 31 |
| '04x | ← 32 | → 33 | ↑ 34 | ↓ 35 | ↔ 36 | ↗ 37 | ↘ 38 | ≃ 39 |
| '05x | ⇐ 40 | ⇒ 41 | ⇑ 42 | ⇓ 43 | ⇔ 44 | ↖ 45 | ↙ 46 | ∝ 47 |
| '06x | ′ 48 | ∞ 49 | ∈ 50 | ∋ 51 | △ 52 | ▽ 53 | / 54 | ∣ 55 |
| '07x | ∀ 56 | ∃ 57 | ¬ 58 | ∅ 59 | ℜ 60 | ℑ 61 | ⊤ 62 | ⊥ 63 |
| '10x | ℵ 64 | $\mathcal{A}$ 65 | $\mathcal{B}$ 66 | $\mathcal{C}$ 67 | $\mathcal{D}$ 68 | $\mathcal{E}$ 69 | $\mathcal{F}$ 70 | $\mathcal{G}$ 71 |
| '11x | $\mathcal{H}$ 72 | $\mathcal{I}$ 73 | $\mathcal{J}$ 74 | $\mathcal{K}$ 75 | $\mathcal{L}$ 76 | $\mathcal{M}$ 77 | $\mathcal{N}$ 78 | $\mathcal{O}$ 79 |
| '12x | $\mathcal{P}$ 80 | $\mathcal{Q}$ 81 | $\mathcal{R}$ 82 | $\mathcal{S}$ 83 | $\mathcal{T}$ 84 | $\mathcal{U}$ 85 | $\mathcal{V}$ 86 | $\mathcal{W}$ 87 |
| '13x | $\mathcal{X}$ 88 | $\mathcal{Y}$ 89 | $\mathcal{Z}$ 90 | ∪ 91 | ∩ 92 | ⊎ 93 | ∧ 94 | ∨ 95 |
| '14x | ⊢ 96 | ⊣ 97 | ⌊ 98 | ⌋ 99 | ⌈ 100 | ⌉ 101 | { 102 | } 103 |
| '15x | ⟨ 104 | ⟩ 105 | ∣ 106 | ∥ 107 | ↕ 108 | ⇕ 109 | \ 110 | ≀ 111 |
| '16x | √ 112 | ∐ 113 | ∇ 114 | ∫ 115 | ⊔ 116 | ⊓ 117 | ⊑ 118 | ⊒ 119 |
| '17x | § 120 | † 121 | ‡ 122 | ¶ 123 | ♣ 124 | ◇ 125 | ♡ 126 | ♠ 127 |

**Font Layout 8:** The font `cmsy10`. The `cmsy` fonts contain many math symbols as well as the calligraphic letters $\mathcal{A} \ldots \mathcal{Z}$ in positions 65–90. The bold face version `cmbsy10` is set up on the same pattern.

| | 0 | 1 | 2 | 3 | 4 | 5 | 6 | 7 |
|---|---|---|---|---|---|---|---|---|
| '00x | Њ 0 | Љ 1 | Џ 2 | Э 3 | I 4 | Є 5 | Ђ 6 | Ћ 7 |
| '01x | њ 8 | љ 9 | џ 10 | э 11 | і 12 | є 13 | ђ 14 | ћ 15 |
| '02x | Ю 16 | Ж 17 | Й 18 | Ё 19 | V 20 | Ѳ 21 | Ѕ 22 | Я 23 |
| '03x | ю 24 | ж 25 | й 26 | ё 27 | ѵ 28 | ѳ 29 | ѕ 30 | я 31 |
| '04x | ¨ 32 | ! 33 | „ 34 | Ѣ 35 | ˘ 36 | % 37 | ′ 38 | ' 39 |
| '05x | ( 40 | ) 41 | ∗ 42 | ѣ 43 | , 44 | - 45 | . 46 | / 47 |
| '06x | 0 48 | 1 49 | 2 50 | 3 51 | 4 52 | 5 53 | 6 54 | 7 55 |
| '07x | 8 56 | 9 57 | : 58 | ; 59 | « 60 | ı 61 | » 62 | ? 63 |
| '10x | ˘ 64 | А 65 | Б 66 | Ц 67 | Д 68 | Е 69 | Ф 70 | Г 71 |
| '11x | Х 72 | И 73 | J 74 | К 75 | Л 76 | М 77 | Н 78 | О 79 |
| '12x | П 80 | Ч 81 | Р 82 | С 83 | Т 84 | У 85 | В 86 | Ш 87 |
| '13x | Ш 88 | Ы 89 | З 90 | [ 91 | " 92 | ] 93 | Ь 94 | Ъ 95 |
| '14x | ' 96 | а 97 | б 98 | ц 99 | д 100 | е 101 | ф 102 | г 103 |
| '15x | х 104 | и 105 | j 106 | к 107 | л 108 | м 109 | н 110 | о 111 |
| '16x | п 112 | ч 113 | р 114 | с 115 | т 116 | у 117 | в 118 | щ 119 |
| '17x | ш 120 | ы 121 | з 122 | – 123 | — 124 | № 125 | ь 126 | ъ 127 |

**Font Layout 9:** The character font `wncyr10`, one of the Cyrillic fonts from the University of Washington.

# 7 Cyrillic fonts

Fonts for the Cyrillic alphabet are not part of the normal TEX/LATEX packages. The American Mathematical Society designed a set in 1980 to be used in reviews of books published in Russian and other Slavic languages in which the titles were to be rendered in the original language. In 1988, the Humanities and Arts Computing Center of the University of Washington redesigned the $\mathcal{A}_{\mathcal{M}}S$ Cyrillic fonts for general purpose Slavic studies, adding the pre-Revolutionary and accented letters. The overall appearance was also greatly enhanced (Layout 9 on the facing page).

The University of Washington Cyrillic fonts all bear the prefix `wncy`, followed by the style designation `r` (upright), `b` (bold), `i` (italic), `sc` (small caps), or `ss` (upright sans serif), and the design size in points.

A Cyrillic font command may be defined with `\newfont` in the normal way. For example, `\newfont{\cyr}{wncyr10}` defines `\cyr` to be a declaration that activates the 10 pt upright Cyrillic font. This command may be called as any other font style or size declaration.

The layout of the Cyrillic fonts has been chosen in such a way that the input text may be entered following the regular English transliteration scheme. Thus Cyrillic С is in position 83 where Latin S is normally situated. Typing S when a Cyrillic font is active outputs the correct equivalent С. Numerals and punctuations are to be found in the standard locations and so may be typed in as usual. 'Санкт-Петербург 10?' is thus generated by `{\cyr Sankt-Peterburg 10?}`.

A better way of enabling the Cyrillic fonts is simply to select font encoding OT2 under NFSS, as illustrated in Section 8.5.2 on page 229. The `.fd` (font definition) files for the Cyrillic fonts have been so set up that the other font attributes fully parallel those of the Latin fonts. This means `wncyr10` has all the same attributes as `cmr10`, except for the encoding: family `cmr`, shape `n`, series `m`. (Of course, if the cm fonts are not the current standard ones, it will require more than just selecting the OT2 encoding to active these Cyrillic fonts.)

Since the Cyrillic alphabet possesses more letters than the Latin, many of them must be transliterated with multi-letter combinations. These are automatically programmed into the fonts using TEX's ligature system. For example, Ch is treated as a ligature for symbol 81 Ч just as fi is for fi in a Latin font. This means that multi-letter transliterations are simply typed in. The input for 'Хрущев' is `{\cyr Khrushchev}`, where Kh → Х and shch → щ. The transliteration scheme is that for English; other languages have their own systems to reproduce the original pronunciation. For example, 'Горбачёв' is *Gorbatschow* in German, *Gorbaciov* in Italian, and *Gorbachev* in English. These other schemes do *not* work with these fonts.

Not all letters can be produced so automatically (for example, the ё in Горбачёв) and for this reason the $\mathcal{A}_{\mathcal{M}}S$ provides a file `cyracc.def` containing macro definitions for accented letters and other special features, such as the hard and soft signs. When these macros are given in a Latin font, additional transliteration symbols appear.

Unfortunately, some of the accent commands in `cyracc.def` will not work with LATEX 2$_\varepsilon$. What is needed is an encoding definition file named `OT2enc.def`, similar to `OT1enc.def` and `T1enc.def`, to define those commands that are encoding-specific with the help of the special definition commands in Section 8.5.9.

## E.8    The font files

### E.8.1    The root names

Every TEX implementation should contain the 75 standard fonts presented in Sections E.3 to E.5 in the various design sizes. The root names of these fonts are summarized here.

| | | | | |
|---|---|---|---|---|
| cmr5 | cmti9 | cmssq8 | cmu10 | cmmi5 |
| cmr6 | cmti10 | cmss8 | cmff10 | cmmi6 |
| cmr7 | cmti12 | cmss9 | cmfi10 | cmmi7 |
| cmr8 | cmbx5 | cmss10 | cmdunh10 | cmmi8 |
| cmr9 | cmbx6 | cmss12 | cmtt8 | cmmi9 |
| cmr10 | cmbx7 | cmss17 | cmtt9 | cmmi10 |
| cmr12 | cmbx8 | cmssqi8 | cmtt10 | cmmi12 |
| cmr17 | cmbx9 | cmssi8 | cmtt12 | cmmib10 |
| cmcsc10 | cmbx10 | cmssi9 | cmtcsc10 | cmsy5 |
| cmsl8 | cmbx12 | cmssi10 | cmsltt10 | cmsy6 |
| cmsl9 | cmb10 | cmssi12 | cmitt10 | cmsy7 |
| cmsl10 | cmfib8 | cmssi17 | cmtex8 | cmsy8 |
| cmsl12 | cmbxsl10 | cmssdc10 | cmtex9 | cmsy9 |
| cmti7 | cmbxti10 | cmssbx10 | cmtex10 | cmsy10 |
| cmti8 | cminch | cmvtt10 | cmex10 | cmbsy10 |

The $\mathcal{A}_{\mathcal{M}}\mathcal{S}$ provides the bold math italic `cmmib` and bold symbol `cmbsy` fonts in design sizes 5–9 pt. The LATEX 2$_\varepsilon$ installation assumes that they are present, although there is no harm done if they are absent.

| | | | | |
|---|---|---|---|---|
| cmmib5 | cmmib6 | cmmib7 | cmmib8 | cmmib9 |
| cmbsy5 | cmbsy6 | cmbsy7 | cmbsy8 | cmbsy9 |

In addition to the standard TEX fonts, there are a number of special logo and LATEX fonts that are also included:

| | | | | |
|---|---|---|---|---|
| lasy5 | lasy8 | lasyb10 | linew10 | logo8 |
| lasy6 | lasy9 | line10 | lcirclew10 | logo9 |
| lasy7 | lasy10 | lcircle10 | logosl10 | logo10 |

The number at the end of the root name is the design size in points. For each of these fonts, there exists a file with the root name and the extension .tfm, for example cmr10.tfm. TeX and LaTeX make use only of these .tfm files during the processing of a text file. They contain information about the size and other characteristics of the font and its symbols, as mentioned on page 393, but nothing about what the symbols look like.

Information about the actual form of the letters and symbols is not needed until the output is sent to the printer by means of a driver program. This information is stored in other files, both in the basic design size as well as in various magnifications.

## .2 Font magnifications

The normal magnification steps for TeX fonts are powers of 1.2 plus $\sqrt{1.2}$. In LaTeX, font sizes are selected by means of the commands in Section 4.1.2, which check to see whether the corresponding font is available in the desired design size, and if not, take a suitable magnification of another design size. LaTeX 2.09 receives its font information from the file lfonts.tex while LaTeX $2_\varepsilon$ uses the font definition files (.fd, Section 8.5.8). Magnified fonts may also be chosen by means of the command

$$\text{\textbackslash newfont\{\textbackslash\{\textit{fnt\_cmd}\}\{\textit{root\_name} scaled \textit{scaling\_factor}\}}$$

which defines \\*fnt_cmd* to be a command that activates the font *root_name* magnified by *scaling_factor*/1000. That is, *scaling_factor* is an integer number equal to 1000 times the magnification. For the design size itself, this is 1000; for the first magnification step, $\sqrt{1.2}$, it is 1095; for the next steps, it is 1200, 1440, .... The TeX command \magstep$n$ may be given for $1.2^n$ and \magstephalf for $\sqrt{1.2}$.

A 10 pt font magnified by 1.2 is not the same as the 12 pt font in its design size, even if the differences are hard to detect, as for example:

12pt unscaled   10pt scaled by 1200.

The differences are more obvious when the multiplication is by $1.2^3$, or a scaling factor of 1728:

17pt unscaled   10pt scaled by 1728.

The magnified fonts may have the same height as the originals, but the characters are blacker and somewhat wider. This is because the fonts with a smaller design size have different relationships between letter height and width and line thickness than the larger fonts. However, when they are magnified to the same height, all other dimensions are increased proportionally. All fonts are fashioned to look their best in their design size.

The full name of the files containing the *pixel patterns* of the fonts depends on the printer resolution and the coding system used. They still possess the original root name of the font, but with an extension that reflects either the scaling factor or the base resolution.  For the most popular laser printers with a resolution of 300 dpi (dots per inch), the extensions are:

| Magn. Factor | Scale Factor | Pixel Coding Source 300pxl | Source 200pxl | Packed Coding |
|---|---|---|---|---|
| 1.0 | 1000 | 1000pxl | 1500pxl | 300pk |
| $\sqrt{1.2}$ | 1095 | 1095pxl | 1643pxl | 329pk |
| 1.2 | 1200 | 1200pxl | 1800pxl | 360pk |
| $1.2^2$ | 1440 | 1440pxl | 2160pxl | 432pk |
| $1.2^3$ | 1728 | 1728pxl | 2592pxl | 518pk |
| $1.2^4$ | 2074 | 2074pxl | 3110pxl | 622pk |
| $1.2^5$ | 2488 | 2488pxl | 3732pxl | 746pk |
| $1.2^6$ | 2986 | 2986pxl | 4479pxl | 896pk |
| $1.2^7$ | 3583 | 3583pxl | 5375pxl | 1075pk |

The pixel file for the 10 pt Roman character set in the magnification $1.2^2$ bears the name `cmr10.1440pxl`, `cmr10.2160pxl`, or `cmr10.432pk`. The difference between the first two is explained thus: all pixel files are designed for a certain printer resolution, and if this was 300 dpi the output will be correct.  The number before the `pxl` is the scaling factor. However, if the pixel files had been originally made up for a printer with 200 dpi resolution, the output will be too small by a factor 2/3.  An additional magnification of 1.5 is needed to correct this.

The packed coding takes the extension .pk preceded by the design resolution in dots per inch.  If this is 300 and the output is sent to a printer of the same resolution, it will be the correct size. If the pixel file has been created for 360 dpi and is sent to the same printer, the output will appear 1.2 times larger than designed, that is, with a magnification of this amount.

On some computer systems, especially PCs, the pixel files are organized in a different manner.  They all bear the same extension, either .pxl or .pk, depending on the coding, but are stored in separate *directories*, one for each magnification. Thus a directory with a name like 360dpi holds all the pixel files for the magnification 1.2 (assuming a printer resolution of 300 dpi).

## E.8.3    Pixel coding

Every character output by a laser printer is made up of a series of tiny dots, called *picture elements* or *pixels*. Their size depends on the printer resolution. If this is

300 dpi, a pixel has a diameter of about 0.08 mm. Below is a blow-up of the letter A in the 10 pt Roman font.

The contents of every box in the picture at the left are stored in the computer either as a 0 or as a 1. The zeros represent the white, empty boxes, and the 1's the black dots. The letter A consists of 28 rows each containing 28 dots. The top two rows are coded as

00000000000001100000000000000
00000000000001111000000000000

while the bottom row is

1111111111000001111111111111

to complete the pixel representation.

Such strings of binary digits, or *bits*, cannot be indefinitely long. A computer normally stores them in blocks of 32, the length of a computer 'word'. Thus the rows in the above example are padded out to 32 bits each by adding 4 extra zeros to each one. If the width of the character is greater than 32 pixels, two or more 32-bit words are needed per row.

A group of 8 bits is called a *byte* in computer language. The 32-bit word thus contains 4 bytes. Our letter A requires 28 words or 112 bytes to store its pattern. An entire font consists of 128 characters, so that the complete pixel file needs something on the order of 14 000 bytes. However, this is not all. Each character needs additional information, as can be demonstrated with the letter *g*:

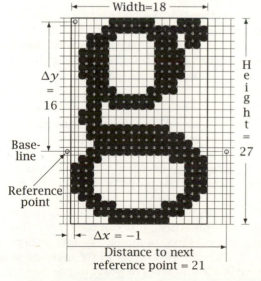

Width=18

Height = 27

Baseline

Reference point

$\Delta y = 16$

$\Delta x = -1$

Distance to next reference point = 21

The pixel pattern for a symbol can be enclosed in a minimal box that just hugs the black dots. This box for the letter *g* is 27 dots high and 18 dots wide. The distance of its baseline from the top row of dots is $\Delta y$, equal to 16 pixels. The reference point for horizontal alignment lies on the baseline a distance $\Delta x$ from the leftmost column of dots; a negative value means that the reference point is to the left of this first column. Here $\Delta x = -1$. Finally, the position for the next character's reference point must also be specified, which for the *g* is 21 pixels further to the right.

These values must be stored in the pixel file for every symbol. Those for the height and width of the minimal box, as well as those for $\Delta y$ and $\Delta x$, are given in pixels and require 16 bits each, a half word. The entry for the distance to the next reference point is given in `tfm` units, that is, the same value as for the character width in the `.tfm` file. A fourth word specifies where the pixel pattern for the symbol begins in the pixel file.

The total of $128 \times 4 = 512$ words of additional information form a sort of table of contents for the 128 characters in one font that appears at the end of the pixel file. Four more words of general font information follow, including design size and magnification. The very first and last words of a pixel file are an identifying 1001. Thus a pixel file consists of the pixel patterns plus 518 words of extra information. Further details are only of interest to writers of `.dvi` driver programs and may be found in the more specialist TEX literature.

The printing procedure would be prohibitively slow if the pixel pattern were transferred to the printer for every single character to be output. In fact, a laser printer possesses its own storage memory, so that the patterns need to be transmitted to it only once for each character. The stored patterns may then be recalled by referring to a code number for that character, consisting of only one byte. These are the *code numbers* shown in the font layouts in Section E.6.

## E.8.4   Packed coding

!

As can be seen from the previous section, pixel files require considerable storage memory, especially at higher magnifications. For example, the pixel file for `cminch` with scaling factor 1440 takes up a total of 705 376 bytes.

For this reason, Tomas Rokicki of Stanford University has developed a compression process to store the pixel information in a much more compact form. The basis of the procedure is that a dot, either black or white, is more often followed by one of the same rather than of the opposite color: the pixels are not distributed randomly but in an ordered manner.

The coding now becomes a series of numbers that specify how many pixels of the same color are to follow. The next number gives the number of pixels of the opposite color, and so on. Of course, the color of the initial pixel must be stated. For the *g* example in the previous section, the starting color is white and the list of numbers begins with

$$5/6/3/3/\underline{5}/14/2/4/4/1/3\dots$$

The symbols thus starts with 5 white pixels, followed by 6 blacks, then by another three whites and three blacks. The last pixel in the first row is white, as are the first four pixels of the second row, hence a total of 5 white pixels now come, spread over two rows. This causes no problems on decoding, since the width of the minimal box is known so that the $\underline{5}$ pixels will be properly split between the two rows.

The number 0 may never appear. An analysis of pixel patterns shows that in more than 90% of the cases, the number of consecutive pixels of one color is less than 14. This means that the sequence numbers may be stored as 4-bit numbers, or *nibbles*, representing the values 0–15. The values 0, 14, and 15 are given special meanings. The zero is used to indicate that the number of pixels of one color is greater than 13 and that the next number continues the sequence with the same color. Since the analysis also demonstrates that in 37% of the cases, one row is followed by an identical row of pixels, the number 15 states that this is the case. Finally, the number 14 indicates that more than two rows have the same pixel pattern, the next number specifying how many rows.

Even the additional information, such as height and width of the minimal box and the position of the reference point, may be stored in a compressed form. Detailed information is only needed for unpacking the process for the .dvi driver. More can be found in Rokicki (1985).

The efficiency of the procedure is enormous. The file cminch.432pk, holding the cminch font in magnification 1.44, requires only 32 644 bytes, less than 5% of the size of the equivalent pixel file. This is an extreme example, for the 75 standard fonts in the first four magnification steps in packed form take up about 20% of the memory they would need in pixel format. The savings are even greater when more (higher) magnifications are present.

Today, the .pxl coded font files are hardly to be found anymore. They have been fully replaced by the .pk coding format.

# Remarks on METAFONT

METAFONT is a program for designing and developing characters fonts, written by the inventor of the TeX program, Donald E. Knuth (Knuth, 1986b, 1986c, 1986d). If METAFONT is available on the computer, the existing fonts may be regenerated with any desired magnification, larger or smaller.

The creation of a totally new set of fonts, such as for Arabic or Hebrew, is feasible, although something that should be left to experts, requiring detailed knowledge about the internal METAFONT language. This is not a book on METAFONT, so no such information will be presented here. We limit ourselves to describing how to create new pixel files for the existing fonts.

How the METAFONT program is called depends on the computer operating system. Once it has been started, it prints to the screen the version number and any extra files that are automatically loaded. Then it waits for a response from the user, prompting with the symbol **. The response must be of the form

    \mode=localfont; mag=*nn*; input *file*

followed by ⟨*return*⟩. The value *nn* of mag= is a decimal number specifying the desired magnification; if it is omitted or set to 1, the design size is taken. The *file* entry to input is the root name of one of the 75 standard fonts from Section E.8.1. As part of the basic implementation of META-FONT there should be 75 files with these names and the extension .mf. These files contain the character definitions as 62 different parameters, which will not be elaborated here. Other .mf files, say for Cyrillic or special character sets, may also be entered in place of *file*.

METAFONT now proceeds to generate the pixel patterns for the selected font in the chosen magnification, printing the font name and the code numbers for the symbols to the screen. Finally, the program prints * and waits for a new user entry. The response end ⟨*return*⟩ terminates the program and restores control to the operating system.

The results of the METAFONT run are two new files, one being the .tfm file for the font, the other bearing the root name and the extension .*xxx*gf, where *gf* stands for *generic font*. The *xxx* reflects the chosen magnification: if this is 1, *xxx* is the printer resolution in dots per inch (dpi). METAFONT obtains the information about the basic printer and its resolution from the command \mode=localfont. In the original version, this resolution was 200 dpi, but at any installation localfont should be changed to portray the local printer characteristics.

The one .tfm file may be used for all magnifications of the same root font. In some places, localfont is modified so that the .tfm file is generated only for the design size, for example, when mag=1 is selected.

It remains now to convert the generic font coding into a form that may be read by a driver, say the packed coding described above. This is carried out with the subsidiary program gftopk. Supposing we have called METAFONT to generate cmr10 in magnification 1.44, for a 300 dpi printer, we now have the file cmr10.432gf. The call

    gftopk cmr10.432gf

does the conversion, creating the packed font file cmr10.432pk.

For older drivers that insist on the original pixel coding, there also exists the subsidiary program gftopxl. For the above example,

    gftopxl cmr10.432gf

creates the file cmr10.1440pxl, following the naming convention described by the table on page 414 and assuming a printer resolution of 300 dpi.

The usual TEX magnification steps are $\sqrt{1.2}$ and integral powers of 1.2. These may be entered into the command line mag= either as a decimal number or as magstep *n* to indicate $1.2^n$. Here *n* must be a whole number. The half step $\sqrt{1.2}$ may be entered as magstep0.5.

METAFONT will permit considerable variations on the basic fonts. The intrepid user who dares to play around with these should be familiar with Knuth (1986d), pages 1–35. In any case, the original .mf files should be left untouched, with any new versions being renamed to something else. The 75 TEX fonts listed on page 412 must remain a standard.

For general information on how to use and exploit the METAFONT program, see *The METAFONT book* (Knuth, 1986b). Warning: playing with METAFONT can become very habit-forming and time consuming!

In accordance with the development of TEX 3.0 for multilingual applications and 256 characters per font, Donald E. Knuth has extended METAFONT to a version 2.0. He now wishes to withdraw from any more new improvements of either of these programs, being prepared merely to correct any definite errors they may contain. To emphasize this decision, he will from now on give version numbers to TeX that converge to $\pi$ (3.14159...) and to METAFONT that approach the value of $e$ (2.71828...). At present, TeX is now at version 3.1415 and METAFONT at 2.71. As a consequence of this decision, any further major developments to these two programs, such as undertaken by user groups, will be under new names, since Donald E. Knuth has kept the copyright to the existing names.

# 0  Extended character sets for TeX 3.0

Proper exploitation of the enhanced capabilities of TeX 3.0 requires new, extended character fonts, since 256 characters per font are now possible instead of the previous 128. The new characters should include accented letters as well as other accents missing from the original fonts.

## 0.1  Limitations and deficiencies of the CM fonts

Most, but not all, of the diacritic marks (accents) used in those European languages based on the Latin alphabet are contained in, or may be generated by, TeX's Computer Modern (CM) fonts. A basic set of naked accents is available to be combined with other letters, such as the acute accent ´ with the letter e to make é. Other combinations may be defined for diacritic marks that are not predefined in TeX or LaTeX. For example, the macros

```
\newcommand{\Dj}{D\hspace{-0.7em}\rule[0.8ex]{0.30em}{0.08ex}%
                 \hspace{0.40em}}
\newcommand{\dj}{d\hspace{-0.35em}\rule[1.2ex]{0.3em}{0.08ex}%
                 \hspace{0.05em}}
```

may be defined for the Croatian symbols Đ and đ, which may be printed with the commands \Dj and \dj. Other diacritic marks, such as the ogonek that appears in Polish and Lithuanian as Ą, ą, Ę, and ę, cannot be formed at all since they are missing from the CM fonts.

Fashioning diacritic characters as a combination of letters and special symbols has one great disadvantage for the TeX processing: words containing such characters cannot take part in the automatic word division since the hyphenation patterns include only pure letters. The accented letters, such as those in German and French and most other languages, must be treated as *single* characters in the hyphenation patterns, and must appear as single letters in the character set.

In addition to diacritic characters, a number of special letters are employed in some European languages, such as ß, Æ, æ, Œ, œ, Ø, and ø, which are provided in standard TeX with the CM fonts (Section 2.5.6).

However, other special letters, such as Ɖ, ŋ, Þ, þ, and ð, are missing completely and cannot be easily constructed from existing ones.

## E.10.2  The Cork extension

At the 1990 International TeX Conference in Cork, Ireland, an extension of the Latin alphabet and its assignments within the 256 character positions was proposed and accepted.  This extension includes the majority of special and diacritic letters in languages based on the Latin alphabet as single characters.  The following languages are completely covered:

> Afrikaans, Albanian, Breton, Catalan, Croatian, Czech, Danish, Dutch, English, Estonian, Faroese, Finnish, French, Frisian, Gaelic, German, Hungarian, Icelandic, Indonesian, Irish, Italian, Madagascan, Norwegian, Polish, Portuguese, Romanian, Romansh, Slovak, Slovene, Sorbian (Upper and Lower), Somali, Spanish, Swahili, Swedish, Turkish.

For all these languages, the special and diacritic letters may be included in hyphenation patterns as single letters for optimal word division by TeX and LaTeX.

The proposed font extension contains most of the accents as separate symbols so that they may be combined with other letters to form further diacritic letters in the same way as in the CM fonts.  Of course, the problems with word division will still be present for these combined letters. The following languages may have all their diacritic letters fashioned as combinations:

> Basque, Esperanto, Latvian, Lithuanian, Maltese, Samoan, Tagalog, and Welsh.

The relationship between single diacritic characters and combined letters is rather variable for these languages.  The extended font contains 6 diacritic letters for the Latvian language, while 18 others must be constructed as combinations.  For Tagalog, the main language of the Philippines, 30 single characters are included, and another 2 must be combined.

Character fonts comforming to the Cork proposal should bear the identifying letters ec in their names for 'Extended Computer' in place of the cm for 'Computer Modern'.

## E.10.3  The DC fonts

The Cork proposal for extending the TeX fonts to 256 characters has been put into practice by Norbert Schwarz, of Bochum, Germany, who has produced the appropriate METAFONT source files.  Font Layout 10

| | 0 | 1 | 2 | 3 | 4 | 5 | 6 | 7 |
|---|---|---|---|---|---|---|---|---|
| '00x | ` 0 | ´ 1 | ^ 2 | ~ 3 | ¨ 4 | ˝ 5 | ° 6 | ˇ 7 |
| '01x | ˘ 8 | ¯ 9 | ˙ 10 | ˏ 11 | ˎ 12 | ‚ 13 | ‹ 14 | › 15 |
| '02x | " 16 | " 17 | „ 18 | « 19 | » 20 | – 21 | — 22 | 23 |
| '03x | 0 24 | 1 25 | J 26 | ff 27 | fi 28 | fl 29 | ffi 30 | ffl 31 |
| '04x | ␣ 32 | ! 33 | " 34 | # 35 | $ 36 | % 37 | & 38 | ' 39 |
| '05x | ( 40 | ) 41 | * 42 | + 43 | , 44 | - 45 | . 46 | / 47 |
| '06x | 0 48 | 1 49 | 2 50 | 3 51 | 4 52 | 5 53 | 6 54 | 7 55 |
| '07x | 8 56 | 9 57 | : 58 | ; 59 | < 60 | = 61 | > 62 | ? 63 |
| '10x | @ 64 | A 65 | B 66 | C 67 | D 68 | E 69 | F 70 | G 71 |
| '11x | H 72 | I 73 | J 74 | K 75 | L 76 | M 77 | N 78 | O 79 |
| '12x | P 80 | Q 81 | R 82 | S 83 | T 84 | U 85 | V 86 | W 87 |
| '13x | X 88 | Y 89 | Z 90 | [ 91 | \ 92 | ] 93 | ^ 94 | _ 95 |
| '14x | ' 96 | a 97 | b 98 | c 99 | d 100 | e 101 | f 102 | g 103 |
| '15x | h 104 | i 105 | j 106 | k 107 | l 108 | m 109 | n 110 | o 111 |
| '16x | p 112 | q 113 | r 114 | s 115 | t 116 | u 117 | v 118 | w 119 |
| '17x | x 120 | y 121 | z 122 | { 123 | \| 124 | } 125 | ~ 126 | - 127 |
| '20x | Ă 128 | Ą 129 | Ć 130 | Č 131 | Ď 132 | Ě 133 | Ę 134 | Ğ 135 |
| '21x | Ĺ 136 | Ľ 137 | Ł 138 | Ń 139 | Ň 140 | Ŋ 141 | Ő 142 | Ŕ 143 |
| '22x | Ř 144 | Ś 145 | Š 146 | Ş 147 | Ť 148 | Ţ 149 | Ű 150 | Ů 151 |
| '23x | Ÿ 152 | Ź 153 | Ž 154 | Ż 155 | IJ 156 | İ 157 | đ 158 | § 159 |
| '24x | ă 160 | ą 161 | ć 162 | č 163 | ď 164 | ě 165 | ę 166 | ğ 167 |
| '25x | ĺ 168 | ľ 169 | ł 170 | ń 171 | ň 172 | ŋ 173 | ő 174 | ŕ 175 |
| '26x | ř 176 | ś 177 | š 178 | ş 179 | ť 180 | ţ 181 | ű 182 | ů 183 |
| '27x | ÿ 184 | ź 185 | ž 186 | ż 187 | ij 188 | ı 189 | ¿ 190 | £ 191 |
| '30x | À 192 | Á 193 | Â 194 | Ã 195 | Ä 196 | Å 197 | Æ 198 | Ç 199 |
| '31x | È 200 | É 201 | Ê 202 | Ë 203 | Ì 204 | Í 205 | Î 206 | Ï 207 |
| '32x | Đ 208 | Ñ 209 | Ò 210 | Ó 211 | Ô 212 | Õ 213 | Ö 214 | Œ 215 |
| '33x | Ø 216 | Ù 217 | Ú 218 | Û 219 | Ü 220 | Ý 221 | Þ 222 | SS 223 |
| '34x | à 224 | á 225 | â 226 | ã 227 | ä 228 | å 229 | æ 230 | ç 231 |
| '35x | è 232 | é 233 | ê 234 | ë 235 | ì 236 | í 237 | î 238 | ï 239 |
| '36x | ð 240 | ñ 241 | ò 242 | ó 243 | ô 244 | õ 245 | ö 246 | œ 247 |
| '37x | ø 248 | ù 249 | ú 250 | û 251 | ü 252 | ý 253 | þ 254 | ß 255 |

**Font Layout 10:** The extended font `dcr10` with T1 coding.

presents the characters and their assignments for the font `dcr10`, the extended version of `cmr10`.

The designation `dc` was selected by Norbert Schwarz to emphasize that this is a preliminary realization of the future `ec` fonts. Some work still needs to be done to fine-tune the design of several symbols. Nevertheless, the choice of characters and their assignments correspond exactly to those of the Cork proposal so that Font Layout 10 may be considered an official model for the EC fonts.

The METAFONT source files are available for the following extended fonts:

| | | | | |
|---|---|---|---|---|
| dcr5 | dcti9 | dcfib10 | dcssi17 | dcdunh9 |
| dcr6 | dcti10 | dcfib12 | dcssbx9 | dcdunh10 |
| dcr7 | dcti12 | dcbxsl5 | dcssbx10 | dcdunh12 |
| dcr8 | dcti17 | dcbxsl6 | dcssbx12 | dcdunh17 |
| dcr9 | dcbx5 | dcbxsl7 | dcssbx17 | dctt8 |
| dcr10 | dcbx6 | dcbxsl8 | dcvtt8 | dctt9 |
| dcr12 | dcbx7 | dcbxsl9 | dcvtt9 | dctt10 |
| dcr17 | dcbx8 | dcbxsl10 | dcvtt10 | dctt12 |
| dccsc10 | dcbx9 | dcbxsl12 | dcvtt12 | dctcsc10 |
| dccsc12 | dcbx10 | dcbxti10 | dcu7 | dctcsc12 |
| dccsc17 | dcbx12 | dcbxti12 | dcu8 | dctcsc17 |
| dcsl5 | dcb5 | dcbxti17 | dcu9 | dcsltt8 |
| dcsl6 | dcb6 | dcss8 | dcu10 | dcsltt9 |
| dcsl7 | dcb7 | dcss9 | dcu12 | dcsltt10 |
| dcsl8 | dcb8 | dcss10 | dcu17 | dcsltt12 |
| dcsl9 | dcb9 | dcss12 | dcff10 | dcitt8 |
| dcsl10 | dcb10 | dcss17 | dcfi10 | dcitt9 |
| dcsl12 | dcb12 | dcssi8 | dcdunh5 | dcitt10 |
| dcsl17 | dcb17 | dcssi9 | dcdunh6 | dcitt12 |
| dcti7 | dcfib8 | dcssi10 | dcdunh7 | dcitt17 |
| dcti8 | dcfib9 | dcssi12 | dcdunh8 | |

Comparing these with the root names of the CM fonts from page 412 and their printed contents in Sections E.3 and E.3.3, one may easily recognize the correspondence. One also sees that the DC fonts exist in many more design sizes than the CM fonts. All the CM text fonts have an equivalent in the DC scheme, except for `cmssq8`, `cmssqi8`, and `cmssdc10`. An extension of the mathematical CM fonts (Section E.5) is not planned.

In contrast to the CM fonts which exhibit various differences in the symbol assignments among them, as illustrated in Layouts 1–4 in Section E.6, the DC fonts *all* have an identical set of symbols with a unique assignment pattern, as presented in Layout 10.

The METAFONT source files for the DC fonts may be obtained from the sources mentioned in Section D.5. Norbert Schwarz has also provided three information files named `doc.tex`, `help.eng`, and `help.ger`, the last two giving advice for running METAFONT in English and German. They explain how the fonts for any desired design size may be generated.

The file doc.tex is a TEX document file that presents the DC character assignments and lists all the languages that are supported; it furthermore indicates which diacritic characters exist as single characters and which may be constructed and to which language(s) they belong (at the time of writing, this is only available in German under the name dok.tex).

## 10.4 Invoking the DC fonts

The DC fonts correspond to the NFSS encoding scheme T1 (Section 8.5.1). The simplest way to activate them in LATEX 2ε is to place

```
\usepackage[T1]{fontenc}
```

in the preamble of the document. All this really does is to make T1 the standard encoding by redefining \encodingdefault to be T1, and it loads the file T1enc.def which redefines the accent and special letter commands by means of the encoding commands of Section 8.5.9. (Since the contents of this file are normally included in the LATEX 2ε format, it is not read in again.)

In future, the DC fonts with their T1 encoding will become the standard, fully replacing the older CM fonts with their variable OT1 coding schemes.

## 10.5 Special character commands

Inspecting Font Layout 10, one notices that the DC fonts contain not only many single characters that are formed out of two CM symbols (like Ä = A + ¨) but also several characters that have no correspondence in the CM font layout at all. The first type is accommodated by internally redefining the action of accent and special character commands. The second set requires new commands that are recognized only when the T1 encoding is active. These are

the ogonek accent \k{o}: ǫ

special letters   \DH = Đ   \DJ = Đ   \NG = Ŋ   \TH = Þ
                      \dh = ð   \dj = đ   \ng = ŋ   \th = þ

special symbols   \guillemotleft = «   \guillemotright = »
                      \guilsinglleft = ‹   \guilsinglright = ›
                      \quotedblbase = „   \quotesinglbase = ‚
                      \textquotedbl = "

When issued in OT1 encoding, these commands print an error message.

**Note:** all of these commands were added in the LATEX 2ε version from December 1, 1994. Any file that makes use of them should therefore contain \NeedsTeXFormat{LaTeX2e}[1994/12/01].

# Command Summary

This appendix contains a brief description of all the LATEX commands, in alphabetical (ASCII) order, neglecting the leading backslash \, along with some TEX commands that have been explained in this book. In the following section, the commands are presented in their logical grouping in a number of tables and figures. At the end, those TEX commands that may not be used during LATEX processing are listed.

## 1    Brief description of the LATEX commands

For each command in the following summary, the section and page number is given where it is introduced and described in detail. The numbers are shown in the form: '(*Section*) – *Page*': for example (2.5.1) – 13 means 'Subsection 2.5.1, page 13'. If these numbers are missing, then the command has not been presented in the book but is only mentioned here.

The following notations may be added to the commands:

[m]  those permitted in math mode only;

[p]  those allowed only in the preamble;

[i]  commands for International LATEX, which has become the standard with the release from December 1, 1991.

Any commands that were added after the first official release of LATEX $2_\varepsilon$ in June 1994 have the date of their first appearance indicated, as for example *(1994/12/01)*. Files containing them should include this or a later date as an optional argument to \NeedsTeXFormat{LaTeX2e}[1994/12/01].

\␣ . . . . . . . . . . . . . . . . . . . . . . . . . (2.1), (3.5.1) – 16, 45

Normal space between words after a command without arguments or after a period that is not the end of a sentence.

! . . . . . . . . . . . . . . . . . . . . . . . . . . (8.4) – 221

> Field separation character within the \index command. For example:
> with \index{command!fragile} one produces an index sub-entry
> 'fragile' under the main entry 'command'.

! ` produces ¡ . . . . . . . . . . . . . . . . . . . . . . (2.5.6) – 21
\! [m] . . . . . . . . . . . . . . . . . . . . . . . (5.5.1) – 140

> In math mode, a negative space of $-1/6$ quad: xx\!x $= xxx$.

" . . . . . . . . . . . . . . . . (2.5.2), (8.4), (B.2) – 20, 222, 311

> 1. In normal text, this produces the double closing quote ".
>
> 2. Literal sign for MakeIndex, in order to print one of the special
>    characters !, @, |, or ". Example: \index{"!} to enter character
>    ! without it being interpreted as a separation character.
>
> 3. Delimiter for a text field in BibTEX. Example:
>    AUTHOR = "Donald E. Knuth".

\" . . . . . . . . . . . . . . . . . . . . . . . . . (2.5.7) – 21

> Produces an umlaut accent: \"{a} = ä.

# . . . . . . . . . . . . . . . . . . . (7.3.2), (7.4.2) – 188, 198

> Argument replacement character in a user-defined command or envi-
> ronment.

## . . . . . . . . . . . . . . . . . . . . . . . . (7.5.7) – 204

> Replacement character for an *internal* argument within a *nested* user-
> defined command or environment.

\# . . . . . . . . . . . . . . . . . . . . . . . . . (2.5.4) – 21

> Command to produce a hash symbol:   \# = #.

$ . . . . . . . . . . . . . . . . . . . . . . . . . . (5.1) – 115

> Toggle character for switching between text and in-line math modes.
> On the first appearance (text to math) it behaves the same as \(
> or \begin{math}, while the second call (math to text) is as \) or
> \end{math}.

\$ . . . . . . . . . . . . . . . . . . . . . . . . . (2.5.4) – 21

> Command to produce a dollar sign:   \$ = $.

% . . . . . . . . . . . . . . . . . . . . . . . . . (4.11) – 113

> Comment character. The rest of the line of text following % is ignored
> by the TEX processing.

\% . . . . . . . . . . . . . . . . . . . . . . . . . (2.5.4) – 21

> Command to produce a per cent sign:   \% = %.

& . . . . . . . . . . . . . . . . . . . . . . . . . . . . (4.8.1) – 95

Indicates a new column in `array` and `tabular` environments.

\& . . . . . . . . . . . . . . . . . . . . . . . . . . . (2.5.4) – 21

Command to produce an ampersand symbol: `\& = &`.

\' . . . . . . . . . . . . . . . . . . . . . . (2.5.7), (4.6.4) – 21,82

1. Command to produce an acute accent: `\'a = á`.

2. Within the `tabbing` environment, a command to jump to the end of the current column.

( ) . . . . . . . . . . . . . . . . . . . . . (6.2), (B.2) – 150, 312

For a picture command in `picture` environment, specifies a coordinate pair. In BIBTEX, an alternative form for the outermost grouping of the entry type.

\( . . . . . . . . . . . . . . . . . . . . . . . . . . . (5.1) – 115

Switches from text to in-line math mode to produce formulas within a line of text. It functions the same as `\begin{math}` and as a $ sign in text mode.

\) . . . . . . . . . . . . . . . . . . . . . . . . . . . (5.1) – 115

Switches back from in-line math mode to text mode. It functions the same as `\end{math}` and as a $ sign in math mode.

\+ . . . . . . . . . . . . . . . . . . . . . . . . . . . (4.6.3) – 81

Within the `tabbing` environment, increments the left margin by one tab stop (moves it to the right).

\, . . . . . . . . . . . . . . . . . . . . (3.5.1), (5.5.1) – 45, 140

Small space, the size of 1/6 quad, for use in text and math mode: `xx\,x = xx x`.

- . . . . . . . . . . . . . . . . . . . . . . . . . . . . (2.5.3) – 20

As -, produces the hyphen - for compound words and word division, as --, the en dash –, and as ---, the em dash —.

\- . . . . . . . . . . . . . . . . . . . . (3.6.1), (4.6.3) – 53, 81

1. Denotes possible word division. If a word contains at least one `\-` the normal word division rules are suspended for that word and division may occur *only* at those locations.

2. Within the `tabbing` environment, decrements the left margin by one tap stop (moves it to the left).

\. . . . . . . . . . . . . . . . . . . . . . . . . . . . (2.5.7) – 21

Command to produce a dot accent: `\.o = ȯ`.

**\/** . . . . . . . . . . . . . . . . . . . . . . (3.5.1), (3.5.1) – 45, 46

Italic correction, the extra space at the end of slanted fonts, or the command to break up ligatures.

**\:** [m] . . . . . . . . . . . . . . . . . . . . . . . . . (5.5.1) – 140

In math mode, a medium space, the size of 2/9 quad:   $xx\backslash:x = xx\,x$.

**\;** [m] . . . . . . . . . . . . . . . . . . . . . . . . . (5.5.1) – 140

In math mode, a large space, the size of 5/18 quad:   $xx\backslash;x = xx\,x$.

**\<** . . . . . . . . . . . . . . . . . . . . . . . . . . (4.6.3) – 81

Within the `tabbing` environment, moves to the left by one tab stop.

**\=** . . . . . . . . . . . . . . . . . . . . . (2.5.7), (4.6.1) – 21, 80

1. Command to produce a macron accent: **\=o** = ō.
2. Within the `tabbing` environment, sets a tab stop at the current position within the line.

**\>** . . . . . . . . . . . . . . . . . . . . . . . . . . (4.6.1) – 80

Within the `tabbing` environment, moves right to the next tab stop.

**?'**   produces ¿ . . . . . . . . . . . . . . . . . . . . (2.5.6) – 21

**@** . . . . . . . . . . . . . . . . . . . . . . . (8.4), (B.2) – 222, 311

1. In MakeIndex, separates an entry in an `\index` command into a lexical (for alphabetization) and printing part.   Example: `\index{sum@$\sum$}` means that the entry appears in the index at the location of the word 'sum' but what is printed is the summation sign $\sum$.
2. In BibTeX, denotes the *entry type*. Example: `@BOOK` indicates that the following literature entries correspond to those of a book.

**\@** . . . . . . . . . . . . . . . . . . . . . . . . . . (3.5.1) – 45

Extra space at the end of a sentence ending with a capital letter.

**[ ]** . . . . . . . . . . . . . . . . . . . . . . . . . . (2.1) – 15

After commands or environment calls, specifies an optional argument.

**\[** . . . . . . . . . . . . . . . . . . . . . . . . . . (5.1) – 116

Switches from text mode to displayed math mode for putting a formula on a line by itself.   Has the same effect as `\begin{displaymath}`.

**\\** [*space*] . . . . . . . . . . . . . . . . . . . . . . (3.5.2) – 48

Ends the current line (without right justifying it). The optional argument [*len*] inserts additional vertical spacing of length *len* before the next line.

The same as `\\` but prevents a page break from occurring between the current and next line.

Switches back from displayed math mode to text mode. Has the same effect as `\end{displaymath}`.

Exponents and superscripts in equations: `x^2` $= x^2$, `x^{-2n}` $= x^{-2n}$.

Command to produce a circumflex accent: `\^o` = ô.

Subscripts in equations: `a_n` $= a_n$, `a_{i,j,k}` $= a_{i,j,k}$.

Command to produce the underbar sign: `t\_v` = t‿v.

1. Command to produce a grave accent: `\'o` = ò.

2. Within the `tabbing` environment, pushes the following text up against the right margin of the line.

1. After a command or environment call, specifies a mandatory argument.

2. Grouping a section of text to create a nameless environment.

3. In BIBTEX, delimiting the name of an entry type, as well as an alternative delimiter for the text field.

Command to produce a left curly brace: `\{` = {.

In MakeIndex, the command character within a `\index` command.

1. After the command `\newcommand{\ii}[1]{\textit{#1}}` has been defined, `\index{entry|ii}` produces the page number for 'entry' in the index in italic type.

2. The cross-reference command `\see` from `makeidx.sty` can be invoked with `\index{bison|see{buffalo}}` to produce cross-references within the index.

\| [m] produces ‖ . . . . . . . . . . . . . . . . . . . . . (5.3.6) – 123
\} . . . . . . . . . . . . . . . . . . . . . . . . . . . . (2.5.4) – 21

> Command to produce a right curly brace: \} = }.

~ . . . . . . . . . . . . . . . . . . . . . . . . . . . . (3.5.1) – 45

> A normal space between words, but without the possibility that the
> line will be broken there. Example: Prof.~Jones ensures that 'Prof.'
> and 'Jones' both remain on the same line.

\~ . . . . . . . . . . . . . . . . . . . . . . . . . . . (2.5.7) – 21

> Command to produce a tilde accent: \~n = ñ.

\a= . . . . . . . . . . . . . . . . . . . . . . . . . . . (4.6.4) – 82

> Produces a macron accent within tabbing environment: \a=o = ō.

\a' . . . . . . . . . . . . . . . . . . . . . . . . . . . (4.6.4) – 82

> Produces an acute accent within tabbing environment: \a'o = ó.

\a' . . . . . . . . . . . . . . . . . . . . . . . . . . . (4.6.4) – 82

> Produces a grave accent within tabbing environment: \a'o = ò.

\AA   produces Å . . . . . . . . . . . . . . . . . . . . (2.5.6) – 21
\aa   produces å . . . . . . . . . . . . . . . . . . . . (2.5.6) – 21
\abovedisplayskip [m] . . . . . . . . . . . . . . . . (5.5.4) – 145

> Vertical space between a *long* displayed equation and the preceding
> line of text. A new value may be assigned with the \setlength
> command:
>
> ```
> \setlength{\abovedisplayskip}{10pt plus2pt minus5pt}
> ```

\abovedisplayshortskip [m] . . . . . . . . . . . . . (5.5.4) – 145

> Vertical space between a *short* displayed equation and the preceding
> line of text. A new value may be assigned with the \setlength
> command as in the above example.

\abstractname [i] . . . . . . . . . . . . . . . . . . . (C.3.3) – 349

> Command for International LaTeX containing the heading for the ab-
> stract. In English, this is 'Abstract' but may be altered for adaptation
> to other languages.

\acute{x} [m] . . . . . . . . . . . . . . . . . . . . . (5.3.9) – 125

> Acute accent over math variable x: \acute{a} = á

\addcontentsline{*file*}{*format*}{*entry*} . . . (3.4.3), (3.4.4) – 43, 44

> Manual addition of *entry* into the list file .toc, .lof, or .lot, according
> to the value of *file*, to be formatted as the heading of a sectioning
> command, as given by *format*, for example
>
> ```
> \addcontentsline{toc}{section}{References}
> ```

`\address{`*sender*`}` . . . . . . . . . . . . . . . . . (A.1) – 296

In the `letter` document class, enters the sender's address. Multiple lines in *sender* are separated by `\\`.

2ε `\addtime{`*secs*`}` . . . . . . . . . . . . . . . . . (8.10.3) – 251

In the `slides` class, if the option `clock` has been selected, a time marker, in minutes, appears at the bottom of the notes. This command adds the specified number of seconds to the marker. See also `\settime`.

`\addtocontents{`*file*`}{`*entry*`}` . . . . . . . . . (3.4.3), (3.4.4) – 43, 44

Manual addition of *entry* into the list file `.toc`, `.lof`, or `.lot`, according to the value of *file*. Example:

```
\addtocontents{lof}{\protect\newpage}
```

`\addtocounter{`*counter*`}{`*number*`}` . . . . . . . . . . (7.1.3) – 182

Adds *number* to the current value of the number stored in *counter*.

`\addtolength{\`*length_name*`}{`*length*`}` . . . . . . . . . (7.2) – 184

Adds the quantity *length* to the current value of the length command `\`*length_name*.

`\addvspace{`*length*`}` . . . . . . . . . . . . . . . . (7.2) – 185

Inserts vertical spacing of amount *length* between paragraphs at the point where the command is given. If other vertical spacing exists, the total will not exceed *length*.

`\AE`  produces Æ . . . . . . . . . . . . . . . . . . (2.5.6) – 21
`\ae`  produces æ  . . . . . . . . . . . . . . . . . (2.5.6) – 21
`\aleph` [m] produces ℵ . . . . . . . . . . . . . . (5.3.6) – 123
`\Alph{`*counter*`}`  . . . . . . . . . . . . . . . . (7.1.4) – 183

Prints the current value of *counter* as a capital letter.

`\alph{`*counter*`}`  . . . . . . . . . . . . . . . . (7.1.4) – 183

Prints the current value of *counter* as a lower case letter.

`\alpha` [m] produces α . . . . . . . . . . . . . . . (5.3.1) – 121
`\alsoname` [i] . . . . . . . . . . . . . . . . . . . (C.3.3) – 350

Command for International LaTeX for use in modified `makeidx` package. It prints the text for a command `\seealso`. In English, this is 'see also' but may be altered for adaptation to other languages. (This command is not standardized!)

`\amalg` [m] produces ⊔⊔ . . . . . . . . . . . . . . . (5.3.3) – 122
`\and` . . . . . . . . . . . . . . . . . . . . . . . . (3.3.1) – 36

Used to separate author names within the `\author` command for generating a title page with `\maketitle`.

`\angle` [m] produces ∠ . . . . . . . . . . . . . . . . . (5.3.6) – 123

`\appendixname` [i] . . . . . . . . . . . . . . . . . . (C.3.3) – 349

> Command for International LATEX containing the heading for the appendix. In English, this is 'Appendix' but may be altered for adaptation to other languages.

`\approx` [m] produces ≈ . . . . . . . . . . . . . . . (5.3.4) – 122

`\arabic{`*counter*`}` . . . . . . . . . . . . . . . . (7.1.4) – 183

> Prints the current value of *counter* as an Arabic number.

`\arccos` [m] . . . . . . . . . . . . . . . . . . . . (5.3.8) – 124

> Command to produce the function name 'arccos' in equations.

`\arcsin` [m] . . . . . . . . . . . . . . . . . . . . (5.3.8) – 124

> Command to produce the function name 'arcsin' in equations.

`\arctan` [m] . . . . . . . . . . . . . . . . . . . . (5.3.8) – 124

> Command to produce the function name 'arctan' in equations.

`\arg` [m] . . . . . . . . . . . . . . . . . . . . . . (5.3.8) – 124

> Command to produce the function name 'arg' in equations.

`\arraycolsep` . . . . . . . . . . . . . . . . . . . . (4.8.2) – 96

> Half the width of the intercolumn spacing in the `array` environment. Value is assigned with the LATEX command `\setlength`:
>
> `\setlength{\arraycolsep}{3mm}`

`\arrayrulewidth` . . . . . . . . . . . . . . . . . (4.8.2) – 96

> The thickness of vertical and horizontal lines in the `array` and `tabular` environments. Its value is assigned to a length with `\setlength`:
>
> `\setlength{\arrayrulewidth}{0.5mm}`

`\arraystretch` . . . . . . . . . . . . . . . . . . . (4.8.2) – 96

> Factor to change the spacing between lines in a table, normal value being 1. Spacing is multiplied by this factor, which is set to a new value with `\renewcommand{\arraystretch}{`*factor*`}`.

`\ast` [m] produces ∗ . . . . . . . . . . . . . . . . . (5.3.3) – 122

`\asymp` [m] produces ≍ . . . . . . . . . . . . . . . (5.3.4) – 122

2ε `\AtBeginDocument{`*code*`}` [p] . . . . . . . . . . . . (C.2.4) – 333

> Stores the *code* to be inserted into the processing stream when `\begin{document}` is executed. Commands that are only allowed in the preamble may be part of *code*. A package might include coding in this way to ensure that it is not overwritten by another package.

Stores the *code* to be inserted into the processing stream when \end{document} is executed. A package might include coding in this way to have additional features printed automatically at the end of the document.

Stores the *code* to be inserted into the processing stream when the current class file has finished being read. May only be given in a class file, or in another file that is read by a class file. May be used by a local configuration file to overwrite defaults in the class file itself.

Stores the *code* to be inserted into the processing stream when the current package file has finished being read. May only be given in a package file, or in another file that is read by a package file. May be used by a local configuration file to overwrite defaults in the package file itself.

Enters the author name(s) for a title page produced by the \maketitle command.

Command to produce an underbar accent: \b{o} = ọ.

In the book class, introduces the material that comes at the end (bibliography, index) by turning off the chapter numbering of the \chapter command.

Macron accent over the math variable $x$: \bar{a} = $\bar{a}$.

Inter-line spacing within a paragraph. Every font has its own internal line spacing. A new value (a rubber length) may be assigned with \setlength:

```
\setlength{\baselineskip}{12pt plus2pt minus1pt}
```

A factor with the normal value of 1 by which the internal length \baselineskip is multiplied to produce the actual inter-line spacing. May be changed with:

```
\renewcommand{\baselinestretch}{factor}
```

The new value takes effect after the next change in font size!

\begin{*envrnmnt*} . . . . . . . . . . . . . . . . . . (2.2) – 17

Start of an environment with the name *envrnmnt*. This command must be coupled with \end{*envrnmnt*} to terminate the environment. The environment name in both these commands must be identical.

\begin{abstract} . . . . . . . . . . . . . . . . . . (3.3.2) – 39

Start of the environment abstract to produce an abstract. With document class article, font size \small and the quotation environment are selected. With report, the abstract appears on a separate page with normal font size and line width. In both cases, the heading **Abstract** is centered above the text.

\begin{appendix} . . . . . . . . . . . . . . . . . . (3.3.4) – 41

Start of the environment appendix to produce an appendix. The main section counter is reset to zero and its numbering appears as capital letters.

\begin{array}[*pos*]{*col*} [m] . . . . . . . (4.8.1), (5.4.3) – 93, 129

Start of the environment array to produce matrices and arrays in math mode. The column definition *col* contains a formatting character for each column. Thus \begin{array}{lcr} produces an array with three columns: one *left justified*, one *centered*, and one *right justified*. The optional parameter *pos* determines how the array is aligned vertically with text outside it on the same line: t with the top line, b with the bottom line, while the default is with the center. See also \begin{tabular}

\begin{center} . . . . . . . . . . . . . . . . . . (4.2.1) – 63

Start of the environment center. Each line of text terminated by \\ appears centered. See also \centering.

\begin{*command_name*} . . . . . . . . . . . . . . . . . . (2.2) – 17

Most declaration commands, such as the font styles and sizes, can be used as environment names. For example, \begin{small} switches to font size \small until the countercommand \end{small} is given.

\begin{description} . . . . . . . . . . . . . . . . . . (4.3.3) – 67

Start of the environment description to produce an indented list with labels. The label text is the argument *label* in the command \item[*label*].

\begin{displaymath} . . . . . . . . . . . . . . . . . . (5.1) – 116

Switches from text to displayed math mode for producing a formula on a line by itself. Functions the same as \[.

\begin{document} . . . . . . . . . . . . . . . . . . (1.5.2) – 12

Start of the outermost environment of a text document. This command terminates the preamble. It is obligatory for every LATEX document, as is its counterpart \end{document} for ending the document.

`\begin{enumerate}` . . . . . . . . . . . . . . . . . (4.3.2) – 66

Start of the environment `enumerate` to produce a numbered, indented listing. The style of numbering depends on the depth of nesting; at the first level, it consists of a running Arabic number that is incremented with each call to `\item`.

`\begin{eqnarray}` . . . . . . . . . . . . . . . . . (5.4.7) – 134

Switches from text to displayed math mode to produce a set of equations or a multi-line formula in the form of a three-column table `{rcl}`. The individual lines of the formula are ended with the command `\\`; the fields within a line are separated by `&` characters. Each line is given a sequential equation number unless the command `\nonumber` appears within it.

`\begin{eqnarray*}` . . . . . . . . . . . . . . . . . (5.4.7) – 134

Is the same as the `eqnarray` environment except that no equation numbers are printed.

`\begin{equation}` . . . . . . . . . . . . . . . . . . (5.1) – 116

Switches from text to displayed math mode to produce a formula on a line by itself including an automatic sequential equation number.

`\begin{figure}[`*loc*`]` . . . . . . . . . . . . . . (6.6.1) – 172

Float environment for entering text for a figure. The optional argument *loc* can be any combination of the letters `h`, `t`, `b`, and `p` to determine the various positioning possibilities. Default is `tbp`. Under LATEX $2_\varepsilon$, the character `!` may additionally be given to ignore all float spacing and number restrictions set by the float style parameters.

`\begin{figure*}[`*loc*`]` . . . . . . . . . . . . . . (6.6.1) – 172

The same as the `figure` environment except that the figure is inserted over the width of two columns when the option `twocolumn` or the command `\twocolumn` has been selected. The standard form `figure` will only fill the width of one column.

$2\varepsilon$ `\begin{filecontents}{`*file_name*`}` [p] . . . . . . . . (C.2.9) – 337

An environment that may be given only before `\documentclass`, it writes its lines literally to a file of the specified name, if that file does not already exist. It also adds comment lines stating its source. In this way, non-standard files may be included in the main document file for shipment to other installations. If a file with the stated name already exists, it is not overwritten, but a warning message is issued.

$2\varepsilon$ `\begin{filecontents*}{`*file_name*`}` [p] . . . . . . . (C.2.9) – 337

Is the same as the `filecontents` environment, except that no comment lines are written to the file. The file will contain exactly the contents of the environment, and nothing more.

\begin{flushleft} . . . . . . . . . . . . . . . . . (4.2.2) – 64

> Start of the flushleft environment in which each line of text is left-justified (flush with the left margin). Lines of text are ended with the command \\. See also \raggedright.

\begin{flushright} . . . . . . . . . . . . . . . . . . (4.2.2) – 64

> Start of the flushright environment in which each line of text is right-justified (flush with the right margin). Lines of text are ended with the command \\. See also \raggedleft.

\begin{fussypar} . . . . . . . . . . . . . . . . . . . (3.6.3) – 54

> In this environment the paragraphs are broken up into lines such that the spacing between words has limited stretchability. This is the standard. See also \fussy. The opposites are sloppypar and \sloppy.

\begin{itemize} . . . . . . . . . . . . . . . . . . . (4.3.1) – 66

> Start of the itemize environment for producing labeled, indented listings. The type of label depends on the depth of nesting; at the first level it is a • generated by each \item command.

\begin{letter}{*recipient*} . . . . . . . . . . . . . . . . . (A.1) – 296

> Start of a letter with the document class letter. Name and address of the *recipient* are given within the second pair of brackets; lines of text within this argument are ended with the command \\.

\begin{list}{*standard_label*}{*list_decl*} . . . . . . . . . (4.4) – 73

> Start of a generalized list environment. The label is defined by *standard_label*, which is generated by each \item command. The desired list declarations are contained in *list_decl* (see page 74).

2ε \begin{lrbox}{\\*boxname*} . . . . . . . . . . . . . . . (4.7.1) – 86

> Functions like the command \sbox. It stores the text of the environment in an LR box named \\*boxname* that has previously been created with \newsavebox{\\*boxname*}. The contents of the box may be printed as often as desired with \usebox{\\*boxname*}.

\begin{math} . . . . . . . . . . . . . . . . . . . . (5.1) – 115

> Switches from text to in-line math mode to produce formulas within a line of text. Has the same effect as \( or $ in text mode.

2.09 \begin{minipage}[*pos*]{*width*} . . . . . . . . . . . . (4.7.3) – 87

> Environment to format text within a 'minipage' of width *width*. Its vertical positioning with respect to the surrounding text is determined by the optional argument *pos*: t for alignment with its top line, b with its bottom line, and centered with no argument.

2ε `\begin{minipage}` [*pos*] [*height*] [*inner_pos*] {*width*}  . . . (4.7.5) – 89

In LATEX 2ε, this environment may have two additional optional arguments: *height* to give the total height, and *inner_pos* to specify how the text is to be positioned inside it. Possible values are t for top, b for bottom, c for centered, and s to be stretched out to fill the whole vertical space. The default is the value of the external positioning *pos* option. The *height* argument may contain the parameters \height, \depth, \width, and \totalheight.

`\begin{note}`  . . . . . . . . . . . . . . . . . . . . (8.10.2) – 250

In slides class, the environment for producing a note for the current slide.  For LATEX 2.09, this is in black and white only.  Notes are numbered with the current slide number followed by a hyphen and running number, for example 8-1, 8-2, etc.

2ε `\begin{overlay}`  . . . . . . . . . . . . . . . . . (8.10.2) – 250

In slides class, the environment for producing an overlay for the current slide. Overlays are numbered with the current slide number followed by a lower case letter, for example 3-a, 3-b, etc.  See also \begin{slide}.

2.09 `\begin{overlay}{`*colors*`}`  . . . . . . . . . . . . . . (8.10.2) – 250

In LATEX 2.09, the overlay environment has an argument specifying the color layers in which it is to be output. Otherwise, it functions as the LATEX 2ε overlay environment.

`\begin{picture}(`*x_dimen,y_dimen*`)`  . . . . . . . . . . . (6.2) – 150

Environment to generate a picture with the width *x_dimen* and height *y_dimen*, where the unit of length has previously been specified by the declaration \unitlength.

`\begin{picture}(`*x_dimen,y_dimen*`)(`*x_offset,y_offset*`)`  . . (6.5.4) – 167

Most general form of the call to the picture environment. The picture is displaced to the left by *x_offset* and downwards by *y_offset*.

`\begin{quotation}`  . . . . . . . . . . . . . . . . . . . (4.2.3) – 64

Start of the quotation environment in which text is indented on both sides relative to the normal page margins.  Paragraphs within the environment are marked with an additional indentation of the first line.

`\begin{quote}` . . . . . . . . . . . . . . . . . . . . . (4.2.3) – 64

The same as the quotation environment except that the first line of a paragraph is not indented but instead additional line spacing comes between paragraphs.

<u>2.09</u> \begin{samepage} . . . . . . . . . . . . . . . . . . . . . . (3.5.5) – 51

> Within this environment page breaks are forbidden within a paragraph or before or after displayed formulas. Since this has never functioned satisfactorily, its use is not encouraged anymore; it is retained only for downward compatibility.

<u>2ε</u> \begin{slide} . . . . . . . . . . . . . . . . . . . . (8.10.2) – 249

> In slides class, the main environment for producing a slide.

<u>2.09</u> \begin{slide}{*colors*} . . . . . . . . . . . . . . . . (8.10.2) – 249

> In LaTeX 2.09, the slide environment has an argument specifying the color layers in which it is to be output. The layers must have been previously specified by a \colors command. Each color may be used as a command, such as \blue, or as an environment \begin{blue} ... \end{blue}. The text of each color is output as a part of a separate color layer.

\begin{sloppypar} . . . . . . . . . . . . . . . . . . . . . . (3.6.3) – 54

> Inside this environment word spacings are allowed to stretch more generously than usual so that paragraphs are broken up into lines with fewer word divisions. See also \sloppy. Countercommands are fussypar and \fussy.

\begin{tabbing} . . . . . . . . . . . . . . . . . . . . . . . (4.6.1) – 80

> Start of the tabbing environment in which special tabbing commands become operational: \= sets a tab stop, \> jumps to the next stop, \< goes back a stop, \\ terminates and starts a new line, \+ sets the left margin one tab stop further, \- moves the left margin back one stop.

\begin{table}[*loc*] . . . . . . . . . . . . . (4.8.4), (6.6.1) – 105, 172

> Float environment for entering text for a table. The optional argument *loc* can be any combination of the letters h, t, b, and p to determine the various positioning possibilities. Default is tbp. Under LaTeX 2ε, the character ! may additionally be given to ignore all float spacing and number restrictions set by the float style parameters.

\begin{table*}[*loc*] . . . . . . . . . . . . . . . . . (6.6.1) – 172

> The same as the table environment except that the table is inserted over the width of two columns when the option twocolumn or the command \twocolumn has been selected. The standard form table will only fill the width of one column.

\begin{tabular}[*pos*]{*cols*} . . . . . . . . . . . . . (4.8.1) – 93

> Start of the tabular environment for producing tables. The argument *cols* contains a formatting character for each column in the table: c for centered text, l for left, r for right justification, or p{*wd*} for a column of width *wd* in which the text may extend over several lines.

When the entry @{*text*} appears between any two of the above column formatting characters, *text* is inserted in every row between those two columns. Where the character | appears, a vertical line is drawn in every row.

The optional argument *pos* specifies how the table is to be vertically aligned with the surrounding text: with no argument, it is centered, otherwise with t the top line, with b the bottom line is aligned with the external baseline.

The text entries of the individual columns are separated by & and the rows are terminated by \\.

\begin{tabular*}{*width*}[*pos*]{*cols*} . . . . . . . . . . (4.8.1) – 93

The same as \begin{tabular} except that the total width of the table is given by the argument *width*. This may only be achieved successfully if there is rubber spacing between the columns. This may be added with @{\extracolsep\fill} somewhere within the *cols* format definition.

\begin{thebibliography}{*sample_label*} . . (4.3.6), (8.3.2) – 71, 217

Environment to generate a list of literature references. The *sample_label* is the longest reference marker that will appear. Each entry in the bibliography starts with the command \bibitem which prints the marker for that entry; lines after the first are indented by an amount equal to the width of *sample_label*.

\begin{theindex} . . . . . . . . . . . . . . . . . . . (8.3.3) – 219

Environment to produce an index register in two-column format. Entries are made with the \item, \subitem, \subsubitem, or \indexspace commands.

\begin{*theorem_type*}[*extra_title*] . . . . . . . . . . . . (4.5) – 79

Environment to invoke a theorem-like structure that has previously been defined by the user with the \newtheorem command. The name of the environment, *theorem_type*, something like theorem or axiom, is the first argument of the \newtheorem command. The *extra_title* is text that added after the name and number of the structure in () parentheses.

\begin{titlepage} . . . . . . . . . . . . . . . . . . (3.3.1) – 36

Environment to produce a title page without a page number. The user has total control over the composition of this page.

\begin{trivlist} . . . . . . . . . . . . . . . . . . (4.4.5) – 78

Environment to generate a trivial list *without* a sample label and list declarations. The parameters \leftmargin, \labelwidth, and \itemsep are all set to 0 pt while \listparindent = \parindent and \parsep = \parskip.

`\begin{verbatim}` . . . . . . . . . . . . . . . . . . . (4.9) – 106

Environment to print out original text, that is, as from a typewriter. Blank lines, line breaking, and commands are all output literally without any interpretation or formatting.

`\begin{verbatim*}` . . . . . . . . . . . . . . . . . (4.9) – 106

The same as the `verbatim` environment except that blanks are printed as ␣ to make them visible.

`\begin{verse}` . . . . . . . . . . . . . . . . . . . (4.2.4) – 65

Environment for setting rhymes, poems, verses, etc. Stanzas are separated by blank lines, individual lines by the `\\` command.

`\belowdisplayskip` [m] . . . . . . . . . . . . . . . (5.5.4) – 145

Vertical spacing between a *long* displayed formula and the following text. A new value may be assigned with the `\setlength` command:

> `\setlength{\belowdisplayskip}{\abovedisplayskip}`

sets `\belowdisplayskip` to the same value as `\abovedisplayskip`. See further examples under `\abovedisplayskip`.

`\belowdisplayshortskip` [m] . . . . . . . . . . . . (5.5.4) – 145

Vertical spacing between a *short* displayed formula and the following text. Value is set with the `\setlength` command as in the above example.

`\beta` [m] produces $\beta$ . . . . . . . . . . . . . . . . (5.3.1) – 121

2.09 `\bezier{`*num*`}`$(x_1,y_1)(x_2,y_2)(x_3,y_3)$ . . . . . . . (6.4.9) – 161

This command can be given within the `picture` environment to draw a quadratic Bézier curve from point $(x_1, y_1)$ to $(x_3, y_3)$, using $(x_2, y_2)$ as the extra Bézier point. The curve is drawn as *num* + 1 dots. This is the same as `\qbezier` except that *num* is mandatory.

In LaTeX 2.09, the option `bezier` must be included in the `\documentstyle` line to enable this command.

2.09 `\bf` . . . . . . . . . . . . . . . . . . . . . . (4.1.5) – 62

Switches to the **Roman, upright, bold** typeface.

2ε `\bfdefault` . . . . . . . . . . . . . . . . . . . (8.5.3) – 229

This command defines the series attribute that is selected with the `\bfseries` command. It may be redefined with `\renewcommand`:

> `\renewcommand{\bfdefault}{b}`

2ε `\bfseries` . . . . . . . . . . . . . . . . (4.1.3), (8.5.2) – 60, 228

This declaration switches to a font in the current family and shape, but with the **bold** series attribute.

`\bibitem[`*label*`]{`*key*`}` *entry_text* . . . . . . (4.3.6), (8.3.2) – 71, 217

> Command to enter the text for a literature reference in the `thebibliography` environment. The reference word *key* is used in the main body of the text with the `\cite` command to refer to this entry. The `\cite` command is replaced either by the optional *label* text or by a standard label, such as a sequential number in square brackets.

`\bibliography{`*file*`}` . . . . . . . . . . . . (8.3.2), (B.1) – 218, 309

> For producing a bibliography with the aid of the BibTeX program; *file* is the root name of one or more files containing the literature databases to be searched.

`\bibliographystyle{`*style*`}` . . . . . . . . . . . . . . (B.1) – 310

> In conjunction with the BibTeX program, this command selects the style in which the bibliography entries are to be written. Choices for *style* are `plain`, `unsrt`, `alpha`, and `abbrv`, where the first is the default. Other non-standard styles may also exist.

`\bibname [i]` . . . . . . . . . . . . . . . . . . . . . (C.3.3) – 350

> Command for International LaTeX containing the heading for the bibliography in `book` and `report` document classes. In English, this is 'Bibliography' but may be altered for adaptation to other languages.

`\big`*br_symbol* `[m]` . . . . . . . . . . . . . . . . . (5.5.3) – 144

> A bracket symbol larger than normal, but smaller than `\Big`. Example: `\big(`.

`\Big`*br_symbol* `[m]` . . . . . . . . . . . . . . . . . (5.5.3) – 144

> A bracket symbol larger than `\big`, but smaller than `\bigg`. Example: `\Big[`.

`\bigcap [m] produces` $\bigcap$ . . . . . . . . . . . . . . . (5.3.7) – 124
`\bigcirc [m] produces` $\bigcirc$ . . . . . . . . . . . . . . (5.3.3) – 122
`\bigcup [m] produces` $\bigcup$ . . . . . . . . . . . . . . . (5.3.7) – 124
`\bigg`*br_symbol* `[m]` . . . . . . . . . . . . . . . . . (5.5.3) – 144

> A bracket symbol larger than `\Big`, but smaller than `\Bigg`. Example: `\bigg|`.

`\Bigg`*br_symbol* `[m]` . . . . . . . . . . . . . . . . . (5.5.3) – 144

> The largest bracket symbol. Example: `\Bigg\langle`.

`\biggl`*br_symbol* `[m]` . . . . . . . . . . . . . . . . . (5.5.3) – 144

> The same as `\bigg` but is also a logical left (opening) bracket.

`\Biggl`*br_symbol* `[m]` . . . . . . . . . . . . . . . . . (5.5.3) – 144

> The same as `\Bigg` but is also a logical left (opening) bracket.

\biggm*br_symbol* [m]  . . . . . . . . . . . . . . . . . (5.5.3) – 144
> The same as \bigg but with larger horizontal spacings on either side (relation operator).

\Biggm*br_symbol* [m]  . . . . . . . . . . . . . . . . . (5.5.3) – 144
> The same as \Bigg but with larger horizontal spacings on either side (relation operator).

\biggr*br_symbol* [m]  . . . . . . . . . . . . . . . . . (5.5.3) – 144
> The same as \bigg but is also a logical right (closing) bracket.

\Biggr*br_symbol* [m]  . . . . . . . . . . . . . . . . . (5.5.3) – 144
> The same as \Bigg but is also a logical right (closing) bracket.

\bigl*br_symbol* [m]  . . . . . . . . . . . . . . . . . (5.5.3) – 144
> The same as \big but is also a logical left (opening) bracket.

\Bigl*br_symbol* [m]  . . . . . . . . . . . . . . . . . (5.5.3) – 144
> The same as \Big but is also a logical left (opening) bracket.

\bigm*br_symbol* [m]  . . . . . . . . . . . . . . . . . (5.5.3) – 144
> The same as \big but with larger horizontal spacings on either side (relation operator).

\Bigm*br_symbol* [m]  . . . . . . . . . . . . . . . . . (5.5.3) – 144
> The same as \Big but with larger horizontal spacings on either side (relation operator).

\bigodot [m] produces $\odot$  . . . . . . . . . . . . . . . . (5.3.7) – 124
\bigoplus [m] produces $\oplus$ . . . . . . . . . . . . . . (5.3.7) – 124
\bigotimes [m] produces $\otimes$ . . . . . . . . . . . . . (5.3.7) – 124
\bigr*br_symbol* [m]  . . . . . . . . . . . . . . . . . (5.5.3) – 144
> The same as \big but is also a logical right (closing) bracket.

\Bigr*br_symbol* [m]  . . . . . . . . . . . . . . . . . (5.5.3) – 144
> The same as \Big but is also a logical right (closing) bracket.

\bigtriangledown [m] produces $\triangledown$ . . . . . . . . . . . (5.3.3) – 122
\bigtriangleup [m] produces $\triangle$ . . . . . . . . . . . . (5.3.3) – 122
\bigskip . . . . . . . . . . . . . . . . . . . . . . . . (3.5.3) – 49
> Inserts large vertical spacing of the amount \bigskipamount. See also \medskip and \smallskip.

\bigskipamount
> Standard value for the amount of vertical spacing that is inserted with the command \bigskip. May be changed with the \setlength command:
>
> ```
> \setlength{\bigskipamount}{5ex plus1.5ex minus2ex}
> ```

`\bigsqcup` [m] produces $\bigsqcup$ . . . . . . . . . . . . . . . (5.3.7) – 124
`\biguplus` [m] produces $\biguplus$ . . . . . . . . . . . . . . . (5.3.7) – 124
`\bigvee` [m] produces $\bigvee$ . . . . . . . . . . . . . . . . (5.3.7) – 124
`\bigwedge` [m] produces $\bigwedge$ . . . . . . . . . . . . . . . (5.3.7) – 124
`\bmod` [m] . . . . . . . . . . . . . . . . . . . . (5.3.8) – 125

> Command to produce the function name 'mod' in the form
> > `a\bmod b` = $a \bmod b$

`\boldmath` . . . . . . . . . . . . . . . . . . . . (5.4.9) – 139

> Switches to bold face for math mode. This command must be given
> in text mode, however, before going into math mode. To set only part
> of a formula in bold face, use `\mbox{\boldmath$...$}` to return
> temporarily to text mode.

`\bot` [m] produces $\bot$ . . . . . . . . . . . . . . . . . (5.3.6) – 123
$\boxed{2\varepsilon}$ `\botfigrule` . . . . . . . . . . . . . . . . . . (6.6.3) – 175

> A command that is executed before a float at the bottom of a page. It
> is normally defined to do nothing, but may be redefined to add a rule
> between the float and the main text. It must not add any net vertical
> spacing.
> > `\renewcommand{\botfigrule}{\vspace*{-.4pt}`
> > `\rule{\columnwidth}{.4pt}}`

`\bottomfraction` . . . . . . . . . . . . . . . . . . (6.6.3) – 174

> Maximum fraction of a page that may be taken up by floats at the
> bottom. May be set to a new value with:
> > `\renewcommand{\bottomfraction}{`*decimal_frac*`}`.

`bottomnumber` . . . . . . . . . . . . . . . . . . . . (6.6.3) – 174

> Maximum number of floats that may appear at the bottom of a page.
> Set to a new number with `\setcounter{bottomnumber}{`*num*`}`.

`\bowtie` [m] produces $\bowtie$ . . . . . . . . . . . . . . . (5.3.4) – 122
`\Box` [m] produces $\Box$ . . . . . . . . . . . . . . . . (5.3.3) – 122
`\breve{`*x*`}` [m] . . . . . . . . . . . . . . . . . . . (5.3.9) – 125

> Breve accent over the math variable *x*: `\breve{a}` = $\breve{a}$.

`\bullet` [m] produces $\bullet$ . . . . . . . . . . . . . . . (5.3.3) – 122

`\c{`*x*`}` . . . . . . . . . . . . . . . . . . . . . (2.5.7) – 21

> Produces a cedilla under *x*: `\c{C}` = Ç.

$\boxed{2.09}$ `\cal` [m] . . . . . . . . . . . . . . . . . . . (5.3.2) – 121

> A declaration in LaTeX 2.09 to select *calligraphic* letters in math mode.
> It has been replaced by the command `\mathcal` in LaTeX $2_\varepsilon$.

`\cap [m]` produces ∩ . . . . . . . . . . . . . . . . . . (5.3.3) – 122

`\caption[`*short_form*`]{`*caption_text*`}` . . . . . . . . . . (6.6.4) – 176

Produces a numbered title or caption with the text *caption_text* within the float environments `figure` or `table`. The *short_form* is the abbreviated text appearing in the list of figures or tables, which is the same as the *caption_text* if it is omitted.

`\captions`*language* . . . . . . . . . . . . . (C.3.3), (D.1.3) – 349, 367

A command used in several language adaptations to redefine the headings of special sections such as 'Chapter' and 'Contents'. It occurs in packages `esperant` and `german` as well as in the `babel` system. This command is normally part of the definition of the `\selectlanguage` command.

`\cc{`*list*`}` . . . . . . . . . . . . . . . . . . . . . . (A.1) – 297

Command within document class `letter` to generate 'cc:', copies, followed by a list of names *list* at the end of the letter.

`\ccname [i]` . . . . . . . . . . . . . . . . . . . . . (C.3.3) – 350

Command in the `letter` document class for International LaTeX containing the word to be printed by the `\cc` command. In English, this is 'cc' but may be altered for adaptation to other languages.

`\cdot [m]` produces · . . . . . . . . . . . . . . . . . . (5.3.3) – 122

`\cdots [m]` produces · · · . . . . . . . . . . . . . . . . (5.2.6) – 119

`\centering` . . . . . . . . . . . . . . . . . . . . . (4.2.1) – 63

Declaration to switch to centered lines of text, each input line being terminated by `\\`. See also `\begin{center}`.

`\centerline{`*text*`}` . . . . . . . . . . . . . . . . . . (4.2.1) – 63

An additional TeX command that sets *text* centered on a horizontal line by itself.

`\chapter[`*short title*`]{`*title*`}` . . . . . . . . . . . . . . . (3.3.3) – 39

Starts a new chapter on a new page, with an automatic sequential chapter number and *title* as header. If the optional *short title* is given, it appears in place of *title* in the table of contents and in the running head at the top of the pages.

`\chapter*{`*title*`}` . . . . . . . . . . . . . . . . . . (3.3.3) – 39

Starts a new chapter on a new page, with *title* as header, but without a chapter number. The entry does not appear in the table of contents.

`\chaptername [i]` . . . . . . . . . . . . . . . . . . . (C.3.3) – 349

Command for International LaTeX containing the chapter heading. In English, this is 'Chapter' but may be altered for adaptation to other languages.

\check{*x*} [m] . . . . . . . . . . . . . . . . . . . . (5.3.9) – 125

Háček accent over the math variable *x*: \check{a} = ǎ.

[2ε] \CheckCommand{\*com_name*}[*narg*][*opt*]{*def*} . . . . . (C.2.5) – 334

Tests that the current definition of \*com_name* is as expected. If not, an error message is issued. This is used to ensure that important commands have not been altered by other packages.

[2ε] \CheckCommand*{\*com_name*}[*narg*][*opt*]{*def*} . . . . (C.2.6) – 334

*(1994/12/01)*

\chi [m] produces χ . . . . . . . . . . . . . . . . . . . (5.3.1) – 121
\circ [m] produces ∘ . . . . . . . . . . . . . . . . . . . (5.3.3) – 122
\circle{*diameter*} . . . . . . . . . . . . . . . . . . . . (6.4.5) – 157

Picture element command to produce a circle with diameter *diameter* in the picture environment. To be used as an argument in a \put or \multiput command.

\circle*{*diameter*} . . . . . . . . . . . . . . . . . . . (6.4.5) – 157

Like \circle but produces a solid circle, filled in black.

\cite[*note*]{*key*} . . . . . . . . . (4.3.6), (8.3.2), (B.1) – 71, 217, 310

Literature citation using the keyword *key* to produce a reference label in the text. The optional *note* text is included with the label.

[2ε] \ClassError{*class_name*}{*error_text*}{*help*} [p] . . . . . (C.2.7) – 335

Writes an error message *error_text* to the monitor and transcript file, labeled with the class name, and halts processing, waiting for a user response as for a LaTeX error. If H⟨*return*⟩ is typed, the *help* text is printed. Both *error_text* and *help* may contain \MessageBreak for a new line, \space for a forced space, and \protect before commands that are to have their names printed literally and not interpreted.

[2ε] \ClassInfo{*class_name*}{*info_text*} [p] . . . . . . . . . (C.2.7) – 336

Is like \ClassWarningNoLine except that the text *info_text* is only written to the transcript file, and not to the monitor.

[2ε] \ClassWarning{*class_name*}{*warning_text*} [p] . . . . . (C.2.7) – 335

Writes *warning_text* to the monitor and transcript file, labeled with the class name and the current line number of the input file. Processing continues. The *warning_text* is formatted in the same way as that for \ClassError.

[2ε] \ClassWarningNoLine{*class_name*}{*warning_text*} [p] . (C.2.7) – 335

Is like \ClassWarning except that the current line number of the input file is not printed.

`\cleardoublepage` . . . . . . . . . . . . . . . . . . (3.5.5) – 51

Ends the current page and outputs all unprocessed floats on to one or more float pages. The next page will be a *right-hand* one, with an odd page number.

`\clearpage` . . . . . . . . . . . . . . . . . . . . (3.5.5) – 51

Ends the current page and outputs all unprocessed floats on to one or more float pages.

`\cline{`*n – m*`}` . . . . . . . . . . . . . . . . . . (4.8.1) – 95

In `tabular` environment, produces a horizontal rule from the beginning of column *n* to the end of column *m*. Example: `\cline{2-5}`.

`\closing{`*regards*`}` . . . . . . . . . . . . . . . . (A.1) – 297

End of the text in the `letter` environment; *regards* stands for the desired terminating text.

`\clubsuit` [m] produces ♣ . . . . . . . . . . . . . . (5.3.6) – 123

[2ε] `\color` *col_spec* . . . . . . . . . . . . . . . . . . (D.3.3) – 383

A command made available with the `color` package. It is a declaration that switches the color in which the text is printed to that specified. It remains in effect until the end of the current environment or until countermanded by another `\color` command. The *col_spec* is either the name of a color defined (or predefined) by `\definecolor` or of the form [*model*]{*specs*}, where the arguments have the same meaning as they do for `\definecolor`. Examples:

    \color[rgb]{0.5,0.5,0}    \color{magenta}

[2ε] `\colorbox` *col_spec*`{`*text*`}` . . . . . . . . . . . . . . (D.3.3) – 383

A command made available with the `color` package. The *text* is set in an LR box with the specified color as the background color. The *col_spec* is the same as for `\color`.

`\columnsep` . . . . . . . . . . . . . . . . . . . . (3.1.1) – 28

Declaration for the amount of inter-column spacing in two-column page formatting. May be changed with the `\setlength` command:

    \setlength{\columnsep}{1pt}

`\columnseprule` . . . . . . . . . . . . . . . . . . (3.1.1) – 28

Declaration for the thickness of the vertical rule separating the columns in two-column page formatting. Value is set with the `\setlength` command:

    \setlength{\columnseprule}{1pt}

Command that appears in the .toc file for every entry in the table of contents, which is read when the `\tableofcontents` command is given. Such commands may be altered or added to the .toc file by means of the text editor. The entry *sec_type* stands for the sectioning level, such as `section`, while *sec_num* is its number (for example, 2.3) and *page* is the page number where the entry appears.

Command for International LaTeX containing the heading for the table of contents. In English, this is 'Contents' but may be altered for adaptation to other languages.

Command to produce the function name 'cos' in formulas.

Command to produce the function name 'cosh' in formulas.

Command to produce the function name 'cot' in formulas.

Command to produce the function name 'coth' in formulas.

Command to produce the function name 'csc' in formulas.

A command that may only be used in the definition of options, especially for default options. It contains the name of the option being processed.

Produces a 'dot under' accent: `\d{o}` = ọ.

Picture element command to produce a dashed frame with width *x_dimen* and height *y_dimen*, using a dash length of *dash* in the `picture` environment. Without the optional *pos*, the contents *text* are centered within the frame, otherwise they are positioned at the left (l), right (r), top (t), or bottom (b), or a combination thereof, such as lt. This command is used as an argument in a `\put` or `\multiput` command.

`\dashv` [m] produces ⊣ . . . . . . . . . . . . . . . . (5.3.6) – 123
`\date{`*date_text*`}` . . . . . . . . . . . . . (3.3.1), (A.1) – 36, 297

1. The command `\maketitle` normally prints the current date on the title page. The declaration `\date` will replace the date with whatever text is given in *date_text*.

2. Prints the text *date_text* instead of the automatic current date in a letter.

`\date`*language* . . . . . . . . . . . . . . (C.3.3), (D.1.3) – 351, 367

A command used in several language adaptations to redefine the `\today` command according to the requirements of *language*. It occurs in packages `esperanto` and `german` as well as in the `babel` system. It may also be used for 'dialects', such a `\dateUSenglish` and `\dateenglish`. This command is normally part of the definition of the `\selectlanguage` command.

⌷2ε⌷ `\dblfigrule` . . . . . . . . . . . . . . . . . . (6.6.3) – 175

A command that is executed after a two-column float at the top of a page. It is normally defined to do nothing, but may be redefined to add a rule between the float and the main text. It must not add any net vertical spacing.

```
\renewcommand{\dblfigrule}{\vspace*{-.4pt}
    \rule{\textwidth}{.4pt}}
```

`\dblfloatpagefraction` . . . . . . . . . . . . . . (6.6.3) – 175

For two-column page formatting, the fraction of a float page that must be filled with floats before a new page is called. New value is assigned with

```
\renewcommand{\dblfloatpagefraction}{decimal_frac}
```

`\dblfloatsep` . . . . . . . . . . . . . . . . . . (6.6.3) – 175

For two-column page formatting, the vertical spacing between floats that extend over both columns. A new value is set with the `\setlength` command:

```
\setlength{\dblfloatsep}{12pt plus 2pt minus 4pt}
```

`\dbltextfloatsep` . . . . . . . . . . . . . . . . . (6.6.3) – 175

For two-column page formatting, the vertical spacing between floats extending over both columns at the top of the page and the following text. A new value is set with the `\setlength` command.

`\dbltopfraction` . . . . . . . . . . . . . . . . . (6.6.3) – 175

For two-column page formatting, the maximum fraction of a page that may be occupied at the top by floats extending over both columns. A new value is assigned with

```
\renewcommand{\dbltopfraction}{decimal_frac}.
```

dbltopnumber . . . . . . . . . . . . . . . . . . . . (6.6.3) – 174

For two-column page formatting, the maximum number of floats that may appear at the top of a page extending over both columns. A new value is assigned with

\setcounter{dbltopnumber}{*num*}.

\ddag produces ‡ . . . . . . . . . . . . . . . . . . (2.5.5) – 21
\ddagger [m] produces ‡ . . . . . . . . . . . . . . . (5.3.3) – 122
\ddot{*x*} [m] . . . . . . . . . . . . . . . . . . . (5.3.9) – 125

A double dot accent in mathematical formulas:  \ddot{a} = *ä*.

\ddots [m] produces ⋰ . . . . . . . . . . . . . . . (5.2.6) – 119

[2ε] \DeclareErrorFont{*code*}{*fam*}{*ser*}{*shp*}{*sz*} [p]  . . (8.5.8) – 233

If no valid font can be found, even after substituting the attributes as given by \DeclareFontSubstitution, the font declared with this command is selected as a last resort.

[2ε] \DeclareFixedFont{\*cmd*}{*code*}{*fam*}{*ser*}{*shp*}{*sz*} [p]
. . . . . . . . . . . . . . . . . . . . . . . . . . . (8.5.4) – 230

Defines \*cmd* to be a font *declaration* that selects a font with the fixed attributes given in the definition.

[2ε] \DeclareFontEncoding{*code*}{*text_set*}{*math_set*} [p]
. . . . . . . . . . . . . . . . . . . . . . . . . . . (8.5.8) – 233

Declares *code* to be the name of a new encoding scheme; *text_set* is a set of commands that is to be executed when switching to text mode, *math_set* a set for math mode.

[2ε] \DeclareFontEncodingDefaults{*text_set*}{*math_set*} [p]
. . . . . . . . . . . . . . . . . . . . . . . . . . . (8.5.8) – 233

Declares the sets of commands to be executed by all encodings when switching to text and math modes; the additional commands specific to each encoding are executed afterwards.

[2ε] \DeclareFontFamily{*code*}{*fam*}{*opt*} [p] . . . . . . . (8.5.8) – 234

Declares *fam* to be a new font family with the encoding *code*; the encoding must previously have been declared. The commands in *opt* are executed every time this family is selected.

[2ε] \DeclareFontShape{*code*}{*fam*}{*ser*}{*shp*}{*def*}{*opt*} [p]
. . . . . . . . . . . . . . . . . . . . . . . . . . . (8.5.8) – 234

Associates external font names with the given font attribute values; the actual definition *def* relates font sizes to font names, as explained on page 234. The commands in *opt* are executed every time this shape is selected.

$\boxed{2_\varepsilon}$ `\DeclareFontSubstitution{`*code*`}{`*fam*`}{`*ser*`}{`*shp*`}` [p]
. . . . . . . . . . . . . . . . . . . . . . . . . . . . . (8.5.8) – 233

Declares the font attributes that are to be substituted in case there is no valid font corresponding to the set of attributes selected. The order of substitution is *shape*, *series*, and *family*; the encoding is never substituted.

$\boxed{2_\varepsilon}$ `\DeclareMathAlphabet{\`*cmd*`}{`*code*`}{`*fam*`}{`*ser*`}{`*shp*`}` [p]
. . . . . . . . . . . . . . . . . . . . . . . . . . . . . (8.5.5) – 231

Defines \\*cmd* to be a math alphabet for setting letters in math mode; the font selected *in all math versions* is that with the specified font attributes. If a different font is to be invoked for certain math versions, they are defined individually with `\SetMathAlphabet` afterwards. However, if the shape attribute is left empty, the alphabet command is indeed created, but remains undefined in *all* versions, requiring an explicit `\SetMathAlphabet` declaration for each one.

$\boxed{2_\varepsilon}$ `\DeclareMathSizes{`*text*`}{`*math_text*`}{`*script*`}{`*sscript*`}` [p]
. . . . . . . . . . . . . . . . . . . . . . . . . . . . . (8.5.6) – 232

Sets the point sizes for the three math styles `\textstyle`, `\scriptstyle`, and `\scriptscriptstyle` when the text is being printed in point size *text*. The unit pt is not included.

$\boxed{2_\varepsilon}$ `\DeclareMathSymbol{\`*symbol*`}{`*type*`}{`*sym_fnt*`}{`*pos*`}` [p]
. . . . . . . . . . . . . . . . . . . . . . . . . . . . . (8.5.6) – 232

Declares \\*symbol* to be a command that prints the character in position *pos* with the symbol font with the internal name *sym_fnt*. This same symbol is printed in all math alphabets, but may be different for other math versions if the symbol font has been `\Set`... to have different attibutes in that math version.

$\boxed{2_\varepsilon}$ `\DeclareMathVersion{`*ver*`}` [p] . . . . . . . . . . . . . (8.5.5) – 231

Declares *ver* to be a new math version for math alphabets and symbol fonts. Initially, the version will use those fonts defined by `\Declare`... commands, which may be redefined for this math version with appropriate `\Set`... commands.

$\boxed{2_\varepsilon}$ `\DeclareOldFontCommand{\`*cmd*`}{`*text_specs*`}{`*math_specs*`}` [p]
. . . . . . . . . . . . . . . . . . . . . . . . . . . . . (8.5.4) – 230

Defines \\*cmd* to be a font *declaration* that invokes *text_specs* in text mode, and *math_specs* in math mode. The new command behaves in math mode as a 2.09 font declaration, although *math_specs* must be a math font command without its argument. It is meant to define commands to be compatible with LaTeX 2.09 and should generally be avoided.

⌐2ε⌐ \DeclareOption{*option*}{*code*} [p]  . . . . . . . . . . (C.2.3) – 332

In a class or package file, this command defines the set of commands
(*code*) that is to be associated with the given *option*. These commands
are executed when \ExecuteOptions or \ProcessOptions is called.
After the latter, all definitions are erased, to save memory. The *code*
is internally stored in a command named \ds@*option*.

⌐2ε⌐ \DeclareOption*{*code*} [p]  . . . . . . . . . . . . . (C.2.3) – 332

In a class or package file, this command defines the default set of
commands that is associated with every undefined option. Special
commands that may be used within *code* are \CurrentOption (the
name of the option) and \OptionNotUsed. Example:

> \DeclareOption*{\InputIfFileExists
>   {\CurrentOption.sty}{}{\OptionNotUsed}}

⌐2ε⌐ \DeclareRobustCommand{\\*cmd*} [*narg*] [*opt*]{*def*} . . . (C.2.5) – 334

Defines or redefines the command \\*cmd* in the same way as
\newcommand except that the result is robust: it may be used in
the argument of another command without a \protect command
before it.

⌐2ε⌐ \DeclareRobustCommand*{\\*cmd*} [*narg*] [*opt*]{*def*}  . . (C.2.6) – 334

The same as \DeclareRobustCommand except that the arguments
to \\*cmd* must be 'short', not containing any new paragraphs.
*(1994/12/01)*

⌐2ε⌐ \DeclareSymbolFont{*sym_fnt*}{*code*}{*fam*}{*ser*}{*shp*} [p]

. . . . . . . . . . . . . . . . . . . . . . . . . . (8.5.6) – 231

Declares the math font with the given attributes to be a symbol font
that may be addressed by other commands with the name *sym_fnt*.
The symbol font applies to all math versions unless redefined with a
\SetSymbolFont command.

⌐2ε⌐ \DeclareSymbolFontAlphabet{\\*cmd*}{*sym_fnt*} [p]

. . . . . . . . . . . . . . . . . . . . . . . . . . (8.5.6) – 232

Defines \\*cmd* to be a math alphabet that uses the font declared with
a \DeclareSymbolFont command to have the internal name *sym_fnt*.
This is preferred over \DeclareMathAlphabet if there is a defined
symbol font with the necessary attributes for the math alphabet.

⌐2ε⌐ \DeclareTextAccent{\\*cmd*}{*code*}{*pos*} [p] . . . . . . (8.5.9) – 236

Defines \\*cmd* to be an accent command when encoding *code* is active;
it uses the symbol in font position *pos* as the accent.

⌐2ε⌐ \DeclareTextAccentDefault{\\*cmd*}{*code*} [p]  . . . . (8.5.9) – 237

Declares the default encoding that is to be taken if the accent command \\*cmd* is called in an encoding for which it is not explicitly
defined. *(1994/12/01)*

[2ε] \DeclareTextCommand{\\*cmd*}{*code*}[*narg*][*opt*]{*def*} [p]
. . . . . . . . . . . . . . . . . . . . . . . . . . (8.5.9) – 236

> Defines \\*cmd* in the same way as \newcommand except the definition
> is only valid when encoding *code* is active.

[2ε] \DeclareTextCommandDefault{\\*cmd*}[*narg*][*opt*]{*def*} [p]
. . . . . . . . . . . . . . . . . . . . . . . . . . (8.5.9) – 237

> Creates a default definition for the command \\*cmd* for all encodings
> for which it is not explicitly defined. *(1994/12/01)*

[2ε] \DeclareTextComposite{\\*cmd*}{*code*}{*let*}{*pos*} [p]
. . . . . . . . . . . . . . . . . . . . . . . . . . (8.5.9) – 236

> Defines \\*cmd* followed by the letter *let* to be the single character in
> font position *pos* when encoding *code* is active. It thus defines the
> action of accent commands in T1 encoding when the accented letter
> exists as a separate symbol. For example:
>
>     \DeclareTextComposite{\'}{T1}{e}{233}
>
> The command must already have been defined for the encoding with
> either \DeclareTextAccent or \DeclareTextCommand (with one ar-
> gument).

[2ε] \DeclareTextCompositeCommand{\\*cmd*}{*code*}{*let*}{*def*} [p]
. . . . . . . . . . . . . . . . . . . . . . . . . . (8.5.9) – 236

> Is the same as \DeclareTextComposite except that any definition
> may be assigned to the command/letter combination, and not just a
> single symbol. *(1994/12/01)*

[2ε] \DeclareTextFontCommand{\\*cmd*}{*font_specs*} [p] . . . (8.5.4) – 230

> Defines \\*cmd* to be a text font command that sets its argument with
> the *font_spec* specifications. Example:
>
>     \DeclareTextFontCommand{\textbf}{\bfseries}

[2ε] \DeclareTextSymbol{\\*cmd*}{*code*}{*pos*} [p] . . . . . . (8.5.9) – 236

> Defines \\*cmd* to print the symbol in font position *pos* when encoding
> *code* is active.

[2ε] \DeclareTextSymbolDefault{\\*cmd*}{*code*} [p] . . . . (8.5.9) – 237

> Declares the default encoding that is to be taken if the symbol com-
> mand \\*cmd* is called in an encoding for which it is not explicitly
> defined. *(1994/12/01)*

[2ε] \definecolor{*name*}{*model*}{*specs*} . . . . . . . . . (D.3.3) – 383

> A command made available with the color package. It associates
> the name of a color (*name*) with the specifications *specs* according
> to a certain *model*. Possible values for *model* are rgb (red, green,

blue), `cmyk` (cyan, magenta, yellow, black), `gray`, and `named`. In each case, *specs* is a comma-separated list of numbers between 0 and 1 specifying the strength of the relevant component. In the case of the `named` model, *specs* is an internal name for the color that is known by the driver program. Examples:

```
\definecolor{litegrn}{cmyk}{0.25,0,0.75.0}
\definecolor{brown}{named}{RawSienna}
```

A number of colors are predefined in all color drivers: `red`, `green`, `blue`, `yellow`, `cyan`, `magenta`, `black`, and `white`.

`\deg [m]` . . . . . . . . . . . . . . . . . . . . . . (5.3.8) – 124

Command to produce the function name 'deg' in formulas.

`2ε` `\DeleteShortVerb{\c}` . . . . . . . . . . . . . . . (8.8.3) – 241

When the standard package `shortvrb` has been loaded, this command counteracts the effects of a previous `\MakeShortVerb{\c}`, allowing the character *c* to have its original meaning once more.

`\Delta [m]` produces $\Delta$ . . . . . . . . . . . . . . . (5.3.1) – 121
`\delta [m]` produces $\delta$ . . . . . . . . . . . . . . . (5.3.1) – 121

`2ε` `\depth` . . . . . . . . . . . . . . . . . . . . . . . (4.7.1) – 85

A length parameter equal to the depth of a box (baseline to bottom); it may only be used in the *width* specification of `\makebox`, `\framebox`, or `\savebox`, or in the *height* specification of a `\parbox` or minipage environment.

```
\framebox[20\depth]{text}
```

`\det [m]` . . . . . . . . . . . . . . . . . . . . . . . (5.3.8) – 124

Command to produce the function name 'det' in formulas. Can be combined with a lower limit by means of the subscript command.

`2ε` `\DH` . . . . . . . . . . . . . . . . . . . . . . . . (E.10.5) – 423

When `T1` encoding is active, prints the character Ð. *(1994/12/01)*

`2ε` `\dh` . . . . . . . . . . . . . . . . . . . . . . . . (E.10.5) – 423

When `T1` encoding is active, prints the character ð. *(1994/12/01)*

`\Diamond [m]` produces ◇ . . . . . . . . . . . . . . . (5.3.3) – 122
`\diamond [m]` produces ◇ . . . . . . . . . . . . . . . (5.3.3) – 122
`\diamondsuit [m]` produces ◆ . . . . . . . . . . . . . (5.3.6) – 123
`\dim [m]` . . . . . . . . . . . . . . . . . . . . . . . (5.3.8) – 124

Command to produce the function name 'dim' in formulas.

`\discretionary{`*before*`}{`*after*`}{`*without*`}` . . . . . . . (3.6.1) – 54

Hyphenation suggestion within a word. The word may be divided such that *before* is at the end of one line, and *after* at the start of the next line. If no division occurs, *without* is printed.

`\displaystyle [m]`  . . . . . . . . . . . . . . . . . . . (5.5.2) – 141

Switches to font size `\displaystyle` as the active font within a math formula.

`\div [m] produces ÷`  . . . . . . . . . . . . . . . . . (5.3.3) – 122

[2ε] `\DJ`  . . . . . . . . . . . . . . . . . . . . . . . . . (E.10.5) – 423

When T1 encoding is active, prints the character Đ. *(1994/12/01)*

[2ε] `\dj`  . . . . . . . . . . . . . . . . . . . . . . . . . (E.10.5) – 423

When T1 encoding is active, prints the character đ. *(1994/12/01)*

[2ε] `\documentclass [`*options*`] {`*class*`} [`*version*`] [p]`  . . . . . . . (3.1) – 25

Normally the first command in a LaTeX document, determining the overall characteristics. Standard values for *class* are:

`article, report, book, letter,` and `slides`

of which only one may be selected. In addition, various options may be chosen, their names separated by commas. Possibilities are:

`10pt, 11pt, 12pt,`
`letterpaper, legalpaper, executivepaper,`
`a4paper, a5paper, b5paper, landscape,`
`onecolumn, twocolumn,`
`oneside, twoside,`
`notitlepage, titlepage,`
`leqno, fleqn, openbib,`
`draft, final`

These and any additional options are all global, meaning that they also apply to any packages specified with a following `\usepackage` command.

The optional *version* is a date, given in the form `yyyy/mm/dd`, as for example `1994/08/01`. If the date of the class file read in is earlier than this, a warning message is printed.

[2.09] `\documentstyle [`*options*`] {`*style*`} [p]`  . . . . . . . . . . . . (3.1) – 25

In LaTeX 2.09, normally the first command in a document, determining the overall characteristics. This command has been replaced in LaTeX 2ε by `\documentclass`, but it may still be issued to initiate the compatibility mode for processing older documents.

`\dot{`*x*`} [m]`  . . . . . . . . . . . . . . . . . . . . . (5.3.9) – 125

A dot accent in mathematical formulas:  `\dot{a}` = *ȧ*.

`\doteq [m] produces ≐`  . . . . . . . . . . . . . . . . (5.3.4) – 122
`\dotfill` . . . . . . . . . . . . . . . . . . . . . . . . . (3.5.1) – 47

Fills up the space in a line with a dotted leader:  . . . . . . . .= `\dotfill`.

\dots produces . . . . . . . . . . . . . . . . . . . . . . . . (5.2.6) – 119
\doublerulesep . . . . . . . . . . . . . . . . . . . . . . (4.8.2) – 96

> The distance between double rules inside the tabular and array environments. New value assigned with \setlength outside of the environment.

\Downarrow [m] produces ⇓ . . . . . . . . . . . . . . . (5.3.5) – 123
\downarrow [m] produces ↓ . . . . . . . . . . . . . . . . (5.3.5) – 123

\ell [m] produces ℓ . . . . . . . . . . . . . . . . . (5.3.6) – 123
\em . . . . . . . . . . . . . . . . . . . . . . . . . . . (4.1.1) – 57

> This declaration switches to an emphatic font, one that has the current family and series, but with a different shape attribute. It normally toggles between an upright and an italic shape.

[2ε] \emph{*text*} . . . . . . . . . . . . . . . . . . . . . . (4.1.1) – 57

> This command sets its argument in an emphatic font, one that has the current family and series, but with a different shape attribute. It normally toggles between an upright and an italic shape. It is equivalent to {\em *text*\/}, that is, it includes the italic correction.

\emptyset [m] produces ∅ . . . . . . . . . . . . . . . (5.3.6) – 123
\encl{*enclosures*} . . . . . . . . . . . . . . . . . . (A.1) – 297

> Command in the document class letter to add the word 'encl:' with the list *enclosures* at the end of a letter. For International LaTeX, the actual word printed is contained in the command \enclname.

\enclname [i] . . . . . . . . . . . . . . . . . . . . (C.3.3) – 350

> Command in the letter document class for International LaTeX containing the word to be printed by the \encl command. In English, this is 'encl' but may be altered for adaptation to other languages.

\end{*environment*} . . . . . . . . . . . . . . . . . . . (2.2) – 17

> Command to terminate an environment started with a command \begin{*environment*}.

[2ε] \enlargethispage{*size*} . . . . . . . . . . . . . . . (3.5.5) – 52

> The \textheight parameter is temporarily increased by the length *size*, in order to improve a bad page break. On the following pages, \textheight will have its normal value once more.

[2ε] \enlargethispage*{*size*} . . . . . . . . . . . . . . . (3.5.5) – 52

> Is the same as \enlargethispage except that any additional spacing between the lines is removed as necessary to maximize the amount of text on the page.

[2ε] `\ensuremath{`*math cmds*`}` . . . . . . . . . . . . . . . . (7.3.1) – 186

Sets *math cmds* in math mode; may be called in both text and math modes. Its main use is to define new commands that require math mode but can be called from either mode.

`\epsilon` [m] produces $\epsilon$ . . . . . . . . . . . . . . . . . . (5.3.1) – 121
`\equiv` [m] produces $\equiv$ . . . . . . . . . . . . . . . . . . (5.3.4) – 122
`\eta` [m] produces $\eta$ . . . . . . . . . . . . . . . . . . . . (5.3.1) – 121
`\evensidemargin` . . . . . . . . . . . . . . . . . . . . . (3.2.4) – 35

Sets the left margin for the even numbered pages. It is effective in the document class book and, when the option twoside has been selected, in the other classes. A new value is assigned with the `\setlength` command:

`\setlength{\evensidemargin}{2.5cm}`

[2ε] `\ExecuteOptions{`*option_list*`}` [p] . . . . . . . . . . . . (C.2.3) – 332

In a class or package file, this command executes all the option definitions in *option_list*. This is normally invoked just prior to `\ProcessOptions` to establish certain options as default.

`\exists` [m] produces $\exists$ . . . . . . . . . . . . . . . . . (5.3.6) – 123
`\exp` [m] . . . . . . . . . . . . . . . . . . . . . . . . . . (5.3.8) – 124

Command to produce the function name 'exp' in formulas.

`\extracolsep{`*extra_width*`}` . . . . . . . . . . . . . . . . (4.8.1) – 94

Tabular command for setting extra spacing between all the following columns in a table. This command is inserted as an @-expression into the column definition field of the tabular environment:

`\begin{tabular}{lr@{\extracolsep{2.5mm}}lcr}`

`\fbox{`*text*`}` produces a frame around $\boxed{text}$ . . . . . . . (4.7.1) – 84
`\fboxrule` . . . . . . . . . . . . . . . . . . . . . . . . . . (4.7.8) – 92

The line thickness for the frames drawn by `\fbox` and `\framebox` commands. A new value is assigned with the `\setlength` command:

`\setlength{\fboxrule}{1pt}`

`\fboxsep` . . . . . . . . . . . . . . . . . . . . . . . . . . (4.7.8) – 92

The distance between the frame and text in the `\fbox` and `\framebox` commands. A new value is assigned with the `\setlength` command:

`\setlength{\fboxsep}{1mm}`

[2ε] `\fcolorbox` *col_spec1 col_spec2*`{`*text*`}` . . . . . . . . . (D.3.3) – 383

A command made available with the color package. Like `\colorbox`, the *text* is set in an LR box with the *col_spec2* as the background color, but with a frame of color *col_spec1* around it. The *col_spec*s are either both defined names or employ the same model. Examples:

`\fcolorbox[rgb]{1,0,0}{0,1,0}{Text}`
`\fcolorbox{red}{green}{Text}`

\figurename [i] . . . . . . . . . . . . . . . . . . (C.3.3) – 350

> Command for International LaTeX containing the name for a figure caption. In English, this is 'Figure' but may be altered for adaptation to other languages.

\fill . . . . . . . . . . . . . . . . . . . . . . . (2.4.2) – 19

> A rubber length with a natural size of zero that can stretch to any size necessary to fill up the horizontal or vertical space available.

\flat [m] produces ♭ . . . . . . . . . . . . . . . . (5.3.6) – 123

\floatpagefraction . . . . . . . . . . . . . . . . (6.6.3) – 175

> The fraction of a float page that must be filled with floats before a new page is called. New value is assigned with
>
> > \renewcommand{\floatpagefraction}{*decimal_frac*}

\floatsep . . . . . . . . . . . . . . . . . . . . . (6.6.3) – 175

> The vertical spacing between floats that appear at the top or bottom of a page. A new value is set with the \setlength command:
>
> > \setlength{\floatsep}{12pt plus 2pt minus 4pt}

\flushbottom . . . . . . . . . . . . . . . . . . . . (3.2.4) – 34

> A declaration that puts vertical spacing between paragraphs so that the last line on every page is at the same position. Standard for the book document class and for the twoside option.

\fnsymbol{*counter*} . . . . . . . . . . . . . . . . (7.1.4) – 183

> Prints the current value of the given *counter* as a 'footnote symbol':
> * † ‡ § ¶ ‖ ** †† ‡‡

[2ε] \fontfamily{*fam*} . . . . . . . . . . . . . . . . (8.5.1) – 225

> This command selects the 'family' of fonts. Possible values of *fam* for standard LaTeX with the Computer Modern fonts are cmr, cmss, cmtt, and cmfi.

[2ε] \fontseries{*ser*} . . . . . . . . . . . . . . . . (8.5.1) – 225

> This command selects the 'series' of fonts within a 'family'. Possible values of *ser* for standard LaTeX are m (medium) and bx (bold extended).

[2ε] \fontshape{*form*} . . . . . . . . . . . . . . . . (8.5.1) – 225

> This command selects the 'shape' of fonts. Possible values of *form* are n (normal), it (italic), sl (slanted), sc (small caps), and u ('unslanted' italic).

[2ε] \fontsize{*sz*}{*line_sp*} . . . . . . . . . . . . . . (8.5.1) – 225

> This command selects the font size. The argument *sz* specifies the size of the characters in points (without the dimension pt) and *line_sp* determines the value of the inter-line spacing (\baselineskip), with an explicit dimension. Example: \fontsize{12}{14pt}.

`\footnote[`*num*`]{`*footnote_text*`}`  . . . . . (4.10.1), (4.10.2) – 107, 108

Produces a footnote containing the text *footnote_tex*. The optional argument *num* will be used as the footnote number in place of the next number in the automatic sequence.

`\footnotemark[`*num*`]`  . . . . . . . . . . . . . . . . (4.10.3) – 109

Produces a footnote marker in the current text. The optional argument *num* will be used as the footnote number in place of the next number in the automatic sequence. May be used within structures where `\footnote` is not normally permitted, such as LR boxes, tables, math formulas.

`\footnoterule` . . . . . . . . . . . . . . . . . . . (4.10.5) – 111

This is an internal command to produce the horizontal rule between the regular text on a page and the footnote text at the bottom. May be changed with

```
\renewcommand{\footnoterule}
{\rule{wdth}{hght}\vspace{-hght}}
```

`\footnotesep`  . . . . . . . . . . . . . . . . . . . . (4.10.5) – 111

The vertical spacing between two footnotes. A new value is assigned with the `\setlength` command:

```
\setlength{\footnotesep}{6.5pt}
```

`\footnotesize` . . . . . . . . . . . . . . . . . . . . . (4.1.2) – 58

Switches to the font size `\footnotesize`, which is smaller than `\small` but larger than `\scriptsize`.

`\footnotetext[`*num*`]{`*footnote_text*`}`  . . . . . . . . . (4.10.3) – 109

Produces a footnote with the text *footnote_text* but without generating a marker in the current text. The marker that is used for the footnote itself at the bottom of the page derives from the current value of the counter `footnote`, which remains unchanged, or from the value of the optional argument *num*. This command may be used together with the `\footnotemark` command to insert footnotes into structures where they are otherwise not allowed, such as LR boxes, tables, and math formulas. The `\footnotetext` command must be given *outside* of that structure.

`\footskip`  . . . . . . . . . . . . . . . . . . . . . . (3.2.4) – 35

The distance from the bottom edge of the text body to the lower edge of the footline. A value is assigned with the `\setlength` command:

```
\setlength{\footskip}{25pt}
```

`\forall [m]` produces ∀  . . . . . . . . . . . . . . . . (5.3.6) – 123
`\frac{`*numerator*`}{`*denominator*`} [m]`  . . . . . . . . . (5.2.3) – 118

Math command for generating fractions.

`\frame{`*text*`}` . . . . . . . . . . . . . . . . . . . . . . (6.4.8) – 161

Produces a frame without any intervening spacing around text. Mainly used as a picture element in a `\put` or `\multiput` command within the `picture` environment.

`\framebox[`*width*`][`*pos*`]{`*text*`}` . . . . . . . . . . . . . . . (4.7.1) – 84

Produces a frame of width *width* around *text*. By default, the text is centered within the frame, but may be left or right justified by giving the optional argument *pos* as l or r. In LATEX2ε, it may also have the value s, to stretch the text to the given width.

`\framebox(`*x_dimen,y_dimen*`)[`*pos*`]{`*text*`}` . . . . . . . . (6.4.2) – 152

Picture element command to produce a frame of width *x_dimen* and height *y_dimen* within the `picture` environment. Without the optional argument *pos*, the text is centered vertically and horizontally. The text may be left or right justified, and/or aligned at the top or bottom, by setting *pos* to a combination of the letters l, r, t, and b, such as tr for top, right. In LATEX2ε, *pos* may also contain s to stretch the text to the full width. The command is to be used as the argument of a `\put` or `\multiput` command.

`\frenchspacing` . . . . . . . . . . . . . . . . . . . . . . . (3.5.1) – 45

After this command has been given, no additional horizontal spacing is inserted at the end of a sentence.   The countercommand is `\nonfrenchspacing`.

|2ε| `\frontmatter` . . . . . . . . . . . . . . . . . . . . . . . . (3.3.5) – 41

In the `book` class, introduces the material that comes at the beginning (preface, table of contents) by turning off the chapter numbering of the `\chapter` command and switching to Roman numbers for the pagination.

`\frown` [m] produces ⌢ . . . . . . . . . . . . . . . . . . (5.3.4) – 122
`\fussy` . . . . . . . . . . . . . . . . . . . . . . . . . . . (3.6.3) – 54

Countercommand of `\sloppy` that allows larger inter-word spacings than normal. After `\fussy` has been given, the normal spacings apply once more.

`\Gamma` [m] produces $\Gamma$ . . . . . . . . . . . . . . . . . . . (5.3.1) – 121
`\gamma` [m] produces $\gamma$ . . . . . . . . . . . . . . . . . . . (5.3.1) – 121
`\gcd` [m] . . . . . . . . . . . . . . . . . . . . . . . . . . (5.3.8) – 124

Command to produce the function name 'gcd' in formulas. A lower limit may be given as a subscript.

Write a \glossaryentry command to the .glo file if \makeglossary
has been issued in the preamble; else it does nothing.

The form in which the entry is written to the .glo file by the \glossary
command.

A command added with the graphpap package for use in the picture
environment. It plots a labeled grid system with the lower left corner
at (*x*,*y*), *lx* wide and *ly* high. Grid lines are drawn every *num* units,
with the fifth ones thicker. If *num* is not specified, it is assumed to
be 10. All arguments must be integers, not decimal fractions.

A grave accent over the math variable *x*:   \grave{a} = à.

When T1 encoding is active, prints the symbol «. *(1994/12/01)*

When T1 encoding is active, prints the symbol ». *(1994/12/01)*

When T1 encoding is active, prints the symbol ‹. *(1994/12/01)*

When T1 encoding is active, prints the symbol ›. *(1994/12/01)*

Hungarian double acute accent:   \H{o} = ő.

Circumflex over the math variable *x*:   \hat{a} = â.

The height of the head at the top of each page. A new value is assigned
with the \setlength command:

```
\setlength{\headheight}{25pt}
```

\headtoname [i] . . . . . . . . . . . . . . . . . . . . . (C.3.3) – 350

Command in the letter document class for International LATEX containing the text that precedes the recipient's name in the headline after the first page. In English, this is 'To' but may be altered for adaptation to other languages.

\headsep . . . . . . . . . . . . . . . . . . . . . . . . (3.2.4) – 35

Vertical spacing between the lower edge of the page head and the top of the main text. A new value is assigned with the \setlength command:

    \setlength{\headsep}{0.25in}

\heartsuit [m] produces ♥ . . . . . . . . . . . . . . (5.3.6) – 123

$\boxed{2\varepsilon}$ \height . . . . . . . . . . . . . . . . . . . . . . (4.7.1) – 85

A length parameter equal to the natural height of a box (distance from the baseline to the top); it may only be used in the *width* specification of \makebox, \framebox, or \savebox, or in the *height* specification of a \parbox or a minipage environment.

    \framebox[6\height]{text}

\hfill . . . . . . . . . . . . . . . . . . . . . . . . . (3.5.1) – 47

A horizontal rubber spacing with a natural length of zero that can be stretched to any value. Used to fill up a horizontal line with blank spacing. This command is an abbreviation for \hspace{\fill}.

\hline . . . . . . . . . . . . . . . . . . . . . . . . . (4.8.1) – 95

Produces a horizontal line in the array and tabular environments over the width of the entire table.

\hoffset . . . . . . . . . . . . . . . . . . . . . . . . 511, 512

Horizontal offset of the output page from the printer border set by the printer driver. This printer border is normally 1 inch from the left edge of the paper. The standard value of \hoffset is 0 pt so that the left reference margin of the page is identical with the printer margin. A new value is assigned with the \setlength command:

    \setlength{\hoffset}{-1in}

\hom [m] . . . . . . . . . . . . . . . . . . . . . . . (5.3.8) – 124

Command to produce the function name 'hom' in formulas.

\hookleftarrow [m] produces ↩ . . . . . . . . . . . (5.3.5) – 123
\hookrightarrow [m] produces ↪ . . . . . . . . . . . (5.3.5) – 123
\hrulefill . . . . . . . . . . . . . . . . . . . . . . (3.5.1) – 47

Fills up the space in a line with a rule: ＿＿＿＿＿＿= \hrulefill.

\hspace{*width*} . . . . . . . . . . . . . . . . . . . . (3.5.1) – 46

Produces horizontal spacing of length *width*. It is ignored if it occurs at the beginning or end of a line.

`\hspace*{`*width*`}` . . . . . . . . . . . . . . . . . (3.5.1) – 46

> Produces horizontal spacing of length *width* even at the beginning or end of a line.

`\huge`  . . . . . . . . . . . . . . . . . . . . . . . (4.1.2) – 58

> Switches to the font size `\huge`, which is smaller than `\Huge` but larger than `\LARGE`.

`\Huge`  . . . . . . . . . . . . . . . . . . . . . . . (4.1.2) – 58

> Switches to the largest font size available `\Huge`, which is larger than `\huge`.

`\hyphenation{`*hyphenation_list*`}` [p]  . . . . . . . . . . (3.6.2) – 54

> Sets up a list of hyphenation exceptions. The *hyphenation_list* consists of a collection of words containing hyphens at the places where word division may occur: `hy-phen-a-tion per-mit-ted`.

`\i`  produces ı  . . . . . . . . . . . . . . . . . (2.5.7) – 22
`\iff` [m] produces ⟺  . . . . . . . . . . . . . . (5.3.5) – 123
[2ε] `\IfFileExists{`*file_name*`}{`*true*`}{`*false*`}`  . . . . . . . (C.2.8) – 336

> Tests if the file *file_name* can be found in the places where LaTeX looks for files; if so, the code *true* is executed; otherwise, *false*. This is like `\InputIfFileExists` except the file is not input.

`\iflanguage{`*language*`}{`*yes_text*`}{`*no_text*`}`  . . . . . . . (D.1.3) – 367

> In the multi-language `babel` system, tests if *language* is the currently selected language and, if so, executes *yes_text*, otherwise *no_text*.

`\ifthenelse{`*test*`}{`*then_text*`}{`*else_text*`}`  . . . . . . . (7.3.5) – 193

> A conditional command available when the standard package `ifthen` has been loaded. If the logical statement *test* evaluates to ⟨*true*⟩ then *then_text* is inserted, otherwise *else_text*. The logical statement may be relational (two numbers with one of `< = >` between them), an even-odd test (`\isodd{`*number*`}`), a comparison of two texts (`\equal{`*text1*`}{`*text2*`}`), a comparison of two lengths (`\lengthtest{`*length1* op *length2*`}`, *op* is one of `< = >`), or a test of a boolean switch (`\boolean{`*switch*`}`). Switches are created with `\newboolean{`*switch*`}` and set with `\setboolean{`*switch*`}{`*value*`}`, where *value* is `true` or `false`. Logical statements may be combined with logical operators `\and`, `\or`, and `\not`, and grouped with `\(` and `\)`.
>
> The tests `\isodd`, `\lengthtest`, and `\boolean` are new to LaTeX 2ε.

`\Im` [m] produces ℑ . . . . . . . . . . . . . . . . . (5.3.6) – 123
`\imath` [m] produces ı  . . . . . . . . . . . . . . . (5.3.6) – 123
`\in` [m] produces ∈ . . . . . . . . . . . . . . . . . (5.3.4) – 122

`\include{`*file*`}` . . . . . . . . . . . . . . . . . . . . . . (8.1.2) – 211

Inserts the contents of the file with the root name *file* and extension `.tex` into the current text at the point where the command appears. A new page is always started! Together with `\includeonly`, this command allows portions of the document to be processed as though the rest of the text were present.

[2ε] `\includegraphics[`*llx,lly*`] [`*urx,ury*`]{`*file_name*`}` . . . . . (D.3.3) – 380

A command made available with the `graphics` package that imports external graphics stored in the file *file_name*. The coordinates of the bounding box are given by *llx*, *lly* (lower left corner) and by *urx*, *ury* (upper right corner). It is the contents of this bounding box that are used for further manipulation: scaling, rotating. It is also the (manipulated) bounding box that is used to reserve space in the text; any graphics that extend beyond the limits of this box will also be printed, but overlapping any other material that may be beside it.

The bounding box coordinates may have units attached to them; the default units are big points `bp` (72 per inch).

If the bounding box coordinates are omitted, the information is obtained in some other manner, depending on the type of graphics file. For an encapsulated PostScript file, this information is taken from the graphics file itself.

If *llx* and *lly* are not specified, they are assumed to be 0. That is, if only one set of optional coordinates are given, they refer to the upper right corner.

[2ε] `\includegraphics*[`*llx,lly*`] [`*urx,ury*`]{`*file_name*`}` . . . . (D.3.3) – 381

The same as `\includegraphics` except that any graphics extending beyond the bounding box are *not* included: the figure is clipped.

`\includeonly{`*file_list*`}` `[p]` . . . . . . . . . . . . . . . . (8.1.2) – 211

Only those files whose names are in *file_list*, separated by commas, will be read in by the `\include` commands. The `\include` commands for other file names are ignored. Nevertheless, all the auxiliary files are read in so that the page and section numbers will be correct, as are the cross-references markers.

`\indent` . . . . . . . . . . . . . . . . . . . . . . . . . . . (3.5.4) – 50

The first line of the *next* paragraph is to be indented.

`\index{`*index_entry*`}` . . . . . . . . . . . . . (8.3.3), (8.4) – 219, 221

Writes a `\indexentry` command to the `.idx` file if the `\makeindex` command has been issued in the preamble; otherwise it does nothing. The MakeIndex program (Section 8.4) can process this file if the entries are in the forms

    `\index{`*main_entry*`}`

\index{*main_entry* ! *sub_entry*}
\index{*main_entry* ! *sub_entry* ! *sub_sub_entry*}

making up a `theindex` environment with the entries alphabetically ordered and organized with \item, \subitem, and \subsubitem commands.

\indexentry{*index_entry*}{*page_number*}  . . . . . . . (8.3.3) – 220

The form in which the entry is written to the .idx file by the \index command.

\indexname [i] . . . . . . . . . . . . . . . . . . . . . . . . (C.3.3) – 350

Command for International LATEX containing the heading for the index. In English, this is 'Index' but may be altered for adaptation to other languages.

\indexspace . . . . . . . . . . . . . . . . . . . . . . . . . (8.3.3) – 219

Command within `theindex` environment to produce a blank line.

\inf [m] . . . . . . . . . . . . . . . . . . . . . . . . . . . (5.3.8) – 124

Command to produce the function name 'inf' in formulas. A lower limit may be set as a subscript.

\infty [m] produces ∞ . . . . . . . . . . . . . . . . . (5.3.6) – 123
\input{*file*}  . . . . . . . . . . . . . . . . . . . . . (8.1.1) – 209

Inserts the contents of the file with the root name *file* and extension .tex into the current text at the point where the command appears. The file that is read in may also contain further \input commands.

$\boxed{2_\varepsilon}$ \InputIfFileExists{*file_name*}{*true*}{*false*}  . . . . . (C.2.8) – 336

Tests if the file *file_name* can be found in the places where LATEX looks for files; if so, the code *true* is executed and the file is input; otherwise, *false* is executed.

\int [m] produces ∫  . . . . . . . . . . . . . . . . . (5.2.5) – 119
\intextsep  . . . . . . . . . . . . . . . . . . . . . . . (6.6.3) – 175

The vertical spacing between floats in the middle of a page and the surrounding text. A new value is assigned with the \setlength command:

        \setlength{\intextsep}{10pt plus2pt minus3pt}

\invisible . . . . . . . . . . . . . . . . . . . . . . . . . (8.10.2) – 250

In `slides` class, a declaration that makes the following text be printed in 'invisible ink', that is, it takes up as much space as though it were there. It remains in effect until the end of the environment, or end of the curly braces, in which it was issued, or until \visible is given. It is used for making overlays.

\iota [m] produces $\iota$ . . . . . . . . . . . . . . . . . . (5.3.1) – 121

2.09 \it . . . . . . . . . . . . . . . . . . . . . (4.1.5) – 62

Switches to the *Roman, italic, medium* typeface.

2ε \itdefault  . . . . . . . . . . . . . . . . (8.5.3) – 229

This command defines the shape attribute that is selected with the \itshape command. It may be redefined with \renewcommand:

    \renewcommand{\itdefault}{it}

\item[*label*]  . . . . . . . . . . . . . . . . (4.3), (4.4.1) – 66, 73

Produces a label and the start of an item text in a list environment. Without the optional argument, the label is generated according to the type of environment, for example, numbers for the enumerate environment. The optional argument inserts *label* in place of this standard item label.

\item{*entry*} . . . . . . . . . . . . . . . . . . . (8.3.3) – 219

Produces a main entry in theindex environment.

\itemindent . . . . . . . . . . . . . . . . . . . . (4.4.2) – 76

The amount by which the label and the text of the first line after each \item is indented in a list environment. The standard value is 0 pt, but a new value may be assigned with the \setlength command:

    \setlength{\itemindent}{1em}

\itemsep . . . . . . . . . . . . . . . . . . . . . (4.4.2) – 74

The amount of vertical spacing in addition to \parsep that is inserted between the \item texts in a list environment. A new value may be assigned with the \setlength command:

    \setlength{\itemsep}{2pt plus1pt minus1pt}

2ε \itshape . . . . . . . . . . . . . . . . . (4.1.3), (8.5.2) – 60, 228

This declaration switches to a font in the current family and series, but with the *italic* shape attribute.


\j  produces ȷ . . . . . . . . . . . . . . . . . . (2.5.7) – 22

\jmath [m] produces $\jmath$ . . . . . . . . . . . . . (5.3.6) – 123

\Join [m] produces ⋈  . . . . . . . . . . . . . . . (5.3.6) – 123

\jot . . . . . . . . . . . . . . . . . . . . . . (5.5.4) – 144

The amount of vertical spacing between the formula lines of an eqnarray or eqnarray* environment. Standard value is 3 pt. A new value may be assigned with the \setlength command:

    \setlength{\jot}{4.5pt}

$\boxed{2\varepsilon}$ **\k{*x*}** . . . . . . . . . . . . . . . . . . . . (E.10.5) – 423

> When T1 encoding is active, prints the ogonek accent \k{A} = A.
> *(1994/12/01)*

**\kappa** [m] produces $\kappa$ . . . . . . . . . . . . . . . . (5.3.1) – 121
**\ker** [m] . . . . . . . . . . . . . . . . . . . . . . (5.3.8) – 124

> Command to produce the function name 'ker' in formulas.

**\kill** . . . . . . . . . . . . . . . . . . . . . . . (4.6.2) – 81

> Removes the preceding sample line in a tabbing environment that
> was given only to set the tabs and not to be printed at this point.

**\L** produces Ł . . . . . . . . . . . . . . . . . . . (2.5.6) – 21
**\l** produces ł . . . . . . . . . . . . . . . . . . . (2.5.6) – 21
**\label{*marker*}** . . . . . . . . . . . . . . . . . . . (8.3.1) – 216

> Sets a marker in the text at this position with the name *marker*. It
> may be referred to either earlier or later in the document with the
> command **\ref{*marker*}** to output the counter that was then current,
> such as the section, equation, or figure number, or with the command
> **\pageref{*marker*}** to print the page number where the marker was
> set.

**\labelenum** *n* . . . . . . . . . . . . . . . . . . . . . (4.3.5) – 69

> A set of commands to produce the standard labels for the nesting
> levels of the enumerate environments, where *n* is one of i, ii, iii,
> or iv. For example,
>
>     \renewcommand{\labelenumii}{\arabic{enumii}.)}
>
> changes the standard labels of the second-level enumerate environ-
> ment to be 1.), 2.), etc.

**\labelitem** *n* . . . . . . . . . . . . . . . . . . . . . (4.3.5) – 69

> A set of commands to produce the standard labels for the nesting
> levels of the itemize environments, where *n* is one of i, ii, iii, or
> iv. For example,
>
>     \renewcommand{\labelitemi}{$\Rightarrow$}
>
> changes the standard labels of the outermost itemize environment
> to ⇒.

**\labelsep** . . . . . . . . . . . . . . . . . . . . . . (4.4.2) – 75

> In a list environment, the distance between the label box and the
> list text. A new value is assigned with the \setlength command:
>
>     \setlength{\labelsep}{5pt}

**\labelwidth** . . . . . . . . . . . . . . . . . . . . . (4.4.2) – 75

> In a list environment, the width of the box reserved for the label. A
> new value is assigned with the \setlength command:
>
>     \setlength{labelwidth}{2.2cm}

In TeX versions 3.0 and later, the set of hyphenation patterns number *num* is made active. The patterns must be previously loaded into the format file by an initex run in which \language{*num*} was given before those patterns were read in.

Switches to the font size \large, which is smaller than \Large but larger than \normalsize.

Switches to the font size \Large, which is smaller than \LARGE but larger than \large.

Switches to the font size \LARGE, which is smaller than \huge but larger than \Large.

Adjusts the size of the bracket symbol *lbrack* to fit the height of the formula between the \left ... \right pair. For example, \left[. If there is to be no matching bracket, the \left and \right commands must still be given to specify the part of the formula to be sized, but the missing bracket is given as a period (for example, \right.).

A command inside the eqnarray environment that outputs its argument as though it had zero width, thus having no effect on the column widths. It is used mainly for the first row of a multi-row formula.

In a list environment, the amount by which the left edge of the text is indented relative to the surrounding text. A new value is assigned with the \setlength command. For nested list environments, different values for the indentation can be specified by adding i ... vi to the declaration name, such as

        \setlength{\leftmarginiii}{0.5cm}

See also . . . . . . . . . . . . . . . . . . . . . . . . (4.3.4) – 67.

\Leftrightarrow [m] produces ⇔ . . . . . . . . . . . (5.3.5) – 123
\leftrightarrow [m] produces ↔ . . . . . . . . . . . (5.3.5) – 123
\leq [m] produces ≤ . . . . . . . . . . . . . . . . . (5.3.4) – 122
\lfloor [m] produces ⌊ . . . . . . . . . . . . . . . . (5.4.1) – 128
\lg [m] . . . . . . . . . . . . . . . . . . . . . . . . . (5.3.8) – 124

Command to produce the function name 'lg' in formulas.

\lhd [m] produces ◁ . . . . . . . . . . . . . . . . . . (5.3.3) – 122
\lim [m] . . . . . . . . . . . . . . . . . . . . . . . . . (5.3.8) – 124

Command to produce the function name 'lim' in formulas. A lower limit may be set as a subscript.

\liminf [m] . . . . . . . . . . . . . . . . . . . . . . . (5.3.8) – 124

Command to produce the function name 'lim inf' in formulas. A lower limit may be set as a subscript.

\limits [m] . . . . . . . . . . . . . . . . . (5.2.5), (5.3.7) – 119, 124

Places the upper and lower limits above and below the appropriate symbols where these would normally go just after them.

\limsup [m] . . . . . . . . . . . . . . . . . . . . . . . (5.3.8) – 124

Command to produce the function name 'lim sup' in formulas. A lower limit may be set as a subscript.

\line($\Delta x, \Delta y$){*length*} . . . . . . . . . . . . . . . (6.4.3) – 155

A picture element command within a picture environment for drawing horizontal and vertical lines of any length as well as slanted lines at a limited number of angles. For horizontal and vertical lines, the *length* argument is the actual length in units of \unitlength. For slanted lines, *length* is the length of the projection on to the x-axis (horizontal displacement). The slope is determined by the ($\Delta x, \Delta y$) arguments, which take on integral values such that $-6 \leq \Delta x \leq 6$ and $-6 \leq \Delta y \leq 6$. This command is the argument of a \put or \multiput command.

\linebreak[$n$] . . . . . . . . . . . . . . . . . . . . . . (3.5.2) – 48

A recommendation to break the line of text at this point such that it fills the horizontal space available (left and right justified). The urgency of the recommendation is given by the integral number $n$ between 0 and 4, with the higher numbers meaning a stronger recommendation. A value of 4 is the same as the command without the optional argument and means an obligatory line break.

\linethickness{*thickness*}  . . . . . . . . . . . . . (6.5.1) – 162

Sets the thickness of the horizontal and vertical lines in the `picture` environment. The argument *thickness* is a length specification with units, for example, `1.2mm`.

\listfigurename [i]  . . . . . . . . . . . . . . . . . . (C.3.3) – 349

Command for International LaTeX containing the heading for the list of figures. In English, this is 'List of Figures' but may be altered for adaptation to other languages.

[2ε] \listfiles [p]  . . . . . . . . . . . . . . . . . . (C.2.9) – 337

When given in the preamble, causes a list of all files read in during the processing to be printed to the monitor and to the transcript file at the end of the run. The list includes version number, date, and any additional information entered with one of the \Provides... commands.

\listoffigures  . . . . . . . . . . . . . . . . . . . . . (3.4.4) – 44

Produces a list of figures with the entries from all the \caption commands in `figure` environments.

\listoftables . . . . . . . . . . . . . . . . . . . . . . (3.4.4) – 44

Produces a list of tables with the entries from all the \caption commands in `table` environments.

\listparindent  . . . . . . . . . . . . . . . . . . . . . (4.4.2) – 75

Depth of indentation for the first line of a paragraph inside a `list` environment. A new value may be assigned with the \setlength command:

    \setlength{\listparindent}{1em}

\listtablename [i]  . . . . . . . . . . . . . . . . . . (C.3.3) – 349

Command for International LaTeX containing the heading for the list of tables. In English, this is 'List of Tables' but may be altered for adaptation to other languages.

\ll [m] produces ≪  . . . . . . . . . . . . . . . . . . (5.3.4) – 122
\ln [m] . . . . . . . . . . . . . . . . . . . . . . . . . (5.3.8) – 124

Command to produce the function name 'ln' in formulas.

[2ε] \LoadClass [*options*] {*class*} [*version*] [p]  . . . . . . . . (C.2.2) – 331

This command may only be invoked within a class file to load another class file. It may only be called once within any class file. The file loaded must have the extension `.cls`. Any options specified in the \documentclass command are *not* passed over as global options.

The optional *version* is a date, given in the form `yyyy/mm/dd`, as for example `1994/08/01`. If the date of the class file is earlier than this, a warning message is printed.

`\location{`*number*`}` . . . . . . . . . . . . . . . . . . (A.1) – 296

> In the `letter` document class, enters the sender's room number. In the standard LATEX `letter` class, *number* is only output if `\address` has not been called. It is intended to be used in company letter classes such as `mpletter`.

`\log [m]` . . . . . . . . . . . . . . . . . . . . . . . (5.3.8) – 124

> Command to produce the function name 'log' in formulas.

`\Longleftarrow [m]` produces ⟸ . . . . . . . . . . (5.3.5) – 123
`\longleftarrow [m]` produces ⟵ . . . . . . . . . . (5.3.5) – 123
`\Longleftrightarrow [m]` produces ⟺ . . . . . . . (5.3.5) – 123
`\longleftrightarrow [m]` produces ⟷ . . . . . . . (5.3.5) – 123
`\longmapsto[m]` produces ⟼ . . . . . . . . . . . (5.3.5) – 123
`\Longrightarrow [m]` produces ⟹ . . . . . . . . . (5.3.5) – 123
`\longrightarrow [m]` produces ⟶ . . . . . . . . . (5.3.5) – 123
`\lq` produces ', identical to the ' symbol.

2ε   `\mainmatter` . . . . . . . . . . . . . . . . . . (3.3.5) – 41

> In the `book` class, introduces the main body of text after the front matter, by resetting the page numbering to 1 with Arabic numbers, and by reactivating the chapter numbering with the `\chapter` command. It undoes the effects of `\frontmatter`.

`\makebox[`*width*`] [`*pos*`]{`*text*`}` . . . . . . . . . . . . . (4.7.1) – 84

> Produces a box of width *width* containing *text* centered horizontally, unless *pos* is given to specify that it is to be left (`l`) or right (`r`) justified. In LATEX 2ε, it may also have the value `s`, to stretch the text to the given width.

`\makebox(`*x_dimen,y_dimen*`) [`*pos*`]{`*text*`}` . . . . . . . . (6.4.2) – 152

> Picture element command to produce a box of width *x_dimen* and height *y_dimen* within the `picture` environment. Without the optional argument *pos*, the text is centered vertically and horizontally. The text may be left or right justified, and/or aligned at the top or bottom, by setting *pos* to a combination of the letters `l`, `r`, `t`, and `b`, such as `tr` for top, right. In LATEX 2ε, *pos* may also contain `s` to stretch the text to the full width. The command is used as the argument of a `\put` or `\multiput` command.

`\makeglossary [p]` . . . . . . . . . . . . . . . . . . (8.3.4) – 221

> Command to activate the `\glossary` commands in the text.

`\makeindex [p]` . . . . . . . . . . . . . . . . . . . (8.3.3) – 220

> Command to activate the `\index` commands in the text.

`\makelabel{`*text*`}` . . . . . . . . . . . . . . *(4.4.1)*, *(7.5.9)* – 74, 205

An internal command that is called by the `\item` command to produce the actual label *text* within a list environment.

`\makelabels` . . . . . . . . . . . . . . . . . . . . . . . *(A.1)* – 299

Produces address labels in the `letter` document class using the entries from the `\begin{letter}` environment.

2ε `\MakeShortVerb{\c}` . . . . . . . . . . . . . . . . . . *(8.8.3)* – 241

When the standard package `shortvrb` has been loaded, this command makes the character *c* a shorthand form for `\verbc`: everything that appears between two occurrences of *c* is printed literally, in typewriter type. With `\DeleteShortVerb{\c}`, the character is restored to its normally meaning. Example:

`\MakeShortVerb{\|}`

`\maketitle` . . . . . . . . . . . . . . . . . . . . . . . *(3.3.1)* – 38

Produces a title page using entries in the `\author` and `\title` commands, and optionally those in the `\date` and `\thanks` commands, if present.

`\mapsto [m]` produces $\mapsto$ . . . . . . . . . . . . . . *(5.3.5)* – 123

`\marginpar [`*left_text*`] {`*right_text*`}` . . . . . . . . . . . *(4.10.6)* – 112

Produces a marginal note at the right of the text containing *right_text*. With two-sided formatting, the marginal note goes into the left margin on the even pages, in which case the optional *left_text* will be written instead. For two-column text, the marginal notes always go into the 'outer' margin, and again *left_text* will be used for the left margin, if present.

`\marginparpush` . . . . . . . . . . . . . . . . . . . . *(4.10.7)* – 113

The minimum vertical separation between two marginal notes. A new value may be assigned with the `\setlength` command, as in the example below.

`\marginparsep` . . . . . . . . . . . . . . . . . . . . . *(4.10.7)* – 113

The spacing between the edge of the text and a marginal note. A new value may be assigned with the `\setlength` command:

`\setlength{\marginparsep}{7pt}`

`\marginparwidth` . . . . . . . . . . . . . . . . . . . . *(4.10.7)* – 113

The width of the box reserved for marginal notes. A new value may be assigned with the `\setlength` command, as in the example above.

`\markboth{`*left_head*`}{`*right_head*`}` . . . . . . . . . . . *(3.2.1)* – 31

Sets the text entries for the left and right page headlines in two-sided formatting when the page style `myheadings` has been selected, or when the automatic entries of page style `headings` are to be manually changed.

\markright{*head*} . . . . . . . . . . . . . . . . . . . . . (3.2.1) – 31

> Sets the text entry for the page headline when the page style myheadings has been selected, or when the automatic entry of page style headings is to be manually changed. In two-sided formatting, only the right headline is set with this command.

[2ε] \mathbf{*text*} [m] . . . . . . . . . . . . . (5.4.2), (8.5.5) – 129, 231

> This command sets *text* in a bold font (\bfseries) within math mode. Spaces are ignored as usual.

[2ε] \mathcal{*text*} [m] . . . . . . (5.3.2), (5.4.2), (8.5.5) – 121, 129, 231

> This command sets *text* in calligraphic letters within math mode. It replaces the \cal declaration in LaTeX 2.09.

\mathindent . . . . . . . . . . . . . . . . . . . . . . . (3.1.1) – 28

> The indentation of displayed formulas from the left margin when the option fleqn has been selected. A new value may be assigned with the \setlength command:
>
> > \setlength{\mathindent}{25pt}

[2ε] \mathit{*text*} [m] . . . . . . . . . . . . (5.4.2), (8.5.5) – 129, 231

> This command sets *text* in a text italic font (\itshape) within math mode. It differs from \mathnormal in that the spacing between the letters is as in regular text. Compare *mathit* and *mathnormal*.

[2ε] \mathnormal{*text*} [m] . . . . . (5.3.1), (5.4.2), (8.5.5) – 121, 129, 231

> This command sets *text* in the normal (italic) math font within math mode.   It replaces the \mit declaration in LaTeX 2.09. In this font, capital Greek letters are also set in italics: $\Gamma\mathnormal{\Gamma}$ = $\Gamma\Gamma$.

[2ε] \mathrm{*text*} [m] . . . . . . . . . . . . (5.4.2), (8.5.5) – 129, 231

> This command sets *text* in a Roman font (\rmfamily) within math mode. Spaces are ignored as usual.

[2ε] \mathsf{*text*} [m] . . . . . . . . . . . . (5.4.2), (8.5.5) – 129, 231

> This command sets *text* in a sans serif font (\sffamily) within math mode. Spaces are ignored as usual.

[2ε] \mathtt{*text*} [m] . . . . . . . . . . . . (5.4.2), (8.5.5) – 129, 231

> This command sets *text* in a typewriter font (\ttfamily) within math mode. Spaces are ignored as usual.

[2ε] \mathversion{*ver*} . . . . . . . . . . . . . . . . (8.5.5) – 230

> Selects the current math version. Possible values are bold and normal; new values may be created with the \DeclareMathVersion command.

\max [m] . . . . . . . . . . . . . . . . . . . . . (5.3.8) – 124

> Command to produce the function name 'max' in formulas. A lower limit may be set as a subscript.

\mbox{*text*} produces an LR box around *text* . . . . . . . (4.7.1) – 84

2*ε* \mddefault . . . . . . . . . . . . . . . . (8.5.3) – 229

> This command defines the series attribute that is selected with the \mdseries command. It may be redefined with \renewcommand:
>
> > \renewcommand{\mddefault}{m}

2*ε* \mdseries . . . . . . . . . . . . . . . (4.1.3), (8.5.2) – 60, 228

> This declaration switches to a font in the current family and shape, **but with the** medium **series attribute.**

\medskip . . . . . . . . . . . . . . . . . . . . . . (3.5.3) – 49

> Inserts large vertical spacing of the amount \medskipamount. See also \bigskip and \smallskip.

\medskipamount

> Standard value for the amount of vertical spacing that is inserted with the command \medskip. May be changed with the \setlength command:
>
> > \setlength{\medskipamount}{3ex plus1ex minus1ex}

2*ε* \MessageBreak . . . . . . . . . . . . . . . . . . (C.2.7) – 335

> Forces a new line in the texts of error, warning, and information messages. These are the only places where it may be invoked, otherwise it does nothing.

\mho [m] produces ℧ . . . . . . . . . . . . . . . . . (5.3.6) – 123
\mid [m] produces | . . . . . . . . . . . . . . . . . (5.3.4) – 122
\min [m] . . . . . . . . . . . . . . . . . . . . . . (5.3.8) – 124

> Command to produce the function name 'min' in formulas. A lower limit may be set as a subscript.

2.09 \mit [m] . . . . . . . . . . . . . . . . . . . . . (5.3.1) – 121

> A declaration in LATEX 2.09 that switches to the font style 'math italic', the standard in math mode. In LATEX 2*ε*, it has been replaced by the command \mathnormal.

\models [m] produces $\models$ . . . . . . . . . . . . . . . . (5.3.4) – 122
\mp [m] produces $\mp$ . . . . . . . . . . . . . . . . . . . (5.3.3) – 122
\mu [m] produces $\mu$ . . . . . . . . . . . . . . . . . . . (5.3.1) – 121
\multicolumn{*n*}{*col*}{*text*} . . . . . . . . . . . . . . (4.8.1) – 95

> Merges the next *n* columns in the array and tabular environments, formatting the text entry *text* according to the single column definition *col*, which may be l, c, r as well as |.

\multiput$(x, y)$$(\Delta x, \Delta y)$$\{n\}\{pic\_elem\}$ . . . . . . . . (6.3) – 151

Multiple positioning command in the picture environment. The object *pic_elem* is placed $n$ times, at $(x, y)$, $(x + \Delta x, y + \Delta y)$, ... $(x + (n-1)\Delta x, y + (n-1)\Delta y)$.

\nabla [m] produces $\nabla$ . . . . . . . . . . . . . . . . (5.3.6) – 123
\name{*sender*} . . . . . . . . . . . . . . . . . . . (A.2) – 300

In the letter document class, enters the sender's name.

\natural [m] produces $\natural$ . . . . . . . . . . . . . . . (5.3.6) – 123
\nearrow [m] produces $\nearrow$ . . . . . . . . . . . . . . (5.3.5) – 123

2ε \NeedsTeXFormat{*format*}[*version*] [p] . . . . . . . . (C.2.1) – 330

Declares the TeX format that is necessary for processing the file. This should be the first statement in the file. At the moment, the only legitimate value for *format* is LaTeX2e. The *version*, if included, must be given as a date in the form yyyy/mm/dd, specifying the earliest possible release date of the format that is consistent with all the features employed in the file. Example:

   \NeedsTeXFormat{LaTeX2e}[1994/06/01]

\neg [m] produces $\neg$ . . . . . . . . . . . . . . . . . (5.3.6) – 123
\neq [m] produces $\neq$ . . . . . . . . . . . . . . . . . (5.3.4) – 123

2ε \newboolean{*switch*} . . . . . . . . . . . . . . . . (7.3.5) – 195

Creates a new boolean switch. The value of the switch is set with \setboolean{*switch*}{*value*}, where *value* is true or false. Its value is tested with \boolean{*switch*}, which may be used as a logical statement in the *test* part of \ifthenelse and \whiledo. Requires the standard LaTeX package ifthen.

2ε \newcommand{*com_name*}[*narg*][*opt*]{*def*} . . . . . . . (7.3) – 185

Defines a user command with the name \*com_name* to be *def*. The first optional argument *narg* ≤ 9 specifies how many variable arguments the command is to have, which appear in the *def* as the replacement characters #1 to #*narg*. If the second optional argument is present, the first argument of the new command is optional, and takes on the value *opt* if it is not explicitly given.

2ε \newcommand*{*com_name*}[*narg*][*opt*]{*def*} . . . . . (C.2.6) – 334

The same as \newcommand except that the arguments to \*com_name* must be 'short', not containing any new paragraphs. *(1994/12/01)*

2.09 \newcommand{*com_name*}[*narg*]{*def*} . . . . . . . . . (7.3) – 185

In LaTeX 2.09, the [*opt*] is missing so that the new command cannot have any optional arguments.

\newcounter{*counter_name*}[*in_counter*] . . . . . . . . (7.1.2) – 182

Establishes a new counter with the name *counter_name*. The optional argument *in_counter* is the name of an existing counter which, when incremented, resets the new counter to zero; that is, the new counter is a sub-counter of *in_counter*.

2ε \newenvironment{*env_name*}[*narg*] [*opt*]{*beg_def*}{*end_def*}

. . . . . . . . . . . . . . . . . . . . . . . . . (7.4) – 196

Defines a user environment with the name *env_name* which has the \begin definition *beg_def* and the \end definition *end_def*. The optional argument *narg* ≤ 9 specifies how many variable arguments the environment is to have, which appear in the *beg_def* as the replacement characters #1 to #*narg*. If the second optional argument is present, the first argument of the \begin command is optional, and takes on the value *opt* if it is not explicitly given.

2ε \newenvironment*{*env_name*}[*narg*] [*opt*]{*beg_def*}{*end_def*}

. . . . . . . . . . . . . . . . . . . . . . . . . (C.2.6) – 334

The same as \newenvironment except that the arguments to \begin{*env_name*} must be 'short', not containing any new paragraphs. *(1994/12/01)*

2.09 \newenvironment{*env_name*}[*narg*]{*beg_def*}{*end_def*}

. . . . . . . . . . . . . . . . . . . . . . . . . (7.4) – 196

In LATEX 2.09, the [*opt*] is missing so that the new \begin command cannot have any optional arguments.

\newfont{\\*font_cmd*}{*font_name* scaled *size*} . . . . . . (4.1.6) – 62

Establishes the relation between the font file name *file_name* (see Section E.8.1) magnified by the scaling factor *size* (Section E.8.2) and a font selection command \\*font_cmd*. After \\*font_cmd* has been called, \baselineskip, the inter-line spacing, still has its previous value.

\newlength{\\*length_cmd*} . . . . . . . . . . . . . . . . (7.2) – 185

Creates a new length command with the name \\*length_cmd* and initializes it to 0 pt. New values may be assigned as for all length commands with the \setlength command:

\setlength{\\*length_cmd*}{*length*}

The quantity *length* must have units (cm, pt, etc.) and may be a rubber length.

\newline . . . . . . . . . . . . . . . . . . . . . . . . (3.5.2) – 48

Terminates and starts a line of text *without* right justifying it.

\newpage . . . . . . . . . . . . . . . . . . . . . . . . (3.5.5) – 50

Terminates and starts a new page, leaving the rest of the page blank.

`\newsavebox{\`*boxname*`}` . . . . . . . . . . . . . . . . . (4.7.1) – 86

Creates a storage box with the name `\`*boxname* in which LR boxes may be saved with the `\savebox` command.

`\newtheorem{`*thrm_type*`}` `[`*num_like*`]` `{`*thrm_title*`}` `[`*in_ctr* `]`   .   (4.5) – 79

Defines a new theorem-like environment named *thrm_type* which when called prints a theorem declaration with the name *thrm_title* in **bold face**, followed by an automatic sequential number, and the actual text of the environment in *italic*. The optional argument *num_like* is the name of another theorem structure which is to share the same numbering counter. The other optional argument *in_ctr* is the name of a sectioning counter, such as `chapter`, which is to reset the theorem counter every time it is incremented. That is, the theorem counter is a sub-counter of *in_ctr*.

2ε `\NG`   . . . . . . . . . . . . . . . . . . . . . . . . (E.10.5) – 423

When T1 encoding is active, prints the character Ŋ. *(1994/12/01)*

2ε `\ng`   . . . . . . . . . . . . . . . . . . . . . . . . (E.10.5) – 423

When T1 encoding is active, prints the character ŋ. *(1994/12/01)*

`\ni` `[m]` produces ∋ . . . . . . . . . . . . . . . . . . (5.3.4) – 122

`\nocite{`*key*`}`   . . . . . . . . . . . . . . . (8.3.2), (B.1) – 218, 310

The entry in the literature database with the key word *key* will be included in the bibliography without any citation (reference) in the text.

2ε `\nocorr`   . . . . . . . . . . . . . . . . . . . . . . (4.1.4) – 61

To be used with font commands `\emph`, `\textsl`, `\textit` to suppress automatic italic correction.

```
\nocorr\emph{emphatic text}   or
\emph{emphatic text\nocorr}
```

`\nofiles` `[p]` . . . . . . . . . . . . . . . . . . . . . . (8.9) – 243

Issued in the preamble, this command suppresses the output of the auxiliary files `.aux`, `.glo`, `.idx`, `.lof`, `.lot`, and `.toc`.

`\noindent`   . . . . . . . . . . . . . . . . . . . . . . (3.5.4) – 50

The first line of the *next* paragraph will *not* be indented.

`\nolimits` `[m]` . . . . . . . . . . . . . . . . . . . . . (5.3.7) – 124

Places the upper and lower limits after the appropriate symbols where these would normally go just above or below them.

`\nolinebreak[`*n*`]`   . . . . . . . . . . . . . . . . . . . (3.5.2) – 49

A recommendation *not* to break the line of text at this point. The urgency of the recommendation is given by the integral number $n$ between 0 and 4, with the higher numbers meaning a stronger recommendation. A value of 4 is the same as the command without the optional argument and means absolutely no line break here.

`\nonfrenchspacing` . . . . . . . . . . . . . . . . . . (3.5.1) – 45

Countermands `\frenchspacing`, switching back to the standard formatting in which extra word spacing is inserted at the end of a sentence.

`\nonumber` [m] . . . . . . . . . . . . . . . . . . . . (5.4.7) – 135

The formula line in an `eqnarry` environment in which this command
appears will *not* contain an equation number.

`\nopagebreak[`*n*`]` . . . . . . . . . . . . . . . . . . (3.5.5) – 50

A recommendation *not* to break the page at this point. The urgency of
the recommendation is given by the integral number *n* between 0 and
4, with the higher numbers meaning a stronger recommendation. A
value of 4 is the same as the command without the optional argument
and means absolutely no page break here.

2ε `\normalcolor` . . . . . . . . . . . . . . . . . . . . (D.3.3) – 383

A command that normally does nothing. However, if the `color` package has been loaded, it resets the color for text to be the color that
was in effect at the end of the preamble, normally black. A `\color`
command in the preamble can alter this 'standard' color.

This command is called by many internal LATEX macros, to reset the
text color when printing headlines and headings. Other packages
should also use it so that they are consistent with the `color` package.

2ε `\normalfont` . . . . . . . . . . . . . . . . (4.1.3), (8.5.2) – 61, 229

This declaration switches to the font with the default family, shape,
and series attributes.

`\normalmarginpar` . . . . . . . . . . . . . . . . . (4.10.6) – 112

Countermands `\reversemarginpar`, switching back to the standard
placement of marginal notes in the 'outer' margin.

`\normalsize` . . . . . . . . . . . . . . . . . . . . . . (4.1.2) – 58

Switches to the font size `\normalsize`, the size selected by the option
in the `\documentclass` or `\documentstyle` commands. It is smaller
than `\large` but larger than `\small`.

`\not` [m] . . . . . . . . . . . . . . . . . . . . . . . (5.3.4) – 123

Changes the following comparison symbol into its negative counterpart:

`\not\cong` = $\not\cong$

`\notesname` [i] . . . . . . . . . . . . . . . . . . . . (C.3.3) – 350

Command for some applications of International LATEX containing the
text for a command `\notes`. In English, this is 'notes' but may be
altered for adaptation to other languages. (This command is not
standardized!)

This command is only used as an *entry* to \addcontentsline. The *sec_num* is the sectioning number and *text* the actual entry into the table of contents for that number.

Sets the left margin for the odd numbered pages in document class book or when the option twoside has been selected for other classes. In all other cases, it sets the left margin for *all* pages. A new value is assigned with the \setlength command:

    \setlength{\evensidemargin}{1.5cm}

Starts a new page and switches from two column to one column page formatting.

In slides class, a command to be issued in the preamble to generate only those notes whose numbers appear in *note_nums*. The command behaves the same as \onlyslides for slides.

In slides class, a command to be issued in the preamble to generate only those slides whose numbers appear in *slide_nums*. The numbers are separated by commas, and may include a range with a hyphen: \onlyslides{4,10-13,23}.

In the letter environment of the letter class, this sets the form of the salutation at the start of the letter text; for example, \opening{Dear George,}.

[2ε]

A command that may only be used in the definition of options, especially default options. It declares the \CurrentOption to be unprocessed. This is used if the processing of a default option should fail, say because some file is missing. LaTeX is then informed that this requested option is still outstanding.

Picture element command to produce an oval with width *x_dimen* and height *y_dimen* in the picture environment. The optional *part* argument may take on values of t, b, l, and r to draw only the top, bottom, left, or right halves of the oval. A combination of these values may be given to draw only a quarter of the oval, such as tl or lt for the top left part. To be used as an argument in a \put or \multiput command.

Produces a horizontal curly brace over the math formula *sub_form*. Any following superscript will be placed centered above the horizontal brace.

$$\overbrace{\text{a+b}} = \overbrace{a + b}$$

$$\overbrace{\text{x+y+z}}^{\{\xi\eta\zeta\}} = \overbrace{x + y + z}^{\xi\eta\zeta}$$

Produces a horizontal bar over the math formula *sub_form*:

$$\overline{\text{a-b}} = \overline{a - b}$$

[2ε]

Writes an error message *error_text* to the monitor and transcript file, labeled with the package name, and halts processing, waiting for a user response as for a LaTeX error. If H⟨return⟩ is typed, the *help* text is printed. Both *error_text* and *help* may contain \MessageBreak for a new line, \space for a forced space, and \protect before commands that are to have their names printed literally and not interpreted.

[2ε]

Is like \PackageWarningNoLine except that the text *info_text* is only written to the transcript file, and not to the monitor.

$\boxed{2\varepsilon}$ \PackageWarning{*pkg_name*}{*warn_text*} [p] . . . . . . (C.2.7) – 335

Writes *warn_text* to the monitor and transcript file, labeled with the package name and the current line number of the input file. Processing continues. The *warn_text* is formatted in the same way as that for \PackageError.

$\boxed{2\varepsilon}$ \PackageWarningNoLine{*pkg_name*}{*warn_text*} [p] . . (C.2.7) – 335

Is like \PackageWarning except that the current line number of the input file is not printed.

\pagebreak[*n*] . . . . . . . . . . . . . . . . . . . (3.5.5) – 50

A recommendation to break the page at this point. The urgency of the recommendation is given by the integral number *n* between 0 and 4, with the higher numbers meaning a stronger recommendation. A value of 4 is the same as the command without the optional argument and means an obligatory page break.

$\boxed{2\varepsilon}$ \pagecolor *col_spec* . . . . . . . . . . . . . . . . . (D.3.3) – 383

A command made available with the color package. Sets the background color starting with the current page. All following pages have the same background color until \pagecolor is called once more. The *col_spec* is the same as for \color.

\pagename [i] . . . . . . . . . . . . . . . . . . . . (C.3.3) – 350

Command in the letter document class for International LATEX containing the text for page numbers after the first page. In English, this is 'Page' but may be altered for adaptation to other languages.

\pagenumbering{*style*} . . . . . . . . . . . . . . . . (3.2.2) – 32

Determines the style of the page numbering and resets the page counter to 1. Possible values for *style* are: arabic, roman, Roman, alph, and Alph.

\pageref{*marker*} . . . . . . . . . . . . . . . . . . (8.3.1) – 216

Prints the number of the page where *marker* has been set by a \label{*marker*} command.

\pagestyle{*style*} [p] . . . . . . . . . . . . . . . . . (3.2) – 31

Determines the page style, that is, the contents of the head and footlines on every page. Possible values for *style* are: plain, empty, headings, and myheadings.

$\boxed{2\varepsilon}$ \paperheight . . . . . . . . . . . . . . . . . . (3.2.4) – 35

The total height of the page as specified by the page size option in the \documentclass command line. With the default lettersize option, this is 11 in; with a4paper, it is 29.7 cm. The additional option landscape interchanges the values of \paperwidth and \paperheight.

$\boxed{2\varepsilon}$ \paperwidth . . . . . . . . . . . . . . . . . . . . . . . . (3.2.4) – 35

> The total width of the page as specified by the page size option in the \documentclass command line. With the default lettersize option, this is 8.5 in; with a4paper, it is 21 cm. The additional option landscape interchanges the values of \paperwidth and \paperheight.

\par . . . . . . . . . . . . . . . . . . . . . . . . . . . . . (3.5.3) – 49

> Ends the current paragraph and begins a new one. This command is equivalent to a blank line.

\paragraph[*short title*]{*title*} . . . . . . . . . . . . . . . . (3.3.3) – 39

> The second last command in the sectioning hierarchy, coming between \subsubsection and \subparagraph. It formats *title* with the current sub-subsection number and an automatic sequential paragraph number. If the optional *short title* is given, it appears in place of *title* in the table of contents.

\paragraph*{*title*} . . . . . . . . . . . . . . . . . . . . . (3.3.3) – 39

> The same as \paragraph but without a number or an entry in the table of contents.

\parallel [m] produces ∥ . . . . . . . . . . . . . . . . (5.3.4) – 122

$\boxed{2.09}$ \parbox[*pos*]{*width*}{*text*} . . . . . . . . . . . . . . . . (4.7.3) – 87

> Produces a vertical box of width *width* in which *text* is set in lines that are left and right justified to this width. The vertical positioning with respect to the surrounding text is determined by the optional argument *pos*: t for alignment with its top line, b with its bottom line, and centered with no argument.

$\boxed{2\varepsilon}$ \parbox[*pos*][*height*][*inner_pos*]{*width*}{*text*} . . . . . (4.7.5) – 89

> In LaTeX $2\varepsilon$, this command may have two additional optional arguments: *height* to give the total height, and *inner_pos* to specify how the text is to be positioned inside it. Possible values are t for top, b for bottom, c for centered, and s to be stretched out to fill the whole vertical space. The default is the value of the external positioning *pos* option. The *height* argument may contain the parameters \height, \depth, \width, and \totalheight.

\parindent . . . . . . . . . . . . . . . . . . . . . . . . . . (3.2.3) – 33

> The amount of indentation for the first line of a paragraph. A new value may be assigned with the \setlength command:
>
>     \setlength{\parindent}{1.5em}

\parsep . . . . . . . . . . . . . . . . . . . . . . . . . . . . (4.4.2) – 74

> The vertical spacing between paragraphs within a list environment. A new value may be assigned with the \setlength command:
>
>     \setlength{\parsep}{2pt plus1pt minus1pt}

The vertical spacing between paragraphs. A new value may be assigned with the `\setlength` command:

`\setlength{\parskip}{3pt plus1pt minus2pt}`

The highest command in the sectioning hierarchy. It begins a new 'Part' with an automatic sequential part number and the heading *title*. The following sectioning numbers are not influenced by the part number. If the optional *short title* is given, it appears in place of *title* in the table of contents.

The same as `\part` but without a number or an entry in the table of contents.

Command for International LATEX containing the part heading. In English, this is 'Part' but may be altered for adaptation to other languages.

The additional vertical spacing at the beginning and/or end of a listing when a blank line precedes or follows the environment commands. A new value may be assigned with the `\setlength` command:

`\setlength{\partopsep}{2pt plus1pt minus1pt}`

Assigns the options in the list *options* to the specified class file, which is later loaded with `\LoadClass`. This command must be called from a class file, or from another file input by a class file. It may be used in the definition of options, or in a configuration file to activate options.

Assigns the options in the list *options* to the specified package file, which is later loaded with `\RequirePackage`. This command may be called from a class or package file. It may be used in the definition of options, or in a configuration file to activate certain options.

Command to produce the function name 'mod' in formulas in the form:

$$y\text{\textbackslash pmod\{a+b\}} = y \quad (\text{mod } a + b)$$

\poptabs . . . . . . . . . . . . . . . . . . . . . . . . (4.6.4) – 82

> Restores the last set of tabular stops in the tabbing environment that has been saved with \pushtabs.

\pounds produces £ . . . . . . . . . . . . . . . . . . (2.5.5) – 21

\Pr [m] . . . . . . . . . . . . . . . . . . . . . . . . . (5.3.8) – 124

> Command to produce the function name 'Pr' in formulas. A lower limit may be set as a subscript.

\prec [m] produces ≺ . . . . . . . . . . . . . . . . (5.3.4) – 122

\preceq [m] produces ≼ . . . . . . . . . . . . . . . (5.3.4) – 122

\prefacename [i] . . . . . . . . . . . . . . . . . . . (C.3.3) – 349

> Command for some applications of International LATEX containing the text for a command \preface. In English, this is 'Preface' but may be altered for adaptation to other languages. (This command is not standardized!)

\prime [m] produces ′ (identical to the ' symbol) . . . . (5.3.6) – 123

\printindex . . . . . . . . . . . . . . . . . . . . . . (8.4) – 221

> A command defined in the makeidx.sty file that generates theindex environment after the program MakeIndex has processed the .idx file.

[2ε] \ProcessOptions [p] . . . . . . . . . . . . . . . . . . (C.2.3) – 332

> In a class or package file, this command processes the requested options by executing the \ds@ commands for each one *in the order in which they were defined.* The \ds@ commands are then erased.

[2ε] \ProcessOptions* [p] . . . . . . . . . . . . . . . . . (C.2.3) – 332

> This is the same as \ProcessOptions except that the \ds@ commands are executed *in the order in which the options were requested.* It is equivalent to the LATEX 2.09 command \@options, which is still maintained for compatibility.

\prod [m] produces ∏ . . . . . . . . . . . . . . . . . (5.3.7) – 124

\propto [m] produces ∝ . . . . . . . . . . . . . . . . (5.3.4) – 122

\protect . . . . . . . . . . . . . . . . . . . . . . . . (2.6) – 23

> Fragile commands may be used in moving arguments when they are preceded by the \protect command. Example:
>
> \section{The \protect\pounds{} Sign}.

[2ε] \providecommand{\*com_name*} [*narg*] [*opt*] {*def*} . . . (7.3.1) – 187

> The same as \newcommand except that if a command with the name \*com_name* already exists, the new definition is ignored.

[2ε] \providecommand*{\*com_name*} [*narg*] [*opt*] {*def*} . . . (C.2.6) – 334

> The same as \providecommand except that the arguments to \*com_name* must be 'short', not containing any new paragraphs. *(1994/12/01)*

2ε \ProvidesClass{*class*}[*version*] [p] . . . . . . . . . . (C.2.1) – 330

> At the beginning of a class file, this statement declares the name of the class and its version, to be checked against the name and version in the \documentclass or \LoadClass command that input it. The *version* specification, if present, consists of three parts: date, version number, and additional information. Example:
>
> \ProvidesClass{thesis}[1995/01/25 v3.8 U of Saigon]

2ε \ProvidesFile{*file_name*}[*version*] . . . . . . . . . . (C.2.1) – 331

> At the beginning of a general file, this statement declares its name and version. No checking is done when the file is read in with \input, but the information is printed out if \listfiles has been activated. This command is not limited to the preamble as the other \Provides.. commands are.

2ε \ProvidesPackage{*class*}[*version*] [p] . . . . . . . . (C.2.1) – 330

> At the beginning of a package file, this statement declares the name of the package and its version, to be checked against the name and version in the \usepackage or \RequirePackage command that input it. The *version* specification, if present, consists of three parts: date, version number, and additional information. Example:
>
> \ProvidesPackage{notes}[1995/02/13 1.2 G. Smith]

2ε \ProvideTextCommand{\*cmd*}{*code*}[*narg*][*opt*]{*def*} [p]
. . . . . . . . . . . . . . . . . . . . . . . . . . . . . (8.5.9) – 236

> Defines \*cmd* in the same way as \providecommand except the definition is only valid when encoding *code* is active. If the command \*cmd* is already defined for that encoding, it is not redefined. *(1994/12/01)*

2ε \ProvideTextCommandDefault{\*cmd*}{*code*}[*narg*][*opt*]{*def*} [p]
. . . . . . . . . . . . . . . . . . . . . . . . . . . . . (8.5.9) – 237

> Is the same as \DeclareTextCommandDefault except that if a default encoding definition already exists for \*cmd*, then no redefinition occurs and the previous definition is retained. *(1994/12/01)*

\ps *text* . . . . . . . . . . . . . . . . . . . . . . . . . (A.1) – 297

> Adds a postscript to a letter in the letter document class.

\Psi [m] produces $\Psi$ . . . . . . . . . . . . . . . . . . (5.3.1) – 121
\psi [m] produces $\psi$ . . . . . . . . . . . . . . . . . . (5.3.1) – 121
\pushtabs . . . . . . . . . . . . . . . . . . . . . . . . (4.6.4) – 82

> Saves the current set of tabulator stops in the tabbing environment. It may be recalled with the \poptabs command.

\put($x, y$){*pic_elem*} . . . . . . . . . . . . . . . . . . (6.3) – 151

> The positioning command within a picture environment. The picture element *pic_elem* is placed with its reference point at the location $(x, y)$.

[2ε] \qbezier[*num*]$(x_1,y_1)(x_2,y_2)(x_3,y_3)$ . . . . . . . (6.4.9) – 161

This command can be given within the picture environment to draw a quadratic Bézier curve from point $(x_1,y_1)$ to $(x_3,y_3)$, using $(x_2,y_2)$ as the extra Bézier point. The curve is drawn as *num* + 1 dots if the optional argument *num* is given, otherwise *num* is calculated automatically to produce a solid line. It is the same as \bezier except that *num* is optional.

\quad . . . . . . . . . . . . . . . . . . . . . . . (3.5.1) – 47

Inserts horizontal spacing of size 1 em.

\qquad . . . . . . . . . . . . . . . . . . . . . . (3.5.1) – 47

Inserts horizontal spacing of size 2 em.

[2ε] \quotedblbase . . . . . . . . . . . . . . . . . . (E.10.5) – 423

When T1 encoding is active, prints the symbol „. *(1994/12/01)*

[2ε] \quotesinglbase . . . . . . . . . . . . . . . . . (E.10.5) – 423

When T1 encoding is active, prints the symbol ‚. *(1994/12/01)*

[2ε] \r{*x*} . . . . . . . . . . . . . . . . . . . . . (2.5.7) – 21

Produces a circle accent: \r{o} = o̊.

\raggedbottom . . . . . . . . . . . . . . . . . . . (3.2.4) – 34

The standard page formatting for article, report, and letter document classes when the twoside option has *not* been selected. The spacing between paragraphs is fixed so that the last line will vary from page to page. The opposite command is \flushbottom.

\raggedleft . . . . . . . . . . . . . . . . . . . . (4.2.2) – 64

After this declaration, the lines of text will only be right justified and the left margin will be uneven. The individual lines are terminated by \\. See also \begin{flushright}.

\raggedright . . . . . . . . . . . . . . . . . . . . (4.2.2) – 64

After this declaration, the lines of text will only be left justified and the right margin will be uneven. The individual lines are terminated by \\. See also \begin{flushleft}.

\raisebox{*lift*}[*height*][*depth*]{*text*} . . . . . . . . . (4.7.2) – 86

An LR box containing *text* is raised an amount *lift* above the current baseline. If *lift* is negative, the box is lowered. The optional arguments state that it is to be treated as though it extended by *height* above and by *depth* below the baseline regardless of its true extents.

Prints the number of the section, equation, figure, or table where *marker* has been set by a \label{*marker*} command.

A command made available with the graphics package that reflects the contents *text* as an LR box such that left and right are reversed.

Command for International LaTeX containing the heading for the bibliography in article document class. In English, this is 'References' but may be altered for adaptation to other languages.

Increases the value of the number stored in *counter* by one, the same as \stepcounter, but also makes the specified counter the relevent one for the \label-\ref cross-referencing commands.

The same as \newcommand except that the command \*com_name* must already exist, otherwise an error message is printed.

The same as \renewcommand except that the arguments to \*com_name* must be 'short', not containing any new paragraphs. *(1994/12/01)*

In LaTeX 2.09, the [*opt*] is missing so that the new command cannot have any optional arguments.

The same as \newenvironment except that the environment *env_name* must already exist, otherwise an error message is printed.

The same as \renewenvironment except that the arguments to \begin{*env_name*} must be 'short', not containing any new paragraphs. *(1994/12/01)*

In LaTeX 2.09, the [*opt*] is missing so that the new \begin command cannot have any optional arguments.

This command is the equivalent of \usepackage within a class or package file. It loads one or more package files with the extension .sty. More than one package may be specified in *packages*, the names being separated by commas. Any *options* listed will be applied to all packages. Furthermore, any options listed in the \documentclass command will also be applied to the package files.

The optional *version* is a date, given in the form yyyy/mm/dd, as for example 1994/08/01. If the date of the package file is earlier than this, a warning message is printed.

A command made available with the graphics package that scales the contents *text* as an LR box such that the horizontal size becomes *h_length* and the vertical size *v_length*. If either size is given as !, the one scale factor is applied to both dimensions.

The same as \resizebox except that the vertical size *v_length* refers to the total heigth plus depth of the LR box.

Changes the placement of marginal notes from the standard (right or 'outer' margin) to the opposite side. Can be countermanded with \normalmarginpar.

Adjusts the size of the bracket symbol *rbrack* to fit the height of the formula between the \left ... \right pair. For example, \right]. If there is to be no matching bracket, the \left and \right commands must still be given to specify the part of the formula to be sized, but the missing bracket is given as a period (for example, \left.).

`\rightmargin` . . . . . . . . . . . . . . . . . . . . . . . . . . . (4.4.2) – 75

> In a `list` environment, the amount by which the right edge of the text is indented relative to the right side of the surrounding text. Standard value is 0 pt. A new value is assigned with the `\setlength` command:
>
> `\setlength{\rightmargin}{0.5cm}`

2.09  `\rm` . . . . . . . . . . . . . . . . . . . . . . . . . . . . . . . . (4.1.5) – 62

> Switches to the Roman, upright, medium typeface (the default).

2ε  `\rmdefault` . . . . . . . . . . . . . . . . . . . . . . . . . . . . (8.5.3) – 229

> This command defines the family attribute that is selected with the `\rmfamily` command. It may be redefined with `\renewcommand`:
>
> `\renewcommand{\rmdefault}{ptm}`

2ε  `\rmfamily` . . . . . . . . . . . . . . . . (4.1.3), (8.5.2) – 60, 228

> This declaration switches to a font in the current series and shape, but with the Roman family attribute.

`\Roman{`*counter*`}` . . . . . . . . . . . . . . . . . . . . . (7.1.4) – 183

> Prints the current value of the *counter* as an upper case Roman numeral.

`\roman{`*counter*`}` . . . . . . . . . . . . . . . . . . . . . (7.1.4) – 183

> Prints the current value of the *counter* as an lower case Roman numeral.

2ε  `\rotatebox{`*angle*`}{`*text*`}` . . . . . . . . . . . . . . . . (D.3.3) – 381

> A command made available with the `graphics` package that rotates the contents *text* as an LR box through the *angle* expressed in degrees. The rotation is counter-clockwise about the left-hand end of the baseline of the box.

`\rq` produces ', identical to the ' symbol.
`\rule[`*lift*`]{`*width*`}{`*height*`}` . . . . . . . . . . . . . . . . . (4.7.6) – 90

> Produces a black rectangle of width *width* and height *height*, raised above the baseline by an amount *lift*, if this optional argument is given. A value of '0 pt' for either the *width* or *height* creates an invisible horizontal or vertical *strut* that may be used to make spacing.

`\S` produces § . . . . . . . . . . . . . . . . . . . . . . . . . (2.5.5) – 21

2ε  `\SS` produces SS . . . . . . . . . . . . . . . . . . . . . . . (2.5.6) – 21

2.09  `\samepage` . . . . . . . . . . . . . . . . . . . . . . . . . . . (3.5.5) – 51

> With this command, page breaks are forbidden within a paragraph or before or after displayed formulas. Since this has never functioned satisfactorily, its use is not encouraged anymore; it is retained only for downward compatibility.

\savebox{\\*boxname*} [*width*] [*pos*] {*text*} . . . . . . . . (4.7.1) – 86

Functions the same as the \makebox command except that the box contents are not output but saved under the name \\*boxname*, which has been previously defined with \newsavebox. The box may be set any place in the text as often as desired with the command \usebox{\\*boxname*}.

\savebox{\\*sub_pic_name*} (*x_dim,y_dim*) [*pos*] {*sub_pic*} . (6.5.3) – 164

In the picture environment, a sub-picture *sub_pic* may be stored as a box of width *x_dim* and height *y_dim* under the name \\*boxname*, which has been previously defined with \newsavebox. The *pos* argument functions as it does for \makebox (picture). The box may be set any place in the picture environment with the command \usebox{\\*boxname*}.

\sb    produces a subscript, identical to the _ symbol.

\sbox{\\*boxname*}{*text*}   . . . . . . . . . . . . . . . . . (4.7.1) – 86

Stores *text* in an LR box named \\*boxname* that has previously been created with \newsavebox{\\*boxname*}. The contents of the box may be printed as often as desired with \usebox{\\*boxname*}.

2.09 \sc . . . . . . . . . . . . . . . . . . . . . . . . (4.1.5) – 62

Switches to the ROMAN, CAPS AND SMALL CAPS, MEDIUM typeface.

2ε \scalebox{*h_scale*} [*v_scale*] {*text*} . . . . . . . . . . (D.3.3) – 381

A command made available with the graphics package that scales the contents *text* as an LR box with the horizontal factor *h_scale* and optionally with the (different) vertical factor *v_scale*. If *v_scale* is missing, it is the same as *h_scale*.

2ε \scdefault   . . . . . . . . . . . . . . . . . . . (8.5.3) – 229

This command defines the shape attribute that is selected with the \scshape command. It may be redefined with \renewcommand:

     \renewcommand{\scdefault}{sc}

\scriptscriptstyle [m] . . . . . . . . . . . . . . . (5.5.2) – 141

Switches to font size \scriptscriptstyle as the active font inside a math formula.

\scriptsize . . . . . . . . . . . . . . . . . . . . (4.1.2) – 58

Switches to the font size \scriptsize, which is smaller than \footnotesize but larger than \tiny.

\scriptstyle [m] . . . . . . . . . . . . . . . . . . (5.5.2) – 141

Switches to font size \scriptstyle as the active font inside a math formula.

$\boxed{2_\varepsilon}$ `\scshape` . . . . . . . . . . . . . . . . . (4.1.3), (8.5.2) – 60, 228

This declaration switches to a font in the current family and series, but with the CAPS AND SMALL CAPS shape attribute.

`\searrow` [m] produces ↘ . . . . . . . . . . . . . . . . (5.3.5) – 123
`\sec` [m] . . . . . . . . . . . . . . . . . . . . . . . (5.3.8) – 124

Command to produce the function name 'sec' in formulas.

`\section`[*short title*]{*title*} . . . . . . . . . . . . . . . (3.3.3) – 39

Begins a new section, formatting *title* with the current chapter number (`book` and `report` classes only) and an automatic sequential section number. If the optional *short title* is given, it appears in place of *title* in the table of contents and the running head at the top of the pages.

`\section`*{*title*} . . . . . . . . . . . . . . . . . . . . (3.3.3) – 39

The same as `\section` but without a number or an entry in the table of contents.

`\see` . . . . . . . . . . . . . . . . . . . . . . . . . (8.4) – 222

A command defined in the file `makeidx.sty` for use with the MakeIndex program. It is called within an `\index` command to refer to another entry in the index register, in the form:

   `\index{`*entry*`|see{`*reference*`}}`
Note: the above text is correct with | in place of \ for |see.

`\seename` [i] . . . . . . . . . . . . . . . . . . . . . (C.3.3) – 350

A command defined in the file `makeidx.sty` for International LATEX containing the text for the command `\see`. In English, this is 'see' but may be altered for adaptation to other languages.

$\boxed{2_\varepsilon}$ `\selectfont` . . . . . . . . . . . . . . . . . . . (8.5.1) – 227

Activates the font with the current set of attributes, making it the current font in which text is set. It should normally follow an attribute selection command. Example:

   `\fontshape{sl}\selectfont`

`\selectlanguage`{*language*} . . . . . . . . (C.3.3), (D.1.3) – 351, 367

Command in multi-language packages such as `esperant`, `german` and in the `babel` system for changing the language. The names of titles, the form of the date command `\today`, special language-specific commands, and the hyphenation patterns (TEX version 3) are all changed. Example:

   `\selectlanguage{english}`

[2ε] `\setboolean{`*switch*`}{`*value*`}` . . . . . . . . . . . . . (7.3.5) – 195

Sets the value of a boolean switch to ⟨*true*⟩ or ⟨*false*⟩, depending on *value*, which must be `true` or `false`. The switch must have been created with `\newboolean{`*switch*`}`. Its value is tested with `\boolean{`*switch*`}`, which may be used as a logical statement in the *test* part of `\ifthenelse` and `\whiledo`. Requires the standard LATEX package `ifthen`.

`\setcounter{`*counter*`}{`*value*`}` . . . . . . . . . . . . . (7.1.3) – 182

Assigns the integral number *value* to the counter *counter*.

`\setlength{\`*length_cmd*`}{`*length_spec*`}` . . . . . . . . (7.2) – 184

The length command with the name `\`*length_cmd* is assigned the length value *length_spec*, which may be a fixed or rubber length. See also . . . . . . . . . . . . . . . . . (2.4.1), (2.4.2) – 19, 19

[2ε] `\SetMathAlphabet{\`*cmd*`}{`*ver*`}{`*code*`}{`*fam*`}{`*ser*`}{`*shp*`}` [p]
. . . . . . . . . . . . . . . . . . . . . . . . . . . . (8.5.5) – 231

Defines the math alphabet that has been declared with `\DeclareMathAlphabet` to take the specified font attibutes in the math version *ver*.

`\setminus` [m] produces \ . . . . . . . . . . . . . . . (5.3.3) – 122

[2ε] `\SetSymbolFont{`*sym_fnt*`}{`*ver*`}{`*code*`}{`*fam*`}{`*ser*`}{`*shp*`}` [p]
. . . . . . . . . . . . . . . . . . . . . . . . . . . . (8.5.6) – 231

Defines the symbol font that has been declared with `\DeclareSymbolFont` to take the specified font attibutes in the math version *ver*.

[2ε] `\settime{`*secs*`}` . . . . . . . . . . . . . . . . . (8.10.3) – 251

In the `slides` class, if the option `clock` has been selected, a time marker, in minutes, appears at the bottom of the notes. This command sets the internal timer to the specified number of seconds. See also `\addtime`.

[2ε] `\settodepth{\`*length_cmd*`}{`*text*`}` . . . . . . . . . . . . (7.2) – 185

The length command with the name `\`*length_cmd* is assigned a value equal to the depth of *text* below the baseline.

[2ε] `\settoheight{\`*length_cmd*`}{`*text*`}` . . . . . . . . . . . . (7.2) – 185

The length command with the name `\`*length_cmd* is assigned a value equal to the height of *text* above the baseline.

`\settowidth{\`*length_cmd*`}{`*text*`}` . . . . . . . . . . . . (7.2) – 185

The length command with the name `\`*length_cmd* is assigned a value equal to the length of *text* as it would be set in an LR box.

2.09 `\sf` . . . . . . . . . . . . . . . . . . . . . . . (4.1.5) – 62

Switches to the sans serif, upright, medium typeface.

2ε `\sfdefault` . . . . . . . . . . . . . . . . . (8.5.3) – 229

This command defines the family attribute that is selected with the `\sffamily` command. It may be redefined with `\renewcommand`:

`\renewcommand{\sfdefault}{phv}`

2ε `\sffamily` . . . . . . . . . . . . . . . (4.1.3), (8.5.2) – 60, 228

This declaration switches to a font in the current series and shape, but with the sans serif family attribute.

`\sharp [m] produces ♯` . . . . . . . . . . . . . . (5.3.6) – 123
`\shortstack[`*pos*`]{`*text*`}` . . . . . . . . . . . . . (6.4.7) – 160

Formats the *text* into a single column, where the individual rows are terminated by `\\`. The optional positioning argument *pos* takes on values of `l` or `r` to set the text left or right justified, otherwise it is centered. Example:

`\shortstack{aa\\bbb\\cc\\x\\yy\\zzz}`

aa
bbb
cc
x
yy
zzz

`\showhyphens{`*word_list*`}` . . . . . . . . . . . . . . . (3.6.5) – 55

Displays on the terminal screen the possible divisions for the words in *word_list*.

`\Sigma [m] produces Σ` . . . . . . . . . . . . . . (5.3.1) – 121
`\sigma [m] produces σ` . . . . . . . . . . . . . . (5.3.1) – 121
`\signature{`*name*`}` . . . . . . . . . . . . . . . . (A.1) – 296

In the `letter` document class, supplies the name of the writer that should go below the signature if this is different from the entry in `\name`.

`\sim [m] produces ~` . . . . . . . . . . . . . . . (5.3.4) – 122
`\simeq [m] produces ≃` . . . . . . . . . . . . . . (5.3.4) – 122
`\sin [m]` . . . . . . . . . . . . . . . . . . . (5.3.8) – 124

Command to produce the function name 'sin' in formulas.

`\sinh [m]` . . . . . . . . . . . . . . . . . . (5.3.8) – 124

Command to produce the function name 'sinh' in formulas.

2.09 `\sl` . . . . . . . . . . . . . . . . . . . . . . . (4.1.5) – 62

Switches to the *Roman, slanted, medium* typeface.

2ε `\sldefault` . . . . . . . . . . . . . . . . . (8.5.3) – 229

This command defines the shape attribute that is selected with the `\slshape` command. It may be redefined with `\renewcommand`:

`\renewcommand{\sldefault}{sl}`

`\sloppy` . . . . . . . . . . . . . . . . . . . . . . (3.6.3) – 54

> After this command has been given, word spacings are allowed to stretch more generously than usual so that paragraphs are broken up into lines with fewer word divisions. It is countermanded by `\fussy`. See also `\begin{sloppypar}`.

$\boxed{2\varepsilon}$ `\slshape` . . . . . . . . . . . . . . . . (4.1.3), (8.5.2) – 60, 228

> This declaration switches to a font in the current family and series, but with the *slanted* shape attribute.

`\small` . . . . . . . . . . . . . . . . . . . . . . . (4.1.2) – 58

> Switches to the font size `\small`, which is smaller than `\normalsize` but larger than `\footnotesize`.

`\smallskip` . . . . . . . . . . . . . . . . . . . . . (3.5.3) – 49

> Inserts large vertical spacing of amount `\smallskipamount`. See also `\medskip` and `\bigskip`.

`\smallskipamount`

> Standard value for the amount of vertical spacing that is inserted with the command `\smallskip`. May be changed with the `\setlength` command:
>
> `\setlength{\smallskipamount}{1ex plus0.5ex minus0.3ex}`

`\smile` [m] produces ⌣ . . . . . . . . . . . . . . . . . (5.3.4) – 122
`\sp` produces a superscript, identical to the ˆ symbol.
`\spadesuit` [m] produces ♠ . . . . . . . . . . . . . . (5.3.6) – 123
`\sqcap` [m] produces ⊓ . . . . . . . . . . . . . . . . . (5.3.3) – 122
`\sqcup` [m] produces ⊔ . . . . . . . . . . . . . . . . . (5.3.3) – 122
`\sqrt`[*n*]{*arg*} [m] . . . . . . . . . . . . . . . . (5.2.4) – 118

> Basic math command to produce a root sign. The height and length of the sign are made to fit the contents *arg*. The optional argument *n* is the degree of the root: `\sqrt[3]{2}` = $\sqrt[3]{2}$, `\sqrt{2}` = $\sqrt{2}$.

`\sqsubset` [m] produces ⊏ . . . . . . . . . . . . . . . . (5.3.4) – 122
`\sqsubseteq` [m] produces ⊑ . . . . . . . . . . . . . . (5.3.4) – 122
`\sqsupset` [m] produces ⊐ . . . . . . . . . . . . . . . (5.3.4) – 122
`\sqsupseteq` [m] produces ⊒ . . . . . . . . . . . . . . (5.3.4) – 122
`\ss` produces ß . . . . . . . . . . . . . . . . . . . . (2.5.6) – 21
`\stackrel`{*upper*}{*lower*} [m] . . . . . . . . . . . . (5.4.5) – 133

> Places one mathematical symbol *upper* on top of another *lower*, such that the upper one appears in a smaller type face:
>
> `\stackrel{\alpha}{\longrightarrow}` = $\stackrel{\alpha}{\longrightarrow}$

`\star` [m] produces ⋆ . . . . . . . . . . . . . . . . . (5.3.3) – 122
`\stepcounter`{*counter*} . . . . . . . . . . . . . . . . (7.1.3) – 182

> Increases the value of the number stored in *counter* by one.

`\stretch{`*decimal_num*`}` . . . . . . . . . . . . . . . (7.2) – 185

>  A rubber length with a natural value of 0 pt but with a stretchability
>  that is *decimal_num* times that of `\fill`.

`\subitem{`*sub_entry*`}` . . . . . . . . . . . . . . . . . (8.3.3) – 219

>  In `theindex` environment, a command to produce a second level entry
>  after an `\item` command.

`\subjectname` [i] . . . . . . . . . . . . . . . . . . . . (C.3.3) – 350

>  Command for International LaTeX for use in modified `letter` docu-
>  ment classes. It prints the text of the `\subject` command. In English,
>  this is 'Subject' but may be altered for adaptation to other languages.
>  (This command is not standardized!)

`\subparagraph[`*short title*`]{`*title*`}` . . . . . . . . . . . . (3.3.3) – 39

>  The last command in the sectioning hierarchy, coming after
>  `\paragraph`. It formats *title* with the current paragraph number
>  and an automatic sequential sub-paragraph number. If the optional
>  *short title* is given, it appears in place of *title* in the table of contents.

`\subparagraph*{`*title*`}` . . . . . . . . . . . . . . . . . (3.3.3) – 39

>  The same as `\subparagraph` but without a number or an entry in the
>  table of contents.

`\subsection[`*short title*`]{`*title*`}` . . . . . . . . . . . . (3.3.3) – 39

>  The command in the sectioning hierarchy that comes between the
>  `\section` and `\subsubsection`. It formats *title* with the current
>  section number and an automatic sequential subsection number. If
>  the optional *short title* is given, it appears in place of *title* in the table
>  of contents.

`\subsection*{`*title*`}` . . . . . . . . . . . . . . . . . . (3.3.3) – 39

>  The same as `\subsection` but without a number or an entry in the
>  table of contents.

`\subsubitem{`*sub_sub_entry*`}` . . . . . . . . . . . . . . (8.3.3) – 219

>  In `theindex` environment, a command to produce a third level entry
>  under a `\subitem` command.

`\subsubsection[`*short form*`]{`*title*`}` . . . . . . . . . . . (3.3.3) – 39

>  The command in the sectioning hierarchy coming between
>  `\subsection` and `\paragraph`. It formats *title* with the current sub-
>  section number and an automatic sequential sub-subsection number.
>  If the optional *short title* is given, it appears in place of *title* in the
>  table of contents.

`\subsubsection*{`*title*`}` . . . . . . . . . . . . . . . . . (3.3.3) – 39

>  The same as `\subsubsection` but without a number or an entry in
>  the table of contents.

> Command to produce the function name 'sup' in formulas. A lower limit may be set as a subscript.

2ε `\suppressfloats[loc]` . . . . . . . . . . . . . . . . . (6.6.2) – 174

> Any floats given between this command and the end of the current page will be suspended at least until the next page. If the optional *loc* is given as one of t or b (not both), only floats with that placement parameter are suspended.

> Produces the symbol in the current character font that is stored under the internal number $n$.

`\t{xy}` . . . . . . . . . . . . . . . . . . . . . . . . . (2.5.7) – 21

> Produces a 'tie-after' accent over two letters: `\t{oo}` = o͡o.

`\tabbingsep` . . . . . . . . . . . . . . . . . . . . . . (4.6.4) – 82

> Determines the spacing between the text *ltext* and the current tabular stop when *ltext*`\'` is given in a `tabbing` environment. A new value may be assigned with the `\setlength` command.

`\tabcolsep` . . . . . . . . . . . . . . . . . . . . . . . (4.8.2) – 96

> Determines the half-column spacing in the `tabular` environment. A new value may be assigned with the `\setlength` command:
>
>     \setlength{\tabcolsep}{3mm}

`\tableofcontents` . . . . . . . . . . . . . . . . . . . . (3.4.2) – 43

> Prints the table of contents from information in the sectioning commands and additional entries.

`\tablename` [i] . . . . . . . . . . . . . . . . . . . . . (C.3.3) – 350

> Command for International LaTeX containing the name for a table caption. In English, this is 'Table' but may be altered for adaptation to other languages.

2ε  \tabularnewline[*len*] . . . . . . . . . . . . . . . . . . (4.8.1) – 96

Terminates a row in the `tabular` or `array` environments, adding vertical spacing *len* if it is specified. This is equivalent to \\[*len*] except that there is no ambiguity as to whether it is terminating a row in the table or a line of text within a column entry. If something like \raggedright is given in the last column, then this command *must* be used in place of \\. *(1994/12/01)*

\tan [m] . . . . . . . . . . . . . . . . . . . . . . (5.3.8) – 124

Command to produce the function name 'tan' in formulas.

\tanh [m]  . . . . . . . . . . . . . . . . . . . . . (5.3.8) – 124

Command to produce the function name 'tanh' in formulas.

\tau [m] produces $\tau$ . . . . . . . . . . . . . . . . (5.3.1) – 121

\telephone{*number*}  . . . . . . . . . . . (A.1), (A.2) – 296, 300

In the `letter` document class, enters the sender's telephone number. In the standard LaTeX `letter.sty`, *number* is only output if \address has not been called. It is intended to be used in company letter styles such as `mpletter`.

\TeX produces TeX . . . . . . . . . . . . . . . . (2.1) – 16

2ε  \text*sym_name*  . . . . . . . . . . . . . . . . . . (8.7) – 238

An alternative means to produce certain special symbols that otherwise are only available in math mode or through ligature combinations:
\textbullet (•); \textemdash (—); \textendash (–);
\textexclamdown (¡); \textperiodcentered (·);
\textquestiondown (¿); \textquotedblleft (");
\textquotedblright ("); \textquoteleft ('); \textquoteright
('); \textvisiblespace (␣)
*(1994/12/01)*

2ε  \textbf{*text*}  . . . . . . . . . . . . . . . . . . (4.1.4) – 61

This command sets its argument in a font in the current family and shape, but with the **bold** series attribute. It is equivalent to {\bfseries *text*}.

2ε  \textcircled{*char*}  . . . . . . . . . . . . . . . . (8.7) – 238

Produces the specified character in a cirlce: \textcircled{s} = Ⓢ. *(1994/12/01)*

2ε  \textcolor *col_spec*{*text*}  . . . . . . . . . . . . . (D.3.3) – 383

A command made available with the `color` package. The *text* is set in the specified color. The *col_spec* is the same as for \color.

Prints an invisible character that may be used to break ligatures:

f\textcompwordmark i = fi
*(1994/12/01)*

The vertical spacing between floats at the top of the page and the following text or between text and floats at the bottom of the page. A new value is set with the \setlength command.

     \setlength{\textfloatsep}{20pt plus 2pt minus 4pt}

The minimum fraction of a page containing text and floats that must be filled with text. A new value is set with

     \renewcommand{\textfraction}{*decimal_frac*}.

The total height reserved for the text on each page, excluding head and footlines. A new value may be assigned with the \setlength command:

     \setlength{\textheight}{45\baselineskip}

This command sets its argument in a font in the current family and series, but with the *italic* shape attribute.  It is equivalent to {\itshape *text*}.

This command sets its argument in a font in the current family and shape, **but with the** medium **series attribute.**  It is equivalent to {\mdseries *text*}.

This command sets its argument in the font with the default family, series, and shape attributes. It is equivalent to {\normalfont *text*}.

When T1 encoding is active, prints the symbol ". *(1994/12/01)*

This command sets its argument in a font in the current series and shape, but with the Roman family attribute.  It is equivalent to {\rmfamily *text*}.

`2ε` \textsc{*text*}  . . . . . . . . . . . . . . . (4.1.4) – 61

This command sets its argument in a font in the current family and series, but with the CAPS AND SMALL CAPS shape attribute.  It is equivalent to {\scshape *text*}.

`2ε` \textsf{*text*}  . . . . . . . . . . . . . . . (4.1.4) – 61

This command sets its argument in a font in the current series and shape, but with the sans serif family attribute.  It is equivalent to {\sffamily *text*}.

`2ε` \textsl{*text*}  . . . . . . . . . . . . . . . (4.1.4) – 61

This command sets its argument in a font in the current family and series, but with the *slanted* shape attribute.  It is equivalent to {\slshape *text*}.

\textstyle [m]  . . . . . . . . . . . . . . . (5.5.2) – 141

Switches to font size \textstyle as the active font inside a math formula.

`2ε` \texttt{*text*}  . . . . . . . . . . . . . . . (4.1.4) – 61

This command sets its argument in a font in the current series and shape, but with the typewriter family attribute.  It is equivalent to {\ttfamily *text*}.

`2ε` \textup{*text*}  . . . . . . . . . . . . . . . (4.1.4) – 61

This command sets its argument in a font in the current family and series, *but with the* upright *shape attribute*.  It is equivalent to {\upshape *text*}.

\textwidth  . . . . . . . . . . . . . . . . (3.2.4) – 35

The total width reserved for the text on a page.  For two-column formatting, this is the width of both columns plus the gap between them. A new value may be assigned with the \setlength command.

`2ε` \TH . . . . . . . . . . . . . . . . . . (E.10.5) – 423

When T1 encoding is active, prints the character Þ.

`2ε` \th . . . . . . . . . . . . . . . . . . (E.10.5) – 423

When T1 encoding is active, prints the character þ.

\thanks{*footnote_text*}  . . . . . . . . . . . . . (3.3.1) – 37

Produces a footnote to an author's name on the title page when \maketitle is called.

\the*counter* . . . . . . . . . . . . . . . . . . (7.1.4) – 183
> Internal commands for formatting and printing the value of the counter, making possible use of other counters. For example, \thesubsection might be defined to be \thesection.\roman{subsection}. A new definition may be made with \renewcommand{\the*counter*}{*def*}.

\Theta [m] produces Θ . . . . . . . . . . . . . . . (5.3.1) – 121
\theta [m] produces θ . . . . . . . . . . . . . . . (5.3.1) – 121
\thicklines . . . . . . . . . . . . . . . . . . (6.5.1) – 162
> In the picture environment, this command sets all the sloping lines and arrows, circles, and ovals to be drawn with thicker than normal lines.

\thinlines . . . . . . . . . . . . . . . . . . (6.5.1) – 162
> In the picture environment, resets the line thickness for sloping lines and arrows, circles, and ovals back to the standard value after \thicklines has been given.

\thispagestyle{*style*} . . . . . . . . . . . . . . . (3.2) – 31
> Changes the page style for the current page only. Possible values for *style* are: plain, empty, headings, and myheadings.

\tilde{*x*} [m] . . . . . . . . . . . . . . . . . (5.3.9) – 125
> Produces a tilde (squiggle) over the math variable *x*:  \tilde{a} = $\tilde{a}$.

\tiny . . . . . . . . . . . . . . . . . . . . . (4.1.2) – 58
> Switches to the smallest font size available \tiny, smaller than \scriptsize.

\times [m] produces × . . . . . . . . . . . . . . (5.3.3) – 122
\title{*text*} . . . . . . . . . . . . . . . . . . (3.3.1) – 36
> Enters the *text* for the title page that is produced by \maketitle.

\to [m] produces → . . . . . . . . . . . . . . . (5.3.5) – 123
\today . . . . . . . . . . . . . . . . . (2.5.9), (C.3.3) – 22, 349
> Prints the current date in the American fashion. This form may be changed to British or to that of other languages by redefining the command with the help of the internal TEX commands \day, \month, and \year.

\top [m] produces ⊤ . . . . . . . . . . . . . . . (5.3.6) – 123
|2ε| \topfigrule . . . . . . . . . . . . . . . . (6.6.3) – 175
> A command that is executed after a float at the top of a page. It is normally defined to do nothing, but may be redefined to add a rule between the float and the main text. It must not add any net vertical spacing.

> ```
> \renewcommand{\topfigrule}{\vspace*{-.4pt}
>   \rule{\columnwidth}{.4pt}}
> ```

`\topfraction` . . . . . . . . . . . . . . . . . . . . . . (6.6.3) – 174

> The maximum fraction of a page that may be occupied at the top by floats at the top of the page. A new value is assigned with
>
> `\renewcommand{\topfraction}{`*decimal_frac*`}`

`\topmargin` . . . . . . . . . . . . . . . . . . . . . . (3.2.4) – 35

> The size of the margin from the top of the page to the page head. A new value may be assigned by the `\setlength` command:
>
> `\setlength{topmargin}{0.5in}`

`topnumber` . . . . . . . . . . . . . . . . . . . . . . . (6.6.3) – 174

> The maximum number of floats that may appear at the top of a page. A new value is assigned with:
>
> `\setcounter{topnumber}{`*num*`}`

`\topsep` . . . . . . . . . . . . . . . . . (4.4.2), (5.5.4) – 74, 145

> The extra vertical spacing, in addition to `\parskip`, inserted at the beginning and end of a listing environment. When document class option `fleqn` has been chosen, it is also inserted at the beginning and end of displayed math formulas. A new value may be assigned with the `\setlength` command:
>
> `\setlength{\topsep}{4pt plus2pt minus2pt}`

`\topskip` . . . . . . . . . . . . . . . . . . . . . . . . (3.2.4) – 35

> The vertical distance from the top of the page body to the baseline of the first line of text. A new value may be assigned with the `\setlength` command:
>
> `\setlength{\topskip}{12pt}`

[2ε] `\totalheight` . . . . . . . . . . . . . . . . . . . . . (4.7.1) – 85

> A length parameter equal to the total natural height of a box (height plus depth); it may only be used in the *width* specification of `\makebox`, `\framebox`, or `\savebox`, or in the *height* specification of a `\parbox` or a `minipage` environment.
>
> `\framebox[6\totalheight]{text}`

`totalnumber` . . . . . . . . . . . . . . . . . . . . . . (6.6.3) – 174

> The total number of floats that may appear on a page regardless of their positions. A new value is assigned with:
>
> `\setcounter{totalnumber}{`*num*`}`

`\triangle` [m] produces △ . . . . . . . . . . . . . . . . (5.3.6) – 123
`\triangleleft` [m] produces ◁ . . . . . . . . . . . . . . (5.3.3) – 122
`\triangleright` [m] produces ▷ . . . . . . . . . . . . . (5.3.3) – 122

[2.09] `\tt` . . . . . . . . . . . . . . . . . . . . . . . . . . (4.1.5) – 62

> Switches to the `typewriter`, `upright`, `medium` typeface.

$\boxed{2_\varepsilon}$ `\ttdefault` . . . . . . . . . . . . . . . . . . . . . (8.5.3) – 229

This command defines the family attribute that is selected with the `\ttfamily` command. It may be redefined with `\renewcommand`:

`\renewcommand{\ttdefault}{pcr}`

$\boxed{2_\varepsilon}$ `\ttfamily` . . . . . . . . . . . . . . . . . (4.1.3), 8.5.2) – 60, 228

This declaration switches to a font in the current series and shape, but with the `typewriter` family attribute.

`\twocolumn[`*text*`]` . . . . . . . . . . . . . . . . . . . . . (3.2.5) – 35

Begins a new page and switches to two-column page format. The optional *text* is set in one column extending over the two columns.

`\typein[\`*cmd*`]{`*message*`}` . . . . . . . . . . . . . . (8.1.3) – 213

Prints the *message* to the terminal screen and stops the program, waiting for a reply from the user. The text of the response is assigned to the LaTeX command named `\@typein`, or to `\`*cmd* if the optional argument has been given. After the return key is pressed, the processing continues. The typed-in text is inserted in place of `\@typein` if the optional argument was not given, otherwise it may be inserted as one pleases with the `\`*cmd* command.

`\typeout{`*message*`}` . . . . . . . . . . . . . . . . . . (8.1.3) – 212

Prints the *message* to the terminal screen and continues the processing. The *message* is also written to the `.log` file.

`\u{`*x*`}` . . . . . . . . . . . . . . . . . . . . . . (2.5.7) – 21

Produces a breve accent: `\u{o}` = ŏ.

`\unboldmath` . . . . . . . . . . . . . . . . . . . . (5.4.9) – 139

Countermands the `\boldmath` command. It must be given outside of the math mode. Afterwards, formulas are set in standard '*math italics*' once more.

`\underbrace{`*sub_form*`}` [m] . . . . . . . . . . . . (5.4.4) – 132

Produces a horizontal curly brace beneath the math formula *sub_form*. Any following subscript will be placed centered below the horizontal brace.

`\underbrace{a+b}`: $\underbrace{a+b}$

`\underbrace{x+y+z}_{\xi\eta\zeta}`: $\underbrace{x+y+z}_{\xi\eta\zeta}$

`\underline{`*text*`}` . . . . . . . . . . . . . . . . . (5.4.4) – 132

Underlines the *text* in both math and normal text modes: `\underline{Text}` = $\underline{\text{Text}}$.

`\unitlength` . . . . . . . . . . . . . . . . . . . . . . . (6.1) – 150

Defines the unit of length for the following `picture` environments. A value is assigned with the `\setlength` command:

> `\setlength{\unitlength}{1.2cm}`

`\unlhd [m]` produces ⊴ . . . . . . . . . . . . . . . (5.3.3) – 122
`\unrhd [m]` produces ⊵ . . . . . . . . . . . . . . . (5.3.3) – 122
`\Uparrow [m]` produces ⇑ . . . . . . . . . . . . . . (5.3.5) – 123
`\uparrow [m]` produces ↑ . . . . . . . . . . . . . . (5.3.5) – 123

2ε `\updefault` . . . . . . . . . . . . . . . . . . . . (8.5.3) – 229

This command defines the shape attribute that is selected with the `\upshape` command. It may be redefined with `\renewcommand`:

> `\renewcommand{\updefault}{n}`

`\Updownarrow [m]` produces ⇕ . . . . . . . . . . . (5.3.5) – 123
`\updownarrow [m]` produces ↕ . . . . . . . . . . . (5.3.5) – 123
`\uplus [m]` produces ⊎ . . . . . . . . . . . . . . . (5.3.3) – 122

2ε `\upshape` . . . . . . . . . . . . . . . . (4.1.3), (8.5.2) – 60, 228

This declaration switches to a font in the current family and series, *but with the* upright *shape attribute.*

`\Upsilon [m]` produces ϒ . . . . . . . . . . . . . . (5.3.1) – 121
`\upsilon [m]` produces υ . . . . . . . . . . . . . . (5.3.1) – 121
`\usebox{\`*boxname*`}` . . . . . . . . . . . . . . . . . (4.7.1) – 86

Inserts into the text the contents of the box that was saved with the `\sbox` or `\savebox` command under the name `\`*boxname*, which has been previously created with the `\newsavebox` command.

`\usecounter{`*counter*`}` . . . . . . . . . . . . . . . . (4.4.1) – 74

Command in the `list` environment that specifies which counter is to be employed in the standard labels with the `\item` commands. This counter is incremented by one with each `\item` call.

2ε `\usefont{`*code*`}{`*fam*`}{`*ser*`}{`*shp*`}` . . . . . . . . . . (8.5.1) – 227

Activates the font with the given set of attributes in the current size. Is equivalent to selecting the given font attributes and then calling `\selectfont`.

2ε `\usepackage[`*options*`]{`*packages*`}[`*version*`] [p]` . . . . . (3.1.2) – 29

Loads one or more package files containing additional LaTeX or TeX definitions. The files have the extension `.sty`. More than one package may be specified in *packages*, the names being separated by commas. Any *options* listed will be applied to all packages. Furthermore, any options listed in the `\documentclass` command will also be applied to the package files.

The optional *version* is a date, given in the form `yyyy/mm/dd`, as for example `1994/08/01`. If the date of the package file is earlier than this, a warning message is printed.

Example:

```
\usepackage{bezier,ifthen}[1994/06/01]
```

`\v{x}` . . . . . . . . . . . . . . . . . . . . . . . . . . . . (2.5.7) – 21

Produces háček accent: `\v{o}` = ǒ.

`\value{counter}` . . . . . . . . . . . . . . . . . . . . . (7.1.3) – 183

The current value of the number stored in *counter* for use with commands than require a number. It does *not* output this number. For example, `\setcounter{counter1}{\value{counter2}}` sets *counter1* to the same value as that of *counter2*.

`\varepsilon` [m] produces $\varepsilon$ . . . . . . . . . . . . . . . (5.3.1) – 121
`\varphi` [m] produces $\varphi$ . . . . . . . . . . . . . . . . (5.3.1) – 121
`\varpi` [m] produces $\varpi$ . . . . . . . . . . . . . . . . . (5.3.1) – 121
`\varrho` [m] produces $\varrho$ . . . . . . . . . . . . . . . . (5.3.1) – 121
`\varsigma` [m] produces $\varsigma$ . . . . . . . . . . . . . . . (5.3.1) – 121
`\vartheta` [m] produces $\vartheta$ . . . . . . . . . . . . . . . (5.3.1) – 121
`\vdash` [m] produces $\vdash$ . . . . . . . . . . . . . . . . . (5.3.6) – 123

`\vdots` [m] produces $\vdots$ . . . . . . . . . . . . . . . . (5.2.6) – 119
`\vec{x}` [m] . . . . . . . . . . . . . . . . . . . . . . . (5.3.9) – 125

A vector symbol over the variable $x$: `\vec{a}` = $\vec{a}$.

`\vector(Δx,Δy){length}` . . . . . . . . . . . . . . . . (6.4.4) – 157

A picture element command within a `picture` environment for drawing horizontal and vertical arrows of any length as well as slanted arrows at a limited number of angles. For horizontal and vertical arrows, the *length* argument is the actual length in units of `\unitlength`. For slanted arrows, *length* is the length of the projection on to the x-axis (horizontal displacement). The slope is determined by the $(\Delta x, \Delta y)$ arguments, which take on integral values such that $-4 \leq \Delta x \leq 4$ and $-4 \leq \Delta y \leq 4$. This command is the argument of a `\put` or `\multiput` command.

`\vee` [m] produces $\vee$ . . . . . . . . . . . . . . . . . . . (5.3.3) – 122
`\verb|source_text|` . . . . . . . . . . . . . . . . . . . . (4.9) – 107

Everything that comes between the |...| symbols is output in the typewriter font exactly as is with no interpretation of special symbols or commands. Any symbol other than * may be used as the switch character, illustrated here as |, as long as it does not appear in *source_text*.

\verb*|*source_text*| . . . . . . . . . . . . . . . . . . . . . (4.9) – 107

> The same as \verb except that blanks are made visible with the symbol ⎵.

\vfill . . . . . . . . . . . . . . . . . . . . . . . . (3.5.3) – 49

> A vertical rubber spacing with a natural length of zero that can be stretched to any value. Used to fill up parts of a page with blank spacing. This command is an abbreviation for \vspace{\fill}.

$\boxed{2\varepsilon}$ \visible . . . . . . . . . . . . . . . . . . . . . . (8.10.2) – 250

> In slides class, a declaration that countermands a previous \invisible command, making text printed again. It remains in effect until the end of the environment, or end of the curly braces, in which it was issued, or until \invisible is given. It is used for making overlays.

\vline . . . . . . . . . . . . . . . . . . . . . . . . . (4.8.1) – 95

> Prints a vertical rule within the column entry of a table in the tabular environment.

\voffset . . . . . . . . . . . . . . . . . . . . . . . . 511, 512

> Vertical offset of the output page from the printer border set by the printer driver. This printer border is normally 1 inch from the top edge of the paper. The standard value of \voffset is 0 pt so that the top reference margin of the page is identical with the printer margin. A new value is assigned with the \setlength command:
>
>     \setlength{\voffset}{-1in}

\vspace{*height*} . . . . . . . . . . . . . . . . . . . (3.5.3) – 49

> Produces vertical spacing of length *height*. It is ignored if it occurs at the beginning or end of a page.

\vspace*{*height*} . . . . . . . . . . . . . . . . . . (3.5.3) – 49

> Produces vertical spacing of length *height* even at the beginning or end of a page.

\wedge [m] produces ∧ . . . . . . . . . . . . . . . . . . (5.3.3) – 122
\whiledo{*test*}{*do_text*} . . . . . . . . . . . . . . . (7.3.5) – 193

> A conditional command available when the standard package ifthen has been loaded. The *do_text* is inserted repeatedly as long as the logical statement *test* evaluates to ⟨true⟩. The logical statement may be relational (two numbers with one of < = > between them), an even-odd test (\isodd{*number*}), a comparison of two texts (\equal{*text1*}{*text2*}), a comparison of two lengths (\lengthtest{*length1* op *length2*}, *op* is one of < = >), or a test of a boolean switch (\boolean{*switch*}). Switches are created with

\newboolean{*switch*} and set with \setboolean{*switch*}{*value*}, where *value* is true or false. Logical statements may be combined with logical operators \and, \or, and \not, and grouped with \( and \).

The tests \isodd, \lengthtest, and \boolean are new to LATEX 2ε.

\widehat{*xyz*} [m] . . . . . . . . . . . . . . . . . . (5.3.9) – 125

Produces a wide \hat symbol over several characters: \widehat{xyz} = $\widehat{xyz}$.

\widetilde{*xyz*} [m] . . . . . . . . . . . . . . . . (5.3.9) – 125

Produces a wide \tilde symbol over several characters: \widetilde{xyz} = $\widetilde{xyz}$.

$\boxed{2\varepsilon}$ \width . . . . . . . . . . . . . . . . . . . . . (4.7.1) – 85

A length parameter equal to the natural width of a box; it may only be used in the *width* specification of \makebox, \framebox, or \savebox, or in the *height* specification of a \parbox or a minipage environment.

\framebox[2\width]{text}

\wp [m] produces $\wp$ . . . . . . . . . . . . . . . . (5.3.6) – 123
\wr [m] produces $\wr$ . . . . . . . . . . . . . . . . (5.3.3) – 122

\Xi [m] produces $\Xi$ . . . . . . . . . . . . . . . . (5.3.1) – 121
\xi [m] produces $\xi$ . . . . . . . . . . . . . . . . (5.3.1) – 121

\zeta [m] produces $\zeta$ . . . . . . . . . . . . . . . (5.3.1) – 121

## F.2    Summary tables and figures

**Table F.1**   LaTeX 2$_\varepsilon$ font attributes   (4.1.3) – p. 60.

| | | |
|---|---|---|
| \rmfamily | \textrm{*text*} | Roman |
| \sffamily | \textsf{*text*} | sans serif |
| \ttfamily | \texttt{*text*} | typewriter |
| \upshape | \textup{*text*} | upright |
| \itshape | \textit{*text*} | *italic* |
| \slshape | \textsl{*text*} | *slanted* |
| \scshape | \textsc{*text*} | Small Caps |
| \mdseries | \textmd{*text*} | medium |
| \bfseries | \textbf{*text*} | **bold face** |

**Table F.2**   LaTeX 2$_\varepsilon$ math alphabet commands   (5.4.2) – p. 129.

| | | |
|---|---|---|
| \mathrm{*text*} | \mathtt{*text*} | \mathbf{*text*} |
| \mathsf{*text*} | \mathit{*text*} | \mathcal{*text*} |
| \mathnormal{*text*} | | |

**Table F.3**   Font sizes   (4.1.2) – p. 58.

| | | | |
|---|---|---|---|
| \tiny | smallest | \Large | larger |
| \scriptsize | very small | \LARGE | even larger |
| \footnotesize | smaller | \huge | still larger |
| \small | small | \Huge | largest |
| \normalsize | normal | | |
| \large | large | | |

**Table F.4**   LaTeX 2.09 font declarations   (4.1.5) – p. 62.

| | | | | | |
|---|---|---|---|---|---|
| \rm | Roman | \it | *Italic* | \sc | Small Caps |
| \bf | **Bold Face** | \sl | *Slanted* | \sf | Sans Serif |
| \tt | Typewriter | \mit | $\Gamma\Pi\Phi$ | \cal | $\mathcal{CAL}$ |

**Table F.5**   Dimensions   (2.4.1) – p. 19.

| | | | |
|---|---|---|---|
| mm | millimeter | bp | big point (1 in = 72 bp) |
| cm | centimeter | dd | (1157 dd = 1238 pt) |
| in | inch (1 in = 2.54 cm) | cc | cicero (1 cc = 12 dd) |
| pt | point (1 in = 72.27 pt) | sp | (1 pt = 63536 sp) |
| pc | pica (1 pc = 12 pt) | | |
| em | The current width of a capital M | | |
| ex | The current height of the letter $x$ | | |

**Table F.6**   Environment names

| | | | | |
|---|---|---|---|---|
| abstract | eqnarray | flushright | picture | tabular* |
| appendix | eqnarray* | fussypar | quotation | thebibliography |
| array | equation | itemize | quote | theindex |
| center | figure | letter | sloppypar | titlepage |
| description | figure* | list | tabbing | trivlist |
| displaymath | filecontents | lrbox | table | verbatim |
| document | filecontents* | math | table* | verbatim* |
| enumerate | flushleft | minipage | tabular | verse |

**Table F.7**   Accents   (2.5.7) – p. 21.

```
ò =\'{o}    ó=\'{o}    ô=\^{o}    ö=\"{o}    õ=\~{o}
ō =\={o}    ȯ=\.{o}    ŏ=\u{o}    ǒ=\v{o}    ő=\H{o}
o͡o=\t{oo}   o̧=\c{o}    o̤=\d{o}    o̲=\b{o}    o̊=\r{o}
```

**Table F.8**   Special letters from other languages   (2.5.6) – p. 21.

```
œ={\oe}  Œ={\OE}  æ={\ae}  Æ={\AE}  å={\aa}  Å ={\AA}  ¡=!`
ø ={\o}   Ø ={\O}   ł ={\l}   Ł ={\L}   ß={\ss}  SS={\SS}  ¿=?`
```
(The commands \r and \SS are only valid for LaTeX 2ε.)

**Table F.9**   Special symbols   (2.5.5) – 21.

```
† \dag   § \S   © \copyright   ‡ \ddag   ¶ \P   £ \pounds
```

**Table F.10**   Command symbols   (2.5.4) – 21.

```
$ \$     % \%     { \{     _ \_     & \&     # \#     } \}
```

**Table F.11**   Greek letters   (5.3.1) – p. 121.

### Lower case letters

| | | | | | | | |
|---|---|---|---|---|---|---|---|
| α | \alpha | θ | \theta | o | o | τ | \tau |
| β | \beta | ϑ | \vartheta | π | \pi | υ | \upsilon |
| γ | \gamma | ι | \iota | ϖ | \varpi | φ | \phi |
| δ | \delta | κ | \kappa | ρ | \rho | φ | \varphi |
| ε | \epsilon | λ | \lambda | ϱ | \varrho | χ | \chi |
| ε | \varepsilon | μ | \mu | σ | \sigma | ψ | \psi |
| ζ | \zeta | ν | \nu | ς | \varsigma | ω | \omega |
| η | \eta | ξ | \xi | | | | |

### Upper case letters

| | | | | | | | |
|---|---|---|---|---|---|---|---|
| Γ | \Gamma | Λ | \Lambda | Σ | \Sigma | Ψ | \Psi |
| Δ | \Delta | Ξ | \Xi | Υ | \Upsilon | Ω | \Omega |
| Θ | \Theta | Π | \Pi | Φ | \Phi | | |

**Table F.12**    Binary operation symbols    (5.3.3) – p. 122.

| | | | | | | | |
|---|---|---|---|---|---|---|---|
| $\pm$ | \pm | $\cap$ | \cap | $\circ$ | \circ | $\bigcirc$ | \bigcirc |
| $\mp$ | \mp | $\cup$ | \cup | $\bullet$ | \bullet | $\Box$ | \Box |
| $\times$ | \times | $\uplus$ | \uplus | $\diamond$ | \diamond | $\Diamond$ | \Diamond |
| $\div$ | \div | $\sqcap$ | \sqcap | $\lhd$ | \lhd | $\triangle$ | \bigtriangleup |
| $\cdot$ | \cdot | $\sqcup$ | \sqcup | $\rhd$ | \rhd | $\bigtriangledown$ | \bigtriangledown |
| $*$ | \ast | $\vee$ | \vee | $\unlhd$ | \unlhd | $\triangleleft$ | \triangleleft |
| $\star$ | \star | $\wedge$ | \wedge | $\unrhd$ | \unrhd | $\triangleright$ | \triangleright |
| $\dagger$ | \dagger | $\oplus$ | \oplus | $\oslash$ | \oslash | $\setminus$ | \setminus |
| $\ddagger$ | \ddagger | $\ominus$ | \ominus | $\odot$ | \odot | $\wr$ | \wr |
| $\amalg$ | \amalg | $\otimes$ | \otimes | | | | |

**Table F.13**    Relational symbols    (5.3.4) – p. 122.

| | | | | | | | | | |
|---|---|---|---|---|---|---|---|---|---|
| $\le$ | \le | \leq | $\ge$ | \ge | \geq | $\neq$ | \neq | $\sim$ | \sim |
| $\ll$ | \ll | | $\gg$ | \gg | | $\doteq$ | \doteq | $\simeq$ | \simeq |
| $\subset$ | \subset | | $\supset$ | \supset | | $\approx$ | \approx | $\asymp$ | \asymp |
| $\subseteq$ | \subseteq | | $\supseteq$ | \supseteq | | $\cong$ | \cong | $\smile$ | \smile |
| $\sqsubset$ | \sqsubset | | $\sqsupset$ | \sqsupset | | $\equiv$ | \equiv | $\frown$ | \frown |
| $\sqsubseteq$ | \sqsubseteq | | $\sqsupseteq$ | \sqsupseteq | | $\propto$ | \propto | $\bowtie$ | \bowtie |
| $\in$ | \in | | $\ni$ | \ni | | $\prec$ | \prec | $\succ$ | \succ |
| $\vdash$ | \vdash | | $\dashv$ | \dashv | | $\preceq$ | \preceq | $\succeq$ | \succeq |
| $\models$ | \models | | $\perp$ | \perp | | $\parallel$ | \parallel \| | $\mid$ | \mid | |

**Table F.14**    Negated relation symbols    (5.3.4) – p. 123.

| | | | | | |
|---|---|---|---|---|---|
| $\not<$ | \not< | $\not>$ | \not> | $\neq$ | \not= |
| $\not\le$ | \not\le | $\not\ge$ | \not\ge | $\not\equiv$ | \not\equiv |
| $\not\prec$ | \not\prec | $\not\succ$ | \not\succ | $\not\sim$ | \not\sim |
| $\not\preceq$ | \not\preceq | $\not\succeq$ | \not\succeq | $\not\simeq$ | \not\simeq |
| $\not\subset$ | \not\subset | $\not\supset$ | \not\supset | $\not\approx$ | \not\approx |
| $\not\subseteq$ | \not\subseteq | $\not\supseteq$ | \not\supseteq | $\not\cong$ | \not\cong |
| $\not\sqsubseteq$ | \not\sqsubseteq | $\not\sqsupseteq$ | \not\sqsupseteq | $\not\asymp$ | \not\asymp |
| $\not\in$ | \not\in | $\notin$ | \notin | | |

**Table F.15**    Brackets    (5.4.1) – p. 128.

| | | | | | | | |
|---|---|---|---|---|---|---|---|
| ( | ( | ) | ) | $\lfloor$ | \lfloor | $\rfloor$ | \rfloor |
| [ | [ | ] | ] | $\lceil$ | \lceil | $\rceil$ | \rceil |
| { | \{ | } | \} | $\langle$ | \langle | $\rangle$ | \rangle |
| \| | \| | $\|$ | \\| | $\uparrow$ | \uparrow | $\Uparrow$ | \Uparrow |
| / | / | \ | \backslash | $\downarrow$ | \downarrow | $\Downarrow$ | \Downarrow |
| | | | | $\updownarrow$ | \updownarrow | $\Updownarrow$ | \Updownarrow |

**Table F.16** Arrows (5.3.5) – p. 123.

| | | | | | |
|---|---|---|---|---|---|
| ← | \leftarrow \gets | ⟵ | \longleftarrow | ↑ | \uparrow |
| ⇐ | \Leftarrow | ⟸ | \Longleftarrow | ⇑ | \Uparrow |
| → | \rightarrow \to | ⟶ | \longrightarrow | ↓ | \downarrow |
| ⇒ | \Rightarrow | ⟹ | \Longrightarrow | ⇓ | \Downarrow |
| ↔ | \leftrightarrow | ⟷ | \longleftrightarrow | ↕ | \updownarrow |
| ⇔ | \Leftrightarrow | ⟺ | \Longleftrightarrow | ⇕ | \Updownarrow |
| ↦ | \mapsto | ⟼ | \longmapsto | ↗ | \nearrow |
| ↩ | \hookleftarrow | ↪ | \hookrightarrow | ↘ | \searrow |
| ↼ | \leftharpoonup | ⇀ | \rightharpoonup | ↙ | \swarrow |
| ↽ | \leftharpoondown | ⇁ | \rightharpoondown | ↖ | \nwarrow |
| ⇌ | \rightleftharpoons | ⇝ | \leadsto | | |

**Table F.17** Miscellaneous symbols (5.3.6) – p. 123.

| | | | | | | | |
|---|---|---|---|---|---|---|---|
| ℵ | \aleph | ′ | \prime | ∀ | \forall | □ | \Box |
| ℏ | \hbar | ∅ | \emptyset | ∃ | \exists | ◊ | \Diamond |
| ι | \imath | ∇ | \nabla | ¬ | \neg | △ | \triangle |
| ȷ | \jmath | √ | \surd | ♭ | \flat | ♣ | \clubsuit |
| ℓ | \ell | ∂ | \partial | ♮ | \natural | ♦ | \diamondsuit |
| ℘ | \wp | ⊤ | \top | ♯ | \sharp | ♥ | \heartsuit |
| ℜ | \Re | ⊥ | \bot | ‖ | \\| | ♠ | \spadesuit |
| ℑ | \Im | ⊢ | \vdash | ∠ | \angle | ⋈ | \Join |
| ℧ | \mho | ⊣ | \dashv | \ | \backslash | ∞ | \infty |

**Table F.18** Mathematical symbols in two sizes (5.3.7) – p. 124.

| | | | | | | | | |
|---|---|---|---|---|---|---|---|---|
| Σ | ∑ | \sum | ∩ | ∩ | \bigcap | ⊙ | ⊙ | \bigodot |
| ∫ | ∫ | \int | ∪ | ∪ | \bigcup | ⊗ | ⊗ | \bigotimes |
| ∮ | ∮ | \oint | ⊔ | ⊔ | \bigsqcup | ⊕ | ⊕ | \bigoplus |
| ∏ | ∏ | \prod | ∨ | ∨ | \bigvee | ⊎ | ⊎ | \biguplus |
| ⊔ | ⊔ | \coprod | ∧ | ∧ | \bigwedge | | | |

**Table F.19** Function names (5.3.8) – p. 124.

| | | | | | | |
|---|---|---|---|---|---|---|
| \arccos | \cosh | \det | \inf | \limsup | \Pr | \tan |
| \arcsin | \cot | \dim | \ker | \ln | \sec | \tanh |
| \arctan | \coth | \exp | \lg | \log | \sin | |
| \arg | \csc | \gcd | \lim | \max | \sinh | |
| \cos | \deg | \hom | \liminf | \min | \sup | |

**Table F.20**  Math accents  (5.3.9) – p. 125.

| | | | |
|---|---|---|---|
| $\hat{a}$ \hat{a} | $\breve{a}$ \breve{a} | $\grave{a}$ \grave{a} | $\bar{a}$ \bar{a} |
| $\check{a}$ \check{a} | $\acute{a}$ \acute{a} | $\tilde{a}$ \tilde{a} | $\vec{a}$ \vec{a} |
| $\dot{a}$ \dot{a} | $\ddot{a}$ \ddot{a} | | |

**Table F.21**  The standard TEX fonts  (Section E.8) – p. 412.

| | | | | |
|---|---|---|---|---|
| cmr5 | cmti9 | cmssq8 | cmu10 | cmmi5 |
| cmr6 | cmti10 | cmss8 | cmff10 | cmmi6 |
| cmr7 | cmti12 | cmss9 | cmfi10 | cmmi7 |
| cmr8 | cmbx5 | cmss10 | cmdunh10 | cmmi8 |
| cmr9 | cmbx6 | cmss12 | cmtt8 | cmmi9 |
| cmr10 | cmbx7 | cmss17 | cmtt9 | cmmi10 |
| cmr12 | cmbx8 | cmssqi8 | cmtt10 | cmmi12 |
| cmr17 | cmbx9 | cmssi8 | cmtt12 | cmmib10 |
| cmcsc10 | cmbx10 | cmssi9 | cmtcsc10 | cmsy5 |
| cmsl8 | cmbx12 | cmssi10 | cmsltt10 | cmsy6 |
| cmsl9 | cmb10 | cmssi12 | cmitt10 | cmsy7 |
| cmsl10 | cmfib8 | cmssi17 | cmtex8 | cmsy8 |
| cmsl12 | cmbxsl10 | cmssdc10 | cmtex9 | cmsy9 |
| cmti7 | cmbxti10 | cmssbx10 | cmtex10 | cmsy10 |
| cmti8 | cminch | cmvtt10 | cmex10 | cmbsy10 |

Extra LATEX fonts

| | | | | |
|---|---|---|---|---|
| lasy5 | lasy8 | lasyb10 | linew10 | logo8 |
| lasy6 | lasy9 | line10 | lcirclew10 | logo9 |
| lasy7 | lasy10 | lcircle10 | logosl10 | logo10 |

Extra fonts from $\mathcal{AMS}$, incorporated in LATEX $2_\varepsilon$

| | | | | |
|---|---|---|---|---|
| cmmib5 | cmmib6 | cmmib7 | cmmib8 | cmmib9 |
| cmbsy5 | cmbsy6 | cmbsy7 | cmbsy8 | cmbsy9 |

**Table F.22**  Magnifications and scaling factors  (Section E.8.2) – p. 414.

| Mag step | Scale factor | Mag step | Scale factor | Mag step | Scale factor |
|---|---|---|---|---|---|
| 1.0 | 1000 | $1.2^2$ | 1440 | $1.2^5$ | 2488 |
| $\sqrt{1.2}$ | 1095 | $1.2^3$ | 1728 | $1.2^6$ | 2986 |
| 1.2 | 1200 | $1.2^4$ | 2074 | $1.2^7$ | 3583 |

The command names underlined in Tables F.12, F.13, F.16, and F.17 can only be used in LATEX $2_\varepsilon$ if the package latexsym has been loaded, or if some other special package that defines them has been included.

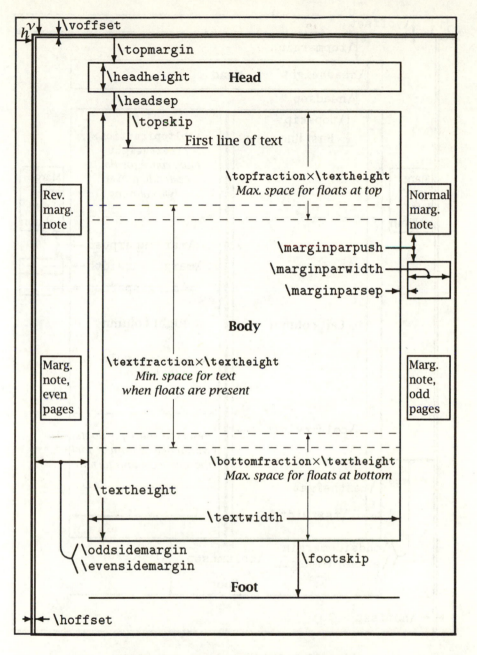

**Figure F.1**   Single column page format
(3.2.4), p. 35 – (4.10.7), p. 113 – (6.6.3), p. 175.

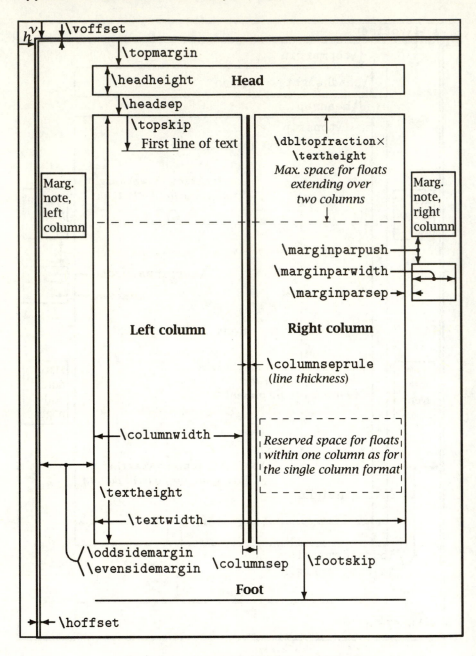

**Figure F.2**   Double column page format
(3.2.4), p. 35 – (3.1.1), p. 28 – (4.10.7), p. 113 – (6.6.3), p. 175.

**Remarks on the page format figures**

The reference margins in the LaTeX processing are shifted from the *logical* margins by the amounts \hoffset and \voffset. These in turn are displaced from the *physical* margins by $h$ and $v$ in the DVI driver. The default values for \hoffset and \voffset are 0 pt, so that the reference margins are equal to the *logical* ones. The usual values for $h$ and $v$ are 1 inch. Thus the logical page margins on the left and at the top are shifted 1 inch from the physical edge of the paper. The user may alter this by changing the values of \hoffset and \voffset.

LaTeX 2ε recognizes the parameters \paperwidth and \paperheight which contain the full dimensions of the paper, including the 1 inch margins. These are set by the paper size option to the class specification.

The parameter \footheight was specified but never used in LaTeX 2.09; it has been dropped from LaTeX 2ε.

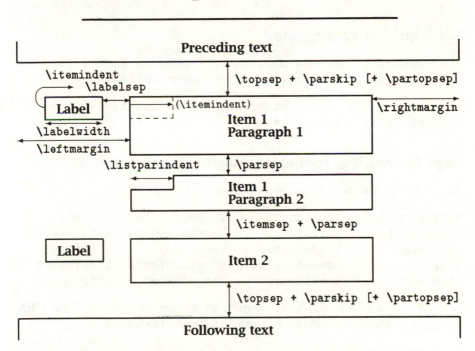

**Figure F.3**   Format of the list environment   (4.4.2) – p. 74.

**Note 1:** The default values for the three parameters \itemindent, \listparindent, \rightmargin are 0 pt.

**Note 2:** The default values in the trivlist environment are 0 pt for \itemindent, \leftmargin, \rightmargin, and \labelwidth; on the other hand, \parsep and \listparindent are assigned the respective values of \parsep and \parindent.

# F.3    Invalid Plain TEX commands

As mentioned in several places in this book, LaTeX is a set of macros, definitions, procedures, auxiliary files, etc., that have been built on top of the more basic Plain TEX format. This means that LaTeX is an extension of Plain TEX, so that all its commands are also available under LaTeX. At least, that is what one might expect.

LaTeX users who are also familiar with the complexity of the TEX system might find it at times useful to resort to that set of more basic commands. This is not recommended for 'normal' users. We have illustrated a few of these commands within this book and they should be sufficient. For the advanced user it is necessary to point out that a number of Plain TEX commands will not function at all under LaTeX, since they have been altered or undefined by the higher-level system. We list these invalid TEX commands according to their logical functionality.

## F.3.1    TEX tabulator commands

The following TEX tabulator commands will not work under LaTeX. They have been replaced by the `tabbing` environment and its commands:

```
\tabs      \tabset    \tabsdone    \cleartabs
\settabs   \tabalign  \+
```

## F.3.2    Page formatting, footnotes, floats

The Plain TEX commands below have been deleted:

```
\advancepageno    \footstrut      \nopagenumbers  \pageno
\dosupereject     \headline       \normalbottom   \plainoutput
\endinsert        \makefootline   \pagebody       \topins
\folio            \makeheadline   \pagecontents   \topinsert
\footline         \midinsert      \pageinsert     \vfootnote
```

Instead one achieves the same results by means of \pagestyle, LaTeX footnote commands, and the `figure` and `table` environments.

## F.3.3    TEX font commands

The Plain TEX font commands

```
\fivei     \fiverm     \fivesy     \fivebf
\seveni    \sevenbf    \sevensy    \teni      \oldstyle
```

are not defined in LaTeX. Similar results may be produced with the typeface and font size commands.

## 3.4   Math commands

All the T<sub>E</sub>X math commands may be applied in L<sup>A</sup>T<sub>E</sub>X with the exceptions of

```
\eqalign     \eqalignno    \leqalingnno
```

which are replaced by the eqnarray and eqnarray* environments.

## 3.5   Miscellaneous

The \beginsection command in Plain T<sub>E</sub>X has been taken over by L<sup>A</sup>T<sub>E</sub>X's sectioning commands. The text is not terminated with \end or with \bye but rather with the command \end{document}. The \centering command in T<sub>E</sub>X has been replaced by a L<sup>A</sup>T<sub>E</sub>X command with the same name. In T<sub>E</sub>X, there is a command \line (for writing a line of text) which conflicts with L<sup>A</sup>T<sub>E</sub>X's command of the same name in the picture environment (to draw a line). Most applications of T<sub>E</sub>X's \line are accomplished with \center, \flushleft, and \flushright in L<sup>A</sup>T<sub>E</sub>X.

The T<sub>E</sub>X command \magnification has been fully removed. It is actually more reasonable and efficient to carry out the magnification as an option to the DVI driver program, provided this is available on your driver. This requires no change to the .tex or .dvi files, altering the printer output directly. Check your driver manual or computer center.

# Bibliography

Abrahams P. W., with Hargreaves K. A. and Berry K. (1990). *TEX for the Impatient*. Reading MA: Addison-Wesley

Botway L. and Biemesderfer C. (1985). *LATEX Command Summary*. Providence RI: TEX Users Group

Eijkhout V. (1992). *TEX by Topic, a TEXnician's Reference*. Wokingham: Addison-Wesley

Goosens M., Mittelbach F. and Samarin A. (1994). *The LATEX Companion*. Reading MA: Addison-Wesley

Knuth D. E. (1984). *The TEXbook*, Computers and Typesetting, Vol. A. Reading MA: Addison-Wesley

Knuth D. E. (1986a). *TEX: The Program*, Computers and Typesetting, Vol. B. Reading MA: Addison-Wesley

Knuth D. E. (1986b). *The METAFONT book*, Computers and Typesetting, Vol. C. Reading MA: Addison-Wesley

Knuth D. E. (1986c). *METAFONT: The Program*, Computers and Typesetting, Vol. D. Reading MA: Addison-Wesley

Knuth D. E. (1986d). *Computer Modern Typefaces*, Computers and Typesetting, Vol. E. Reading MA: Addison-Wesley

Kopka H. (1994). *LATEX, Band 1, eine Einführung*. Bonn: Addison-Wesley

Kopka H. (1995). *LATEX, Band 2, Ergänzungen, mit einer Einführung in METAFONT*. Bonn: Addison-Wesley

Lamport L. (1985). *LATEX—A Document Preparation System*. Reading MA: Addison-Wesley

Lamport L. (1994). *LATEX—A Document Preparation System*, 2nd edn. for LATEX 2$_\varepsilon$. Reading MA: Addison-Wesley

Rokicki T. (1985). Packed (PK) font file format. *TUGboat*, **6**(3), 115–20

Samuel A. L. (1985). *First Grade TEX: A Beginner's TEX Manual*. Providence, RI: TEX Users Group

Schwarz N. (1990). *Introduction to TEX*. Reading MA: Addison-Wesley

Snow W. (1992). *TEX for the Beginner*. Reading MA: Addison-Wesley

Spivak M. (1985). *PCTEX Manual*. Mill Valley CA: Personal TEX

Spivak M. (1986). *The Joy of TEX*. Providence RI: American Mathematical Society

TEX Users Group (1980–1991). *TUGboat*, Vols 1–12. Providence RI: TEX Users Group

Urban M. (1986). *An Introduction to LATEX*. Providence RI: TEX Users Group

Wichura M. J. (1987). *The PiCTEX Manual*. Providence RI: TEX Users Group

# Index

For purposes of alphabetization, the backslash character \ is ignored at the start of an entry. Otherwise, the ordering is by the ASCII sequence.

Bold page numbers indicate the place where the command or concept is introduced, explained, or defined. Italic page numbers refer to the Command Index, Appendix F. Slanted page numbers are from the Summary Tables and Figures, Section F.2.

The keyword index is set up with main and two sub-entries. If a keyword cannot be found as a main entry, one should try to find it as a sub-entry to some more general term. Such major topics are

> bibliographic database, box, command, command (user-defined), cross-reference, environment, environment (user-defined), error messages, file, float, fonts, footnote, formula, hyphenation, LaTeX, letter, line breaking, lists, page breaking, picture, programming, sectioning, spacing, style parameter, slides, symbols, tabbing, table, table examples, TeX, text.